Intimacy and Developing Personal Relationships in the Virtual World

Rejani Thudalikunnil Gopalan
Gujarat Forensic Sciences University, India

A volume in the Advances in Human and Social Aspects of Technology (AHSAT) Book Series

IGI Global
DISSEMINATOR OF KNOWLEDGE

Published in the United States of America by
IGI Global
Information Science Reference (an imprint of IGI Global)
701 E. Chocolate Avenue
Hershey PA, USA 17033
Tel: 717-533-8845
Fax: 717-533-8661
E-mail: cust@igi-global.com
Web site: http://www.igi-global.com

Library of Congress Cataloging-in-Publication Data

Names: Gopalan, Rejani Thudalikunnil, 1974- editor.
Title: Intimacy and developing personal relationships in the virtual world / Rejani Thudalikunnil Gopalan, editor.
Description: Hershey : Information Science Reference, [2018]
Identifiers: LCCN 2017026833| ISBN 9781522540472 (hardcover) | ISBN 9781522540489 (ebook)
Subjects: LCSH: Virtual reality--Social aspects. | Interpersonal relations.
Classification: LCC HM851 .I58925 2018 | DDC 302--dc23 LC record available at https://lccn.loc.gov/2017026833

This book is published in the IGI Global book series Advances in Human and Social Aspects of Technology (AHSAT) (ISSN: 2328-1316; eISSN: 2328-1324)

British Cataloguing in Publication Data
A Cataloguing in Publication record for this book is available from the British Library.

For electronic access to this publication, please contact: eresources@igi-global.com.

Advances in Human and Social Aspects of Technology (AHSAT) Book Series

Ashish Dwivedi
The University of Hull, UK

ISSN:2328-1316
EISSN:2328-1324

Mission

In recent years, the societal impact of technology has been noted as we become increasingly more connected and are presented with more digital tools and devices. With the popularity of digital devices such as cell phones and tablets, it is crucial to consider the implications of our digital dependence and the presence of technology in our everyday lives.

The **Advances in Human and Social Aspects of Technology (AHSAT) Book Series** seeks to explore the ways in which society and human beings have been affected by technology and how the technological revolution has changed the way we conduct our lives as well as our behavior. The AHSAT book series aims to publish the most cutting-edge research on human behavior and interaction with technology and the ways in which the digital age is changing society.

Coverage

- Public Access to ICTs
- Human Development and Technology
- Digital Identity
- Philosophy of technology
- Technoself
- Technology and Freedom of Speech
- End-User Computing
- Human Rights and Digitization
- Cultural Influence of ICTs
- ICTs and social change

IGI Global is currently accepting manuscripts for publication within this series. To submit a proposal for a volume in this series, please contact our Acquisition Editors at Acquisitions@igi-global.com or visit: http://www.igi-global.com/publish/.

The Advances in Human and Social Aspects of Technology (AHSAT) Book Series (ISSN 2328-1316) is published by IGI Global, 701 E. Chocolate Avenue, Hershey, PA 17033-1240, USA, www.igi-global.com. This series is composed of titles available for purchase individually; each title is edited to be contextually exclusive from any other title within the series. For pricing and ordering information please visit http://www.igi-global.com/book-series/advances-human-social-aspects-technology/37145. Postmaster: Send all address changes to above address.

Titles in this Series

For a list of additional titles in this series, please visit: www.igi-global.com/book-series

Handbook of Research on Civic Engagement and Social Change in Contemporary Society
Susheel Chhabra (Periyar Management and Computer College, India)
Information Science Reference • copyright 2018 • 445pp • H/C (ISBN: 9781522541974) • US $245.00 (our price)

Corporate and Global Standardization Initiatives in Contemporary Society
Kai Jakobs (RWTH Aachen University, Germany)
Information Science Reference • copyright 2018 • 394pp • H/C (ISBN: 9781522553205) • US $205.00 (our price)

Computational Psychoanalysis and Formal Bi-Logic Frameworks
Giuseppe Iurato (Independent Researcher, Italy)
Information Science Reference • copyright 2018 • 332pp • H/C (ISBN: 9781522541288) • US $215.00 (our price)

Psychological, Social, and Cultural Aspects of Internet Addiction
Bahadir Bozoglan (IF Weinheim Institute, Germany)
Information Science Reference • copyright 2018 • 390pp • H/C (ISBN: 9781522534778) • US $200.00 (our price)

Experience-Based Human-Computer Interactions Emerging Research and Opportunities
Petr Sosnin (Ulyanovsk State Technical University, Russia)
Information Science Reference • copyright 2018 • 294pp • H/C (ISBN: 9781522529873) • US $165.00 (our price)

Technology-Enhanced Human Interaction in Modern Society
Francisco Vicente Cipolla-Ficarra (Latin Association of Human-Computer Interaction, Spain & International Association of Interactive Communication, Italy) Maria Valeria Ficarra (Latin Association of Human-Computer Interaction, Spain & International Association of Interactive Communication, Italy) Miguel Cipolla-Ficarra (International Association of Interactive Communication, Italy) Alejandra Quiroga (Universidad Nacional de La Pampa, Argentina) Jacqueline Alma (Electronic Arts – Vancouver, Canada) and Jim Carré (University of The Netherlands Antilles, Curaçao)
Information Science Reference • copyright 2018 • 319pp • H/C (ISBN: 9781522534372) • US $205.00 (our price)

HCI Challenges and Privacy Preservation in Big Data Security
Daphne Lopez (VIT University, India) and M.A. Saleem Durai (VIT University, India)
Information Science Reference • copyright 2018 • 275pp • H/C (ISBN: 9781522528630) • US $215.00 (our price)

IGI Global
DISSEMINATOR OF KNOWLEDGE

701 East Chocolate Avenue, Hershey, PA 17033, USA
Tel: 717-533-8845 x100 • Fax: 717-533-8661
E-Mail: cust@igi-global.com • www.igi-global.com

Table of Contents

Preface xiv

Acknowledgment xix

Chapter 1
Changes in Online Subjectivity: Artificial Users, Subject Fragmentarization, and Multimodal Interaction 1
Zdenek Smutny, University of Economics, Prague, Czech Republic
Vaclav Janoscik, Academy of Performing Arts in Prague, Czech Republic

Chapter 2
Psychological Benefits and Detrimental Effects of Online Social Networking 21
Irem Metin Orta, Atilim University, Turkey
Müge Çelik Örücü, TED University, Turkey

Chapter 3
Relational Body Identities: Body Image Control Through Self-Portraits – A Revision of the Body Image Control in Photos Questionnaire 40
Valentina Boursier, University of Naples Federico II, Italy
Valentina Manna, Association for Social Promotion Roots in Action, Italy

Chapter 4
Desired Speed of Reply During Text-Based Communication via Smartphones: A Survey of Young Japanese Adults 64
Yuuki Kato, Sagami Women's University, Japan
Shogo Kato, Tokyo Woman's Christian University, Japan
Yasuyuki Ozawa, Meisei University, Japan

Chapter 5
Public Relations and Advertising in the Context of E-Sports 84
Tina Tomazic, University of Maribor, Slovenia
Luka Druks, University of Maribor, Slovenia
Noemia Bessa Vilela, Universidade Portucalense (UPT), Portugal

Chapter 6
Social Media and TV Watching Metrics 96
Gülşah Sari, Abant Izzet Baysal University, Turkey

Chapter 7
Facebook Depression or Facebook Contentment: The Relation Between Facebook Use and Well-Being 104
Jessica J. Joseph, Mount Royal University, Canada
Malinda Desjarlais, Mount Royal University, Canada
Lucijana Herceg, Mount Royal University, Canada

Chapter 8
Offending, Victimization, Forensic Investigation, and Prevention of Cyberstalking 126
Rejani Thudalikunnil Gopalan, Gujarat Forensic Sciences University, India

Chapter 9
Cyberbullying 153
Michelle F. Wright, Pennsylvania State University, USA

Chapter 10
Internet Addiction and Online Gaming: An Emerging Epidemic of the Twenty-First Century? 174
Tanay Maiti, Christian Medical College, India

Chapter 11
Cybersex 201
Aman Choudhary, Independent Researcher, India

Chapter 12
The Effect of Social Networks on Relationships Outside the Network 213
Tami Seifert, Kibbutzim College of Education, Technology, and the Arts, Israel
Idit Miara, Kibbutzim College of Education, Technology, and the Arts, Israel

Chapter 13
Romantic Relationships, Online Dating, and Mental Health Issues 236
Tejaswini Bhave, Deenanth Mangeshkar Hospital and Research Center, India

Chapter 14
Impact of Online Dating, Cyber Stalking, Cybersex, and Pornography on Mental Health 244
Rejani Thudalikunnil Gopalan, Gujarat Forensic Sciences University, India

Chapter 15
Empowering Technology Use to Promote Virtual Violence Prevention in Higher Education Context 272
Miftachul Huda, Universiti Teknologi Malaysia, Malaysia
Aminudin Hehsan, Universiti Teknologi Malaysia, Malaysia
Singgih Basuki, Sunan Kalijaga State Islamic University, Indonesia
Budi Rismayadi, Buana Perjuangan University, Indonesia
Kamarul Azmi Jasmi, Universiti Teknologi Malaysia, Malaysia
Bushrah Basiron, Universiti Teknologi Malaysia, Malaysia
Mohd Ismail Mustari, Universiti Teknologi Malaysia, Malaysia

Compilation of References 292

About the Contributors 347

Index 353

Detailed Table of Contents

Preface xiv

Acknowledgment xix

Chapter 1
Changes in Online Subjectivity: Artificial Users, Subject Fragmentarization, and Multimodal Interaction 1
Zdenek Smutny, University of Economics, Prague, Czech Republic
Vaclav Janoscik, Academy of Performing Arts in Prague, Czech Republic

Human subjectivity is deeply affected by the environment as mediated by the Internet. As users within this environment, people are not only affected by their entrance into it, but their subjectivity evolves along with the trends of online networking. The subjectivity of people is affected by (their networking with) human and artificial users of the environment and the possibility of influencing user's subjectivity is also given by other specific aspects of the environment. This chapter focuses on three areas: artificial users, subject and its fragmentarization, and multimodal interaction. Findings in conceptualizing change in terms of subjectivity are based within the poststructuralist philosophical tradition. There is applied the phenomenon known as the "death of the author," proclaimed in late 1960s, to the situation of the contemporary user to uncover changes in online subjectivity. The chapter also presents examples of implications of such changes at the level of interactions and distribution of messages and the role of artificial users in these processes within online marketing.

Chapter 2
Psychological Benefits and Detrimental Effects of Online Social Networking 21
Irem Metin Orta, Atilim University, Turkey
Müge Çelik Örücü, TED University, Turkey

With the growing prevalence of wireless communication technologies, social networking sites (SNSs) such as Facebook, Twitter, etc. have become an important venues for interpersonal communication. This chapter provides a detailed overview of the current literature on online social networking with respect to its beneficial and detrimental effects on psychological wellbeing. In particular, it provides empirical evidence for the associations of SNS use with depression, self-esteem, loneliness, subjective wellbeing, social anxiety, attachment, personality traits, and addiction. Furthermore, it identifies the characteristics of individuals who are more prone to social networking, and presents possible mediators and moderators playing a role in the relationship between social networking and mental health. The chapter overall provides a comprehensive guideline to parents, researchers, educators, healthcare, and communication professionals to the issue of online social networking from a psychological perspective.

Chapter 3
Relational Body Identities: Body Image Control Through Self-Portraits – A Revision of the Body Image Control in Photos Questionnaire 40
Valentina Boursier, University of Naples Federico II, Italy
Valentina Manna, Association for Social Promotion Roots in Action, Italy

Self-portrayal is one of the most popular online activities, especially among adolescents and young adults. The selfie-craze explosion through photo-sharing represent a new task for adolescents' researchers, but few instruments explore how adolescents can control their body image through self-portraits. One of these is the body image control in photos questionnaire. The aim of this chapter is to develop and validate a revised short version of the BICPQ, administered to 1220 Italian adolescents. The establishment of a cut-off procedure is proposed for screening purposes to identify at-risk and problematic users. Moreover, differences by gender and age are explored and discussed.

Chapter 4
Desired Speed of Reply During Text-Based Communication via Smartphones: A Survey of Young Japanese Adults 64
Yuuki Kato, Sagami Women's University, Japan
Shogo Kato, Tokyo Woman's Christian University, Japan
Yasuyuki Ozawa, Meisei University, Japan

Text-based forms of communication have long been communicated via PCs and more recently via mobile phones and smartphones. This chapter has tried to explore how the speed of text message exchanges has become a nonverbal cue in the asynchronous communications that occurs via mobile phones and smartphones. This chapter presents the investigation of the speed of exchange relevant to the LINE text-messenger application. Specifically, the authors surveyed Japanese university students who provided free-response descriptions of situations when (a) a quick reply is preferred and (b) a late reply is acceptable. The main finding was that judging when a quick reply is preferred and when a late reply is acceptable is overwhelmingly influenced by the convenience of the sender (who is waiting for a reply) over the convenience of the recipient who will reply.

Chapter 5
Public Relations and Advertising in the Context of E-Sports 84
Tina Tomazic, University of Maribor, Slovenia
Luka Druks, University of Maribor, Slovenia
Noemia Bessa Vilela, Universidade Portucalense (UPT), Portugal

E-sports within the gaming industry characterize an economic sector that is engaged in the developing, marketing, and sale of video games. They represent many opportunities for advertising and public relations, which are very important to increase the visibility of e-sports. The use of both has proved far more effective, because it allowed a rapid increase in their popularity. The aim of this chapter is to compare the use of public relations and advertising in e-sports and to determine their appropriateness. So, the relationship between public relations, advertising, and e-sports is developed and researched for the first time here. The authors used qualitative comparative analysis between public relations and advertising in the context of e-sports based on Natus Vincere, one of the most important Ukrainian organizations in the gaming industry. The rise of the gaming industry and recent success of e-sports demonstrate the profitable economic potentials of gaming spectatorship.

Chapter 6
Social Media and TV Watching Metrics 96
Gülşah Sari, Abant Izzet Baysal University, Turkey

In this chapter, in order to measure the relation between social media and television, the inside sequence published in Turkish television series during the broadcasting period of 2016-2017 was examined. The reason for the selection of this directory is that 39 episodes are broadcast throughout the episode, and the high interest in social media is a high percentage of TV ratings. The study looked at the follow-up measures in social media that were used to help measure social media in-line monitoring. The Kimola firm is one of the companies that conducts research on this subject. In the study, Kimola presented its published series of 39 episodes published in the series. As a result of this study, it shows that social media have an increasing role in the effect of watching television.

Chapter 7
Facebook Depression or Facebook Contentment: The Relation Between Facebook Use and Well-Being 104
Jessica J. Joseph, Mount Royal University, Canada
Malinda Desjarlais, Mount Royal University, Canada
Lucijana Herceg, Mount Royal University, Canada

Within the literature, Facebook has received much attention in order to understand the potential positive and negative effects associated with using the social networking site. The current chapter provides a discussion of the empirical support for the differential outcomes associated with actively posting and chatting on Facebook vs. passively browsing Facebook, as well as the underlying mechanisms for the effects. Specifically, the current chapter will discuss two perspectives related to the differential effects of active and passive Facebook use: Facebook contentment (a wellbeing enhancing effect) and Facebook depression (a wellbeing diminishing effect). The authors also discuss the extension of the results to other social media platforms and provide suggestions for future research.

Chapter 8
Offending, Victimization, Forensic Investigation, and Prevention of Cyberstalking 126
Rejani Thudalikunnil Gopalan, Gujarat Forensic Sciences University, India

The term cyberstalking has been used to describe a variety of behaviors that involve repeated threats and/or harassment by the use of electronic mail or other computer-based communication that would make a reasonable person afraid or concerned for their safety. It is growing fast and creating problems, especially psychologically. This chapter mainly focused on its definition, typologies, characteristics of victims and offenders, forensic investigation, and its prevention. There is not much agreement on the definition of cyberstalking as it appeared recently due to technological advancement. Many of the researches were done on university students and the prevalence of cyberstalking among general population and special groups are not much known. But researches repeatedly confirm it as a growing issue. Technical advancements and thorough knowledge on technical details among researchers from different backgrounds poses a big problem to its complete understanding and prevention. Future research needs to focus on all these aspects.

Chapter 9
Cyberbullying 153
Michelle F. Wright, Pennsylvania State University, USA

Cyberbullying has become a major focus of not only youths, educators, and researchers, but also among the general population, due to high profile cases of cyberbullying victimization involving suicide and the increasing prevalence of these behaviors. The purpose of this chapter is to examine cyberbullying among children and adolescents, referred to as "youths" throughout the chapter. An extension of traditional bullying, cyberbullying is a form of bullying which takes place by means of electronic technologies, such as email, instant messaging, social networking websites, and text messaging through mobile devices. Drawing on research from a variety of disciplines, such as psychology, education, social work, sociology, and computer science, this chapter describes the definition of cyberbullying, the electronic technologies used, the prevalence rates, characteristics and risk factors, negative psychosocial and academic difficulties, theoretical frameworks, recommendations, and future directions.

Chapter 10
Internet Addiction and Online Gaming: An Emerging Epidemic of the Twenty-First Century?....... 174
Tanay Maiti, Christian Medical College, India

Internet addiction has gradually turned a medium of gaming and other leisure activities shifting from its original intention to fasten the communication and help in the researches. The excessive usage of internet and nature of its usage has been found to be similar with psycho-addictive substance addiction with similar neurobiological basis. Inclusion of gambling disorder into DSM 5 further strengthens the emerging concept of behavioral addiction. Various worldwide researches also support the upsurge of such problem. The clinical presentation and management options are mostly based on the behavioral principles learned from the substance abuse problems. However, large-scale randomized trails and epidemiological studies are definitely needed to understand this twenty-first century problem.

Chapter 11
Cybersex.. 201
Aman Choudhary, Independent Researcher, India

Cybersex is often used as a collective term for all sorts of sexually related entertainment, information, and personal contact offers available in computer networks respective "in cyberspace." It is also understood to be a computer-mediated interpersonal interaction in which the participants are sexually motivated, meaning they are seeking sexual arousal and satisfaction. Types are virtual-reality-based cybersex, video-based cybersex, and text-based cybersex. From a technical perspective, two sub-forms of text-based cybersex are differentiated: tinysex and erotic chat. This chapter focuses on various forms of cybersex from commercialization to self-exhibitionism and voyeurism has been explained in terms of commercial and personal cybersex aided by MUD. The chapter concludes with an evaluative view that despite being considered advantageous in a recreative and imaginative alternative for sexual satisfaction, cybersex increases problems an individual goes through along with the family, friends, and other relationships simultaneously elevating infidelity component in stable relationships.

Chapter 12
The Effect of Social Networks on Relationships Outside the Network 213
Tami Seifert, Kibbutzim College of Education, Technology, and the Arts, Israel
Idit Miara, Kibbutzim College of Education, Technology, and the Arts, Israel

This chapter examines the impact of three different aspects of romantic discourse on social networks: romance, identity, and privacy. Qualitative research focused on the influence of the social networks on the opinions and interpersonal behavior of 11 single academics, aged 30-45 years old, men and women who used Facebook as a means for meeting potential romantic partners. The research employed semi-structured in-depth interviews to elicit qualitative data. Results indicate that an intimate, romantic setting cannot exist on the social network. Most users enhanced their identity in order to appear more attractive online. Most of the interviewees clearly felt that they needed to control the exposure of their personal details, and there was a clear indication that privacy does not exist online: it seems to be impossible to limit exposure of the published contents to specific selected audiences. Online romantic relationships are a metonymy for rapidly changing values and social norms in a dynamic global reality.

Chapter 13
Romantic Relationships, Online Dating, and Mental Health Issues 236
Tejaswini Bhave, Deenanth Mangeshkar Hospital and Research Center, India

This chapter attempts to present the overview of mental health issues associated with online dating and online romantic relationships with relevant research background. It briefly cautions about the possible risks involved in the world of online dating platforms and later delves into mental health concerns that can emerge out of experiences while selecting a potential partner online, developing a romantic relationship, and being involved in a romantic relationship online. It also discusses safety measures that need to be taken before and while being active on such online dating sites. The chapter draws attention to the specific role of mental health professionals that is needed while dealing with victims of online scams and abuse.

Chapter 14
Impact of Online Dating, Cyber Stalking, Cybersex, and Pornography on Mental Health................ 244
Rejani Thudalikunnil Gopalan, Gujarat Forensic Sciences University, India

Online behavior varies according to the purpose and situations and many get involved in intimate relations, like in online dating, which have an impact on the person and his mental health. The chapter focused on the impact of online dating, cyber stalking, cybersex, and pornography on mental health. Though many studied the online dating among adolescents and adults, that of old age group is not yet fully explored especially about their sexual needs. It is worth exploring factors related to risky sexual behaviors among gay and bisexual individuals. Online dating for mentally ill people is an under-researched area. Cyberstalking is an important issue, especially among adolescents and young adults, and cybersex and cyber pornography threatens the safety and mental health in addition to the problems of addiction and child trafficking, and it is linked with high sexual risk behaviors and sex crimes. It is necessary to develop tailored psychotherapeutic and pharmacological interventions by taking into account the complexity and heterogeneity of the problems.

Chapter 15
Empowering Technology Use to Promote Virtual Violence Prevention in Higher Education Context 272
Miftachul Huda, Universiti Teknologi Malaysia, Malaysia
Aminudin Hehsan, Universiti Teknologi Malaysia, Malaysia
Singgih Basuki, Sunan Kalijaga State Islamic University, Indonesia
Budi Rismayadi, Buana Perjuangan University, Indonesia
Kamarul Azmi Jasmi, Universiti Teknologi Malaysia, Malaysia
Bushrah Basiron, Universiti Teknologi Malaysia, Malaysia
Mohd Ismail Mustari, Universiti Teknologi Malaysia, Malaysia

This chapter aims to explore the pattern to use technology as an attempt to promote virtual violence prevention. A literature review from referred journals and books was conducted. The findings reveal that technology use, in particular an effort to solve the emerging issues of violence promotes the solution with an innovative approach designed in HE. With technology use in attempting violence prevention insights, an innovative way to strengthen technology use wisely with underlying the compassionate skills to promote the preventive action of violent forms is needed. Attempts to promote virtual violence prevention in higher education should be combined with empowering technology use to focus comprehensively on encouraging diverse learners with personal and social awareness in digital interaction. This chapter is expected to contribute in dealing with exploring the systematic approach in nurturing the self-awareness and social concern in digital interaction to be potentially applied in HE.

Compilation of References 292

About the Contributors 347

Index 353

Preface

Cyber psychology focuses on interaction between computers and human behavior, which include a wide range of aspects such as cognitive functions, online behavior, addict behaviors, and crimes. Nowadays computers have an important place in our life and the issues related to virtual world also affecting thoughts and behaviors of children and adults. The issues such as, online relationships, online dating and sex are important domains of research. An internet relationship is a relationship between people who have met online, and in many cases know each other only via the Internet. It is an emerging area and existing literature is not yet reached to public at large.

Previous books on cyber Psychology either focused on cognitive aspects, technological aspects or human behaviors, so this research book focus on a comprehensive understanding intimacy and developing personal relationships in the Virtual world on social, Psychological and legal perspectives. This book addressed the difficulties and challenges due to online intimacy and relationships and it discussed about different aspects of online intimacy, romantic and extramarital relationships, mental health issues due to online relations and break ups, sexual intimacy, and related topics. It has fifteen chapters from eminent researchers of eleven countries.

The first chapter discussed about the changes in online subjectivity. Human subjectivity is deeply affected by the environment as mediated by the Internet. As users within this environment, people are not only affected by their entrance into it, but their subjectivity evolves along with the trends of online networking. The subjectivity of people is affected by (their networking with) human and artificial users of the environment and the possibility of influencing user's subjectivity is also given by other specific aspects of the environment. This chapter focuses on three areas: artificial users, subject and its fragmentarization and multimodal interaction. Findings in conceptualizing change in terms of subjectivity are based within the poststructuralist philosophical tradition. There is applied the phenomenon known as the "death of the author," proclaimed in late 1960's, to the situation of the contemporary user to uncover changes in online subjectivity. The chapter also presents examples of implications of such changes at the level of interactions and distribution of messages and the role of artificial users in these processes within online marketing. It is a well written chapter and explained in detail about issues of subjectivity and would give a comprehensive knowledge about it.

The second chapter dealt with psychological benefits and detrimental Effects of online social networking and it is another well written chapter. With the growing prevalence of wireless communication technologies, social networking sites (SNSs) such as Facebook, Twitter, etc. have become an important venues for interpersonal communication. This chapter provides a detailed overview of the current literature on online social networking with respect to its beneficial and detrimental effects on psychological well-being. In particular, it provides empirical evidence for the associations of SNS use with depression, self-esteem, loneliness, subjective well-being, social anxiety, attachment, personality traits and addiction. Furthermore, it identifies the characteristics of individuals who are more prone to social networking, and presents possible mediators and moderators playing role in the relationship between social networking and mental health. The chapter overall provides a comprehensive guideline to parents, researchers, educators, health care and communication professionals to the issue of online social networking from a psychological perspective.

The third chapter explored about body image and attempted to develop and validate revised version of questionnaire related to this. Self-portrayal is one of the most popular online activities, especially among adolescents and young adults. The selfie-craze explosion through photo-sharing represent a new task for adolescents' researchers but few instruments explore how adolescents can control their body image through self-portraits. One of this is the Body Image Control in Photos questionnaire. The aim of this study is to develop and validate a revised short version of the BICPQ, administered to 1220 Italian adolescents. The establishment of a cut-off procedure is proposed for screening purpose to identify at risk and problematic users. Moreover, differences by gender and age are explored and discussed. Hope that this tool will be a valuable one in future researches.

Fourth chapter focused on the desired speed of reply during text-based communication via smartphones and it was conducted among young Japanese adults. Text-based forms of communication have long been communicated via PCs and more recently increasingly via mobile phones and smartphones. This chapter has tried to explore the speed of text message exchanges has become a nonverbal cue in the asynchronous communications that occurs via mobile phones and smartphones. This chapter presents the investigation of the speed of exchange relevant to the LINE text-messenger application. Specifically, the authors surveyed Japanese university students who provided free-response descriptions of situations when: (a) a quick reply is preferred and; (b) a late reply is acceptable. The main finding was that judging when a quick reply is preferred and when a late reply is acceptable is overwhelmingly influenced by the convenience of the sender (who is waiting for a reply) over the convenience of the recipient who will reply.

Fifth chapter explored the public relations and advertising in the context of E-sports and it is an interesting study in the area of E-sports. E-sports within the gaming industry characterize an economic sector that is engaged in the developing, marketing and sale of video games. They represent many opportunities for advertising and public relations, which are very important to increase the visibility of e-sports. The use of both has proved far more effective, because it allowed a rapid increase in their popularity. The aim of this chapter is to compare the use of public relations and advertising in e-sports and to determine their appropriateness. So, the relationship between public relations, advertising and e-sports is developed and researched for the first time here. The authors used qualitative comparative analysis between public relations and advertising in the context of e-sports based on Natus Vincere, one of the most important Ukrainian organizations in the gaming industry. The rise of the gaming industry and recent success of e-sports demonstrate the profitable economic potentials of gaming spectatorship.

The sixth chapter examined the relation of social media and TV watching metrics. In this study, in order to measure the relation between social media and television, the inside sequence published in Turkish television series during the broadcasting period of 2016-2017 was examined. The reason for the selection of this directory is that 39 episodes are broadcast throughout the episode, and the high interest in social media is a high percentage of TV ratings. The study looked at the follow-up measures in social media that were used to help measure social media in-line monitoring. The Kimola firm is one of the companies that conduct research on this subject in our country. In the study, Kimola presented its published series of 39 episodes published in the series. As a result of this study, it shows that social media have an increasing role in the effect of watching television.

Chapters 7-14 mainly focused on the mental health problems related to virtual activities such as Facebook, cyberstalking, cyber bullying, internet addictions and online gaming cybersex, social networking, romantic relations, online behaviors such as online dating, cyber sex, and cyber pornography. Etiological factors, risk factors, prevention and intervention of each problem are described in detail.

Chapter 7 concentrated on relation between Facebook use and wellbeing. Within the literature, Facebook has received much attention in order to understand the potential positive and negative effects associated with using the social networking site. The current chapter provides a discussion of the empirical support for the differential outcomes associated with actively posting and chatting on Facebook versus passively browsing Facebook, as well as the underlying mechanisms for the effects. Specifically, the current chapter discussed two perspectives related to the differential effects of active and passive Facebook use: Facebook Contentment (a well-being enhancing effect) and Facebook Depression (a well-being diminishing effect). The authors also discussed the extension of the results to other social media platforms and provide suggestions for future research.

The eighth chapter emphasized the problems related to cyberstalking. The term "cyberstalking" has been used to describe a variety of behaviors that involve repeated threats and/or harassment by the use of electronic mail or other computer-based communication that would make a reasonable person afraid or concerned for their safety. It is growing fast and creating problems especially psychologically. This paper mainly focused on is definition, typologies, characteristics of victims and offenders, forensic investigation and its prevention. The author concluded that there is not much agreement on the definition of cyberstalking as it appeared recently due to technological advancement. Many of the researches were conducted among university students and the prevalence of cyberstalking among general population and special groups are not much known but researches repeatedly confirmed it as growing issue. The information on vulnerable groups and individuals to cyberstalking is still at preliminary level as same as our understanding of offenders. Technical advancements and thorough knowledge on technical details among researchers from different backgrounds poses a big problem to its complete understanding and prevention. Future researches needs to focus on all these aspects.

Chapter 9 discussed about cyberbullying. It has become a major focus of not only youths, educators, and researchers, but also among the general population, due to high profile cases of cyberbullying victimization involving suicide and the increasing prevalence of these behaviors. The purpose of this chapter is to examine cyberbullying among children and adolescents, referred to as "youths" throughout the chapter. An extension of traditional bullying, cyberbullying is a form of bullying which takes place by means of electronic technologies, such as email, instant messaging, social networking websites, and text messaging through mobile devices. Drawing on research from a variety of disciplines, such as psychology, education, social work, sociology, and computer science, this chapter describes the definition of cyberbullying, the electronic technologies used, the prevalence rates, characteristics and risk factors, negative psychosocial and academic difficulties, theoretical frameworks, recommendations, and future directions. The chapter tried to cover various aspects related to cyberbullying.

Chapter 10 discussed in detail about internet addiction and online gaming. The excessive usage of internet and nature of its usage has soon found to be similar with psycho addictive substance addiction with similar neurobiological basis. Inclusion of gambling disorder into DSM 5 further strengthens the emerging concept of behavioral addiction. The author pointed out that various worldwide researches also supports the upsurge of such problem. The clinical presentation and management options are mostly based on the behavioral principles learned from the substance abuse problems, however large scale randomized trails and epidemiological studies are definitely the future need to understand this '21st century' problem.

The eleventh chapter discussed cybersex. It is often used as a collective term for all sorts of sexually-related entertainment, information and personal contact offers available in computer Networks respective "in cyberspace". It is also understood to be a computer-mediated interpersonal interaction in which the participants are sexually motivated, meaning they are seeking sexual arousal and satisfaction. Accordingly, based on the technical conditions under which it takes place, three forms of cybersex: virtual reality-based cybersex, video- based cybersex and text-based cybersex. From a technical perspective, two sub-forms of text-based cybersex are differentiated: tinysex and hot chat. This chapter focuses on various forms of cybersex from commercialization to self exhibitionism and voyeurism has been explained in terms of commercial and personal cyber sex aided by MUD. It is solely a social happening where solitary fantasizing and/or use of erotica do not have to include an active partner, but within the course of cybersexual interactions the participants must continually adapt to one another, they experience consent, rapport, and enthusiasm as well as rejection, misunderstanding or violation of personal boundaries. The chapter concludes with an evaluative view that despite being considered advantageous in recreative and imaginative alternative for sexual satisfaction, cybersex increases problems an individual goes through along with the family, friends and other relationships simultaneously elevating infidelity component in stable relationships. The individual is pronc to lose self-esteem which causes a wide range of other social problems such as guilt, low self-esteem and criminal activities of sexual origin.

The thirteenth focused on the romantic relationships, online dating and mental health issues. The chapter attempts to present the overview of mental health issues associated with online dating and online romantic relationships with relevant research background. Firstly it briefly cautions about the possible risks involved in the world of online dating platforms and later delves into mental health concerns that can emerge out of experiences while selecting a potential partner online, developing a romantic relationship and being involved in a romantic relationship online. It also discusses safety measures that need to be taken before and while being active on such online dating sites. The chapter draws attention to the specific role of mental health professionals that is needed while dealing with victims of online scams and abuse.

The fourteenth chapter focused on the Impact of online dating, cyber stalking, Cybersex and Pornography on mental health issues. Online behavior varies according to the purpose and situations and many get involved in intimate relations, like in online dating and it will have an impact on the person and his mental health especially interactions related to internet dating, cybersex, social networking relationships, and online gaming. The chapter focused on impact of online dating, cyber stalking, Cybersex and Pornography on mental health. Though many studied the online dating among adolescents and adults, that of old age group is not yet fully explored especially about their sexual needs. Internet plays lot many roles for gay and bisexual population and it is worth to explore factors related to risky sexual behaviors. Online dating for mentally ill people is an under researched area. It is important to explore how is it useful, how well it is affecting their treatment, relapse preventions and recovery, how do they reacts to break ups of online partners and their coping strategies and this will throw new lights on prevention and intervention strategies. Cyberstalking is an important issue especially among adolescents and young adults and how do they react to these situations are also equally important factor for vulnerability to mental illness. Cybersex and cyber pornography threats the safety and mental health in addition to the problems of addiction and child trafficking and it is linked with high sexual risk behaviors and sex crimes.

Online behaviors are prone to addictive disorders and other psychiatric comorbidities, hence it is necessary to develop tailored psychotherapeutic and pharmacological interventions by taking into account the complexity and heterogeneity of the problems. Future studies to intensify the search for understanding of online behaviors, its prevalence, causes and risks, prevention and interventions.

Chapter 15 dealt with the use of technology to promote virtual violence Prevention in higher education context. This chapter aimed to explore the pattern to use technology in particular way as an attempt to promote the virtual violence prevention. Literature review from referred journals and books was conducted. The findings reveal that technology use in particular effort to solve the emergence issues of violence entails to point out promoting the solution with an innovative approach designed in HE. With technology use in attempting violence prevention insights, any form in the issue of violence is needed an innovative way to strengthen technology use wisely with underlying the compassionate skills to promote the preventive action of violent forms. Attempts to promote virtual violence prevention in higher education context should be combined with empowering technology use to focus comprehensively on encouraging diverse learners with personal and social awareness in digital interaction. This chapter is expected to contribute in dealing with exploring the systematic approach in nurturing the self-awareness and social concern in digital interaction to be potentially applied in HE.

The research works cited in this book is referenced according to APA guidelines.

The target audience of this book is composed of professionals and researchers working in the mental health area such as clinicians (especially Psychiatrists, Clinical Psychologists, Pediatricians), academicians, special educators, social workers, Psychiatric nurses, rehabilitation centres, lawyers, and students in the area of mental health. It will be useful for Universities, hospitals, and the public. Moreover, this book will provide deep knowledge on various online behaviours and intimacy issues. I am hopeful that this book would be helpful to understand how cyber world and technology affects relationships, mental health and human behavior. The collection of fifteen chapters from researchers from eleven countries would definitely enrich our comprehensive understanding on intimacy and developing personal relationships in the Virtual world.

Acknowledgment

I express my heartfelt thanks to all authors, reviewers, and editorial members for their active contribution and collaboration to make this book a reality. I am especially thankful to team of IGI Global for the constant support and encouragement.

I thank my family members for being supportive. Special thanks to my son Hari Krishnan for his constant support, encouragement, and sacrifices.

Chapter 1
Changes in Online Subjectivity:
Artificial Users, Subject Fragmentarization, and Multimodal Interaction

Zdenek Smutny
University of Economics, Prague, Czech Republic

Vaclav Janoscik
Academy of Performing Arts in Prague, Czech Republic

ABSTRACT

Human subjectivity is deeply affected by the environment as mediated by the Internet. As users within this environment, people are not only affected by their entrance into it, but their subjectivity evolves along with the trends of online networking. The subjectivity of people is affected by (their networking with) human and artificial users of the environment and the possibility of influencing user's subjectivity is also given by other specific aspects of the environment. This chapter focuses on three areas: artificial users, subject and its fragmentarization, and multimodal interaction. Findings in conceptualizing change in terms of subjectivity are based within the poststructuralist philosophical tradition. There is applied the phenomenon known as the "death of the author," proclaimed in late 1960s, to the situation of the contemporary user to uncover changes in online subjectivity. The chapter also presents examples of implications of such changes at the level of interactions and distribution of messages and the role of artificial users in these processes within online marketing.

INTRODUCTION

The chapter springs from the cross-disciplinary intersection of informatics and philosophy. From this standpoint, the chapter provides a description of certain features present in online behaviours and relations within the context of the framework of subjectivity, as articulated in philosophy. Understanding of the subject is focused on its ability to create new environments and to become an agent in them. In the information society, the subject is connected with the massive development of information and communication technologies (ICT), including Internet-based technologies and services. This paper analyses and discusses the impact of these technologies on human life, both current and future, which finds itself in a new Internet-mediated environment.

DOI: 10.4018/978-1-5225-4047-2.ch001

The starting point of presented considerations is the philosophical approach to the subject and the reflection of these ideas in current ICT developments, including the adoption of these technologies by society. Conceptualizing the interrelation between the subject and the Internet-mediated online environment can orient us in today's socio-economical world, which is pervaded by the phenomenon of the Internet. On this basis, it is discussed socio-economic impacts of selected phenomena (e.g. fragmentarization or multimodality of interaction) that are associated with the subject and its environment. To present socio-economic consequences, examples from the field of online marketing were chosen.

The chapter is divided into several comprehensive sections. This section provides an introduction to the issue, including definitions of important terms used in the text of this chapter. The next section deals with the philosophical aspects of the subject. It is defined the subject of environment, its connection with the online or virtual environment (interaction), and possibilities of distribution and interpretation compared to such possibilities in the physical environment. On this basis, it is possible to identify the role of the Internet-based services (e.g. social media) user, both in its self-creation (subjectivity) and in its processing of communications, including further distribution through other services. It is also possible to present consequences in relevant field of online marketing in the third section. The conclusion summarizes the most interesting points and ideas.

DEFINITIONS OF IMPORTANT TERMS

The emergence of the information society represents an important qualitative shift, with significant implications for the future development of society. It was created new platform – it is a shared and continuously re-formed new environment designed for human and human made artificial agents (named e.g. software agents, softbots or simply bots). This environment is in various fields named in different ways, e.g.: cyberspace, online environment(s), Internet-mediated environment(s), virtual environment(s), virtual world(s). Each designation emphasizes another feature or aspect which is associated with a given environment. As appropriate designation for needs of this chapter was chosen virtual environment.

The most appropriate and sufficiently general explanation of this term is that it is an environment that consists of Internet-based services mediated by computers interconnected via networks (Internet). It is in accordance with a similar approach applies for virtual conversation, teams, products, organizations, etc. For example, virtual conversation is defined as communications that take place over computer networks, in which there is an essential element utilizing ICT for mediating such communications and cooperation among otherwise physically distant entities (Davidow, 1993; DeSanctis & Monge, 1999). Virtual conversation can be dynamically changed, e.g. resources can be added or removed according to the objective – so-called switching. (Mowshowitz, 1999; Mowshowitz & Kawaguchi, 2005). Virtual teams for instance, are formed as user-selected networks using the principle of switching. Relevant individuals are chosen while others are excluded, "switched off".

To summarize, the features of the virtual environment are as follows: It is an environment composed of various Internet-based services, which are mediated by ICT (including Internet). A clear definition is important, because the term itself is not strictly defined or established in the current literature (Schroeder, 2007), and might lead to confusion or conflation with other terms, such as cyberspace, virtual reality, virtuality, etc. Additional definitions of terms can be found at the end of the chapter in section *Key terms and definitions*.

For users, both human and artificial, it is used and promoted the common term subject. It can be preliminarily defined as an actor of relationships in the virtual environment (e.g. use of services, content creation, sharing and reproduction). The general conditions of the possibility of the existence and the behaviours of these actors form the concept of subjectivity. In the chapter are described the outlines and the transformation of these conditions in the current Internet-mediated virtual environment.

The chapter traces the concept of subject and subjectivity within the philosophical context, with special regard to insights, which can be seen as precursors of the virtual environment. It will be shown how this topic – including the unprecedented convergence of humans and artificial intelligence – is in certain sense anticipated by the philosophical treatment of subjectivity. What is presented as a subject can be provisionally defined as an agent (or user) within the environment, thus an entity with the capability of using, alternating or creating contents within a certain medial field, here represented by the virtual environment.

THEORETICAL BACKGROUND

From philosophical perspective, this chapter aims:

1. At introducing "the dispute over the subject" that will recapitulate recent developments of the concept. Such course of argument will also prevent oversimplification.
2. More specifically, the authors will argue against linear development of the subject. They reject both the simple, modern constitution of the concept (Enlightenment) and its alleged end (Postmodernity). Rather, this chapter will explain the deeper roots of the term itself and its ongoing persistence.
3. Nevertheless, what animates the issue most acutely with respect to the virtual environment is precisely the critique of the subject, which will be summarized mainly with respect to the mutual conditionality of the subject and its environment.
4. From this perspective, this intercommunity between agents and environment has importance in the context of language. It is in this context that the functional view of the reciprocal relationship between the subject and the virtual environment will be introduced.

The Dispute Over the Subject

The concept of the subject forms one of the key problems and never-ending controversies not only within the history of philosophy, but in other disciplines as well. This general dispute can be summarized with the help of Vincent Descombes, who, in his seminal monograph, describes it as "the European dispute over the subject" (Descombes, 2004). Despite its "awkward results," this debate still interacts with the grand theories of the Twentieth Century, such as analytic philosophy, phenomenology, existentialism, structuralism, and hermeneutics (Ricoeur, 1992). In the framework of this dispute one can distinguish "supporters" and "opponents" of the term subject. The latter tried to show how the subject is divided, fragmented, opaque and helpless. Therefore, they claim that the idea of the subject is entirely "fictitious". Meanwhile, the supporters of the concept, although generally accepting the critique of the subject`s dividedness or helplessness, still hold onto the concept as a necessary cornerstone of their theories and disciplines. The conclusion of this dialectic is an agreement on the side of the critique of a "transparent" or "sovereign" subject, and strife around its necessity or fictitiousness (Descombes, 2004). Aim of this chapter is precisely to take this dead end as a point of departure that can conceptualize the subject as both necessary and fictitious: a necessary fiction (Ricoeur, 1992; 1990). Therefore, it represents an agent that needs to be "necessarily" presupposed. Which means, on the other hand, that is fictive. It is presupposed so that one can conceive of its environment as something intentionally evolving, with respect not only to intentions as such, but moreover with respect to the agency of certain subjects.

Together with Descombes, one may in a certain sense situate present situation with respect to subject at the end of the "dispute over the subject". Such perspective accepts the critique of the subject but still maintains its role, however post-metaphysical or non-essential, e.g. as defined without any a priori inherent attributes. Its only condition is its ability to enter, form, and affect relationships with other subjects and act within such framework. This dynamic of the concept of the subject achieved its pinnacle within the postmodern or poststructuralist critique; therefore, one has to address the outcomes of this critique. Some of its positions rejected even this free possibility of entering into interaction in terms of the determinism of language, power or other structures (Barthes, 1977; Foucault, 1977). However, these critiques were known far earlier.

By reopening the "dispute over the subject" this chapter wants to present an alternative to some oversimplified conceptions concerning the notion's development. It differs firstly with the linear perspective, which posits the birth of subject (Enlightenment) and its death (Postmodernity). Such a dynamic may suggest the subject as a solely historically conditioned form, which had to be invented in Enlightenment or by modern science, later to have been outdated in the radical critique during 1960's. Yet, transformations of subjectivity are ongoing throughout the entire history of philosophy through series of nuanced steps, which cannot be simply identified as birth or death. However, despite positing this dynamic, one should not undermine the foundational acts (Aristotle, 1996; Judovitz, 1988; Kant, 2009) or the critical challenges (Barthes, 1977; Foucault, 1977; Deleuze & Guattari 1994).

Where does the subject as a philosophical term come from? Alain de Libera in his grand project *Archéologie du sujet* (Libera, 2007; 2008) is maps precisely this "birth of the subject". He rejects the notion of a discontinuity between the modern idea of the subject and previously-existing, traditions present in the Middle Ages. Contrarywise, he traces its development in a terminological shift that had taken place within the Second Scholastic Period. Specifically, this profound change in Latin word *subjectum* takes place in the work of Thomas Aquinas. Originally in Latin works this term had been a translation of Aristotle`s term *hypokeimenon*, which means a passive base. In the Greek tradition, it was conceived of as an important metaphysical element, a material predisposition of all things, as opposed to substance, which manifests an active form of things. Each object had to have its base, *hypokeimenon*, to which other elements were attributed. But exactly because of this process of attribution the term subject shifts to the field of theory of soul and theory of agency. The problem of scholastic is: to what can we "attribute" the ability of action, the capacity to initiate the causal nexus. The subject seemed to be the answer.

Similarly to the birth, the end – or more emphatically the death – of the subject needs to be unveiled. The authors here contend that it does not form a specific event in the linear scheme; rather, it presents the pinnacle of certain tendencies, which have been inherent to the notion since far earlier in its development. One can exemplify this with reference to Foucault's attack on the subject (Foucault, 1977), respectively on the author (Burke, 2008) and the human (Foucault, 2012). This attack is a particular critique of certain hidden presuppositions and transformations of the concept and not a wholesale liquidation of authorship or the subject itself (Derrida, 1991). Such critique of the term (regardless of whether it is from the structuralist or poststructuralist position) does not mean its elimination, but rather a utilization of its division, fragmentarization, opacity, or lack of freedom.

Critique of the Subject

Let us examine the critique in detail. Although profoundly revised (Libera, 2007), it initiated other philosophical developments of the term, as an example one can think of diverse accounts of environment determinism. Generally, postmodernity endeavoured to grasp a new position for the human being, within the actual reality and intellectual development of Western societies. In the Structuralist scope the subject was even determined by the grid of meaning formed by language, power, or otherwise (Barthes, 1977; Foucault, 1977). In their view any message is coded within this framework, which preconditions any meaning we wish to express and any action we want to take. This thesis is revised within the post-structuralist stage of the critique. It attempts to introduce a dialectical relationship between the subject and its environment. For Roland Barthes, the interrelation finds its expression in the in transferability of the individual (subject) to the general (structure) (Barthes, 1981). Another break from the Postmodern perspective is presented by the theory of communicative action, developed by Jürgen Habermas (Habermas, 1985), or the hermeneutics of the subject (Ricoeur, 1992; Gadamer, 2004). The most radical attitude towards the problem of subject seems to be speculative realism and even more particularly object-oriented ontology (Harman, 2013), which aims at equalizing all the things in our world as objects, completely omitting the position of any subject. In this case the relationship between the subject and its environment is fundamentally overturned. Generally speaking, from perspective of these conceptualizations the individual is emancipated from and non-reducible to the general, be it either structure or environment. Nonetheless, as a concept, conditioning by the environment has not disappeared; it has been shifted to more nuanced efforts to unmask apparatuses of power (Foucault, 1975) or the logocentrism of our culture (Derrida, 1997), both of which structure our thought and action.

The outcomes of this "dispute over the subject" can, in this perspective, be summarized as conversion between the deterministic relation and mutual conditioning. The subject, therefore, is conditioned by language and/or environment in its ability to act and communicate. But, conversely, the environment and the world in general reflect the nature and possibilities of the individuals (e.g. subjects). Hence one can return to the initial recourse of Vincent Descombes: the subject is a necessary fiction, which is to say that the concept is essential for forming the environment, which by its nature is defined as a user-based environment. On the other hand, the subject itself has no solid or essential basis; it is not defined as existing for itself, but only within its relation to its environment.

Following section aims to show how the virtual environment appropriately fits the conceptual perspective developed above. Subjects of the virtual environment are necessary elements in forming a defining that sphere. But also, they are not simply given as such. Today we are uncertain whether they represent human or artificial users; they are qualified merely by their ability to act in the virtual environment.

Interrelation Between the Subject and the Environment

The major aspect of the critique in question here was influenced by the so-called linguistic turn (Habermas, 1994; Burns, 2002; Seigel, 1994). One can exemplify this relation with the structuralist recourse to language as a determining grid, only within which meaning or a subject is possible. The poststructuralists, and even the postmodernists, aim in the opposite direction: they support the radical irreducibility of the particular-subject as individual to the general-subject as role.

This controversy between subject and language (environment) can be summarized or even reconciled with help of Czech philosopher Zdenek Vasicek and his post-mortem book, *How are the philosophies being formed*. He argues that language is a static basis of speech (parole), which includes individual choice, accent, hierarchization, and interpretation. Thus, it is connected with the subject (and) the individual (Vasicek, 2012). Language in his reckoning is in no way a structuralistic determinant, nor does it accord with the poststructuralistic firm rejection of transferability of particular subject and general environment. Vasicek forms the interconnection functionally; the subject chooses, accents, hierarchizes, and interprets. That does not mean s/he controls the language. The relation of subject to language (or subject to environment) is, in practice of course, supra-individual, unconscious and, moreover, dialectical. That means that if we consider ourselves as part of a whole, our position and relations within the framework will form our identity (Vasicek, 2012). This conception of interrelation between subject and environment naturally follows various theories focused on their interdependency; consider, for instance, Deleuze and Guattari with their geophilosophy or Foucault's term, heterotopia (Deleuze & Guattari 1994; Foucault, 1984).

In this respect the authors of this chapter aim at attaining a perspective on the virtual environment by reviewing a particular philosophical tradition. To be specific, it has been already unveiled how important it is not only to omit any essential definitions of the subject, but also how appropriate it is to define it with respect to its position within the environment. This attitude can be considered as a necessary condition for tracing, and comparing the interactions between artificial and human users.

This section summarizes the issue with reference to the mutual constitution of the subject and its environment. Our identification with the aforementioned framework directs us to hypothesize that our subjectivity is changed within the development of the environment. As users, we are affected by a plurality of relations (e.g. fragmentarization, multimodal interaction) and by new subjects entering into these relations.

It should be apparent by now how useful this metaphilosophy (e.g. the critique of philosophical language) is to the study of the virtual environment, especially with respect to the problem of artificial users. More precisely, the perspective of Zdenek Vasicek is of significant importance to the whole concept of subjectivity in virtual environment. The virtual environment has topology like network and the environment is dynamically construed through the interaction of its users. On the other hand, the subject itself is formed through its position within the environment and is thus influenced by perspectives of other users. Users move in circles, where articulation is superseded by determination, which always is already a re-determination. Figure 1 shows the reflection of philosophical ideas into the technological understanding of the relationship between user and the virtual environment of the network.

Figure 1. Relationship between subject and environment at the philosophical and technological level
Source: Authors.

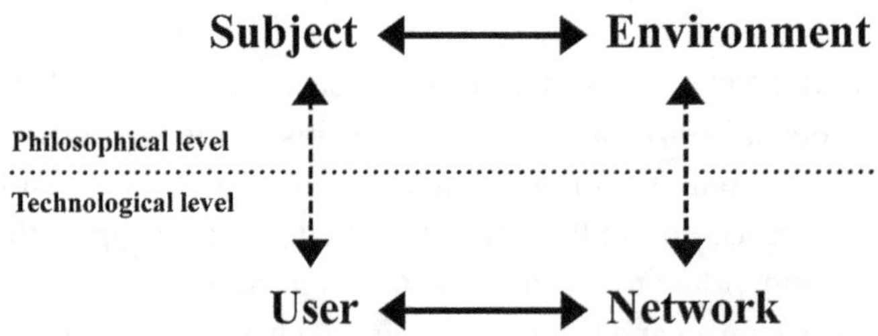

ONLINE SUBJECTIVITY

In the previous section is made an excursion into the evolution of approaches towards the subject in philosophy and development of subjectivity. This section deal with these various approaches, conceptualizing the subject further with respect to the human-constituted environment, where a qualitative change has led to the application of ICT to human life. In sociology arose broad field of Science, Technology and Society (STS) in 1980s that brings together several theories, which build on poststructuralist philosophical tradition and allow to model the relationship between human and technology. Individual theories differ in particular understanding of what or who may be denoted as a subject or focus on a relationship of subject and object and significance of the environment (system) in shaping the relationship.

The STS deals with social structures that affect technological development and also how these technologies affect the social structures. Examples of such (social) constructivist frameworks are well-known approaches such as Actor-Network Theory (ANT) and the Social Construction of Technology (SCOT) from late 1980s or Social Shaping of Technology (SST) from 1990s (Williams & David, 1996; Latour, 1987; Trevor & Bijker, 1986). In the 1990s, these theories and concepts also inspired other fields such as informatics, which overlaps with the following fields: information systems, information technology, computer science and information science (Gammack, Hobbs, & Pigott, 2006). The Western concept of social informatics in its early stages builds on similarly constructed strategies or approaches to modeling sociotechnical interaction (Kling, 2000; Smutny, 2016) and sociotechnical research (Davenport, 2008).

This chapter does not want to deal with the problems of the interaction of society and technology, which is both theoretically and practically extensively addressed, even in discourses mentioned above. Rather, the authors want to address solely the issue of subjectivity in the newly-constructed virtual environment. In the following discussion authors' point of view starts with the interactions that occur in this environment and their features.

There is a need to move away from an intuitive point of view that explicitly deals with the human on one side and the artificial on the other, where the latter is seen as a tool. The goal of this section is to place the artificial – human-created – into a new position. But the authors do not want to go as far as ANT, which formed a heterogeneous network of actors (e.g. humans, ideas, organizations, products); rather, the authors aim to present a homogeneous network of interacting subjects in the environment of Internet-based services (e.g. social media, multimodal online navigation, mobile application, web portal), including both human and artificial agents, while preserving the relationship between the subject and object. Therefore, the authors argue for a convergence of human and artificial agents in the virtual environment; which is to say, their equivalence at the level of interaction and being in this environment. Our subject within the environment is not only human (which is the currently preferred view); with an eye to the future, it is increasingly necessary to emphasize the role of artificial agents and their equivalence with humans with regard to interactions in this environment. This shift in the stage of development of online subjectivity will be presented in this section. In addition, it is highlighted issues associated with the fragmentarization of the subject in this environment, including a comparison with philosophical aspects of the concept of subject and the related implications for the socio-economic environment.

The Convergence of Human and Artificial Users in the Virtual Environment

From the time when man first created machines, he desired that these machines be intelligent and therefore close to man. Since the 1950's we have witnessed the development of artificial intelligence as a field of study. Initial optimism that such machines (robots) would be able to think or at least act like people (Darrach, 1970; Eason, 2014) was replaced by more nuanced conceptualizations of limited intelligence, where the "intelligent" behaviour of the machine is restricted by the environment (for example, robots can behave intelligently only in the artificial environment of the laboratory). Therefore, machines are, as of yet, not able to interact to the same extent as man in the physical environment (reality). This issue is addressed at the transdisciplinary level by cognitive science. Its efforts are predominantly associated with machines in the physical environment (in which the biological human resides) or man-modified environments (e.g. cities, factories).

With the development of ICT and wide-spread internet accessibility, however, implicitly comes a new qualitative jump in the form of a new artificial environment: the virtual environment. This shared environment unites its users (agents, actors) in a new way: it is common to both man and machine (as both humans and software alike use Internet-based services) and also creates a superstructure upon the physical environment. This has been achieved thanks to proximity of cognitive abilities of both types of users in the virtual environment. On the one hand, there is a man who is "cognitively cut" (e.g. he is limited by the capabilities of the service and computer-mediated communications) and is immersed in the level of weak virtuality – see (Horrocks, 2000); on the other hand, there is, for example, a bot (artificial user) cognitively adapted to the environment, because the bot as well as the environment is created by man, and these creations are not diametrically different with respect to their complexity. It can be said that human and artificial users in the virtual environment are closest, in terms of the results of their interactions. This is, of course, not a full equivalence; yet, it does represent the closest proximity in terms of the possibilities of the users and their resulting behaviors.

Despite these conclusions, the two types of users possess different interface of the environment, although the resulting behavior may be equivalent. While the human sees and accesses the Internet-based service through the (graphical) user interface (UI), the artificial user accesses it either via an application programming interface (API) or via the UI, in the form of the return code from the server. Access to certain services is adapted to the cognitive capabilities of its users, but the resulting change in the level of service is the same. Human users access graphical interface of diverse services (e.g. via web browser). On the other hand artificial users process the code itself (e.g. HTML, XML) mediated through the service (e.g. via API). It is obvious that with the development of internet technologies (web semantization towards Web 3.0) there exist just these efforts to include artificial users in the virtual environment and open them up to new opportunities for interaction.

In the philosophical tradition, the subject is not a certain substance; rather, it is fragmented and conditioned by its environment. It is enclosed in a constant cycle of redetermination: subject inside the environment and vice versa the environment within the subject. In a similar manner new media theorist employ fluid ontology in order to outline the interdependence and non-substantiality of objects within virtual worlds (Manovich, 2001). On general level this course of argument can be summarized as extending these theories to the field of our online subjectivity.

The virtual environment is created by the interaction/communication of its users, which also determines these users as their subjects. Enaction approach emphasizes how the subject enacts its own situation in the environment in which it interacts. The subject in the virtual environment also changes, fragmenting its behavior according to the service that it currently uses. Both human and artificial users meet all of these criteria; for example a bot can use diverse Internet-based services, take specific (preprogramed) position within. Thus these bots involve their own identity that defines their action.

In this section were presented two arguments (cognitive – the equivalence of performed actions, thus cognitive abilities; and philosophical – the issue of fragmentarization and the related dialectics of actor-environment mutual redetermination) stressing the similarities in behavior of human and artificial users. On this basis, it is possible to identify the subjects of the virtual environment, because there are parallels with the above philosophical approaches to the subject. More specifically, it can be point out that within virtual environment it cannot be ignored that artificial users enter the environment, whether it in form of user or organizer of environment content. It is obvious that subject`s ability to act in the environment (e.g. produce, use, and mediate contents) is an essential for defining the subject of virtual environment.

Multimodal Interaction of Subjects

The subject stirs within the virtual environment, which consists of Internet-based services – limited worlds with their own rules and delineated courses of actions. Particular services are restricted for specific sorts of users (e.g. communication via specific API for artificial users; professional orientation of Internet-based service to specific group of human users). This reflects not only the divide between humans and artificial users but also their individual properties (for instance age, specialization, and knowledge of the environment). Given the plurality of such intersecting fields it is apparent how the concept of the fragmentized subject is at work here. With reference to Vincent Descombes, it can be posited that precisely this idea of the fragmentized subject is can be considered the denouement of Twentieth Century philosophy.

While the phenomenon of the construction of personal identities online is somewhat salient (Floridi, 2011; Elwell, 2014), our inquiry is focused solely on subjectivity, where there are important and implicit multimodal interactions that apply equally for human and artificial users. Thinking about subjectivity in the virtual environment, it can be noted that contemporary human users are in situation where anybody can acquire not only different but completely disparate roles and even identities within the numerous of Internet-based services (in each service they can represent someone else, or they can even possess multiple profiles in a single network). Moreover, this identity can be undertaken as imagined, fabricated or even forged according to the options that a particular service allows – human cannot, for instance, realize telepresence via Twitter and this feature along with all other possibilities of the service conditions our interaction within the channel.

The nature of the service is not the only basis of such fragmentarization. The diversity of intentions motivating users to join certain services leads to additional plurality of online identities, which correspond to diversified identities that the users have already acquired in their lives outside the virtual environment. The management of identities require diverse modes of agency within different services, such as full frame networks (e.g. Facebook, Google), professional groups (e.g. LinkedIn, Academia.edu), dating services (e.g. Badoo), and last but not least social bookmarking services (e.g. Reddit, Digg). Figure 2 shows mentioned view coming from the platform toward the individual Internet-based services.

From what is observed, it can be coined the term multimodal interaction. Subjects are dragged into dissociated fields where they establish different identities and thus frameworks of multimodal interactions. Thus, this mere possibility evolves into a necessity on the part of human users. With respect to artificial users it might be tempted to subdue their agency and whole existence to the intention of their

Figure 2. Each platform (e.g. made by Apple, Google, Microsoft) offers its own ways of interacting through the interface. These interfaces are used by individual Internet-based services and determine which users will use particular service. Human user uses multiple services across platforms, and his or her subjectivity is influenced by the environment of each service and its users (subjects of the environment including bots).
Source: Authors.

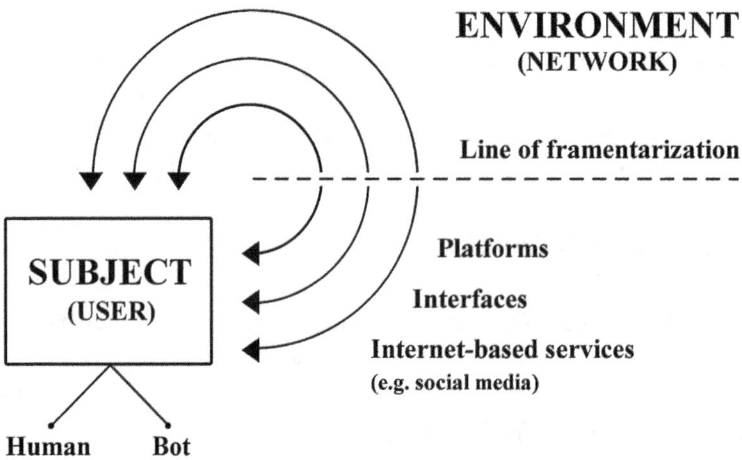

creator (generally human). This view may further lead us to grasp them as mere instruments expanding our communication, like the web browser does. Indeed, there is initial intention behind created bots. Nonetheless, it is obvious that their interactions do not purely replicate their original setup, but rather involve communication and agency of its own, very often indistinguishable from those of human users. Characteristic examples of such self-standing activities run by bots are algorithms based on machine learning. That means there are artificial subjects, who can themselves change or set anew relevant operations according to interaction in course of time – see also (Caschera, D'Ulizia, Ferri, & Grifoni, 2012).

Now it can be seen that the initial intention is realized within regular communication in the networks inhabited by humans as well as bots. In other words, we are trapped in a loop where we fabricate artificial means of communication, but on the other hand these "instruments" are operating within the process of communication, thus obtaining the status of subjects. Moreover, from the cognitive perspective their potential agency is very close to that of human users. Finally, not even subjugation to someone else's intention is the criterion for principal difference between artificial and human users. It can be seen in the case of a person's identity being stolen (Moncura, Orzecha, & Nevilleb, 2016), where even human users can be turned into instruments of other subject's intentions.

Illustrative Examples of Socio-Economic Consequences in the Field of Online Marketing

Multimodality of interactions, which is a product of the fragmentarization of the subject, solidifies the previously argued equivalence of human and artificial users of Internet-based services. This raises crucial questions about activities in the socio-economic environment. These questions revolve around a central ambiguity: between users that companies want to address and those who are actually addressed.

This has implications for our assessment concerning online interaction and subjectivity (e.g. whether we are dealing with human or artificial user, or who is the originator of the meaning). This problem will only be exacerbated with ongoing web semantization (Web 3.0). It involves deepening the availability of virtual environment to artificial actors.

These contemporary conditions considerably affect communication in virtual environment, concerning not only individuals but also organizations, whose decisions have an impact on the socio-economic environment. So, companies are faced with basic questions that require new responses and an associated new view of the environment, which is constantly evolving and combining the human and the artificial, resulting in a new quality. Several of those questions are as follows:

- What kind of interactions do companies deal with?
- Which aspects of these interactions would they like to evaluate?
- Whom do the companies want to address with their communications (e.g. marketing) in the virtual environment?

In a physical environment, the human is the only agent or subject – all attention is focused on him, no matter whether it is positioned on the level of marketing management or marketing activities themselves. However, based on presented discussion of the essence of the subject in the virtual environment, there is a fundamental change – an artificial agent can be also proclaimed as a subject of this environment. For example, according to the study (Chu, Gianvecchio, Wang, & Jajodia, 2010), bots initiated 14% of the total amount of communication on Twitter and a further 37.5% were assisted by bots (bot-assisted human or human-assisted bot). It can be expected that this trend will continue. In addition, recognizing artificial and human actor is not trivial (Schmitz Yanenko, & Hebing, 2012; Laukyte, 2017).

Marketing activities are most often evaluated via Internet, where artificial agents process data collection in order to manage these activities. There is much malpractice in the obtaining of data for decision-making or for the marketing activities (e.g. harvesting of private user data, spreading of /mis/ information) (Boshmaf, Muslukhov, Beznosov, & Ripeanu, 2013). In these cases, the human is unwittingly replaced with an artificial agent for the purpose of fulfilling the will of someone else. Once in the service of another party, the victim's identity (or identities in multiple services) is then misused, for example, by the dissemination of certain compromising messages, initiating a specific action (botnet attack), or a continuous acquisition of personal data of close friends for financial gain. In some cases it is very difficult to distinguish actions performed by the human and artificial users. There is the overall reason for the tension and dubiety of subject in virtual environment.

It is important to recognize the radical change in (the perception of) subjectivity that human and artificial users that use Internet-based services are undergoing. The message, which is being communicated online, is no longer dependent on its producer but rather on the subsequent interpretation by a subject in this environment. Moreover, the web contents are conditioned by interactions across different services, where such communication is distributed and where each service creates unique set of possibilities. Consider as an example familiar situation where particular messages are extended by comments and discussion or forwarding channels, where their meaning can be influenced or even reversed – see Appendix. But hierarchization of network contacts, ads reflecting personal data of a user, using cookies or even tagging and bookmarking are also instances of interpretive and distributive function.

The producer (e.g. the subject in a particular Internet-based service) in fact does not produce the content or original meaning of a message, which is further communicated to other subjects in other services. Rather such production becomes a distributional and interpretative function, which determines and delimits the audience and therefore the potential spreading of the communication. For example, reactions to a particular message/communication within a particular service (e.g. Facebook) determine (and limit) its recipients, both human and artificial, and the potential for the spread of communication, in the sense that both types of users effectively become distribution mechanisms independent on the original author. Thus, users can spread and change the message by other channels and services, in the same manner in which bots can be programed to redirect or multiply certain contents or even instrumentalized human users can disseminate certain information, as exemplified by the phenomenon of click farms. Each of these distribution agents (re)determines again the possible recipients and also creates new interpretive possibilities, by means of supplementation or reinterpretation (e.g. retweet with additional content) – see Appendix.

There is a fundamental misunderstanding concerning the subjectivity within virtual environment. Companies manage their marketing activities based on an evaluation of the interaction of all users, but they want to target only the human user who possesses and controls financial resources. However, in this evaluation they use inappropriate data concerning subjects. Misinterpretation that comes to our mind as first consists in confusing the online subject with human users, while, as have been already argued, in fact they inhere bots as well. Companies attempt to target people across services (Facebook, Twitter, Google, Adwords, etc.) on the basis of the data obtained. They completely disregard the amount of artificial agents that have significant influence on marketing strategies. One of the few remarks in this respect may be found in the work (Srnicek, 2017) of political theorist Nick Srnicek.

Companies are spending ineffectively when they cannot differentiate between prospective customers and bots, between authentic preferences and mere click fraud, when they evaluate relevant interaction (sharing rate, number of views, presence, click rate, feedback, number of fans and many other statistics). Ad campaigns are targeting also artificial users without any prospective of financial or symbolic profit. Spreading their online contents through fraud channels might be even harmful to their marketing (e.g. when unintentionally using click farms the contents are viewed only to their fraud contacts, moreover in case of Facebook these clicks cannot be removed by the original user who posted the ad or other content).

Change of perspective consists in the fact that companies should target not only for a certain group of people (human users), but also a certain group of artificial users (e.g. search bots). The reason of this is the ability of artificial users of Internet-based services being subject of the virtual environment and thus change the subjectivity of other subjects, including human users. It can be seen, that even artificial user can influence the decisions of man (e.g. on what website navigate) and also to be part of (and to build) his or her "social" network within fragmented human user communicates.

Due to the constitution of the subject in the virtual environment and its consequences vis-à-vis the socio-economic activities of man, it is necessary to grasp this environment from inside and shift our implicit understanding of the subject as it still heavily relies on the physical world, where important agents (users, actors) are only people. There is a need to raise general awareness towards artificial agents, see also (Guilbeault, 2016). Their presence profoundly affects our behaviour and even our online subjectivity in virtual environment.

Besides implications for commercial activities in the environment of Internet-based services, it can be pointed to other related issues affecting agents, such as collaboration between human agents in this environment (Bainbridge, 2012), ethical issues (Laukyte, 2017; Schroeder, 2007), or the challenges of multimodal human-computer interaction (Turk 2014; Jaimesa & Nicu, 2007).

CONCLUSION

The chapter focused on the interactions that take place within virtual environment, as well as man's coexistence with contemporary ICT. The authors grounded their analysis philosophically with help of certain dominant theories of subjectivity, illuminating the mutual character constituting both subject and environment. Such course of thought permitted them to conceptualize current conditions of virtual environment by emphasizing the role of the subject and its constitution. From this perspective, it is introduced artificial users, usually referred to as bots. In the core of the argumentation the authors argued against their conceptualization as mere instruments. While, conversely, elevating their status to subject, the authors offered two arguments; the first is based on the cognitive abilities of human and artificial users in this environment and the second on the necessary philosophical predisposition of the subject as such.

The authors consider ongoing changes in online subjectivity as landmark turnover in coexistence of the human his and technology. This major shift can be seen in respect to the proximity of human and artificial users in this environment, not only in terms of activities performed but also with respect to cognitive capabilities, e.g. the possibility of intelligent behaviour of both users in the environment. Furthermore, concerning the problem of the constitution of the subject within the virtual environment, the authors advanced the notion of the fragmentarization based in multimodal interaction and the resulting implications, which will be important for subsequent developments of ICT and its role in society.

The chapter endeavoured to exemplify this issue within the realm of online marketing. Here it can be already observed the growing importance of artificial users, namely the increased amount of interaction assisted, controlled or generated by bots. Despite this rise, bots are still not considered as subjects (by organizations or managers) and are therefore regarded with insufficient attention. More precisely the companies are focused on bots in terms of marketing and spreading their advertisement but they don't take the artificial agents into account as prospective users (to whom they direct their marketing or about whom they mine user data and evaluate them). From standpoint of this chapter, it is apparent that we need to take into account different types of subjects, including bots, when considering agency within the virtual environment. It can occur to misrepresenting of evaluation on the basis of past interactions, which are affected by artificial users of Internet-based services, that do not provide any value for the company. On the other hand, there are also artificial users that can be important for online marketing activities (e.g. search bots), because they influence subjectivity of human users.

This course of action inheres the presumption of multimodality of interaction (and fragmentarization). It provides us with new dynamic concerning subjectivity tied to the environment and the user as its interpretation and distribution mechanism. As a result, it should be aware of potential miscommunication (e.g. an action in a particular service addressing an inappropriate subject), and of the interpretative role of both human and artificial users.

It is apparent that the possibilities of subjectivity in the virtual environment are fundamentally evolving. Changes are taking place not only in relation to other media, but also within its own logic. Let us express the radical nature of this transformation with the help of a historical parallel. At the end of 1960s, profound intellectual and social changes urged a rethinking of the very subjectivity of the writer and author. The medium of literature and, to some extent, the creation of meaning as such were no longer seen as the domain of authorial intentionality, but rather as a sphere of its absence. Roland Barthes asserts that the author does not create, but rather records the story, the meaning of which is controlled by the reader (Barthes, 1977). Similarly Michel Foucault, although his object of study is precisely the authorial function, also fundamentally challenges the very meaning of the text and the author's power over it (Foucault, 1977). Both Foucault and Barthes proclaimed in the late 1960s the famous "death of the author". From a contemporary perspective, it can be understood the rhetorical momentum of this concept: it is not the destruction of the author's position; rather, it is a radical change of how can be think about the conditions surrounding the entity acting as the author.

In a parallel to this moment of intellectual history, it can be proposed to echo this theme by forwarding the "death of the user". In this way the authors want to underline the seriousness and the possible consequences of changes that the authors have noticed in the development of user subjectivity: the rise of artificial users and their intelligence (in a restricted environment), which not only can create imitations and alternatives to human users, but through communication interfaces and other mechanisms shapes our own communication in the virtual environment; the multimodality of user interaction within the field of Internet-based services; the related fragmentarization of identities; and tensions between concurrent media channels. These are the practices and trends that inspired us to rethink the implicitly shared ideas about online subjectivity of users. Against traditional conception of usership it can be argued that they, the users, cannot be defined by free interaction with the meaning and content they communicate through the various Internet-based services. There are not those who simply "use" these services. Rather they enter complex web of relationships that have decisive power over their options and actual decisions, in which they have to deal with rising role of artificially processed and even created contents.

Nonetheless, contemporary human and artificial agents still retain certain "user" roles, which potentially connect different services by providing a self-identical subject, similar to the way Foucault sees the author as merely a mechanism of distribution and interpretation of texts. Paralleling Foucault, it can be concluded that the traditional "user" (e.g. human agent who engage in the free production and distribution of online contents) is essentially dead. This death, however, does not mean the non-existence of users and authors, as Foucault and Barthes also argued. Rather, it only means to indicate the extent of the fundamental shifts in online subjectivity.

The community of users flooded by posts, shares, retweets or likes depreciates any information ("Medium is message"). "Death of the user" might be indeed certain recreation of an author. Nonetheless he is not to become new individual creator of authoritative meaning. He must incline to the fragmentized nature of the environment; his distributional (rather than creative) function; and he definitely will involve artificial users to certain extent. From our point of view the online subjectivity in the virtual environment does not need new options for the user. It strives for redefinition or clarification of authorial position.

The authors course of argument involves many prospective directions for further research. What the authors tried to establish in this chapter is conceptual basis within the cross-disciplinary intersection of philosophy and informatics. It is essential for all such endeavors to elaborate a notion of subjectivity and its constitution within the field of the virtual environment that includes consideration of its fragmentarization, multimodal interaction, and the problem of artificial users. On such grounds, the subject is conceptualized non-substantially. On one hand it is necessary for carefully considering the nature of the virtual environment, as it essentially is a user-based environment. Online subjectivity is increasingly becoming to be connected with artificial users, thus it is becoming fictive. Therefore, it can be concluded it to be a necessary fiction, a term that can be viewed as a major benefit to the philosophical tradition summarized above. On a practical level, this renewed concept revises evaluation of artificial users and the resulting socio-economic implications. If marketing, for instance, aims to deal with subject-buyers, they would benefit from an underlying theoretical background for assessing whom they engage with. More specifically, a new conception of the online subject can provide insight into the nature of online interactions (e.g. identifying fake interactions), and, on the other hand, it can suggest more nuanced models of the distributive and interpretative potential of users (for example sharing patterns within social networks). New and changing conditions of online subjectivity are promoting new forms, conditions and relationships for respective subjects.

REFERENCES

Aristotle. (1999). *Nicomachean Ethics*. Indianapolis, IN: Hackett Publishing.

Bainbridge, W. S. (2012). eAnarchy. *Futures*, *44*(9), 823–831. doi:10.1016/j.futures.2012.07.003

Barthes, R. (1977). *Image-Music-Text*. London: Fontana Press.

Barthes, R. (1981). *Camera Lucida*. New York: Hill and Wang.

Boshmaf, Y., Muslukhov, I., Beznosov, K., & Ripeanu, M. (2013). Design and analysis of a social botnet. *International Journal of Computer and Telecommunications Networking*, *57*(2), 556–578. doi:10.1016/j.comnet.2012.06.006

Burke, S. (2008). *The Death and Return of the Author: Criticism and Subjectivity in Barthes, Foucault and Derrida*. Edinburg, UK: Edinburg University Press.

Burns, R. M. (2002). Language, tradition, and the self in the generation of meaning. *History of European Ideas*, *28*(1-2), 51–75. doi:10.1016/S0191-6599(02)00008-6

Caschera, M. C., D'Ulizia, A., Ferri, F., & Grifoni, P. (2012). Towards Evolutionary Multimodal Interaction. In P. Herrero, H. Panetto, R. Meersman, & T. Dillon (Eds.), *On the Move to Meaningful Internet Systems: OTM 2012 Workshops*. Berlin: Springer; doi:10.1007/978-3-642-33618-8_80

Chu, Z., Gianvecchio, S., Wang, H., & Jajodia, S. (2010). Who is tweeting on Twitter: human, bot, or cyborg? In *Proceedings of the 26th Annual Computer Security Applications Conference* (pp. 21-30). New York: ACM. 10.1145/1920261.1920265

Darrach, B. (1970). Meet Shaky: The first electronic person. *Life Magazine*, *69*(21), 58B–68B.

Davenport, E. (2008). Social informatics and sociotechnical research – a view from the UK. *Journal of Information Science*, *34*(4), 519–530. doi:10.1177/0165551508091011

Davidow, W. H., & Michael, S. M. (1993). *The Virtual Corporation: Structuring and Revitalizing the Corporation for the 21st Century*. New York: Harper Business.

Day, R. E. (2011). Death of the User: Reconceptualizing Subjects, Objects, and Their Relations. *Journal of the Association for Information Science and Technology*, *62*(1), 78–88. doi:10.1002/asi.21422

Deleuze, G., & Guattari, F. (1994). *What is Philosophy?* London: Verso.

Derrida, J. (1991). "Eating Well," or the Calculation of the Subject. In E. Cadava, P. Connor, & J. L. Nancy (Eds.), *Who comes after subject* (pp. 96–119). New York: Routlege.

Derrida, J. (1997). *Of Grammatology*. Baltimore, MD: Johns Hopkins University Press.

DeSanctis, G., & Monge, P. (1999). Introduction to the Special Issue: Communication Processes for Virtual Organizations. *Organization Science*, *10*(6), 693–703. doi:10.1287/orsc.10.6.693

Descombes, V. (2004). *Le Complément de Sujet, Enquête sur le fait d'agir de soi-même*. Paris: Gallimard.

Eason, K. (2014). Afterword: The past, present and future of sociotechnical systems theory. *Applied Ergonomics*, *45*(2), 213–220. doi:10.1016/j.apergo.2013.09.017 PMID:24183568

Elwell, S. J. (2014). The transmediated self: Life between the digital and the analog. *Convergence (London)*, *20*(2), 233–249. doi:10.1177/1354856513501423

Floridi, L. (2011). The Construction of Personal Identities Online. *Minds and Machines*, *21*(4), 477–479. doi:10.100711023-011-9254-y

Foucault, M. (1975). *Discipline and Punish: the Birth of the Prison*. New York: Random House.

Foucault, M. (1977). What is an Author? In D. F. Bouchard (Ed.), *Language, Counter-Memory, Practice* (pp. 124–127). New York: Cornell University Press.

Foucault, M. (1984). Of Other Spaces, Heterotopias. *Architecture, Mouvement, Continuité*, *5*, 46–49.

Foucault, M. (2012). *Order of Things*. London: Routlege.

Gadamer, H. G. (2004). *Truth and Method*. London: Continuum.

Gammack, J., Hobbs, V., & Pigott, D. (2006). *The Book of Informatics*. South Melbourne: Thomson.

Guilbeault, D. (2016). Growing Bot Security: An Ecological View of Bot Agency. *International Journal of Communication*, *10*, 5003–5021.

Habermas, J. (1985). The Theory of Communicative Action: Vol. 1. *Reason and the Rationali-zation of Society*. Boston: Beacon Press.

Habermas, J. (1994). Philosophy and Science as Literature? In J. Habermas (Ed.), *Postmetaphysical Thinking: Philosophical Essays* (pp. 205-228). MIT Press.

Harman, G. (2013). *Tool-Being: Heidegger and the Metaphysics of Objects*. Chicago: Open Court.

Horrocks, C. (2000). *Marshall McLuhan and virtuality*. Cambridge: Icon Books.

Jaimesa, A., & Nicu, S. (2007). Multimodal human–computer interaction: A survey. *Computer Vision and Image Understanding*, *108*(1-2), 116–134. doi:10.1016/j.cviu.2006.10.019

Judovitz, D. (1988). *Subjectivity and representation in Descartes: The origins of modernity*. Cambridge, UK: Cambridge University.

Kant, I. (2009). *An Answer to the Question: What is Enlightenment?* London: Penguin.

Kling, R. (2000). Learning About Information Technologies and Social Change: The Contribution of Social Informatics. *The Information Society*, *16*(3), 217–232. doi:10.1080/01972240050133661

Latour, B. (1987). *Science in action: How to follow scientists and engineers through society*. Cambridge, MA: Harvard University Press.

Laukyte, M. (2017). Artificial agents among us: Should we recognize them as agents proper? *Ethics and Information Technology*, *19*(1), 1–17. doi:10.100710676-016-9411-3

Lévy, P. (1997). *Cyberculture. Rapport au Conseil de l'Europe dans le cadre du projet "Nouvelles technologie: coopération culturelle et communication"*. Paris: Odile Jacob.

Libera, A. (2007). *Archéologie du sujet, I. Naissance du sujet*. Paris: Vrin.

Libera, A. (2008). *Archéologie du sujet, II. Quette de l'Identité*. Paris: Vrin.

Manovich, L. (2001). *The Language of New Media*. Cambridge: MIT Press.

Moncura, W., Orzecha, K. M., & Nevilleb, F. G. (2016). Fraping, social norms and online representations of self. *Computers in Human Behavior*, *63*, 125–131. doi:10.1016/j.chb.2016.05.042

Mowshowitz, A. (1999). The switching principle in virtual organization. In P. Sieber & J. Griese (Eds.), *Organizational Virtualness and Electronic Commerce* (pp. 9–20). Simova Verlag.

Mowshowitz, A., & Kawaguchi, A. (2005). Quantifying the switching model of virtual organization. *Journal of Information Technology Theory and Application*, *6*(4), 53–74.

Pinch, T., & Bijker, W. (1986). Science, relativism and the new sociology of technology: Reply to Russell. *Social Studies of Science*, *16*(2), 347–360. doi:10.1177/0306312786016002009

Ricoeur, P. (1990). *Time and Narrative*. Chicago: University of Chicago Press.

Ricoeur, P. (1992). *Oneself as another*. Chicago: University of Chicago Press.

Schmitz, A., Yanenko, O., & Hebing, M. (2012). Identifying artificial actors in E-dating: A probabilistic segmentation based on interactional pattern analysis. In W. Gaul, A. Geyer-Schulz, L. Schmidt-Thieme, & J. Kunze (Eds.), *Challenges at the Interface of Data Analysis, Computer Science, and Optimization. Studies in Classification, Data Analysis, and Knowledge Organization* (pp. 319–327). Berlin: Springer. doi:10.1007/978-3-642-24466-7_33

Schroeder, R. (2007). An overview of ethical and social issues in shared virtual environments. *Futures*, *39*(6), 704–717. doi:10.1016/j.futures.2006.11.009

Seigel, J. (1994). The human subject as a language-effect. *History of European Ideas*, *18*(4), 481–495. doi:10.1016/0191-6599(94)90081-7

Smutny, Z. (2016). Social informatics as a concept: Widening the discourse. *Journal of Information Science*, *42*(5), 681–710. doi:10.1177/0165551515608731

Srnicek, N. (2017). *Platform Capitalism*. Cambridge, UK: Polity Press.

Turk, M. (2014). Multimodal interaction: A review. *Pattern Recognition Letters*, *36*(2), 189–195. doi:10.1016/j.patrec.2013.07.003

Vasicek, Z. (2012). *Jak se delaji filosofie* [How are the philosophies being formed]. Prague: Triada.

Williams, R., & Edge, D. (1996). The social shaping of technology. *Research Policy*, *25*(6), 865–899. doi:10.1016/0048-7333(96)00885-2

ADDITIONAL READING

Alvarado, L. X. B., & Alvarez, S. P. C. (2016). Subjetividades On-Line: Entre la Vigilancia y la Autoreferencia Global [Subjectivities On-line: Between Global Monitoring and Self-Reference]. *Sociologia y Tecnociencia*, *2*(6), 17–29.

Bratton, B. H. (2016). *The Stack: On Software and Sovereignty*. Cambridge: MIT Press. doi:10.7551/mitpress/9780262029575.001.0001

Malik, S., & Avanessian, A. (2016). *Genealogies of Speculation: Materialism and Subjectivity since Structuralism*. London: Bloomsbury Academic.

Pasquinelli, M. (2016). Abnormal Encephalization in the Age of Machine Learning. *e-flux*, 75(September). Retrieved March 17, 2017, from http://www.e-flux.com/journal/75/67133/abnormal-encephalization-in-the-age-of-machine-learning/

Tiqqun. (2012). *Preliminary Materials for a Theory of the Young-Girl*. Cambridge: MIT Press.

Tsvetkova, M., Yasseri, T., Meyer, E. T., Pickering, J. B., Engen, V., Walland, P., . . . Bravos, G. (2015). *Understanding human-machine networks: A cross-disciplinary survey*. Retrieved March 17, 2017, from https://arxiv.org/abs/1511.05324

Whitehead, N. L., & Wesch, M. (2012). *Human No More: Digital Subjectivities, Unhuman Subjects & the End of Anthropology*. Colorado: University Press of Colorado.

KEY TERMS AND DEFINITIONS

Internet-Based Services: Services mediated by computers interconnected via networks (internet). Services (e.g., social media, multimodal online navigation, mobile application, web portal) are provided to human and artificial users.

Subject: It can be defined as an agent (or user) within the environment, thus an entity with the capability of using, alternating, or creating contents within a certain medial field, here represented by the virtual environment.

Subjectivity: It can be understood as the condition of being a user of an environment. Human subjectivity is individual experience, which is always unique and influenced by the environment and the users (other actors) in the environment in which the subject resides (in the virtual environment, these could be human but also artificial users). Online subjectivity emphasizes the need to be available/to be present/to be online.

Virtual Environment: It is an environment composed of various Internet-based services, which are mediated by ICT.

Virtual Reality: It is an environment that offers strong virtuality (immersion). Immersive and interactive (realistic) environment is generated by computer technologies.

APPENDIX

Figure 3 shows an example of distributive function of the subject in the virtual environment. Original photo was published by Jason Ward (March 3, 2015). The original communication referred to what can be seen in nature (1). Further communications have new dimensions. Most often, it is a remaking of the original photo and the communications shift to new positions: (2) mockery of president Putin, who was presented in Russian media that can do anything; (3) plane crash with Harrison Ford and the parallels to the film character of Indiana Jones. New impetuses towards creativity of "new" authors: inverse perspective (4), marketing communication of Coca-Cola company (5). Some communications are addressed to a specific "community" – e.g. library at the University of Oxford presents the image from a medieval book, where is captured a similar phenomenon.
Although in the example is given the emphasis on the visualized information, equally significant and also simpler is to change a text of a message (e.g. comment, description of a photo), what can do artificial user. It can be also found an innumerable reflection of this communication in other Internet-based services (Facebook, Google+, and others).

Figure 3. Example of subject distributive function on Twitter
Source: Authors.

The original photo: *ABSOLUTLEY INCREDIBLE photo by Martin Le-May. Green Woodpecker and Weasel. Apparently the Woodpecker escaped.*

Example of remaking: *Putin was not missing. He was busy riding that woodpecker, remember???*

Example of remaking when actor Harrison Ford crashed with a plane: *"Fly Yes, Land No!" - Indiana Jones*

Example of remaking: *New sensational photo! Woodpecker taking a rest on the way back, riding on the weasel.*

Example of remaking by Coca-Cola in Serbia: *Pogon na #radost #WeaselPecker*

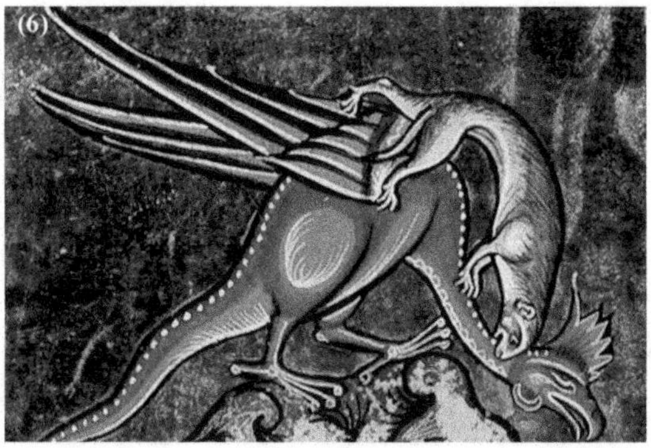

Reaction of library at the University of Oxford: *We're not at all surprised to see weasels on other animals: #weaselpecker #medievalmemes*

Chapter 2
Psychological Benefits and Detrimental Effects of Online Social Networking

Irem Metin Orta
Atilim University, Turkey

Müge Çelik Örücü
TED University, Turkey

ABSTRACT

With the growing prevalence of wireless communication technologies, social networking sites (SNSs) such as Facebook, Twitter, etc. have become an important venues for interpersonal communication. This chapter provides a detailed overview of the current literature on online social networking with respect to its beneficial and detrimental effects on psychological wellbeing. In particular, it provides empirical evidence for the associations of SNS use with depression, self-esteem, loneliness, subjective wellbeing, social anxiety, attachment, personality traits, and addiction. Furthermore, it identifies the characteristics of individuals who are more prone to social networking, and presents possible mediators and moderators playing a role in the relationship between social networking and mental health. The chapter overall provides a comprehensive guideline to parents, researchers, educators, healthcare, and communication professionals to the issue of online social networking from a psychological perspective.

INTRODUCTION

Online social networking plays an important role in the way people communicate and interact. It has benefits for children and adolescents such as socialization, communication, increased learning opportunities, and assessing health information, however it has also some detrimental effects such as cyberbullying, online harassment, and sexting (O'Keefe & Clark-Pearson, 2011). The statistics show that there were 2.34 billion social network users worldwide in 2016 and the number is expected to reach to 2.95 billion by 2020 (Statista Facts on Social Networks, 2017). The average social media user spent 1.7 h per day

DOI: 10.4018/978-1-5225-4047-2.ch002

on social media in the USA and 1.5 h in the UK, with social media users in the Philippines having the highest daily use at 3.7 h. (Statista, 2017).

The growing popularity of online social network sites such as Facebook, MySpace, Twitter has attracted the attention of many scholars, and they have shown particular interest in understanding the psychological correlates of SNS use. Accordingly, this chapter aims to provide a detailed overview of the current literature with respect to the benefits and detrimental effects of online social networking on psychological well-being. To do so, it reviews current empirical evidence for the associations of SNS use with various mental health outcomes including depression, self-esteem, loneliness, subjective well-being, social anxiety, attachment, personality traits and addiction. Furthermore, it identifies the intrapersonal characteristics of individuals who show more tendency to use SNSs. Thus, this chapter would contribute to parents, researchers, educators, healthcare and communication professionals in providing theoretical information and practical implications of online social networking.

Throughout this chapter, several issues are addressed. First, a general introduction to the definition and history of online social networking is given and the emergent interest in this concept is discussed. Second, the empirical research focusing on the relationship between online social networking and psychological variables are systematically reviewed. A comprehensive search is conducted to gain understanding of theexisting literature about the benefits and detrimental consequences of online social networking. For this purpose, SSCI, EBSCOhost, Psych ARTICLES, Scopus, and ProQuest electronic databases are consulted for the literature search using several keywords such as *social networking, psychological well-being, mental health, self-esteem, depression, anxiety, loneliness, personality, addiction, attachment etc*. The priority is given to the articles published in the last decade. Finally, practical implications and suggestions for future research are proposed through addressing plausible moderators and mediators in relation to social networking.

BACKGROUND

Social networking websites (SNSs) have become important venues for interpersonal communication and relationships. SNSs are virtual groups where personal information via profiles are shared, meet with other people based on common interests, and contact with people by writing messages or adding them as friends (Krämer & Winter, 2008; Kuss & Griffiths, 2011). The history of social networking sites dates back to 1997, when individuals are linked via six degrees of separation (Boyd & Ellison, 2007), then, the society is viewed as becoming increasingly inter-connected. Without considering time and space, individuals connect with one another online and SNSs have become an important leisure activity for many people (Kuss & Griffiths, 2017).

The sites may have different orientations related with work (i.e. LinkedIn), romantic relationship (i.e. Friendster), sharing interests (i. e. Myspace) or social connection (i.e. Facebook) (Ellison, Steinfield, & Lampe, 2007). The most popular networking sites are respectively Facebook, Whatsapp, Youtube, Facebook Messenger, WeChat, QQ, Instagram, Qzone, Tumble, Twitter, etc (Statista Facts on Social Networks, 2017). In 2004, Facebook was launched as an online community for students at Harvard University (Byod & Ellison, 2007) and has since become the world's most popular SNS. Currently, Facebook is the most dominant SNS in the U.S with 1.97 billion registered users (Statista Facts on Social Networks, 2017). One reason Facebook is the most popular social networking site is the convenience it provides for users (Kuss& Griffiths, 2017). Social information is easily shared and can be stored among members, therefore comments and feedbacks are given.

Social networking is considered as a way of being and relating with others (Kuss & Griffiths, 2017). Especially for young adults, technology is an essential part of their lives. It is such a lifestyle that necessitates them to connect everytime. This has two important consequences. First one is the maintenance of the status quo and second one is the need not to miss out and to stay up to date (Kuss & Griffiths, 2017). Given the substantial importance and prevalence of SNSs in the lives of young people today, it is of crucial importance to understand the psychological correlates of SNS use. Thus, the following section of the chapter reviews the empirical research focusing on the psychological benefits and detrimental effects of online social networking.

MAIN FOCUS OF THE CHAPTER

The popularity of SNSs has raised questions among scholars about their potential impact on mental health (O'Keefe & Clark-Pearson, 2011). Research on social media typically focuses on its benefits; considerably less is known about the dark side of social networking sites. Social networking and online communication in general is linked to psychological well-being such as increase in self-esteem, sense of belongingness, self-disclosure, and emotional supportas well as decreases in social anxiety and social isolation (see Best, Manktelow, & Taylor, 2014 for a review). On the other side, the frequent use of social media is linked to unmet need for mental health support, poor mental health, higher levels of psychological distress and suicidal ideation (Sampasa-Kanyinga & Lewis, 2015; Kim, 2016).

Accordingly, there is an increased interest in the well-being of students at school and potential problems related with students' use of socio-digital technologies (i.e.,the mobile devices, computers, social media, and the internet). In addition to the contribution of social activities to the creativity of individuals, there is a threat of being addicted to or having compulsive behavior which may result in general and school-related mental health problems. To illustrate, researchers have revealed that there is a reciprocal relationship between excessive use of digital technologies and school burnout among adolescent groups (Salmela-Aro, Upadyaya, Hakkarainen, Lonka & Alho, 2016). That is, school burnout is associated with later excessive online social activities, which in turn is related with later school burnout.

Social Networking and Depression

The majority of empirical studies have linked the prolonged use of SNS with higher levels of depression (see Pantic, 2014 for a review). As defined by American Academy of Pediatrics (2011), "Facebook depression" is a phenomena in which teens spend frequent time on SNSs and exhibit symptoms of depression (Jelenchick, Eickhoff, & Moreno, 2013; O'Keefe & Clarke-Pearson, 2011). Thus, the existing research provide promoting evidence for Facebook depression. For instance, research has shown that the time spent on social networking is positively correlated with depressive symptoms among high school students (Pantic, Damjanovic, Todorovic, Topalovic, Bojovic-Jovic, Ristic, & Pantic, 2012) and young adults (Rosen, Whaling, Rab, Carrier, & Cheever, 2013). Several mechanisms might underlie the relationship between social networking and depression.

First, individual's less social engagement and less interaction with others as a result of internet use might explain this relationship (Kraut, Patterson, Lundmark, Kiesler, Mukopadhyay, & Scherlis, 1998).

As stated previously, the time spent on internet has considerably increased with the technological advances, which in turn influences the quality of interpersonal communication and interaction within the family and social environment (Pantic, 2014). A longitudinal study by Kraut and his colleagues (1998) has shown that as the time spent online increases, the communication with family members and the size of local social circle decreases. This situation further leads to feelings of depression and loneliness. Indeed, the online communication is shallower than everyday face-to-face communications (Pantic, 2014) and internet use replaces stronger ties with weaker ties in social relationships (Kraut, Patterson, Lundmark, Kiesler, Mukopadhyay, & Scherlis, 1998). This might explain the negative impact of internet use, in particular, social networking on psychological well-being.

Second, increased levels of screen viewing and decreased levels of outdoor physical activities might explain the link between online social networking and depression (Pantic, Damjanovic, Todorovic, Topalovic, Bojovic-Jovic, Ristic, & Pantic, 2012). For instance, a longitudinal study with a 10-year follow up (Lucas, Mekary, Pan, Mirzaei, O'Reilly, Willett, ... & Ascherio, 2011) has shown that older adults who are most physically active (more than 90 min/a day) and spend less time on TV (0-5 hours/a week) report lowest level of depression than those who are less physically active (less than 10 min/ a day) and spend more time on TV (more than 21 hours/ a week). From this finding, it can be argued that as the time spent on physical activity decreases and/or the time spent on watching TV increases, the risk of developing depression increases (Lucas, Mekary, Pan, Mirzaei, O'Reilly, Willett, ... & Ascherio, 2011).

Third, individuals' incorrect perceptions regarding the lives of online friends might account for the relationship between online social networking and depressive symptoms. For instance, Chou and Edge (2012) have shown that people who spend more time on Facebook are more likely to perceive others as happier and having better lives than themselves. In constrast, people who spend more time on going out with friends are less likely to have these perceptions. Furthermore, people who have more friends on Facebook tend to more perceive the life as fair and less perceive others as happier; however, people who have personally unknown Facebook friends tend to have more perceptions of others having better lives than themselves. It is argued that with a greater extent of social networks, Facebook users tend to employ heuristics (i.e. availability heuristic) when they make judgments or form impressions about others (Chou & Edge, 2012). In addition, they tend to attribute others' actions more to stable personal disposition than situational factors (i.e. correspondence bias) especially when they do not know the person well. These distorted perceptions, in turn, might increase people's vulnerability for developing depression (Pantic, Damjanovic, Todorovic, Topalovic, Bojovic-Jovic, Ristic, & Pantic, 2012).

The existing research also point that the type of use and the quality of social interactions are important determinants for developing depression. For instance, Davila and his colleagues (2012) have shown that depression is not associated with the quantity (frequency) but the quality of online social interactions (how positive or negative it is). In particular, people with less positive and more negative interactions in social networking report more depressive symptoms over time. Furthermore, greater use of Facebook activities for impression management and less online friends are linked to more depressive symptoms (Rosen, Whaling, Rab, Carrier, & Cheever, 2013).

Some of the studies however reveal no significant relationship between SNS use and depression among older adolescents and young adults (Jelenchick, Eickhoff, & Moreno, 2013; Kross, Verduyn, Demiralp, Park, & Lee, 2013; Simoncic, Kuhlman, Vargas, Houchins, & Lopez-Duran, 2014). Interestingly, in one study, the relationship becomes significant when it is moderated by sex and personality trait (Simoncic, Kuhlman, Vargas, Houchins, & Lopez-Duran, 2014). That is, increased Facebook activity is linked to lower levels of depressive symptoms only among young female adults with high neuroticism scores. It is argued that SNS use may be beneficial for vulnerable individuals, in particular, for females high in neuroticismin terms of promoting adaptive social interactions (Simoncic, Kuhlman, Vargas, Houchins, & Lopez-Duran, 2014). The negative association between online communication and depression is also supported by a study conducted by Bessiere, Pressman, Kiesler and Kraut (2010). In their study, researchers reveal that people who use the internet for health-related purposes show small increase in depression whereas those who use the internet for the purpose of communication with family and friends show declines in depression. It is argued that the use of SNSs not extensively may strengthen social ties with family members and close friends, and thus contributes to individual's mental health (Bessiere, Pressman, Kiesler,& Kraut, 2010).

Besides, SNSs, specifically Facebook, can be used for early detection and assessment of depression (Park, Lee, Kwak, Cha & Jeong, 2013). Since depressive prone individuals are more likely to use depression related Facebook activities, the identification of early symptoms may predict future depression. In a study, researchers have examined the social network determinants of depressive symptoms which distinguish depressed individuals from those who are not depressed (Park, Lee, Kwak, Cha, & Jeong, 2013). As a result, depressive symptoms are positively correlated with individuals' Facebook activities such as accumulated app points and number of viewed tips, and negatively correlated with the number of friends and location tags. Supporting findings of other studies (Chou & Edge, 2012; Rosen, Whaling, Rab, Carrier, & Cheever, 2013), having more online friends might protect individuals from developing depression.

In addition to Facebook, depression is found to be common among users of Tumble, which is also a widely used SNS (Cavazos-Rehg, Krauss, Sowles, Connolly, Rosas, Bharadwaj, ... & Bierut, 2017). Popular depression-related Tumblr accounts are monitored in order to gain a better understanding of the depression, self harm, and suicidal content that is being shared on Tumblr. Posts are randomly selected by the research team and coded based on predetermined topics. Common themes are found as self-loathing, loneliness/feeling unloved, self-harm and suicide. Cavazos-Rehg's study (2017) is an important first step at better understanding the displayed depression-related references on Tumblr. Considering the depression and suicidal content observed on Tumblr, the findings suggest a need for suicide prevention efforts to intervene on Tumblr and this platform can be used in a strategic way (Cavazos-Rehg, Krauss, Sowles, Connolly, Rosas, Bharadwaj, ... & Bierut, 2017).

Social Networking and Self-Esteem

The relationship between online social networking and signs and symptoms of depression might also be explained by changes in self-esteem (Pantic, Damjanovic, Todorovic, Topalovic, Bojovic-Jovic, Ristic, & Pantic, 2012). Self-esteem, the evaluative aspect of the self, is a belief in one's capacity, worth and significance (Coopersmith, 1981). The systematic review of recent research shows mixed findings about the relationship between SNS use and self-esteem (see Pantic, 2014 for a review). In particular, Gonzales and Hancock (2011) propose two different theoretical explanations for the possible impact of social networking on individual's self-esteem. First, based on *objective self-awareness theory* (Duval & Wicklund, 1972), researchers suggest that conscious awareness of one's self (i.e. through mirror, photoor autobiographical information) influences impressions of the self negatively. Extending this rationale to SNSs, viewing one's personal profile containing self-descriptions and pictures may increase self-awareness, thus diminish one's self-esteem.

Second, based on *the hyperpersonal model* (Walther, 1996), researchers state that online communication enables individuals present one's positive (or preferred) aspects of personality which in turn may enhance one's self-esteem (Gonzales & Hancock, 2011). Supporting the process of *selective self-presentation*, researchers have shown that attention to one's own profile (i.e. viewing and updating information) influences impressions of the self positively (Gonzales & Hancock, 2011). As Krämer and Winter (2008) state, SNSs are ideal venues for managing self-presentation, andaccordingly, the modifiable nature of self-presentation in computer-mediated communication enhances one's self-esteem (Gonzales & Hancock, 2011).

In a related vein, a group of researchers has shown that positive feedback on the profiles of networking sites enhances adolescents' social self-esteem (Valkenburg, Peter, & Schouten, 2006). That is, adolescents who receive positive feedback on their profiles report more positive evaluations for their physical appearance, romantic attractiveness and for their ability to form close relationships. However, adolescents who receive negative feedback on their profiles report more negative self-evaluations on these dimensions. These findings can be explained by adolescents engagement of *imaginative audience behavior* (Elkind & Bowen,1979). In general, adolescents think that they are watched and evaluated by others, thus they are overly concerned with their self-presentations. Accordingly, as shown by researchers (Valkenburg, Peter, & Schouten, 2006), the feedback received on profiles in SNSs may affect individual'slevel ofself-esteem either positively or negatively.

Even though a few studies have revealed no relationship between self-esteem and SNS use (Krämer &Winter, 2008; Wilson, Fornasier, & White, 2010), other studies have demonstrated that people with low self-esteem tend to spend more time online (Joinson, 2004; Mehdizadeh, 2010). For instance, those individuals prefer online communication more than face-to-face communication (Joinson, 2004). In addition, people's level of self-esteem is negatively correlated with time spent on online ('Facebook') activities and their narcissism scores are positively correlated with self-promotion content of these activities (Mehdizadeh, 2010). From these findings, it can be argued that lower levels of self-esteem predicts more social networking since it provides benefits to individuals in terms of enhancing their psychological well-being (Ellison, Steinfield, & Lampe, 2007).

Besides, a study conducted by Fioravanti, Dettore, and Casale (2012) show that female adolescents' preferences for an online social interaction (POSI) partially mediates the relationship between self-esteem and internet addiction. That is, low levels of esteem predicts internet addiction directly and indirectly through higher levels of POSI. More interestingly, *the opportunity to escape from the real world* appears as an important characteristics of computer-mediated communication in the relation between self-esteem and POSI. Even though the findings of aforementioned studies link low self-esteem to higher frequency of SNS use, given the cross-sectional nature of thestudies, no causal inferences can be drawn with regard to these relationships.

Social Networking and Subjective Well-Being

Subjective well-being (SWB) in general is comprised of affective (i.e. positive and negative affect) and cognitive components (i.e. satisfaction with life) (Pavot & Diener, 2004). The existing literature has yielded mixed results for the relationship between social networking and subjective well-being. For instance, a study has shown that as the use of Facebook increases, people report more negative feelings and less satisfaction with their lives over time even when the level of loneliness is controlled (Kross,

Verduyn, Demiralp, Park, & Lee, 2013). Similarly, Bevan, Gomez, and Sparks (2014) also reveal that the time spent on SNSs is negatively correlated with the quality of life. In contrast, direct interaction with others (face-to-face or phone) is associated with increases in affective well-being (Kross, Verduyn, Demiralp, Park, & Lee, 2013).

On the other side, researchers have shown that the intensity of Facebook use among young adults is correlated with increased life satisfaction scores (Valenzuela, Park, & Kee, 2009), and positive feedback on the profiles of friend networking sites enhances adolescents' life satisfaction via social self-esteem (Valkenburg, Peter, & Schouten, 2006). From these finding, it can be argued that positive evaluations received on a SNS profile enhances individual's self-esteem, which in turn reflects upon on subjective well-being. Supporting this notion, researchers has shown that the Facebook use provides benefits especially for individuals with lower levels of self-esteem and life satisfaction (Ellison, Steinfield, & Lampe, 2007).

In another study, Fox and Moreland (2015) have formed a focus group from Facebook users to understand individuals' negative psychological and relational experiences tied to the SNSs and their utilization (e.g., connectivity, visibility, accessibility, persistence, and social feedback). As a result, five themes related to Facebook stressors have emerged as managing inappropriate or annoying content, being attached, lack of privacy and control, social comparison and jealousy, and relationship tension and conflict. Results also demonstrate that despite having experiences of negative emotions, Facebook users still feel pressured to connect the site frequently due to the fear of missing out and to keep up with relationships. Even though users state that Facebook is unimportant, they later report significant unpleasant events associated with Facebook (Fox & Moreland, 2015).

Considering psychological well-being, scholars have introduced new concepts in relation to social networking. For instance, recent research (Oberst, Wegmann, Stodt, Brand & Chamarro, 2017; Buglass, Binder, Betts & Underwood, 2017) suggests that high engagement in social networking is partially due to what has been named the *fear of missing out* (FOMO). FOMO is a pervasive apprehension that others might be having rewarding experiences from which one is absent (Przybylski, Murayama, DeHaan & Gladwell, 2013). Researchers have shown that higher levels of FOMO is related with greater engagement with Facebook and decreases in mood, well-being, and life satisfaction as well as inappropriate social networking (Przybylski, Murayama, DeHaan, & Gladwell, 2013).

Furthermore, '*nomophobia*' has been defined as no mobile phone phobia, i.e., *the fear of being without one's mobile phone* (Bragazzi & Del Puente, 2014). Researchers have called for nomophobia to be included in the DSM-5, and the following criteria have been outlined to contribute to this problem constellation:

... regular and time-consuming use, feelings of anxiety when the phone is not available, 'ringxiety' (repeatedly checking one's phone for messages, sometimes leading to phantom ring tones), constant availability, preference for mobile communication over face to face communication, and financial problems as a consequence of use (Bragazzi & Del Puente, 2014).

Another presentation of ringxiety is '*phantom vibration syndrome*', defined as *perceived vibration from a cellphone that is not vibrating (Drouin, Kaiser, & Miller, 2012).*

Social Networking, Loneliness, Social Anxiety, and Attachment

Researchers have proposed that feelings of loneliness increases people's tendency to use Facebook (Clayton, Osborne, Miller, & Oberle, 2013; Kross Verduyn, Demiralp, Park, & Lee, 2013). In particular, individuals who perceive themselves lonely tend to use SNSs to connect with others. In a study by Bonetti, Campbell and Gilmore (2010), researchers examined how much time children and adolescents with and without feelings of loneliness and/or social anxiety spend communicating online, the topics they choose, the purpose of communication and the partners they engage with. The results show that as the feelings of loneliness increases, the frequency of online communication about personal and intimate topics increases. In addition, the most common motives for online communication reported by lonely and socially anxious people appears to be social compensation, meeting new people, belonging to a group and relaxing. Supporting the previous findings (i.e. Caplan, 2003; 2007), lonely and socially anxious people prefer online communication more since it provides them an opportunity to compensate for their poorer social skillsto meet new people (Bonetti, Campbell, & Gilmore, 2010). In particular, they state that they do not feel as shy, feel more relaxed and venture more in online communication.

Accordingly, direct interaction with others using Facebook is associated with lower levels of loneliness and greater feelings of social capital (Burke, Marlow & Lento, 2010; Lou, Yan, Nickerson, & McMorris, 2012). In contrast, spending time passively in SNS such as viewing friends' content is correlated with higher levels of loneliness and lower feelings of social capital. Nevertheless, there are mixed findings regarding the causality of the relationships in the related literature. Kraut and his colleagues (1998) suggest that initial levels of loneliness may not predict changes in internet use and the direction of causality may be from the use of internet to declines in psychological well-being. Thus, the directionality of the relationship between loneliness and social networking remains unclear.

Research suggests that online communication may be beneficial for those who have high social anxiety. Accordingly, a number of scholars have shown that social anxiety predicts individual's emotional attachment to Facebook and their connections with others using Facebook (Clayton, Osborne, Miller, & Oberle, 2013). It indicates that socially anxious people prefer to use Facebook for social interaction, and integrate the social network site into their daily lives. Based on past findings (Caplan, 2007; Ebeling-Witte, Frank & Lester, 2007; Kim, LaRose & Peng, 2009), it can be argued that individuals with social anxiety and perceived loneliness have deficient social skills, and since they perceive greater control over self-presentation online, they feel more comfortable in online communication than face-to-facecommunication. Accordingly, it is shown that a person's preference for online social interaction (POSI) mediates the relationship between level of loneliness or social anxiety and negative outcomes resulting from internet use (Caplan, 2003; 2007).

In a related vein, for individuals high in attachment anxiety and/or avoidance, Facebook offers advantages over face-to-face interactions. By managing their self-presentation, anxious individuals may feel more confident in maintaining interpersonal relationships. For people who desire closeness but anticipate and fear rejection, being able to carefully manage self-presentation could be a particularly attractive feature of Facebook (Buote, Wood, & Pratt, 2009). The relationships between attachment anxiety and avoidance and Facebook use are examined by researchers (Oldmeadow, Quinn & Kowert, 2013). When adults feel negative emotions and have high attachment anxiety, it is found that they use Facebook more frequently, as they are more worried about how others see them on Facebook. In contrast, high attachment avoidance is related to less Facebook use, less openness and less positive attitudes towards Facebook. When social skills are controlled, the relationships remain the same. Findings make the scholars consider that Facebook may serve attachment functions and provide a basis for understanding how online communication be related to attachment styles (Oldmeadow, Quinn, & Kowert, 2013). Another way in which Facebook may appeal to individuals with attachment issues is by providing a sense of belonging to a social network. SNSa are also found to increase belongingness among adults (Oldmeadow, Quinn, & Kowert, 2013).

In a study by Gentzler, Oberhauser, Westerman and Nadorff (2011), college students are asked to report on their use of electronic communication with a parent whom they stated as their closest family member. Results indicate that students who report more frequent phone conversations with parents also report more satisfying, intimate, and supportive parental relationships, but those students who use a SNS to communicate with parents report higher levels of loneliness, anxious attachment, as well as conflict within the parental relationship. The findings offer new evidence on how electronic communication technology with parents is related to adjustment in college students. To better understand the young adults' use of technology to communicate in today's society, further research with longitudinal designs is needed (Gentzler Oberhauser, Westerman, & Nadorff, 2011).

Social Networking and Cyberbullying

Another dark side of SNS is that, it can have harmful consequences for users such as cyberbullying, stalking, and online harassment. Cyberbullying refers to:

... the transmission by electronic means of demeaning, distressing, threatening and abusive messages and images which target a particular individual or a group of individuals (Kyriacou, 2017).

Messages, images, recordings which can be sent directly or indirectly to the victim and to the cyberbully's peer group, are forms of cyberbullying. It is an electronic or internet bullying in which individuals intentionally harm a victim via electronic means (Bonanno & Hymel, 2013). A range of other terms has been used to describe the phenomenon including: cyberharassment, cybervictimisation, online harassment and electronic bullying (Beran, Rinaldi, Bickham & Rich, 2012; Brown, Demaray& Secord, 2014).

Unlike traditional or face-to-face forms of bullying, anonymity and invisibility of the perpetrators are important characteristics of cyberbullying (Bonanno & Hymel, 2013). According to Dempsey, Sulkowski, Nichols and Storch (2009), cyberbullying may be particularly harmful to victims for several reasons. First, cyberbullying is hard to escape, as it can occur across settings. Second, the aggressors remain anonymous. As the aggressors do not have direct contact with the victim, feeling empathy or remorse is rare among them. Third, in a short time frame due to the use of technology, the aggressor reaches large audiences. Finally, chances of intervention is reduced due to less adult supervision.

Cyberbullying is related to various mental health outcomes. For instance, Bonanno and Hymel (2013) have shown cyber victimization to be related to depression and suicidal ideation in a sample of 8th to 10th grade students. Similarly, Olenik-Shemesh, Heiman and Eden(2012) have found that cyber victimization is related to both loneliness and depressive mood among young adults. These studies indicate that cyberbullying puts young individuals at risk for internalizing problems. Weight-based cyberbullying is also prevalent among youth and adolescents, and may have lasting negative psychological effects on the victims (Anderson, Bresnahan, & Musatics, 2014). Furthermore, cyberbullying may have physical effects on victims such as weight loss or gain, substance abuse, headache, abdominal pain and sleeping problems. In the related literature, there is not a clear understanding considering gender and developmental differences in experiences of cyber victimization. Inconsistent findings related with gender may result from a number of factors, including researchers examining different age groups, in different countries, and at different reference time periods in the assessments (Brown, Demaray, & Secord, 2014).

Social Networking and Addiction

People engage in a variety of activities in SNS, some of which may potentially be addictive. Rather than becoming addicted to a substance, some users may develop an addiction to some specific online activities. There are five different types of internet addiction, namely computer addiction (i.e., computer game addiction), information overload (i.e., web surfing addiction), net compulsions (i.e., online gambling or online shopping addiction), cybersexual addiction (i.e., online pornography or online sex addiction), and cyber-relationship addiction (i.e., an addiction to online relationships)(Kuss & Griffiths, 2011). SNS addiction falls in the last category since the individuals are motivated to use SNSs to establish and maintain online relationships. Even though some scholars (i.e. Griffiths, 2012) argue that they are not synonymous, the term SNS addiction is sometimes used interchangebly with "Facebook addiction".

Research into social networking addiction fall into one of four types:

1. Self-perception studies of social networking addiction,
2. Studies of social networking addiction utilizing a social networking addiction scale,
3. Studies examining the relationship between social networking and other online addictions, and
4. Studies examining social networking addiction and interpersonal relationships (Griffiths, Kuss & Demetrovics, 2014).

Although the concept of social networking addiction is controversial, some people may experience addiction-like symptoms as a result of excessive use.

Besides, social media supported gambling activities has been found to increase recently. The particular concern is with respect to the possible potential of early age gambling involvement, and development of positive attitudes and/or behavioral intentions toward gambling. In their study, King, Delfabbro, Kaptsis and Zwaans (2014) have examined adolescents' involvement in gambling activities on social media, and tried to find out the indicators of pathological gambling risk. Results have shown that a significant proportion of young people engage in a range of gambling activities in social media. Having a history of engagement in gambling activities, adolescents seem to be at greater risk of pathological gambling. Need for regulation and monitoring of gambling activity are highlighted with the findings. There is also a need for further research on the potential risks of early exposure to gambling activities (King, Delfabbro, Kaptsis, & Zwaans, 2014).

Social Networking, Personality, and Gender Differences

As studies are conducted for understanding the benefits and negative consequences of SNS usage, personality types, traits or disorders have also become the center of attention. Rosen and his colleagues (2013) have examined the impact of the use of specific technologies and media on clinical symptoms of mood disorders and personality disorders. Among these disorders, greater facebook use and using it for impression management motivation and larger number of online friends are found to be related with narcissism and histrionic disorder. Furthermore, Weisskirch and Delevi (2011) have introduced the term sexting, sending text messages with sexual content, as one of the diagnostic criterion for histrionic personality disorder.

Carpenter (2012) has investigated the effect of Facebook activity on antisocial personality behaviors and identified certain antisocial behaviors including taking revenge on negative remarks around oneself, carefully reading others' announcements to check whether they are discussing them, and looking for more social bolster than one gives to others. In the increasing use of SNSs, users' personality traits may be important factors leading them to engage in social media. The related literature in particular suggests that BigFive factors such as extraversion, emotional stability and openness to experience are related to SNS use. In a study done by Correa, Hinsley and De Zuniga (2010) when socio-demographics and life satisfaction variables are controlled, extraversion and openness to experiences are positively whereas emotional stability is negatively related to social media use. These findings differ by gender and age. Extraverted men and women are both likely to be more frequent users of social media tools, while only men with greater degrees of emotional instability are more regular users. The relationship between extraversion and social media use is particularly important among young adults. Conversely, openness to new experiences emerges as an important personality factor in relation with social media use for olderadults (Correa, Hinsley, & De Zuniga, 2010).

Another personality trait, conscientiousness, refers to a person's work ethic, orderliness and thoroughness (Costa & McCrae, 1992), and scholars has suggested that conscientious individuals are inclined to avoid SNS as they promote procrastination and serve as a distraction from more important tasks (Butt & Phillips, 2008). In contrast, people who are high in sociability have positive attitudes towards SNS and show willingness to join SNS (Hughes, Rowe, Batey & Lee, 2012). Agreeableness has been included in several studies relating to internet and social media usage, and has generally been found to be unrelated (Correa, Hinsley, & De Zuniga, 2010; Amichai-Hamburger, & Vinitzky, 2010)

Researchers have also investigated gender differences with regard to the frequency of and motivations for SNS use. Despite a study showing more positive attitudes toward and more use of SNSs at workplace among males (Andreassen, Torscheim, & Pallesen, 2014), considerable research has shown greater social networking among females (Barker, 2009; Bonetti, Campbell, & Gilmore, 2010; Simoncic, Kuhlman, Vargas, Houchins, & Lopez-Duran, 2014; Fioravanti, Dettore, & Casale, 2012; Hargittai, 2008). For instance, Barker (2009) reports that teenage girls show higher overall use of SNSs than boys, and mostly use SNSs for relational purposes (i.e. communication with peers). However, teenage boys mostly use SNSs for social compensation and learning purposesas well as for social identity gratifications. It is argued that social networking may provide social support and peer group belongingness that teenage boys especially need in periods of life transition (Barker, 2009).

In accordance with gender role expectations, researchers have shown that men are more likely to use SNSs for networking, making new friends and finding potential dates, whereas women use them for relationship maintenance (Muscanell & Guadagno, 2012). Similarly, Bonetti and his colleagues (2010) reveal that girls are more involved in online communication for relational purposes than boys. Besides, researchers report more risk taking attitudes among men as compared to women in social networking (Fogel & Nehmad, 2008). That is, men display more private information (telephone number, home address, etc.), and women show greater concern for privacy and less identity information disclosure than men in social networking websites.

CONCLUSION

General Practical Implications

This chapter explains the benefits and detrimental consequences of online social networking from a psychological perspective. To do so, it reviews a growing body of research about online social networking and various indicators of psychological well-being. Overall, the findings show mixed evidence of the links between SNS use and mental health outcomes. While some studies have revealed the beneficial impact of SNS use on mental health including enhanced self-esteem, life satisfaction, sense of belongingness, and reduced social anxiety and loneliness, considerable research has shown its detrimental impact including increased depression, addiction, cyberbullying as well as reduced self-esteem and subjective well-being. Besides, higher engagement in social networking is linked to various types of phobias including FOMO and nomophobia.

Even though this chapter focuses on only certain areas of mental health, the findings presented above provide several implications for research and practice on the impact of SNS use. Taken together, existing findings support that online social networking undermines psychological well-being of adolescents and young adults. Given the prevalence of social media use among this population, it is imperative for scholars to take necessary steps to prevent possible negative consequences of social networking. One way to reduce the potential risk of developing addiction especially among lonely and socially anxious teenagers is monitoring and educating them on appropriate use of online communication tools (O'Keeffe, & Clarke-Pearson, 2011; Subrahmanyam & Lin, 2007). Future studies may wish to include preventive efforts for adolescents and young adults. Scholars may also focus in their future research on identifying signs of possible psychopathological behaviors related of abuse of SNSs (Barbera, Paglia & Valsavoia, 2009).

Limitations and Avenues for Future Research

This chapter concentrates on the psychological correlates of the use of different online SNSs which has a *different patterns of use, user characteristics and social functions* (Wilson, Gosling, & Graham, 2012). To illustrate, Facebook is based on creating and updating personal profiles, while Twitter is based on posting and reading short-messages (Pantic, 2014). Given the variability of SNSs, it is important for scholars to question the generalizability of their findings (Kross Verduyn, Demiralp, Park, & Lee, 2013). Since the research field is relatively young, studies investigating social networking unsurprisingly suffer from a number of methodological problems (Kuss & Griffiths, 2011; Pantic, 2014). For instance, most studies comprise small and unrepresentative samples. For future studies, researchers should select larger samples which represent broader populations across cultures and especially in SNS research, scholars should focus on populations at risk for developing SNS addiction. In current literature, studies use several different psychometric scales (Pantic, 2014). By using more reliable and valid measures in future research, it would be more possible to make generalizations (Griffiths, Kuss, & Demetrovics, 2014).

The vast majority of previous research on social networking and mental health outcomes are cross-sectional in nature, which does not allow for causal inferences. Therefore, it remains unclear whether social networking or mental health outcome is the cause or the effect (Pantic, 2014). To illustrate, it is possible that individuals using SNSs show poor psychological well-being or those individuals with poor psychological well-being show more tendency to use SNSs. Given the cross-sectional nature of past research, it is imperative for scholars to continue with longitudinal studies to identify the temporality and causality of these relationships (Pantic, 2014).Besides, there are limited studies that examine the possible mediators or moderators that play role in the relationship between online social networking and mental health (i.e. Kim, 2016; Simoncic, Kuhlman, Vargas, Houchins, & Lopez-Duran, 2014). Future studies would therefore do well to investigate the differential role of certain factors such as family or school atmosphere or social support on various mental health issues.

In summary, this chapter basically is just a starting point for future studies on social networking by reviewing the current literature with respect to the benefits and detrimental effects of online social networking. Taken all together, the findings suggest that the associations among social networking and psychological well-being are complex and warrant in-depth consideration by scholars and practitioners.

REFERENCES

Amichai-Hamburger, Y., & Vinitzky, G. (2010). Social network use and personality. *Computers in Human Behavior*, *26*(6), 1289–1295. doi:10.1016/j.chb.2010.03.018

Anderson, J., Bresnahan, M., & Musatics, C. (2014). Combating weight-based cyberbullying on Facebook with the dissenter effect. *Cyberpsychology, Behavior, and Social Networking*, *17*(5), 281–286. doi:10.1089/cyber.2013.0370 PMID:24690025

Andreassen, S. C., Torscheim, T., & Pallesen, S. (2014). Predictors of use of social network sites at work: A specific type of cyberloafing. *Journal of Computer-Mediated Communication*, *19*(4), 906–921. doi:10.1111/jcc4.12085

Barbera, L. D., Paglia, L. F., & Valsavoia, R. (2009). Social network and addiction. *Studies in Health Technology and Informatics*, *144*, 33–36. PMID:19592725

Barker, V. (2009). Older adolescents' motivations for social network site use: The influence of gender, group identity, and collective self-esteem. *Cyberpsychology & Behavior*, *12*(2), 209–213. doi:10.1089/cpb.2008.0228 PMID:19250021

Beran, T. N., Rinaldi, C., Bickham, D. S., & Rich, M. (2012). Evidence for the need to support adolescents dealing with harassment and cyber-harassment: Prevalence, progression, and impact. *School Psychology International*, *33*(5), 562–576. doi:10.1177/0143034312446976

Bessiere, K., Pressman, S., Kiesler, S., & Kraut, R. (2010). Effects of internet use on health and depression: A longitudinal study. *Journal of Medical Internet Research*, *12*(1), e6. doi:10.2196/jmir.1149 PMID:20228047

Best, P., Manktelow, R., & Taylor, B. (2014). Online communication, social media and adolescent wellbeing:A systematic narrative review. *Children and Youth Services Review*, *41*, 27–36. doi:10.1016/j.childyouth.2014.03.001

Bevan, J. L., Gomez, R., & Sparks, L. (2014). Disclosures about important life events on Facebook: Relationships with stress and quality of life. *Computers in Human Behavior*, *39*, 246–253. 246-253.doi.org/10.1016/j.chb.2014.07.021. doi:10.1016/j.chb.2014.07.021

Bonanno, R. A., & Hymel, S. (2013). Cyber bullying and internalizing difficulties: Above and beyond the impact of traditional forms of bullying. *Journal of Youth and Adolescence*, *42*(5), 685–697. doi:10.100710964-013-9937-1 PMID:23512485

Bonetti, L., Campbell, M. A., & Gilmore, L. (2010). The Relationship of loneliness and social anxiety with children's and adolescents' online communication. *Cyberpsychology, Behavior, and Social Networking, 13*(3), 279-285. doi: 10.1089=cyber.2009.0215

Boyd, D. M. &Ellison, N. B. (2007). Social network sites: Definition, history, and scholarship. *Journal of Computer-Mediated Communication, 13*(1), 210-230. doi: 6101.2007.00393.x10.1111/j.1083

Bragazzi, N. L., & Del Puente, G. (2014). A proposal for including nomophobia in the new DSM-V. *Psychology Research and Behavior Management*, *7*, 155. doi:10.2147/PRBM.S41386 PMID:24876797

Brown, C. F., Demaray, M. K., & Secord, S. M. (2014). Cyber victimization in middle school and relations to social emotional outcomes. *Computers in Human Behavior*, *35*, 12–21. doi:10.1016/j.chb.2014.02.014

Buglass, S. L., Binder, J. F., Betts, L. R., & Underwood, J. D. (2017). Motivators of online vulnerability: The impact of social network site use and FOMO. *Computers in Human Behavior*, *66*, 248–255. doi:10.1016/j.chb.2016.09.055

Buote, V. M., Wood, E., & Pratt, M. (2009). Exploring similarities and differences between online and offline friendships: The role of attachment style. *Computers in Human Behavior*, *25*(2), 560–567. doi:10.1016/j.chb.2008.12.022

Burke, M., Marlow, C., & Lento, T. (2010). Social network activity and social well-being. *Postgraduate Medical Journal*, *85*, 455–459.

Butt, S., & Phillips, J. G. (2008). Personality and self reported mobile phone use. *Computers in Human Behavior*, *24*(2), 346–360. doi:10.1016/j.chb.2007.01.019

Caplan, S. E. (2003). Preference for online social interaction: A theory of problematic Internet useand psychosocial well-being. *Communication Research*, *30*(6), 625–648. doi:10.1177/0093650203257842

Caplan, S. E. (2007). Relation among loneliness, social anxiety, andproblematic internet use. *Cyberpsychology & Behavior*, *10*(2), 234–242. doi:10.1089/cpb.2006.9963 PMID:17474841

Carpenter, C. J. (2012). Narcissism on Facebook: Self-promotional and anti-social behavior. *Personality and Individual Differences*, *52*(4), 482–486. doi:10.1016/j.paid.2011.11.011

Cavazos-Rehg, P. A., Krauss, M. J., Sowles, S. J., Connolly, S., Rosas, C., Bharadwaj, M., ... Bierut, L. J. (2016). An analysis of depression, self-harm, and suicidal ideation content on Tumblr. *Crisis*, *38*(1), 44–52. doi:10.1027/0227-5910/a000409 PMID:27445014

Chou, H. G., & Edge, N. (2012). "They are happier and having better lives than i am": The impact of using Facebook on perceptions of others' lives. *Cyberpsychology, Behavior, and Social Networking*, *15*(2), 117–122. doi:10.1089/cyber.2011.0324 PMID:22165917

Clayton, R. B., Osborne, R. E., Miller, B. K., & Oberle, C. D. (2013). Loneliness, anxiousness, and substance use as predictors of Facebook use. *Computers in Human Behavior, 29*(3), 687–693. doi:10.1016/j.chb.2012.12.002

Coopersmith, S. (1981). *Self-esteem inventories.* Palo Alto, CA: Consulting Psychologists Press.

Correa, T., Hinsley, A. W., & De Zuniga, H. G. (2010). Who interacts on the Web?: The intersection of users' personality and social media use. *Computers in Human Behavior, 26*(2), 247–253. doi:10.1016/j.chb.2009.09.003

Costa, P. T., & McCrae, R. R. (1992). *NEO PI-R professional manual.* Odessa, FL: Psychological Assessment Resources.

Davila, J., Hershenberg, R., Feinstein, B. A., Gorman, K., Bhatia, V., & Starr, L. R. (2012). Frequency and quality of social networking among young adults: Associations with depressive symptoms, rumination, and corumination. *Psychology of Popular Media Culture, 1*(2), 72–86. doi:10.1037/a0027512 PMID:24490122

Dempsey, A. G., Sulkowski, M. L., Nichols, R., & Storch, E. A. (2009). Differences between peer victimization in cyber and physical settings and associated psychosocial adjustment in early adolescence. *Psychology in the Schools, 46*(10), 962–972. doi:10.1002/pits.20437

Drouin, M., Kaiser, D. H., & Miller, D. A. (2012). Phantom vibrations among undergraduates: Prevalence and associated psychological characteristics. *Computers in Human Behavior, 28*(4), 1490–1496. doi:10.1016/j.chb.2012.03.013

Duval, S., & Wicklund, R. A. (1972). *A theory of objective self awareness.* Oxford, UK: Academic Press.

Ebeling-Witte, S., Frank, M. L., & Lester, D. (2007). Shyness, internet use, andpersonality. *Cyberpsychology & Behavior, 10*(5), 713–716. doi:10.1089/cpb.2007.9964 PMID:17927542

Elkind, D., & Bowen, R. (1979). Imaginary audience behavior in children and adolescents. *Developmental Psychology, 15*(1), 38–44. doi:10.1037/0012-1649.15.1.38

Ellison, N. B., Steinfield, C., & Lampe, C. (2007). The benefits of Facebook "friends": Social capital and college students' use of online social network sites. *Journal of Computer-Mediated Communication, 12*(4), 1143–1168. doi:10.1111/j.1083-6101.2007.00367.x

Fioravanti, G., Dettore, D., & Casale, S. (2012). Adolescent internet addiction: Testing the association between self-esteem, the perception of internet attributes, and preference for online social ınteractions. *Cyberpsychology, Behavior, and Social Networking, 15*(6), 318–323. doi:10.1089/cyber.2011.0358 PMID:22703038

Fogel, J., & Nehmad, E. (2009). Internet social network communities: Risk taking, trust, and privacy concerns. *Computers in Human Behavior, 25*(1), 153–160. doi:10.1016/j.chb.2008.08.006

Fox, J., & Moreland, J. J. (2015). The dark side of social networking sites: An exploration of the relational and psychological stressors associated with Facebook use and affordances. *Computers in Human Behavior, 45*, 168–176. doi:10.1016/j.chb.2014.11.083

Gentzler, A. L., Oberhauser, A. M., Westerman, D., & Nadorff, D. K. (2011). College students' use of electronic communication with parents: Links to loneliness, attachment, and relationship quality. *Cyberpsychology, Behavior, and Social Networking*, *14*(1-2), 71–74. doi:10.1089/cyber.2009.0409 PMID:20973676

Gonzales, A. L., & Hancock, J. T. (2011). Mirror, mirror on my Facebook wall: Effects of exposure to Facebook on self-esteem. *Cyberpsychology, Behavior, and Social Networking*, *14*(1-2), 79–83. doi:10.1089/cyber.2009.0411 PMID:21329447

Griffiths, M. D. (2012). Facebook addiction: Concerns, criticisms and recommendations. *Psychological Reports*, *110*(2), 518–520. doi:10.2466/01.07.18.PR0.110.2.518-520 PMID:22662405

Griffiths, M. D., Kuss, D. J., & Demetrovics, Z. (2014). Social networking addiction: An overview of preliminary findings. *Behavioral addictions: Criteria, evidence and treatment*, 119-141. doi:10.1016/B978-0-12-407724-9.00006-9

Hargittai, E. (2008). Whose space? Differences among users and non-users of social netwrok sites. *Journal of Computer-Mediated Communication*, *13*(1), 276–297. doi:10.1111/j.1083-6101.2007.00396.x

Hughes, D. J., Rowe, M., Batey, M., & Lee, A. (2012). A tale of two sites: Twitter vs. Facebook and the personality predictors of social media usage. *Computers in Human Behavior*, *28*(2), 561–569. doi:10.1016/j.chb.2011.11.001

Jelenchick, L. A., Eickhoff, J. C., & Moreno, M. A. (2013). Facebook depression?"Social networking site use and depression in older adolescents. *The Journal of Adolescent Health*, *52*(1), 128–130. doi:10.1016/j.jadohealth.2012.05.008 PMID:23260846

Joinson, A. N. (2004). Self-esteem, interpersonal risk, and preference for e-mail to face-to-face communication. *Cyberpsychology & Behavior*, *7*(4), 472–478. doi:10.1089/cpb.2004.7.472 PMID:15331035

Kim, H. H. (2016). The impact of online social networking on adolescent psychological well-being (WB): A population-level analysis of Korean school aged-children. *International Journal of Adolescence and Youth*, 1–13. doi:10.1080/02673843.2016.1197135

Kim, J., LaRose, R., & Peng, W. (2009). Loneliness as the cause and the effect of problematic internet use: The relationship between internet use and psychological well-being. *CyberPsychology & Behavior, 12*(4), 451-455. doi: 10.1089=cpb.2008.0327

King, D. L., Delfabbro, P. H., Kaptsis, D., & Zwaans, T. (2014). Adolescent simulated gambling via digital and social media: An emerging problem. *Computers in Human Behavior*, *31*, 305–313. doi:10.1016/j.chb.2013.10.048

Krämer, N. C., & Winter, S. (2008). Impression management 2.0: The relationship of self-esteem, extroversion, self-efficacy, and self-presentation within social networking sites. *Journal of Media Psychology*, *20*(3), 106–116. doi:10.1027/1864-1105.20.3.106

Kraut, R., Patterson, M., Lundmark, V., Kiesler, S., Mukopadhyay, T., & Scherlis, W. (1998). Internet Paradox: A social technology that reduces social involvement and psychological well-being? *The American Psychologist*, *53*(9), 1017–1031. doi:10.1037/0003-066X.53.9.1017 PMID:9841579

Kross, E., Verduyn, P., Demiralp, E., Park, J., Lee, S. D., Lin, N., ... Ybarra, O. (2013). Facebook use predicts declines in subjective well-being in young adults. *PLoS One*, *8*(8), e69841. doi:10.1371/journal.pone.0069841 PMID:23967061

Kuss, D. J., & Griffiths, M. D. (2011). Online social networking and addiction: A review of the psychological literature. *International Journal of Environmental Research and Public Health*, *8*(12), 3528–3552. doi:10.3390/ijerph8093528 PMID:22016701

Kuss, D. J., & Griffiths, M. D. (2017). Social networking sites and addiction: Ten lessons learned. *International Journal of Environmental Research and Public Health*, *14*(3), 311. doi:10.3390/ijerph14030311 PMID:28304359

Kyriacou, C. (2017). Dealing with cyberbullying by pupils. In All Party Parliamentary Group on Bullying (Ed.), *Evidence presented at meetings of the All Party Parliamentary Group on Bullying 2011-2016* (pp. 21-22). London: All Party Parliamentary Group on Bullying.

Lou, L. L., Yan, Z., Nickerson, A., & McMorris, R. (2012). An examination of the reciprocal relationship of loneliness and Facebook use among first-year college students. *Journal of Educational Computing Research*, *46*(1), 105–117. doi:10.2190/EC.46.1.e

Lucas, M., Mekary, R., Pan, A., Mirzaei, F., O'Reilly, É. J., Willett, W. C., ... Ascherio, A. (2011). Relation between clinical depression risk and physical activity and time spent watching television in older women: A 10-year prospective follow-up study. *American Journal of Epidemiology*, *174*(9), 1017–1027. doi:10.1093/aje/kwr218 PMID:21984659

Mehdizadeh, S. (2010). Self-presentation 2.0: Narcissism and self-esteem on Facebook. *CyberPsychology, Behavior, and Social Networking, 13*(4), 357-364. doi: 10.1089=cyber.2009.0257

Muscanell, N. L., & Guadagno, R. E. (2012). Make new friends or keep the old: Gender and personality differences in social networking use. *Computers in Human Behavior*, *28*(1), 107–112. doi:10.1016/j.chb.2011.08.016

O'Keeffe, G. S., & Clarke-Pearson, K. (2011). The impact of social media on children, adolescents, and families. *Pediatrics*, *127*(4), 800–804. doi:10.1542/peds.2011-0054 PMID:21444588

Oberst, U., Wegmann, E., Stodt, B., Brand, M., & Chamarro, A. (2017). Negative consequences from heavy social networking in adolescents: The mediating role of fear of missing out. *Journal of Adolescence*, *55*, 51–60. doi:10.1016/j.adolescence.2016.12.008 PMID:28033503

Oldmeadow, J. A., Quinn, S., & Kowert, R. (2013). Attachment style, social skills, and Facebook use amongst adults. *Computers in Human Behavior*, *29*(3), 1142–1149. doi:10.1016/j.chb.2012.10.006

Olenik-Shemesh, D., Heiman, T., & Eden, S. (2012). Cyberbullying victimisation in adolescence: Relationships with loneliness and depressive mood. *Emotional & Behavioural Difficulties*, *17*(3-4), 361–374. doi:10.1080/13632752.2012.704227

Pantic, I. (2014). Online social networking and mental health. *Cyberpsychology, Behavior, and Social Networking*, *17*(10), 652–657. doi:10.1089/cyber.2014.0070 PMID:25192305

Pantic, I., Damjanovic, A., Todorovic, J., Topalovic, D., Bojovic-Jovic, D., Ristic, S., & Pantic, S. (2012). Association between online social networking and depression in high-school students: Behavioral physiology viewpoint. *Psychiatria Danubina*, *24*, 90–93. PMID:22447092

Park, S., Lee, S. W., Kwak, J., Cha, M., & Jeong, B. (2013). Activities on Facebook reveal the depressive state of users. *Journal of Medical Internet Research*, *15*(10), 1–15. doi:10.2196/jmir.2718 PMID:24084314

Pavot, W., & Diener, E. (2004). The subjective evaluation of well-being in adulthood: Findings andimplications. *Ageing International*, *29*(2), 113–135. doi:10.100712126-004-1013-4

Przybylski, A. K., Murayama, K., DeHaan, C. R., & Gladwell, V. (2013). Motivational, emotional, and behavioral correlates of fear of missing out. *Computers in Human Behavior*, *29*(4), 1841–1848. doi:10.1016/j.chb.2013.02.014

Rosen, L. D., Whaling, K., Rab, S., Carrier, L. M., & Cheever, N. A. (2013). Is Facebook creating "iDisorders"? The link between clinical symptoms of psychiatric disorders and technology use, attitudes and anxiety. *Computers in Human Behavior*, *29*(3), 1243–1254. doi:10.1016/j.chb.2012.11.012

Salmela-Aro, K., Upadyaya, K., Hakkarainen, K., Lonka, K., & Alho, K. (2017). The dark side of Internet use: Two longitudinal studies of excessive Internet use, depressive symptoms, school burnout and engagement among Finnish early and late adolescents. *Journal of Youth and Adolescence*, *46*(2), 343–357. doi:10.100710964-016-0494-2 PMID:27138172

Sampasa-Kanyinga, H., & Lewis, R. F. (2015). Frequent use of social network sites is associated with poor psychological functioning among children and adolescents. *Cyberpsychology, Behavior, and Social Networking*, *18*(7), 380–385. doi:10.1089/cyber.2015.0055 PMID:26167836

Simoncic, T. E., Kuhlman, K. R., Vargas, I., Houchins, S., & Lopez-Duran, N. L. (2014). Facebook use and depressive symptomatology: Investigating the role of neuroticism and extraversion in youth. *Computers in Human Behavior*, *40*, 1–5. doi:10.1016/j.chb.2014.07.039 PMID:25861155

Statista. Average Numbers of Hours Per Day Spent by Social Media Users on all Social Media Channels as of 4th Quarter 2015, by Country. (n.d.). Available online: https://www.statista.com/statistics/270229/usage-duration-of-social-networks-by-country/

Statista Facts on Social Networks. (n.d.). Available online: https://www.statista.com/topics/1164/social-networks/

Subrahmanyam, K., & Lin, G. (2007). Adolescents on the net: Internet use and well-being. *Adolescence*, *42*(168), 659–677. PMID:18229503

Valenzuela, S., Park, N., & Kee, K. F. (2009). Is there social capital in a social network site? Facebook use and college students' life satisfaction, trust and participation. *Journal of Computer-Mediated Communication*, *14*(4), 875–901. doi:10.1111/j.1083-6101.2009.01474.x

Valkenburg, P. M., Peter, J., & Schouten, A. P. (2006). Friend networking sites and their relationship to adolescents' well-being and social self-esteem. *Cyberpsychology & Behavior*, *9*(5), 584–590. doi:10.1089/cpb.2006.9.584 PMID:17034326

Walther, J. B. (1996). Computer-mediated communication: Impersonal, interpersonal, and hyperpersonal interaction. *Communication Research, 23*(1), 3–43. doi:10.1177/009365096023001001

Weisskirch, R. S., & Delevi, R. (2011). 'Sexting' and adult romantic attachment. *Computers in Human Behavior, 27*(5), 1697–1701. doi:10.1016/j.chb.2011.02.008

Wilson, K., Fornasier, S., & White, K. M. (2010). Psychological predictors of young adults' use of social networking sites. *CyberPsychology, Behavior, and Social Networking, 13*(2), 173-177. doi: 10.1089=cyber.2009.0094

Wilson, R. E., Gosling, S. D., & Graham, L. T. (2012). A review of Facebook research in the social sciences. *Perspectives on Psychological Science, 7*(3), 203–220. doi:10.1177/1745691612442904 PMID:26168459

KEY TERMS AND DEFINITIONS

Addiction: A chronic disorder with biological, psychological, social, and environmental factors influencing its development and maintenance.

Attachment: Emotional bond or connectedness between two people, especially child and the caregiver.

Cyberbullying: A kind of harassment that occurs on the internet or either by cell phones or other devices.

Depression: A mood disorder marked by emotional, mental, and physical symptoms such as feelings of sadness, hopelessness, or pessimism, lowered self-esteem, reduced energy and vitality, slowness of thought.

Loneliness: An unpleasant emotional response to isolation.

Personality: Individual differences in characteristic patterns of thinking, feeling, and behaving.

Self-Esteem: A person's overall sense of self-worth or personal value.

Social Anxiety: Nervousness in social situations.

Social Networking Site: An online platform that allows users to create a public profile and interact with other users on the website.

Subjective Well-Being: A term used for people's own judgements over the quality of their lives and includes both emotional and cognitive aspects.

Chapter 3
Relational Body Identities:
Body Image Control Through Self-Portraits - A Revision of the Body Image Control in Photos Questionnaire

Valentina Boursier
University of Naples Federico II, Italy

Valentina Manna
Association for Social Promotion Roots in Action, Italy

ABSTRACT

Self-portrayal is one of the most popular online activities, especially among adolescents and young adults. The selfie-craze explosion through photo-sharing represent a new task for adolescents' researchers, but few instruments explore how adolescents can control their body image through self-portraits. One of these is the body image control in photos questionnaire. The aim of this chapter is to develop and validate a revised short version of the BICPQ, administered to 1220 Italian adolescents. The establishment of a cut-off procedure is proposed for screening purposes to identify at-risk and problematic users. Moreover, differences by gender and age are explored and discussed.

INTRODUCTION

Self-portrayal is one of the most popular online activities, especially among adolescents and young adults (Lenhart, Purcell, Smith, & Zickuhr, 2010): 93 million selfies are taken each day by smartphone users, and online photo sharing in 2014 was about 880 billion (Lee & Sung, 2016).

The Internet anonymity despite the hyper-visibility, as well as the intensified and rapid control over the interactions through the web, let people use the public net-space for private or social identity purposes (Valkenburg, Schouten & Peter, 2005). For examples, people can modify their self-portraits to be posted online in order to resemble closely to social ideals (Siibak & Hernwall, 2011), by taking advantages of a positive self-image's presentation on social networks (McAndrew & Jeong, 2012). Thus, the Internet provides a virtual space in which a great amount of control can be applied over one's own external appearance, by improving or manipulating it based on the others' feedbacks. These aspects represent basic

DOI: 10.4018/978-1-5225-4047-2.ch003

components in the analysis of the personal and interpersonal body-identities construction for the new generation: the so-called "millennials". Indeed, the self-portrait's approval may function as a part of their self-definition and self-confidence, especially during the adolescence transition, due to the modeling role of interpersonal relationships on one's body image and self-construction, nowadays also carried on through the web medium. Considering the selfie-craze explosion and the widespread use of the Social Networking Sites (SNS) in everyday life, and taking in account the specificity of the adolescence, as a stage of life during which the body identity construction and the relational interactions represent core elements, the authors question the use of self-portraits as an instrument to control the body image and the social identity, by providing a tool for measuring the problematic use of body image control through photos.

BACKGROUND

The identity construction is a personal and psychological process that involves body indwelling and, profoundly, the connection with primary emotional and relational experiences. At the same time, it represents a public process involving both the individual ''identity announcement" and the ''identity placement" provided by the others, who endorse the claimed identity (Stone, 1981). Certainly, the identity construction and the *new* body integration represent phase-specific developmental tasks during the adolescence (Zhao, Grasmuck, & Martin, 2008). On one hand, body transformations require such a kind of process; on the other hand, the experience of *who I am* is deeply related to *the way I look* and to *the group I belong to*, as they suggest what the *other* see and reflect about *me*. As a result, one's own body image is strongly influenced by self-esteem and self-evaluation, and strictly linked to the evaluation provided by the others. Moreover, it can be powerfully affected by cultural messages and societal/media standards of appearance and attractiveness. For this reason, research investigating the process of identity construction in adolescence is increasingly exploring the Internet environment (Pelosi, Zorzi & Corsano, 2014), which constitutes a key context for interpersonal relationships and self-presentation.

Additionally, the opportunities to establish and maintain relationships on the Internet have multiplied in the last few years. Social networking sites (SNS) and smartphone apps have rapidly expanded virtual and real relationships formation through the web medium. Thus, the use of social media has become an increasingly popular leisure activity in many countries (Kuss & Griffiths, 2011). People visit social media sites engaging in different types of entertainment and social/interpersonal activities such as playing games, socializing, passing time, communicating, and posting pictures (Allen, Ryan, Gray, Mclnerney & Waters, 2014; Ryan, Chester, Reece, & Xenos, 2014). Given the recent worldwide proliferation of SNS and the over-expanding numbers of adolescents joining up, these sites and apps presumably play an integral role in adolescents' life. Although this has quickly become a normal modern phenomenon (Valkenburg, Peter, & Schouten, 2006), concerns have been raised regarding the potential addictive use of social media (Andreassen & Pallesen, 2014; Andreassen, 2015, Griffiths, Kuss & Demetrovics, 2014). At the same time, the impact of social media usage on one's self-view has been explored (de Vries, 2014), as well as the relationship between SNS addiction, self esteem and narcissism which has been recently demonstrated, especially in girls and young women (Andreassen, Pallesen & Griffiths, 2017).

Many image-centered social media platforms like Instagram and tumblr, and apps such as Snapchat and WhatsApp, are growing in numbers of users and importance. Recently, Kuss and Griffiths (2017) stated that SNS increasingly represent *a Way of Being* and a potential form of addiction too, as data diffusion clearly shows: in 2016, the most popular social networking site was Facebook with 1.712 million active users and 136,000 photos uploaded every minute. In 2016 Instagram, launched in 2010 as a specific picture sharing SNS, have registered 500 million active users. In 2011, Snapchat was launched as a SNS that allows users to message and connect with others by using a smartphone to send photos, texts, videos; in 2016 it had 200 million users, becoming very popular among the youngest. In 2016, Twitter had 313 million active users, making it the most successful microblogging site to date. Social networking can include instant messaging, like the most popular messaging services such as WhatsApp and Facebook Messenger with 1.000 million active users each. Obviously, the Internet, Apps and SNS use and misuse present many opportunities and risks for the adolescents (Livingston, 2008; Boursier & Manna, in press).

MAIN FOCUS OF THE CHAPTER

Issues, Controversies, Problems

In face-to-face interactions, corporal body encounters prevent people from claiming identities different from the visible part of their physical characteristics. The advent of the Internet has changed the traditional conditions of the identity production.

Disembodied online encounters enable people to hide their undesired physical features, and anonymity allows individuals to re-create their biography and personality. In other words, the disembodied and anonymous online environment makes it possible for people to reinvent themselves through the production of new identities (Zhao, Grasmuck, & Martin, 2008).

Thus, disembodiment and anonymity can create a technologically mediated environment in which a new mode of identity production emerges (Bargh, McKenna & Fitzsimons, 2002; McKenna, Green, & Gleason, 2002). Particularly significant in the adolescent's self-construction is the role of interpersonal feedbacks as results of self-presentation that the nowadays millennials mainly realize through photographic material posted online (Zhao, Grasmuck, & Martin, 2008). Indeed, self-presentation is one of the major motives driving activity in SNS (Krämer & Winter, 2008) and the numbers of selfie diffusion refer about a huge phenomenon all over the world.

How strategic one's self-image management could be (Rui & Stefanone, 2013) and which advantages/disadvantages can arise from selfie posting activities?

A previous (Manna & Boursier, 2015a) study has highlighted the large dissemination of this activity among Italian adolescents (aged between 13 and 18 years) and the adolescent's expectancies towards the selfie practice, that probably encourage this ordinary practice. The link between selfie posting and self-presentation, self-confidence, and self-attractiveness (the last especially for boys) contributes to define the way adolescents use selfie.

The advantages of a positive self-image presentation on social networks has been discussed (McAndrew & Jeong, 2012), as well as the risk of a *google-related self-confidence*. The awareness of being evaluated by other users through one's own profile-appearance, can be associated with self-objectification (de Vries & Peter 2013), as significant predictor of objectified body consciousness and shame, for both women and men (Manago Ward, Lemm, Reed, & Seabrook, 2015). Moreover, the increasing use of social networking sites is changing the components of one's image that can be judged salient during the appearance comparison process. It seems that, even though Facebook has been strongly associated with body image concerns (Tiggemann & Miller 2010), women upload to their SNS profiles above all portrait pictures, rather than full-bodied ones (Haferkamp, Eimler, Papadakis & Kruck, 2012). This practice provides them many opportunities to make face, skin, and hair-related comparisons than body comparisons. However, many social media and virtual places perpetuate and promote stereotypical ideals of beauty, especially for the feminine one (Slater, Tiggemann, Hawkins & Werchon, 2011). In this perspective, it has been demonstrated that the SNS use is associated with a greater internalization of thin ideal, appearance comparison and weight dissatisfaction, especially for high school girls (Tiggemann & Miller, 2010; Tiggemann & Slater, 2013). It could be alarming that girls who spend more time on Facebook frequently checking their own profile, have a higher determination for thinness and a greater body dissatisfaction (Fardouly & Vartanian, 2015). Similarly alarming is that, if compared with those girls who did not share self-images on social media, girls who regularly share them report significantly higher overvaluation of the shape and the weight, body dissatisfaction, diet restraint, and internalization of the thin ideal (McLean, Paxton, Wertheim, & Masters, 2015). In the same vein, it has been demonstrated that spending more time on MySpace and Facebook is associated with increased body surveillance, greater endorsement of the thin ideal, more frequent appearance comparisons, and decreased weight satisfaction among girls, younger and older adolescents (Tiggemann & Miller, 2010; Tiggemann & Slater, 2013; 2014). A recent review by Holland and Tiggeman (2016) about the impact of the SNS use on body image and disordered eating outcomes, highlighted that specific SNS activities, such as viewing and uploading photos or seeking negative feedbacks via status updates, can be particularly problematic. Furthermore, appearance-based social comparison often mediates the relationship between SNS use, body image and eating concerns. Particularly, Meier and Gray (2014) determined that the amount of time spent engaging in Facebook "photo activity" (e.g., posting photos, viewing friends' photos) is related to body image concerns, more than the total time spent on Facebook.

Haferkamp and Kramer (2011) showed that both men and women have a decrease in body satisfaction after being exposed to attractive Facebook profiles. Similarly, DeVries et al. (2014) demonstrate that SNS use has been associated to a greater investment on the body appearance and the desire for cosmetic surgery across the genders, with no significant differences and that the SNS use is related to men and women's body image in the same manner and to the same extent (de Vries, Peter, de Graaf, & Nikken, 2016). Likewise, Facebook involvement seems to be a significant predictor of objectified body consciousness and body shame across gender (Manago, Ward, Lemm, Reed, & Seabrook, 2015).

Furthermore, although it is assumed that posting selfies is a gendered process (Albury, 2015), and recent research suggest that women tend to post more selfies than men (Sorokowska, Oleszkiewicz, Frackowiak, Pisanski, Chmiel, & Sorokowski, 2016; Sorokowski, Sorokowska, Oleszkiewicz, Frackowiak, Huk, & Pisanski, 2015), it seems problematic to define if gender is a significant predictor of selfie behaviors. However, gender moderates the relationship between the need for popularity and the selfie posting: the former particularly influences men's selfie posting (Kim & Chock, 2015).

Despite the selfie-craze explosion among adolescents, there is still a lack of instruments specifically exploring how teenagers can control their body image through self-portraits. Measures usually employed in the analysis of the body image only converge on the assessment of body image concerns and appearance-related social comparisons. How SNS users select and edit photographic material in order to improve their physical body image represent a specific and actual topic, barely explored until now.

Indeed, the debate around how the use of social media can impact one's self-view, have not deepened how the selfie practice interconnects with the adolescent task of integrating the sexual body within the identity and the intimate relationships (vis-à-vis or virtual ones). A pioneer study in this direction has been conducted in Italy by Pelosi et al. (2014) through the development of a self-report measure named "Body Image Control in Photos Questionnaire" (BICP, 30 items). Based on the assumption that social networks are ideal places for adolescents to discover their evolutionary processes (Riva, 2010) and face the body mentalization, where the exposure of their bodies assumes greater relevance, the authors developed a tool to evaluate the self-presentation of body image through photographs on Facebook. The measure considers seven steps in photo management that let an increasing control of body image: Aesthetic preparation, Preparation during the taking of photos, Checking of camera's display, Image elaboration through image editing programs, Photo selection, Privacy level, Selection of photos to tag. The scale, which showed a good internal reliability ($\alpha = .819$), highlighted the presence of 5 factors in the Body Image Control in Photos: 1) a control over the negative body image; 2) a control over the positive body image; 3) the control over self-portraits; 4) the control via technological image editing; 5) the control over tagging of photos.

However, relevant aspects such as the use of self-portraits to satisfy the need of surveillance on one's own body, or the importance of confirming and conveying sexual attractiveness through photos, have been excluded from this and other recent researches on the topic. Yet little is known about the quality of the Selfie experience among adolescents, whilst the lack of consensual definition around the self-portraits world led to inconsistencies in the assessment criteria. Particularly, no information are available about a possible cut-off threshold for identifying a problematic use of self-portraits to over control one's own body image. Moreover, empirical data are needed about potential correlations between the Selfie practice and other social media net-activities, such as the problematic use of Internet or Smartphones. Finally, recently published studies provided interesting but yet conflicting results about the role of gender and age on this phenomenon.

Aims

The focus in the current study is to validate a short and reliable instrument to identify maladaptive use of the self-portraits to control over the body image conveyed via social media - with special reference to Facebook - among preadolescents and adolescents. We aimed to:

- Evaluate the psychometric properties of a promising risk measure;
- Establish a cut-off threshold for defining "problematic" teen-use of the self-portraits to control over their body image;
- Estimate the prevalence of potential problematic users and define their typical profile;
- Verify the role of gender and age;
- Explore the interconnections among the phenomenon and other relevant research areas around *e*-adolescence, such as sexual dimensions and social media activities.

Participants

We involved 1220 participants aged 11-19 years (M = 14.14; SD = 2.519), recruited in 12 secondary schools (I and II grade) from culturally-different Naples areas (South Italy), equally distributed for gender (53.9% males and 46.1% females). All participants were Caucasian from Italian families. They all participated voluntary in the research and were informed about the confidentiality of the data and their anonymous treatment.

Measures

Data was collected via a self-report anonymous questionnaire administered to participants in groups during the school-time. It comprised five sections:

1. Sociodemographics;
2. Mobile phone/social networks/apps usage patterns;
3. The Body Surveillance scale (McKinley & Hyde, 1996; Dakanalis, Di Mattei, Bagliacca, Prunas, Sarno, Riva, & Zanetti, 2012);
4. A revised-short version of the Body Image Control in Photos Questionnaire (BICPQ: Pelosi, Zorzi, & Corsano, 2014);
5. A collection of measures to evaluate the overall experience about social media, with reference to the Smartphone (Cuestionario de Experiencias Relacionadas con el Móvil - CERM: Sánchez-Carbonell, Beranuy, Castellana, Chamarro & Oberst, 2008; Beranuy Fargues, Chamarro Lusar, Graner Jordania & Carbonell Sánchez, 2009; Boursier & Manna, in press), the Internet (Internet Related Problem Scale – IRPS: Armstrong, Phillips,&Saling, 2000; Boies, Cooper, & Osborne, 2004; Boursier & Manna, in press), the frequency of Selfie practice and the expectations about it (Weisskirchet &Delevi, 2011; Dir, Cyders & Coskunpinar, 2013; Manna & Boursier, 2015b), and the representation about one's own Sexual Self (Deutsch, 2012; Manna & Boursier, 2017). All measures were adapted into Italian.
   a. The recorded socio-demographics were: gender; age (categorizing pupils into preadolescents 11–13 years: 47%, and adolescents 14–19 years: 53%); school year and school location (Town borough).
   b. Under the section about mobile phone/social networks/apps usage patterns, participants were asked to indicate:
      i. If they have a smartphone;
      ii. Why they use smartphones (to make phone calls, to message, to exchange photos/videos, to surf the Internet);
      iii. Which social networks and apps they use to exchange messages and photos/videos.
   c. The Body Surveillance Scale is a subscale (8 items) of the Objectified Body Consciousness Scale, specifically assessing the interiorization of the observer's perspective, i.e. the degree to which the subject assumes himself/herself as an object to be evaluated based on his/her physical aspect.
   d. In BICPQ, participants were asked to use a 5-point Likert scale to indicate, "How often has this happened to you?"; statements refer to behaviors and habits around the managing of participants' self-portraits or photos immortalizing them and circulating on social media.
   e. To this study aims, a variation of the Body Image Control in Photos Questionnaire was introduced: we reduced the length of the questionnaire by selecting from each factor the items with higher factor loadings and recovering some items, excluded by the authors along their analysis, which referred to the sexual components of the control over body image through photos, particularly relevant to our research purposes. As a result, we obtained a 16-items short version of the BICPQ with the aim of discussing and analyzing a more comprehensive perspective on the phenomenon, by taking in account the identity and sexual challenges of adolescence.

f. The last section included the following measures:
   i. CERM is a measure developed to assess intra- and interpersonal conflicts related to the mobile use, referring both to behavioral and emotional aspects of this phenomenon;
   ii. IRPS is adopted to analyze thoughts, feelings and experiences related to the Internet use, in order to identify maladaptive use of the web;
   iii. The Selfie Frequency Scale is an original 19 items tool developed to quantify how often adolescents do selfie;
   iv. The Selfie Expectancies Scale is an original 34 items instrument, which analyzes the expectancies towards the Selfie, i.e. the individuals' beliefs/perceptions of what the outcomes of the Selfie practice might be: positive expectancies are important and consistent predictors of engagement in specific risk behaviors. It includes 7 factors as multidimensional components of the construct: F1 Worries, i.e. possible negative consequences of Selfie on the self and on familial and couple relationships; F2 Virtual related anguishes, specifically referring to the potential negative consequences related to the "on-line" features of Selfie; F3 Sexual desire, in terms of feelings of excitement and sexual phantasy, related to Selfie; F4 Ordinary practice, stating the ordinary nature of Selfie as an ubiquitin component of modern adolescents' life; F5 Self confidence, referring to the narcissistic nature of Selfie as an instrument to reinforce the self esteem; F6 Self presentation related to the use of Selfie as a way to present oneself to the others (here a risk of self manipulation should be considered); F7 Perceived risks, referring to the perception of Selfie as somehow dangerous.
   v. The Sexual Self scale measures the understanding and perceptions of oneself as a sexual person. It includes two factors, particularly interesting for our research purposes, i.e. F1: sexual self attractiveness(measuring the perception of the Self as attractive from a sexual perspective) and F2: body care (including items referring to the care of the body from a health and physical point of view).

ANALYSIS

The factorial properties and structure of our revised-short version of BICPQ (BICPQ-rev) were firstly explored and verified among a sample of 712 adolescents by EFA and CFA in Mplus 6.11 (Muthén & Muthén, 2010). Due to the non-normal distribution of the sample, we employed Robust Maximum Likehood with oblique Geomin rotation. The factorial solution was identified according to the criteria of minimal factorial saturation (at least 0.30), residuals analysis and avoiding high cross-loadings (Fabrigar, Wegener, MacCallum, & Strahan, 1999). It is supported by scree-plot analysis, Bartlett's test of sphericity and KMO measure of sampling adequacy. In order to verify the emerged structure solution and test the dimensionality of our version of BICPQ, a Confirmatory Factor Analysis (CFA) was used with Robust Maximum Likehood. To further verify the construct validity, we also conducted a 2nd order CFA highlighting the existence of a single implicit psychological construct. The overall model fit was evaluated by CFI, RMSEA (90% CI), TLI and SRMR. Secondly, the sample was extended to 580 preadolescents and the factorial solution was confirmed also on this group. Internal reliability was calculated among the whole sample through Cronbach's α, item-total correlations and factor correlations, also evaluating the internal coherence of each factor. Convergent validity was assessed by bivariate correlations between BICPQ-rev and Body Surveillance ($p<.001$).

We also applied a tentative statistical establishment of a cut-off score on the whole sample of pre-adolescents and adolescents, by referring to the criteria used in literature on problematic mobile phone use (Lopez-Fernandez, Honrubia-Serrano, Freixa-Blanxart, & Gibson, 2014): the 15th, 80th, and 90th percentiles are used to classify occasional, habitual, at risk, and problematic use respectively. Then, an equivalent subsample of non-problematic users was randomly extracted to compare them with the group of problematic users and obtain the profile of a typical problematic user, by means of descriptive and ANOVA. One-way ANOVAs were also used to evaluate the role of gender and age on the whole sample. Finally, correlations between the BICPQ-rev and other measures of problematic use around the web were carried on (scales adopted: CERM, IRPS, Selfie Frequency, Selfie Expectancies, Sexual Self) to explore the interconnections among the phenomenon and other relevant areas around e-adolescence.

RESULTS

EFA yielded all factor loadings greater than 0.3. A five-factor solution of the 16items BICPQ-rev was tested with CFA. The model provided a good fit to the data ($\chi 2=180.512$df=94 p .0000; CFI=0.966; TLI=0.956; RMSEA=0.040 [0.031–0.049]; Probability RMSEA <=.05: 0.969, SRMR=0.034).

The obtained solution (Table 1) is quite different from the original version, by revealing the central role of sexual and relational dimensions in controlling the body image via self-portrait:

Factor 1 – Self-ie: This factor specifically refers to the dimension of selfie portraits;
Factor 2 – To Whom: It deals with the privacy restrictions applied to moderate relational exchanges via photos;
Factor 3 – The Others and My Positive Image: Refers to the ways positive image of self is presented to the others;
Factor 4 – Selfie Sexual Attractiveness: Includes items referring to sexualized dimensions of self-photo portraits;
Factor 5 – The Others and My Negative Image: Refers to the ways negative image of the self is preserved from the others' view.

The scale showed an excellent reliability ($\alpha=.891$), with strong inter-correlations among its factors (ranging from $r=.248$ to $r=.869$. Bivariate correlations indicated that BICPQ-rev and Body Surveillance subscale assess interrelated, yet distinct, constructs ($r=.439$), thus confirming the convergent validity of the tool. (Table 2)

Our sample revealed a widespread Internet use: 97.8% participants have a smartphone, used to surf the Internet (87.2%), with special reference to Facebook for exchanging messages (68.6%) or photos (64.9%). We registered a mean of 2.45 for BICPQ-rev scores among participants (SD=.798). Our participants mainly show the need of controlling their negative image to be showed to others (F5: M=2.86; SD=1.12), i.e. as it appears on the social media. Secondly, the control over one's own positive image (M = 2.65; SD = 2.50) and the managing of identity aspects via selfies (M = 2.60; SD = 2.60) seem to be relevant matters to our participants. The findings show interconnection between the identity and relational aspects conveyed via photos on social media.

Following Lopez-Fernandez and colleagues (2014), we established the score of 55 as a cut-off for identifying problematic users. The categories of occasional, habitual, at risk and problematic user correspond to scores of 0-24, 25-50, 51-55 and more than 55 respectively. Results revealed that 16.6% participants were occasional users, 64.4% habitual users,9.5% were at risk of problematic use and 9.5%problematic users (within the range of other risk measures for related activities, e.g. Internet or Smartphone use: Boursier & Manna, in press). Findings are quite worrying if we sum at risk and problematic users, obtaining 19% participants showing potential excessive control on the body image.

Then, a subsample non-problematic users (n=115) was randomly extracted to be compared with problematic users. Considering the smartphones/apps/social networks use, a clear profile of BICP problematic users was not observed: the latter do not differ in the *way* they use a specific social media tool but in the *privacy control* hey apply to their body image, as a tool to mark the intimacy borders around their virtual self within virtual relationships. Indeed, they show scores higher than their group average (M=3.87) on the same items that appears to be challenging for the non-problematic users, *but* on the factor "To whom" (F2), where their scores are much higher. Thus, they show a specific tendency to limit the view on their body image to specific people.

Interestingly, problematic and non-problematic users share the same controversial aspects with special reference to the issue, "I practice in front of the mirror to find how to look good in photos" (M=1; SD =.000) and about the Selfie Sexual Attractiveness. These dimensions seem to be a matter problematic within the whole sample. In other words, the differentiation between what could be considered as problematic and what "non-problematic" on this area appear really subtle.

Thus, in what ways do problematic and non-problematic users properly differ? ANOVA's results (Table 3) reveal that the problematic users show higher score on *all* items and factors, thus suggesting that the difference between the two groups may consist in a *quantitative* and not qualitative point of view for what strictly concerning the control over body image through photos. And, what about the comprehensive experience these groups have about social media and close issues? The results from the correlations with the other scales (Table 4) suggest that people that apply a problematic control over their body images via self-portrait also have a problematic relation with the Smartphone (r =.448) and with the Internet (r =.349), thus, with the virtual world in general. Moreover, they also show a major tendency to the objectification of their body (r =.439), to have care of it (r =.245) and to believe in their sexual attractiveness (r=.223). Thus, the body seems to be used as an object or a sexualized tool.

Moreover, problematic and non-problematic users greatly differ in their peculiar experience with the Selfie practice. Indeed, the problematic BICP users do Selfie more frequently, suggesting a compulsive attitudes towards the practice, and they have more worries and virtual-related anguishes. Whereas, the non-problematic BICP users have more positive expectancies towards Selfie, that is, in their view, an ordinary practice to strengthen self-confidence and present themselves to others. Thus, they show the advantages of a positive self-image's presentation on social networks and of the use of social media to impact one's self-view. Finally, our findings suggest a relevant role played by gender and age: problematic users are mostly preadolescents (59.1%) and clearly female (70.4%), having a smartphone in almost all cases (97.5%). The mean BICP score was 2.71 (SD=.817) for girls and 2.29 (SD=.795) for boys. Relevant gender differences were found on several factors via ANOVAs (Table 5), revealing a major condition of risk among girls. Indeed, they apply a greater control both on their positive and negative image conveyed via self-portraits, and show a greater tendency to use Selfie as a practice to manage identity issues. On the contrary, boys most attribute to the Selfie a sexualized dimension dealing with the self-attractiveness. Relevant differences based on age were also registered between adolescents and

Figure 1. Full model

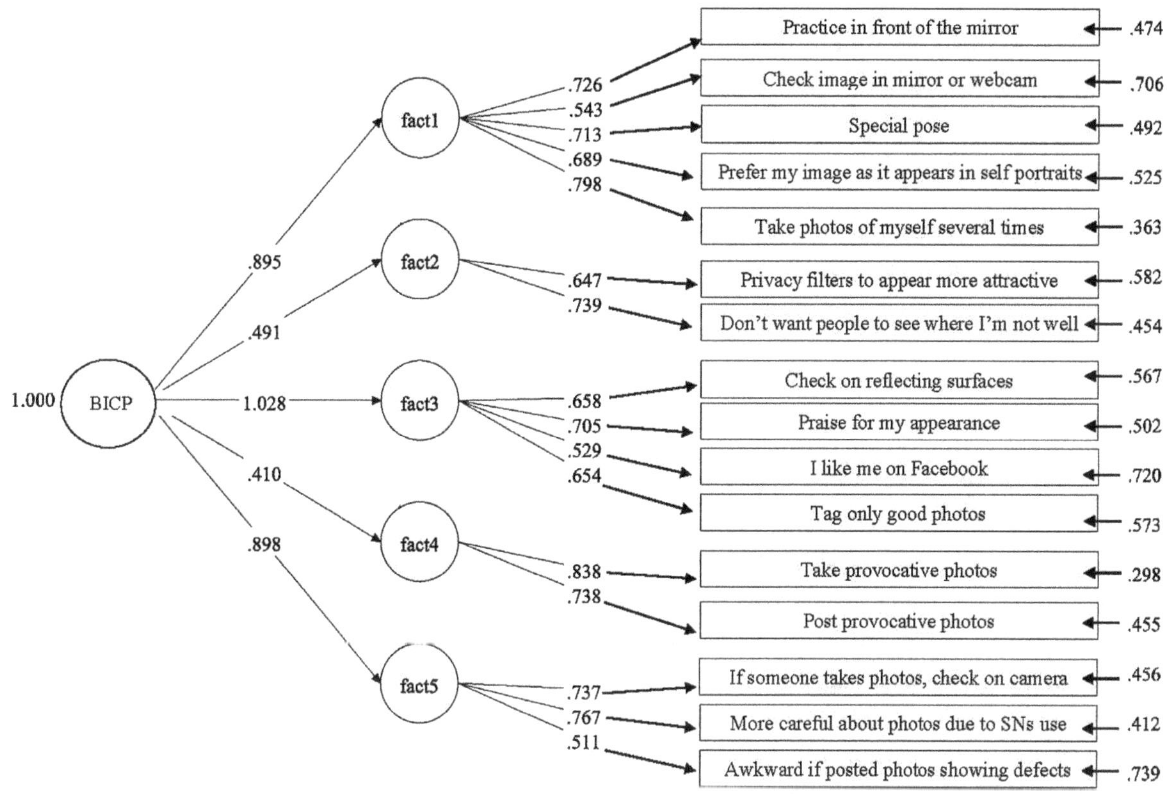

preadolescents (Table 6): the younger is the participant, the more problematic is his/her tendency to control over the body image via self-portraits, with special reference to identity aspects related to the selfie practice (Figure 1). This is confirmed by the data registered about some behaviors that appear more typical of preadolescents, such as practicing in front of the mirror, checking their own image in the camera, preferring self-portraits rather than photos taken by others, taking several photos before selecting one and do not wanting people to see photos where they are not well.

FUTURE RESEARCH DIRECTIONS

This study has some limitations to be considered when interpreting the reported findings:

- Participants were recruited using a non-probability sampling technique, which potentially limits the external validity of the findings. However, to the best of the authors' knowledge, there are no data available on this issue in this context taking in account the mentioned need for the establishment of a cut-off and for the comparison by gender and age;
- Data were entirely collected using self-report questionnaires, which may produce potential biases (e.g., social desirability biases) but at the same time provide several advantages, such as: inter-

pretability, richness of information, motivation to report and sheer practicality (Paulhus & Vazire, 2007);

- This is a situate study, i.e. locally based: in the future it would be interesting to compare different Italian regions to verify the existence of differences between North and South Italy, considering that Italy is a Country with strong territorial differences. Cross-cultural research should also be conducted in the future.

Besides these potential limitations, the present study has some key strengths. It provides a short and psychometrically valid measure to assess the problematic control over body image through photos, and given the strong psychometrics of the instrument, researchers are encouraged to consider adopting this tool to assess the way preadolescents/adolescents use SNS as place to manage their own body images in relation with the others. Thus, future research on this specific topic are suggested.

CONCLUSION

Focusing on the widespread use of the public net-space for private or social identity purposes and on the possibilities provided by social networks to apply a great amount of control over one's own external appearance, this study contributed to the ongoing debate regards the use of photos on SNS to improve and manipulate the body image. The theme was explored with special reference to adolescence, as a stage of life during which the body-identities construction and the relational interactions are strongly interconnected in determining the self-definition and self-confidence.

Moreover, taking in account the selfie-craze explosion and the widespread use of the SNS, a specific contribution to the reflection about the use of self-portraits as an instrument to control the body image and the social identity has been proposed and here expanded. Indeed, authors included aspects related to the development of the adolescent Sexual Self and to the risk of an objectification of the body as key components to be considered when focusing on these issues.

Moving from this debate, this study presented the validation of a psychometric tool to assess the problematic use of body image control through photos on Facebook among Italian preadolescents/adolescents, that overcomes the shortcomings of extant instruments and researches. To the best of the authors' knowledge, this is the first study to provide empirical information about the measurement of a cut-off threshold for preadolescents/adolescents.

The proposed 5-factors model fitted the data adequately, highlighting the existence of interconnected dimensions of the control applied over Body Image through photos, dealing with positive and negative aspects of the Self as exposed to the others' view. These results, together with good sensitivity and reliability, could indicate the utility of the scale to measure whether a preadolescent/adolescent could develop an *over control* of the Body Image on social media via self-portraits.

Compared with the original version of the instrument here adopted, this revised version of the BICPQ reveals the central role of sexual and relational dimensions in controlling the body image via self-portrait, in addiction to the other dimensions already highlighted by a previous study in the Italian context.

Indeed, this new model of BICP proposes a more comprehensive framework, taking in account the key role of sexuality, surveillance over the body and expectancies in the adolescents' experiences of their own body. What is here defined probably represents a more complete operationalization of the BICP.

In this perspective, the problematic relation with the manipulation of body images defines a continuous (not dichotomous) measure which can identify lower, medium or higher level of risky net use.

The estimated prevalence of preadolescents/adolescents classified as problematic users, by using the cut off procedure, was 9.5%, which is within the range of other risk behaviors related to the use of Social Media (Boursier & Manna, in press).

Our findings also show some advantages of a positive self-image's presentation on social networks and of the use of social media to impact one's self-view. Finally, they suggest a relevant role played by gender and age: showing that problematic users are mostly preadolescents (59.1%) and clearly female (70.4%). The study also highlighted a gendered tendency to use Selfie as a practice to manage identity issues, particularly spread among girls, with boys more interested in the sexualized dimension dealing with the self-attractiveness. These results partially support and partially contradict previous international studies, thus suggesting to promote preventive programs which should take in account the five dimensions emerged as relevant in determining the amount of control over body image, to be differentiated by gender and age.

REFERENCES

Albury, K. (2015). Selfiesl Selfies, Sexts and Sneaky Hats: Young People's Understandings of Gendered Practices of Self-Representation. *International Journal of Communication*, *9*, 12.

Allen, K. A., Ryan, T., Gray, D. L., McInerney, D. M., & Waters, L. (2014). Social media use and social connectedness in adolescents: The positives and the potential pitfalls. *The Educational and Developmental Psychologist*, *31*(1), 18–31. doi:10.1017/edp.2014.2

Andreassen, C. S. (2015). Online social network site addiction: A comprehensive review. *Current Addiction Reports*, *2*(2), 175–184. doi:10.100740429-015-0056-9

Andreassen, C. S., & Pallesen, S. (2014). Social network site addiction – An overview. *Current Pharmaceutical Design*, *20*(25), 4053–4061. doi:10.2174/13816128113199990616 PMID:24001298

Andreassen, C. S., Pallesen, S., & Griffiths, M. D. (2017). The relationship between addictive use of social media, narcissism, and self-esteem: Findings from a large national survey. *Addictive Behaviors*, *64*, 287–293. doi:10.1016/j.addbeh.2016.03.006 PMID:27072491

Armstrong, L., Phillips, J. G., & Saling, L. L. (2000). Potential determinants of heavier internet usage. *International Journal of Human-Computer Studies*, *53*(4), 537–550. doi:10.1006/ijhc.2000.0400

Bargh, J. A., McKenna, K. Y., & Fitzsimons, G. M. (2002). Can you see the real me? Activation and expression of the "true self" on the Internet. *The Journal of Social Issues*, *58*(1), 33–48. doi:10.1111/1540-4560.00247

BeranuyFargues, M., ChamarroLusar, A., GranerJordania, C., & Carbonell Sánchez, X. (2009). Validación de dos escalas breves para evaluar la adicción a Internet y el abuso de móvil. *Psicothema*, *21*(3).

Boies, S. C., Cooper, A., & Osborne, C. S. (2004). Variations in Internet-related problems and psychosocial functioning in online sexual activities: Implications for social and sexual development of young adults. *Cyberpsychology & Behavior*, *7*(2), 207–230. doi:10.1089/109493104323024474 PMID:15140364

Boursier, V., & Manna, V. (in press). Problematic linkages in adolescents. Italian adaptation of a measure for Internet-related problems. In B. Bozoglan (Ed.), *Psychological, Social, and Cultural Aspects of Internet Addiction*. Hershey, PA: IGI Global.

Dakanalis, A., Di Mattei, V. E., Bagliacca, E. P., Prunas, A., Sarno, L., Riva, G., & Zanetti, M. A. (2012). Disordered eating behaviors among Italian men: Objectifying media and sexual orientation differences. *Eating Disorders*, *20*(5), 356–367. doi:10.1080/10640266.2012.715514 PMID:22985233

de Vries, D. A., Peter, J., de Graaf, H., & Nikken, P. (2016). Adolescents' social network site use, peer appearance-related feedback, and body dissatisfaction: Testing a mediation model. *Journal of Youth and Adolescence*, *45*(1), 211–224. doi:10.100710964-015-0266-4 PMID:25788122

Deutsch, A. R. (2012). *A test of a conceptual model of sexual self-concept and its relation to other dimensions of sexuality* (Unpublished doctoral dissertation). The University of Nebraska, Lincoln, NE.

deVries, D. A. (2014). *Social media and online self-presentation: Effects on how we see ourselves and our bodies* (Unpublished doctoral dissertation). University of Amsterdam.

deVries, D. A., & Peter, J. (2013). Women on display: The effect of portraying the self online on women's self-objectification. *Computers in Human Behavior*, *29*(4), 1483–1489. doi:10.1016/j.chb.2013.01.015

Dir, A. L., Cyders, M. A., & Coskunpinar, A. (2013). From the bar to the bed via mobile phone: A first test of the role of problematic alcohol use, sexting, and impulsivity-related traits in sexual hookups. *Computers in Human Behavior*, *29*(4), 1664–1670. doi:10.1016/j.chb.2013.01.039

Fabrigar, L. R., Wegener, D. T., MacCallum, R. C., & Strahan, E. J. (1999). Evaluating the use of exploratory factor analysis in psychological research. *Psychological Methods*, *4*(3), 272–299. doi:10.1037/1082-989X.4.3.272

Fardouly, J., & Vartanian, L. R. (2015). Negative comparisons about one's appearance mediate the relationship between Facebook usage and body image concerns. *Body Image*, *12*, 82–88. doi:10.1016/j.bodyim.2014.10.004 PMID:25462886

Griffiths, M. D., Kuss, D. J., & Demetrovics, Z. (2014). Social networking addiction: An overview of preliminary findings. In K. P. Rosenberg & L. C. Feder (Eds.), *Behavioral addictions: Criteria, evidence, and treatment* (pp. 119–141). London: Academic Press. doi:10.1016/B978-0-12-407724-9.00006-9

Haferkamp, N., Eimler, S. C., Papadakis, A. M., & Kruck, J. V. (2012). Men are from Mars, women are from Venus? Examining gender differences in self-presentation on social networking sites. *Cyberpsychology, Behavior, and Social Networking*, *15*(2), 91–98. doi:10.1089/cyber.2011.0151 PMID:22132897

Haferkamp, N., & Krämer, N. C. (2011). Social comparison 2.0: Examining the effects of online profiles on social-networking sites. *Cyberpsychology, Behavior, and Social Networking*, *14*(5), 309–314. doi:10.1089/cyber.2010.0120 PMID:21117976

Holland, G., & Tiggemann, M. (2016). A systematic review of the impact of the use of social networking sites on body image and disordered eating outcomes. *Body Image*, *17*, 100–110. doi:10.1016/j.bodyim.2016.02.008 PMID:26995158

Kim, J. W., & Chock, T. M. (2015). Body image 2.0: Associations between social grooming on Facebook and body image concerns. *Computers in Human Behavior*, *48*, 331–339. doi:10.1016/j.chb.2015.01.009

Krämer, N. C., & Winter, S. (2008). Impression management 2.0: The relationship of self-esteem, extraversion, self-efficacy, and self-presentation within social networking sites. *Journal of Media Psychology*, *20*(3), 106–116. doi:10.1027/1864-1105.20.3.106

Kuss, D. J., & Griffiths, M. D. (2011). Online social networking and addiction—a review of the psychological literature. *International Journal of Environmental Research and Public Health*, *8*(9), 3528–3552. doi:10.3390/ijerph8093528 PMID:22016701

Kuss, D. J., & Griffiths, M. D. (2017). Social networking sites and addiction: Ten lessons learned. *International Journal of Environmental Research and Public Health*, *14*(3), 311. doi:10.3390/ijerph14030311 PMID:28304359

Lee, J. A., & Sung, Y. (2016). Hide-and-seek: Narcissism and "Selfie"-related behavior. *Cyberpsychology, Behavior, and Social Networking*, *19*(5), 347–351. doi:10.1089/cyber.2015.0486 PMID:27028460

Lenhart, A., Purcell, K., Smith, A., & Zickuhr, K. (2010). *Social Media & Mobile Internet Use among Teens and Young Adults. Pew internet & American life project.* Washington, DC: Millennials.

Livingstone, S. (2008). Taking risky opportunities in youthful content creation: Teenagers' use of social networking sites for intimacy, privacy and self-expression. *New Media & Society*, *10*(3), 393–411. doi:10.1177/1461444808089415

Lopez-Fernandez, O., Honrubia-Serrano, L., Freixa-Blanxart, M., & Gibson, W. (2014). Prevalence of problematic mobile phone use in British adolescents. *Cyberpsychology, Behavior, and Social Networking*, *17*(2), 91–98. doi:10.1089/cyber.2012.0260 PMID:23981147

Manago, A. M., Ward, L. M., Lemm, K. M., Reed, L., & Seabrook, R. (2015). Facebook involvement, objectified body consciousness, body shame, and sexual assertiveness in college women and men. *Sex Roles*, *72*(1-2), 1–14. doi:10.100711199-014-0441-1

Manna, V., & Boursier, V. (2015a, September). *Selfie and Sexting: risky opportunities for teens on web and apps. Some preliminary results.* Paper presented at 17th National Meeting of the Italian Association of Psychology, Section of Clinical and Dynamic Psychology, Milazzo, Italy.

Manna, V., & Boursier, V. (2015b, November). *Social media connectedness, sexual exploration and self-presentation. Measuring adolescents' expectancies towards sexting and selfie.* Paper presented at the 8th International and 13th National Congress of Clinical Psychology, Granada, Spain.

Manna, V., & Boursier, V. (2017, July). *I am a sexual person: measuring sexual self-concept and attitudes towards sexuality among adolescents. An Italian study.* Paper presented at the 15th European Congress of Psychology, Amsterdam, The Netherlands.

McAndrew, F. T., & Jeong, H. S. (2012). Who does what on Facebook? Age, sex, and relationship status as predictors of Facebook use. *Computers in Human Behavior*, *28*(6), 2359–2365. doi:10.1016/j.chb.2012.07.007

McKenna, K. Y., Green, A. S., & Gleason, M. E. (2002). Relationship formation on the Internet: What's the big attraction? *The Journal of Social Issues, 58*(1), 9–31. doi:10.1111/1540-4560.00246

McKinley, N. M., & Hyde, J. S. (1996). The objectified body consciousness scale development and validation. *Psychology of Women Quarterly, 20*(2), 181–215. doi:10.1111/j.1471-6402.1996.tb00467.x

McLean, S. A., Paxton, S. J., Wertheim, E. H., & Masters, J. (2015). Photoshopping the selfie: Self photo editing and photo investment are associated with body dissatisfaction in adolescent girls. *International Journal of Eating Disorders, 48*(8), 1132–1140. doi:10.1002/eat.22449 PMID:26311205

Meier, E. P., & Gray, J. (2014). Facebook photo activity associated with body image disturbance in adolescent girls. *Cyberpsychology, Behavior, and Social Networking, 17*(4), 199–206. doi:10.1089/cyber.2013.0305 PMID:24237288

Muthen, L. K., & Muthén, B. O. (2010). Mplus user's guide, v. 6.1. Los Angeles, CA: Muthen and Muthen, UCLA.

Paulhus, D. L., & Vazire, S. (2007). The self-report method. Handbook of Research Methods in Personality Psychology, 1, 224-239.

Pelosi, A., Zorzi, G., & Corsano, P. (2014). The Body Image Control in Photos questionnaire (BICP). *BPA-Applied Psychology Bulletin (Bollettino di Psicologia Applicata), 62*(269).

Riva, G. (2016). *I social network.* Bologna, Italy: Il mulino.

Rui, J. R., & Stefanone, M. A. (2013). Strategic image management online: Self-presentation, self-esteem and social network perspectives. *Information Communication and Society, 16*(8), 1286–1305. doi:10.1080/1369118X.2013.763834

Ryan, T., Chester, A., Reece, J., & Xenos, S. (2014). The uses and abuses of Facebook: A review of Facebook addiction. *Journal of Behavioral Addictions, 3*(3), 133–148. doi:10.1556/JBA.3.2014.016 PMID:25317337

Sánchez-Carbonell, X., Beranuy, M., Castellana, M., Chamarro, A., & Oberst, U. (2008). La adicción a Internet y al móvil:¿ moda o trastorno? *Adicciones, 20*(2), 149. doi:10.20882/adicciones.279 PMID:18551228

Siibak, A., &Hernwall, P. (2011). 'Looking like my favourite Barbie': Online Gender Construction of Tween Girls in Estonia and in Sweden. *Studies of Transition States and Societies, 3.*

Slater, A., Tiggemann, M., Hawkins, K., & Werchon, D. (2011). Just one click: A content analysis of advertisements on teen web sites. *The Journal of Adolescent Health, 50*(4), 339–345. doi:10.1016/j.jadohealth.2011.08.003 PMID:22443836

Sorokowska, A., Oleszkiewicz, A., Frackowiak, T., Pisanski, K., Chmiel, A., & Sorokowski, P. (2016). Selfies and personality: Who posts self-portrait photographs? *Personality and Individual Differences, 90*, 119–123. doi:10.1016/j.paid.2015.10.037

Sorokowski, P., Sorokowska, A., Oleszkiewicz, A., Frackowiak, T., Huk, A., & Pisanski, K. (2015). Selfie posting behaviors are associated with narcissism among men. *Personality and Individual Differences*, *85*, 123–127. doi:10.1016/j.paid.2015.05.004

Stone, G. (1981). Appearance and the self: A slightly revised version. In G. Stone & H. A. Farberman (Eds.), *Social psychology through symbolic interaction* (2nd ed.; pp. 187–202). New York, NY: Wiley.

Tiggemann, M., & Miller, J. (2010). The Internet and adolescent girls' weight satisfaction and drive for thinness. *Sex Roles*, *63*(1-2), 79–90. doi:10.100711199-010-9789-z

Tiggemann, M., & Slater, A. (2013). NetGirls: The Internet, Facebook, and body image concern in adolescent girls. *International Journal of Eating Disorders*, *46*(6), 630–633. doi:10.1002/eat.22141 PMID:23712456

Tiggemann, M., & Slater, A. (2014). NetTweens: The Internet and body image concerns in preteenage girls. *The Journal of Early Adolescence*, *34*(5), 606–620. doi:10.1177/0272431613501083

Valkenburg, P. M., Peter, J., & Schouten, A. P. (2006). Friend networking sites and their relationship to adolescents' well-being and social self-esteem. *Cyberpsychology & Behavior*, *9*(5), 584–590. doi:10.1089/cpb.2006.9.584 PMID:17034326

Valkenburg, P. M., Schouten, A. P., & Peter, J. (2005). Adolescents' identity experiments on the Internet. *New Media & Society*, *7*(3), 383–402. doi:10.1177/1461444805052282

Weisskirch, R. S., & Delevi, R. (2011). "Sexting" and adult romantic attachment. *Computers in Human Behavior*, *27*(5), 1697–1701. doi:10.1016/j.chb.2011.02.008

Zhao, S., Grasmuck, S., & Martin, J. (2008). Identity construction on Facebook: Digital empowerment in anchored relationships. *Computers in Human Behavior*, *24*(5), 1816–1836. doi:10.1016/j.chb.2008.02.012

KEY TERMS AND DEFINITIONS

Body Control Image in Photos: The possibility of checking, manipulating, and adjusting one's own body image as it appears in photos. It is related to the opportunities given by photo editing programs and apps of applying effects or selecting photos to be shared on the social network sites.

Confirmatory Factor Analysis (CFA): A statistical method used to test whether measures of a construct are consistent with a researcher's understanding of the nature of that construct. The objective of confirmatory factor analysis is to test whether the data fit a hypothesized measurement model.

Cut Off Value: It is a statistical term referring to a critical value of a measure, assumed as a discriminant score to distinguish ranges within a sample.

Exploratory Factor Analysis (EFA): A statistical method used to uncover the underlying structure of a relatively large set of variables. It is commonly used by researchers when developing a scale to identify a set of latent constructs underlying a battery of measured variables.

Risk Measure: An instrument useful to statistically assess the probability of developing a problematic behavior. It allows the researcher to identify populations at risk and distinguish them from non-at-risk ones.

Scale: A collection of questions used to measure a particular research topic. The responses of a scale can be combined together into a single measure (a latent variable). The items of a scale can be dichotomous (e.g., yes/no, agree/disagree, correct/incorrect) or polytomous as in a Likert-scale (e.g., disagree strongly/disagree/neutral/agree/agree strongly).

Self-Portrait: A representation of a person that is drawn, painted, photographed, or sculpted by the person himself/herself. With regards to social media, it often turns into "selfie" (i.e., a self-portrait photograph, typically taken with a digital camera or camera phone held in the hand or supported by a selfie stick). Selfies are usually shared on social networking services.

APPENDIX

Table 1. Results from exploratory factor analysis

Items	F1	F2	F3	F4	F5	Original Collocation	Item-tot Correlation	α if Item Removed
Factor 1: Self-ie								
Faccio prove davanti allo specchio per capire come uscire bene in foto [I practice in front of the mirror to see how I may come out in a photo]	.579	-.019	.316	-.023	-.087	Self-portraits	.635	.881
Mi scatto foto allo specchio o con la webcam per controllare la mia immagine mentre la immortalo [I take photos in front of the mirror or with the webcam, so that I may check my image]	.441	.020	.029	.198	.007	Self-portraits	.510	.886
Quando mi scattano una foto mi metto in una posa particolare o utilizzo una particolare espressione perché so che così vengo meglio [When someone takes a photo of me, I adopt a special pose or expression to look better]	.754	-.015	-.076	-.011	.106	Negative body image control	.644	.881
Mi preferisco nelle foto scattate da me perché so come fare per venire meglio [I prefer my image as it appears in self portraits, because I know how to make it look better]	.623	.025	.061	.04	.096	Self-portraits	.613	.882
Mi scatto fotografie più volte per ottenere una bella immagine da caricare sul profilo [I take photos of myself several times, until I obtain the image that makes me appear more attractive, in order to post it on my FB profile]	.473	.000	.279	-.005	-.006	Removed	.711	.878
Factor 2: To Whom								
Inserisco dei filtri privacy per mostrare solo a determinate persone fotografie in cui sono più attraente [I use privacy filters in order to show photos in which I appear more attractive only to certain people]	-.002	2.17	.004	-.003	-.001	Removed	.345	.891
Inserisco filtri privacy perché non voglio che determinate persone vedano foto in cui non sono uscito/a bene [I use privacy filters because I don't want some people to see photos in which I have not come out very well]	.027	.456	-.124	.127	.154	Removed	.397	.890
Factor 3: The Others and my Positive Image								
Se mi trovo in una situazione in cui c'è qualcuno che scatta fotografie, mi controllo spesso allo specchio o su altre superfici riflettenti nel caso dovessi rientrare nell'inquadratura [If someone around me is taking photos, I often check how I look in mirrors or other reflecting surfaces, in case I am in the picture]	.221	.031	.392	.030	.142	Positive body image control	.610	.882
Carico fotografie scegliendo tra quelle che spero riceveranno dei commenti positivi sul mio aspetto [I post those photos which I hope will receive praise for my appearance]	.021	-.002	.649	.090	.154	Positive body image control	.657	.880
Sono soddisfatto/a di come appare il mio aspetto fisico su Facebook e/o altri social [I like how my body looks on FB]	.029	.002	.418	.196	.011	Removed	.508	.886
Guardandomi nelle foto caricate da altri mi taggo solo in quelle in cui mi piaccio [I check how I appear in photos posted by others, and I tag only those in which I look good]	.098	-.012	.480	.054	.157	Removed	.633	.881
Factor 4: Selfie Sexual Attractiveness								
Ho fatto foto provocanti per attirare l'attenzione su di me [I take provocative photos in order to attract others' attention to me]	-.023	-.027	.039	.778	.031	Removed	.373	.890
Ho messo su Facebook e/o altri social delle foto in atteggiamenti provocanti per farmi notare [I have posted provocative photos on FB, in order to attract attention to myself]	.015	.015	-.023	.870	-.034	Removed	.335	.891
Factor 5: The Others and my Negative Image								
Se so che le foto che mi scattano verranno pubblicate su Facebook e/o altri social, controllo sulla fotocamera come sono uscito/a [When I notice that someone is taking photos in which will be posted on FB or other SNs, I check on the camera display how I have come out]	.120	.010	.202	-.031	.574	Removed	.624	.881
Da quando ho Facebook e/o altri social sto più attento/a a come esco in foto [Since I started using FB and/or others SNs, I am more careful about I come out in photos]	-.025	.012	.255	-.060	.486	Positive body image control	.658	.880
Scoprire che qualcuno ha caricato foto che ritraggono un mio difetto fisico mi provoca disagio [I feel awkward if I notice that someone has posted photos that show my body's defects]	-.029	-.058	.011	-.005	.772	Self-portraits	.446	.888
Cronbach's alfa: .891	.736	.646	.732	.765	.712	Self-portraits		

Table 2. Correlations among BICPQ-rev factors and body surveillance

Correlations	BICP	BICP-F1	BICP-F2	BICP-F3	BICP-F4	BICP-F5	SURVEILLANCE
BICP	1						
BICP-F1 – *Self-ie*	.867**	1					
BICP-F2 – *To whom*	.506**	.248**	1				
BICP-F3 – *The others and my Positive Image*	.869**	.670**	.318**	1			
BICP-F4 - *Selfie sexual attractiveness*	.449**	.304**	.270**	.313**	1		
BICP-F5 – *The others and my Negative Image*	.810**	.606**	.298**	.678**	.263**	1	
SURVEILLANCE	.439**	.424**	.251**	.340**	.205**	.424**	1

** The correlation is significant at level 0.01 (2-codes).

Table 3. One-way ANOVAs: Problematic and non-problematic users

		Mean	SD		Sum of Squares	Mean Square	F	Sig.
Practice in front of the mirror	Non Problematic	1.00	.000	Between groups	.000	.000	54.318	.000
	Problematic	1.00	.000	Within groups	.000	.000		
Check my image in mirror or webcam	Non Problematic	1.69	1.08	Between groups	161.952	161.95	93.864	.000
	Problematic	3.37	1.50	Within groups	393.391	1.725		
Special pose	Non Problematic	2.59	1.34	Between groups	212.352	212.35	177.66	.000
	Problematic	4.51	.765	Within groups	272.522	1.195		
Prefer my image as it appears in self portraits	Non Problematic	2.72	1.41	Between groups	153.584	153.58	102.73	.000
	Problematic	4.36	.997	Within groups	339.350	1.495		
Take photos of myself several times	Non Problematic	1.31	.730	Between groups	55.018	55.018	42.626	.000
	Problematic	2.29	1.43	Within groups	291.702	1.291		
Privacy filters to appear more attractive	Non Problematic	2.24	1.25	Between groups	199.113	199.11	140.14	.000
	Problematic	4.10	1.12	Within groups	323.930	1.421		
Don't want people to see where I am not very well	Non Problematic	2.63	1.25	Between groups	234.017	234.01	232.68	.000
	Problematic	4.64	.665	Within groups	229.304	1.006		
Check on reflecting surfaces	Non Problematic	2.36	1.29	Between groups	227.719	227.71	188.10	.000
	Problematic	4.36	.867	Within groups	272.378	1.211		
Praise for my appearance	Non Problematic	2.79	1.39	Between groups	152.678	152.67	105.06	.000
	Problematic	4.43	.992	Within groups	326.979	1.453		
I like me on FB	Non Problematic	2.74	1.42	Between groups	166.795	166.79	118.13	.000
	Problematic	4.47	.911	Within groups	313.451	1.412		
Tag only good	Non Problematic	2.65	1.26	Between groups	123.979	123.97	98.665	.000
	Problematic	4.13	.960	Within groups	280.216	1.257		
Take provocative photos	Non Problematic	1.71	1.20	Between groups	87.522	87.522	42.111	.000
	Problematic	2.96	1.64	Within groups	465.557	2.078		
Post provocative photos	Non Problematic	2.30	1.35	Between groups	251.798	251.79	195.17	.000
	Problematic	4.41	.878	Within groups	288.980	1.290		
If notice someone taking photos, check on camera	Non Problematic	1.29	.743	Between groups	41.729	41.729	34.975	.000
	Problematic	2.15	1.34	Within groups	267.262	1.193		
More careful about photos due to SNs use	Non Problematic	2.63	1.23	Between groups	93.707	93.707	63.811	.000
	Problematic	3.92	1.19	Within groups	326.008	1.469		

continued on following page

Table 3. Continued

		Mean	SD		Sum of Squares	Mean Square	F	Sig.
Awkward if posted photos showing defects	Non Problematic	1.84	1.21	Between groups	170.235	170.23	95.046	.000
	Problematic	3.57	1.44	Within groups	401.203	1.791		
F1 – Self-ie	Non Problematic	2.34	.919	Between groups	198.462	198.46	340.36	.000
	Problematic	4.20	.565	Within groups	132.944	.583		
F2 – To whom	Non Problematic	1.78	1.07	Between groups	125.186	125.18	94.119	.000
	Problematic	3.26	1.22	Within groups	300.599	1.330		
F3 – The others and my Positive Image	Non Problematic	2.37	.936	Between groups	202.683	202.68	346.11	.000
	Problematic	4.252	.5416	Within groups	133.517	.586		
F4 - Selfie sexual attractiveness	Non Problematic	1.300	.6063	Between groups	47.935	47.935	48.481	.000
	Problematic	2.213	1.268	Within groups	225.430	.989		
F5 - The others and my Negative Image	Non Problematic	2.694	1.128	Between groups	142.505	142.50	168.63	.000
	Problematic	4.275	.6511	Within groups	190.980	.845		
Body Image Control in Photos	Non Problematic	2.218	.7204	Between groups	155.917	155.91	495.53	.000
	Problematic	3.865	.3319	Within groups	71.739	.315		
CERM	Non Problematic	2.30	.717	Between groups	23.156	23.156	39.679	.000
	Problematic	2.93	.807	Within groups	131.886	.584		
IRPS	Non Problematic	2.33	.811	Between groups	13.635	13.635	21.322	.000
	Problematic	2.81	.787	Within groups	145.802	.639		
Body Surveillance	Non Problematic	4.20	.994	Between groups	22.676	22.676	21.238	.000
	Problematic	4.83	1.06	Within groups	238.098	1.068		
Selfie Frequency	Non Problematic	2.36	.512	Between groups	21.406	21.406	77.827	.000
	Problematic	2.98	.535	Within groups	62.436	.275		
Selfie Expectancies	Non Problematic	2.92	.470	Between groups	9.148	9.148	33.874	.000
	Problematic	2.52	.564	Within groups	61.575	.270		
Selfie Expectancies F1 - Worries	Non Problematic	1.65	.823	Between groups	6.088	6.088	7.705	.006
	Problematic	1.98	.950	Within groups	180.143	.790		
Selfie Expectancies F2 - Virtual anguishes	Non Problematic	2.62	1.20	Between groups	9.433	9.433	5.542	.019
	Problematic	3.03	1.40	Within groups	386.388	1.702		
Selfie Expectancies F3 – Sexual desire	Non Problematic	3.01	1.13	Between groups	18.298	18.298	11.874	.001
	Problematic	2.44	1.33	Within groups	349.805	1.541		
Selfie Expectancies F4 – Ordinary practice	Non Problematic	3.55	.946	Between groups	70.214	70.214	80.992	.000
	Problematic	2.45	.915	Within groups	197.661	.867		
Selfie Expectancies F5 – Self confidence	Non Problematic	3.78	.957	Between groups	92.006	92.006	85.851	.000
	Problematic	2.52	1.10	Within groups	243.276	1.072		
Selfie Expectancies F6 – Self presentation	Non Problematic	2.37	.810	Between groups	.024	.024	.031	.003
	Problematic	2.35	.948	Within groups	176.795	.779		
Selfie Expectancies F7 – Perceived risks	Non Problematic	1.65	.823	Between groups	6.088	6.088	7.705	.006
	Problematic	1.98	.950	Within groups	180.143	.790		
Sexual Self	Non Problematic	2.28	.772	Between groups	42.810	21.405	35.552	.000
	Problematic	2.64	.781	Within groups	724.286	.602		
Sexual Self F1 – Sexual Self attractiveness	Non Problematic	3.01	.874	Between groups	14.206	14.206	17.665	.000
	Problematic	3.51	.918	Within groups	183.352	.804		
Sexual Self F2 – Body care	Non Problematic	4.01	1.11	Between groups	9.621	9.621	11.914	.001
	Problematic	4.42	.616	Within groups	184.110	.808		

Table 4. Correlations between BICPQ and other scale

Correlations	BICP	CERM	IRPS	FREQ	SE	SE-F1	SE-F2	SE-F3	SE-F4	SE-F5	SE-F6	SE-F7	SS	SS-F1	SS-F2
BICP	1														
CERM	.448**	1													
IRPS	.349**	.740**	1												
SELFIE FREQUENCY	.513**	.347**	.184**	1											
SELFIE EXPECTANCIES	-.300**	-.134**	-112**	-.338**	1										
S. EXPECT.-F1 *Worries*	.174**	.222**	.254**	.064	.378**	1									
S. EXPECT.-F2 *Virtual anguishes*	.170**	.149**	.136**	.067	.512**	.442**	1								
S. EXPECT.-F3 *Sexual desire*	.210**	-.153**	-.163**	-.261**	.420**	-.181**	-.009	1							
S. EXPECT.-F4*Ordinary practice*	-.088**	-.048	-.041	-.130**	.450**	.003	.009	.196**	1						
S. EXPECT.-F5 *Self confidence*	-.529**	-351**	-.301**	-.413**	.582**	-.162**	-.107**	.358**	.120**	1					
S. EXPECT.-F6 *Self presentation*	-.431**	-.292**	-.291**	-.311**	.558**	-.145**	-.051	.333**	.168**	.611**	1				
S. EXPECT.-F7 *Perceived risks*	-.007	.085*	.089*	-.111**	.398**	.329**	.370**	-.096*	-.008	-.047	-114**	1			
SEXUAL SELF	.162**	-.108**	-.139**	.187**	-.208**	-.029	-.028	-.125**	-.092*	-.181**	-.160**	-.108**	1		
S. SELF-F1 Sex. *self attractiveness*	.223**	-.078**	-.093**	.185**	-.224**	-.044	-.099*	-.178**	-.039	-.168**	-.137**	-.125**	.850**	1	
SEXUAL SELF-F2 – *Body care*	.245**	-.100**	-.135**	.097*	-.090*	.004	.081*	.003	-.123**	-.114**	-.114**	-.031	.713**	.239**	1

** The correlation is significant at level 0.01 (2-codes).

Table 5. One-way ANOVAs by gender

		Mean	SD		Sum of Squares	Mean Square	F	Sig.
Practice in front of the mirror	Males	2.11	1.21	Between groups	176.094	88.047	54.318	.000
	Females	2.88	1.33	Within groups	1940.293	1.621		
Check my image in mirror or webcam	Males	1.82	1.15	Between groups	24.046	12.023	8.342	.000
	Females	2.09	1.25	Within groups	1719.376	1.441		
Special pose	Males	2.63	1.35	Between groups	93.678	46.839	25.817	.000
	Females	3.17	1.34	Within groups	2168.038	1.814		
Prefer my image as it appears in self portraits	Males	2.55	1.36	Between groups	181.509	90.755	48.612	.000
	Females	3.32	1.37	Within groups	2227.240	1.867		
Take photos of myself several times	Males	2.44	1.32	Between groups	209.469	104.73	58.746	.000
	Females	3.28	1.34	Within groups	2116.215	1.783		
Privacy filters to appear more attractive	Males	2.01	1.30	Between groups	2.312	1.156	.645	.003
	Females	2.51	1.37	Within groups	2111.603	1.793		

continued on following page

Table 5. Continued

		Mean	SD		Sum of Squares	Mean Square	F	Sig.
Don't want some people to see where I am not very well	Males	2.00	1.30	Between groups	14.959	7.480	4.149	.016
	Females	2.22	1.38	Within groups	2139.737	1.803		
Check on reflecting surfaces	Males	2.26	1.26	Between groups	62.579	31.290	18.444	.000
	Females	2.71	1.34	Within groups	2020.443	1.696		
Praise for my appearance	Males	2.48	1.30	Between groups	42.293	21.146	11.805	.000
	Females	2.85	1.38	Within groups	2106.630	1.791		
I like me on FB	Males	2.85	1.32	Between groups	7.749	3.875	2.306	.003
	Females	2.80	1.26	Within groups	1979.617	1.680		
Tag only good	Males	2.44	1.36	Between groups	82.928	41.464	21.173	.000
	Females	2.96	1.44	Within groups	2320.596	1.958		
Take provocative photos	Males	1.58	1.00	Between groups	23.593	11.796	14.823	.000
	Females	1.30	.739	Within groups	941.454	.796		
Post provocative photos	Males	1.53	.976	Between groups	22.076	11.038	14.485	.000
	Females	1.26	.739	Within groups	896.129	.762		
If notice someone taking photos, check on the camera	Males	2.71	1.37	Between groups	127.153	63.577	33.234	.000
	Females	3.36	1.39	Within groups	2268.793	1.913		
More careful about image in photos due to SNs use	Males	2.63	1.36	Between groups	92.659	46.330	23.747	.000
	Females	3.17	1.43	Within groups	2274.848	1.951		
Awkward if posted photos showing defects	Males	2.47	1.29	Between groups	71.987	35.993	20.417	.000
	Females	2.96	1.36	Within groups	2076.665	1.763		
F1 – Self-ie	Males	2.31	.948	Between groups	123.798	61.899	64.001	.000
	Females	2.94	1.02	Within groups	1159.610	.967		
F2 – To whom	Males	2.01	1.14	Between groups	4.651	2.325	1.725	.003
	Females	2.11	1.18	Within groups	1609.756	1.348		
F3 – The others and my Positive Image	Males	2.50	.958	Between groups	37.961	18.980	19.269	.000
	Females	2.83	1.03	Within groups	1183.000	.985		
F4 - Selfie sexual attractiveness	Males	1.55	.883	Between groups	22.631	11.316	17.937	.000
	Females	1.28	.679	Within groups	758.295	.631		
F5 - The others and my Negative Image	Males	2.60	1.05	Between groups	96.899	48.450	41.018	.000
	Females	3.16	1.12	Within groups	1415.048	1.181		
Body Image Control in Photos	Males	2.28	.772	Between groups	42.810	21.405	35.552	.000
	Females	2.64	.781	Within groups	724.286	.602		

Table 6. One-way ANOVAs by age

		Mean	SD		Sum of Squares	Mean Square	F	Sig.
Practice in front of the mirror	Preadolescents	2.59	1.37	Between groups	18.513	18.513	10.572	.001
	Adolescents	2.34	1.27	Within groups	2097.874	1.751		
Check my image in mirror or webcam	Preadolescents	2.03	1.27	Between groups	8.731	8.731	6.010	.014
	Adolescents	1.86	1.14	Within groups	1734.691	1.453		
Special pose	Preadolescents	2.95	1.41	Between groups	6.344	6.344	3.364	.067
	Adolescents	2.81	1.33	Within groups	2255.372	1.886		
Prefer my image as it appears in self portraits	Preadolescents	3.07	1.42	Between groups	29.627	29.627	14.869	.000
	Adolescents	2.75	1.39	Within groups	2379.122	1.993		
Take photos of myself several times	Preadolescents	2.94	1.43	Between groups	13.234	13.234	6.799	.009
	Adolescents	2.73	1.36	Within groups	2312.451	1.947		
Privacy filters to appear more attractive	Preadolescents	2.02	1.35	Between groups	.062	.062	.035	.852
	Adolescents	2.00	1.32	Within groups	2113.853	1.793		
Don't want some people to see where I am not well	Preadolescents	2.19	1.37	Between groups	7.402	7.402	4.095	.043
	Adolescents	2.03	1.32	Within groups	2147.294	1.807		
Check on reflecting surfaces	Preadolescents	2.54	1.35	Between groups	6.495	6.495	3.728	.054
	Adolescents	2.39	1.29	Within groups	2076.527	1.742		
Praise for my appearance	Preadolescents	2.63	1.38	Between groups	.403	.403	.221	.639
	Adolescents	2.67	1.32	Within groups	2148.520	1.825		
I like me on FB	Preadolescents	2.84	1.39	Between groups	.213	.213	.127	.722
	Adolescents	2.81	1.20	Within groups	1987.153	1.685		
Tag only good	Preadolescents	2.68	1.45	Between groups	.001	.001	.000	.984
	Adolescents	2.68	1.39	Within groups	2403.524	2.027		
Take provocative photos	Preadolescents	1.43	.907	Between groups	.461	.461	.566	.452
	Adolescents	1.46	.899	Within groups	964.586	.815		
Post provocative photos	Preadolescents	1.38	.899	Between groups	.459	.459	.588	.443
	Adolescents	1.42	.868	Within groups	917.746	.780		
If notice someone taking photos, check on the cam	Preadolescents	3.05	1.46	Between groups	1.981	1.981	.982	.322
	Adolescents	2.97	1.38	Within groups	2393.966	2.017		
More careful about image in photos due to SNs use	Preadolescents	2.90	1.47	Between groups	.700	.700	.345	.557
	Adolescents	2.85	1.37	Within groups	2366.807	2.028		
Awkward if posted photos showing defects	Preadolescents	2.71	1.35	Between groups	.194	.194	.107	.744
	Adolescents	2.68	1.34	Within groups	2148.458	1.822		
F1 – Self-ie	Preadolescents	2.71	1.06	Between groups	14.810	14.810	14.009	.000
	Adolescents	2.49	.989	Within groups	1268.598	1.057		
F2 – To whom	Preadolescents	2.09	1.16	Between groups	1.826	1.826	1.353	.245
	Adolescents	2.02	1.15	Within groups	1612.581	1.349		

continued on following page

Table 6. Continued

		Mean	SD		Sum of Squares	Mean Square	F	Sig.
F3 – The others and my Positive Image	Preadolescents	2.66	1.07	Between groups	.158	.158	.155	.694
	Adolescents	2.64	.942	Within groups	1220.803	1.016		
F4 - Selfie sexual attractiveness	Preadolescents	1.40	.810	Between groups	.541	.541	.834	.361
	Adolescents	1.44	.801	Within groups	780.385	.649		
F5 - The others and my Negative Image	Preadolescents	2.88	1.12	Between groups	.637	.637	.506	.477
	Adolescents	2.83	1.11	Within groups	1511.309	1.260		
Body Image Control in Photos	Preadolescents	2.49	.834	Between groups	2.437	2.437	3.837	.050
	Adolescents	2.40	.761	Within groups	764.659	.635		

Chapter 4
Desired Speed of Reply During Text-Based Communication via Smartphones:
A Survey of Young Japanese Adults

Yuuki Kato
Sagami Women's University, Japan

Shogo Kato
Tokyo Woman's Christian University, Japan

Yasuyuki Ozawa
Meisei University, Japan

ABSTRACT

Text-based forms of communication have long been communicated via PCs and more recently via mobile phones and smartphones. This chapter has tried to explore how the speed of text message exchanges has become a nonverbal cue in the asynchronous communications that occurs via mobile phones and smartphones. This chapter presents the investigation of the speed of exchange relevant to the LINE text-messenger application. Specifically, the authors surveyed Japanese university students who provided free-response descriptions of situations when (a) a quick reply is preferred and (b) a late reply is acceptable. The main finding was that judging when a quick reply is preferred and when a late reply is acceptable is overwhelmingly influenced by the convenience of the sender (who is waiting for a reply) over the convenience of the recipient who will reply.

INTRODUCTION

Reports in recent years have indicated that slow replies during text message exchanges via smartphones have caused problems among young people in Japan, in some cases progressing to bullying and even homicide (Schreiber, 2015). The speed of exchange of text messages thus strongly influences the emotions of young smart phone users (Kato & Kato, 2015). In this chapter, we focus on significance of the speed of exchange (interaction) during text-based communication via smartphones.

DOI: 10.4018/978-1-5225-4047-2.ch004

Text-Based Communication on Smartphones in Japan

When communication tools such as e-mail first became widely popular, they were mainly used with PCs. In the latter half of the 1990s, the short message service (SMS) and mobile access to the Internet became available on mobile phones. Since Apple's release of the iPhone in 2007 (2008 in Japan), the penetration rate of smartphones has continued to increase rapidly. According to the *White Paper 2015: Information and Communication in Japan* (Ministry of Internal Affairs and Communications, 2015), the share of smartphones in Japan in 2014 was 94.5% among those in their 20s and 92.4% among those in their 30s, and smartphones have become the dominant mobile terminal, replacing conventional mobile phones, especially among the younger generation. About ten years ago, voice calls and SMS were the main method of communication for mobile phones, with Internet use still limited on these devices. However, with the rapid spread of smart phones in recent years, various communication tools such as social media can be easily accessed through Internet applications. The modern smartphone allows for selective utilization of various communication tools according to the user's intent and circumstances.

In addition to conventional communication tools like SMS, social media such as Twitter and Facebook are also used for everyday communication via smartphones. Previously, social media was primarily PC-based but has become more common on smartphones with the emergence of easy-to-use applications. In fact, the high affinity between the smartphone and social media has rapidly increased utilization rates for both. Against this background, text over IP messaging applications have become more common as well.

Globally, the most popular of these messaging applications is WhatsApp, which was created in the United States in 2009 (Ahad & Lim, 2014; Church & Oliveira, 2013; O'Hara, Massimi, Harper, Rubens, & Morris, 2014). There are currently around 900 million active users of WhatsApp, with the number of downloads in first or second place in many countries, mostly in Europe, the United States, Southeast Asia, and South America (Statista, 2016). In Japan, Thailand, and Taiwan, however, the most-downloaded social media/messenger application is LINE (Statista, 2016). This was released in June 2011, following the Great East Japan Earthquake of March 2011, with the aim of creating an application where users can easily communicate even in the event of a disaster. One year after its launch, LINE reached 50 million users, and currently has about 212 million active users, as well as the seventh-highest adoption rate among messaging applications worldwide. In Japan, LINE has come to replace traditional mobile text messages (including SMS), especially among young people (Ministry of Internal Affairs and Communications, 2016).

Socio-Emotional Aspects of Text-Based Communication

Early studies of Internet-related psychology have cited a lack of nonverbal cues and visual anonymity as characteristics of PC text-based communication, such as e-mail and electronic bulletin boards (e.g., Daft & Lengel, 1984; Kiesler, Siegel, & McGuire, 1984; Short, Williams, & Christie, 1976). A number of studies on computer-mediated communication (CMC) have discussed two characteristics of text-based CMC exchanges: the absence of facial expressions and gestures, which are included during face-to-face conversation, and the absence of nonverbal cues such as tone of voice. These characteristics form the basis of various models and theories in CMC research conducted prior to the 1990s. For example, the *social presence model* posits that when media conveys little nonverbal information, the sense of the other party as an actual person becomes less distinct, resulting in cold, impersonal communication (Short,

Williams, & Christie, 1976). In media selection, the *media richness theory* recommends using rich media that can transmit sufficient information for unequivocal communication (Daft & Lengel, 1984; Daft & Lengel, 1986). The *cuelessness model* explains that communication tends to become task-oriented rather than socioemotional due to the lack of nonverbal cues in CMC (Rutter, 1984; Rutter, 1987; Rutter, Stephenson, & Dewey, 1981). Alternatively, the *reduced social cues approach* (Kiesler, Siegel, & McGuire, 1984; Sproull, & Kiesler, 1986) argues that the lack of nonverbal cues in CMC causes depersonalization among communication partners, resulting in uninhibited communication in which features that fall outside of social norms (e.g., framing (Dyer, Green, Pitts, & Millward, 1995) are more likely to occur (McGuire, Kiesler, & Siegel, 1987; Siegel, Dubrovsky, Kiesler, & McGuire, 1986). As indicated above (especially in early CMC studies), CMC is considered inferior to face-to-face communication and likely to contribute to emotional difficulties due to the lack of the many nonverbal cues available in face-to-face communication (Joinson, McKenna, Postmes, & Reips, 2007).

However, subsequent CMC studies have shown many examples of socioemotional communication that can deepen personal relationships, even using text message exchanges that contain few nonverbal cues (Walther, 1992; Walther, Anderson, & Park, 1994; Walther & Burgoon, 1992). For instance, more self-disclosure is thought to occur in CMC (Joinson, 2001; Matheson, 1991; Matheson & Zanna, 1988). With few nonverbal cues, visual anonymity is preserved and de-individuation occurs, which decreases the restraint typically exercised in face-to-face communication (Matheson, 1991; Matheson & Zanna, 1988). Also, according to the *hyperpersonal model*, with its fewer nonverbal cues, CMC permits interactions that are closer to the idealized self (Walther, 1996). For example, users can make controlled, selective presentations of themselves to the other party in a way that makes it easier to create a favorable impression (Walther, 1996). Although these studies showed examples of the skillful employment of minimal nonverbal cues in CMC, they also provided evidence that CMC increases difficulties in communication because it lacks the abundant nonverbal information that exists during face-to-face communication (Walther & Tidwell, 1995).

Most early CMC research focused on Internet-mediated communication with PCs. However, many people now use mobile phones and smartphones to communicate over the Internet, which differs from PC-based Internet communication (Scott, Kato, Kato, & Liu, 2012). For example, in text-based communication via mobile phones, emoji and emoticons are used more frequently than in PC-based communication; thus, email sent from a mobile phone might be more likely to transmit emotions than email sent from a PC (Scott, Coursaris, Kato, & Kato, 2009).

Additionally, compared with PC-based communication, there is a notable trend toward quick, on-demand interactions when using mobile phone text-messaging applications (Kato, Kato, & Chida, 2012; 2013). Specifically, in communication via mobile phones, responders may at times feel pressured to reply quickly and the senders waiting for a response that is delayed may begin to feel anxious and frustrated. In fact, the lack of nonverbal information in text-based communication has been the subject of much CMC research. However, now that mobile phone communication has come to play a major role in communication today, response time can be thought of as conveying important nonverbal information. For example, a "slow" response alone might convey negative emotion as nonverbal information (Kato & Kato, 2015). Although many previous studies have focused on emoticons, pictograms, and message content as contributing factors to social emotional interactions, few studies have examined how the speed of the exchange affects users' emotions.

Speed of Exchange in Text Messaging

Internet technology has dramatically accelerated the speed of message-based interactions. For example, in contrast to paper mail, e-mail text messages can be sent instantly by a simple operation without regard to geographical location. However, PC-based email requires a sender sitting in front of a PC to send a message and a recipient who must use a PC and activate its email program before receiving the message. This means that, despite its fast speed, e-mail is asynchronous communication that does not enable "anywhere anytime" real-time communication (Tyler & Tang, 2003). In contrast, those carrying mobile phones and smartphones can communicate at nearly real-time speed with not only voice calls, but text messaging as well. Therefore, faster exchange speed is now in demand for text-based communication methods (e.g., text messaging) that were once asynchronous (Kato & Kato, 2015; Kato, Kato, & Chida, 2012; 2013). This is especially noticeable among the younger generation. For example, Kato (2015) investigated whether "digital natives" (i.e., the tech-savvy generation whose members grew up familiar with computers and the Internet (Prensky, 2001a; 2001b) feel uncomfortable engaging in mobile communication with "digital immigrants" (i.e., older people whose main means of pre-Internet-era communication involved face-to-face meetings, landline telephones, postal mail, and fax machines). Kato found that many students were uncomfortable when text-messaging with older people because they felt the replies were late.

Now that text-based communication has come to demand rapid exchanges between parties, many young people pay avid attention to incoming messages, checking the standby screens of their mobile phones and smartphones often. According to some surveys on private use of mobile phones and smartphones during classes at Japanese universities, the main purpose of private smartphone use during class is communication (Kato & Kato, 2016a; 2016b). In fact, many college students check that they have received a message, even during class, and immediately respond to them. These studies also suggest the great importance of speed of interaction in mobile communication, particularly for today's younger generation. Of course, not all young people share this viewpoint, but there seems to be a shared recognition among them that a rapid response is necessary even during inherently asynchronous communications via mobile phones and smartphones.

With the spread of smartphones, the main tool for text-based communication among young people in Japan has shifted from mobile phone text-messaging (e.g., SMS) to LINE text messaging because it is an instant messenger application that allows for quick, simple exchanges. Today, LINE is used on a daily basis by many in Japan. However, in the same way as mobile phone text messaging, LINE is an asynchronous text-based communication tool that was never intended for real-time communication such as face-to-face or telephone conversations. For instance, LINE users do not interact while they bathe and sleep and generally avoid LINE usage during class. Also, asynchronous communication allows users to reply at any time without interrupting the other party, unlike a voice call. Even though faster replies are needed in text-based communication that occurs via mobile devices, an immediate response is impossible in some situations. Given that senders must sometimes wait a long time for a reply, users should consider the recipient's situation when a reply is delayed. In reality, the sender wants the recipient to reply quickly, and the recipient sometimes feels pressure to respond quickly. Although faster exchanges of text-based messages would be convenient and efficient, we believe it places psychological burden on users. In particular, a frequent topic in Japan is "LINE fatigue," the psychological burden caused by the perceived need for a fast exchange of LINE text messages. Therefore, we need to understand the specific situations where LINE users do and do not expect a quick reply from the other party.

OBJECTIVE

The objective of the study was to explore LINE application to identify the kinds of situations where the sender hopes for a quick reply and the kinds of situations where a speedy reply is or is not needed. We conducted a survey of Japanese college students who used LINE on a daily basis to obtain free-response written descriptions of situations where they desire a quick reply and those where they would accept a slower one.

METHOD

Participants

Participants of this questionnaire survey were 123 first-year university students (63 men, 60 women) enrolled at universities in the Tokyo area. We conducted this survey in computer rooms where each participant had the use of one desktop computer. The survey took place in October 2016. Prior to this survey, we confirmed that all participants owned smartphones and regularly used LINE text messaging via the device.

Procedure

The survey contained the following questions:

1. When LINE text messaging, in what kinds of situations do you want a quick reply from the other party?
2. When LINE text messaging, in what kinds of situations do you tolerate a slow reply from the other party?

For each question, participants were asked to provide a free description based on their day-to-day experience using LINE. Central monitors located between the participants' desktop computers presented the two questions and requested that each answer be typed in a Microsoft Word 2010 file located on the desktop computers. Participants who completed the survey submitted their Word files to a shared folder accessible to the authors.

RESULTS

Categories Extracted From Responses

Most participants provided multiple situations for both when a quick reply is preferred and when a late reply is acceptable. Therefore, we counted the number of situations when a quick reply is preferred (394 situations) and when a late reply is acceptable (332 situations). Next, three authors independently examined the content of each of these situations. After these individual examinations, they compared the results jointly and then determined the following major categories. The subcategories of each category will be described later.

- *Types of Recipient*
- *Topics of Interaction*
- *Interaction Styles*
- *Status of Senders (survey participants waiting for a reply)*
- *Status of Recipients (who send a reply)*

More detailed responses were elicited for the situation when a late reply is acceptable than for when a quick reply is preferred. Therefore, we added two additional categories for when a late reply is acceptable:

- *Specific Status of Senders (survey participants waiting for a reply)*
- *Specific Status of Recipients (who send a reply)*

In the first of these categories, *Types of Recipient* relates to recipients of LINE text-messages sent by the participants, and we extracted five recipient subcategories from the survey responses: (a) family and relatives; (b) friends; (c) part-time colleagues and bosses; (d) romantic partners or persons for whom they have romantic feelings; and (c) persons that the participant dislikes or is not interested in.

The *Topics of Interaction* category relates to topics currently being exchanged via LINE text-messaging, and we extracted twelve topic subcategories:

1. Meetings and appointments;
2. Schedule adjustments;
3. School (classes);
4. School (other than classes);
5. Fun and interesting topics;
6. Advice on important or serious matters;
7. Part-time jobs;
8. Clerical communication matters;
9. Decision-making;
10. Information gathering;
11. Unimportant chat and;
12. Thanks and greetings.

The *Interaction Styles* category relates to styles of LINE interaction, such as Q&A, the current atmosphere of exchanges, and progressive stages of exchanges. We extracted eight subcategories:

1. When the sender asked a question;
2. When the recipient asked the sender a question;
3. When the sender initiated the interaction by sending a message;
4. When the recipient initiated the interaction by sending a message;
5. Ongoing interaction;
6. Interaction using a LINE app sticker;

7. Interaction using LINE app group functions, and;
8. Interaction about no particular topic.

The *Status of Senders* category relates to the mental state of the participant senders who are waiting for a reply and the situations they face. We extracted nine subcategories:

1. When the sender feels pleasure or joy;
2. When the sender feels sad or lonely;
3. When the sender feels angry or irritated;
4. When the sender is in trouble;
5. When the sender has an emergency;
6. When the sender has free time;
7. When the sender is busy;
8. When the sender needs an immediate reply, and;
9. When the sender does not need an immediate reply.

The *Status of Recipients* category relates to the mental state of recipients who send a reply and the situations they face. We extracted nine subcategories:

1. When the recipient feels pleasure or joy;
2. When the recipient feels sad or lonely;
3. When the recipient feels angry or irritated;
4. When the recipient is in trouble;
5. When the recipient has an emergency;
6. When the recipient has free time;
7. When the recipient is busy;
8. When the recipient needs an immediate reply from the sender;
9. When the recipient does not need an immediate reply from the sender.

The *Specific Status of Senders* category relates to specific situations faced by senders waiting for a reply. We extracted seven subcategories based on participants' responses to situations when a late reply is acceptable:

1. The sender is in class;
2. The sender is engaged in a part-time job;
3. The sender is on the move;
4. The sender is eating;
5. The sender is bathing;
6. The sender is sleeping, and;
7. The sender is with someone.

The *Specific Status of Recipients* category relates to specific situations faced by recipients who send a reply. We extracted seven subcategories based on participants' responses to situations when a late reply is acceptable:

1. The recipient is in class;
2. The recipient is engaged in a part-time job;
3. The recipient is on the move;
4. The recipient is eating;
5. The recipient is bathing;
6. The recipient is sleeping, and;
7. The recipient is with someone.

Response Classification by Category and Subcategory

We counted the number of responses related to each of the above categories and subcategories. For example, the response "When I asked my friend about homework for the lecture that we are both taking" was classified as follows: subcategory "friends" under the category *Types of Recipient;* subcategory "schools (classes)" under the category *Topics of Interaction;* and subcategory "when the participant asked the other party a question" under the category *Interaction Styles.* Table 1 shows the results for situations when a quick reply is preferred and Table 2 shows the results for situations when a late reply

Table 1. Classification of situations when a quick reply is preferred

Groups and Categories	*n*	%[a]	%[b]	%[c]
Type of Recipients	**52**			**13.2**
Friends	18	4.6	34.6	
Part-time colleagues and bosses	13	3.3	25.0	
Romantic partners or persons for whom they have romantic feelings	12	3.0	23.1	
Family and relatives	7	1.8	13.5	
Persons that the participant dislikes or is not interested in	2	0.5	3.8	
Not applicable	342	86.8		
Total	394	100.0		
Topics of Interactions	**227**			**57.6**
Meetings and appointments	61	15.5	26.9	
Schedule adjustments	49	12.4	21.6	
Advice in important or serious matters	29	7.4	12.8	
Information gathering	26	6.6	11.5	
School (classes)	19	4.8	8.4	
Clerical communication matter	14	3.6	6.2	
Part-time jobs	13	3.3	5.7	
Decision-making	9	2.3	4.0	
School (other than classes)	2	0.5	0.9	
Fun and interesting topics	2	0.5	0.9	
Unimportant chat	2	0.5	0.9	
Thanks and greetings	1	0.3	0.4	

continued on following page

Table 1. Continued

Groups and Categories	*n*	%[a]	%[b]	%[c]
Not applicable	167	42.4		
Total	394	100.0		
Interaction Styles	**15**			**3.8**
When the sender asked a question	6	1.5	40.0	
Ongoing interaction	4	1.0	26.7	
When the sender initiated interaction by sending a message	2	0.5	13.3	
When the recipient initiated interaction by sending a message	2	0.5	13.3	
Interaction using LINE app group functions	1	0.3	6.7	
Not applicable	379	96.2		
Total	394	100.0		
Status of Senders	**121**			**30.7**
When the sender needs an immediate reply	45	11.4	37.2	
When the sender has an emergency	41	10.4	33.9	
When the sender is in trouble	11	2.8	9.1	
When the sender has free time	10	2.5	8.3	
When the sender is busy	7	1.8	5.8	
When the sender feels pleasure or joy	4	1.0	3.3	
When the sender feels angry or irritated	2	0.5	1.7	
When the sender feels sad or lonely	1	0.3	0.8	
Not applicable	273	69.3		
Total	394	100.0		
Status of Recipients	**36**			**9.1**
When the recipient needs an immediate reply from the sender	18	4.6	50.0	
When the recipient has an emergency	11	2.8	30.6	
When the recipient has free time	3	0.8	8.3	
When the recipient feels pleasure or joy	2	0.5	5.6	
When the recipient feels angry or irritated	1	0.3	2.8	
When the recipient is busy	1	0.3	2.8	
Not applicable	358	90.9		
Total	394	100.0		

Note. Number = the number of responses mentioning the relevant category or subcategory.

[a]The number of responses mentioning the relevant subcategory divided by the total number of responses (N = 394).

[b]The number of responses mentioning the relevant category divided by the total number of responses, excluding the number of answers classified "Not applicable."

[c]The number of responses mentioning the relevant category divided by the total number of responses (N = 394).

is acceptable. In both situations—when a quick reply is preferred and when a late reply is acceptable—most answers were given for the category *Topics of Interaction.* Also, more answers were given for the mental state of the senders and the situations senders face than for categories related to the mental states of the recipients and the situations they face. In fact, desiring a quick reply from the recipient seemed to be based on the sender's own convenience. Therefore, for situations when a late reply is acceptable, we reanalyzed the extent to which each sender's convenience and the recipient's convenience were included.

Table 2. Classification of situations when a late reply is acceptable

Groups and Categories	*n*	%[a]	%[b]	%[c]
Type of Recipients	**28**			**8.4**
Persons that the participant dislikes or is not interested in	12	3.6	42.9	
Friends	8	2.4	28.6	
Part-time colleagues and bosses	5	1.5	17.9	
Family and relatives	3	0.9	10.7	
Not applicable	304	91.6		
Total	332	100.0		
Topics of Interactions	**109**			**32.8**
Unimportant chat	80	24.1	73.4	
Schedule adjustments	14	4.2	12.8	
Clerical communication matters	5	1.5	4.6	
Thanks and greetings	5	1.5	4.6	
Advice on important or serious matters	3	0.9	2.8	
Fun and interesting topics	1	0.3	0.9	
School (classes)	1	0.3	0.9	
Not applicable	223	67.2		
Total	332	100.0		
Interaction Styles	**33**			**9.9**
Interaction using LINE app group function	19	5.7	57.6	
Interaction about no particular topic	10	3.0	30.3	
When the sender asks a question	2	0.6	6.1	
When the sender initiated the interaction by sending a message	2	0.6	6.1	
Not applicable	299	90.1		
Total	332	100.0		
Status of Senders	**92**			**27.7**
When the sender needs an urgent reply	34	10.2	37.0	
When the sender is busy	24	7.2	26.1	
When the sender has free time	15	4.5	16.3	
When the sender is in trouble	11	3.3	12.0	
When the sender is angry or irritated	4	1.2	4.3	
When the sender feels pleasure or joy	4	1.2	4.3	
Not applicable	240	72.3		
Total	332	100.0		
Status of Recipients	**17**			**5.1**
When the recipient is busy	11	3.3	64.7	
When the recipient feels angry or irritated	4	1.2	23.5	
When the recipient has an emergency	1	0.3	5.9	
When the recipient feels pleasure or joy	1	0.3	5.9	
Not applicable	315	94.9		
Total	332	100.0		

continued on following page

Table 2. Continued

Groups and Categories	n	%[a]	%[b]	%[c]
Specific Status of Senders	**44**			**13.3**
When the sender is sleeping	22	6.6	50.0	
When the sender is in class	6	1.8	13.6	
When the sender is engaged in a part-time job	5	1.5	11.4	
When the sender is eating	5	1.5	11.4	
When the sender is bathing	3	0.9	6.8	
When the sender is with someone	2	0.6	4.5	
When the sender is on the move	1	0.3	2.3	
Not applicable	288	86.7		
Total	332	100.0		
Specific Status of Recipients	**10**			**3.0**
When the recipient is sleeping	8	2.4	80.0	
When the recipient is on the move	1	0.3	10.0	
When the recipient is engaged in a part-time job	1	0.3	10.0	
Not applicable	322	97.0		
Total	332	100.0		

Note. Number = The number of responses mentioning the relevant category or subcategory.
[a]The number of responses mentioning the relevant subcategory divided by the total number of responses (N = 332).
[b]The number of responses mentioning the relevant subcategory divided by the total number of responses, excluding the number of responses classified "not applicable."
[c]The number of responses mentioning the relevant category divided by the total number of responses (N = 332).

In this reanalysis, we directly reconfirmed the meaning and content of all 332 answers independently from the category results described above. These responses were divided into the sender's convenience or the recipient's convenience. After two authors conducted this classification individually, the results of the classification were decided by consensus. Table 3 shows the results of this classification. The results indicate that judging when a quick reply is preferred and when a late reply is acceptable is overwhelmingly influenced by the convenience of the sender (who is waiting for a reply) over the convenience of the recipient who will reply.

Table 3. Classification of the sender's convenience and the recipient's convenience in situations when a late reply is acceptable

Groups and Categories for Convenience	n	%[a]	%[b]	%[c]
Sender's Convenience and Recipient's Convenience	**175**			**52.7**
Sender's convenience	156	47.0	89.1	
Recipient's convenience	19	5.7	10.9	
Not applicable	157	47.3		
Total	332	100.0		

Note. Number = The number of responses mentioning the relevant category or subcategory.
[a]The number of responses mentioning the relevant subcategory divided by the total number of responses (N = 332).
[b]The number of responses mentioning the relevant subcategory divided by the total number of responses, excluding the number of responses classified "not applicable."
[c]The number of responses mentioning the relevant category divided by the total number of responses (N = 332).

DISCUSSION

Text-based forms of communication now occur via PCs, mobile phones, and smartphones. Previous CMC research has pointed out that socioemotional interaction is possible, by devising content or using emoticons, even in text-based communication that lacks nonverbal cues (Walther, 1992; Walther, Anderson, & Park, 1994; Walther & Burgoon, 1992). However, we believe that nonverbal cues now exist in communication via mobile phones and smartphones, not only through the ingenuities described in most conventional PC-based CMC research, but also by the speed of exchange in sending text messages (Kato & Kato, 2015; Kato, Kato, & Chida, 2012; 2013). For example, consciously adjusting one's speed of reply can convey nonverbal communicative intent to the other party. A deliberately delayed reply can be mistaken for an unavoidably delayed reply and, as such, the sender waiting for a reply might interpret the speed of reply as intentional nonverbal information by the recipient. Thus, in communication by mobile phone or smartphone, a slow reply might make the sender uneasy or irritated. In Japan, disturbing cases such as bullying are occurring more frequently and even a murder in 2015 was partly attributed to a late reply to a LINE text message (Schreiber, 2015). Accordingly, reply speed is thought to be a major factor in the emotional aspects of text-based communication via mobile phones or smartphones.

In this study, we focused on the highly popular LINE text messenger application in Japan to investigate speed of exchange. In our sample of young adults, there was a clear finding that the speed required for text-based interactions ultimately depends on the convenience of the senders who are waiting for a reply. Particularly in situations when a late reply is acceptable, many more mentions were made of the senders' convenience rather than the recipient's convenience. In traditional landline voice calls, communication is not established if a recipient does not answer the call due to inconvenience or absence, so the exchange does not actually begin until both parties have acknowledged that real-time communication is possible. Conversely, communication by text messaging begins when a message is sent, because senders tend to expect recipients to read the message soon after it is sent and reply quickly. Because most people carry mobile phones and smartphones today, it is commonly expected that when a message arrives, the user will naturally notice it and be able to respond at once. This unfounded belief indicates there is little concern about the recipient's situation at the time of sending. The findings of this study support this lack of understanding. That is, most situations when a late reply was judged acceptable were based on the convenience of the senders themselves (e.g., when senders are sleeping). However, few of the survey responses considered the situation of the recipients. Many users might unconsciously believe that when they themselves are in a situation when they can exchange text messages, then the other party naturally must also be in the same situation. We believe this perception is one of the reasons why a late reply often causes problems.

The above results were discussed from the viewpoint of convenience of senders and the convenience of recipients. Both for when a quick reply is preferred and when a late reply is acceptable, the *Topics of Interaction* subcategories were most frequently mentioned. In other words, topics of interaction were most relevant to the required speed of reply. In particular, a quick reply is preferred for the topics of "meetings and appointments" and "schedule adjustments" and a late reply is acceptable for the topic "unimportant chat." Thus, we consider that exchanges requiring fast replies are task-oriented interactions and exchanges when late replies are acceptable are social-oriented interactions. As shown in previous CMC research (Luor, Lu, Wu, & Tao, 2010; Rutter, 1984; Rutter, 1987; Rutter, Stephenson, & Dewey, 1981; Siegel, Dubrovsky, Kiesler, & McGuire, 1986), compared with task-oriented exchanges, communication partners in social-oriented exchanges tend to strive to maintain good personal relationships, paying attention to each other's emotions. In task-oriented interactions, losing social emotional consideration for each other and requesting fast exchanges can lead to problems. Especially in task-oriented exchanges, users' recognition that mobile devices can communicate "anytime and anywhere" can greatly affect the speed of exchange. In addition, "advice on important or serious matters" was deemed a topic that required a quick reply. In such situations, a late reply might result in the sender feeling ignored or feeling that the recipient does not care about the sender or the issue at hand. In other words, a fast reply can reflect the other party's degree of concern.

Although this study takes a valuable first step in examining the desired speed of reply in text messaging, there are several limitations that must be addressed. Firstly, the data included only undergraduate students at Japanese universities. Thus, it is unclear whether the current findings can be generalized to users of various ages from other countries and cultural backgrounds. Future research should include subjects with diverse socio-demographic characteristics. Secondly, this study used a cross-sectional design. Future research should consider a longitudinal study to examine individuals' evolving behavior in text messaging over an extended time period. Finally, this study found that the most frequently mentioned situations related to the desired speed of reply depended on the topics of interaction. As each answer about the topics was very specific to the respondent and therefore difficult to factor, we placed answers into one of twelve rough subcategories. A research plan dedicated to the relationship between the topics discussed in text messaging and desired speed should be implemented in the future.

FUTURE RESEARCH DIRECTIONS

In this study we presented a detailed categorization of situations when a quick reply is preferred and a late reply is acceptable in text-based forms of communication using the LINE application. The results summarize the participants' free-description responses to the questionnaire items. Future research is needed to clarify the weight of each category obtained in this study by creating questionnaire items based on each category and participants rating each item.

This study did not specifically address how long a wait constitutes a quick reply and how long a late reply constitutes. Instead, wait time was left to the judgment of the survey participants. In the future, we hope to clarify what wait time or times constitute a late reply.

Our findings do not suggest that users need to have fast exchange speeds. Text-based communication is asynchronous, which offers users the advantage of communicating at their convenience. More than ever, education is needed to help users understand this feature. Elucidating the best way to carry out education is a direction for our future work.

CONCLUSION

This chapter focused on the LINE text-messenger application to investigate speed of exchange. Specifically, we conducted a survey of Japanese university students who provided free-text descriptions of situations when they would prefer a quick reply and when a late reply would be acceptable. Our main finding was that judging when a quick reply is preferred and when a late reply is acceptable is overwhelmingly influenced by the convenience of the sender (who is waiting for a reply) over the convenience of the recipient who will reply.

ACKNOWLEDGMENT

This research was supported by JSPS (Japan Society for the Promotion of Science) Grants-in-Aid for Scientific Research [grant number 15K01089]; and JSPS Grants-in-Aid for Scientific Research [grant number 15K01095].

REFERENCES

Ahad, A. D., & Lim, S. M. A. (2014). Convenience or nuisance?: The 'WhatsApp' dilemma. *Procedia: Social and Behavioral Sciences*, *155*(6), 189–196. doi:10.1016/j.sbspro.2014.10.278

Church, K., & Oliveira, R. (2013). What's up with whatsapp?: Comparing mobile instant messaging behaviors with traditional SMS. *Proceedings of the 15th international conference on Human-computer interaction with mobile devices and services*, 352-361. 10.1145/2493190.2493225

Daft, R. L., & Lengel, R. H. (1984). Information richness: A new approach to managerial behavior and organizational design. *Research in Organizational Behavior*, *6*, 191–233.

Daft, R. L., & Lengel, R. H. (1986). Organizational information requirements, media richness and structural design. *Management Science*, *32*(5), 554–571. doi:10.1287/mnsc.32.5.554

Dyer, R., Green, R., Pitts, M., & Millward, G. (1995). What's the flaming problem? CMC - deindividuation or disinhibiting? In M. A. R. Kirby, A. J. Dix, & J. E. Finlay (Eds.), *People and computers X* (pp. 289–302). Cambridge, UK: Cambridge University Press.

Joinson, A. N. (2001). Self-disclosure in computer-mediated communication: The role of self-awareness and visual anonymity. *European Journal of Social Psychology*, *31*(2), 177–192. doi:10.1002/ejsp.36

Joinson, A. N., McKenna, K., Postmes, T., & Reips, U. D. (Eds.). (2007). *The oxford handbook of Internet psychology*. Oxford, UK: Oxford University Press.

Kato, Y. (2015). A generation gap on mobile phone communication: The sense of discomfort experienced by digital natives when communicating with digital immigrants. *Journal of Information and Media Studies*, *1*, 31–44.

Kato, Y., & Kato, S. (2015). Reply speed to mobile text messages among Japanese college students: When a quick reply is preferred and a late reply is acceptable. *Computers in Human Behavior*, *44*, 209–219. doi:10.1016/j.chb.2014.11.047

Kato, Y., & Kato, S. (2016a). Mobile phone use during class at a Japanese women's college. In M. N. Yildiz & J. Keengwe (Eds.), *Handbook of Research on Media Literacy in the Digital Age* (pp. 436–455). Hershey, PA: IGI Global. doi:10.4018/978-1-4666-9667-9.ch021

Kato, Y., & Kato, S. (2016b). Mobile phone placement during lectures and dependency on LINE and text messaging: Survey of students at a women's university in Japan. *Journal of Socio-Informatics*, *8*(1), 28–40.

Kato, Y., Kato, S., & Chida, K. (2012). Reply timing and emotional strategy in mobile text communications of Japanese young people: replies to messages conveying four different emotions. In S. D. Long (Ed.), *Virtual Work and Human Interaction Research* (pp. 99–114). Hershey, PA: IGI Global. doi:10.4018/978-1-4666-0963-1.ch006

Kato, Y., Kato, S., & Chida, K. (2013). Reply timing as emotional strategy in mobile text communications of Japanese young people: focusing on perceptual gaps between senders and recipients. In J. E. Pelet & P. Papadopoulou (Eds.), *User Behavior in Ubiquitous Online Environments* (pp. 1–18). Hershey, PA: IGI Global.

Kiesler, S., Siegel, J., & McGuire, T. W. (1984). Social psychological aspects of computer mediated communication. *The American Psychologist*, *39*(10), 1123–1134. doi:10.1037/0003-066X.39.10.1123

Luor, T., Lu, H. P., Wu, L. L., & Tao, Y. H. (2010). The effect of emoticon in simplex and complex task-oriented communication: An empirical study of Instant Messaging. *Computers in Human Behavior*, *26*(5), 889–895. doi:10.1016/j.chb.2010.02.003

Matheson, K. (1991). Social cues in computer-mediated negotiations: Gender makes a difference. *Computers in Human Behavior*, *7*(3), 137–145. doi:10.1016/0747-5632(91)90003-J

Matheson, K., & Zanna, M. P. (1988). The impact of computer-mediated communication on self-awareness. *Computers in Human Behavior*, *4*(3), 221–233. doi:10.1016/0747-5632(88)90015-5

McGuire, T. W., Kiesler, S., & Siegel, J. (1987). Group and computer-mediated discussion effects in risk decision making. *Journal of Personality and Social Psychology*, *52*(5), 917–930. doi:10.1037/0022-3514.52.5.917

Ministry of Internal Affairs and Communications. (2015). *White paper 2015: Information and communications in Japan*. Retrieved November 12, 2016, from http://www.soumu.go.jp/johotsusintokei/whitepaper/eng/WP2015/2015-index.html/

Ministry of Internal Affairs and Communications. (2016). *White paper 2016: Information and communications in Japan*. Retrieved January 15, 2015, from http://www.soumu.go.jp/johotsusintokei/whitepaper/eng/WP2016/2016-index.html/

O'Hara, K., Massimi, M., Harper, R., Rubens, S., & Morris, J. (2014). Everyday dwelling with WhatsApp. *Proceedings of the 17th ACM conference on Computer supported cooperative work & social computing*, 1131-1143.

Prensky, M. (2001a). Digital natives, digital immigrants. *On the Horizon*, *9*(5), 1–6. doi:10.1108/10748120110424816

Prensky, M. (2001b). Digital natives, digital immigrants, part II: Do they really think differently? *On the Horizon*, *9*(6), 1–6. doi:10.1108/10748120110424843

Rutter, D. R. (1984). *Looking and seeing the role of visual communication in social interaction*. Chichester, UK: John Wiley & Sons.

Rutter, D. R. (1987). *Communicating by telephone*. Oxford, UK: Pergamon Press.

Rutter, D. R., Stephenson, G. M., & Dewey, M. E. (1981). Visual communication and the content and style of conversation. *British Journal of Social Psychology*, *20*(1), 41–52. doi:10.1111/j.2044-8309.1981.tb00472.x PMID:7237005

Schreiber, M. (2015). Seeking blame in a Kawasaki teen's death. *The Japan Times*. Retrieved January 15, 2017, from http://www.japantimes.co.jp/news/2015/03/14/national/media-national/seeking-blame-kawasaki-teens-death/#.WYVJGYTyiUk

Scott, D. J., Coursaris, C. K., Kato, Y., & Kato, S. (2009). The exchange of emotional context in business communications: A comparison of PC and mobile email users. In M. M. Head & E. Li (Eds.), Mobile and ubiquitous commerce: Advanced e-business methods: volume 4 of advances in electronic business series (pp. 201-219). Hershey, PA: IGI Global.

Scott, D. J., Kato, Y., Kato, S., & Liu, S. (2012). Comparing computer and mobile phone use by American and Japanese university students. *Proceedings of World Conference on E-Learning in Corporate, Government, Healthcare, and Higher Education (E-Learn) 2012*, 1912-1917.

Short, J. A., Williams, E., & Christie, B. (1976). *The social psychology of telecommunications*. London: Wiley.

Siegel, J., Dubrovsky, V., Kiesler, S., & McGuire, T. W. (1986). Group processes in computer-mediated communication. *Organizational Behavior and Human Decision Processes*, *37*(2), 157–187. doi:10.1016/0749-5978(86)90050-6

Sproull, L., & Kiesler, S. (1986). Reducing social context cues: Electronic mail in organizational communication. *Management Science*, *32*(11), 1492–1512. doi:10.1287/mnsc.32.11.1492

Statista. (2016). *Most popular global mobile messenger apps 2016*. Retrieved January 10, 2017, from http://www.statista.com/statistics/258749/most-popular-global-mobile-messenger-apps/

Tyler, J. R., & Tang, J. C. (2003). When can I expect an email response? A study of rhythms in email usage. *Proceedings of the Eighth European Conference on Computer Supported Cooperative Work (ECSCW2003)*, 239-258. 10.1007/978-94-010-0068-0_13

Walther, J. B. (1992). Interpersonal effects in computer-mediated interaction: A relational perspective. *Communication Research*, *19*(1), 52–90. doi:10.1177/009365092019001003

Walther, J. B. (1996). Computer-mediated communication impersonal, interpersonal, and hyperpersonal interaction. *Communication Research*, *23*(1), 3–43. doi:10.1177/009365096023001001

Walther, J. B., Anderson, J. F., & Park, D. W. (1994). Interpersonal effects in computer-mediated interaction: A meta-analysis of social and antisocial communication. *Communication Research*, *21*(4), 460–487. doi:10.1177/009365094021004002

Walther, J. B., & Burgoon, J. K. (1992). Relational communication in computer-mediated interaction. *Human Communication Research*, *19*(1), 50–88. doi:10.1111/j.1468-2958.1992.tb00295.x

Walther, J. B., & Tidwell, L. C. (1995). Nonverbal cues in computer-mediated communication, and the effect of chronemics on relational communication. *Journal of Organizational Computing and Electronic Commerce*, *5*(4), 355–378. doi:10.1080/10919399509540258

ADDITIONAL READING

Amali, I. O. O., Bello, M. B., & Hassan, I. (2012). A survey of University of Ilorin students' use of mobile phone in lecture rooms and its implications in education for Nigeria development. *Journal of Education and Practice*, *3*(10), 1–6.

Barak, M., Lipson, A., & Lerman, S. (2006). Wireless laptops as means for promoting active learning in large lecture halls. *Journal of Research on Technology in Education*, *38*(3), 245–263. doi:10.1080/15391523.2006.10782459

Baron, N. S. (2008). *Always on: Language in an online and mobile world*. Oxford, NY: Oxford University Press. doi:10.1093/acprof:oso/9780195313055.001.0001

Bennett, S., Maton, K., & Kervin, L. (2008). The 'digital natives' debate: A critical review of the evidence. *British Journal of Educational Technology*, *39*(5), 775–786. doi:10.1111/j.1467-8535.2007.00793.x

Campbell, S. (2006). Perceptions of mobile phone in college classrooms: Ringing, cheating, and classroom policies. *Communication Education*, *55*(3), 280–294. doi:10.1080/03634520600748573

Demb, A., Erickson, D., & Hawkins-Wilding, S. (2004). The laptop alternative: Student's reactions and strategic implications. *Computers & Education*, *43*(4), 383–401. doi:10.1016/j.compedu.2003.08.008

Derks, D., Bos, A. E. R., & Von Grumbkow, J. (2007). Emoticons and social interaction on the Internet: The importance of social context. *Computers in Human Behavior*, *23*(1), 842–849. doi:10.1016/j.chb.2004.11.013

Derks, D., Bos, A. E. R., & Von Grumbkow, J. (2008). Emoticons in computer-mediated communication: Social motives and social context. *Cyberpsychology & Behavior*, *11*(1), 99–101. doi:10.1089/cpb.2007.9926 PMID:18275321

Derks, D., Fischer, A. H., & Bos, A. E. R. (2008). The role of emoticon in computer-mediated communication: A review. *Computers in Human Behavior*, *24*(8), 766–785. doi:10.1016/j.chb.2007.04.004

Dresner, E., & Herring, S. C. (2010). Functions of the non-verbal in CMC: Emoticons and illocutionary force. *Communication Theory*, *20*(3), 249–268. doi:10.1111/j.1468-2885.2010.01362.x

Fang, B. (2009). From distraction to engagement: Wireless devices in the classroom. *EDUCAUSE Quarterly*, *32*(4), 1–10.

Fried, C. B. (2008). In-class laptop use and its effects on student learning. *Computers & Education*, *50*(3), 906–914. doi:10.1016/j.compedu.2006.09.006

Hall, J. A., & Pennington, N. (2013). Self-monitoring, honesty, and cue use on Facebook: The relationship with user extraversion and conscientiousness. *Computers in Human Behavior*, *29*(4), 1556–1564. doi:10.1016/j.chb.2013.01.001

Hammer, R., Ronen, M., Sharon, A., Lankry, T., Huberman, Y., & Zamtsov, V. (2010). Mobile culture in college lectures: Instructors' and students' perspectives. *Interdisciplinary Journal of E-Learning and Learning Objects*, *6*, 293–304. doi:10.28945/1316

Hembrooke, H., & Gay, G. (2003). The laptop and the lecture: The effects of multitasking in learning environments. *Journal of Computing in Higher Education*, *15*(1), 46–64. doi:10.1007/BF02940852

Huffaker, D. A., & Calvert, S. L. (2005). Gender, identity, and language use in teenage blogs. *Journal of Computer-Mediated Communication*, *10*(2). http://onlinelibrary.wiley.com/doi/10.1111/j.1083-6101.2005.tb00238.x/full Retrieved January 10, 2010

Kato, Y., Kato, S., & Akahori, K. (2007). Effects of emotional cues transmitted in e-mail communication on the emotions experienced by senders and receivers. *Computers in Human Behavior*, *23*(4), 1894–1905. doi:10.1016/j.chb.2005.11.005

Kaye, L. K., Malone, S. A., & Wall, H. J. (2017). Emojis: Insights, affordances, and possibilities for psychological science. *Trends in Cognitive Sciences*, *21*(2), 66–68. doi:10.1016/j.tics.2016.10.007 PMID:28107838

Lee, C. (2003). *How does instant messaging affect interaction between the genders?* Stanford, CA: The Mercury Project for Instant Messaging Studies at Stanford University. Retrieved January 10, 2015, from http://www.stanford.edu/class/pwr3-25/group2/projects/lee.html

Lo, S. K. (2008). The nonverbal communication functions of emoticons in computer-mediated communication. *Cyberpsychology & Behavior*, *11*(5), 595–597. doi:10.1089/cpb.2007.0132 PMID:18817486

Marengo, D., Giannotta, F., & Settanni, M. (2017). Assessing personality using emoji: An exploratory study. *Personality and Individual Differences*, *112*, 74–78. doi:10.1016/j.paid.2017.02.037

McCoy, B. R. (2013). Digital distractions in the classroom: Student classroom use of digital devices for non-class related purposes. *Journal of Medical Education*, *4*(4), 5–14.

Palfrey, J., & Gasser, U. (2008). *Born digital: Understanding the first generation of digital natives*. New York, NY: Basic Books.

Reid, D. J., & Reid, F. J. M. (2007). Text or talk? Social anxiety, loneliness, and divergent preferences for cell phone use. *Cyberpsychology & Behavior*, *10*(3), 424–435. doi:10.1089/cpb.2006.9936 PMID:17594267

Rezabek, L. L., & Cochenour, J. J. (1998). Visual cues in computer-mediated communication: Supplementing text with emoticons. *Journal of Visual Literacy*, *18*(2), 201–215. doi:10.1080/23796529.1998.11674539

Rice, R. E., & Love, G. (1987). Electronic emotion: Socioemotional content in a computer-mediated communication network. *Communication Research*, *14*(1), 85–108. doi:10.1177/009365087014001005

Riva, G. (2002). The sociocognitive psychology of computer-mediated communication: The present and future of technology-based interactions. *Cyberpsychology & Behavior*, *5*(6), 581–598. doi:10.1089/109493102321018222 PMID:12556121

Ross, C., Orr, E. S., Sisic, M., Arseneault, J. M., Simmering, M. G., & Orr, R. R. (2009). Personality and motivations associated with Facebook use. *Computers in Human Behavior*, *25*(2), 578–586. doi:10.1016/j.chb.2008.12.024

Savicki, V., & Kelley, M. (2000). Computer mediated communication: Gender and group composition. *Cyberpsychology & Behavior*, *3*(5), 817–826. doi:10.1089/10949310050191791

Singh, N., Chopra, N., & Kaur, J. (2014). A study to analyze relationship between psychological behavioral factors on WhatsApp addiction among youth in Jalandhar District in Punjab. *European Journal of Business and Management*, *6*(37), 269–274.

Thompsen, P. A., & Fougler, D. A. (1996). Effects of pictographs and quoting on flaming in electronic mail. *Computers in Human Behavior*, *12*(2), 225–243. doi:10.1016/0747-5632(96)00004-0

Timmers, M., Fischer, A. H., & Manstead, A. S. R. (1998). Gender differences in motives for regulating emotions. *Personality and Social Psychology Bulletin*, *24*(9), 974–985. doi:10.1177/0146167298249005

Tossell, C. C., Kortum, P., Shepard, C., Barg-Walkow, L. H., Rahmati, A., & Zhong, L. (2012). A longitudinal study of emoticon use in text messaging from smartphones. *Computers in Human Behavior*, *28*(2), 659–663. doi:10.1016/j.chb.2011.11.012

Walther, J. B., & D'Addario, K. P. (2001). The impacts of emoticons on message interpretation in computer-mediated communication. *Social Science Computer Review*, *19*(3), 324–347. doi:10.1177/089443930101900307

Witmer, D. F., & Katzman, S. L. (1997). On-line smilies: Does gender make a difference in the use of graphic accents? *Journal of Computer-Mediated Communication*, *2*(4). http://jcmc.indiana.edu/vol2/issue4/witmer1.html Retrieved January 10, 2010

Wolf, A. (2000). Emotional expression online: Gender differences in emoticon use. *Cyberpsychology & Behavior*, *3*(5), 827–833. doi:10.1089/10949310050191809

KEY TERMS AND DEFINITIONS

Communication Tools in Japan: Currently in Japan, communication tools that can be used with smartphones include mobile email, Twitter, and LINE. The most-used social media in Japan is LINE, followed by Twitter and then Facebook.

Digital Immigrants: Digital immigrants are the generations preceding digital natives, who initially used traditional media before gradually adopting new information/communications technologies and services as they became available.

Digital Natives: Digital natives are born into an information/communications technology environment where the internet, email, and mobile phones are commonly used.

LINE Application: LINE is an instant messenger that is similar to other internet-based messengers, such as WhatsApp, and is the most-downloaded social media/messenger application in Japan. The application was released in June 2011, following the Great East Japan Earthquake of March 2011, with the aim of creating an application where users can easily communicate even in the event of a disaster. In Japan, LINE has come to replace traditional mobile text messaging services (including SMS), especially among young people.

LINE's Read Receipt Status: LINE's read receipt function automatically informs the sender that the recipient has read the message.

LINE's Unread Receipt Status: LINE's unread receipt function automatically informs the sender that the recipient has not read the message.

Speed of Reply: Although LINE can easily exchange text messages, its users typically expect faster replies than with cellphone text messaging. In fact, the act of periodically checking one's smartphone for incoming messages happens daily.

Stickers: The sticker is a newer graphical element similar to emoji or emoticons that conveys emotional state, attitude, and opinion and is a small illustration that is sent in place of a message. The sticker originated as an attachment in LINE, but by 2013, Facebook Messenger was equipped with similar features, followed by Facebook timeline in 2014. In 2016, iMessage for iPhone added sticker functionality.

Chapter 5
Public Relations and Advertising in the Context of E-Sports

Tina Tomazic
University of Maribor, Slovenia

Luka Druks
University of Maribor, Slovenia

Noemia Bessa Vilela
Universidade Portucalense (UPT), Portugal

ABSTRACT

E-sports within the gaming industry characterize an economic sector that is engaged in the developing, marketing, and sale of video games. They represent many opportunities for advertising and public relations, which are very important to increase the visibility of e-sports. The use of both has proved far more effective, because it allowed a rapid increase in their popularity. The aim of this chapter is to compare the use of public relations and advertising in e-sports and to determine their appropriateness. So, the relationship between public relations, advertising, and e-sports is developed and researched for the first time here. The authors used qualitative comparative analysis between public relations and advertising in the context of e-sports based on Natus Vincere, one of the most important Ukrainian organizations in the gaming industry. The rise of the gaming industry and recent success of e-sports demonstrate the profitable economic potentials of gaming spectatorship.

INTRODUCTION

Videogames are one of the fastest growing media industries worldwide, and playing video games is a form of expression. Hutchins (2008) showed, that the extraordinary global growth of the computer games industry and gaming activities and cultures over the past decade are representative of the speed and character of social and cultural transformation in the second modernity. The World Cyber Games (WCG) represents a logical yet radical extension, integrating the organizational, physical and technological bases of competition. This arrangement has been made possible by the Information Technology (IT) revolution

DOI: 10.4018/978-1-5225-4047-2.ch005

and rapid expansion in the availability, capabilities and popularity of interactive digital communications technologies. Changes in the scale and capacity of transport and communications technologies, as well as the interrelated standardization and codification of pre-sport pastimes, created fundamental transformations in the structure and appearance of both. Unusually, modern media and sport were born.

The aim of this work is to compare the use of public relations and advertising in the "gaming" industry and e-sports. In this article, the relationship between public relations, advertising and e-sports is developed and researched for the first time. Namely, the gaming industry represents an economic sector that is engaged in the developing, marketing and sale of videogames. A further objective is to present the organization Natus Vincere (NV), one of the most important Ukrainian organizations in the field of the gaming industry and, in the latter case, to determine the appropriateness of the use of public relations and advertising in e-sports. The advertising and public relations was presented in one of the most successful e-sport organizations in the world. The advertising is mainly for insight into the advertising sponsors of NV and advertising the organization as a brand (e.g. selling T-shirts). The authors looked at how public relations work within the e-sports organization NV, and how effective they are. the Qualitative comparative analysis was used to analyze the causal contribution between public relations and advertising to find the crucial differences and to determine which logical conclusions a data set supports in the context of e-sports in the example of the NV organization.

The main limitation is the fact that there are very few scientific papers on the topic of advertising and public relations in e-sports. It is supposed that the advertising in e-sports must become suitable and effective, so that more frequent use of public relations will bring e-sports growing popularity and, thus, the more frequent occurrence of traditional media (the example is South Korea).

It has been considered, that advertising is more suitable and effective than public relations or publicity in e-sports. Due to the poor visibility of e-sport in most countries around the world, this is also a reason for the poor publicity and lack of interest of traditional media for the transmission of e-sports events. In some countries, such as South Korea, e-sports have almost the status of traditional sports, such as football. It is also believed that the application of public relations in the e-sports would contribute to the increasing popularity of e-sports and, therefore, the breakthrough in the traditional media. This applies to the regions or continents (for example Europe), in which e-sports are not so well known or popular.

DEVELOPMENT OF E-SPORTS

Taylor (2012) argued, that e-sports represent an increasingly popular and profitable array of organizations, communities, and sets of practices, all of which place tremendous value on audiences; for example, playing games competitively, in front of a crowd, represents the legitimization of gaming as a spectator sport. E-sports involve the enactment of videogames as a spectator-driven sport, carried out through promotional activities.

Hutchins (2008) and Taylor (2015) showed, that electronic sport (e-sport), or sport as media, signifies the seamless interpenetration of media content, sport and networked information and communications technologies, and represents an increasingly popular and profitable range of communities, organizations, and sets of practices, all of which place tremendous value on audiences; for example, playing games competitively, in front of a crowd, represents the legitimization of gaming as a spectator sport. However, organized competitive gaming is treated as much more than a passing fad; instead representing the emergence of a new phenomenon, e-sport.

The growing e-sports industry is intended to fulfil a number of international and domestic strategic goals (Szablewicz, 2016). However, e-sport has been an important subsidiary element that has helped increase the mainstream saturation of online game players. Pechi (2008) argued, that the popularity of e-sport operates to merge different social interest groups, industry players and online game consumers. The example is South Korea. In 1999, the South Korean government started to offer support to the e-sport game industry. They supported e-sport by organizing different social groups to promote positive public awareness of online gameplay. The Ministry of Culture and Tourism has worked closely with the Korean Association of E-Sport to produce an official system that verifies professional players and certifies standards for game titles of professional e-sport. So called 'pro-leaguers', professional players, can earn around US$ 1 million per year. The government encourages South Korean people to play games in public spaces to increase the visibility of e-sport. Staying on the case of South Korea, the rise of game broadcasting in e-sport reveals another industry dynamic of the South Korean online gaming industry responding to media globalization. High broadband penetration offers South Korean game consumers the ability to watch e-sport games in a convenient media environment. Two media channels, Ongame.net and MBC Game, broadcast game competitions live through cable and Internet services. The popularity of e-sport leads to the rise of new media companies such as World of Cyber Game (WCG) and World of E-Sport Game, Inc. (WEG). The e-sport culture is a local attempt to connect South Korea to the world through global media consumption of online games.

As Hutchins (2008) argued, the strength of the media sport concept is its accessibility, signifying a shift in cultural and historical sensibilities, which has resulted in a seemingly natural relationship existing between the media and sports industries.

E-SPORTS TODAY

E-sports today increasingly follow, and are even closer to, the popular trends of the traditional sports, such as football and basketball. The crowd of fans who are willing to sit in front of the computer or live and be attended by high-quality production is increasing. The quality production includes the experts who analyzed the match and commentators who make the transmission more interesting. Offline-events today even have judges who will ensure that everything is done according to the rules. Also, selected venues of offline-events are growing, especially in the eastern region: South Korea, China and Thailand, and some other countries, have already come so far as to have venues which are intended only for e-sports, and they have appointed Stadia. Even in Europe and North America they already have venues dedicated to e-sports, but these are merely studios. But this does not mean that the western region lags behind the east. The scene of the so-called Season 3 World Finals Games League of Legends will be the famous Staples Center, home base of the world-famous Basketball Team the LA Lakers and LA Kings Hockey Team.

Taylor (2015) showed, that most major e-sports organizations, such as Natus Vincere, WCG, Major League Gaming (MLG), and the Electronic Sports World Cup (ESWC), as well as game companies such as Valve (makers of Defense of the Ancients 2), Blizzard (Starcraft 2) and Riot (League of Legends), engage extensively in media production practices that often deliberately invoke mainstream spectator sports as a way of delivering content to digitally mediated audiences. This content includes live Tournament casts, interviews with players, replays and highlight reels of both online and Tournament-based games, and promotional documentaries – representing an increasing (and increasingly popular) range of video commodities through which to push e-sports to broader audiences.

Today, the most popular games are the League of Legends (LoL), Defense of the Ancients 2 (DotA2), Starcraft 2, Call of Duty, Counter Strike: Global Offensive, Street Fighter and Tekken. The first three are particularly outstanding. According to Jin (2010), even the League has since shifted almost entirely toward computer-based games such as Starcraft 2 and League of Legends, which carry broader appeal to audiences in Korea, where e-sports are significantly more established.

League of Legends is one of the Multiplayer Online Battle Arena genres (MOBA) and has been developed by the US Company Riot Games. The game is free, but developers are serving with micro transactions; they offer additional products that are not essential to play the game. It is primarily for skins, which are only visually exciting, and do not offer the player any advantage when playing games. Free of charge, the simplicity and popularity of the genre have carried the game quickly to being among the most popular in the world. The peculiarity of this game is that, since the popularity reached so far, the company decided to start their own exclusive League called the League Championship Series. The League for the professional player represents the real meaning of videogames, because of which they manage to qualify and, for at least a few months, receive a monthly salary of two thousand dollars per player. In addition, they even get 30 thousand dollars to rent a house (League of Legends, 2015). League of Legends is by far the biggest entity in the pro-gaming sector because, in 2013, the World Championships boasted 32 million viewers. The numbers shatter the notion that videogame streams can rival TV in terms of scale and reach (McCormick, 2013). Even Dota 2 is a free game that belongs to the MOBA genre and is the successor to the successful Blizzard's video game DotA. It was developed by the company Valve, which used a different system and organizes an exclusive and prestigious Tournament annually called The International, in which only the best compete (Dota 2, 2015). Finally, there is the game StarCraft 2. Although the scene is the most developed in South Korea, it does not mean that the rest of the world is not popular. In this game prize funds are smaller, because the play is not teamed, but amounts are still very high.

The best professional players have celebrity status. In the eastern region, the euphoria of the celebrity players is still higher than in the West. Not only in offline-events are autographs awarded to the fans, but they are also online, followed by a multitude of fans on social media platforms and livestream. The most popular players suddenly have more than 50 thousand spectators. This represents a great benefit to them, and some earn even more than 5 thousand euros per month. In the US, professional players are granted the status of real professional athletes, which is similar to the status of NBA, NFL players and others. This is a significant step because, in the first place, this means no more problems with visas. The absolute record for the number of fans of the Spanish individual player games League of Legends is Carlos 'ocelote' Santiago Rodriguez, who has more than 220 thousand Facebook fans. Such a large number of fans is not only in the context of e-sports, but also for other areas. According to Crawford (2015), the Sports Team or Club a fan follows is made up of multiple elements and a complex history, which allows the fan to see in the object of their fandom what they value in themselves; it becomes a mirror to them and, hence, as such, they feel part of the Club they follow. This is why sports fans often use the first-person pronoun when referring to the Club or Team they follow, such as ''we won on Saturday'', and by attending games, singing, chanting, buying the team shirt, or wearing a lucky item of clothing, fans feel they have an influence, possibly even some degree of control, of the Club they (literally) support. It is their Club.

The popularity of e-sports has helped the development of the "live stream platform" greatly, which also allows each fan to live part of their playing various videogames online, or watch their favorite player. It's not necessarily that the most popular streamers are only professional players. There are many examples that the streamer is an entertainer and he has, with his character, gained a lot of fans. For some, entertainer represents their profession. The maximum platform applies to Twitch.tv, which has more than 34 million viewers per month. These platforms could be used by the organizers of Tournaments and Leagues (Twitch.tv, 2016).

The global e-Sports audience is 134 million strong, and growing. Thirteen percent (13%) of live-stream viewers watch e-Sports. Almost half of e-Sports viewers in the U.S. use Twitch.tv, the world's largest live streaming site for game content. Roughly the same amount of e-Sports viewers participate in some type of competitive gaming, mostly through online platforms. Investment in innovative business models, platforms and derivative businesses further spurs growth in competitive gaming. Asia still leads the global e-Sports market with $374 million in annual revenues (61%). In the coming years, we expect to see the fruits of the continued investment in North America, Western and Eastern Europe by game companies like Riot Games and Wargaming (Superdata, 2016).

THE RELATION OF PUBLIC RELATIONS, ADVERTISING AND E-SPORTS

Not only traditional sports, but also e-sport are shaped increasingly by the media, spectacularized by commerce, employed to deliver audiences to sponsors and, ultimately, linked to the technological opportunities afforded by various media delivery forms (English, 2016; Miller, Lawrence, McKay, & Rowe, 2001).

Public Relations (PR) and advertising in e-sports are used for different purposes. They share the fact that the vast majority are used only in digital media. Digital media allow to organizations cheaper innovation and creativity to implement PR and advertising campaigns. Moreover, the target public and target market on a daily basis use different digital media. Typical for e-sports organizations is that they do not use advertising and PR-agencies and do everything within the organization so as to reduce the costs. Recently, agencies have already started emerging that are specialized in e-sports. However, the common aim of the advertising and PR in e-sports is to increase the visibility of e-sports in the world.

Advertisers are different, and in recent times there are not only companies, organizations or individuals who are in any sense related to e-sports. On the web they often choose to lease the advertising space in the form of pictorial banners and other major image ads on various websites that are related to e-sports (blogs, websites, organizations, news portals on the topic of e-sports, etc.) or advertising time in the form of video ads, mainly on livestream platforms. There are two types of video ads on the livestream platforms which are common; it is a form of contextual advertising. The first type of video ad production triggers the replay of the ad whenever it wishes. These ads are not integrated into pre-prepared production since they depend randomly on the location of the viewer. By playing this form of art, the broadcaster earns according to the number of viewers at that time. In the second type, the difference is that production plays the desired results that advertise the sponsors. Sponsors pre-paid the advertising and the advertising is being used only in large-offline events. Common to both is that it is impossible to skip them. Advertising in e-sports is, in the great majority, brand advertising of companies or organizations that have a commercial function. Companies in e-sports are almost always included in advertising with the sponsoring of organizations and Tournaments or Leagues. There is a symbiosis between all players, because the organization and the organizers of Leagues and Tournaments allow the advertising space and time to their sponsors and vice versa. E.g. logo, web site and other information of a sponsor occur in the production, website, social media and clothes of organizations or Tournaments and Leagues. In return, the organizations returned the favor to sponsors and organizers. The offline events also represent a great opportunity to advertise, where sponsors set up stalls and are in direct contact with the target market. The effectiveness of advertising is measured by the market and advertising goals that have been set. But, according to Van Dreunen (2011), advertising is not part of this business history, because it is an indirect revenue stream.

The great majority of the organizations are using PR in e-sports. The main purpose is the continuous and immediate two-way communication with the users through the website and social media. There is no need to issue a press release to be published the next day in the newspapers. Thus, companies, organizations and individuals (professional players) maintain a certain image and reputation that must first be created and then maintained. Surprisingly, it often happens that one of the major e-sports organizations must resolve a scandal or problem to maintain their reputation. With PR the organizations mainly maintain contact with their fans 24 hours a day, 7 days a week. There are available to them news (results, new players, go players, etc.) either on the website of the organization, a news portal for e-sports, or on the social networks. The real breakthrough for the PR failed recently. Thematic e-sports articles began to appear more frequently on the website of the US business magazine Forbes (www.forbes.com), and the largest sports site in the world ESPN (espn.go.com). One of the most popular US e-sports organizations has managed an excellent PR-move, Team Solo Mid (www.solomid.net). CBS (American Broadcasting) made a live reality show from their "gaming". The show is aired once a week on the Internet and called GameCribs (Gamespot, 2016).

In e-sports is also the very interesting area of theming. According to Crawford (2015), theming is evident in many areas of society, most obviously in fast-food restaurants and theme parks, but can also be seen in the sports industry, which also includes e-sports. Standardized products, such as t-shirts, mugs, and scarves, are given a (perceived) added value by the application of a brand or theme. This is significant in a culture industry that has increasingly seen a hyper commodification and disconnection from its working class roots and origins. Sports brands, themes, and even stadia, become purchasable, for the right price. In an industry where fans' influence and control is becoming less apparent, capitalism profits by selling consumers a sense of control, influence, and support. Sports-themed videogames therefore represent the most rationalized version of this; which is both a key example and a metaphor of the wider capitalist sports industry. Here, gamers are sold pre-packaged elements of a sport, in a standardized and formulaic format which, in each iteration, gets tweaked slightly and given a veneer of individuality. Here, the gamer gets to experience a sense of control of a world normally outside their reach. The videogame turns the unquantifiable into rationalized calculations and code, to give the gamer the sensation of control and direction they lack in relation to the sports they follow, as well as other aspects of the capitalist society in which they live. According to Superdata (2016), brand owners and advertisers are expected to adapt to emergent forms of entertainment, which will grow sponsorship deals across the segment. Following the lead of early movers, we anticipate an increase in ad spending by consumer packaged goods, automotive and technology brands.

Competitive gaming is a spectacular phenomenon that is changing game publishing. Valued at $621 million, most of the worldwide revenues today come from advertisers and corporate sponsors. But e-sports also offer publishers an opportunity to expand the touchpoints around their games and give fans news way to engage with their favorite characters and enter into a deeper experience. Competitive gaming is a marketing strategy, not a revenue driver (Superdata, 2016). It is believed that, in addition to traditional marketing efforts, organizing events and streaming content improves awareness and retention.

STATUS OF E-SPORT ORGANIZATION- EXAMPLE ON NATUS VINCERE ORGANIZATION

Natus Vincere (NV) is a Ukrainian e-sport organization, which is considered one of the most successful in the world. Natus Vincere derives from Latin words and means "born to win" (Natus Vincere, 2016). Since their establishment in early January 2010, they have been attended by over 50 Tournaments in more than 20 different countries on three different continents and all won more than € 1.1 million, mainly through the games Dota 2 and Counter Strike 1.6. With great successes they have acquired a large number of fans who followed them massly on social networks (Facebook, Twitter), and monitor livestreams of their favorite players regularly. The biggest success was when, in 2011 in Cologne in Germany, they won first place in the Tournament The International 1 and all won a little less than € 800,000. In addition, fans are necessary to gain sponsors who are, first and foremost, the key to the survival, success and visibility of each e-sports organization.

The organization NV has gained suitable sponsors because of its reputation: Alienware ("gaming" branch of the American company Dell), SteelSeries (Danish manufacturer of peripheral devices, which is one of the largest in the "gaming" area), Kingston (US manufacturers of RAM, USB sticks, hard disks and memory cards) and some others. The organization NV is currently active in five different games: Counter Strike: Global Offensive, Dota 2, Fifa, StarCraft 2 and World of Tanks. When searching for new teams results or quality of players are crucial. This is not the only important factor in the selection of the teams, market value plays big part in the selection of the team. The market value of certain teams represents a videogame and the existing base of fans. NV is one of the few e-sports organizations which managed excellent results and innovative communication with fans, and the "gaming" organization changed into one of the leading brands in the e-sports due to their successes.

The goals of the organization are: The promotion and development of e-sports, to create a global e-sports Academy based on identifying young people with high potential and the necessary characteristics to become professional gamers, to create successful, socially and physically-developed gamers who are able to achieve goals in all aspects of life, and the admission of e-sports as an official sport and sectioned competition in the Olympic Games (at this point we could place a parallel with a traditional sport, according to Miller *et al.* (2001). Traditional sport is the most universal aspect of popular culture and is characterized commonly as the global culture industry par excellence, and cultural commentators find evidence of his new phenomenon in international sports media spectacles, such as the Olympic games, too.

USE OF PUBLIC RELATIONS IN NATUS VINCERE

The main objective of the communication for the organization NV is to increase the number of fans worldwide. Today, on Facebook, they have nearly 200,000 fans and 50,000 followers on Twitter. The following communication goal is that these fans who form their online community engage in various activities of the organization and in its teams. It is essential that the public has an active fan, which means that it is not only following the publication on social networks, but also participates in various promotions (e.g. Prize). NV often implemented various promotions and contests which draw fans to the fact that more time is devoted to trademarks. The next goal is to strengthen the membership trademarks of NV and data collection. Many applications for consolidation of affiliation trademarks are also socializing with fans on the offline-events. By consolidating the membership, the profit is increasing with the growth in the sales of NV features (e.g. T-shirts, mice, keyboards, headsets, etc.).

To achieve the objectives of NV they use the social networks Facebook and Twitter in conjunction with its website, and livestream platform Twitch.tv. On Facebook and Twitter they publish short summaries of press releases regularly; by clicking links they lead to the entire message on their website. Press releases are news about teams or players, the acquisition of new players, teams, sponsors, interviews, coverage and online-offline-events. So, they inform their fans constantly, from which they can get immediate feedback via commenting, sharing or liking.

For PR they do not only apply their profiles on social networks and their websites, but sponsors of significant announcements share their profiles on social networks and websites. Many times it happens that the summarized message, published news e-sports page, or the organization itself has previously sent a message to the public. The organization NV has often appeared on Ukrainian television, and in conjunction with the Tournaments they have visited.

The organization does not communicate with their fans only as a whole, but each player is also personally in touch with their fans on Facebook and Twitter. Twitch.tv represents a special form of communication. Among streaming viewers it can communicate continuously with the streamers by interacting over streams (video and audio), or chat rooms. Sponsors often use players as the face of PR-campaigns.

THE SIGNIFICANCE OF ADVERTISING IN NATUS VINCERE

In NV there are two types of advertising. The first is branding of NV and other sponsors through advertising this organization. The main objective that is common to both types is to increase the profits for the organization and sponsors. The organization also sells the advertising space to third parties for an extra income.

The organization does not advertise with the purchase of advertising space for achieving the advertising goals. They advertise mainly with the product line NV (jerseys of the team) and peripheral devices of NV. NV is one of the few organizations that have, in conjunction with its sponsors SteelSeries, its line of peripherals. The key to such advertising has a strong brand, because consumers do not buy only jerseys or headphones. The brand NV is additional value in the form of characteristic color, logo and key winning mentality.

As already mentioned, in the case of SteelSeries, the sponsors also have a very important role in advertising the brand of the organization. Sponsors regularly include the organization NV in their advertising campaigns in several different ways:

- The promotion of the organization NV on social networks and websites of the sponsors;
- Players are involved in the development of new products or services. From players they acquire opinions, for example, what do they think about the form of a new mouse?
- The use of players and brands in various advertisements, products and product packaging. E.g. headsets, keyboards, mice, mouse pads from SteelSeries with a color and logo of the organization NV. Kingston, for example, uses the organization's logo on the packaging; and
- The invitation of the players to the exclusive Tournaments and promotions (e.g. Facebook promotions, video ads), organized by the aforementioned sponsors of NV.

In return, the organization advertises its sponsors. The website of the organization NV has a special place for advertising, intended solely for advertising sponsors.

All multimedia contents (e.g. YouTube Videos, Facebook promotions) that are created by an organization also includes the logos of all sponsors. All the videos on the YouTube channel NV begin with a presentation of all the sponsors, sometimes with a short advertisement in many of them. On Twitch.tv the players must use graphics with all sponsors. These graphics can be located on the streamer's screen or below in the description of the profile.

It is also very important for sponsors that viewers on the stream and live could see the players with their products. Most players during streaming used the camera so viewers can see with which mouse, keyboard, headset and pad they play. In the offline-events the players wear the jerseys, which present all the sponsors. They use SteelSeries peripheral devices and sometimes Alienware notebooks. They use the concept of traditional sports. When a consumer sees his favorite football player in a jersey and new football boots with his name, he wants it himself. It's similar in the e-sports; when a fan sees a player from the organization NV wear a jersey or use a SteelSeries headset, he wants it himself, because this shows loyalty to the Club.

COMPARISON OF PUBLIC RELATIONS AND ADVERTISING IN THE CASE OF THE NATUS VINCERE ORGANIZATION

Both types of communication are used several times a day and it would be difficult to say that one of them is very abundant. In most cases they even overlap completely. In the case of the organization NV we can see that the common goal of PR and advertising is increasing the brand awareness of the organization. To achieve this objective, two types of communication are using the digital media; they rely mainly on community, created on Facebook, Twitter and Forums, which are the result of prolonged PR and advertising. In general the claim is that advertising is expensive and PR is cheap. In NV it was evident that they do not devote financial resources for advertising and for PR. This allows them primarily the loyal crowd of fans on the social networks, and also a symbiosis with the sponsors, because they benefit one to another. Of course, sponsors are not doing this for free. Sponsors, such as Alienware, SteelSeries and Kingston, are aware that, in terms of the organization's visibility, they get a lot. Most fans of NV are regular gamers and, consequently, represent target audiences and a target market for PR and advertising sponsors. Achieving the target public, in conjunction with the organization NV, is much cheaper than if they advertise or use PR on their own.

The Table 1 summarizes the findings of qualitative comparative analysis between PR and advertising in the context of e-sports on the example of the organization NV.

CONCLUSION

The popularity of e-sports is growing, so the e-sport has made impressive progress in a relatively short period of time. Starts for e-sports are being enabled by the sponsors, which enabled for organizations the regular employment by playing video games. At the beginning these were the only companies that have been linked directly to e-sports, for example, game developers, manufacturers of computers or peripherals. E-sports have enabled them to have direct contact with the target audience which, in this

Table 1. Public relations and advertising in the context of e-sports on the example of the organization Natus Vincere

	PR	Advertising
The Financial Aspect	The organization since its establishment has not yet invested money in any PR campaign. The entire PR, which the organization carries out daily, is running free through their profiles and the profiles of sponsors and partners in the social networks. The base of fans that the organization has represents the cornerstone of communications. The content they generate on a daily basis must be the most unique, interesting and viral (the viral effect is the one that people create themselves) in order to attract both existing fans, as well as potential new ones. To create new contents, they use mainly YouTube and Twitch. With the PR the organization presents and expands its story of success and winning mentality. The primary objective of the use of PR is not to increase the earnings, but to increase the brand awareness. However, increasing the brand awareness of NV indirectly also affect higher income from increasing the sales of NV products and attracting new sponsors.	As with PR, the organization also does not invest money in advertising in advertising campaigns. They are prospering because they use exclusively their own advertising space and the space of its sponsors and partners. The organization often creates advertising campaigns for their sponsors. Sponsors then have these advertising campaigns implemented in their network, but the organization can also support through its network. Thus, both will save a lot of money, which would otherwise be spent to achieve the target market. In addition, the advertising organizations have the same goal as the PR has, but there is another target of increasing the earnings, e.g. increasing the sales of team jerseys or other products of NV brands and their sponsors.
Media Usage	The organization carries out PR in the vast majority in digital media. They are using digital media because of the possibility of an immediate transmission of a communication, possibility of interaction with fans, which is the key to the success of the organization, and because it is free. Increasingly, the publication of the major successes of the organization appears on Ukrainian television.	Also, at this point the PR and advertising are similar, since they are both carried in digital media. A computer and an internet connection represent a condition for e-sports, so there is no surprise that the focus is mainly on advertising the target market.
Efficacy	Visibility of organizations with skillful and effective use of PR is one of the leading requirements in e-sports. Based on all these considerations, the use of PR is to increase the visibility of e-sports and can be very effective.	In addition, to the fact that advertising is effective by increasing brand awareness, they are also increasing the profits from year to year. Of course, it doesn't present a bigger profit only for the organization but also for their sponsors.

Source: Own.

case, represents the fans and players of videogames, and the target market. Today such companies still represent the majority, but a trend of integration of enterprises has appeared that are not associated with e-sports.They are aware that e-sports are not only more appealing to computer enthusiasts, but are becoming "mainstream". By becoming so popular, however, they attract a crowd, which represents the potential consumers. The companies Pringles, Adidas, MasterCard and Coca Cola have joined this trend recently. Especially it impresses the fact that the economic crisis has no effect on e-sports and the "gaming" industry as prize funds and cash contributions grow from year to year. It's probably only a matter of time until all "gaming" organizations begin to appoint major sponsors, as is already customary in traditional sports.

As was argued, at the beginning, advertising represents too high a cost and risk, while a well-planned PR-campaign can be carried out free of charge and with great effect. The implementation of a PR-campaign can be long-term, because first a fan base has to be created that will pose significant target audiences. The next finding is that the use of Public Relations in e-sports contributes to the increasing popularity of e-sports and, thus, also a breakthrough in the traditional media. This applies to the country or regions (US, Europe), in which e-sports are not so well known or popular which can be seen from the example of the organization NV. An important finding is also that both the PR and advertising are very important to increase the visibility of e-sports and to complement each other. The using of both has proved far more effective, because it allows a rapid increase in the popularity of e-sports. It will be very interesting to monitor the integration of Coca Cola in e-sports as they are known for excellent PR and advertising campaigns, which could bring the e-sports to a whole new level of visibility.

For many countries, the e-sports are still a relatively unknown concept. Due to the poor visibility of e-sports in most countries around the world, this is also responsible for the poor publicity and lack of interest of traditional media for the transmission of e-sports events. In some countries, such as South Korea, e-sports have almost the status of conventional sports, such as football. These countries could lack strong and large communities, which could take e-sports to a higher level. Of course, the fact that no company is associated with e-sports does not help. Companies in this field are not aware of them and this represents a serious risk. The organization of a Tournament which would have a big enough prize pool would contribute greatly to the visibility of e-sports in the country. Very cheaply it could increase visibility with the creation of the inter-faculty league's most popular videogames in the world - League of Legends. The websites and profiles on social networks would be used for PR and advertising. This would create a large enough community to which would follow also the sponsors. The profit would be by broadcasting the ads on Twitch.tv, since all matches were streamed with commentary. Nevertheless, advertising e-sports should become a suitable and effective way to encourage more frequent use of Public Relations, bringing increasing popularity of the e-sport, and, thus, also a higher frequency of traditional media (e.g. South Korea).

In many ways, competitive gaming seems, to resemble traditional sports. But to think that a new phenomenon like e-sports can be described in terms of the old is to misunderstand it entirely. The intersection of technology, fandom and interactive entertainment is presenting us with new ways of sharing experiences on a global scale and, with 134 million e-sports enthusiasts worldwide, this is no longer a niche activity, but a shift in the way people consume games. North America and Europe are nascent but fast-growing markets. Since 2011, e-sports have been growing in the west exponentially. In addition to live-streaming sites and online console devices, organizations like Major League Gaming in the US and the Electronic Sports League in Europe have helped provide the necessary infrastructure for the space to thrive (Superdata, 2016). However, the rise of the gaming industry, and the recent success of the e-sports, demonstrate the lucrative economic potentials of gaming spectatorship.

REFERENCES

Crawford, G. (2015). Is it in the Game? Reconsidering Play Spaces, Game Definitions, Theming, and Sports Videogames. *Games and Culture,* 1-22. Retrieved August 1, 2015, from http://blog.dota2.com/?l=english

English, P. (2016). Twitter's diffusion in sports journalism: Role models, laggards and followers of the social media innovation. *New Media & Society*, *18*(3), 484–501. doi:10.1177/1461444814544886

Gamespot. (n.d.). Retrieved July 26, 2016, from http://www.gamespot.com/

Hutchins, B. (2008). Signs of meta-change in second modernity: The growth of e-sport and the World Cyber Games. *New Media & Society*, *10*(6), 851–869. doi:10.1177/1461444808096248

League of Legends. (n.d.). Retrieved August 1, 2015, from http://gameinfo.eune.leagueoflegends.com/en/game-info/get-started/what-is-lol/

McCormick, R. (2013). *League of Legends' eSports finals watched by 32 million people*. Retrieved June 8, 2016, from http://www.theverge.com/2013/11/19/5123724/league-of-legends-world-championship-32-million-viewers

Miller, T., Lawrence, G. A., McKay, J., & Rowe, D. (2001). *Globalization and Sport: Playing the World*. London: SAGE Publications Ltd.

Natus Vincere. (n.d.). Retrieved July 21, 2016, from http://navi-gaming.com/en

Peichi, C. (2008). New Media for Social Change: Globalisation and the Online Gaming Industries of South Korea and Singapore. *Science, Technology & Society*, *13*(2), 303–323. doi:10.1177/097172180801300207

Superdata. (2016). *Playable media & games market research*. Retrieved June 8, 2016, from https://www.superdataresearch.com/

Szablewicz, M. (2016). A Realm of Mere Representation? "Live" E-Sports Spectacles and the Crafting of China's Digital Gaming Image. *Games and Culture*, *11*(3), 256–274. doi:10.1177/1555412015595298

Taylor, N. (2015). Play to the camera: Video ethnography, spectatorship, and e-sports. *Convergence (London)*, •••, 1–16.

Taylor, T. L. (2012). *Raising the Stakes: The Professionalization of Computer Gaming*. Cambridge, MA: The MIT Press.

Twitch.tv. (n.d.). Retrieved June 1, 2016, from http://www.twitch.tv/p/about

Van Dreunen, J. (2011). *A Business History of Video Games: Revenue Models from 1980 to Today. The Game Behind the Video Game: Business, Regulation, and Society in the Gaming Industry*. New Brunswick, NJ: Academic Press.

Chapter 6
Social Media and TV Watching Metrics

Gülşah Sari
Abant Izzet Baysal University, Turkey

ABSTRACT

In this chapter, in order to measure the relation between social media and television, the inside sequence published in Turkish television series during the broadcasting period of 2016-2017 was examined. The reason for the selection of this directory is that 39 episodes are broadcast throughout the episode, and the high interest in social media is a high percentage of TV ratings. The study looked at the follow-up measures in social media that were used to help measure social media in-line monitoring. The Kimola firm is one of the companies that conducts research on this subject. In the study, Kimola presented its published series of 39 episodes published in the series. As a result of this study, it shows that social media have an increasing role in the effect of watching television.

1. SOCIAL MEDIA

There is a lot of research on networking. Castells is an important one among those working in the field. Castells (2013), points out that by the end of the 1990s, the Internet's communications power has led to another technological change towards the widespread use of computerized computing through inter-connected computing devices that emerge in a wide variety of formats from discrete microcomputers and mainframes to new developments in telecommunications and computing. In the last quarter of the century, the formation and spread of computerized networks of the Internet, the internet, have changed the structure of the new medium of communication, the architecture of the network, the culture and the form of communication of those connected to the network forever. The architecture of the network is open; Support the widespread access of the CAM; That social inequalities are emerging strongly in the field of electronics despite the restrictions imposed by the government, or by commercial restrictions. On the other hand, the openness of the system is also a result of the continuous renewal and free access process initiated by the first computer hackers who find hundreds of thousands of netten people and those who have adopted the network as a hobby.

DOI: 10.4018/978-1-5225-4047-2.ch006

According to Blossom (2009), the terminology used to define how individuals are using today's publishing tools to influence other people can be quite confusing. Blossom points out that people refer to Web 2.0, user-generated content, social networking, and other terms to try to encompass the movement toward people becoming influential publishers on the Web and beyond. All of these terms and others have their place in describing useful tools for people to publish to the world. He finds that the term "social media" serves as a good umbrella for encompassing all of the available technologies that will not be limited to a specific application of publishing or a particular era of publishing. As discussed earlier, social media has been with us from the first human utterances and will be with us long after the Internet has been supplanted by other forms of global communications that empower individuals to be influential publishers.

It is seen that various definitions have been made for social media through studies on internet based network technology and social media. According to Lincoln (2009), social media is more about the ideas that you share, collaborate on, create and participate in rather than observe. Also according to Kara (2013), social media is the whole of web-based applications that operate on the basis of web 2.0 and user-generated content. Büyükaslan (2015), describe social media as an environment in which many activities carried out in a social network where many sharing is made, daily shopping is performed, food is ordered, banking transactions are done, chat is played with the closest friends, acquaintances and acquaintances, movies are played together and the classical definition of social concept. From these definitions, social media is the name given to the dialogue that people have made with each other over the internet, the sharing they have done and the many activities that have been carried out.

Gündüz and Pembecioğlu (2015), points out that, the concept of social media has emerged as the Internet has enabled mutual data communication at the Web 2.0 level. Along with the development of the social media, the movement of knowledge and news has become a structure that needs to be addressed at very different speeds and dimensions. Also Kuyucu (2015), says that social media, which started to be used as an alternative to traditional media but succeeded in taking away the power of setting the agenda of the traditional media as the usage area developed, allows the individuals to discuss concepts unlimitedly. The communication that passes through the audit screen in the traditional media is made more freely in the social media. In this context, social media allows individuals to freely express concepts as they wish.

According to Shabir and others (2014), social media is most recent form of media and having many features and characteristics. It have many facilities on same channel like as communicating, texting, images sharing, audio and video sharing, fast publishing, linking with all over world, direct connecting. It is also cheapest fast access to the world so it is very important for all age of peoples. Its use is increasing day by day with high rate in all over the world. Majority of youth is shifting speedily from electronic media like as television viewers and radio listeners to the social media among all age of group.

Social media, the product of the last 35 years, does not end its development. Kara (2013), admits that almost every day a new application is added to the network, and few of them end their assets. According to the social media research conducted by the Pew Research Center, only 14 social media sites have been closed to date. One hundred and ninety eight people are still members. When many social sharing sites select users who use a specific geographic mass or language as the target audience, the user groups can become completely different from the more cosmopolitan or originally targeted audience, depending on the increase in the number of members of the site. For example, a Turkish-speaking Turkish Orkut social-sharing site was initially a social network that began to spread in English in the United States, but eventually became a social network of Brazilian members.

According to Shabir and others (2014), social media is recent and most favorite form of media. it is a useful tool for youth so its use is essential to get information and knowledge when youth going to connect the social media should keep in mind that basic purpose to usage and always remember that they are going to share the information or links are not only for their gratification and interest but also for all their contacts and friends community, so be carefully utilize with social responsibility, ethically, religiously and politically appropriate links should be share.

2. SOCIAL MEDIA AND TV WATCHING

It is seen that the concept of freedom provided by the use of media is a very effective advantage especially when we consider it in terms of television audience. Gündüz and Pembecioğlu (2015), point out that the tendency of the young population to spend time with TV is a declining structure compared to the mobile technology, internet and social media interest, as well as an important data supported by the researches. Of course, it is natural that such young and dynamic enthusiasts tend to watch prime time content, high-profile sequences or movies from the internet. According to Cheng and others (2016), social media introduce a new approach for TV viewers to interact with the TV shows as well as with other viewers about the shows. They pointed out that the likes, shares, comments of Facebook allow viewers to share their opinions and to show support for their favorite TV shows. In a way it enables fans to participate in discussion whilst watching the shows on TV.

Leyla and Majnun, one of the most watched comedy series in Turkey in recent years, seems to be supportive of our assertion when we evaluate the viewing, sharing and commenting on the internet. The announcement following the removal of the series from the national TRT broadcast of the directory also shows that the index is more viewed on the internet and that this population is much higher than the actual rating of the index. Solutions such as Tivibu, which basically focus on television as the point of view of the series and other programs and produce different alternatives in this direction, have options such as recording and watching first, and the freedom and indispensable superiority of the internet is obvious. From a point of view, the accessibility of publications can be said to precede the traceability of publications.

Today, many TV viewers watch the series especially from the internet. Most importantly, today's media user is the sole source of social media. Altan (2015), points out another important point is the interaction of classical media such as radio and television with social media. This interaction also brings with it the continual renewal of the mainstream media in the alternative media light.

According to Çetinkaya (2014), today, the development of new communication tools, the technological convergence and the new communication possibilities between networks, digitized television publishing has become a monologous mass communication process, an interactive, multidimensional and mutual communication process. In the past, television It was only a monitored object, but it has become an object of experience at the same time. In particular, the social media, which has entered our lives through the development of internet technologies and social networks, has also led to a change in television watching habits of television viewers. Now, television viewing behavior, which only takes place in the living rooms and is limited to the room in which they are located, confronts as an experience shared with the whole world. This development and change has led to the necessity of changing the monitoring measurement methods.

While social media encompasses areas where the mainstream media is insufficient to satisfy Altan (2015), says that the needs of today's media users, it also obliges them to harmonize their classic traditions. Thus, a highly interactive transmission system is established in which all mass media refer to the virtual media.

Çetinkaya (2014), explains that the intensive use of social media by audiences has led to the emergence of a new concept called "Social Television" (Social TV). The concept of social TV can be defined as technology that promotes social interaction and communication in relation to a television program or in the context of television viewing. Thanks to this technology, users can use voice communication and / or text messages and recommendation, scoring etc. about the program. Behaviors directly on the television screen or using side tools. This situation has made Social TV a new investment tool for both operators and researchers. Social TV has created a living room where the cyberspace plays an increasing role in interacting with the audience around the program. The concept of social TV is not only IPTV, Cable TV, etc. Not defined by the television technology infrastructure, but can also be defined for computers, tablets and smart mobile devices.

3. SOCIAL MEDIA AND TELEVISION MONITORING MEASUREMENT: SERIES OF ICERDE

In this study, in order to measure the relationship between social media and television, the Turkish TV series published in Turkey will be examined in *İçerde* which is published in the publication period of 2016-2017. The reason for the selection of this directory is that 39 episodes are broadcast throughout the episode, and the high interest in social media is a high percentage of TV ratings. In Table 1, there is an order according to the viewing rates of the most watched series published in December in the national channels in Turkey. *İçerde* is the second row.

The study looked at the follow-up measures in social media that were used to help measure social media in-line monitoring. The Kimola firm is one of the companies that conduct research on this subject in Turkey. In the study, Kimola presented his published series of 39 episodes published in the series.

Çetinkaya (2014), explains that Kimola and similar companies broadcast their tweets through their own algorithms, retweet, copy-paste, content filtering, total number of tweets after first tweet, tweets according to gender distribution, And share it with customers and the public. Kimola, which measures social rating in Turkey, has caused a great resonance and controversy in the marketing sector, which shows the gap between 'Behzat Ç' and 'Leyla and Majnun' series published by Kimola Analytics on social media popularity and traditional rating results.

According to Table 2, only 14 weeks for 39 weeks were not in the first place. In 25 weeks, the inside line got the first place on Social TV as the most tweeted series.

According to the tableware Kimola company's table (Table 3), Twitter's instant agenda "trend topic" in the 39-week sequence of the inside line is looked at.

According to this table, the series had an average course for 39 weeks. However, it could be a trend topic by taking the first four positions in twenty sections of the index. These ratios are calculated by looking at the number of tweets that people have put together with the hashtags in the series. According to these rates, the index is said to be a popular series with a high number of viewers.

Table 1. The most watched programs in the EU Group in December

Row	Program	Channel	Total Rating	Number of Broadcast	Rating of Episode
1	Diriliş Ertuğrul	TRT 1	48,57	3	16,19
2	İçerde	SHOW TV	36,98	3	12,33
3	Anne	STAR TV	30,55	3	10,18
4	Eşkıya Dünyaya Hükümdar Olmaz	ATV	28,43	3	9,48
5	Vatanım Sensin	KANAL D	35,13	4	8,78
6	Cesur ve Güzel	STAR TV	31,90	4	7,98
7	O Ses Çocuklar	TV 8	7,13	1	7,13
8	O Ses Türkiye	TV 8	75,69	11	6,88
9	Kalbimdeki Deniz	FOX TV	26,64	4	6,66
10	Güldür Güldür Show	SHOW TV	25,84	4	6,46
11	Kara Sevda	STAR TV	19,35	3	6,45
12	No: 309	FOX TV	15,53	3	5,18
13	Arka Sokaklar	KANAL D	19,40	4	4,85
14	Hayat Şarkısı	KANAL D	14,23	3	4,74
15	Kırgın Çiçekler	ATV	14,19	3	4,73
16	Kiralık Aşk	STAR TV	18,57	4	4,64
17	Bodrum Masalı	KANAL D	13,62	3	4,54
18	Aşk Laftan Anlamaz	SHOW TV	17,53	4	4,38
19	Poyraz Karayel	KANAL D	13,05	3	4,35
20	O Hayat Benim	FOX TV	12,54	3	4,18
21	Seviyor Sevmiyor	ATV	12,37	3	4,12
22	Seksenler	TRT 1	15,64	4	3,91
23	Demet Akbağ ile Çok Aramızda	SHOW TV	11,67	3	3,89
24	Aşk ve Mavi	ATV	15,50	4	3,88
25	Paramparça	STAR	7,39	2	3,70

Source: http://www.reytingsonuclari.com/2017/1/aralik-ayi-aylik-reyting-sonuclari-h2235.html

4. CONCLUSION

Social media is a mass media tool whose value is increasing according to the number of users. Nowadays, users with high number of users are Facebook, Twitter, Instagram, Youtube. Social media has been added to audience measurements used in traditional media. With the help of social media, series producers can follow the audience with the hashtags displayed on the screen during the program, talk about the audience during the week during which the section is broadcast, and even increase the watching rates of their programs. With the help of these social networks, viewers have the opportunity to meet and chat on the same platform with other viewers of the series and share their comments on the series. Even the producers for the next episodes of the series are asking the audience questions in the calculations they open, and in response to the estimated answers, they invite the audience to the set of series and meet the players. This study focuses on the limitations of social media measurement. For this one of the national channels

Table 2. Social TV ratings between September 19, 2016 and June 19, 2017

Date	Ranking	Time, Number of Tweets/Min *	Share Ratio %**
19.09.16	1	22:05, 1008	40.2
26.09.16	1	22:45, 565	45.22
03.10.16	1	22:45, 409	41.24
10.10.16	1	23:30, 691	44.20
17.10.16	1	23:45, 815	45.18
24.10.16	1	21:15, 300	36.62
31.10.16	1	23:35, 270	39.58
07.11.16	1	23:35, 498	50.41
14.11.16	1	23:50, 847	50.58
21.11.16	1	23:40, 310	40.22
28.11.16	1	23:30, 595	43.47
05.12.16	1	23:35, 617	42.87
12.12.16	1	23:55, 426	33.05
19.12.16	1	23:45, 185	27.72
26.12.16	1	23:25, 270	36.47
02.01.17	5	23:00, 29	8.73
09.01.17	1	21:25, 121	31.03
16.01.17	1	21:55, 147	23.29
23.01.17	2	23:20, 150	20.91
30.01.17	2	23:25, 156	20.45
06.02.17	2	23:30, 156	17.54
13.02.17	1	23.35, 192	22.61
20.02.17	2	21:50, 131	22.96
27.02.17	2	21:45, 87	12.54
06.03.17	2	23:20, 164	19.04
13.03.17	1	23.30, 174	16.09
20.03.17	-	-	-
27.03.17	-	-	-
03.04.17	3	22:50, 175	14.33
10.04.17	3	23:35, 178	11.94
17.04.17	3	23:25, 212	13.49
24.04.17	1	21:45, 261	23.85
01.05.17	3	00:00, 103	14.41
08.05.17	2	23:45, 417	21.54
15.05.17	2	23:45, 438	22.31
22.05.17	1	23.30, 1644	44.47
29.05.17	1	22:05, 821	34.41
05.06.17	2	23:25, 431	26.89
12.06.17	1	23.40, 903	41.62
19.06.17	1	00:00, 1723	52.39

Source: http://kimola.com/tr/portal/tv-yayinlari/

* The minute that we share the most about publications, the density of sharing at this minute.

** Percentage of share numbers on posts across all Social TV shares.

Table 3.

Date	# /Row	Topic	Category	Peak Performance	Share Ratio
19.09.16	3	#içerde	TV	22:05 650 tweet/min	%5.34
26.09.16	15	#içerde	TV	23:15 291 tweet/ min	%2.14
03.10.16	4	#içerde	TV	22.45 279 tweet/ min	%4.36
10.10.16	4	#içerdeyim	TV	23.30 392 tweet/ min	%6.76
17.10.16	4	#içerdeyim	TV	23.45 604 tweet/ min	%5.82
24.10.16	3	#içerdeki	TV	21:15 148 tweet/ min	%6.17
31.10.16	4	#içerdemisin	TV	23:35 161 tweet/ min	%5.57
07.11.16	1	#içerdemi	TV	23:35 463 tweet/ min	%12.02
14.11.16	2	#MestanıKimÖldürdü	TV	23:50 294 tweet/ min	%6.58
21.11.16	2	#içerdeler	TV	23:40 252 tweet/ min	%5.91
28.11.16	8	#içerde	TV	23.30 291 tweet/ min	%3.16
05.12.16	2	#benkimim	TV	23:35 595 tweet/ min	%7.82
12.12.16	-				
19.12.16	20	#patronkim	TV	23:45 60 tweet/ min	%1.50
26.12.16	3	#iyimiyiz	TV	23:25 200 tweet/ min	%5.81
02.01.17	-				
09.01.17	18	#içerde	TV	21:25 88 tweet/ min	%1.36
16.01.17	4	#melekikimkurtaracak	TV	21:55 104 tweet/ min	%3.62
23.01.17	2	#umutiçin	TV	23:20 134 tweet/ min	%4.15
30.01.17	10	#oyuniçindeoyun	TV	23:25 125 tweet/ min	%2.47
06.02.17	14	#nefesnefese	TV	23:30 146 tweet/ min	%2.23
13.02.17	3	#kardeşim	TV	23:35 163 tweet/ min	%4.81
20.02.17	5	#kimkazanacak	TV	21:45 118 tweet/ min	%3.24
27.02.17	13	#güçlüoynayankazansın	TV	21:45 85 tweet/ min	%1.94
06.03.17	4	#yolunsonu	TV	23:20 213 tweet/ min	%5.29
13.03.17	9	#filmbaşlıyor	TV	23:30 179 tweet/ min	%2.67
20.03.17	17	#benimmahallem	TV	23:25 81 tweet/ min	%1.78
27.03.17	12	#içerde	TV	22:50 123 tweet/ min	%2.04
03.04.17	5	#filminsonu	TV	22:50 162 tweet/ min	%3.90
10.04.17	18	#enbüyüksır	TV	23:35 175 tweet/ min	%1.19
17.04.17	19	#kardeşim	TV	23:25 154 tweet/ min	%1.37
24.04.17	3	#obirmelek	TV	21:45 290 tweet/ min	%5.82
01.05.17	----				
08.05.17	9	#hesapgünü	TV	23:45 301 tweet/ min	%2.66
15.05.17	-------				
22.05.17	1	#içerdeyizabi	TV	23:30 1266 tweet/ min	%14.86
29.05.17	4	#YılmazBrothers	TV	22:05 874 tweet/ min	%8.97
05.06.17	-------				
12.06.17	3	#kardeşleriçerde	TV	23:40 614 tweet/ min	%6.84
19.06.17	3	#SonKezİçerdeyiz	TV	23:25 506 tweet/ min	%7.69

Source: http://kimola.com/tr/portal/tv-yayinlari

in Turkey, one of the television series with the most number of viewers was chosen as a sample. Such an application has been seen in the Instagram account of the insider list subject to review. As a result of the analysis, it shows that social media will have an increasing role in the effect of watching television.

REFERENCES

Altan, H. Z. (2015). Sosyal Medyanın Kullanımlar ve Doyumlar Haritası: Youtube, Facebook ve Twitter. In Sosyal Medya Araştırmaları 2: Sosyalleşen Olgular. Konya: Çizgi Publication.

Blossom, J. (2009). *Content Nation: Surviving and Thriving as Social Media Changes Our Work, Our Lives, and Our Future*. Wiley Publishing.

Büyükaslan, A. (2015). Sosyalleşmenin Boyutu. In Sosyal Medya Araştırmaları 2: Sosyalleşen Olgular. Konya: Çizgi Publication.

Castells, M. (2013). Enformasyon Çağı: Ekonomi, Toplum ve Kültür Birinci Cilt: Ağ Toplumunun Yükselişi. Istanbul Bilgi University Publication.

Çetinkaya, A. (2015). Sosyal Medya ve Televizyon İzleme Ölçümü. In Sosyal Medya Araştırmaları 2: Sosyalleşen Olgular. Konya: Çizgi Publication.

Cheng, M., Wu, Y., & Chen, M. (2016). Television Meets Facebook: The Correlation between TV Ratings and Social Media. *American Journal of Industrial and Business Management*, *6*(03), 282–290. doi:10.4236/ajibm.2016.63026

Gündüz, U., & Pembecioğlu, N. (2015). Sosyal Medya: Mizah, Muhalefet ve Direniş Pratikleri. In Sosyal Medya Araştırmaları 2: Sosyalleşen Olgular. Konya: Çizgi Publication.

Kara, T. (2013). *Sosyal Medya Endüstrisi. Beta Publication*.

Kuyucu, M. (2015). Sosyal Medyada Mahremiyet: Türkiye'deki Twitter Kullanıcılarının Mahremiyet Anlayışı. In Sosyal Medya Araştırmaları 2: Sosyalleşen Olgular. Konya: Çizgi Publication.

Lincoln, S. R. (2009). *Mastering Web 2.0: Transform Your Business Using Key Website and Social Media Tools*. Kogan Page.

Shabir, G., Hameed, Y. M. Y., Safdar, G., & Gilani, S. M. F. S. (2014). The Impact of Social Media on Youth: A Case Study of Bahawalpur City. *Asian Journal of Social Sciences & Humanities*, *3*(4), 132–151.

Chapter 7
Facebook Depression or Facebook Contentment:
The Relation Between Facebook Use and Well-Being

Jessica J. Joseph
Mount Royal University, Canada

Malinda Desjarlais
Mount Royal University, Canada

Lucijana Herceg
Mount Royal University, Canada

ABSTRACT

Within the literature, Facebook has received much attention in order to understand the potential positive and negative effects associated with using the social networking site. The current chapter provides a discussion of the empirical support for the differential outcomes associated with actively posting and chatting on Facebook vs. passively browsing Facebook, as well as the underlying mechanisms for the effects. Specifically, the current chapter will discuss two perspectives related to the differential effects of active and passive Facebook use: Facebook contentment (a wellbeing enhancing effect) and Facebook depression (a wellbeing diminishing effect). The authors also discuss the extension of the results to other social media platforms and provide suggestions for future research.

INTRODUCTION

Social networking sites are rapidly changing the way that people interact with one another, and have the potential to influence psychosocial functioning and emotional distress. Of the variety of social networking sites that exist, Facebook has rapidly gained popularity since its induction to the general public in 2005. Facebook users create online profiles containing personal information about the self that are broadcasted to other online users, which can be updated with additional information at the discretion

DOI: 10.4018/978-1-5225-4047-2.ch007

of the profile owner. The information shared is also open to the reception of quantitative or qualitative feedback from Facebook friends.

Subjective well-being is a phenomenon that is comprised of people's personal evaluations of their lives, including emotional responses to life events, as well as a personal assessment of one's overall satisfaction with life (Diener, Suh, Lucus, & Smith, 1999). Research on the social aspects of well-being has revealed that interpersonal relationships and social engagement are associated with positive affect and enhancements in subjective well-being (see Diener, Suh, Lucas, & Smith, 1999 for review). With the opportunity to stay connected with others online, Facebook may benefit subjective well-being, resulting in a potential for "Facebook Contentment". However, not all aspects of being social enhance subjective well-being; for example, if a person compares him/herself to others who are doing better off than he/she is, then subjective well-being is reduced (Michalos, 1985). Similar emotional distress may arise when negative feedback is received for information about oneself that is shared on Facebook. In either case, Facebook users are at risk of "Facebook Depression".

Overall, this chapter will synthesize the current literature regarding Facebook and its relation to psychosocial functioning, which may aid in the advancement of research, increase in public awareness, policy development, and clinical applications. The chapter is divided into the following sections. First, the chapter will summarize statistics about the frequency of Facebook's use and its most popular users. Second, the authors will synthesize the literature examining the relationship for active and passive Facebook use separately with subjective well-being and present theoretical background to explain these associations to support the potential for Facebook Contentment and Facebook Depression, respectively. Third, a summary of the literature regarding the effects of posting selfies will be provided, and the authors will present an evidence-based argument that active Facebook use is not always positive when considering selfie-posting behavior. Fourth, the authors will evaluate the uniqueness of the findings related to Facebook in comparison to offline interactions and other social networking sites, which highlights the real but rather small magnitude of effect Facebook has on social interactions and mental health. Finally, the gaps in the literature will be discussed and future research suggested.

AN OVERVIEW OF FACEBOOK USE AND USERS

Internationally, over 1.7 billion people visit Facebook every month, with over 1.2 billion visits every day, and 85% of the logins occurring outside of North America (Stats, 2016). In relation to North American use, in November of 2016, the Pew Research Centre reported that Facebook remains the most popular social networking platform in the United States by an overwhelming margin (Greenwood, Perrin, & Duggan, 2016). Furthermore, in a 2015 study conducted by Forum Research on social media usage, Facebook remained the top social network in Canada, with 59% of respondents indicating they use Facebook and visit about nine times each week (McKinnon, 2015). On average, Facebook users are comprised of young adults between the ages of 18 and 39, with female users being slightly more common than male users (Greenwood, Perrin, & Duggan, 2016).

While on Facebook, users are able to create a personal profile, known as the Facebook 'Timeline' that contains an amalgamation of image and text-based information about the user, which can then be shared with the user's Facebook 'friends'. In the context of Facebook, 'friends' consist of a combination of close friends and acquaintances met offline, and family members, for which the average ranges from around 150 (Ellison, Steinfield, & Lampe, 2007) to over 400 friends (Manago, Taylor, & Greenfield,

2012). Young adults often turn to Facebook to aid in the maintenance of their relationships (e.g., to post or send messages, stay in touch with friends), to pass time, or for entertainment purposes (e.g., to see other people's pictures and read their profiles; Davis, 2012; Sheldon, 2008; Smith, 2011). Therefore, users can interact with Facebook in a passive or active fashion. First, Facebook is often used to *observe* Facebook friends by anonymously scrolling through the newsfeed, or browsing friends' photos/timelines, without any form of direct communication with their Facebook friends. This type of Facebook behaviour is regarded as passive Facebook use or surveillance (Ryan & Xenos, 2011). Second, during active use, individuals communicate with others by *sharing* text-based information or photos when directly messaging friends, posting status updates, sharing memories, posting on timelines, or reacting to others' posts.

The taking and sharing of selfies, a specific type of image shared on Facebook (Weiser, 2015), falls under the umbrella of active Facebook use. A selfie consists of a photograph of one's self alone or with others that is taken with a camera held at arm's length or pointed at a mirror (Sorokowski, Sorokowska, Oleszkiewicz, Frackowiak, Huk, & Pisanski, 2015). Selfies are shared as a means for communication, to attract attention from others, for entertainment, and to archive memories (Sung, Lee, Kim, & Choi, 2016). According to American surveys of 18 to 24 year old participants, 98% took selfies, 46% had shared selfies within the past day, and 69% tended to share selfies three to 20 times daily (Katz & Crocker, 2015). There are mixed findings regarding who frequently posts selfies. On the one hand, there is some support that frequent selfie-posters tend to be those who score high on narcissism (Moon, Lee, Lee, Choi, & Sung, 2016; Weiser, 2015) or extroversion (Kim & Chock, 2017; Sorokowska, Oleszkiewicz, Frackowiak, Pisanski, Chmiel, & Sorokowski, 2016), as well as adolescents and younger adults (Dhir, Pallesen, Torsheim, & Andreassen, 2016). On the other hand, researchers have also reported no such relationships between behaviour and characteristics of the poster (Barry, Doucette, Loflin, Rivera-Hudson, & Herrington, 2017; Sung, Lee, Kim, & Choi, 2016). Given the increasing popularity of selfies, it is important to consider the effect of this Facebook activity on its own.

Taking into account how and why Facebook is being used, there are potential consequences for subjective well-being. The following sections present an overview of subjective well-being, and outlines why active (including selfie posting behaviour) and passive Facebook use may influence well-being in a positive (Facebook Contentment) or negative (Facebook Depression) way.

FACEBOOK USE AND SUBJECTIVE WELL-BEING

Facebook provides opportunities for users to disclose personal information about themselves, to receive reactions from others, and to compare how they are doing relative to their Facebook friends. These activities have the potential to contribute to subjective well-being by influencing feelings of social connectedness and self-esteem. Social connectedness is characterized as the feelings of belonging and staying in touch with ongoing social relationships (Van Baren, IJsselsteijn, Markopoulos, Romero, & De Ruyter, 2004). Self-esteem is considered as the level of value you place on yourself, which is influenced by the reactions of and comparison with others (Argyle, 2008). The popularity of Facebook has given rise to a body of research investigating the association between Facebook use and well-being or one of its related constructs (e.g., depression, life satisfaction, and loneliness), which has uncovered inconsistent results. On the one hand, spending more time on Facebook was associated with increases in depressive symptoms (Steers, Wickham, & Acitelli, 2014), as well as feeling lonely (Lou, Yan, Nickerson, & McMorris, 2012), ostracized from their friends (Tobin, Vanman, Verreynne, & Saeri, 2015), and less satisfied in their own lives (Blachnio, Przepiorka, & Pantic, 2016; Valenzuela, Halpern, & Katz, 2014). In fact, when Facebook users take a break from using the social networking site, it enhances both the cognitive and emotional aspects of subjective well-being (Tromholt, 2016). On the other hand, research also supports that more time spent on Facebook enhances life satisfaction (Valenzuela, Park, & Kee, 2009), self-esteem (Burke, Kraut, & Marlow, 2011), and psychological well-being (Burke & Kraut, 2016; Liu & Yu, 2013). Still, others report no relationship between time spent on Facebook and depressive symptoms (Jelenchick, Eickhoff, & Moreno, 2013), or life satisfaction (Glynn, Huge, & Hoffman, 2012). The challenge with measuring Facebook use as a single dimension is that it may cancel out the effects associated with different activities. While activities directed at the sharing of information may enhance social connectedness and has the potential for Facebook Contentment, the viewing of others' posts may elicit negative feelings because of social comparison, which increases the risk for Facebook Depression. Therefore, the following sections present a synthesis of the literature for active and passive Facebook use and explains their unique association with subjective well-being.

Facebook Contentment and Active Facebook Use

Active Facebook use is characterized by making social contributions while on Facebook, including broadcasting information about one's self and writing what's on a person's mind (through posting photos, status updates, or sharing links, memories, or memes), communicating with others (by writing on friends' timelines, and sending messages on Facebook), and providing feedback to others [by liking, commenting, and reacting to friends' Facebook posts (Burke, Kraut, & Marlow, 2011; Verduyn, Lee, Park, Shablack, Orvell, Bayer, & Kross, 2015). It should be noted that social networking activities usually involve the sharing of authentic information and content without malicious intent (Fox & Moreland, 2015; Reinecke & Trepte, 2014), and thus a discussion of false identities and cyberbullying or similar contexts are considered beyond the scope of the chapter. Typical active Facebook use has the potential then for Facebook Contentment, a phenomenon suggested by the authors that emphasizes the positive consequences for psychosocial functioning associated with the use of Facebook (and other social networking sites). In other words, active Facebook use results in enhanced subjective well-being and related constructs. In support of this principle, active use is typically associated with heightened subjective well-being (Kim & Lee, 2011). Greater active use is also correlated with enhancements in social well-being (Burke, Marlow, & Lento, 2010), and self-esteem (Csepeli & Nagyfi, 2014), as well as decreases in depression (Frison & Eggermont, 2016), and loneliness (Ryan & Xenos, 2011).

Social connectedness, a key underlying mechanism for enhanced mental health in general (Baumeister & Leary, 1995), has been put forward as the variable that links active Facebook use and subjective well-being. When considering social connectedness in the context of traditional offline interactions, those with greater subjective well-being also report greater levels of social connectedness (Baumeister & Leary, 1995), and social support (Helliwell, Huang, & Harris, 2009). In a three-year longitudinal study of over 1700 adolescents, researchers found that youth who reported higher levels of social connectedness would subsequently report higher well-being, but there was no support for a reciprocal relation (Jose, Ryan, & Pryor, 2012). These benefits of social connectedness also extend to online social interactions. In particular, individuals who are more active on Facebook report greater social connectedness (Köbler, Riedl, Vetter, Leimeister, & Krcmar, 2010), social capital (Burke, Kraut, & Marlow, 2011), and social support (Wright, Rosenberg, Egbert, Ploeger, Bernard, & King, 2013). In addition, when researchers test the features that fall under the classification of active Facebook separately, only certain active behaviours enhance users' life satisfaction. In a longitudinal study, Wenninger, Krasnova, and Buxmann (2014) measured each active component separately (i.e., posting, chatting, liking, and commenting), as well as users' life satisfaction over the course of one week. Posting on and chatting with friends via Facebook were associated with increases in users' life satisfaction over the course of one week, while liking and commenting on friends' posts were not related to life satisfaction. Therefore, only the specific Facebook features that enabled users to make social contributions, that are required for enhancements in subjective well-being, actually contributed to life satisfaction.

There is also direct empirical support for social connectedness as a mediating factor that explains the positive association between actively posting on Facebook and users' subjective well-being. Correlational studies indicate that the feelings of social connectedness that occur when actively using Facebook are associated with decreases in depressive symptoms (Grieve, Indian, Witteveen, Tolan, & Marrington, 2013). Similarly, Frison and Eggermont (2016) identified that for females, actively interacting with friends either publicly or privately while on Facebook led to the perception of being supported by friends, which then decreased depressive mood. Since correlational studies can only support a relationship between variables, and cannot distinguish the directionality of the effect between Facebook use and social connectedness, Deters and Mehl (2013) conducted an experimental study to investigate the proposed directional effect that Facebook use leads to increases in feelings of connectedness. In their study, participants in the experimental condition were asked to post on Facebook more frequently than they typically would, while their control counterparts were instructed to use Facebook as usual over the course of one week. The results indicated that the Facebook users in the experimental (active) condition experienced decreases in loneliness, which was attributed to feeling more connected to their friends.

In sum, the findings from the research centered on active Facebook use provides overwhelming support for Facebook Contentment. More specifically, the studies suggest the following two principles: (1) the phenomenon of Facebook Contentment is an accurate depiction of what users experience when they are engaging in active behaviour on Facebook; and (2) social connectedness is the causal link between active use and subjective well-being. It can then be inferred that when users log onto Facebook and utilize the features that enable them to make active social contributions such as sharing information about themselves, or communicating with friends, the feelings of social connectedness that result resemble feelings that occur during traditional offline interactions, and consequently so do the enhancements in subjective well-being.

Facebook Depression and Passive Facebook Use

In general, researchers and society have become concerned with the potential harmful effects elicited by Facebook use. This has led to the introduction of Facebook Depression. In the current literature, Facebook Depression refers to a phenomenon where users experience increases in depression and loneliness, and decreases in self-esteem and psychological well-being as a result of spending too much time on Facebook (Kross, Verduyn, Demiralp, Park, Lee, Lin, … Ybarra, 2013; O'Keeffe & Clarke-Pearson, 2011). Facebook Depression is not an overarching result of Facebook use; rather, the negative effects of Facebook have been associated only with passive use. Passively observing friends on Facebook is negatively associated with several constructs that are related to subjective well-being, including increased loneliness (Ryan & Xenos, 2011), and depression (Frison & Eggermont, 2016), as well as decreased social well-being (Burke, Marlow, & Lento, 2010), and life satisfaction (Wenninger, Krasnova, & Buxmann, 2014). In fact, in an experimental study by Verduyn et al. (2015), participants in the passive experimental condition were asked to use Facebook solely passively (i.e., scrolling through Facebook with no posting or interacting) for 10 consecutive minutes. Although there was no change in well-being immediately following Facebook use, participants reported decreases in affective well-being at the end of the day. Even after controlling for the changes in affective well-being that occurred via passive use, the reverse path (affective well-being resulting in higher levels of passive use) was not significant.

What is it about passive Facebook use that would be detrimental to subjective well-being? Social comparisons are a rather automatic consequence of being social (Festinger, 1954). Festinger's (1954) social comparison theory postulates that individuals engage in self-evaluation by comparing themselves to those who are similar. Social comparison provides individuals with the ability to gather information to evaluate their own capacities and characteristics so they can develop stable and accurate evaluations about the self. During social comparison, individuals gain social information, think about social information and then react to the comparative information (Diener, Suh, Lucas, & Smith, 1999). Building on social comparison theory, Suls, Martin, and Wheeler (2002) argued that social comparison can be both upward and downward, and that there are differences in the outcomes of social comparison depending on whether the evaluator is engaging in upward or downward social comparison. Upward social comparisons (aka negative social comparison) refer to instances where the targets of social comparison are doing better than oneself (Suls, Martin, & Wheeler, 2002). Michalos (1985) postulated that a person's subjective well-being depends on the discrepancy between a person's current life circumstances compared to a standard set by comparing him/herself to others' current life circumstances. If the target(s) that a person compares him/herself with is perceived to be more successful, happier, wealthier, more attractive than him/herself, then there is a tendency to develop a negative self-image and exhibit decreases in subjective well-being (Michalos, 1985). On the other hand, a person can also compare him/herself to a target who appears to be worse off. This downward social comparison (aka positive social comparison) is typically associated with a more positive self-image and increased subjective well-being (Suls, Martin, & Wheeler, 2002).

Facebook users do compare themselves to their Facebook friends (Feinstein, Hershenberg, Bhatia, Latack, Meuwly, & Davila, 2013; Joseph & Desjarlais, 2017; Vogel, Rose, Roberts, & Eckles, 2014). And, the more time users spend on Facebook, the more likely they are to negatively compare themselves to others, which often leaves users feeling as though their friends are doing better off in life than they are (Chou & Edge, 2012; de Vries & Kühne, 2015). Similar to offline contexts, the act of negatively socially comparing while on Facebook is associated with increases in depressive symptoms (Nesi & Prinstein, 2015; Steers, Wickham, & Acitelli, 2014). The challenges associated with negative social comparison online are only evident for passive Facebook use. Scrolling through Facebook has been associated with increases in negative social comparison and thus decreases in users' self-esteem (Vogel, Rose, Roberts, & Eckles, 2014), and increases in feelings of envy (Appel, Crusius, & Gerlach, 2015; Krasnova, Wenninger, Widjaja, & Buxmann, 2013). Furthermore, passive use is not related to users' depressive symptoms unless the browsing Facebook has led to feelings of envy (Tandoc, Ferrucci, & Duffy, 2015).

Negative social comparison in the context of Facebook is especially troublesome because when people are comparing themselves to others on Facebook, they may not actually be comparing themselves to a realistic target. In general, people are concerned about the way they are perceived by others (Goffman, 1959), and thus attempt to manage the impressions others on Facebook form and their evaluations by presenting oneself to others in a positive and socially desirable way (Zhao, Grasmuck, & Martin, 2008). Applications that enable users to touch up their photographs with filters, thus promoting users to hide their flaws (Walther, 2007), have become increasingly popular (Lup, Trub, & Rosenthal, 2015). As such, the information visible while scrolling through Facebook probably is comprised of images and statements that represent users' idealized selves (Manago, Graham, Greenfield, & Salimkhan, 2008). Thus, if social comparison occurs while passively using Facebook, and the information posted on Facebook sets a standard for a level of unrealistic perfection, then users find themselves comparing to an unrealistic target. It is not surprising then that users feel as though they do not measure up to their friends.

In conclusion, the literature regarding passive use support a real risk for Facebook Depression. Consistent with social comparison theory, negatively comparing one's self to Facebook friends, and the feelings of envy that ensue, appear to be driving the negative association between passive Facebook use and subjective well-being. Due to selective presentation and impression management strategies common on Facebook, users need to be cautious they do not get wrapped up in a fantasy where everyone else's lives are near perfection.

SELFIES: THE POTENTIAL FOR FACEBOOK CONTENTMENT AND FACEBOOK DEPRESSION

As aforementioned, active Facebook use is positively associated with subjective well-being and related constructs. However, within the literature on the psychological effects of Facebook use, a specific type of active behavior has not received attention - that is, the posting of a specific type of photo, the selfie. Unlike active Facebook activities in general or other specific active behaviors (posting and instant messaging), sharing selfies has disparate effects on subjective well-being. Selfie-posting behavior may lead to enhanced subjective well-being through self-disclosure and positive reactions from others. On the other hand, sharing selfies can deflate self-esteem when the photos receive negative attention. Since there is limited research explicitly investigating the link between selfie-posting behavior and subjective well-being, the authors can only postulate the potential for Facebook Contentment and Facebook Depression.

Facebook Contentment: Selfies Facilitate Connections With Others

Intimate friendships have implications for adolescent psychosocial adjustment and the quality of future relationships. For example, a lack of close friends has been associated with feelings of loneliness, alienation, depression and low self-esteem among adolescents (Buhrmester, 1990; Cohen & Willis, 1985), as well as life satisfaction during adulthood (Marion, Laursen, Zettergren, & Bergman, 2013). Learning to maintain close relationships prepares adolescents for adult intimate relationships (Sullivan, 1953), such that high-quality adolescent friendships are related to greater adult romantic relationship commitment (De Goede, Branje, van Duin, VanderValk, & Meeus, 2012). Self-disclosure, or the sharing of personal thoughts, feelings, and experiences, is an important feature of adolescent and adult intimate friendships (Berndt, 1989).

Social networking sites are providing users with the ability to meet these social needs. Valkenburg and Peter (2009; 2011) formulated the Internet-enhanced self-disclosure hypothesis, which postulates that online interactions stimulate online self-disclosure and in turn enhances closeness with friends. Therefore, Facebook may offer users a comfortable environment for sharing information, including anonymity, accessibility, asynchrony, and the absence of nonverbal cues. In direct support of the Internet-enhanced self-disclosure hypothesis, Valkenburg and Peter (2009) found that the relationship between online communication and friendship quality was fully mediated by self-disclosure. Other studies have also provided support for portions of the hypothesis. Specifically, more frequent use has been associated with greater online self-disclosure (Desjarlais & Joseph, 2017). Moreover, online disclosure consistently has been associated with increases in friendship quality (see Desjarlais, Gilmour, Sinclair, Howell & West, 2015 for a review), which then enhances users' well-being (Valkenburg & Peter, 2007, 2009).

When asking about people's motivations for posting selfies, they do indicate that some selfies are shared as a means to communicate with others. Instead of posting notes that one is starting a new job, is on a vacation, or feeling upset, the poster can share a selfie of him/herself in her new uniform, sitting on a beach relaxing in the sun, or visually crying. As a snapshot of one's life, selfies offer a medium to express emotions and reveal insights (Wortham, 2013). In this context, the intention for posting the selfie is not to present the best polished self, but rather to share honest information, natural insights, and emotions with friends, family, and acquaintances in an effort to build intimacy (Choi, Sung, Lee, & Choi, 2017; Diefenbach & Christoforakos, 2017). Group selfies also provide information about the poster through social cues, such as relationships with others and behaviour in a group (Wang, Yang, & Haigh, 2017). In terms of the outcomes of such disclosure activities, results suggest that self-disclosure through selfies may open the line of communication, earn sympathy, and result in positive emotional experiences for posters (Diefenbach & Christoforakos, 2017). Therefore, it is reasonable to postulate that the selfie contributes to connections made with friends and family, supporting the Facebook Contentment perspective.

Facebook Depression: Selfies May Deflate Self-Esteem

In general, people are concerned about the way they are perceived by others, and as such, their reactions can raise or deflate self-esteem (Goffman, 1959). Compliments, praise, and indications of liking serve to enhance self-esteem, whereas criticism and rejection deflate it. In order to elicit esteem-enhancing reactions, people attempt to manage the impressions others form and their evaluations by presenting oneself to others in a positive and socially desirable way both offline (Walther, 2007) and online (Hart, 2017). People often put work into selfies in order to present the best image of themselves. They have worked on finding the right angle, and will edit the pictures before posting in order to present one's ideal self (Hart, 2017). In interviews regarding social media use, adolescent girls indicated that editing photographs and making oneself look good on social media has become a necessity (Chua & Chang, 2016). All admitted to using filters and editing photos with software to, for example, brighten the skin, conceal facial imperfections, and enhance colors. One-third of the girls went so far as to change their facial features, including modifying their face line, and altering the size of their eyes and noses. According to one teen, the purpose of putting so much effort into perfecting the selfie is so posters can share pictures that meet the standard and to impress their friends (Chua & Chang, 2016). Consistent with this, attention seeking has been acknowledged as a driving motivation behind the taking and sharing of selfies. People post selfies with a desire to attract attention, to be acknowledged by others, to gain self-confidence from others' reactions, and to receive affirmation from others (Sung, Lee, Kim, & Choi, 2016).

Individuals seem to place high importance on the number of likes and followers they receive, believing that the numbers are more important than comments, and that the numbers serve as an indication of peer attention, benchmark against peers, and their position in their peer group (Chua & Chang, 2016). By manipulating the number of likes individuals receive, Burrow and Rainone (2017) examined the extent to which self-esteem was sensitive to the number of likes received on selfies posted to a mock Facebook site, and if this depended on individuals' sense of purpose. They did find that for those reporting a lower sense of purpose in life, the number of likes was positively associated with self-esteem; whereas, there was no relationship between the number of likes and self-esteem among those with a greater sense of purpose. Other researchers have argued that frequent likes may affirm the ideal self that one presented in a selfie and make an individual feel good about him/herself, thereby increasing self-esteem (Bazarova & Choi, 2014; Shin, Kim, Im, & Chong, 2017). On the positive side, selfies do generate a high number of likes compared to natural pictures (Souza, de Las Casas, Flores, Youn, Cha, Quercia, & Almeida, 2015). So long as selfies receive a high number of likes, self-esteem may be boosted.

However, other research regarding selfie-posting does not suggest such esteem-enhancing effects, which is particularly concerning for girls and women given that they exhibit higher selfie-posting frequency as compared to males (Dhir, Pallesen, Torsheim, & Andreassen, 2016; Sorokowska, Frackowiak, Karwowski, Rusicka, & Oleszkiewicz, 2016; Weiser, 2015). With the exception of a few studies (Barry, Doucette, H., Loflin, Rivera-Hudson, & Herrington, 2017; McCain, Borg, Rothenberg, Churillo, Weiler, & Campbell, 2016), research tends to suggest a negative association between selfies and self-esteem for the profile owner. In an experimental study, participants who took selfies, whether they were saved or posted to social media, showed decreases in self-esteem (Shin, Kim, Im, & Chong, 2017). In general, selective self-enhancement is negatively related to self-esteem and well-being (Robins & Beer, 2001), and instead, it is the honest self-presentation that enhances perceived social support and thereby has positive implications for subjective well-being (Kim & Lee, 2011). Adolescent girls believe that insecurity and low self-esteem are the root of the need to edit photographs to perfection (Chua & Chang, 2016). Furthermore, there is also increasing support for a link between selfies and self-esteem related to body image. For adolescent girls, sharing selfies correlated with over-evaluation of shape and weight, body dissatisfaction, and thin idealization (McLean, Paxton, Wertheim, & Masters, 2015).

Shin and colleagues (2017) argued that taking and sharing selfies may hinder self-esteem because of heightened self-awareness that one does not meet social standards. Specifically, according to objective self-awareness theory (proposed by Duval & Wicklund, 1972), self-awareness increases when individuals view images of themselves, which leads people to become more anxious about others' judgments about themselves, and make social standards and norms more salient. Since people often think they do not meet social standards when self-awareness is heightened (Gonzales & Hancock, 2011), there is the possibility that taking selfies would lower self-esteem. In fact, in one experiment, participants were instructed to take a selfie or a picture of an object using their own smartphone and then either post it on social media or save it (Shin, Kim, Im, & Chong, 2017). Those who were instructed to take a selfie, especially those who also posted it, showed heightened concern for other people's judgments and reactions to themselves compared to those instructed to take a picture of an object. This supports the objective self-awareness theory, suggesting that people became more socially sensitive after taking a selfie.

Although selfies do grab the attention of viewers over other types of photographs on social media sites (Ford, 2016; Souza, de Las Casas, Flores, Youn, Cha, Quercia, & Almeida, 2015), the attention may not be as positive as one hoped. Placing importance on the reactions of others may be detrimental to subjective well-being, given that selfies are not perceived in the best light. There is a clear preference for non-selfie, natural pictures of the self over selfies (Diefenbach & Christoforakos, 2017). Furthermore, the negative perceptions that people have of those who post selfies may translate into the quantitative and qualitative feedback selfies receive, and thereby influence one's self-esteem. In a study of perceived positive and negative aspects, people indicated that selfies are fake, a threat to self-esteem through the receipt of negative reactions, and result in negative impressions by others (Diefenbach & Christoforakos, 2017). Selfies are regarded as an inauthentic way of showing off (Lobinger & Branter, 2015). Consistently, selfie-posters are judged as being narcissistic, with males judged more harshly than females, and external raters assume posters are motivated to seek attention (Diefenbach & Christoforakos, 2017; Krämer, Feurstein, Kluck, Meier, Rother, & Winter, 2017; Re, Wang, He, & Rule, 2016; Sung, Lee, Kim, & Choi, 2016). Even though these comments come from people who post their own selfies, they justify their own selfie-posting behavior with the belief that their self-portraits are more authentic and self-ironic (i.e., selfie-bias; Diefenbach & Christoforakos, 2017).

In conclusion, on the one hand selfies may have positive implications for subjective well-being by establishing and maintaining relationships online. Alternatively, there is much more support for the risk of decreasing self-esteem, and thus for Facebook Depression, simply by taking selfies. The negative perceptions the public holds for selfie posters in general can translate to negative reactions posted online for all Facebook friends to see. In effect, the attempt to manage others' impressions and evaluations may be to no avail.

IS FACEBOOK UNIQUE?

Facebook facilitates communication with friends and family, social comparisons, and feedback from others, resulting in both positive and negative consequences for users' subjective well-being. These social factors and the associated ramifications, however, are not novel to Facebook. That is, Facebook is not the only setting in which people are able to acquire information about their friends and broadcast information about oneself; instead, individuals may socialize within a multitude of social networking sites as well as offline settings. In a study by the Pew Research Center (2017), the most-widely used of the major social media platforms after Facebook were Instagram, LinkedIn, and Twitter, with just under a third of Americans using each of these sites. In addition, roughly half of Instagram users and 40% of Twitter users visit these sites at least once a day. Also considered among the most popular social media sites is Snapchat (Duggan, 2015). The following provides an overview of the unique features and audiences for three other popular social media platforms - Twitter, Instagram, and Snapchat.

Twitter is a micro-blogging social media platform that restricts users' posts (known as tweets) to 140 characters. Users can and do typically follow other individuals with whom they do not have a relationship, such as celebrities, politicians, and organizations (Jin & Phua, 2014). On Instagram, users are also likely to interact with others they do not know in real life, but to a lesser degree than Twitter. Instagram provides users with a platform to take photos, edit them using a series of filters, and share them to their profile instantaneously (Ting, Wong, de Run, & Lau, 2015). Other users have the ability to follow individuals on Instagram, which allows the follower to view the owner's profile and photos, and for recently uploaded pictures to appear in the follower's Instagram newsfeed. Unlike Facebook where friending gives both partners access to each other's profiles, the action of following someone on Instagram does not automatically result in reciprocal following. Having followers as opposed to friends creates more acceptability and opportunity to view strangers' posts. In contrast, Snapchat is a photo-sharing application where users can send snaps (i.e., pictures and short videos that can include text and drawings) with friends that dissolve after a few seconds (Vaterlaus, Barnett, Roche, & Young, 2016). Therefore, in contrast to Facebook where posts are long lasting and often visible to a large audience, information shared on Snapchat is transitory and relatively private and thereby reducing the need to self-censor. In effect, communication via snaps has been viewed as more intimate (Utz, Muscanell, & Khalid, 2015).

There are relatively few studies investigating the psychosocial outcomes of Twitter, Instagram, or Snapchat use. Of the research that is available, these social media platforms do appear to have similar outcomes as Facebook. It is argued that people do use Twitter to connect with others by staying updated about the lives of friends and acquaintances (Boyd, 2009), and that Twitter activity may be related to decreases in loneliness (Pittman, 2015) and increased feelings of camaraderie (Chen, 2011). Moreover, the multitude and variety of people being followed can increase social capital (Phua, Jin, & Kim, 2017). Similarly, social interaction is a key motivation for using Instagram (Lee, Lee, Moon, & Sung, 2015), and Instagram activity has been associated with positive effects for social capital (Phua, Jin, & Kim, 2017) and happiness (Pittman & Reich, 2016). However, there is a potential for negative effects on self-esteem when using Instagram that mirror Facebook. The combination of frequent selfie-posting by users (Hu, Manikonda, & Kambhampati, 2014), the ubiquitous selective self-presentation (Lee, Lee, Moon, & Sung, 2015; Ridgway & Clayton, 2016), and the frequent use for surveillance purposes (Sheldon & Bryant, 2016) may give rise to negative social comparison and decreased self-esteem. In contrast, Snapchat may offer the most positive outcomes of the social media platforms when considering social connectedness. From interviews of young adults for perceptions of how Snapchat behaviors influenced their interpersonal relationships, it was clear that Snapchat was praised for being a valuable communication tool (Vaterlaus, Barnett, Roche, & Young, 2016). Users felt that the ability to present messages using a combination of picture and text allowed for better understanding of the emotional context of the conversation (i.e., emotion can be shown in a picture and attached with a text message). Young adults indicated that Snapchat provided a way to remain close with their most important friends.

In addition to social networking sites, Facebook users still do interact with their friends face-to-face. Adolescents use social media predominantly to supplement rather than replace offline interactions with friends (Valkenburg & Peter, 2011). Social connections, social support, and social comparison are all associated with face-to-face social interactions in the same fashion as was discussed in the context of Facebook (Berkman & Glass, 2000). The socialization that occurs on Facebook, and other social networking sites, mirror those in offline settings. Thus, the increases and decreases in subjective well-being associated with sharing information, social connectedness, and social comparison are something that people experience regularly, and regardless of whether they use Facebook or any other social networking sites. What is different when face-to-face however, is the presence of verbal cues and body language. So although someone may present only the most positive and socially desirable information, his/her body language, clothing, tone of voice, eye contact, and so on when face-to-face may inadvertently reveal the truth. It may be then that the ability to selectively present and filter personal information posted on social networking sites make the negative effects in subjective well-being more salient online compared to offline interactions.

FUTURE RESEARCH DIRECTIONS

This chapter presented a review of the literature pertaining to Facebook, its features, and subjective well-being. The vast majority of research reviewed in the current chapter is cross-sectional and correlational. While this research can reveal the relationship between variables (e.g., passive use and poorer subjective well-being, or selfie-posting frequency and decreased self-esteem), the directionality and causal links among variables are speculative. Facebook Contentment and Facebook Depression present the perspective that Facebook use leads to increases and decreases for subjective well-being, respectively. However, it is equally plausible that those with already strong connections with friends turn to Facebook to share information. Alternatively, people with emotional distress may be inclined to view others' successes in Facebook without posting their own feelings of failures, which results in negative social comparison. Although there have been a few longitudinal studies that examined the directional effects of Facebook use, they were at the end of day (Verduyn, Lee, Park, Shablack, Orvell, Bayer, & Kross, 2015) or end of the week (Deters & Mehl, 2013). Examining relationships over a greater span of time would provide information on the long-term effects of Facebook use and provide perspective on just how detrimental or facilitating activities are for subjective well-being. In addition, a few studies have involved experimental manipulations of activity engagement to investigate causal implications (Deters & Mehl, 2013; Shin, Kim, Im, & Chong, 2017; Verduyn, Lee, Park, Shablack, Orvell, Bayer, & Kross, 2015). Similar research is needed to assess the relationship between selfies and subjective well-being. Specifically, it is relatively unknown whether the negative perceptions associated with selfie posting translate into the quantitative or qualitative feedback that a selfie poster receives, and whether this information has any meaningful long-term effects for the target.

Longitudinal studies are also necessary to evaluate the practical significance of the relation between Facebook activity engagement and subjective well-being, or related constructs. Although passive Facebook use and selfie-posting are correlated with decreased subjective well-being and self-esteem, respectively, there is no evidence to suggest a major concern for users. On the other hand, however, Facebook use may have additive effects over time, ultimately resulting in decreases in subjective well-being to levels that would significantly affect an individual's psychosocial functioning. The questions that arise then are: Does passive Facebook use or sharing selfies over time lead to depression at a clinical level? Moreover, does this effect exist after controlling for overall mental health? Therefore, longitudinal research would be valuable for understanding any reciprocal relationships between use and psychosocial functioning as well as additive effects.

Furthermore, research investigating who is most affected by using Facebook and posting selfies is scarce. While some studies suggest that females may be most at risk (Dhir, Pallesen, Torsheim, & Andreassen, 2016; Weiser, 2015), there are other factors that also need attention. For instance, given the fact that cultural values and expectations are important factors that influence subjective well-being (Diener, Oishi, & Lucas, 2003) and social relationships (Kim, Sherman, & Taylor, 2008), it may be that the effects for subjective well-being derived from using Facebook and posting selfies are culturally dependent. In addition, researchers have identified that individuals who are shy or socially anxious may exhibit benefits from online interactions in general (social compensation hypothesis; Valkenburg & Peter, 2007). Last, people who have particular expectations of their Facebook friends regarding the content and frequency of feedback to postings may also exhibit the largest effects to self-esteem. Although Facebook users typically report receiving the amount of feedback they expect (Joseph, 2017), there is evidence that sharing information online without receiving a response leads to feeling ostracized (Smith & Williams, 2004). Thus, it is plausible that how using Facebook and posting selfies affect subjective well-being depends on cultural values, current level of shyness, or expectations of other users.

CONCLUSION

What is clear across the current Facebook literature is that Facebook serves as a double-edged sword - a communication medium that could lead to feelings of inadequacy and envy, but at the same time facilitate social relationships. Offering support for the Facebook Contentment perspective, active Facebook use often correlated with enhancements in subjective well-being through feelings of social connectedness. This was true for active use in general and when examining activities that resulted in some level of self-disclosure. In contrast, selfie-posting behavior, when driven by attention seeking motives, presents consequences that are more negative. Similarly, passive Facebook use typically was associated with emotional distress as a function of negative social comparison, which supports the risk for Facebook Depression. It should be noted that the mediating factors in the associations between active and passive Facebook use with subjective well-being (i.e., self-disclosure, jealousy, negative social comparison, feedback from others, and selective presentation) are not unique to Facebook. People engaged in these social activities prior to the advent of the Internet and social media, and will continue to engage in these when they move on to the next popular social media platform. Therefore, more longitudinal and experimental studies are required to truly understand the significance of active and passive Facebook (or any other social media) use for long-term changes in mental health.

ACKNOWLEDGMENT

This research received no specific grant from any funding agency in the public, commercial, or not-for-profit sectors.

REFERENCES

Appel, H., Crusius, J., & Gerlach, A. L. (2015). Social comparison, envy, and depression on Facebook: A study looking at the effects of high comparison standards on depressed individuals. *Journal of Social and Clinical Psychology*, *34*(4), 277–289. doi:10.1521/jscp.2015.34.4.277

Argyle, M. (2008). *Social encounters: Contributions to social interaction*. Aldine Transaction.

Barry, C. T., Doucette, H., Loflin, D. C., Rivera-Hudson, N., & Herrington, L. L. (2017). 'Let me take a selfie': Associations between self-photography, narcissism, and self-esteem. *Psychology of Popular Media Culture*, *6*(1), 48–60. doi:10.1037/ppm0000089

Baumeister, R. F., & Leary, M. R. (1995). The need to belong: Desire for interpersonal attachments as a fundamental human motivation. *Psychological Bulletin*, *117*(3), 497–529. doi:10.1037/0033-2909.117.3.497 PMID:7777651

Bazarova, N. N., & Choi, Y. H. (2014). Self-disclosure in social media: Extending the functional approach to disclosure motivations and characteristics on social network sites. *Journal of Communication*, *64*(4), 635–657. doi:10.1111/jcom.12106

Berkman, L. F., & Glass, T. (2000). Social integration, social networks, social support, and health. *Social Epidemiology*, *1*, 137–173. doi:10.1016/S0277-9536(00)00065-4

Berndt, T. J. (1989). Obtaining support from friends during childhood and adolescence. In D. Belle (Ed.), *Children's Social Networks and Social Supports* (pp. 308–331). Oxford, UK: John Wiley & Sons.

Błachnio, A., Przepiorka, A., & Pantic, I. (2016). Association between Facebook addiction, self-esteem and life satisfaction: A cross-sectional study. *Computers in Human Behavior*, *55*, 701–705. doi:10.1016/j.chb.2015.10.026

Boyd, D. (2009, August 16). Twitter: "pointless babble" or peripheral awareness + social grooming? [Web log post]. Retrieved from http://www.zephoria.org/thoughts/archives/2009/08/16/twitter_pointle.html

Buhrmester, D. (1990). Intimacy of friendship, interpersonal competence, and adjustment during preadolescence and adolescence. *Child Development*, *61*(4), 1101–1111. doi:10.2307/1130878 PMID:2209180

Burke, M., Kraut, R., & Marlow, C. (2011). Social capital on Facebook: Differentiating uses and users. In *Proceedings of the 29th Annual Conference on Human Factors in Computing Systems* (pp. 571–580). New York: ACM Press. 10.1145/1978942.1979023

Burke, M., & Kraut, R. E. (2016). The relationship between Facebook use and well-being depends on communication type and tie strength. *Journal of Computer-Mediated Communication*, *21*(4), 265–281. doi:10.1111/jcc4.12162

Burke, M., Marlow, C., & Lento, T. (2010, April). Social network activity and social well-being. In *Proceedings of the 28th International Conference on Human Factors in Computing Systems*. New York: ACM.

Burrow, A. L., & Rainone, N. (2017). How many likes did I get?: Purpose moderates links between positive social media feedback and self-esteem. *Journal of Experimental Social Psychology*, *69*, 232–236. doi:10.1016/j.jesp.2016.09.005

Chen, G. M. (2011). Tweet this: A uses and gratifications perspective on how active Twitter use gratifies a need to connect with others. *Computers in Human Behavior*, *27*(2), 755–762. doi:10.1016/j.chb.2010.10.023

Choi, T. R., Sung, Y., Lee, J., & Choi, S. M. (2017). Get behind my selfies: The big five traits and social networking behaviors through selfies. *Personality and Individual Differences*, *10*, 998–1001. doi:10.1016/j.paid.2016.12.057

Chou, H. T. G., & Edge, N. (2012). "They are happier and having better lives than I am": The impact of using Facebook on perceptions of others' lives. *Cyberpsychology, Behavior, and Social Networking*, *15*(2), 117–121. doi:10.1089/cyber.2011.0324 PMID:22165917

Chua, T. H., & Chang, L. (2016). Follow me and like my beautiful selfies: Singapore teenage girls' engagement in self-presentation and peer comparison on social media. *Computers in Human Behavior*, *55*, 190–197. doi:10.1016/j.chb.2015.09.011

Cohen, S., & Willis, T. A. (1985). Stress, social support, and the buffering hypothesis. *Psychological Bulletin*, *98*(2), 310–357. doi:10.1037/0033-2909.98.2.310 PMID:3901065

Csepeli, G., & Nagyfi, R. (2014). Facebook diagnostics: Detection of mental health problems based on online traces. *European Journal of Mental Health*, *9*(2), 220–230. doi:10.5708/EJMH.9.2014.2.5

Davis, K. (2012). Friendship 2.0: Adolescents' experiences of belonging and self-disclosure online. *Journal of Adolescence*, *35*(6), 1527–1536. doi:10.1016/j.adolescence.2012.02.013 PMID:22475444

De Goede, I. H., Branje, S., van Duin, J., VanderValk, I. E., & Meeus, W. (2012). Romantic relationship commitment and its linkages with commitment to parents and friends during adolescence. *Social Development, 21*(3), 425–442. doi:10.1111/j.1467-9507.2011.00633.x

de Vries, D. A., & Kühne, R. (2015). Facebook and self-perception: Individual susceptibility to negative social comparison on Facebook. *Personality and Individual Differences, 86*, 217–221. doi:10.1016/j.paid.2015.05.029

Desjarlais, M., Gilmour, J., Sinclair, J., Howell, K. B., & West, A. (2015). Predictors and social consequences of online interactive self-disclosure: A literature review from 2002 to 2014. *Cyberpsychology, Behavior, and Social Networking, 18*(12), 718–725. doi:10.1089/cyber.2015.0109 PMID:26652672

Desjarlais, M., & Joseph, J. J. (2017). Socially interactive and passive technologies enhance friendship quality: An investigation of the mediating roles of online and offline self-disclosure. *Cyberpsychology, Behavior, and Social Networking, 20*(5), 286–291. doi:10.1089/cyber.2016.0363 PMID:28418718

Deters, F. G., & Mehl, M. R. (2013). Does posting Facebook status updates increase or decrease loneliness? An online social networking experiment. *Social Psychological & Personality Science, 4*(5), 579–586. doi:10.1177/1948550612469233 PMID:24224070

Dhir, A., Pallesen, S., Torsheim, T., & Andreassen, C. S. (2016). Do age and gender differences exist in selfie-related behaviours? *Computers in Human Behavior, 63*, 549–555. doi:10.1016/j.chb.2016.05.053

Diefenbach, S., & Christoforakos, L. (2017). The selfie paradox: Nobody seems to like them yet everyone has reasons to take them. An exploration of psychological functions of selfies in self-presentation. *Frontiers in Psychology, 8*. doi:10.3389/fpsyg.2017.00007 PMID:28144225

Diener, E., Oishi, S., & Lucas, R. E. (2003). Personality, culture, and subjective well-being: Emotional and cognitive evaluations of life. *Annual Review of Psychology, 54*(1), 403–425. doi:10.1146/annurev.psych.54.101601.145056 PMID:12172000

Diener, E., Suh, E. M., Lucas, R. E., & Smith, H. L. (1999). Subjective well-being: Three decades of progress. *Psychological Bulletin, 125*(2), 276–302. doi:10.1037/0033-2909.125.2.276

Duggan, M. (2015). Mobile messaging and social media 2015. *The Pew Research Center*. Retrieved from http://www.pewinternet.org/2015/08/19/mobilemessaging-and-social media-2015-main-findings/

Duval, S., & Wicklund, R. A. (1972). *A theory of objective self awareness*. New York: Academic Press.

Ellison, N. B., Steinfield, C., & Lampe, C. (2007). The benefits of Facebook 'friends': Social capital and college students' use of online social network sites. *Journal of Computer-Mediated Communication, 12*(4), 1143–1168. doi:10.1111/j.1083-6101.2007.00367.x

Feinstein, B. A., Hershenberg, R., Bhatia, V., Latack, J. A., Meuwly, N., & Davila, J. (2013). Negative social comparison on Facebook and depressive symptoms: Rumination as a mechanism. *Psychology of Popular Media Culture, 2*(3), 161–170. doi:10.1037/a0033111

Festinger, L. (1954). A theory of social comparison processes. *Human Relations, 7*, 117-140. doi: 10.1177001872675400700202

Ford, N. (2016). *Do selfies grab our attention? Areas of interest and scan paths of Instagram profiles* (Unpublished honour's thesis). Mount Royal University, Canada.

Fox, J., & Moreland, J. J. (2015). The dark side of social networking sites: An exploration of the relational and psychological stressors associated with Facebook use and affordances. *Computers in Human Behavior*, *45*, 168–176. doi:10.1016/j.chb.2014.11.083

Frison, E., & Eggermont, S. (2016). Exploring the relationships between different types of Facebook use, perceived online social support, and adolescents' depressed mood. *Social Science Computer Review*, *34*(2), 153–171. doi:10.1177/0894439314567449

Glynn, C. J., Huge, M. E., & Hoffman, L. H. (2012). All the news that's fit to post: A profile of news use on social networking sites. *Computers in Human Behavior*, *28*(1), 113–119. doi:10.1016/j.chb.2011.08.017

Goffman, E. (1959). *The presentation of self in everyday life*. Westminster, MD: Random House.

Gonzales, A. L., & Hancock, J. T. (2011). Mirror, mirror on my Facebook wall: Effects of exposure to Facebook on self-esteem. *Cyberpsychology, Behavior, and Social Networking*, *14*(1-2), 79–83. doi:10.1089/cyber.2009.0411 PMID:21329447

Greenwood, S., Perrin, A., & Duggan, M. (2016, November 11). Social media update 2016: Facebook usage and engagement is on the rise while adoption of other platforms holds steady. *Pew Research Center*. Retrieved from http://www.pewinternet.org/2016/11/11/social-media-update-2016/

Grieve, R., Indian, M., Witteveen, L., Tolan, G. A., & Marrington, J. (2013). Face-to-face or Facebook: Can social connectedness be derived online? *Computers in Human Behavior*, *29*(3), 604–609. doi:10.1016/j.chb.2012.11.017

Hart, M. (2017). Being naked on the Internet: Young people's selfies as intimate edgework. *Journal of Youth Studies*, *20*(3), 301–315. doi:10.1080/13676261.2016.1212164

Helliwell, J. F., Huang, H., & Harris, A. (2009). International differences in the determinants of life satisfaction. In R. Tridip, E. Somanathan, & D. Bhaskar (Eds.), *New and enduring themes in development economics* (pp. 3–40). Singapore: World Scientific. doi:10.1142/9789812839428_0001

Hu, Y., Manikonda, L., & Kambhampati, S. (2014). What we instagram: A first analysis of instagram photo content and user types. In *Proceedings of AAAI International Conference on Web and Social Media.* (pp. 595-598). Ann Arbor, MI: AAAI. Retrieved from http://www.aaai.org/ocs/index.php/ICWSM/ICWSM14/paper/viewFile/8118/8087

Jelenchick, L. A., Eickhoff, J. C., & Moreno, M. A. (2013). "Facebook depression?" Social networking site use and depression in older adolescents. *The Journal of Adolescent Health*, *52*(1), 128–130. doi:10.1016/j.jadohealth.2012.05.008 PMID:23260846

Jin, S. A. A., & Phua, J. (2014). Following celebrities' tweets about brands: The impact of Twitter-based electronic word-of-mouth on consumers' source credibility perception, buying intention, and social identification with celebrities. *Journal of Advertising*, *43*(2), 181–195. doi:10.1080/00913367.2013.827606

Jose, P. E., Ryan, N., & Pryor, J. (2012). Does social connectedness promote a greater sense of well-being in adolescence over time? *Journal of Research on Adolescence*, *22*(2), 235–251. doi:10.1111/j.1532-7795.2012.00783.x

Joseph, J. J. (2017). *Examining mediating and moderating factors in the relationship between Facebook use and subjective well-being* (Unpublished honour's thesis). Mount Royal University, Canada.

Joseph, J. J., & Desjarlais, M. (2017, April). *The relationship between Facebook and subjective well-being: The mediating roles of social comparison and social connectedness.* Poster presented at the 49th Banff International Conference on Behavioural Science, Banff, AB.

Katz, J. E., & Crocker, E. T. (2015). Selfiesl Selfies and photo messaging as visual conversation: Reports from the United States, United Kingdom and China. *International Journal of Communication*, *9*, 1861–1872. Retrieved from http://ijoc.org/index.php/ijoc/article/view/3180/1405

Kim, H. S., Sherman, D. K., & Taylor, S. E. (2008). Culture and social support. *The American Psychologist*, *63*(6), 518–526. doi:10.1037/0003-066X PMID:18793039

Kim, J., & Lee, J. R. (2011). The Facebook paths to happiness: Effects of the number of Facebook friends and self-presentation. *Cyberpsychology, Behavior, and Social Networking*, *14*(6), 359–364. doi:10.1089/cyber.2010.0374 PMID:21117983

Kim, J. W., & Chock, T. M. (2017). Personality traits and psychological motivations predicting selfie posting behaviors on social networking sites. *Telematics and Informatics*, *34*(5), 560–571. doi:10.1016/j.tele.2016.11.006

Köbler, F., Riedl, C., Vetter, C., Leimeister, J. M., & Krcmar, H. (2010). Social connectedness on Facebook – An explorative study on status message usage. In *Proceedings of the 16th Americas Conference on Information Systems* (*Vol. 247*, pp. 12-15). Lima, Peru: Academic Press.

Krämer, N. C., Feurstein, M., Kluck, J. P., Meier, Y., Rother, M., & Winter, S. (2017). Beware of selfies: The impact of photo type on impression formation based on social networking profiles. *Frontiers in Psychology*, *8*. doi:10.3389/fpsyg.2017.00188 PMID:28261129

Krasnova, H., Wenninger, H., Widjaja, T., & Buxmann, P. (2013). *Envy on Facebook: A hidden threat to users' life satisfaction?* Paper presented at the 11th International Conference on Wirtschaftsinformatik (WI), Leipzig, Germany.

Kross, E., Verduyn, P., Demiralp, E., Park, J., Lee, D. S., Lin, N., ... Ybarra, O. (2013). Facebook use predicts declines in subjective well-being in young adults. *PLoS One*, *8*(8), e69841. doi:10.1371/journal.pone.0069841 PMID:23967061

Lee, E., Lee, J., Moon, J. H., & Sung, Y. (2015). Pictures speak louder than words: Motivations for using Instagram. *Cyberpsychology, Behavior, and Social Networking*, *18*(9), 552–556. doi:10.1089/cyber.2015.0157 PMID:26348817

Liu, C. Y., & Yu, C. P. (2013). Can Facebook use induce well-being? *Cyberpsychology, Behavior, and Social Networking*, *16*(9), 674–678. doi:10.1089/cyber.2012.0301 PMID:24028138

Lobinger, K., & Brantner, C. (2015). Selfiesl In the eye of the beholder: Subjective views on the authenticity of selfies. *International Journal of Communication*, *9*, 1848–1860.

Lou, L. L., Yan, Z., Nickerson, A., & McMorris, R. (2012). An examination of the reciprocal relationship of loneliness and Facebook use among first-year college students. *Journal of Educational Computing Research*, *46*(1), 105–117. doi:10.2190/EC.46.1.e

Lup, K., Trub, L., & Rosenthal, L. (2015). Instagram# instasad?: Exploring associations among instagram use, depressive symptoms, negative social comparison, and strangers followed. *Cyberpsychology, Behavior, and Social Networking*, *18*(5), 247–252. doi:10.1089/cyber.2014.0560 PMID:25965859

Manago, A. M., Graham, M. B., Greenfield, P. M., & Salimkhan, G. (2008). Self-presentation and gender on MySpace. *Journal of Applied Developmental Psychology*, *29*(6), 446–458. doi:10.1016/j.appdev.2008.07.001

Manago, A. M., Taylor, T., & Greenfield, P. M. (2012). Me and my 400 friends: The anatomy of college students' Facebook networks, their communication patterns, and well-being. *Developmental Psychology*, *48*(2), 369–380. doi:10.1037/a0026338 PMID:22288367

Marion, D., Laursen, B., Zettergren, P., & Bergman, L. R. (2013). Predicting life satisfaction during middle adulthood from peer relationships during mid-adolescence. *Journal of Youth and Adolescence*, *42*(8), 1299–1307. doi:10.100710964-013-9969-6 PMID:23771820

McCain, J. L., Borg, Z. G., Rothenberg, A. H., Churillo, K. M., Weiler, P., & Campbell, W. K. (2016). Personality and selfies: Narcissism and the dark triad. *Computers in Human Behavior*, *64*, 126–133. doi:10.1016/j.chb.2016.06.050

McKinnon, M. (2015, January 12). 2015 Canadian social media usage statistics. *Canadians Internet*. Retrieved from http://canadiansinternet.com/2015-canadian-social-media-usage-statistics/

McLean, S. A., Paxton, S. J., Wertheim, E. H., & Masters, J. (2015). Photoshopping the selfie: Self photo editing and photo investment are associated with body dissatisfaction in adolescent girls. *International Journal of Eating Disorders*, *48*(8), 1132–1140. doi:10.1002/eat.22449 PMID:26311205

Michalos, A. C. (1985). Multiple discrepancies theory (MDT). *Social Indicators Research*, *16*(4), 347–413. doi:10.1007/BF00333288

Moon, J. H., Lee, E., Lee, J., Choi, T. R., & Sung, Y. (2016). The role of narcissism in self-promotion on Instagram. *Personality and Individual Differences*, *10*, 122–125. doi:10.1016/j.paid.2016.05.042

Nesi, J., & Prinstein, M. J. (2015). Using social media for social comparison and feedback-seeking: Gender and popularity moderate associations with depressive symptoms. *Journal of Abnormal Child Psychology*, *43*(8), 1427–1438. doi:10.100710802-015-0020-0 PMID:25899879

O'Keeffe, G. S., & Clarke-Pearson, K. (2011). The impact of social media on children, adolescents, and families. *Pediatrics*, *127*(4), 800–804. doi:10.1542/peds.2011-0054 PMID:21444588

Pew Research Center. (2017, January 12). Social media fact sheet. *Pew Research Center*. Retrieved from http://www.pewinternet.org/fact-sheet/social-media/

Phua, J., Jin, S. V., & Kim, J. (2017). Uses and gratifications of social networking sites for bridging and bonding social capital: A comparison of Facebook, Twitter, Instagram, and Snapchat. *Computers in Human Behavior*, *72*, 115–122. doi:10.1016/j.chb.2017.02.041

Pittman, M. (2015). Creating, consuming, and connecting: Examining the relationship between social media engagement and loneliness. *The Journal of Social Media in Society*, *4*, 66–98. Retrieved from http://www.thejsms.org/tsmri/index.php/TSMRI/article/view/92

Pittman, M., & Reich, B. (2016). Social media and loneliness: Why an Instagram picture may be worth more than a thousand Twitter words. *Computers in Human Behavior*, *62*, 155–167. doi:10.1016/j.chb.2016.03.084

Re, D. E., Wang, S. A., He, J. C., & Rule, N. O. (2016). Selfie indulgence: Self-favoring biases in perceptions of selfies. *Social Psychological & Personality Science*, *7*(6), 588–596. doi:10.1177/1948550616644299

Reinecke, L., & Trepte, S. (2014). Authenticity and well-being on social network sites: A two-wave longitudinal study on the effects of online authenticity and the positivity bias in SNS communication. *Computers in Human Behavior*, *30*, 95–102. doi:10.1016/j.chb.2013.07.030

Ridgway, J. L., & Clayton, R. B. (2016). Instagram unfiltered: Exploring associations of body image satisfaction, Instagram #selfie posting, and negative romantic relationship outcomes. *Cyberpsychology, Behavior, and Social Networking*, *19*(1), 2–7. doi:10.1089/cyber.2015.0433 PMID:26779659

Robins, R. W., & Beer, J. S. (2001). Positive illusions about the self: Short-term benefits and long-term costs. *Journal of Personality and Social Psychology*, *80*(2), 340–352. doi:10.1037/0022-3514.80.2.340 PMID:11220450

Ryan, T., & Xenos, S. (2011). Who uses Facebook? An investigation into the relationship between the Big Five, shyness, narcissism, loneliness, and Facebook usage. *Computers in Human Behavior*, *27*(5), 1658–1664. doi:10.1016/j.chb.2011.02.004

Sheldon, P. (2008). The relationship between unwillingness-to-communicate and students' Facebook use. *Journal of Media Psychology*, *20*(2), 67–75. doi:10.1027/1864-1105.20.2.67

Sheldon, P., & Bryant, K. (2016). Instagram: Motives for its use and relationship to narcissism and contextual age. *Computers in Human Behavior*, *58*, 89–97. doi:10.1016/j.chb.2015.12.059

Shin, Y., Kim, M., Im, C., & Chong, S. C. (2017). Selfie and self: The effect of selfies on self-esteem and social sensitivity. *Personality and Individual Differences*, *111*, 139–145. doi:10.1016/j.paid.2017.02.004

Smith, A. (2011, November 15). Why Americans use social media friends. *Pew Research Center*. Retrieved from http://www.pewinternet.org/2011/11/15/why-americans-use-social-media/

Smith, A., & Williams, K. D. (2004). R U there? Ostracism by cell phone text messages. *Group Dynamics*, *8*(4), 291–301. doi:10.1037/1089-2699.8.4.291

Sorokowska, A., Oleszkiewicz, A., Frackowiak, T., Pisanski, K., Chmiel, A., & Sorokowski, P. (2016). Selfies and personality: Who posts self-portrait photographs? *Personality and Individual Differences*, *90*, 119–123. doi:10.1016/j.paid.2015.10.037

Sorokowski, P., Sorokowska, A., Frackowiak, T., Karwowski, M., Rusicka, I., & Oleszkiewicz, A. (2016). Sex differences in online selfie posting behaviors predict histrionic personality scores among men but not women. *Computers in Human Behavior*, *59*, 368–373. doi:10.1016/j.chb.2016.02.033

Sorokowski, P., Sorokowska, A., Oleszkiewicz, A., Frackowiak, T., Huk, A., & Pisanski, K. (2015). Selfie posting behaviors are associated with narcissism among men. *Personality and Individual Differences*, *85*, 123–127. doi:10.1016/j.paid.2015.05.004

Souza, F., de Las Casas, D., Flores, V., Youn, S., Cha, M., Quercia, D., & Almeida, V. (2015). Dawn of the selfie era: The whos, wheres, and hows of selfies on Instagram. In *Proceedings of the 2015 ACM Conference on Online Social Networks* (pp. 221-231). Palo Alto, CA: ACM Press. 10.1145/2817946.2817948

Stats (2016, September 30). Stats. *Facebook Newsroom.* Retrieved from http://newsroom.fb.com/company-info/

Steers, M. L. N., Wickham, R. E., & Acitelli, L. K. (2014). Seeing everyone else's highlight reels: How Facebook usage is linked to depressive symptoms. *Journal of Social and Clinical Psychology*, *33*(8), 701–731. doi:10.1521/jscp.2014.33.8.701

Sullivan, H. S. (1953b). Preadolescence. In H. S. Perry & M. L. Gawel (Eds.), *The Interpersonal Theory of Psychiatry* (pp. 245–262). New York: Norton.

Suls, J., Martin, R., & Wheeler, L. (2002). Social comparison: Why, with whom, and with what effect? *Current Directions in Psychological Science*, *11*(5), 159–163. doi:10.1111/1467-8721.00191

Sung, Y., Lcc, J., Kim, E., & Choi, S. M. (2016). Why we post selfies: Understanding motivations for posting pictures of oneself. *Personality and Individual Differences*, *97*, 260–265. doi:10.1016/j.paid.2016.03.032

Tandoc, E. C. Jr, Ferrucci, P., & Duffy, M. (2015). Facebook use, envy, and depression among college students: Is facebooking depressing? *Computers in Human Behavior*, *43*, 139–146. doi:10.1016/j.chb.2014.10.053

Ting, H., Wong, W. P. M., de Run, E. C., & Lau, S. Y. C. (2015). Beliefs about the use of Instagram: An exploratory study. *International Journal of Business and Innovation*, *2*, 15–31.

Tobin, S. J., Vanman, E. J., Verreynne, M., & Saeri, A. K. (2015). Threats to belonging on Facebook: Lurking and ostracism. *Social Influence*, *10*(1), 31–42. doi:10.1080/15534510.2014.893924

Tromholt, M. (2016). The Facebook experiment: Quitting Facebook leads to higher levels of well-being. *Cyberpsychology, Behavior, and Social Networking*, *19*(11), 661–666. doi:10.1089/cyber.2016.0259 PMID:27831756

Utz, S., Muscanell, N., & Khalid, C. (2015). Snapchat elicits more jealousy than Facebook: A comparison of Snapchat and Facebook use. *Cyberpsychology, Behavior, and Social Networking*, *18*(3), 141–146. doi:10.1089/cyber.2014.0479 PMID:25667961

Valenzuela, S., Halpern, D., & Katz, J. E. (2014). Social network sites, marriage well-being and divorce: Survey and state-level evidence from the United States. *Computers in Human Behavior*, *36*, 94–101. doi:10.1016/j.chb.2014.03.034

Valenzuela, S., Park, N., & Kee, K. F. (2009). Is there social capital in a social network site?: Facebook use and college students' life satisfaction, trust, and participation. *Journal of Computer-Mediated Communication*, *14*(4), 875–901. doi:10.1111/j.1083-6101.2009.01474.x

Valkenburg, P. M., & Peter, J. (2007). Online communication and adolescent well-being: Testing the stimulation versus the displacement hypothesis. *Journal of Computer-Mediated Communication*, *12*(4), 1169–1182. doi:10.1111/j.1083-6101.2007.00368.x

Valkenburg, P. M., & Peter, J. (2009). Social consequences of the Internet for adolescents a decade of research. *Current Directions in Psychological Science*, *18*(1), 1–5. doi:10.1111/j.1467-8721.2009.01595.x

Valkenburg, P. M., & Peter, J. (2011). Online communication among adolescents: An integrated model of its attraction, opportunities, and risks. *The Journal of Adolescent Health*, *48*(2), 121–127. doi:10.1016/j.jadohealth.2010.08.020 PMID:21257109

Van Baren, J., IJsselsteijn, W. A., Markopoulos, P., Romero, N., & De Ruyter, B. (2004). Measuring affective benefits and costs of awareness systems supporting intimate social networks. In Nijholt, A., & Nishida, T. (Eds.), *Proceedings of the 3rd Workshop on Social Intelligence Design* (*Vol. 2*, pp. 13-19). Academic Press.

Vaterlaus, J. M., Barnett, K., Roche, C., & Young, J. A. (2016). "Snapchat is more personal": An exploratory study on Snapchat behaviors and young adult interpersonal relationships. *Computers in Human Behavior*, *62*, 594–601. doi:10.1016/j.chb.2016.04.029

Verduyn, P., Lee, D. S., Park, J., Shablack, H., Orvell, A., Bayer, J., & Kross, E. (2015). Passive Facebook usage undermines affective well-being: Experimental and longitudinal evidence. *Journal of Experimental Psychology: General, 144*, 480-488. doi: 2062/10.1037/xge0000057

Vogel, E. A., Rose, J. P., Roberts, L. R., & Eckles, K. (2014). Social comparison, social media, and self-esteem. *Psychology of Popular Media Culture*, *3*(4), 206–222. doi:10.1037/ppm0000047

Walther, J. B. (2007). Selective self-presentation in computer-mediated communication: Hyperpersonal dimensions of technology, language, and cognition. *Computers in Human Behavior*, *23*(5), 2538–2557. doi:10.1016/j.chb.2006.05.002

Wang, R., Yang, F., & Haigh, M. M. (2017). Let me take a selfie: Exploring the psychological effects of posting and viewing selfies and groupies on social media. *Telematics and Informatics*, *34*(4), 274–283. doi:10.1016/j.tele.2016.07.004

Weiser, E. B. (2015). #Me: Narcissism and its facets as predictors of selfie-posting frequency. *Personality and Individual Differences*, *86*, 477–481. doi:10.1016/j.paid.2015.07.007

Wenninger, H., Krasnova, H., & Buxmann, P. (2014). Activity matters: Investigating the influence of Facebook on life satisfaction of teenage users. In M. Avital, J. M. Leimeister, & U. Schultze (Eds.), *Twenty Second European Conference on Information Systems* (pp. 1–18). Tel Aviv, Israel: ECIS.

Wortham, J. (2013, October 19). My Selfie, Myself. *The New York Times*. Retrieved from http://www.nytimes.com/2013/10/20/sunday-review/my-selfie-myself.html

Wright, K. B., Rosenberg, J., Egbert, N., Ploeger, N. A., Bernard, D. R., & King, S. (2013). Communication competence, social support, and depression among college students: A model of Facebook and face-to-face support network influence. *Journal of Health Communication*, *18*(1), 41–57. doi:10.1080/10810730.2012.688250 PMID:23030518

Zhao, S., Grasmuck, S., & Martin, J. (2008). Identity construction on Facebook: Digital empowerment in anchored relationships. *Computers in Human Behavior*, *24*(5), 1816–1836. doi:10.1016/j.chb.2008.02.012

KEY TERMS AND DEFINITIONS

Active Facebook Use: An approach by which Facebook users interact with other users through sharing textual and pictorial information, sending messages, and reacting to others' posts.

Facebook Contentment: A phenomenon related to Facebook use that is characterized by positive outcomes for psychological functioning and wellbeing.

Facebook Depression: A phenomenon related to Facebook use that is characterized by negative outcomes for psychological functioning and wellbeing.

Negative Social Comparison: Instances where the targets of social comparison appear to be doing better than oneself.

Passive Facebook Use: An approach by which Facebook users surveil others through scrolling the newsfeed, and browsing timelines.

Positive Social Comparison: Instances where the targets of social comparison appear to be doing worse than oneself.

Self-Esteem: A global self-evaluation of one's own self-worth or value.

Selfie: A photograph of oneself, alone or with others, taken with a smartphone held at arm's length or pointed at a mirror.

Social Connectedness: Feelings of belonging and staying in touch with ongoing social relationships.

Subjective Wellbeing: The evaluation of one's own life including an assessment of overall life satisfaction and emotional responses to life events.

Chapter 8
Offending, Victimization, Forensic Investigation, and Prevention of Cyberstalking

Rejani Thudalikunnil Gopalan
Gujarat Forensic Sciences University, India

ABSTRACT

The term cyberstalking has been used to describe a variety of behaviors that involve repeated threats and/or harassment by the use of electronic mail or other computer-based communication that would make a reasonable person afraid or concerned for their safety. It is growing fast and creating problems, especially psychologically. This chapter mainly focused on its definition, typologies, characteristics of victims and offenders, forensic investigation, and its prevention. There is not much agreement on the definition of cyberstalking as it appeared recently due to technological advancement. Many of the researches were done on university students and the prevalence of cyberstalking among general population and special groups are not much known. But researches repeatedly confirm it as a growing issue. Technical advancements and thorough knowledge on technical details among researchers from different backgrounds poses a big problem to its complete understanding and prevention. Future research needs to focus on all these aspects.

DEFINITION AND TYPOLOGIES

Stalking can be defined as recurring unwelcome attention which causes people to fear for their own safety and for the safety of those closest to them (Baum, Catalano, Rand, & Rose, 2009). Stalking is an assembly of behaviors involving recurring and persistent attempts to impose on another person unwanted communication and/or contact. These behaviors include repeated phone calls or letters as well as pursuit, approach, threats or assault by the perpetrator (Pathé, 2002). Being stalked includes being repetitively followed in a manner that causes a reasonable person to fear for his or her safety. The definition has two aspects that are behavioral and emotional. The behavioral represents the repeated pursuit of behaviors as experienced by the victims. Second is the emotional issues suffered by the victim in terms of fear,

DOI: 10.4018/978-1-5225-4047-2.ch008

anxiety and distress. Stalking physically takes place in spatial proximity to the victim and increases the potential physical harm to the victim and, therefore, heightened fear of the realization of its probability (Reyns, 2010).

Cyberstalking is an electronic crime involving a perpetrator using the internet or other high tech communication devices to take advantage of systematic weaknesses, or to exploit a person's vulnerability, including stalking a person online (Stambaugh, Beaupre, Baker, Cassaday, & Williams, 2001). It is harassment on the Internet using various modes of transmission such as electronic mail (e-mail), chat rooms, newsgroups, mail exploders, and the World Wide Web (Deirmenjian, 1999). The term "cyberstalking" has been used to describe a variety of behaviors that involve: (a) repeated threats and/or harassment; (b) by the use of electronic mail or other computer-based communication; (c) that would make a reasonable person afraid or concerned for their safety (Fisher, Cullen, & Turner, 2000; U.S. Department of Justice, 2000). According to Petherick (2001), it is which is simply an extension of the physical form of stalking, is where the electronic mediums such as the Internet are used to pursue, harass or contact another in an unsolicited fashion. Cyber stalking doesn't involve any physical contact yet stalking through the internet has found favor among the offenders for certain advantages available like, ease of communication access to personal information and anonymity (Verma, 2016). As per Bocij and McFarlane (2002), cyber stalking is a group of behaviors in which an individual, group of individuals or organization uses information technology to harass one or more individuals. Such behavior may include, but are not limited to, the transmission of threats and false accusations, identity theft, data theft, damage to data or equipment, computer monitoring and the solicitation of minors for sexual purposes. Harassment is defined as:

a course of action that a reasonable person, in possession of the same information, would think causes another reasonable person to suffer emotional distress.

Any of the following categories may constitute the perpetration of cyberstalking: persistent unwanted contact, repeated unwanted harassment, persistent and unwanted sexual advances, or implied threats or acts of violence. The main difference between stalking and cyber stalking stems from the methods of perusal occupied. Cyber stalking adheres to the repeated pursuit of a victim by exploiting various electronic communicative avenues. These online behaviors are facilitated by technological innovations that liberate potential stalkers of the spatial restriction of their recurring perusal (Reyns, Henson, & Fisher, 2011; Reyns, 2010).

There are three primary ways of cyber stalking depending on the use of the internet:

1. **E-Mail Stalking:** This is direct communication through e-mail characterized by threatening, hateful, or obscene nature, or even send spam or viruses to harass others.
2. **Internet Stalking:** There is global communication through the Internet and the domain is more wide and public in comparison to e-mail stalking. Here stalkers can use a wide range of activities to harass their victims.
3. **Computer Stalking:** This is unauthorized control of another person's computer. In this type of stalking, the stalker exploits the working of the Internet and the Windows operating system in order to to assume control over the computer of the targeted victim (Ogilvie, 2000).

A number of typologies concerning stalking have been proposed by researchers. Zona et al., (1993) reported about three kinds of stalkers — erotomanics, love obsessionals and simple obsessionals. *Ero-*

tomanics have the delusional belief that the target of interest, usually of higher status, is in love with the stalker. Cases involving *love obsessionals* are characterized by the absence of an existing relationship between the stalker and the victim (usually celebrities), yet the stalker has a fanatical love towards the subject. These stalkers tend to suffer from schizophrenia, or bipolar disorder, or some other psychiatric illness. The final group is the *simple obsessional,* where the stalker is usually an ex-partner of the victim and may wish to rekindle the relationship or may harass the victim for revenge. Harmon et al. (1995) classified stalkers in to two based on the nature of the attachment between victim and stalker (classified as affectionate/amorous or persecutory/angry), and the nature of the prior relationship between stalker and victim (i.e. personal, professional, employment, media, acquaintance, none and unknown). It was noted that *amorous/affectionate* harassers usually suffered from erotomanic features, and that the majority of stalkers of ex-intimates had narcissistic and paranoid personality traits. *Persecutory/angry* harassers not only stalked individuals but also large institutions who had wronged them (real or imagined) (Mullen, Pathé, & Purcell, 2000).

Wright et al. (1996) classified stalkers in to *domestic* or *nondomestic (*nature of the relationship between the victim and stalker), *nondelusional* or *delusional (*the content of the communications), *low, medium, high (*the level of risk to the victim in terms of aggression), *infatuation, possession, anger/retaliation, other (*the motive of the stalker) and *legal, suicide, psychiatric, other(*the outcome of the case for the stalker). Their system was developed from crime scene and common forensic findings, stalking cases, anecdotal reviews, newspaper accounts of stalking, as well as interviews with victims of stalkers.

Attempt was made to categorize stalkers based on psychiatric evaluation and Kienlen et al. (1997) divided stalkers into *psychotic* (with symptoms that ranged from schizophrenia, delusional disorder with erotomanic features, bipolar disorder) and *non-psychotic* (with disorders that ranged from mood disorder, alcohol and drug abuse, and personality disorder). Based on the stalkers' predominant motivation and the context in which stalking occurred, information about the nature of the prior relationship with the victim, and finally, a psychiatric diagnosis, Mullen et al. (1999) classified five types of stalkers:

1. **The Rejected Stalker:** Has had an intimate relationship with the victim (although occasionally the victim may be a family member or close friend), and views the termination of the relationship as unacceptable. Their behavior is characterized by a mixture of revenge and desire for reconciliation.
2. **Intimacy Seekers:** Attempt to bring to fruition a relationship with a person who has engaged their desires, and who they may also mistakenly perceive reciprocates that affection.
3. **Incompetent Suitors:** Tend to seek to develop relationships but they fail to abide by social rules governing courtship. They are usually intellectually limited and/or socially incompetent.
4. **Resentful Stalkers:** Harass their victims with the specific intention of causing fear and apprehension out of a desire for retribution for some actual or supposed injury or humiliation.
5. **Predatory Stalkers:** Are those who stalk for information gathering purposes or fantasy rehearsal in preparation for a sexual attack.

Ellison (1999) has classified cyber stalking as either "direct" or "indirect" based on the type of electronic communication used to stalk the victim and the extent to which the communication is private or public. Direct cyber stalking includes the use of pagers, cell phones and e-mail to send messages of hate, obscenities, and threats to intimidate a victim and it is the most common form of cyber stalking and most common way in which stalking begins (Wallace, 2000).

McFarlane and Bocij (2003) identified four categories of offenders:

1. **Vindictive Cyberstalkers:** Are characterized by relentless harassment of their victim without a specific reason. They are frequently suffering from psychological disorders.
2. **Composed Cyberstalkers:** Aim to cause constant annoyance and irritation to the targeted victim. They have no desire to establish a relationship with their victim, and are motivated to cause them distress.
3. **Intimate Cyberstalkers:** Are characterized by the desire to attract the attention or affection of their victim. They usually have detailed knowledge of the person being targeted.
4. **Collective Cyberstalkers:** Consist of a group of individuals harassing their victims through the use of communication technology.

Spitzberg and Cupach, (2007) classified eight categories of stalking and obsessive relational intrusion (ORI) behaviors such as:

1. **Hyper-Intimacy:** Typical courtship activities, but taken to an excessive level.
2. **Mediated Contacts:** All forms of communication efforts performed through technologies, including email, instant message (IM), the Internet, cell phones, etc. ·
3. **Interactional Contacts:** Activities oriented toward face-to-face or proximal conversation. This includes behaviors oriented toward direct contact such as physical approaches, appearing at various places, pursuing common activities and locations, etc.
4. **Pursuit and Surveillance:** The systematic attempt to secure knowledge or information about the victim without the victim's awareness. Following, watching, and/or monitoring the person or the person's behaviors. ·
5. **Invasion:** Activities that involve the violation of normatively prescribed personal and legal boundaries, such as the theft of information, breaking and entering into a person's premises, and trespassing, etc.
6. **Harassment and Intimidation:** Variety of aggressive verbal or nonverbal activities designed to bother, annoy, or otherwise stress the victim such as insults, seeking to harm the person's reputation, spreading rumors, calling non-stop, etc.
7. **Coercion and Threat:** Implicit or explicit suggestion of potential harm that may befall the victim. Threats may be against loved ones, pets, property, colleagues, the victim, or even to the pursuer (e.g., threatening to commit suicide), etc.
8. **Physical Aggression and Violence:** Involves vandalism, use of a weapon, assault, injury, attempted suicide and suicide, attempted rape and rape, and attempted homicide and homicide.

Though many typologies are available, each has its own merits and demerits and it is important how well these typologies help in detection and prevention of cyberstalking.

PREVALENCE

The prevalence of cyber stalking varies according to types. Mitchell, Becker-Blease, and Finkelhor (2005) found that individuals reported being victimized while using online sites in two forms, sexual and nonsexual. One method is harassment, which can be accomplished by:

... posting defamatory or embarrassing personal information about others, impersonating others online, stalking people online, threatening violence, and physical and emotional abuse.

Kennedy and Taylor (2010) conducted an anonymous, self-report surveys were completed polling experiences with harassment, stalking, and sexual assault and it was found that the majority of victimization types were reported infrequently, while rates of sexual assault overall were quite high compared to prior research. Types of victimization varied by where they were occurring: online or offline. Acts such as verbal harassment, pestering, unwanted behaviors, and sexual harassment were all fairly prevalent online, while other victimizations, such as being threatened or stalked, occurred more offline.

Mitchell, Finkelhor, and Wolak (2001) surveyed 1,501 frequent internet users between the ages of 10-17 (63% were 14 or older) and found that nearly one-fifth of the sample had been sexually solicited, which meant that an individual had made requests for sex, discussed sex when it was unwanted, or consensually discussed sex. It was also found that females and those who were between the ages of 14 and 17 were solicited at higher rates than those aged 10 to 13, while those between the ages of 10 and 13 reported being distressed by the solicitations more frequently than older teens. Mitchell, Finkelhor and Wolak (2007) reported that risk factors for solicitations were being female, using chat rooms frequently, talking about sex frequently online, revealing personal information, and being abused offline.

In a study among university students, Spitzberg and Hoobler (2002) reported that 59 percent of respondents felt that they had been cyberstalked, of which 19.6 percent felt threatened or were in fear for their personal safety. In another study of offline and online stalking, 11 percent of participants had been harassed. The majority of complainants were female (61 percent) and ages ranged from 17 to 42, with 55 percent aged 20 or younger (Burgess & Baker, 2002). It was reported that CyberAngels (a well-known Internet safety organization) receives some 500 complaints of cyberstalking each day, of which up to 100 represent legitimate cases and another Internet safety organization (Working to Halt Online Abuse) reports receiving an average of 100 cases per week (Dean, 2000; WHOA, 2001) which indicated it as a significant problem.

In an online survey of 6,379 participants involving users of the German social network StudiVZ, the prevalence of cyberstalking was estimated to be 6.3%. In various aspects, cyberstalking was comparable to offline stalking such as cyberstalking occurred most often in the context of ex-partner relationships; most of the victims were female and the majority of the perpetrators were male. The prevalence of cyberstalking is considerable. However, if stringent definition criteria comparable to those of offline stalking are applied, it is not a mass phenomenon (Dreßing, Bailer, Anders, Wagner, & Gallas, 2014). Previous studies also reported high prevalence rate of stalking. The lifetime prevalence of stalking was estimated at 4.5 percent of adults surveyed, translating into roughly 10 million people having been stalked at some point in their life (Basile, Swahn, Chen, & Saltzman, 2006). In an another study on a sample of 16,507 adults aged 18 and over, the lifetime stalking victimization rate for women was 16 percent and 5 percent for men (Black, Basile, Breiding, Smith, Walters, Merrick, Chen, & Stevens, 2011). In a meta-analysis of 103 research studies of stalking related incidents involving 70,000 individuals, authors found approximately three fourths of the perpetrators had some type of relationship with the victims and nearly half of all occurrences occurred between past romantic partners (Spitzberg, 2002). Overall, it is predicted nearly one in every five people will become a victim of stalking in their lifetimes, and women are almost two and a half times more likely than men to be victims (Spitzberg, 2002). In another meta-analysis of 175 research studies on stalking, representing over 120,000 cases, Spitzberg and Cupach (2007) reported 25% of the sample experienced stalking. Alexy, Burgess, Baker, and Smoyak (2005) have surveyed 756 students across 2 universities and reported 4 percent of their sample had been cyberstalked (32% of the total stalking cases). Sheridan and Grant, (2007) found 7 percent self-reported cyberstalking victimization was 7 percent and purely online was 4 percent and Paullet et al., (2009) reported 13 percent among 302 students at a mid-Atlantic university.

Cyber stalking often happens to celebrities and politicians because of the nature of work and in one study in New Zealand reported that politicians felt they (and their families) had become more exposed as a result of the Internet. Half of MPs had been personally approached by their harassers, 48% had been directly threatened and 15% had been attacked. Some of these incidents were serious, involving weapons such as guns, Molotov cocktails and blunt instruments (Every-Palmer, Barry-Walsh, & Pathé, 2015). In a recent study, the prevalence of cyberstalking among Italian nurses was 23.3% and 42.7% had to change their lifestyle and work. The cyberstalker was predominantly male (52%) and, in 49% of cases, was a patient. The victims reported moderate anxiety levels and depression and increased levels of depression in nurses experienced in computer use, website managers or blogs, and a negative correlation between anxiety level and experienced nurses. The cyberstalking is a phenomenon that occurs frequently among nurses. The nurse-patient relationship plays a central role in the development of the phenomenon and the victims reported stress-related disorders that affect working life. These preliminary results could sensitize hospital managers, politics and anti-violence centers in order to develop resolutive strategies (Comparcini, Simonetti, Lupo, Galli, Bocij, & Cicolini, 2016).

RISK FACTORS

Bocij and McFarlane (2003) pointed out how technology can encourage individuals to harass others. The central argument made is that technology both enables and invites participation in criminal or anti-social behavior from individuals who would not normally take part in such activities. One way in which this can be explained is by suggesting that some of the social and technological characteristics of the Internet act together in order to lower inhibitions and establish new norms. For instance, the anonymity offered by the Internet enables people to participate in activities such as encouraging violence against others with little fear of retaliation. In addition, by allowing a cyber stalker to harm another person at a distance, the victim is effectively depersonalized. In this way it can be argued that some of those who sympathize with the goals of far-right organizations may be reluctant to act in the offline world but more willing to act in the online world.

Social networking web site is a virtual environment where people can connect with each other and it is often used as a channel for harassment and intimidation. More victims reported to having been tracked down through social networks than on dating sites. Victims also can be tracked through search engines, online forums, message boards, chat rooms or electronic mail. In the case of cyber stalking, perpetrators were likely to be strangers, resulting in unclear motives for the harassment. It cannot be said that social networking is the cause of cyberstalking but it do facilitate (Hill, 2010; Smith, 2011).

Risk of Being Victim

Studies have found many factors related with being a victim of cyber stalking such as gender, age, social actors, and relationship status with offender. Studies have noticed that mostly cyberstalking victims are females (Bjorklund, Häkkänen-Nyholm, Sheridan, & Roberts, 2010; Reyns, Henson, & Fisher, 2011;

Baum, Catalano, Rand, & Rose, 2009; Henson, Reyns, & Fisher, 2011; Spitzberg, 2002). Hitchcock (2000) reported that 90% of off-line stalking victims are female. Majority of the victims are females of average socioeconomic status with most victims between the ages of 18 and 29 (Goode, 1995; Brownstein, 2000; McCann, 2000; Sinwelski & Vinton, 2001). Stalking has become a problem to women and children on a larger part in comparison to men. Women are threatened, vandalized, assaulted when it comes to real world but the same things happen when cyber stalking takes place. Obscenity also adds up with the, threatens and harassment. No doubt men also become the prey of the same but its lower when it comes to females. Children also undergo the same trauma by adult predators and pedophiles. The victim is normally a person who is less thorough regarding internet services and its applications. The stalker is generally a person who is a paranoid with no self-esteem. But the traits differ from one stalker to another. Some harass to seek revenge or some do so for their own pleasure. While some just to do it for playing a mischief (Amita, 2016).

Relationship status with offender is a crucial factor in determining the risk for being a victim. Zona, et al. (1993) reported, 65% of off-line victims had a previous relationship with their stalker and up to 51% by Working to Halt Online Abuse (2003). Baum et al (2009) noted that 75% of victims were stalked by a known person, most commonly a neighbor, co-inhabitant, or past romantic partner/companion. Ending the relation, ill will, rage, and revenge were the most frequent reasons for cyberstalking (Baum, Catalano, Rand, & Rose, 2009; Spitzberg, 2002). But some argue that cyber stalking begins during a relationship and continues, even after it's termination, the stalker using his/her intimate knowledge of the victim's personal life as an aid in commission of the crime (Logan & Walker, 2009). McEwan, Mullen, and MacKenzie (2009) found that the type of prior relationship between stalker and victim is strongly associated with persistence, with prior acquaintances the most persistent, and strangers least. Being aged over 30, sending the victim unsolicited materials, and having an intimacy seeking or resentful motivation was also associated with greater persistence, as was the presence of psychosis. Lyndon, Bonds-Raacke and Cratty (2011) reported abundant anecdotes and warnings of inappropriate behaviors on social networking sites, particularly about Facebook. They studied whether individuals obsessively monitor or harass their ex-partners on Facebook (related to general "Facebook stalking") and, if so, whether those individuals would also engage in cyber obsessional pursuit (COP) and obsessive relational pursuit (ORI), which are categories of cyberstalking and stalking (Covert Provocation, Public Harassment, and Venting). They found that each category of Facebook harassment was related to perpetration of COP and ORI. Additionally, participants who engaged in COP were almost six times more likely to also perpetrate ORI. If participants admitted to engaging in some types of stalking behaviors, they did so online, offline, and on Facebook. Though studies reported that victims are known to the perpetrator, some studies also found that offenders are strangers to victims, never ever romantically involved or had any biological relationship (Sissing, 2013).

Victim's victim's past deviant internet behavior such as downloading pirated media, contacting someonein a threatening manner, and sending sexual images predicted high risk for victimization. Individuals who engaged in deviant onlinebehavior were found to be 14 times more likely to be victims of cyberstalking (Reyns, Henson, & Fisher, 2011). Marcum, Ricketts, and Higgins (2010) have conducted a survey to 100-level courses at a mid-sized university in the northeast, which questioned respondent on their Internet behaviors and experiences during the high school senior and college freshman time period. The findings of the study indicated that participating in behaviors that increased exposure to motivated offenders and target suitability in turn increased the likelihood of victimization for both genders.

Cyber stalking may cause victims to alter their lifestyles in terms of interpersonal, professional and general social functioning. For instance, victims may change their personal contact information such as telephone numbers, e-mail addresses or even their names. Moreover, they may remove their contact details from public portals, change their daily routines, suspend previously enjoyed activities, find new jobs and schools for their children, relocate and or end communication with family, friends or 66 colleagues. Naturally, victims squander a lot of energy, time and money in achieving the above-mentioned changes (Drahokoupilová, 2007).

Studies have indicated that females are more prone to cyberstalking especially youngsters and it do affect their life significantly.

Risk of Being Offender

Though many cyberstalkers maintain their anonymity by using internet technologies to conceal their actions (Wykes, 2007; Harrison, 2006), many factors related with offenders such as gender, social and mental characteristics, and pathology. Studies have reported that most of the cyberstalkers on both online and offline are males (Bjorklund, Häkkänen-Nyholm, Sheridan, & Roberts, 2010; Meloy & Gothard, 1995; Mullen, Pathé, & Purcell, 1999; Working to Halt Online Abuse, 2003). It ranges from 68% to 91.8%. When a victim was male, the offender was also male 41.3% of the time, female 42.5% of the time, and unknown 16.1% of the time; when a victim was a female; the offender was male 66.9% of the time, female 23.5% of the time, and unknown 9.3% of the time (Baum, Catalano, Rand, & Rose, 2009). Cyberstalkers are between the ages of 19 and 30 (Bjorklund, Häkkänen-Nyholm, Sheridan, & Roberts, 2010) and belongs to diverse socioeconomic backgrounds with either underemployment or unemployment (Meloy, 1996). It is also noted that most offenders stalked victims of the same ethnicity (Baum, Catalano, Rand, & Rose, 2009). Though studies have reported male as perpetrator, women admitted greater frequencies of cyberstalking perpetration than males in one study signaling that further research on frequency and motivation for cyberstalking among the sexes is necessary (Strawhun & Huss, 2013).

Studies have reported that many psychological factors are related with cyberstalkers. Off-line stalkers were above intelligence and older in comparison to other criminal offenders (McCann, 2000). Cyber stalkers have similar characteristics to the off-line stalkers and most of them are motivated to control the victim (Jenson, 1996; Ogilvie, 2000; Report on Cyberstalking, 1999). Factors such as social isolation, maladjustment and emotional immaturity, along with an inability to cope with failed relationships are common with off-line stalking groups (Kamphuis & Emmelkamp, 2000). Childhood sexual maltreatment predicted cyber and overt stalking for men and women and for men, narcissistic vulnerability and its interaction with sexual abuse predicted stalking behavior while for women, insecure attachment (for cyber and overt stalking) and alcohol expectancies (for cyber stalking) predicted stalking behavior (Ménard & Pincus, 2012).

Morrison (2001) examined the factors associated with violent/aggressive behavior in stalkers using a sample of 100 Canadian cases of persons charged with criminal harassment (more commonly known as stalking). Results revealed that the typical profile of a "simple obsessional" type of stalker was a middle-aged male, single or separated/estranged, with a history of emotional and/or anger management problems. The most common initial strategies used by the victims to cope with the stalkers were oriented towards legal resources. Initial legal remedies, including court orders or police warnings, seemed to be ineffective as a strategy to stop stalking given that most stalkers chose to ignore them. The study also provided partial support for a preliminary model of predictors of violent/aggressive behavior in stalkers.

Stalkers with previous violent behaviors, strong negative emotions, and obsessional tendencies toward the victim may be most at risk of future violent and aggressive acts.

Mullen, et al. (1999) claims the majority of simple obsessional stalkers have some form of personality disorder and as a group have the greatest potential to become violent. Testimonies from stalking victims consistently revealed how personable, caring, and charismatic offenders seemed at first, but how those initially appealing features quickly transformed. Once an offender had won over his/her victim, the need to control emerged and behavior including outward acts of jealousy, aggression and threats, and mental abuse was displayed (Cox & Speziale, 2009). Prior attachment, jealousy, and violence issues within relationships are significant predictors of cyberstalking-related behaviors (Strawhun & Huss, 2013). Zona et al. (1993) reported that the love obsessional stalkers are those who have never met their victim. The erotomanic group is the smallest among stalkers and is motivated by the belief that the victim is in love with them, as a result of active delusions. Sheridan and Grant (2007) observed that cyberstalking was less likely to be perpetrated by ex-partners and was more often engaged by acquaintance or strangers.

It is also noted that cyberstalking has been connected to pedophilia. Of adults to stalk children on the internet, 74% were 20-49 years old and 95% were males (Alexy, Burgess, & Baker, 2005). Many studies have observed that offenders showed a tendency to display low to medium mental impairment when entering the criminal justice system, as well as nonconforming psychological states of being and antisocial behaviors (Prins, 2005; Kamphuis & Emmelkamp, 2005).

Rosenfeld (2003) was the first to conduct an empirical study on the relationship between stalkers and recidivism and it was found that half of the offenders repeated the offence. Personality disorder, particularly those that involve antisocial, borderline, or narcissistic behaviors, which are collectively referred to as "Cluster B" personality disorders, combination of a personality disorder and a history of substance abuse raised the risk of re-offending even higher. This is consistent with the findings associated with other criminal offender groups. Based on experience, those offenders with a history of mental illness and substance abuse have a higher than normal probability of re-offending (Pittaro, 2007).

Mainly offenders are found to be males, who may or may not have psychological disorders. Though many researches were conducted, clarity on many aspects related to offending is not clear.

THEORIES

Many theories were put forward to explain cyberstalking such as evolutionary theory, relational goal theory, and psychodynamic approaches. According to evolutionary approach, stalking evolved as one strategy among an armament of strategies for solving historically recurrent problems of mating and within gender competition (Duntley & Buss, 2012). As per Relational Goal Theory obsessive relational pursuers link the goal of having a particular relationship to higher-order goals such as happiness and self-worth (Spitzberg & Cupach, 2007). In the case of stalking, perpetrator goal is to make relation with victim as their happiness and self-worth depends on it. If this goal (i.e., relationship) becomes blocked, the individual experiences strain, frustration, and anger. They respond to this frustration by excessively ruminating about their failed objective. They will not stop until they feel they have achieved their goal and they believe the more persistent and intense methods of pursuit will eventually lead them to success. Attachment theory and object relations theory are used to explain stalking under paradigm of psychodynamic approach. Attachment theories suggest that those who stalk tend to have attachment issues stemming from childhood disruptions such as the loss of a caregiver, an emotionally or physically absent caregiver, or childhood emotional, physical, and/or sexual abuse In the cases of stalking, individuals with insecure-anxious attachment issues have the propensity to resort to stalking and other threatening behaviors in order to preserve or mend the bond and reduce the anxiety they experience from the rejection or abandonment. Likewise, the more unavailable or emotionally distant the object of pursuit gets the more intense and desperate the attempts become to try to reform the attachment (Kienlen, 1998; Meloy, 1998; Patton, Nobles, & Fox, 2010).

Another theory used to explain cyberstalking is the lifestyle exposure theory which suggests that the likelihood of victimization is dependent on lifestyle. This proposes that any change in the habitual activities of an individual or group, be it potential victims or wrongdoers, is enough to increase or decrease exposure to risk as well as present opportunities for victimization. The lifestyle exposure theory permits the predictability of victimization or potential victimization when lifestyle is taken into account. In other words, patterns, routines and daily schedules are exploited to the benefit of the perpetrator. In this way, not only can high risk individuals of cyber stalking be identified and targeted by cyber stalkers but also by protective agents concerned by the matter at hand (Davis, 2005).

The routine activity theory is based on the observations by Cohen and Felson pertaining crime to a product of the recurrent, routine activities and structuring of everyday life (SAGE dictionary of Criminology, 2006). In its original conception, the theory was designed to explain the volume and distribution of violent crimes or that of theft – cases in which both the victim and offender are physically present at the scene of the crime (Davis, 2005). The Routine activity theory was used to explore whether there is an increased risk while using online sites and whether the use of social networking sites should be deemed a risky act that may lead to various types of victimization. It looks for a convergence in time and location of motivated offenders, targets that are deemed suitable by the offender and a lack of guardianship over desired persons or things (De Coster, Estes, & Mueller, 1999).

Rational choice theory suggests that individuals, which in this case would be cyber stalkers, freely choose to commit a crime after weighing the prospective rewards against the potential risks. Since rational choice theory assumes that cyber stalkers will calculate the risks before committing a crime, it also assumes that such behaviors could be deterred if the risks were certain and the punishment was severe (Barkan, 2006).

Not a single theory is fully explaining the complexity of cyberstalking, more theories are yet to come in future.

FORENSIC INVESTIGATION

Cybercrime offending can be technically complex and legally intricate. Rapid advancements in the functionality of information communication technologies (ICTs) and innate disparities between systems of law globally are stark challenges for first responders, investigating authorities, forensic interrogators, prosecuting agencies, and administrators of criminal justice (Brown, 2015). Many cybercrimes are sophisticated and well-conceived, requiring police to apply technological expertise and deductive reasoning to unravel complex 'modus operandi' and substantiate elements of an offence and many cybercrime offenders have evaded prosecution due to weaknesses in substantive criminal laws that do not address technological means of offending (Bromby, 2006; Downing, 2005).

Criminal profiles are widely used in investigations to link together different crimes, to narrow down lists of suspects and to aid the process of investigation (Rogers, 2003). Offender profiling is a forensic technique used in criminal investigations for analyzing, assessing, and interpreting the physical evidence, the crime scene, the nature of the offence and the way it was committed. This aims to create a profile of the demographic and behavioral characteristics (e.g., gender, age, background, psychological disorders, guilt, anger) of an offender against the characteristics of those who have previously committed similar crimes. Profiles help build a bigger picture and reconstruct the crime, when there are too many unknowns (Kocsis, 2006; Turvey, 2011). Criminal profiling in simple terms is defined as:

A technique for identifying the major personality and behavioural characteristics of an individual based upon an analysis of the crimes he or she has committed (Douglas, Ressler, Burgess, & Hartman,1986).

Criminal Profiling in Prosecution Profiles have been proved useful in court in helping keep evidence in a case and proving a connection between one or several crimes and an offender (Ingram, 1998).

Criminal profiling models have two main approaches – inductive, where statistical information about committed crimes is used to generalize the behavior exhibited by these crimes, and deductive, where offender characteristics are derived from the specific case. It relies on data from criminal databases to identify a generalized behavioral pattern and personality traits of a typical offender in specific kind of cases (e.g., rape, serial homicides). After identifying a behavioral pattern or specific characteristics of a typical offender, the investigator can use criminal databases or records related to the defined characteristics to develop a group of potential suspects (Rogers, 2003). This method is less methodological and possibility of having errors caused by variable levels of honesty and perception bias of questionnaire respondents, or by case studies being taken from a wide range of time and increased possibility of unpredictable external influences on the case (Turvey, 2012). A deductive method takes a more personal approach, as it examines every case contextually and it relates to case-based investigation. It analyses evidence from the case in question focusing on specific behavioral and personality traits, and uses it to develop a profile of the specific characteristics of the probable offender (Turvey, 2012; 2011). It looks the case more in detail but it lacks access to a real case with the appropriate amount of case detail.

Profiling of cyber stalkers is difficult as it involves complex and sometimes unpredictable behaviours (Burmerster, Henry, & Kermes, 2005). Sheridan and Grant (2007) reported that cyberstalking is not fundamentally different from offline stalking and Bocij (2003) noticed many similarities and differences among offline stalkers. Though attempts are made to build profile like Barnes (2013) builds a cyberstalking victim profile in terms of their daily activities, relationship with technology, behaviour online, age group, lack of many studies and clarity is preventing to form a formal profile of cyberstalker and victim.

Digital forensics is a branch of forensic science, which encompasses the discovery, acquisition and investigation of information associated with digital devices. Originally used as a synonym for computer forensics, the term digital forensics has expanded to involve the investigation of any device capable of storing information in digital form. Digital forensics investigations have a variety of applications and the use of forensic techniques in the digital domain is increasingly an essential element of high-tech investigations, but also to support or refute the theory of a case in traditional civil and criminal investigations (Brown, 2015). The utility of Behavioural Evidence Analysis (BEA) has gained attention in the field of Digital Forensics in recent years. BEA is a deductive, case-based investigative strategy that analyses evidence from a specific case focusing on certain behavioral and personality traits to derive characteristics of the probable offender which is consisted of four steps: equivocal forensic analysis, victimology, crime scene characteristics, and offender characteristics. Victimology focuses on the reasons for being targeted, offender motivations and their relation with victim, and the traits of victims (e.g., physical characteristics, marital status, personal lifestyle). Crime scene characteristics explore motives and behavioral decisions of the offender and giving more evidence. Offender characteristics focus on the behavioral and personality characteristics of the offender to make a profile and equivocal forensic analysis reviews the case evidence scientifically, thoroughly and objectively to develop theories that are justified by actual facts (Turvey, 2011; Casey, 2011; Karmen, 2012). Recently, Rogers (2015) proposed a model which incorporates BEA into the process of digital forensics investigation which included six phases such as Case classification, context analysis, data collection, statistical analysis, timeline analysis/visualization, and decision/opinion.

Mutawa, Bryce, Franqueira, and Marrington (2015) explored the use of BEA for the investigation of cases of the possession and dissemination of Sexually Exploitative Imagery of Children (SEIC) and found that integrating BEA in digital investigations can greatly assist the investigator in assessing the reliability of digital evidence and the strength of associated conclusions. This can produce a more detailed reconstruction of evidence that can inform sentencing and prosecution in court. It can also assist in mapping and understanding offending behavior and the dynamics of offences. In another study on the utility of BEA for analyzing cyberstalking cases in terms of understanding the behavioral and motivational dimensions of offending, and the way in which digital evidence can be interpreted, the authors found that BEA helps to focus an investigation, enables better understanding and interpretation of victim and offender behavior, and assists in inferring traits of the offender from available digital evidence. These benefits can help investigators to build a stronger case, reduce time wasted to mistakes, and to exclude suspects wrongly accused in cyberstalking cases (Mutawa, Bryce, Franqueira, & Marrington, 2016). More studies are required to understand the use of BEA in digital investigation.

Criminal profiling and use of BEA are different methods aid in the criminal investigation and many methods are required for the effective investigation on cyber stalking as not much scientific information is available on cyberstalking. Profiling can help deal with extensive suspect pools and abundance of digital traces to investigate, leading to a successful case conclusion in less time or where otherwise none would be possible. However, the extent to which it can be applied to cybercrime altogether is not clear. There have been thorough attempts to profile hackers and other cybercriminals, suggesting that this should also be possible for cyber stalkers. There are studies that investigate application of existing profiling techniques and criminal typologies to cyberstalking. Most of these attempts have little to offer to real-life forensic investigations, and only have an academic significance. They cover cyber stalker profiling very broadly, only offering approximate typologies or templates and little detail. There is also little to no consideration to technical aspects of the crime. A possible reason for that is problematic access to detailed cases and hence the use of inductive methods by researchers, which, as a statistics-based method, offers little detail to the profile. Another problem is the lack of consideration for digital forensic investigation models and what profiling can offer to a real investigation, carried out according to such a methodology (Silde, 2013).

PREVENTION

The prevention of cyberstalking needs to be done with public education, and law and enforcement. Educating the public about cyberstalking and promoting multi—agency awareness campaigns would reduce the risk of being victim (Stambaugh, Beaupre, Icove, Baker, Cassaday, & Williams, 2000; Baum, Catalano, Rand, & Rose, 2009). Educating about the risk of adding strangers as friends, engaging in deviant activities (e.g., surfing sites depicting pornographic images), and associating online with deviant peers, educating on internet security measures and use these techniques to help control access to personal information on sites such as Facebook and Myspace are helpful in reducing the chance of victimization. Adults monitoring children and youth's internet use and making guidelines for them are also useful (Reyns, Henson, & Fisher, 2011; Henson, Reyns, & Fisher, 2011; Marcum, Ricketts, & Higgins, 2010). Several studies of Internet use by adolescents have found that increasing numbers of young people are experiencing the following types of victimization while using computer-mediated communication (CMC) methods: unwanted exposure to sexual material, sexual solicitation, and unwanted nonsexual harassment (Mitchell, Finkelhor, & Wolak, 2003; 2007; O'Connell, Barrow, & Sange, 2002). Many students recommended appropriate prevention, education, and intervention strategies, mainly offline programs at the college level to battle cyberstalking (White & Carmody, 2014). Tokunaga and Aune (2015) reported that victims used seven general management tactics of which ignore/avoidance, active technological disassociation, and help seeking were the most common and using technology to move away from pursuers was reported as the most effective tactic for managing the unwanted relational pursuit. It is also suggested that victims' management responses were associated with the type of behaviors experienced.

It can be seen that addressing cyberstalking involves a variety of different approaches, including personal prevention strategies, legislative interventions, and technological solutions to current technological flaws. However, the first step in effectively responding to cyberstalking in particular and Internet-based crime in general, is to ensure that the understanding of the Internet is derived from a realistic appreciation of the nature of the new technologies themselves, rather than being rooted in a pre-Internet conception of information exchange mechanisms. Whilst it can be argued that some cybercrimes are not different from real world crimes in as much as they reflect the same range of offensive and dangerous behaviors, it also needs to be acknowledged that the Internet can magnify, distort, and ignore the attributes of the real world in ways we urgently need to address. Cyberstalking provides an illuminating example of cybercrime. The extent to which cyberstalking can be regulated and responded to by the criminal justice system depends in many respects upon the extent to which it emulates traditional stalking behaviors in the physical world. The new technologies are so different from the old that the old ways may no longer hold good, and we may need to reassess our thinking about the nature of the possible intervention strategies. In sum, while some of the traditional strategies will remain applicable in addressing cyberstalking, new and innovative legislative, technical, and investigative counter measures will almost certainly be necessary (Thapa & Kumar, 2011).

Bocij (2004) suggested few recommendations to prevent cyberstalking such as controlling information and communicative technology. Controlling information means controlling their personal information to ensure that it does not become accessible to others. The more active an individual is in the online realm, the more information is likely to be available to others and by controlling access to personal information, the danger posed by cyber stalkers is reduced. Communicative technology indicates that individuals should be thoroughly familiarized themselves with the particular site and its security measures before joining it which help them to understand the potential dangers implement security measures to protect their online security. He also gave three rules to online behavior such as one should behave appropriately when interacting in communicative technology, avoid any arguments and personal attacks within cyber space and personal information should not be disclosed to online platforms.

It is also important to educate the victims about cyberstalking, and encourage seeking legal help and also mental health services to reduce the distress associated with stalking. The involvement and law and enforcement and ensuring punishment for cybercrimes including cyber stalking would be beneficial.

The laws should be updated with new developments in technology and crimes related to it. It is also important to protect oneself from cyber harassment and stalking and many suggestions available for the same. Hitchcock (2000) listed suggestions regarding staying safe online which are as follows:

1. Use your primary e-mail account only for messages to and from people you know and trust.
2. Get a free e-mail account from someplace like Hotmail, Juno, or Excite, and so forth, and use that for all of your other online activities.
3. When you select an e-mail username or chat nickname, create something gender-neutral and like nothing you have elsewhere or have had before. Try not to use your name.
4. Do not fill out profiles for your e-mail account, chat rooms, IM (instant messaging), and so forth.
5. Do set your options in chat or IM to block all users except for those on your buddy list.
6. Do learn how to use filtering to keep unwanted e-mail messages from coming to your e-mailbox.
7. If you are being harassed online, try not to fight back. This is what the harasser wants—a reaction from you. If you do and the harassment escalates, do the following:
    a. Contact the harasser and politely ask them to leave you alone.
    b. Contact their ISP and forward the harassing messages.
    c. If harassment escalates, contact your local police.
    d. If they cannot help, try the State Police, District Attorney's office and/or State Attorney General.
    e. Contact a victims group, such as WHOA, SafetyED or CyberAngels.

GENERAL GUIDELINES FOR ONLINE INTERACTION SAFETY

Prevention

- Online identity. The information available on the net that allows someone to build a picture of them so consider using a gender neutral nickname may be safer than using a real name and makes it harder for potential cyber stalkers to access potential victims. Using pseudonyms in adult chat rooms and using gender-neutral names in other forms may be helpful.
- Being wary about what information you provide online, whether it is on a FaceBook or MySpace profile, in a blog, on a bulletin board, in the course of chat or in response to an online marketer's offer of an amazing deal. Once posted, forever online. Be attentive when making online posts by assuming that everything posted will be permanently recorded in cyber space. Even if an account is deleted, anyone on the Internet can easily print and save the posts, such as photos, contact information or status updates made.
- Personal information should remain personal. The more information posted online, the more at risk an individual may become to cyber stalking. It is important to be cautious about including personal mobile phone numbers in email footers.
- Know and manage online friends. Often communicative platforms are used to gain large numbers of friends – known and unknown to the user and there are tools on these communicative platforms which allow for the management of profiles. For instance, an Internet user can share certain information with certain friends or have multiple online pages that vary in content and magnitude. Adding strangers to social media risk for stalking.

- Use strong passwords. Passwords which are long, complex and alphanumeric are advisable as they are more difficult to figure out. It is always better to have different password for each online account occupied. Passwords should also be changed regularly, also make sure of not using a pet's name as a password and not sharing passwords with friends or colleagues.
- Use discretion when selecting profile pictures. Assume that people will use the information and pictures gained from profiles destructively. For instance, an already provocative picture could be further altered to humiliate and degrade the victim.
- Apply caution when clicking on links. It is suggested that Internet users be very careful when clicking on links as they may contain viruses or malware.
- Protection of laptops, personal computers - including use of passwords, caution in downloading potential spyware and attention to keeping virus protection up to date.
- Consider creating an additional e-mail account. The creation of an additional email account may be beneficial, in that all the online activity and interaction in the communicative technology can be linked to this delegated account as opposed to a personal one.
- Do not allow any site to scan an e-mail address book. Often, on joining a social network, a request is sent out to enter the individual's e-mail address and password in order to find out if there are any contacts that are also active on the same social network. This process allows for the social network to send an email to everyone ever e-mailed, informing them of the individual's participation in that specific social network.
- While making e-mail id, don't use full name and living place instead use a first name or surname as the user name identity.
- Be cautious of using of e-mail signature as it may expose full name, position and contact details so it is to be included when necessary and to known recipients and remove the contact details of the e-mail signature when sending e-mails to unknown recipients.
- Use blind carbon copy (BCC) when sending an e-mail to multiple recipients so that each recipient only sees his or her e-mail address.
- Regularly delete personal messages or encrypt old as it may prevent stalker to gain more information regarding the victim.
- As youngsters spend more time on online and often feel a sense of belonging to online communities which may put them on high risk for stalking, hence education and awareness about cyber stalking are must for them.
- Younger Internet users are encouraged to work securely from wireless networks and cautioned to choose networks that have a network security key and to connect to a standard or wired network that offers the best protection.
- Warn young users against becoming victim to cyber stalkers with intimate and romantic motives and are cautioned to avoid flirtation with unknown online friends. The participation in 'harmless' flirtation may give a potential cyber stalker the wrong indication of interest.
- Victims who are under the age of eighteen should tell their parents or another adult they trust about any harassments or threats.
- Experts suggest that in cases where the offender is known, victims should send the stalker a clear written warning. Specifically, victims should communicate that the contact is unwanted, and ask the perpetrator to cease sending communications of any kind. Victims should do this only once. Then, no matter the response, victims under no circumstances ever communicate with the stalker again.

- Victims should save copies of this communication in both electronic and hard copy for if the harassment continues; the victim may wish to file a complaint with the stalker's Internet service provider, as well as with their own service provider.
- Many Internet service provides offer tools that filter or block communications from specific individuals.
- As soon as individuals suspect they are victims on online harassment or cyber stalking, they should start collecting all evidence and document all contact made by the stalker. Save all email, postings or other communications in both electronic and hard-copy form. If possible, save all of the header information from e-mail and newsgroup postings. Record the dates and times of any contact with the stalker.
- Victims may also want to start a log of each communication explaining the situation in more detail. Victims may want to document how the harassment is affecting their lives and what steps they have taken to stop the harassment.
- Victims may want to file a report with local law enforcement or contact their local prosecutor's office to see what charges, if any, can be pursued. Victims should save copies of police reports and record all contact with low enforcement officials and the prosecutor's office.
- Victims who are being continually harassed may want to consider changing their e-mail address, Internet service provider, a home phone number, and should examine the possibility of using encryption software or privacy protection programs.
- Under no circumstances should victims agree to meet with the perpetrator face to face to work it out, or talk. No contact should ever be made with the stalker. Meeting a stalker in person can be very dangerous.
- Prevention of cyber stalking for business users should focus on two key roles: protecting the public from becoming victims of cyber stalking by employees through business resources and protecting the business and its staff from becoming victims of cyber stalking.
- Business owners can control their resources by means of an Acceptable Use Policy (AUP). An AUP clearly sets out how a company's Information Communication Technology (ICT) resources can be used as well as any prohibited behaviours and practices. The AUP should also list any penalties for the misuse of business facilities.
- Business owners can implement regular software audits. This involves the regular checks of computer systems to make sure that no pornography or private software is stored.
- Business owners can place controls on the use of company facilities for e-mails and web browsing in order to monitor the use of the Internet.
- It is necessary to take proper precautions when marketing a business online and to be done in secure and safe ways such as using a specialized e-mail address to advertise the business, avoid giving out any personal contact details, avoid publicizing personal and private information and avoid unhealthy rivalry and competition, including bad mouthing and slandering other business competitors.

(Bocij, 2004; Communication Technologies, nd; Miller & Morris, 2012; Online Privacy…nd; Small & Vorgan, 2008; Social Networking…,nd; Sissing, 2013; Thape & Kumar, 2011).

Intervention

Bocij (2004) warns that an offensive e-mail or online argument does not constitute a valid case of cyber stalking. So the first step in dealing with cyber stalking is establishing whether or not cyber stalking is actually taking place Understanding the concept of cyberstalking and legal definition of cyber stalking in concerned countries would be useful to decide upon the interventions. The decision whether or not to contact the cyber stalker is a difficult one and needs to be carefully considered. The decision to ignore the cyber stalker may cause him to lose interest or the cyber stalker may decide to retaliate and increase the cyber stalking behaviour. Similarly, the same results can be produced if the cyber stalker is contacted, confronted and asked to stop the behaviour. This plea to stop the cyber stalking may come across as weakness which further fuels the cyber stalker's destructive behaviour. In some situations it may be necessary for the victim to contact the cyber stalker to ask him to stop the cyber stalking behaviour. If an individual decides to do this, research suggests that this request should only be made once and subsequently all contact with the cyber stalker should seize. If the victim continues to entertain the cyber stalker, this behaviour is not only counterproductive but also dangerous in terms of escalation of the cyber stalking behavior (Bocij, 2004; Sissing, 2013).

Once it is understood that cyberstalking is happening, it is important to gather as much evidence as possible. It is suggested that all the evidence be saved on an external device such as an external hard drive or data disk and all the cyber-stalking-related communication should be saved as the cyber stalker's ISP or even identity may be traced. The victims may also make use of "screen grabber" applications to record and save cyber stalking messages. Make use of the security options available within social networks, e-mail facilities or cell phones to block the cyber stalkers. Also, increase cyber security measures on any online forums. After increasing online security measures, efforts should be made to search for the victim's name on the Internet via major search engines such as Google or Yahoo with full name in order to check how much personal information is available to the public and consider deleting this information. It is important for the victim to find a supportive personal safety network of friends, family, and resources and always let this trusted network know of their whereabouts. Security measures at home, in a vehicle and at work, cyber safety measures, memorizing emergency numbers and keep them on speed dial, keep their cell phone charged, not accepting private calls and blocking the cyber stalker's number are a must. Victims should consider notifying his or her Internet service and they may take action depending on their internal policies. In addition to this, victims should make sure that the cyber stalker has no opportunity to download any programs that aid in monitoring their online activity. Victims can also purchase software to block, squelch, or ignore unwanted electronic communication and it would be advisable to contact one's Internet Service Provider since most ISPs have established policies in the online agreement prohibiting such abuse of services The ISP can immediately terminate the offender's service for violating this policy without fear of legal recourse by the offender However, the reality of the situation is that most ISPs have concentrated more on helping its customers avoid spam, unwanted pop-ups, and virus protection rather than protecting against online harassment Legal actions against perpetrator can be considered. IT specialists should seek to develop new and innovative ways to increase the traceability of online predators and make the necessary efforts to launch awareness programmes aimed at the various criminal justice role players as well as local communities to better equip them with knowledge and knowhow regarding IT vigilance (Bocij, 2004; Donovan & Bernier, 2009; Sissing, 2013; Hutton & Haantz, 2003).

Al-Khateeb, Epiphaniou, Zhraa, Barnes, and Short (2017) suggested that most offences were communicated through private channels such as emails and/or mobile texts/calls. A significant number of victims did not report this to their service provider because they did not know they could. While Police were recognized as the first-point-of-contact in such cases, 41.6% of our sample did not contact the Police due to reasons such as fear of escalation, guilt/sympathy and self-blaming. Experiences from those who have reported offences to service providers demonstrate that no or very little support was offered. Overall, the majority of participants shared the view that third-party intervention is required on their behalf in order to mitigate risks associated with cyberstalking. An independent specialist anti-stalking organization was a popular choice to act on their behalf followed by the Police and network providers. Incidents are taking place on channels owned and controlled by large, cross-border international companies providing mobile services, webmail and social networking. The lack of support offered to victims in many cases of cyberstalking can be identified as Corporate Social Irresponsibility (CSI). Awareness should be raised as regarding service providers' liability and social responsibility towards adopting better strategies.

Law enforcement officials have suggested that to prevent being a victim, people choose screen names that are gender and age ambiguous and if possible, avoid posting personal information in web profiles. Most importantly, be extremely cautious when meeting with an individual that was met online. It suggests that if a meeting is to take place that it is done in a public location and it is strongly advisable to bring a friend along. To aid in the investigation, cyber stalking victims should be advised to inform the perpetrator that the communication is unwanted and should cease immediately. It is also advisable to save all unaltered and unedited communication from the perpetrator that could be used as prosecutorial evidence (Petrocelli, 2005 in Pittaro, 2007).

Online support groups such as Working to Halt Online Abuse (WHOA) (http://www.haltabuse.org), CyberAngels (http://www.cyberangels.com), WiredPatrol (http://www.wiredpatrol.org), Web Police (http://www.intergov.org), and Network for Surviving Stalking (http://www.nss.org.uk), are informative and give a platform to express their anger, sadness and personal experiences to cyberstalking. Victims would be benefited from joining such groups. Unfortunately, there are several obstacles to treating this disorder. First, finding a qualified mental health professional that acknowledges this condition and specializes in this type of treatment may be a cumbersome task to accomplish (King, 1996). The literature on cyber stalking is scarce at best and the studies that have been done have been based on comparatively small sample populations. From what has been researched, it is doubtful that mental health professionals even have a general understanding of cyber stalking behaviors and are less likely to know how to approach and treat this particular offender. The Internet is one of the most resourceful advancements in technology to have ever been created by humankind, but it also has a malevolent side to it that cannot be discounted. Clinicians have only recently begun to understand the dangers associated with the Internet (Pittaro, 2007).

CONCLUSION

There is not much agreement on the definition of cyberstalking as it appeared recently due to technological advancement. Many of the researches were conducted among university students and the prevalence of cyberstalking among general population and special groups are not much known but researches repeatedly confirm it as growing issue but less information on nature and extent of cyber stalking happening.

There is not much agreement or lack of universally accepted definitions leads to varied prevalence rates of cyberstalking. The information on vulnerable groups and individuals to cyberstalking is still not enough as same as our understanding of offenders. There is concern regarding the use of profiling and typologies in actual criminal investigation. Technical advancements and thorough knowledge on technical details among researchers from different backgrounds poses a big problem to its complete understanding and prevention. All these are preventing to make a much authentic preventive and intervention guidelines. Future researchers need to focus on all these aspects.

Though many prevention techniques are advised, it suffers from limitations too. For example, the idea that changing one's username "prevents" cyberstalking seems misleading—it does not get at the root of the problem, and may in fact buy into cyberstalker mentality (Baer, 2010). According to Cavelty (2014), current approaches to cyber-security are not working and the reason for this is a multi-dimensional and multi-faceted security dilemma. The threat arising from cyberspace to (national) security is a possible disruption to a specific way of life, one building on information technologies and critical functions of infrastructures, with relatively little consideration for humans directly. This non-focus on people makes it easier for state actors to militarize cyber-security and (re-)assert their power in cyberspace, thereby overriding the different security needs of human beings in that space. Paradoxically, the use of cyberspace as a tool for national security, both in the dimension of war fighting and the dimension of mass-surveillance, has detrimental effects on the level of cyber-security globally. A solution out of this dilemma is a cyber-security policy that is decidedly anti-vulnerability and at the same time based on strong considerations for privacy and data protection. Such a security would have to be informed by an ethics of the info sphere that is based on the dignity of information related to human beings.

The concept of cyber resilience has emerged in recent years in response to the recognition that cyber security is more than just risk management. Cyber resilience is the goal of organizations, institutions and governments across the world and yet the emerging literature is somewhat fragmented due to the lack of a common approach to the subject. This limits the possibility of effective collaboration across public, private and governmental actors in their efforts to build and maintain cyber resilience. In response to this limitation, and to calls for a more strategically focused approach, this paper offers a knowledge-based view of cyber security management that explains how an organization can build, assess, and maintain cyber resilience (Ferdinand, 2015).

As mentioned by Maple, Short, and Brown (2011), one clear message from the data collected is that many of the victims of cyber harassment are frustrated with the lack of help and support they feel is available. The key sources they want to be able to act are the Police and Service Providers, both in terms of providing actions that can stop on going harassment and also in providing support to those affected in dealing with its effects. This adds to the growing debate of whether legislative change is required to allow the police and encourage service providers to provide the help people need in cases of cyber harassment and if so, exactly what changes those should be.

Current understanding on cyber staking indicates that we still need to go a long way to understand its prevalence, causes, risks, prevention and intervention effectiveness.

REFERENCES

Al-Khateeb, H. M., Epiphaniou, G., Alhaboby, Z. A., Barnes, J., & Short, E. (2017). Cyberstalking: Investigating formal intervention and the role of Corporate Social Responsibility. *Telematics and Informatics*, *34*(4), 339–349. doi:10.1016/j.tele.2016.08.016

Al Mutawa, N., Bryce, J., & Marrington, A.(2015). *Behavioural evidence analysis applied to digital forensics: an empirical analysis of child pornography cases using P2P networks*. Academic Press. 10.1109/ARES.2015.49

Al Mutawa, N., Bryce, J., Franqueira, V. N. L., & Marrington, A. (2016). Forensic investigation of cyberstalking cases using Behavioural Evidence Analysis. *Digital Investigation*, *16*, S96–S103. doi:10.1016/j.diin.2016.01.012

Alexy, E. M., Burgess, A. W., Baker, T., & Smoyak, S. A. (2005). Perceptions of cyberstalking among college students. *Brief Treatment and Crisis Intervention*, *5*(3), 279–289. doi:10.1093/brief-treatment/mhi020

Amita, V. (2016). *Cyber Crimes & Law*. Central Law Publication. Retrieved from http://www.legalindia.com/cyber-stalking-the-impact-of-its-legislative-provisions-in-india/

Baer, M. (2010). Cyberstalking and the Internet Landscape We Have Created. *Virginia Journal of Law & Technology.*, *15*(154), 153–174.

Barkan, S. (2006). *Criminology: A sociological understanding* (3rd ed.). Upper Saddle River, NJ: Prentice Hall.

Basile, K. C., Swahn, M., Chen, J., & Saltzman, L. (2006). Stalking in the United States: Recent national prevalence estimates. *American Journal of Preventive Medicine*, *31*(2), 172–175. doi:10.1016/j.amepre.2006.03.028 PMID:16829335

Baum, K., Catalano, S., Rand, M., & Rose, K. (2009). *Stalking victimization in the United States*. Washington, DC: U.S. Department of Justice.

Baum, K., Catalano, S., Rand, M., & Rose, K. (2009). *Stalking victimization in the United States*. Washington, DC: U.S. Department of Justice.

Björklund, K., Häkkänen-Nyholm, H., Sheridan, L., & Roberts, K. (2010). The Prevalence of Stalking Among Finnish University Students. *Journal of Interpersonal Violence*, *25*(4), 684–698. doi:10.1177/0886260509334405 PMID:20065315

Black, M. C., Basile, K. C., Breiding, M. J., Smith, S. G., Walters, M. L., Merrick, M. T., ... Stevens, M. R. (2011). *National Intimate Partner and Sexual Violence Survey, 2010 summary report*. Atlanta, GA: National Center for Injury Prevention and Control of the Centers for Disease Control and Prevention.

Bocij, P. (2003). Victims of cyberstalking: An exploratory study of harassment perpetrated via the Internet. *First Monday*, *8*(10). doi:10.5210/fm.v8i10.1086

Bocij, P. (2004). *Cyberstalking: Harassment in the Internet age and how to protect your family*. Westport, CT: Praeger Publishers.

Bocij, P., & McFarlane, L. (2002). Online harassment: Towards a definition of cyberstalking. *Prison Service Journal*, *139*, 31–38.

Bocij, P., & McFarlane, L. (2003). The Internet: A Discussion of Some New and Emerging Threats to Young People. *The Police Journal*, *76*(1), 3–13. doi:10.1177/0032258X0307600102

Bocij, P., & McFarlane, L. (2003). Cyberstalking: The Technology of Hate.*The Police Journal: Theory. Practice and Principles*, *76*(3), 204–221. doi:10.1350/pojo.76.3.204.19442

Bromby, M. (2006). Security against Crime: Technologies for Detecting and Preventing Crime. *International Review of Law Computers & Technology*, *20*(1-2), 1–5. doi:10.1080/13600860600818235

Brown, C. S. D. (2015). Cyber-Attacks, Retaliation and Risk: Legal and Technical Implications for Nation-States and Private Entities. In J. L. Richet (Ed.), *Cybersecurity Policies and Strategies for Cyberwarfare Prevention* (pp. 166–203). Hershey, PA: IGI Global. doi:10.4018/978-1-4666-8456-0.ch008

Brownstein, A. (2000). In the campus shadows, women are stalkers as well as the stalked. *The Chronicle of Higher Education*, *47*(15), 4042.

Burgess, A. W., & Baker, T. (2002). Cyberstalking. In J. Boon & L. Sheridan (Eds.), *Stalking and psychosexual obsession: Psychological perspectives for prevention, policing and treatment*. Chichester, UK: Wiley. doi:10.1002/9780470713037.ch12

Burmester, M., Henry, P., & Kermes, L. S. (2005). Tracking Cyberstalkers: A Cryptographic Approach. ACM SIGCAS Computers and Society, 35(3).

Cameron, S., & Brown, D. (2015). Investigating and Prosecuting Cyber Crime: Forensic Dependencies and Barriers to Justice. *International Journal of Cyber Criminology*, *9*(1), 55–119.

Casey, E. (2011). Investigative reconstruction with digital evidence. In E. Casey & B. E. Turvey (Eds.), *Digital evidence and computer crime: forensic science, computers and the internet* (pp. 255–273). Academic Press.

Cavelty, D. M. (2014). Breaking the cyber-security dilemma: Aligning security needs and removing vulnerabilities. *Science and Engineering Ethics*, *20*(3), 701–715. doi:10.100711948-014-9551-y PMID:24781874

Comparcini, D., Simonetti, V., Lupo, R., Galli, F., Bocij, P., & Cicolini, G. (2016). Cyberstalking among Italian nurses: a large multicentric study. *Prof Inferm*, *69*(3), 150-158. doi: 10.7429 / pi.2016.693150

Cox, L., & Speziale, B. (2009). Survivors of stalking. *Affilia*, *24*(1), 5–18. doi:10.1177/0886109908326815

Curtis, L. F. (2012). *Virtual vs. reality: an examination of the nature of stalking and cyberstalking* (Master Thesis). Retrieved from http://citeseerx.ist.psu.edu/viewdoc/download?doi=10.1.1.467.5711&rep=rep1&type=pdf

Davis, L. (2005). *Victimology in South Africa*. Pretoria: Van Schaik.

De Coster, S., Estes, S., & Mueller, C. (1999). Routine activities and sexual harassment in the workplace. *Work and Occupations*, *26*(1), 21–49. doi:10.1177/0730888499026001003

Dean, K. (2000). The Epidemic of Cyberstalking. *Wired News*. Retrieved from http://www.wired.com/news/politics/0,1283,35728,00.html

Deirmenjian, J. (1999). Stalking in Cyberspace. *The Journal of the American Academy of Psychiatry and the Law*, *27*(3), 407–413. PMID:10509940

Donovan, F., & Bernier, K. (2009). *Cyber crime fighters: Tales from the trenches*. Indianapolis, IN: Que Publishing.

Douglas, J. E., Ressler, R. K., Burgess, A. W., & Hartman, C. R. (1986). Criminal Profiling from Crime Scene Analysis. *Behavioral Sciences & the Law*, *4*(4), 401–421. doi:10.1002/bsl.2370040405

Downing, R. W. (2005). Shoring Up the Weakest Link: What Lawmakers Around the World Need to Consider in Developing Comprehensive Laws to Combat Cybercrime. *Columbia Journal of Transnational Law*, *43*, 741–762.

Drahokoupilová, J. (2007). *Cyberstalking*. Available at: http://heinonline.org/HOL/Page?handle=hein.journals/mujlt1&div=36&g_sent=1&collection=journals

Dreßing, H., Bailer, J., Anders, A., Wagner, H., & Gallas, C. (2014). Cyberstalking in a large sample of social network users: Prevalence, characteristics, and impact upon victims. *Cyberpsychology, Behavior, and Social Networking*, *17*(2), 61–67. doi:10.1089/cyber.2012.0231 PMID:24106979

Duntley, J. D., & Buss, D. M. (2012). The evolution of stalking. *Sex Roles*, *66*(5-6), 311–327. doi:10.100711199-010-9832-0

Ellison, L. (1999). *Cyberspace 1999: Criminal, criminal justice and the internet*. Fourteenth BI LETA Conference, York, UK. Retrieved from http://www.bileta.ac.uk/99papers/ellison.htm

Ellison, L., & Akdeniz, Y. (1998). *Cyber-Stalking: the Regulation of Harassment on the Internet. In Criminal Law Review* (pp. 29–48). Crime, Criminal Justice and the Internet.

Epiphaniou, G., Alhaboby, Z. A., Barnes, J., & Short, E. (2017). Cyberstalking: Investigating formal intervention and the role of Corporate Social Responsibility. *Telematics and Informatics*, *34*(4), 339–349. doi:10.1016/j.tele.2016.08.016

Every-Palmer, S., Barry-Walsh, J., & Pathé, M. (2015). Harassment, stalking, threats and attacks targeting New Zealand politicians: A mental health issue. *The Australian and New Zealand Journal of Psychiatry*, *49*(7), 634–641. doi:10.1177/0004867415583700 PMID:25954019

Ferdinand, J. (2015). Building organisational cyber resilience: A strategic knowledge-based view of cyber securitymanagement. *Journal of Business Continuity & Emergency Planning*, *9*(2), 185–195. PMID:26642176

Fisher, B. S., Cullen, F. T., & Turner, M. G. (2000). *The sexual victimization of college women*. Washington, DC: National Institute of Justice, Bureau of Justice Statistics. doi:10.1037/e377652004-001

Goode, M. (1995). Stalking: Crime of the nineties? *Criminal Law Journal*, *19*, 21–31.

Harmon, R. B., Rosner, R., & Owens, H. (1995). Obsessional harassment and erotomania in a criminal court population. *Journal of Forensic Sciences*, *40*(2), 188–196. doi:10.1520/JFS15339J PMID:7602275

Harrison, C. (2006). Cyberspace and child abuse images. *Affilia*, *21*(4), 365–379.

Henson, B., Reyns, B. W., & Fisher, B. S. (2011). Security in the 21st century. *Criminal Justice Review*, *36*(3), 253–268.

Henson, B., Reyns, B. W., & Fisher, B. S. (2011). Security in the 21st century. *Criminal Justice Review*, *36*(3), 253–268. doi:10.1177/0734016811399421

Hill, A.L., Rand, D.G., Nowak, M.A., & Christakis, N.A. (2010). Emotions as infectious diseases in a large social network: the SISa model. *Proceeding of Biological Science*, *277*(1701), 3827–3835. doi: 10.1098/rspb.2010.1217

Hitchcock, J. A. (2000). Cyberstalking. *Link-Up*, *17*(4). Retrieved from http://www.infotoday.com/lu/ju100/hitchcock.htm

Hutton, S., & Haantz, S. (2003). *Cyber stalking*. Retrieved from http://www.nw3c.org

Ingram, S. (1998). If the Profile Fits: Admitting Criminal Psychological Profiles into Evidence in Criminal Trials. *Journal of Urban and Contemporary Law*, *54*, 239–266.

Jenson, B. (1996). *Cyberstalking: Crime, enforcement and personal responsibility of the on-line world.* S.G.R. MacMillan. Retrieved from http://www.sgrm.com/art-8.htm

Kamphuis, J. H., & Emmelkamp, P. M. G. (2000). Stalking—A contemporary challenge for forensic and clinical psychiatry. *The British Journal of Psychiatry*, *176*(03), 206–209. doi:10.1192/bjp.176.3.206 PMID:10755065

Karmen, A. (2012). *Crime victims: an introduction to victimology.* Cengage Learning.

Kennedy, M. A., & Taylor, M. A. (2010). Online Harassment and Victimization of College Students. *Justice Policy Journal*, *7*, 1–21.

Kienlen, K. K. (1998). Developmental and social antecedents of stalking. In J. R. Meloy (Ed.), *The psychology of stalking: Clinical and forensic perspectives* (pp. 52–65). San Diego, CA: Elsevier Science. doi:10.1016/B978-012490560-3/50022-0

Kienlen, K. K., Birmingham, D. L., Solberg, K. B., & O'Regan, J. T. (1997). A comparative study of psychotic and nonpsychotic stalking. *The Journal of the American Academy of Psychiatry and the Law*, *25*(3), 317–334. PMID:9323658

King, S. A. (1996). *Is the Internet Addictive, or Are Addicts Using the Internet?* Retrieved February 18, 2006, from Web site: http://webpages.charter.net/stormking/iad.html

Kocsis, R. N. (2006). *What Is Criminal Profiling?* Springer. doi:10.1007/978-1- 59745-109-3_1

Logan, T., & Walker, R. (2009). Partner stalking. *Trauma, Violence & Abuse*, *10*(3), 247–270. doi:10.1177/1524838009334461 PMID:19433407

Lyndon, A., Bonds-Raacke, J., & Cratty, A. D. (2011). College students' Facebook stalking of ex-partners. *Cyberpsychology, Behavior, and Social Networking*, *14*(12), 711–716. doi:10.1089/cyber.2010.0588 PMID:21732735

Maple, C., Short, E., & Brown, A. (2011). *Cyberstalking in the United Kingdom An Analysis of the ECHO Pilot Survey*. Retrieved from http://paladinservice.co.uk/wp-content/uploads/2013/12/ECHO_Pilot_Final-Cyberstalking-in-the-UK-University-of-Bedfordshire.pdf

Marcum, C. D., Ricketts, M. L., & Higgins, G. E. (2010). Assessing sex experiences of online victimization: An examination of adolescent online behaviors utilizing Routine Activity Theory. *Criminal Justice Review*, *35*(4), 412–437. doi:10.1177/0734016809360331

McCann, J. T. (2000). A descriptive study of child and adolescent obsessional followers. *Journal of Forensic Sciences*, *45*(1), 195–199. doi:10.1520/JFS14660J PMID:10641939

McEwan, T. E., Mullen, P. E., & MacKenzie, R. (2009). A study of the predictors of persistence in stalking situations. *Law and Human Behavior*, *33*(2), 149–158. doi:10.100710979-008-9141-0 PMID:18626757

McFarlane, L., & Bocij, P. (2003). An exploration of predatory behavior in cyberspace: Towards a typology of cyberstalkers. *First Monday*, *8*(9), 1–12. doi:10.5210/fm.v8i9.1076

Meloy, J. R. (1996). Stalking (obsessional following): A review of some preliminary studies. *Aggression and Violent Behavior*, *1*(2), 147–162. doi:10.1016/1359-1789(95)00013-5

Meloy, J. R. (1998). The Psychology of stalking. In J. R. Meloy (Ed.), *The psychology of stalking: Clinical and forensic perspectives* (pp. 2–21). San Diego, CA: Elsevier Science. doi:10.1016/B978-012490560-3/50020-7

Meloy, J. R., & Gothard, S. (1995). Demographic and clinical comparison of obsessional followers and offenders with mental disorders. *The American Journal of Psychiatry*, *152*(2), 25826. PMID:7840361

Ménard, K. S., & Pincus, A. L. (2012). Predicting overt and cyber stalking perpetration by male and female college students. *Journal of Interpersonal Violence*, *27*(11), 2183–2207. doi:10.1177/0886260511432144 PMID:22203630

Ménard, K. S., & Pincus, A. L. (2012). Predicting overt and cyber stalking perpetration by male and female college students. *Journal of Interpersonal Violence*, *27*(11), 2183–2207. doi:10.1177/0886260511432144 PMID:22203630

Miller, B. N., & Morris, R. G. 2012. Cyber-related violence. In Violent offenders: Theory, research, policy and practice. London: Jones & Bartlett Learning.

Miller, G. (1999). Gore to release cyberstalking report, call for tougher laws. *Latimes.com*. Retrieved from http://www. latimes.com/news/ploitics/elect2000/pres/gore

Mitchell, K., Becker-Blease, K., & Finkelhor, D. (2005). Inventory of problematic Internet experiences encountered in clinical practice. *Professional Psychology*, *36*(5), 498–509. doi:10.1037/0735-7028.36.5.498

Mitchell, K., Finkelhor, D., & Wolak, J. (2001). Risk factors for and impact of online sexual solicitation of youth. *Journal of the American Medical Association*, *285*(23), 3011–3014. doi:10.1001/jama.285.23.3011 PMID:11410100

Mitchell, K., Finkelhor, D., & Wolak, J. (2003). The exposure of youth to unwanted sexual material on the Internet: A national survey of risk, impact and prevention. *Youth & Society*, *34*(3), 300–358. doi:10.1177/0044118X02250123

Mitchell, K., Finkelhor, D., & Wolak, J. (2007). Youth Internet users at risk for the more serious online sexual solicitations. *American Journal of Preventive Medicine*, *32*(6), 532–537. doi:10.1016/j.amepre.2007.02.001 PMID:17533070

Morrison, K. (2001). Predicting Violent Behavior in Stalkers: A Preliminary Investigation of Canadian Cases in Criminal Harassment. *Journal of Forensic Sciences*, *46*(6), 1403-1410. 10.1520/JFS15163J

Mullen, P. E., Pathé, M., & Purcell, R. (2000). *Stalkers and their victims*. Cambridge, UK: Cambridge University Press. doi:10.1017/CBO9781139106863

Mullen, P. E., Pathé, M., Purcell, R., & Stuart, G. W. (1999). A study of stalkers. *The American Journal of Psychiatry*, *156*, 1244–1249. PMID:10450267

O'Connell, R., Barrow, C., & Sange, S. (2002). *Young peoples use of chat rooms: Implications for policy strategies and programs of education*. Retrieved November 1, 2005, from http://www.uclan.ac.uk/host/cru/ publications.htm

Ogilvie, E. (2000). *Cyberstalking, trends and ıssues in crime and criminal justice*. Retrieved from http://www.aic. gov.au

Pathé, M. (2002). *Surviving stalking*. London: Cambridge University Press. doi:10.1017/CBO9780511544200

Pathé, M., & Mullen, P. E. (2002). The victim of stalking. In J. Boon & L. Sheridan (Eds.), *Stalking and Psychosexual Obsession: Psychological Perspectives for Prevention, Policing and Treatment* (pp. 1–22). West Sussex, UK: Wiley. doi:10.1002/9780470713037.ch1

Patton, C. L., Nobles, M. R., & Fox, K. A. (2010). Look who's stalking: Obsessive pursuit and attachment theory. *Journal of Criminal Justice*, *38*(3), 282–290. doi:10.1016/j.jcrimjus.2010.02.013

Paullet, K. L., Rota, D. R., & Swan, T. T. (2009). Cyberstalking: An exploratory study of students at a mid-Atlantic university. *Issues in Information Systems*, *2*, 640–649.

Petherick, W. (2001). *Cyberstalking: Obsessional pursuit and the digital criminal*. Retrieved from http://www.crimelibrary.com/criminology/cyberstalking/index.html

Petrocelli, J. (2005). Cyber stalking. *Law and Order*, *53*(12), 56–58.

Prins, H. (2005). Mental disorder and violent crime: A problematic relationship. *Probation Journal*, *52*(4), 333–357. doi:10.1177/0264550505058033

Report on Cyberstalking. (1999, August). *Cyberstalking: A new challenge for law enforcement and ındustry*. A Report from the Attorney General to The Vice President. Retrieved from http://www.usdoj.gov/criminal/ cybercrime/cyberstalking.htm

Reyns, B. W. (2010). A situational crime prevention approach to cyberstalking victimization: Preventive tactics for Internet users and online place managers. *Crime Prevention and Community Safety*, *12*(2), 99–118. doi:10.1057/cpcs.2009.22

Reyns, B. W., Henson, B., & Fisher, B. S. (2011). Being pursued online: Applying cyberlifestyle- routine activities theory to cyberstalking victimization. *Criminal Justice and Behavior*, *38*(11), 1149–1169. doi:10.1177/0093854811421448

Rogers, M.K. (2015). Psychological profiling as an investigative tool for digital forensics. *Digital Forensics Threatscaes and Best Practices*, 45-58. DOI:10.1016/B978-0-12-804526-8.00003-4

Rogers, M. (2003). The role of criminal profiling in the computer forensics process. *Computers & Security*, *22*, 292-298. doi: 10.1016/s0167-4048(03)00405-x

Sheridan, L., & Grant, T. (2007). Is cyberstalking different? *Psychology, Crime & Law*, *13*(6), 627–670. doi:10.1080/10683160701340528

Silde, A. (2013). *Profiling the Cyberstalker* (Master Thesis). Retrieved from file:///C:/Users/HP/Downloads/67-1-209-1-10-20140623%20(5).pdf

Sinwelski, S., & Vinton, L. (2001). Stalking: The constant threat of violence. *Affilia*, *16*(1), 46–65. doi:10.1177/08861090122094136

Sissing, S. K. (2013). *A criminological exploration of cyber stalking in South Africa* (Master Thesis). Retrieved from http://uir.unisa.ac.za/bitstream/handle/10500/13067/dissertation_sissing_sk.pdf?sequence=1

Smith, H. J., Dinev, T., & Xu, H. (2011). Information privacy research: An interdisciplinary review. *Management Information Systems Quarterly*, *35*(4), 989–1015. doi:10.2307/41409970

Spitzberg, B. H. (2002). The tactical topography of stalking victimization and management. *Trauma, Violence & Abuse*, *3*(4), 261–288. doi:10.1177/1524838002237330

Spitzberg, B. H., & Cupach, W. R. (2007). The state of the art of stalking: Taking stock of the emerging literature. *Aggression and Violent Behavior*, *12*(1), 64–86. doi:10.1016/j.avb.2006.05.001

Spitzberg, B. H., & Hoobler, G. (2002). Cyberstalking and the technologies of interpersonal terrorism. *New Media & Society*, *4*(1), 71–92. doi:10.1177/14614440222226271

Spitzner, L. (2002). *Honeypots: Tracking hackers*. Addison Wesley.

Stambaugh, H., Beaupre, D., Icove, D., Baker, R., Cassaday, W., & Williams, W. (2000). *State and local law enforcement needs to combat electronic crime.* U.S. Department of Justice, Office of Justice Programs, National Institute of Justice. Retrieved from U.S. Government website: https://www.ncjrs.gov/pdffiles1/nij/183451.pdf

Stambaugh, H., Beaupre, D., Icove, D., Baker, R., Cassaday, W., & Williams, W. (2001). *Electronic crime needs assessment for state and local law enforcement.* Retrieved September 1, 2005 from http://www.ojp.usdoj.gov/nij/pubs-sum/186276.htm

Stephenson, P. R., & Walter, R. D. (2011). *Toward cyber crime assessment.* Cyberstalking 6th Annual symposium on information assurance (ASIA'11)

Strawhun, J., Adams, N., & Huss, M. T. (2013). The assessment of cyberstalking: An expanded examination including social networking, attachment, jealousy, and anger in relation to violence and abuse. *Violence and Victims, 28*(4), 715–730. doi:10.1891/0886-6708.11-00145 PMID:24047049

Thapa, A., & Kumar, R. (2011). Cyber staking: crime and challenge at the cyberspace. *International Journal of Computing and Business Research, 2*(1).

Tokunaga, R. S., & Aune, K. S. (2015). Cyber-Defense: A Taxonomy of Tactics for Managing Cyberstalking. *Journal of Interpersonal Violence, 32*(10), 1451–1475. doi:10.1177/0886260515589564

Turvey, B. E. (2011). A history of criminal profiling. In B. E. Turvey (Ed.), *Criminal profiling: An introduction to behavioural evidence analysis* (pp. 3–40). Oxford, UK: Elsevier.

U.S. Department of Justice. (2000). *The electronic frontier: The challenge of unlawful conduct involving the use of the Internet.* Report of the President's Working Group on Unlawful Conduct on the Internet. Washington, DC: Author. Retrieved March 20, 2003, from http://www. usdoj.gov/criminal/cybercrime/unlawful.htm

Verma, S. K., & Raman Mittal, R. (2004). *Legal Dimension of Cyberspace.* New Delhi: Indian Law Institute.

Wallace, B. (2000). Stalkers find a new tool—The Internet e-mail is increasingly used to threaten and harass, authorities say. *SFGate News.* Retrieved from http://sfgate.com/cgi-bin/article_cgi?file=/chronicle/archive/2000/07/10/MN39633.DTL

White, W. E., & Carmody, D. (2014). Preventing Online Victimization College Students' Views on Intervention and Prevention. *Journal of Interpersonal Violence.* doi:10.1177/0886260515625501

Working to Halt Online Abuse. (2011). *Online Harassment/Cyberstalking Statistics.* Retrieved from http://www.haltabuse.org/resources/stats/index.shtml

Working to Halt Online Abuse (WHO). (2003). *Online harassment statistics.* Retrieved May 25, 2007 from http://www.haltabuse.org/resources/stats/index. shtml

Wright, J. A., Burgess, A. G., Burgess, A. W., Laszlo, A. T., McCrary, G. O., & Douglas, J. E. (1996). A typology of interpersonal stalking. *Journal of Interpersonal Violence, 11*(4), 487–502. doi:10.1177/088626096011004003

Wykes, M. (2007). Constructing crime: Culture, stalking, celebrity and cyber. *Crime, Media, Culture, 3*(2), 158–174. doi:10.1177/1741659007078541

Zona, M. A., Sharma, K. K., & Lane, A. J. (1993). Comparative study of erotomanic and obsessional subjects in a forensic sample. *Journal of Forensic Sciences, 38*(4), 894–903. PMID:8355005

Chapter 9
Cyberbullying

Michelle F. Wright
Pennsylvania State University, USA

ABSTRACT

Cyberbullying has become a major focus of not only youths, educators, and researchers, but also among the general population, due to high profile cases of cyberbullying victimization involving suicide and the increasing prevalence of these behaviors. The purpose of this chapter is to examine cyberbullying among children and adolescents, referred to as "youths" throughout the chapter. An extension of traditional bullying, cyberbullying is a form of bullying which takes place by means of electronic technologies, such as email, instant messaging, social networking websites, and text messaging through mobile devices. Drawing on research from a variety of disciplines, such as psychology, education, social work, sociology, and computer science, this chapter describes the definition of cyberbullying, the electronic technologies used, the prevalence rates, characteristics and risk factors, negative psychosocial and academic difficulties, theoretical frameworks, recommendations, and future directions.

INTRODUCTION

Millions of youths use electronic technologies, such as mobile phones and the Internet, daily (Lenhart, 2015). These technologies allow youths many opportunities, such as the ability to communicate with just about anyone, quick access to information for leisure and homework purposes, and entertainment (e.g., watching videos). Despite the positives associated with electronic technology use, many youths are at risk for exposure to problematic online situations. Such situations might involve viewing unwanted electronic content through videos, images, and text, which contains gory or sexually graphic content. Problematic online situations also include experiencing identity theft and being targeted by sexual predators. Cyberbullying is another risk associated with youths' electronic technology use.

Defined as an extension of traditional bullying, cyberbullying involves being targeted by negative and unwanted behaviors via electronic technologies, including email, instant messaging, social networking websites, and text messages via mobile phones (Bauman, Underwood, & Card, 2013; Grigg, 2012). The anonymity of the cyber context allows cyberbullies greater flexibility to harm their victims without having to witness the reactions of the victims and/or experience any negative consequences as a result of their

DOI: 10.4018/978-1-5225-4047-2.ch009

actions (Wright, 2014b). Cyberbullies' ability to remain anonymous is made possible by the ability to mask or hide their identity in cyberspace. Because youths can remain anonymous online, anonymity can trigger the online disinhibition effect. The online disinhibition effect is when youths do or say something to others that they typically would never do or say in the offline world (Suler, 2004; Wright, 2014). Another component of electronic technologies is the rapid transmission of communication. Because electronic technologies have such a feature, many cyberbullies can target their victims more quickly. For example, a rumor in the offline world might take several hours to spread around school, while in the online world, this rumor could take a matter of minutes to spread to various classmates. Bullies can often target victims as often as they want as it is difficult to escape bullying in the online world as the behaviors can follow the person almost anywhere there is electronic technology access. Although it is possible to have many bystanders for traditional school bullying, cyberbullying has the potential to reach an audience of millions. These individuals can then perpetuate the cycle of cyberbullying by further sharing cyberbullying content (e.g., videos, pictures) with others.

The aim of this chapter is to review the topic of cyberbullying among youths, who might include children and adolescents from elementary school to high school. The literature reviewed includes studies from various disciplines, such as psychology, education, media studies, communication, social work, sociology, computer science, information technology, and gender studies. These studies might also include cross-sectional, longitudinal, qualitative, quantitative, and mixed-methods research designs. The chapter also draws on various studies across the world to conceptualize cyberbullying as a global health concern. The chapter includes seven sections, including:

1. **Background:** Contains the definition of cyberbullying, the various characteristic behaviors), the various electronic technologies, the prevalence rates of cyberbullying, and the role of anonymity in perpetrating cyberbullying.
2. **Youths' Characteristics and Risk Factors:** Reviews the factors associated with youth's involvement in cyberbullying as perpetrators and/or victims.
3. **Negative Psychosocial and Academic Outcomes:** Explains research findings regarding the psychological, social, behavioral, and academic consequences associated with youths' cyberbullying involvement.
4. **Theoretical Framework:** Provides an overview of the social cognitive theory and the online disinhibition effect, and their application to cyberbullying.
5. **Solutions and Recommendations:** Describes suggestions for prevention and intervention programs aimed at reducing cyberbullying involvement among youths, and public policy recommendations.
6. **Future Research Directions:** Explains various recommendations for future research aimed at understanding youths' involvement in cyberbullying.
7. **Conclusion:** Highlights closing remarks regarding the current nature of the literature on cyberbullying.

BACKGROUND

Smith and colleagues (2013) defined cyberbullying as youths' use of electronic technologies to harass, embarrass, and intimidate others with hostile intent. The "hostile intent" portion of the definition is a requirement for a particular behavior or behaviors to qualify as cyberbullying. Cyberbullying can also include repetition and an imbalance of power between the perpetrator and the victim, similar to the traditional face-to-face bullying definition. In cyberbullying, the bully might target the victim multiple times by sharing a humiliating and embarrassing video or text message to one person or multiple people (Bauman, Underwood, & Card, 2013). It might also include only sending a message to someone once. Another opportunity for repetitiveness might be sending a video or a text message to one person and then that particular person shares the content again with another person or multiple people, who then again share the content with someone else. Repetitiveness of cyberbullying captures the potentially cyclic nature of this form of bullying.

The electronic technology component of the cyberbullying definition separates this form of bullying from traditional face-to-face bullying (Curelaru, Iacob, & Abalasi, 2009). Examples of cyberbullying include sending unkind, mean, and/or nasty text messages, chat program messages, and emails, theft of identity information, pretending to be someone else, making anonymous phone calls, sharing secrets about the victim by posting or sending the secret to someone else, tricking someone to share a secret and then spreading the secret around, spreading nasty and/or untrue rumors using social networking websites, threatening to harm someone in the offline world, or uploading an embarrassing picture or video of a video who does not want to image shared (Bauman, Underwood, & Card, 2013). Many cyberbullying behaviors are similar to those perpetrate or experienced in the offline world, such as experiencing/perpetrating harassment, insults, verbal attacks, teasing, physical threats, social exclusion, gossip, humiliation.

Cyberbullying behaviors can occur through a variety of technologies, such as social networking websites, text messages via mobile phones, chat programs, online gaming, creation of a defamatory website against someone, and making fake social networking profiles using someone else's identity (Rideout, Roberts, & Foehr, 2005). Another type of cyberbullying includes happy slapping, which involves a group of people who insult another person at random while filming the incident via a mobile phone and then posting the images or videos online for others to watch. Flaming is another type of cyberbullying behavior, and it involves posting a provocative or offensive message in a public forum with the desire of provoking a hostile response or triggering an argument with other members of the forum. The most frequently utilized technologies to harm others include gaming consoles, instant messaging tools, and social networking websites (Ybarra & Mitchell, 2007).

The prevalence rates of cyberbullying among youths has been frequently examined. In one study, 3,767 middle school students (aged 11-14) were surveyed to examine their involvement in cyberbullying (Kowalski & Limber, 2007). Of this sample, 11% reported that they were cyberbullied at least once, 4% had bullied other youths, and 7% were involved as both perpetrator and victim. Higher prevalence rates were found by Patchin and Hinduja (2006). They found that 29% of the youths in their sample reported having experienced cyber victimization and 47% indicated that they were cyber bystanders. With an older sample of youths, grades 9th through 12th, Goebert and colleagues (2011) found that 56.1% of youths in their sample from the state of Hawaii reported that they were victims of cyberbullying. Taking into account the potential of cyberbullying experiences to extend from middle school to high school, Hinduja and Patchin (2012) surveyed youths in grades 6th through 12th. They found that 4.9% of their sample perpetrated cyberbullying in the past 30 days. Although differences in prevalence rates are the result of variations in sampling techniques and measurement techniques, it is important to understand these rates as they suggest that cyberbullying is a growing concern among children and adolescents. Cyberbullying is not just a problem localized to youths in the United States. Instead, it is a global problem with increasing evidence that cyberbullying occurs in Canada, Europe, Australia, Africa, Asia, and South America.

Cyberbullying in Canada

In comparison to cyberbullying prevalence rates in the United States, rates of youths' involvement in these behaviors is lower in Canada. In particular, Cappadocia and colleagues (2013) found that 2.1% of youths in their sample of 10th graders reported that they were perpetrators of cyberbullying, 1.9% reported being cyber victims, and 0.6% explained that they were both cyberbullies and cyber victims. Slightly higher rates were found in another sample of Canadian adolescents in the 8th through 10th grades (Bonnanno & Hymel, 2013). Bonnanno and Hymel found that 6% of their sample reported that they were cyberbullies, 5.8% reported that they were cyber victims only, and 5% indicated that they were both cyberbullies and cyber victims.

Cyberbullying in Europe

Using a sample of 22,544 Swedish youths, between the ages of 15 and 18, Laftman and colleagues (2013) found that 5% of their sample were cyber victims, 4% were cyberbullies, and 2% were both cyber victims and cyberbullies. In a slightly younger sample of Swedish adolescents, 7th through 9th graders, Beckman and colleagues (2012) found that 1.9% of their sample were cyber victims, 2.9% were classified as cyberbullies, and 0.6% were cyberbullies and cyber victims. Cyberbullying has also been documented in Ireland in a sample of 876 12 through 17 year olds (Corcoran, Connolly, & O'Moore, 2012). Rates were 6% for cyber victimization among this group of Irish youths. Italian youths typically report higher levels of cyberbullying involvement when compared to youths in Northern and Western Europe. In one study, Brighi et al. (2012) found that 12.5% of the Italian youths in their sample of 2,326, with an average age of 13.9 years, were classified as cyber victims. Similar rates have been found among German youths. In this research, Festl and colleagues (2013) found that 13% of their sample of 276 13 through 19 year olds were classified as cyberbullies and 11% were classified as cybervictims. Olenik-Shemesh et al. (2010) found that 16.5% of their participants ($N = 242$; 13-16 year olds) were cyber victims. The rate of Israeli adolescents identified as cyber victims or witnesses of cyberbullying was 32.4% of the sample ($N = 355$; 13 to 17 year olds; Lazuras, Barkoukis, Ourda, & Tsorbatzoudis, 2013).

Research has also been conducted with Turkish youths. In this research, Yimaz (2011) found that 18% of the 756 7th graders in the study reported that they were victimized by cyberbullying and 6% reported that they were perpetrators of cyberbullying. Rates were much higher in Erdur-Baker's (2010) study. She found that 32% of the 276 youths, ages 14 to 18 years, in her study reported that they were cyber victims. Ayas and Horzum (2012) found that 19% of youths in the sample of 12 to 14 year olds had perpetrated cyberbullying. Slightly higher rates of cyberbullying perpetration were reported among Aricak et al.'s (2008) sample of 269 Turkish secondary school students. Of these students, 36% admitted that they had cyberbullied someone at least once.

Cyberbullying in Asia

Research on cyberbullying among Asian countries has been slower to develop than research in the United States, Canada, and Europe. In this research, Huang and Chou (2010) found that 63.4% of the 545 Taiwanese youths in their sample had witnessed cyberbullying, 34.9% were classified as cyber victims, and 20.4% were classified as cyberbullies. Jang and colleagues (2014) surveyed 3,238 Korean adolescents, with findings revealing that 43% were classified as being involved in cyberbullying. Similar rates have been found among adolescents in China, with 34.8% in one sample ($N = 1,438$) reporting that they were cyberbullies and 56.9% as cyber victims (Zhou, Tang, Tian, Wei, Zhang, & Morrison, 2013). Focusing exclusively on Facebook cyberbullying, Kwan and Skoric (2013) reported that 59.4% of Singaporean adolescents in their study experienced cyber victimization through this social media website, while 56.9% perpetrated cyberbullying. In addition, Wong and colleagues (2014) found that 12.2% of adolescents in their sample ($N = 1,912$) were cyber victims and 13.1% were classified as cyberbullying perpetrators.

Cross-Cultural Differences in Cyberbullying Involvement

Research on the cross-cultural differences in cyberbullying typically classified countries according to an independent self-construal or an interdependent self-construal. To have an independent self-construal view, the self is viewed as separate from the social context. On the other hand, someone with an interdependent self-construal views themselves within the context of their society. Typically people from Western countries, like the United States, Canada, and the United Kingdom, reinforce and prime people to behave in ways aligned with an independent self-construal, while people from Eastern countries, like China, Korea, and Japan, are reinforced and primed for behavior consistently in regards to an independent self-construal. Differences in these self-construals affect people's social behaviors, particularly bullying and cyberbullying. Therefore, independent and interdependent self-construal's have been used to explain these behaviors. In this research, youths from the United States typically reported higher rates of cyberbullying involvement, either as perpetrators or victims, when compared to Japanese youths (Barlett, Gentile, Anderson, Suzuki, Sakamoto, Yamaoka, & Katsura, 2013). Similar patterns have also been found among Austrian and Japanese youths (Strohmeier, Aoyama, Gradinger, & Toda, 2013). In other research, Chinese youths reported less cyberbullying perpetration when compared to Canadian youths (Li, 2008) but more cyberbullying victimization than Canadian youths (Li, 2006). Other research comparing East Asian youths from Canada with Canadian youths, Shapka and Law (2013) found that East Asian youths engaged in cyberbullying more for proactive reasons (i.e., to obtain a goal), while Canadian youths reported cyberbullying perpetration for reactive reasons (i.e., response to provocation). Wright and colleagues (2015) found that Indian youths reported higher levels of cyberbullying involvement than youths from China and Japan, with Indian boys reporting the highest rates of cyberbullying involvement. Conducted in European countries, Genta and colleagues (2012) compared rates of cyberbullying perpetration among youths in Italy, Spain, and England. The findings revealed that Italian boys perpetrated more cyberbullying than boys from Span and England.

YOUTHS' CHARACTERISTICS AND RISK FACTORS FOR CYBERBULLYING

Despite differences in the estimates of cyberbullying rates, these studies provided evidence that cyberbullying is an experience that is reported among youths. With the recognition that cyberbullying is something to be concerned about among youths, researchers began to direct their attention to the characteristics and risk factors related to youths' involvement in cyberbullying.

Age was one of the first risk factors to receive attention. Findings from this research indicated that cyberbullying victimization peaked in early adolescences and that high school adolescents were more likely to perpetrated cyberbullying (Williams & Guerra, 2007). In addition, physical forms of cyberbullying, such as hacking, also peaked in middle school but generally declined in high school. On the other hand, Wade and Beran (2011) concluded that cyberbullying involvement was highest among 9th graders in their study when compared to middle school students.

Other research has focused on gender as a predictor of youths' cyberbullying involvement. Findings from this research indicated that boys were more often the perpetrators of cyberbullying when compared to girls (Boulton, Lloyd, Down, & Marx, 2012; Li, 2007; Ybarra, Diener-West, & Leaf, 2007). In contrast, other research (e.g., Dehue, Bolman, & Vollink, 2008; Pornari & Wood, 2010) has revealed that girls were more often cyberbullies than boys. In some studies, girls reported that they were more often victimized by cyberbullying in comparison to boys (Hinduja & Patchin, 2007; Kowalski & Limber, 2007). Contrary to these findings, some research (e.g., Huang & Chou, 2010; Sjurso, Fandrem, & Roland, 2016) has found that boys were more often cyber victims when compared to girls. Other studies (e.g., Stoll & Block, 2015; Wright & Li, 2013b) have revealed no gender differences in youths' involvement in cyberbullying.

Researchers have also directed their attention to considering youths' offline experience of perpetrators and victims of traditional school bullying as risk factors for youths' involvement in cyberbullying. These studies have considered the role of victim and perpetrator in both the face-to-face and cyber contexts. In these studies, positive associations are found between cyberbullying perpetration and traditional face-to-face bullying perpetration, cyber victimization and traditional face-to-face victimization, and-cyberbullying perpetration and traditional face-to-face victimization (Barlett & Gentile, 2012; Mitchell, Ybarra, & Finkelhor, 2007; Wright & Li, 2013a; Wright & Li, 2013b).

Another risk factor associated with youths' cyberbullying involvement is their use of electronic technology. The underlying conclusion in this research is that any exposure to electronic technology can increase youths' risk of cyberbullying. Higher use of the internet is associated positively with both the perpetration and victimization by cyber victimization (Ang, 2016; Aricak, Siyahhan, Uzunhasanoglu, Saribeyoglu, Ciplak, Yilmaz, & Memmedov, 2008). Compared with nonvictims, cyber victims spend more time using instant messaging tools, email, blogging sites, and online gaming (Smith, Mahdavi, Carvalho, Fisher, Russell, & Tippett, 2008). A possible explanation for the connection between electronic technology use and cyberbullying involvement is the likelihood that these youths disclose more personal information online, including geographical location (Ybarra, Diener-West, & Leaf, 2007). Disclosing this information puts them at risk for cyber victimization.

Internalizing problems, like depression and loneliness, as well as externalizing problems, like alcohol use, are also associated with youths' involvement in cyberbullying. To explain such relationships, researchers propose that victims' coping abilities are diminished or ineffective, which makes them vulnerable to cyberbullying (Cappadocia, Craig, & Pepler, 2013; Mitchell, Ybarra, & Finkelhor, 2007). Furthermore, Cappadocia and colleagues (2013) and Wright (in press) found that alcohol and drug use were each related positively to cyberbullying perpetration.

Researchers have also identified other variables that are linked to youths' cyberbullying involvement. Normative beliefs are the beliefs that a specific set of behavior, in this case cyberbullying, is an acceptable form of behavior. In this research, youths with higher normative beliefs concerning face-to-face bullying and cyberbullying were related positively to cyberbullying perpetration (e.g., Burton, Florell, & Wygant, 2013; Wright, 2014b). Therefore, cyberbullies believe that cyberbullying is an acceptable form of behavior to engage in. Pro victim attitudes, defined as the belief that bullying is unacceptable and that defending victims is valuable, is another factor related to cyberbullying. Holding lower levels of pro victim attitudes is associated positively with cyberbullying perpetration (Sevcikova, Machackova, Wright, Dedkova, &Cerna, 2015). In addition, youths with lower levels of peer attachment, less self-control, and empathy, and greater moral disengagement were each related positively to cyberbullying perpetration (e.g.,Wright, Kamble, Lei, Li, Aoyama, & Shruti, 2015).

Many of the studies on the characteristics and risk factors associated with cyberbullying involvement utilize cross-sectional research designs. Consequently, it is difficult to make understand the long-term associations of these characteristics and risk factors associated with cyberbullying involvement. Fanti and colleagues (2012) conducted a longitudinal study investigating youths' exposure to violent media and their callous and unemotional traits in relation to cyberbullying involvement one year later. Findings revealed that media violence exposure related to greater cyber victimization. Perceived levels of stress from parents, peers, and academics also have a role in adolescents' perpetration of cyberbullying one year later (Wright, 2014a).

In sum, there are a variety of characteristics and risk factors that make youths vulnerable to cyberbullying. Moving away from individual-related characteristics and risk factors, other researchers have examined the role of parents, schools, and teachers in youths' cyberbullying involvement.

Parents as Risk Factors

Parenting styles are linked to youths' involvement in cyberbullying. In particular, youths who are bully-victims often have parents who utilize indifferent-uninvolved parenting styles and inconsistent monitoring of their activities increases youths' involvement in cyberbullying (Totura, MacKinnon-Lewis, Gesten, Gadd, Divine, Dunham, & Kamboukos, 2009). Neglectful parenting, or sometimes referred to as indifferent-uninvolved parenting, increased youths' involvement in cyberbullying in comparison to uninvolved youths (Dehue, Bolman, Vollink, & Pouwelse, 2012). Indifferent-uninvolved parents are often emotionally distance from their children, engage in little or no supervision, show little warmth and affection toward their children, place fewer demands on their children's behaviors, might and intentionally avoid their children. Cyber victimization was also increased among children who reported that their parents engaged in authoritarian parenting styles. Authoritarian parenting style is defined as parents who have high levels of demands and low levels of responsiveness. These parents have very high expectation but they display very low levels of warmth or nurturance.

Another aspect of parenting is the use of parental monitoring. The cyber context provides another opportunity for parents to monitor their children's online activity. In this research, Mason (2008) found that 50% of the children in his study reported that their parents monitored their online activities. One study explored the differences between what parents report in terms of how often they monitor their children's online activities and how often their children reported being monitored (McQuade, Colt, & Meyer, 2009). McQuade et al. found that 93% of parents in their study reported that they set limits on their children's online activities. However, only 37% of their children reported that their parents had given them rules regarding their online activities. These findings might indicate that parents overestimate the amount of monitoring they engage in or that the strategies they do implement are ineffective. Just like in the offline world, parents have an important role in protecting their children against online risks. Additional attention should be given to how parents navigate conversations with their children about online risks and opportunities.

Other research has focused on the role of parental monitoring and parental mediation in relation to reducing youths' risk of cyberbullying involvement. Wright (2015) found that when youths reported more technology mediation by their parents they reported lower levels of cyber victimization and the associated negative adjustment difficulties. To explain these connections, Wright explains that parents who monitor their children's electronic technology use might have more opportunities to engage in discussions on the risks associated with cyberbullying involvement. Parents might also convey, during these discussions, that cyberbullying is unacceptable. Such a proposal is supported by the literature as Hinduja and Patchin (2013) and Wright (2013a) found that youths who were concerned with being punished for negative online behaviors were much less likely to perpetrate cyberbullying. One study found little support that parental monitoring was helpful for preventing cyberbullying involvement. In this study, Aoyama and colleagues (2011) did not find that parental mediation and monitoring of their children's online activities were related to their children's cyberbullying perpetration and victimization. Aoyama et al. explained that many parents lack the technological skills to effectively monitor their children's online activities, which makes it difficult for them to know when and how to intervene in these activities. Another potential explanation might be that parents implement rules for electronic technology use that they do not follow-up on. Not following through with these rules can give the impression that parents are unconcerned with appropriate online behaviors, increasing the risk of engaging in cyberbullying. Failing to enforce rules might also indicate that parents do not often update strategies as their children become more independent electronic technology users. Research findings support this proposal as many parents report that they are not sure as to what type of online activities to discuss with their children (Rosen, 2007). When parents are not sure how to talk to their children about online activities, then it might lead many parents to not discuss appropriate online behaviors with their children.

There is also some research which investigates other family characteristics in relation to youths' cyberbullying involvement. Family income, parental education, and marital status of caregivers were unrelated to youths' involvement in cyberbullying (Ybarra & Mitchell, 2004). Other research indicates that parental unemployment increased youths' risk of cyberbullying perpetration and victimization (Arslan, Savaser, Hallett, & Balci, 2012).

Schools as Risk Factors

Schools' role in monitoring and punishing youth's involvement in cyberbullying is a topic of great debate about school districts, parents, authorities, and researchers. This is because many of the cases involving cyberbullying are carried out off school groups, making it difficult for schools to be aware of such cases (deLara, 2012; Mason, 2008). However, many incidences of cyberbullying involve youths who attend the same school, making the schools' role in handling such incidences complex. Because cyberbullies and cyber victims might attend the same school, it is possible that knowledge of a cyberbullying incidence could spread throughout the school, leading to negative interactions between youths while on school grounds. These negative interactions could disrupt the learning process.

Regardless of the extent to which cyberbullying incidences can "spill over" onto school grounds, many administrators, teachers, and school districts have very different perceptions and awareness of cyberbullying. Some of these individuals might not even perceive cyberbullying as a significant event, warranting attention (Kochenderfer-Ladd & Pelletier, 2008). It is problematic when administrators and teachers do not perceive cyberbullying as problematic because electronic technology and digital communication are embedded in the lives of the youths they teach. Furthermore, these administrators and teachers are often not likely to perceive any form of covert bullying behavior as serious and harmful as physical bullying (Sahin, 2010). They are often not likely to understand the consequences associated with relational bullying and cyberbullying. This could lead to the decision not to help youths who experience these behaviors or dealing with the situation by minimizing it. Teacher training might not properly inform teachers on how to deal with and recognize cyberbullying, making teachers' ability to intervene difficult. Cassidy et al. (2012a) found that many Canadian teachers were unfamiliar with newer technologies. Being unfamiliar with newer technologies made it difficult for these teachers to deal with cyberbullying as they were often unsure of how to respond to the incidence or of how to implement strategies to address the incident. Evn when teachers were concerned with cyberbullying, their school district did not have policies and programs in place to deal with these behaviors (Cassidy, Brown, & Jackson, 2012b). This made it difficult for teachers to implement solutions and strategies.

Other research has revealed that teachers were often willing to participate in prevention programs aimed at reducing traditional face-to-face bullying but not cyberbullying prevention programs (Tangen & Campbell, 2010). This could be a product of few empirically and theoretical driven cyberbullying prevention programs or that administrators and teachers do not consider cyberbullying an important enough issue to warrant attention. Recognizing the importance of implementing policies and training programs on cyberbullying is important because youths' involvement in these behaviors has the potential to impact the learning environment (Shariff & Hoff, 2007).

Educators require training to increase their awareness of cyberbullying, with the hope of developing policies at the school level to reduce these behaviors. When teachers are more confident about their abilities and have a stronger commitment to their school, they are more likely to learn about cyberbullying, and have a greater awareness of these behaviors and knowledge to deal effectively with it (Eden, Heiman, & Olenik-Shemesh, 2013). Such awareness and knowledge prevent children's and adolescents' cyberbullying perpetration and victimization. Furthermore, when teachers feel more confident, they intervene in cyberbullying incidences more often, which protects adolescents' from experiencing these behaviors (Elledge, Williford, Boulton, DePaolis, Little, & Salmivalli, 2013). Unfortunately, teachers' motivation for learning about cyberbullying decreases from elementary school to middle school, which is problematic as cyberbullying involvement usually increases in these years (Ybarra & Mitchell, 2007). Therefore, there is a need for educator training programs aimed at raising awareness of cyberbullying, particularly in the middle school years.

Youths' involvement in cyberbullying are less likely to perceive their school and teachers positively when compared to uninvolved youths (Bayar & Ucanok, 2012). Some youths might experience cyberbullying and fear that their classmates could be responsible. This decreases these youths' concentration on learning, thereby reducing their academic attainment and performance (Eden, Heiman, & Olenik-Shemesh, 2013). Lower school commitment and perceptions of a negative school climate increase children's and adolescents' engagement in cyberbullying as they feel less connected to their school (Williams & Guerra, 2007). Youths' involvement in cyberbullying is linked to poor academic functioning (Wright, in press).

Peer interactions are present in both the offline and online world. Through these interactions, youths learn about the social norms dictating acceptable and unacceptable behaviors within the peer group, and consequently they engage in more of the acceptable behaviors, even if they are negative. In this line of research, cyberbullying involvement is highest among classrooms in which these behaviors are elevated (Festl, Schwarkow, & Quandt, 2013). Something about the classroom climate might be driving the levels of cyberbullying behaviors within a particular classroom. Furthermore, believing that one's friends engaged in cyberbullying also increases youths' risk of perpetrating cyberbullying (Hinduja & Patch, 2013). Peer contagion might potentially explain these relationships. What this means is that one's friends "spread" negative online behaviors to others within their social network (Sijtsema, Ashwin, Simona, & Gina, 2014).

Another peer-related variable associated with cyberbullying involvement is peer attachment. Peer attachment is defined as the closeness that youths feel with their same or similarly aged peers. Lower levels of peer attachment were associated positively with cyberbullying perpetration and victimization (Burton, Florell, & Wygant, 2013). When youths have poor peer attachment, they are likely to believe that their peers will not be there for them when they need it. This belief promotes negative interactions with peers. Cyberbullying involvement is higher when youths' experience peer rejection, whether perceived rejection or peer-reported rejection (Sevcikova, Machackova, Wright, Dedkova, & Cerna, 2015; Wright & Li, 2013b). Wright and Li (2012) argue that peer rejection triggers negative emotional responses that leads to cyberbullying perpetration and victimization.

Cyberbullying perpetration might also be used to maintain and boost youths' social standing among their peer group, both online and offline. Wright (2014c) found that higher levels of perceived popularity, a reputational type of popularity in the peer group, was associated positively with cyberbullying perpetration six months later. With the prominent role of electronic technologies in youths' lives, Wright proposes that they might utilize these technologies as a tool for the promotion and maintenance of their social standing. The literature in this section suggests that it is important to consider the role of schools and peers in youths' cyberbullying involvement.

NEGATIVE PSYCHOSOCIAL AND ACADEMIC OUTCOMES THE OUTCOMES ASSOCIATED WITH YOUTHS' INVOLVEMENT IN CYBERBULLYING

Concerns with cyberbullying involvement among youths were triggered by the associated negative psychosocial and academic outcomes. A potential research for these linkages is that cyberbullying disrupts youths' emotional experiences, making them more vulnerable to negative outcomes, due to ineffective coping strategies. Cyber victims are more likely than nonvictims to report lower levels of global happiness, general school happiness, school satisfaction, family satisfaction, and self-satisfaction (Toledano, Werch, & Wiens, 2015). In addition, cyber victims report more feelings of anger, sadness, and fear in comparison to noninvolved children and adolescents (Dehue, Bolman, & Vollink, 2008; Machackova, Dedkova, Sevcikova, & Cerna, 2013; Patchin & Hinduja, 2006).

Cyberbullying involvement also impacts youths' academic performance. In this literature, both cyber victims and cyberbullies are at an increased risk for difficulties at school, including academic problems, less motivation for school, poor academic performance, lower academic attainment, and more school absences (Belae & Hall, 2007; Yousef & Bellamy, 2015). Lower school functioning also relates to cyberbullying perpetration and cyber victimization (Wright, in press). Cyberbullies and cyber victims experience the lower levels of school functioning when compared to cyberbullies, cyber victims, and uninvolved youths.

Internalizing and externalizing problems are both associated with youths' cyberbullying involvement (e.g., Mitchell, Ybarra, & Finkelhor, 2007; Patchin & Hinduja, 2006; Wright, 2014b; Ybarra, Diener-West, & Leaf, 2007). Cyberbullies and cyber victims both experience suicidal thoughts and attempt suicide more often than uninvolved youths (Bauman, Toomey, & Walker 2013). Similar results were found by Beckman and colleagues (2012). Beckman and colleagues also found that cyberbullying involvement increased youths' risk for experiencing mental health problems. Other research suggests that these youths are also at risk for psychiatric and psychosomatic problems (Sourander, Brunstein, Ikonen, Lindroos, Luntamo, Koskelainen, Ristkari, & Helenius, 2010).

A limitation associated with the research on the psychosocial and behavioral consequences related to youths' cyberbullying involvement is that researchers do not account for youths' involvement in traditional face-to-face bullying. It is important to account for youths' involvement in traditional face-to-face bullying because this experience is associated with similar consequences as cyberbullying and due to the high correlation between the two (Williams & Guerra, 2007; Wright & Li, 2013b). One study accounted for traditional face-to-face bullying involvement and the findings suggested that cyberbullying perpetration and victimization might have worse psychological consequences when compared to the face-to-face bullying perpetration and victimization, after controlling for face-to-face bullying and victimization (Bonanno & Hymel, 2013).

Given the high correlation between cyberbullying and traditional face-to-face bullying involvement, some researchers have focused on the combined effects of these experiences on youths' psychosocial and behavioral outcomes. In this research, victims of both traditional face-to-face bullying and cyberbullying reported higher levels of internalizing symptoms when compared to youths who experienced only one type of victimization (Gradinger, Strohmeier, & Spiel, 2009).

The research reviewed in this section suggests that a combination of various bullying experiences, whether online or offline, exacerbates youths' experience of depression, anxiety, and loneliness. These findings indicate the importance of considering youths' involvement in various bullying behaviors to better understand the best ways to intervene.

THEORETICAL FRAMEWORKS

In this section, two theories will be presented, along with their application to cyberbullying involvement among youths. These theories include the social cognitive theory and the online disinhibition effect.

According to the social cognitive theory, parents and/or friends serve as important models of behaviors that are observed and replicated by youths (Hinduja & Patchin, 2008; Mouttapa, Valente, Gallaher, Rohrbach, & Unger, 2004). This theory has been extensively applied to youths' involvement in aggressive behaviors, including cyberbullying (Barlett & Gentile, 2012). According to Olweus (1993), children's aggressive behaviors are learned or modeled by someone who was stronger than the observer. The effects of the model on the observer depended on the observer's positive evaluation of the model. These perceptions have the potential to increase the likelihood of reducing children's inhibition for aggressive behaviors and increase aggressive acts, particularly when the model is rewarded for acting aggressively. In regard to cyberbullying, youths observe various incidences of successful cyberbullying acts (Barlett & Gentile, 2012). The more often they are exposed to these acts the greater the likelihood that they believe cyberbullying is acceptable, normative, and tolerable. The anonymity offered by the cyber context increases the chance that little or no immediate consequences occur after cyberbullying perpetration. When youths are positively reinforced for cyberbullying behaviors, adolescents held greater positive attitudes toward these behaviors (Barlett & Gentile, 2012). These attitudes relate to future perpetration of cyberbullying behaviors (Wright & Li, 2013a; Wright & Li, 2013b).

The online disinhibition effect theory refers to the likelihood that the characteristics of the cyber context will increase the likelihood that youths engage in different ways online than they would offline (Suler, 2004). The cyber context allows people to loosen, reduce, or dismiss the typical social restrictions and inhibitions present in normal face-to-face interactions (Mason, 2008). The literature supports the premise that people behave differently in cyberspace than in the offline world. Research indicates that people are likely to be blunter when communicating with others via electronic technologies (McKenna & Bargh, 2000). In online communication, there are more misunderstanding, heightened hostility, and increase in aggressive behaviors via electronic technologies when compared to face-to-face communication. It is also possible for communications through some electronic technologies might to not see emotional reactions. Not being able to see someone's emotional reactions in cyberspace prevents people from modulating their own behaviors because they are not able to witness the consequences of their actions, like they could in the offline world (Kowalski & Limber, 2007). Cyberbullying often occurs because cyberbullies cannot witness the cyber victims' reactions nor are their many opportunities to experience social disapproval, punishment, or other consequences. Many cyberbullies recognize the ease of engaging in aggressive behaviors through electronic technologies, which could potentially lead their behaviors to become more disinhibited over time, especially when they receive positive reinforcement for their behavior and are not able to recognize the consequences of their behaviors (Hinduja & Patchin, 2010; Wright, 2014a). Deindividuation, the process of not being accountable for one's actions, also occurs as a result of the online disinhibition effect (Joinson, 1998). Being able to remain anonymous through electronic technologies reduces youths' accountability for their online interactions. Coupling the reduction of accountability with the anonymity of the cyber context, might make it easier for youths to disengage from others, leading to increases in harmful online behaviors (Wright, 2014a).

SOLUTIONS AND RECOMMENDATIONS

Cyberbullying is a public health concern, warranting attention by all members of our communities, including educators, researchers, parents, and youths themselves. It is also important for education curriculum to include digital literacy skills training and citizenship in both the online and offline worlds (Cassidy, Brown, & Jackson, 2012b). Such curriculum should also focus on the positive uses of electronic technology, building empathy for negative online interactions, self-esteem, and social skills. To also improve school climate, administrators and teachers should learn students' names, praise good behavior, and stay technologically informed and up-to-date (Hinduja & Patchin, 2012).

Schools and parents should partner to help address cyberbullying. Parents should also increase their awareness and knowledge of electronic technologies (Cassidy, Brown, & Jackson, 2012a; Diamanduros & Downs, 2011). Increasing one's knowledge of electronic technologies can help parents understand the importance of technology in their children's lives and to recognize the risk and opportunities of their children's electronic technology use. Parents can also implement more effective monitoring strategies when they are more knowledge about electronic technologies and cyberbullying. Parents are encouraged to engage in open dialogue with children about appropriate electronic technology use.

FUTURE RESEARCH DIRECTIONS

There are some noticeable future directions for research on youths' involvement in cyberbullying. Anonymity is associated with youths' perpetration of cyberbullying involvement, but little attention has been given to this topic. Future research should focus on youths' perceptions of anonymous acts online and which factors might motivate them to engage in anonymous forms of cyberbullying. This research should also examine anonymous forms of cyberbullying versus non-anonymous forms of cyberbullying to better understand the motivators underlying these behaviors. This research should also investigate whether coping strategies and psychosocial adjustment difficulties vary as a function of whether cyberbullying was anonymous or non-anonymous. Additional investigations should be undertaken to understand the long-term impact of cyberbullying involvement among youths. Intervention and prevention programs could be developed which specific consideration to the specific age group identified as at the most risk for cyberbullying involvement.

CONCLUSION

The literature in this chapter provides a firm foundation for understanding youths' involvement in cyberbullying and the next directions for intervention, prevention, public policy, and research. The review suggests that much of the earlier research on cyberbullying focused on the prevalence rates of these behaviors. Current shifts in this research has changed the focus to understanding the causes and consequences of youths' involvement in cyberbullying. Although this research is still in its early stages in comparison to the literature on traditional face-to-face bullying, many of the published studies on cyberbullying focus on individual predictors of youths' involvement in these behaviors. More consideration is needed to understand the role of parents, schools, peers, and communities in youths' cyberbullying perpetration and victimization. Follow-up research on cyberbullying is important as this negative behavior impacts many aspects of our society, potentially undermining ethical and moral values. Consequently, it is imperative that we unite and do our part to reduce children's and adolescents' involvement in cyberbullying together.

SUMMARY

The purpose of this literature review was to summarize research on cyberbullying involvement among youths by providing a description and definition, information about the characteristics and risk factors, the negative adjustment outcomes associated with the involvement in these behaviors, and theoretical frameworks. The studies reviewed in this chapter utilize cross-sectional, longitudinal, qualitative, quantitative, and mixed-methods research designs. Studies with various youths from across the world were also reviewed to shed more light on the cross-cultural research on youths' cyberbullying involvement. This cross-cultural research also provides support about youths' cyberbullying involvement being a global phenomenon.

REFERENCES

Ang, R. P. (2016). Cyberbullying: Its prevention and intervention strategies. In D. Sibnath (Ed.), *Child safety, welfare and well-being: Issues and challenges* (pp. 25–38). Springer. doi:10.1007/978-81-322-2425-9_3

Aoyama, I., Utsumi, S., & Hasegawa, M. (2011). Cyberbullying in Japan: Cases, government reports, adolescent relational aggression and parental monitoring roles. In Q. Li, D. Cross, & P. K. Smith (Eds.), *Bullying in the global playground: Research from an international perspective.* Oxford, UK: Wiley-Blackwell.

Aricak, T., Siyahhan, S., Uzunhasanoglu, A., Saribeyoglu, S., Ciplak, S., Yilmaz, N., & Memmedov, C. (2008). Cyberbullying among Turkish adolescents. *Cyberpsychology & Behavior*, *11*(3), 253–261. doi:10.1089/cpb.2007.0016 PMID:18537493

Arslan, S., Savaser, S., Hallett, V., & Balci, S. (2012). Cyberbullying among primary school students in Turkey: Self-reported prevalence and associations with home and school life. *Cyberpsychology, Behavior, and Social Networking*, *15*(10), 527–533. doi:10.1089/cyber.2012.0207 PMID:23002988

Ayas, T., & Horzum, M. B. (2010). *Cyberbullying / victim scale development study*. Retrieved from: http://www.akademikbakis.org

Barlett, C. P., & Gentile, D. A. (2012). Long-term psychological predictors of cyber-bullying in late adolescence. *Psychology of Popular Media Culture*, *2*, 123–135. doi:10.1037/a0028113

Barlett, C. P., Gentile, D. A., Anderson, C. A., Suzuki, K., Sakamoto, A., Yamaoka, A., & Katsura, R. (2013). Cross-cultural differences in cyberbullying behavior: A short-term longitudinal study. *Journal of Cross-Cultural Psychology*, *45*(2), 300–313. doi:10.1177/0022022113504622

Bauman, S., Toomey, R. B., & Walker, J. L. (2013). Associations among bullying, cyberbullying, and suicide in high school students. *Journal of Adolescence*, *36*(2), 341–350. doi:10.1016/j.adolescence.2012.12.001 PMID:23332116

Bauman, S., Underwood, M. K., & Card, N. A. (2013). Definitions: Another perspective and a proposal for beginning with cyberaggression. In S. Bauman, D. Cross, & J. Walker (Eds.), *Principles of cyberbullying research: Definitions, measures, methodology* (pp. 26–40). New York, NY: Routledge.

Bayar, Y., & Ucanok, Z. (2012). School social climate and generalized peer perception in traditional and cyberbullying status. *Educational Sciences: Theory and Practice*, *12*, 2352–2358.

Beckman, L., Hagquist, C., & Hellstrom, L. (2012). Does the association with psychosomatic health problems differ between cyberbullying and traditional bullying? *Emotional & Behavioural Difficulties*, *17*(3-4), 421–434. doi:10.1080/13632752.2012.704228

Bonanno, R. A., & Hymel, S. (2013). Cyber bullying and internalizing difficulties: Above and beyond the impact of traditional forms of bullying. *Journal of Youth and Adolescence*, *42*(5), 685–697. doi:10.100710964-013-9937-1 PMID:23512485

Boulton, M., Lloyd, J., Down, J., & Marx, H. (2012). Predicting undergraduates' self-reported engagement in traditional and cyberbullying from attitudes. *Cyberpsychology, Behavior, and Social Networking*, *15*(3), 141–147. doi:10.1089/cyber.2011.0369 PMID:22304402

Brighi, A., Guarini, A., Melotti, G., Galli, S., & Genta, M. L. (2012). Predictors of victimisation across direct bullying, indirect bullying and cyberbullying. *Emotional & Behavioural Difficulties*, *17*(3-4), 375–388. doi:10.1080/13632752.2012.704684

Burton, K. A., Florell, D., & Wygant, D. B. (2013). The role of peer attachment and normative beliefs about aggression on traditional bullying and cyberbullying. *Psychology in the Schools*, *50*(2), 103–114. doi:10.1002/pits.21663

Cappadocia, M. C., Craig, W. M., & Pepler, D. (2013). Cyberbullying: Prevalence, stability and risk factors during adolescence. *Canadian Journal of School Psychology*, *28*(2), 171–192. doi:10.1177/0829573513491212

Cassidy, W., Brown, K., & Jackson, M. (2012a). "Making kind cool": Parents' suggestions for preventing cyber bullying and fostering cyber kindness. *Journal of Educational Computing Research*, *46*(4), 415–436. doi:10.2190/EC.46.4.f

Cassidy, W., Brown, K., & Jackson, M. (2012b). "Under the radar": Educators and cyberbullying in schools. *School Psychology International*, *33*(5), 520–532. doi:10.1177/0143034312445245

Corcoran, L., Connolly, I., & O'Moore, M. (2012). Cyberbullying in Irish schools: An investigation of personality and self-concept. *The Irish Journal of Psychology*, *33*(4), 153–165. doi:10.1080/03033910.2012.677995

Curelaru, M., Iacob, I., & Abalasei, B. (2009). *School bullying: Definition, characteristics, and intervention strategies*. Lumean Publishing House.

Dehue, F., Bolman, C., & Vollink, T. (2008). Cyberbullying: Youngsters' experiences and parental perception. *CyberPscyhology& Behavior*, *11*(2), 217–223. doi:10.1089/cpb.2007.0008 PMID:18422417

Dehue, F., Bolman, C., Vollink, T., & Pouwelse, M. (2012). Cyberbullying and traditional bullying in relation to adolescents' perceptions of parenting. *Journal of Cyber Therapy and Rehabilitation*, *5*, 25–34.

deLara, E. W. (2012). Why adolescents don't disclose incidents of bullying and harassment. *Journal of School Violence*, *11*(4), 288–305. doi:10.1080/15388220.2012.705931

Diamanduros, T., & Downs, E. (2011). Creating a safe school environment: How to prevent cyberbullying at your school. *Library Media Connection*, *30*(2), 36–38.

Eden, S., Heiman, T., & Olenik-Shemesh, D. (2013). Teachers' perceptions, beliefs and concerns about cyberbullying. *British Journal of Educational Technology*, *44*(6), 1036–1052. doi:10.1111/j.1467-8535.2012.01363.x

Elledge, L. C., Williford, A., Boulton, A. J., DePaolis, K. J., Little, T. D., & Salmivalli, C. (2013). Individual and contextual predictors of cyberbullying: The influence of children's provictim attitudes and teachers' ability to intervene. *Journal of Youth and Adolescence*, *42*(5), 698–710. doi:10.100710964-013-9920-x PMID:23371005

Erdur-Baker, O. (2010). Cyberbullying and its correlation to traditional bullying, gender and frequent and risky usage of internet-mediated communication tools. *New Media & Society*, *12*(1), 109–125. doi:10.1177/1461444809341260

Fanti, K. A., Demetriou, A. G., & Hawa, V. V. (2012). A longitudinal study of cyberbullying: Examining risk and protective factors. *European Journal of Developmental Psychology*, *8*(2), 168–181. doi:10.1080/17405629.2011.643169

Festl, R., Schwarkow, M., & Quandt, T. (2013). Peer influence, internet use and cyberbullying: A comparison of different context effects among German adolescents. *Journal of Children and Media*, *7*(4), 446–462. doi:10.1080/17482798.2013.781514

Goebert, D., Else, I., Matsu, C., Chung-Do, J., & Chang, J. Y. (2011). The impact of cyberbullying on substance use and mental health in a multiethnic sample. *Maternal and Child Health Journal, 15*(8), 1282–1286. doi:10.100710995-010-0672-x PMID:20824318

Gradinger, P., Strohmeier, D., & Spiel, C. (2009). Traditional bullying and cyberbullying. *The Journal of Psychology, 217*, 205–213.

Grigg, D. W. (2012). Definitional constructs of cyberbullying and cyber aggression from a triagnulatory overview: A preliminary study into elements. *Journal of Aggression, Conflict and Peace Research, 4*(4), 202–215. doi:10.1108/17596591211270699

Hinduja, S., & Patchin, J. W. (2007). Offline consequences of online victimization. *Journal of School Violence, 6*(3), 89–112. doi:10.1300/J202v06n03_06

Hinduja, S., & Patchin, J. W. (2008). Cyberbullying: An exploratory analysis of factors related to offending and victimization. *Deviant Behavior, 29*(2), 129–156. doi:10.1080/01639620701457816

Hinduja, S., & Patchin, J. W. (2010). Bullying, cyberbullying, and suicide. *Archives of Suicide Research, 14*(3), 206–221. doi:10.1080/13811118.2010.494133 PMID:20658375

Hinduja, S., & Patchin, J. W. (2012). Cyberbullying: Neither and epidemic nor a rarity. *European Journal of Developmental Psychology, 9*(5), 539–543. doi:10.1080/17405629.2012.706448

Hinduja, S., & Patchin, J. W. (2013). Social influences on cyberbullying behaviors among middle and high school students. *Journal of Youth and Adolescence, 42*(5), 711–722. doi:10.100710964-012-9902-4 PMID:23296318

Huang, Y., & Chou, C. (2010). An analysis of multiple factors of cyberbullying among junior high school students in Taiwan. *Computers in Human Behavior, 26*(6), 1581–1590. doi:10.1016/j.chb.2010.06.005

Jang, H., Song, J., & Kim, R. (2014). Does the offline bully-victimization influence cyberbullying behavior among youths? Application of general strain theory. *Computers in Human Behavior, 31*, 85–93. doi:10.1016/j.chb.2013.10.007

Joinson, A. (1998). Causes and implications of behavior on the Internet. In J. Gackenbach (Ed.), *Psychology and the Internet: Intrapersonal, interpersonal, and transpersonal implications* (pp. 43–60). San Diego, CA: Academic Press.

Kochenderfer-Ladd, B., & Pelletier, M. (2008). Teachers' views and beliefs about bullying: Influences on classroom management strategies and students' coping with peer victimization. *Journal of School Psychology, 46*(4), 431–453. doi:10.1016/j.jsp.2007.07.005 PMID:19083367

Kowalski, R. M., & Limber, S. P. (2007). Electronic bullying among middle school students. *The Journal of Adolescent Health, 41*(6), 22–30. doi:10.1016/j.jadohealth.2007.08.017 PMID:18047942

Kwan, G. C. E., & Skoric, M. M. (2013). Facebook bullying: An extension of battles in school. *Computers in Human Behavior, 29*(1), 16–25. doi:10.1016/j.chb.2012.07.014

Laftman, S. B., Modin, B., & Ostberg, V. (2013). Cyberbullying and subjective health: A large-scale study of students in Stockholm, Sweden. *Children and Youth Services Review, 35*(1), 112–119. doi:10.1016/j.childyouth.2012.10.020

Lazuras, L., Barkoukis, V., Ourda, D., & Tsorbatzoudis, H. (2013). A process model of cyberbullying in adolescence. *Computers in Human Behavior*, *29*(3), 881–887. doi:10.1016/j.chb.2012.12.015

Lenhart, A. (2015). *Teens, social media & technology overview 2015*. Retrieved from: http://www.pewinternet.org/2015/04/09/teens-social-media-technology-2015/

Li, Q. (2007). Bullying in the new playground: Research into cyberbullying and cybervictimization. *Australian Journal of Educational Technology*, *23*, 435–454.

Li, Q. (2008). A cross-cultural comparison of adolescents' experience related to cyberbullying. *Educational Research*, *50*(3), 223–234. doi:10.1080/00131880802309333

Machackova, H., Dedkova, L., & Mezulanikova, K. (2015). Brief report: The bystander effect in cyberbullying incidents. *Journal of Adolescence*, *43*, 96–99. doi:10.1016/j.adolescence.2015.05.010 PMID:26070168

Machackova, H., Dedkova, L., Sevcikova, A., & Cerna, A. (2013). Bystanders' support of cyberbullied schoolmates. *Journal of Community & Applied Social Psychology*, *23*(1), 25–36. doi:10.1002/casp.2135

Mason, K. (2008). Cyberbullying: A preliminary assessment for school personnel. *Psychology in the Schools*, *45*(4), 323–348. doi:10.1002/pits.20301

McKenna, K. Y. A., & Bargh, J. A. (2000). Plan 9 from cyberspace: The implications of the internet for personality and social psychology. *Personality and Social Psychology Review*, *4*(1), 57–75. doi:10.1207/S15327957PSPR0401_6

McQuade, C. S., Colt, P. J., & Meyer, B. N. (2009). *Cyber bullying: Protecting kids and adults from online bullies*. Westport, CT: Praeger.

Mitchell, K. J., Ybarra, M., & Finkelhor, D. (2007). The relative importance of online victimization in understanding depression, delinquency, and substance use. *Child Maltreatment*, *12*(4), 314–324. doi:10.1177/1077559507305996 PMID:17954938

Mouttapa, M., Valente, T., Gallagher, P., Rohrbach, L. A., & Unger, J. B. (2004). Social network predictor of bullying and victimization. *Adolescence*, *39*, 315–335. PMID:15563041

Olweus, D. (1993). *Bullying at school. What we know and what we can do*. Malden, MA: Blackwell Publishing.

Patchin, J. W., & Hinduja, S. (2006). Bullies move beyond the schoolyard: A preliminary look at cyberbullying. *Youth Violence and Juvenile Justice*, *4*(2), 148–169. doi:10.1177/1541204006286288

Perren, S., Dooley, J., Shaw, T., & Cross, D. (2010). Bullying in school and cyberspace: Associations with depressive symptoms in Swiss and Australian adolescents. *Child and Adolescent Psychiatry and Mental Health*, *4*(1), 1–10. doi:10.1186/1753-2000-4-28 PMID:21092266

Pornari, C. D., & Wood, J. (2010). Peer and cyber aggression in secondary school students: The role of moral disengagement, hostile attribution bias, and outcome expectancies. *Aggressive Behavior*, *36*(2), 81–94. doi:10.1002/ab.20336 PMID:20035548

Rideout, V. J., Roberts, D. F., &Foehr, U. G. (2005). *Generation M: Media in the lives of 8-18-year-olds: Executive summary.* Menlo Park, CA: Henry J. Kaiser Family Foundation.

Rosen, L. D. (2007). *Me, Myspace, and I: Parenting the Net Generation.* New York: Palgrave Macmillan.

Sahin, M. (2010). Teachers' perceptions of bullying in high schools: A Turkish study. *Social Behavior and Personality, 38*(1), 127–142. doi:10.2224bp.2010.38.1.127

Sevcikova, A., Machackova, H., Wright, M. F., Dedkova, L., & Cerna, A. (2015). Social support seeking in relation to parental attachment and peer relationships among victims of cyberbullying. *Australian Journal of Guidance & Counselling, 15,* 1–13. doi:10.1017/jgc.2015.1

Shapka, J. D., & Law, D. M. (2013). Does one size fit all? Ethnic differences in parenting behaviors and motivations for adolescent engagement in cyberbullying. *Journal of Youth and Adolescence, 42*(5), 723–738. doi:10.100710964-013-9928-2 PMID:23479327

Shariff, S., & Hoff, D. L. (2007). Cyber bullying: Clarifying legal boundaries for school supervision in cyberspace. *International Journal of Cyber Criminology, 1,* 76–118.

Sijtsema, J. J., Ashwin, R. J., Simona, C. S., & Gina, G. (2014). Friendship selection and influence in bullying and defending. *Effects of moral disengagement. Developmental Psychology, 50*(8), 2093–2104. doi:10.1037/a0037145 PMID:24911569

Sjurso, I. R., Fandream, H., & Roland, E. (2016). Emotional problems in traditional and cyber victimization. *Journal of School Violence, 15*(1), 114–131. doi:10.1080/15388220.2014.996718

Smith, P. K., Del Barrio, C., & Tokunaga, R. S. (2013). Definitions of bullying and cyberbullying: How useful are the terms? In S. Bauman, D. Cross, & J. Walker (Eds.), *Principles of cyberbullying research: Definitions, measures, methodology* (pp. 26–40). New York, NY: Routledge.

Smith, P. K., Mahdavi, J., Carvalho, M., Fisher, S., Russell, S., & Tippett, N. (2008). Cyberbullying: Its nature and impact in secondary school pupils. *Journal of Child Psychology and Psychiatry, and Allied Disciplines, 49*(4), 376–385. doi:10.1111/j.1469-7610.2007.01846.x PMID:18363945

Sourander, A., Brunstein, A., Ikonen, M., Lindroos, J., Luntamo, T., Koskelainen, M., ... Helenius, H. (2010). Psychosocial risk factors associated with cyberbullying among adolescents: A population-based study. *Archives of General Psychiatry, 67*(7), 720–728. doi:10.1001/archgenpsychiatry.2010.79 PMID:20603453

Stoll, L. C., & Block, R. Jr. (2015). Intersectionality and cyberbullying: A study of cybervictimization in a Midwestern high school. *Computers in Human Behavior, 52,* 387–391. doi:10.1016/j.chb.2015.06.010

Strohmeier, D., Aoyama, I., Gradinger, P., & Toda, Y. (2013). Cybervictimization and cyberaggression in Eastern and Western countries: Challenges of constructing a cross-cultural appropriate scale. In S. Bauman, D. Cross, & J. L. Walker (Eds.), *Principles of cyberbullying research: Definitions, measures, and methodology* (pp. 202–221). New York: Routledge.

Suler, J. (2004). The online disinhibition effect. *Cyberpsychology & Behavior, 7*(3), 321–326. doi:10.1089/1094931041291295 PMID:15257832

Tangen, D., & Campbell, M. (2010). Cyberbullying prevention: One primary school's approach. *Australian Journal of Guidance & Counselling, 20*(02), 225–234. doi:10.1375/ajgc.20.2.225

Toledano, S., Werch, B. L., & Wiens, B. A. (2015). Domain-specific self-concept in relation to traditional and cyber peer aggression. *Journal of School Violence, 14*(4), 405–423. doi:10.1080/15388220.2014.935386

Totura, C. M. W., MacKinnon-Lewis, C., Gesten, E. L., Gadd, R., Divine, K. P., Dunham, S., & Kamboukos, D. (2009). Bullying and victimization among boys and girls in middle school: The influence of perceived family and school contexts. *The Journal of Early Adolescence, 29*(4), 571–609. doi:10.1177/0272431608324190

Wade, A., & Beran, T. (2011). Cyberbullying: The new era of bullying. *Canadian Journal of School Psychology, 26*(1), 44–61. doi:10.1177/0829573510396318

Wong, D. S., Chan, H. C. O., & Cheng, C. H. (2014). Cyberbullying perpetration and victimization among adolescents in Hong Kong. *Children and Youth Services Review, 36*, 133–140. doi:10.1016/j.childyouth.2013.11.006

Wright, M. F. (2013). The relationship between young adults' beliefs about anonymity and subsequent cyber aggression. *Cyberpsychology, Behavior, and Social Networking, 16*(12), 858–862. doi:10.1089/cyber.2013.0009 PMID:23849002

Wright, M. F. (2014a). Cyber victimization and perceived stress: Linkages to late adolescents' cyber aggression and psychological functioning. *Youth & Society*.

Wright, M. F. (2014b). Predictors of anonymous cyber aggression: The role of adolescents' beliefs about anonymity, aggression, and the permanency of digital content. *Cyberpsychology, Behavior, and Social Networking, 17*(7), 431–438. doi:10.1089/cyber.2013.0457 PMID:24724731

Wright, M. F. (2014c). Longitudinal investigation of the associations between adolescents' popularity and cyber social behaviors. *Journal of School Violence, 13*(3), 291–314. doi:10.1080/15388220.2013.849201

Wright, M. F. (2015). Cyber victimization and adjustment difficulties: The mediation of Chinese and American adolescents' digital technology usage. *Cyberpsychology (Brno), 1*(1), 1. Retrieved from http://cyberpsychology.eu/view.php?cisloclanku=2015051102&article=1

Wright, M. F. (in press). Adolescents' cyber aggression perpetration and cyber victimization: The longitudinal associations with school functioning. *Social Psychology of Education*.

Wright, M. F., Kamble, S., Lei, K., Li, Z., Aoyama, I., & Shruti, S. (2015). Peer attachment and cyberbullying involvement among Chinese, Indian, and Japanese adolescents. *Societies (Basel, Switzerland), 5*(4), 339–353. doi:10.3390oc5020339

Wright, M. F., & Li, Y. (2012). Kicking the digital dog: A longitudinal investigation of young adults' victimization and cyber-displaced aggression. *Cyberpsychology, Behavior, and Social Networking, 15*(9), 448–454. doi:10.1089/cyber.2012.0061 PMID:22974350

Wright, M. F., & Li, Y. (2013a). Normative beliefs about aggression and cyber aggression among young adults: A longitudinal investigation. *Aggressive Behavior*, *39*(3), 161–170. doi:10.1002/ab.21470 PMID:23440595

Wright, M. F., & Li, Y. (2013b). The association between cyber victimization and subsequent cyber aggression: The moderating effect of peer rejection. *Journal of Youth and Adolescence*, *42*(5), 662–674. doi:10.100710964-012-9903-3 PMID:23299177

Ybarra, M. L., Diener-West, M., & Leaf, P. (2007). Examining the overlap in internet harassment and school bullying: Implications for school intervention. *The Journal of Adolescent Health*, *1*(6), 42–50. doi:10.1016/j.jadohealth.2007.09.004 PMID:18047944

Ybarra, M. L., & Mitchell, K. J. (2004). Online aggressor/targets, aggressors, and targets: A comparison of associated youth characteristics. *Journal of Child Psychology and Psychiatry, and Allied Disciplines*, *45*(7), 1308–1316. doi:10.1111/j.1469-7610.2004.00328.x PMID:15335350

Yousef, W. S. M., & Bellamy, A. (2015). The impact of cyberbullying on the self-esteem and academic functioning of Arab American middle and high school students. *Electronic Journal of Research in Educational Psychology*, *23*(3), 463–482.

Zhou, Z., Tang, H., Tian, Y., Wei, H., Zhang, F., & Morrison, C. M. (2013). Cyberbullying and its risk factors among Chinese high school students. *School Psychology International*, *34*(6), 630–647. doi:10.1177/0143034313479692

ADDITIONAL READING

Bauman, S. (2011). *Cyberbullying: What counselors need to know*. Alexandria, VA: American Counseling Association.

Bauman, S., Cross, D., & Walker, J. (2013). *Principles of cyberbullying research: Definitions, measures, and methodology*. New York, NY: Routledge.

Hinduja, S., & Patchin, J. W. (2015). *Bullying beyond the schoolyard: Preventing and responding to cyberbullying*. Thousand Oaks, CA: Sage Publications.

Li, Q., Cross, D., & Smith, P. K. (2012). *Cyberbullying in the global playground*. Malden, MA: Blackwell Publishing. doi:10.1002/9781119954484

Menesini, E., & Spiel, C. (2012). *Cyberbullying: Development, consequences, risk and protective factors*. New York, NY: Psychology Press.

Tokunaga, R. S. (2010). Following you home from school: A critical review and synthesis of research on cyberbullying victimization. *Computers in Human Behavior*, *26*(3), 277–287. doi:10.1016/j.chb.2009.11.014

Wright, M. F. (2016). *A social-ecological approach to cyberbullying*. Hauppauge, NY: NOVA Publisher.

KEY TERMS AND DEFINITIONS

Anonymity: The quality of being unknown or unacknowledged.

Anxiety: A mental health disorder which includes symptoms of worry, anxiety, and/or fear that are intense enough to disrupt one's daily activities.

Collectivism: A cultural value that stressed the importance of the group over individual goals and cohesion within social groups.

Cyberbullying: Children's and adolescents' usage of electronic technologies to hostilely and intentionally harass, embarrass, and intimidate others.

Empathy: The ability to understand or feel what another person is experiencing or feeling.

Externalizing Difficulties: Includes children's and adolescents' failure to control their behaviors.

Individualism: The belief that each person is more important than the needs of the whole group or society.

Loneliness: An unpleasant emotional response to isolation or lack of companionship.

Normative Belief: Beliefs about the acceptability and tolerability of a behavior.

Parental Mediation and Monitoring: The strategies that parents use to manage the relationship between their children and media.

Parenting Style: The standard strategies that parents use in their child rearing.

Peer Attachment: The internalization of the knowledge that their peers will be available and responsive.

Peer Contagion: The transmission or transfer of deviant behavior from one adolescent to another.

Pro-Victim Attitudes: The belief that bullying is unacceptable and that defending victims is valuable.

Social Exclusion: The process involving individuals or groups of people block or deny someone from the group.

Traditional Face-to-Face Bullying: The use of strength or influence to intimidate or physically harm someone.

Chapter 10
Internet Addiction and Online Gaming:
An Emerging Epidemic of the Twenty-First Century?

Tanay Maiti
Christian Medical College, India

ABSTRACT

Internet addiction has gradually turned a medium of gaming and other leisure activities shifting from its original intention to fasten the communication and help in the researches. The excessive usage of internet and nature of its usage has been found to be similar with psycho-addictive substance addiction with similar neurobiological basis. Inclusion of gambling disorder into DSM 5 further strengthens the emerging concept of behavioral addiction. Various worldwide researches also support the upsurge of such problem. The clinical presentation and management options are mostly based on the behavioral principles learned from the substance abuse problems. However, large-scale randomized trails and epidemiological studies are definitely needed to understand this twenty-first century problem.

INTRODUCTION

The Internet itself is a neutral device originally designed to facilitate research among academic and military agencies. However, how some people have come to use this communication medium has created a stir among the mental health community by great discussion of Internet addiction. Addictive use of the Internet is a new and rapidly growing phenomenon.

According to the Pew Research Center (2003), Internet use in the United States alone has grown from just less than half of American adults in 2000 to about 59% of adults at the end of 2002, and studies suggest that nearly 6% of online users suffer from Internet addiction (Greenfield, 1999). Since then, over the last few decades increased presentation of such problems occasionally as a sole complaint has been observed worldwide over various settings. More than the earlier existing controversies, online gaming and over use of internet is more of a real-life problem over the question of its rarity.

DOI: 10.4018/978-1-5225-4047-2.ch010

ADDICTION NEUROBIOLOGY

The neurobiological model of any disorder generally explains the disorder from genetic aspects, neuroanatomical regions related to the functions, receptor and synaptic systems, signal transduction and proteins related to it. Family and twin studies have persistently showed up to 60% of heritability among first degree relatives. Trait factors like impulsivity risk taking behavior, stress responsivity and even chances of co morbidity seemed to be having higher genetic inheritance. Various genes like OPRM1, OPRK1, DRD2, DRD3, DRD4, tryptophan hydroxylase 1 and 2, MAO A, COMT, GABA receptor alpha1, beta1 and alpha6, CYP 2D6, ADH1B,1C etc. have been identified to be having potential roles in various psychoactive substance abuse. From vulnerability to relapse genes has been observed to have prominent roles in addiction behavior. Ventral tegmental area(VTA), Nucleus Accumbens (NA) and Prefrontal Cortex(PFC) has remained part of the postulated reward pathway and their significance has been proved persistently in functional imaging.

BIO-PSYCHO-SOCIAL MODEL OF ADDICTION

Since George Engel proposed his revolutionary biopsychosocial model of illnesses, the psychological factors and social stressors has remained a matter of discussion and search for other modifiable factors have been proved effective. The role of psychological and social factors has been found to have immense role in addiction and substance abuse specially because of their role in management and chance to modify certain 'set behavior/patterns'.

There are many individual (personal vulnerability) factors that may be involved in the acquisition, development and maintenance of behavioral addictions (e.g. personality traits, biological and genetic predispositions, unconscious motivations, learning and conditioning effects, thoughts, beliefs, and attitudes), although some factors are more personal (e.g. financial motivation and economic pressures in the case of gambling addiction).

Addiction is an incredibly complex behavior and always results from an interaction and interplay between many factors including the person's biological and/or genetic predisposition, their psychological constitution (personality factors, unconscious motivations, attitudes, expectations, beliefs, etc.), their social environment (situational characteristics such as accessibility and availability of the activity, the advertising of the activity) and the nature of the activity itself (i.e. structural characteristics such as the size of the stake or jackpot in gambling). This 'global' view of addiction highlights the interconnected processes and integration between individual differences (i.e. personal vulnerability), situational factors, structural characteristics, and the resulting addictive pattern of behavior. There are many individual (personal vulnerability and traits) factors that may work as predisposing factors, whereas the development and maintenance of behavioral addictions might occur over factors like; unconscious motivations, learning and conditioning effects, personal thoughts, cultural beliefs and attitudes, although some factors are more personal or situational(e.g. financial motivation and economic pressures in the case of gambling addiction).

Psychosocial factors such as low self-esteem, loneliness, depression, high anxiety, and stress all appear to be common among those with behavioral addictions (Griffiths, 2015).

BEHAVIORAL ADDICTION

According to DSM-IV, the essential feature of behavioral addictions is the failure to resist an impulse, drive, or temptation to perform an act that is harmful to the person or to others. Each behavioral addiction is characterized by a recurrent pattern of behavior in one specific domain. The repetitive engagement in such pattern of behaviors which affects one's functioning much similarly like addiction to psychoactive substances. Behavioral and substance addictions have many similarities in natural history, phenomenology, and adverse consequences. Both have onset in adolescence and young adulthood and higher rates in these age groups than among older adults (Chambers & Potenza, 2003) including natural histories that may exhibit chronic, relapsing patterns, but with many people recovering on their own without formal treatment (Slutske, 2006).

The diagnostic criteria for other behavioral addiction has been proposed also, including compulsive buying (Black, 1996), Internet addiction (Ko, Yen, Yen, Chen, & Chen, 2009), video/computer game addiction (Porter, Starcevic, Berle, & Fenech, 2010), sexual addiction (Goodman, 1992) etc.

CLASSIFICATORY SYSTEM AND BEHAVIORAL ADDICTION

In 2013, the criteria for problem gambling (now called 'Gambling Disorder') were included in the newly published fifth edition of the Diagnostic and Statistical Manual for Mental Disorders (DSM-5), and for the very first time, problem gambling or any behavioral 'addiction' was included in the section 'Substance-related and Addiction Disorders' (in the place of earlier section of impulse control disorders as it was been included in DSM III). Over clinical discussion and individual views, DSM 5 is first to include behavioral addiction in the classificatory systems. There had also been debates about whether or not 'Internet Addiction Disorder' should have been included in the DSM-5. As a result of these debates, the Substance Use Disorder Work Group recommended that the DSM-5 include 'Internet Gaming Disorder' (IGD) in Section three (Emerging Measures and Models) which needs 'further research' before possible inclusion in future editions. Other than gambling and gaming, no other behavior (sex, work, exercise, love etc.) has yet to be classified as a genuine addiction by established medical and/or psychiatric organizations. Lack of national level data/registry is certainly a prominent hindrance to understand the community prevalence and henceforth to argue for inclusion of other behavioral addictions. Further large-scale community based research and understanding the phenomenology will surely help to understand the nature of various types of behavioral addictions and common links among them.

EVOLUTION OF CONCEPT OF BEHAVIORAL AND INTERNET ADDICTION

In ancient Greece, where organized gaming was part and parcel of daily life, Emperor Commodus possessed hedonistic and irresponsible gambling habits that may have contributed to the decline of the Roman Empire (Hekster, 2002). In the era modern psychiatry, in the 1812 edition of the first American text on mental illness, Benjamin Rush, the founder of the American Psychiatric Association, called attention to the potentially pathological nature of excessive sexual desire (Rush, 1812). But it was not until

2010 that the Diagnostic and Statistical Manual Work Group for the *Diagnostic and Statistical Manual of Mental Disorders,* Fifth Edition (*DSM-5*), added the term *behavioral addictions* to the set of official psychiatric diagnoses. However, the term 'internet addiction' was first proposed by Ivan Goldberg for pathological internet use in 1993 (Kuss, 2014). Caplan later replaced the term to "problematic internet use"(PIU) mentioning that social isolation plays a greater role in behavioral symptoms of PIU than does the presence of psychopathology (Caplan, 2007).

TYPES OF ONLINE GAMING

The main objective of playing videogames is to entertain users via interactive systems that have now been developed across multiple platforms (e.g., personal computer, game consoles, mobile phones, and tablets). Consequently, there are thousands types of online videogames have emerged in the virtual word, which include:

1. Massively multiplayer online role-playing games (MMORPGs), such as World of Warcraft (WoW);
2. Multiplayer online battle arena (MOBA) games, such as League of Legends (LoL); and
3. First-person shooter (FPS) games such as action games like Battlefield (BT), Counter Strike (CS), and Call of Duty (CoD).
4. There are also Bsocial videogames, such as Angry Birds, which are usually very simple and quick to play and have been developed to play via social networks and smartphones (Carbonell, Torres-Rodríguez, & Fuster, 2016).

However, such classification may become less important due to the way new games are evolving. Newer games have begun to incorporate multiple genres and game modes simultaneously: action games (survival, shooter, platform, etc.), simulation games (vehicle, life, and construction simulation), role-playing games (MMORPGs), strategy games (MOBA, wargames, etc.), adventure games, sports games, cooperative games, and casual games. videogames are becoming more realistic and complete, offering users immersive playability.

TYPES OF INTERENT ADDICTION

Young (1998) further categorized five specific types of internet addiction:

1. Cyber sexual addiction or cyber porn;
2. Cyber relationship addiction to online friendships that replace real-life situations;
3. Netcompulsions to online gambling, auctions,
4. Information overload leading to compulsive web surfing; and
5. Addiction to computer game playing or programming (Young, 1998).

PREVALENCE

There were about 42 million active internet users in urban India in 2008 as compared to 5 million in 2000 (Goel, Subramanyam, & Kamath, 2013). Reports reveals that there were about 137 million internet users in India in 2013 and further suggest India as world's second largest in internet use after China in the near future. There is considerable variance in the prevalence rates reported across studies for internet addiction with rates between 0.3% and 38% being re-ported (Kuss, 2013). 1.5% in Greece (Simons, Dafouli, Braimiotis, Mouzas, & Angelopoulos, 2008), 1.6% in Finland (Ko, Yen, Chen, Wang, Chen, & Yen, 2014) while high rates of 5.3% being reported in Riyadh, Saudi Arabia (Al-Hantoushi & Al-Abdullateef, 2014). In another study that used a modified version of the Minnesota Impulsive Disorders Inventory, 4% of US high school adolescents were identified as being addicted to the internet (Ko, Yen, Yen, Chen, & Chen, 2012). Higher prevalence rates have been re-ported in adolescents, with studies demonstrating 8% prevalence in China (Yu, & Shek, 2013) and 10.7% in South Korea (Kim, Ryu, Chon, Yeun, Choi, Seo, & Nam, 2006).

ETIOLOGY: TEMPERAMENT, PERSONALITY FACTORS, AND PSYCHOPATHOLOGY

Why some people likes internet more than 'usual' than the 'usual population'? what appeals them extra? Zuret has pointed out that fun, engaging, collaborative, opportunity to build community, challenging, can play any time, meet new people – all at one's fingertips mostly turns very lucrative. Working in hierarchy, opportunity to be imaginative, opportunity to create – build games also add on into that.

Role of various demographic details has also been looked into by Griffiths et al where variables like gender, age, marital status, nationality, education level, occupation have been evaluated against popular online game Ever quest, where they examined playing frequency (i.e., amount of time spent playing the game a week), playing history (i.e., how long they had been playing the game, who they played the game with, whether they had ever gender swapped their game character), the favorite and least favorite aspects of playing the game, and what they sacrifice (if anything) to play the game. Results showed that 81% of online game players were male, and that the mean age of players was 27.9 years of age. For many players, the social aspects of the game were the most important factor in playing. A small minority of players appear to play excessively (over 80 h a week), and results suggest that a small minority sacrifice important activities in order to play (e.g., sleep, time with family and/or partner, work, or schooling) (Griffiths & Whitty, 2010). There is also increasing convergence between online gaming and other online activities such as gambling, activities that are primarily based on positive and negative reinforcement. Other similar characteristics include the following:

1. High sociability;
2. Multiplayer features;
3. Potential for high immersion in virtual environments;
4. Creation of one's own virtual identity and/or character development; and
5. Possibility of infinite duration within a 24/7 environment (Griffiths & Nuyens, 2017; King Delfabbro, & Griffiths, 2010; Wood, Griffiths, Chappell, & Davies, 2004).

All five of these things can be found in online gambling too.

The playing of massively multiplayer online role-playing games (MMORPGs) is now a highly popular leisure activity. Studies have been set out to explore the attitudes, experiences, and feelings of online gamers. Study involving various countries with different ethnic origins have found 6 main themes emerged from the analyses of the interview transcripts:

1. Online gaming and integration into day-to-day lives;
2. Online gaming, excessive play, and problems;
3. Addiction;
4. Psychosocial impact;
5. Gaming, dissociation, and time loss; and
6. Gaming and the alleviation of negative emotions.

These findings specifically showed how gamers used MMORPGs to alleviate negative feelings and provided detailed descriptions of personal problems that had arisen while playing such games (Hussian & Griffiths, 2009). Lam and colleagues looked into several factors are predictive of problematic Internet use, including personality traits, parenting and familial factors, alcohol use, and social anxiety. They concluded that although internet-addicted individuals have difficulty suppressing their excessive online behaviors in real life, further research is needed to understand detailed pathophysiological and cognitive mechanisms responsible for Internet addiction. On the other end, a south east Asian study involving various kind of college students like medicine, dental, nursing, pharmacology and agriculture has shown (using Internet addiction test (IAT) and Duke Health profile tool) no statistically significant correlation between IAT score and psychopathologies.

ONLINE VIDEO GAME ADDICTION FRAMEWORK

To organize a structured literature review, a model following Venkatesh and Bala's (2008) framework for analyzing Technology Acceptance Model (TAM) research worth to be discussed. In the proposed framework, it is important to note that current literature does not clearly articulate the causal relationship between psychosocial problems and video game addiction. As such, psychosocial problems are expressed with a bidirectional relationship with online video game addiction, showing the comorbidity identified in medical literature rather than as outcomes.

RISK FACTORS

Selective important risk factors in addiction to online videogames (Rodriguez & Griffiths, 2017):

1. Biological factors
    a. Vulnerability to addictions
    b. Deficits in neurotransmitters
    c. Psychiatric comorbidity: depression, anxiety, ADHD, ASD, etc.
2. Personality and psychological vulnerability factors

Figure 1.
Source: Venkatesh & Bala, 2008.

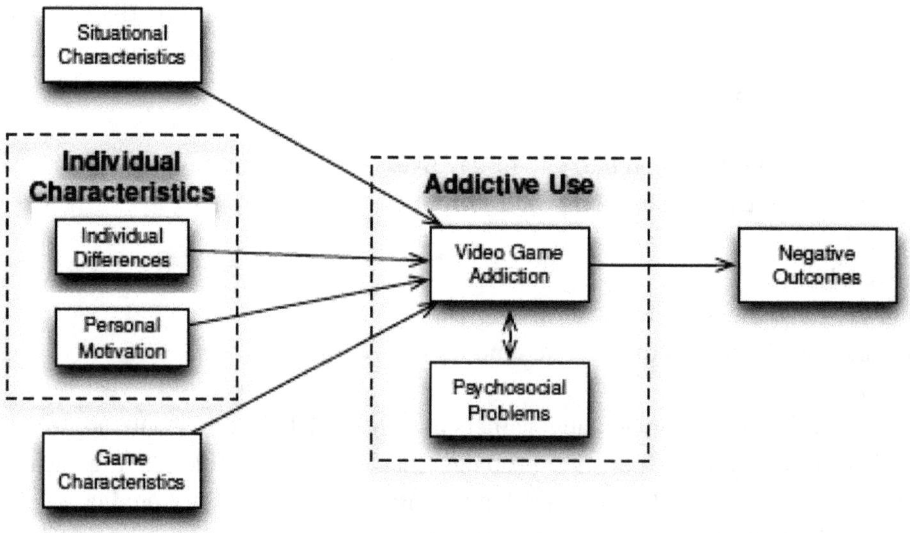

   a. Immaturity
   b. Unconsolidated identity
   c. Low self-esteem and indecision
   d. Lack of self-control
   e. Frustration
   f. Low resilience
   g. High sensation search
   h. Deficit of social skills, inhibition and extreme shyness
3. Environmental factors
   a. Family environment: conflictive, poor communication and affection, lack of supervision and family cohesion, etc.
   b. School environment with low performance, demotivation, etc.
   c. Poor social environment
4. Stress factors
   a. Grief
   b. Major crises
   c. Drastic life changes

NOSOLOGY AND DIAGNOSTIC STATUS

Young (1996) characterized Internet addiction as staying online for pleasure averaging 38 hours or more per week, largely in chat rooms, and concluded that Internet addiction can shatter families, relationships and careers (Young, 1996).

Criteria for Problematic Internet Use Include (Young, 1999):

1. Preoccupation with Internet
2. Need for longer amounts of time online
3. Repeated attempts to reduce Internet use
4. Withdrawal when reducing Internet use
5. Time management issues
6. Environmental distress (family, school, work, friends)
7. Deception around time spent online
8. Mood modification through Internet use

Broader diagnostic criteria for problematic internet use as proposed by Shapira (Shapira, Lessing, Goldsmith, Szabo, Lazoritz, Gold, & Stein, 2003):

1. Maladaptive preoccupation with internet use, as indicated by at least one of:
    a. Preoccupation experienced as irresistible.
    b. Excessive use of periods longer than planned.
2. With clinically significant distress or impairment.
3. Not occurring during the period of mania or hypomania.

Whereas, Beard et al.(2001) recommends that the following diagnostics criteria are required for a diagnosis of internet addiction viz:

1. Feeling preoccupied with the Internet;
2. Need to use the internet with- increased amounts of time in order to achieve satisfaction;
3. Unsuccessful efforts to control, cut back, or stop inter-net use;
4. Restless, moody, depressed, or irritable when attempting to cut down or stop internet use;
5. Staying online longer than originally intended. Additionally, at least one of the following must be present;
6. Jeopardized or risked the loss of a significant relationship, job, educational or career opportunity because of the internet;
7. Lying to family members, therapist, or others to conceal the extent of involvement with the inter-net and;
8. Using the internet as a way of escaping from problems or of relieving a dysphoric mood (e.g., feelings of helplessness, guilt, anxiety, depression).

Finally, the DSM 5 criteria.

Repetitive use of Internet-based games, about which 5 out of following 9 criteria must be met within one year:

1. Preoccupation or obsession with Internet games.
2. Withdrawal symptoms when not playing Internet games.
3. A build-up of tolerance–more time needs to be spent.
4. Tried to stop or curb playing, but has failed to do so.
5. Had a loss of interest in other life activities, such as hobbies.

6. Continued overuse even with the knowledge of impact.
7. Lied to others about his or her Internet game usage.
8. Uses Internet games to relieve anxiety or guilt.
9. Lost or put at risk & opportunity or relationship (DSM 5, 2013).

CLINICAL FEATURES AND RED FLAGS

Warning Signs

How to identify when the internet use is turning or what could be the identifiable red flags when oneself/ caregiver needs to get cautious about the overuse:

- **Preoccupation With the Game:** The psychological and affective involvement is often remains the prominent feature where the individual lives in the internet or his gaming world.
- **Lying or Hiding Gaming Issues:** The individual often keeps his gaming behavior as 'personal life' and remains secretive about it to family members.
- **Defensiveness and Anger:** Individual remains defensive and turns angry when anybody enquires about his/her online activities.
- **Loss of Interest in Other Activities:** Individual often neglects academic, occupational or outdoor activities for the sake of internet life.
- **Psychological Withdrawal:** Frequent irritability and other anxiety symptoms are prominent when internet access is not available.
- **Using Gaming as Escape:** The setbacks in life or other frustration including relationship breakup often takes individual in the internet world where he/she finds the needed solace.

ASSESSMENT

Using Young's internet addiction criteria (Young,1998):

The Internet Addiction Test (IAT) (Widyanto, 2004)

This was a 20-item likert scale that measured the severity of self-reported compulsive use of the internet. Total internet addiction scale scores were calculated, with possible scores for the sum of 20 items ranging from 20-100. According to Young's criteria, total IAT scores 20-39 represent average users with complete control of their internet use 40-69 represent over-users with frequent problems caused by their internet use, 70-100 represent internet addicts with significant problems caused by their internet use. This was used to determine the presence or absence of internet ad-diction in the adolescents. The original questionnaire is in English and was used for the study.

According to Turel et al. (2011b) Behavioural and Technology Addiction can be categorized into three groups which can be applied to Video Game Addiction as well, like:

1. Unidimensional measures that are Obsessive-Compulsive Disorder based. For example, Van Rooij et al (2011) adopt Compulsive Internet Use Scale (CIUS; Meerkerk, Van Den Eijnden, Vermulst, & Garretsen, 2009) in the context of online gaming.
2. Unidimensional constructs developed to measure the core symptoms, which are generally based on DSM-IV's Pathological Gambling diagnosis questionnaire, categorized as an Impulse Control Disorder. e.g. Charlton and Daforth (2007); Chou and Ting (2003); Griffiths and Hunt (1998). These are mostly the recently developed ones keeping online gaming in the mindset.
3. Multidimensional or composite constructs that are composed of different scales. Haagsma et al (2013) develop a new scale based on Caplan's (2010) General Problematic Internet Use Scale (GPIUS), where video game addiction has been seen through the structural model of relationships between different dimensions.

Assessment Of Pathological Internet Use (Young,1999) as proposed should be seen in following domains:

- Applications
- Emotions
- Cognitions
- Life Events

As these remains the prominent areas where the lives of online gamers move around.

COMPLICATIONS: NEGATIVE CONSEQUENCES OF ADDICTIVE USE OF THE INTERNET

The hallmark consequence of substance dependence is the medical implication involved, such as cirrhosis of the liver due to alcoholism, or increased risk of stroke due to cocaine use. However, the physical risk factors involved with an addiction to the Internet are comparatively minimal yet notable. While time is not a direct function in defining Internet addiction, generally addicted users are likely to use the Internet anywhere from forty to eighty hours per week, with single sessions that could last up to twenty hours. To accommodate such excessive use, sleep patterns are typically disrupted due to late night log-ins. The patient typically stays up past normal bedtime hours and may report staying on-line until two, three, or four in the morning with the reality of having to wake for work or school at six a.m. In extreme cases, caffeine pills are used to facilitate longer Internet sessions. Such sleep deprivation causes excessive fatigue often making academic or occupational functioning impaired and may decrease one's immune system, leaving the patient vulnerable to disease. Additionally, the sedentary act of prolonged computer use may result in a lack of proper exercise and lead to an increased risk for carpal tunnel syndrome, back strain, or eyestrain. While the physical side-effects of utilizing the Internet are mild compared to chemical dependency, addictive use of the Internet will result in similar familial, academic, and occupational impairment (Young, 1999).

Familial Problems

The scope of relationship problems caused by Internet addiction has been undermined by its current popularity and advanced utility. Young (1996) found that serious relationship problems among majority, including marriages, dating relationships, parent-child relationships, and close friendships have been prominent to be seriously disrupted by online-behavior or "net binges." Marriages appear to be the most affected as Internet use interferes with responsibilities and obligations at home, and it is typically the spouse who takes on these neglected chores and often feels like a "Cyber-widow." Addicted on-line users tend to use the Internet as an excuse to avoid needed but reluctantly performed daily chores such as doing the laundry, cutting the lawn, or going grocery shopping. Those boring tasks are ignored along with important activities such as caring for children, going to banks etc. Loved ones first rationalize the obsessed Internet user's behavior as "a phase" in hopes that the attraction will soon disappear. However, when addictive behavior continues, arguments about the increased volume of time and energy spent online soon take place, but such complaints are often deflected as part of the denial by the users. Addictive use is also evidenced by anger outbursts at others who question such behavior. Matrimonial lawyers even have reported seeing a rise in divorce cases due to the formation of such Cyberaffairs (Quittner, 1997). Individuals may form on-line relationships which with time will over-shadow time the actual spent with real life people. The chances and ability to carry out romantic and sexual relationships over on-line methods will further deteriorate the situation. The patient will continue to emotionally and socially withdraw from the marriage, exerting more effort to maintain recently discovered on-line "lovers" which certainly creates distrust and over time will hurt the quality of once stable relationships.

Academic Problems

The Internet has been touted as a premiere educational tool driving schools to integrate Internet services among their classroom environments. But while questioning its educational value, Young (1996) found that fifty-eight percent of students reported a decline in study habits, a significant drop in grades, missed classes, or being placed on probation due to excessive Internet use.

Although the merits of the Internet make it an ideal research tool, students often surf irrelevant web sites, engage in chat room gossip, converse with Internet pen pals for really long hours, and play interactive games at the cost of productive activity. In a survey by counselors at the University of Texas at Austin found that of the 531 valid responses, 14% met criteria for Internet addiction. At the University of Maryland at College Park's Counseling Center Internet addiction support group was initiated, where academic impairment and poor integration in extracurricular activities due to excessive Internet use on campus was addressed (Murphey, 1996).

Occupational Problems

Internet misuse among employees is a serious concern among their managers and supervisors. One survey with nearly 1,000 companies revealed that more than 50% of executives believed that time surfing the Internet for non-business purposes is undermining their employees' effectiveness on the job (Robert Half International, 1996). New monitoring devices are being created and updated every other day only to further confirm and strengthen the boss's suspicion. There is growing availability of such monitoring software as employers not only fear poor productivity, but they need to stop the use of valuable network resources for non-business related purposes (Newborne, 1997). The benefits of the Internet use such as assisting employees with anything from market research to business communication outweigh the negatives for any company, yet there is a definite and real concern for prominent distractions for many. Any misuse of time in the workplace creates a problem for managers, especially when the misuse happens with a regular and unavoidable tool/mode. Employers often stay uncertain how to approach Internet addiction among workers; further increasing conflicts, job suspensions, or termination from employment instead of making a referral to the company's Employee Assistance Program (Young, 1996).

PSYCHIATRIC CO MORBIDITY

Research on internet addiction had demonstrated that greater use of the internet is associated with social and psychological variables such as depression (Muller, Glaesmer, Brähler, Woelfling, & Beutel, 2014), loneliness (Petry, 2013), low self-esteem and life satisfaction (Nalwa, 2003), sensation or novelty seeking (Tonioni, 2012) and mental health problems (Kim, La Rose, & Peng, 2009). Inter-net addiction has now been officially recognized as a psychiatric disorder in the latest classification issued by the American Psychiatric Association (DSM-5).

High prevalence of major depression, adjustment disorder with depressive reaction, dissociative identity disorder and borderline personality disorder have been seen to be high prevalence along with online gaming addiction behavior and comorbid psychiatric pathology in 90% of 30 PIU-patients, also mostly depressive, anxiety and personality disorders (Kratzer & Hegerl, 2008); Wildt, 2010).

PHYSICAL HAZARDS

Though, comparing to various physical hazards caused by psychoactive substances, the physical effects of excessive internet use are mild, but following symptoms/problems need to be taken care of:

- Eye ache
- Refractive errors
- Back strain
- Back ache, spondylitis
- Carpal tunnel syndrome

INTERNET ADDICTION AND INDIAN RESEARCH

In the past few decades the internet use and nature of internet use have been changed markedly in India also and scientific research are not sparse from the subcontinent. Nalwa et al (2003) took part in a cross sectional multi centric study over various other countries(US, UK and China) and reported its emerging trend among the Indian population. Yadav et al.(2012) reported internet addiction of upto 12% among high school students(n=552) in a cross sectional study. Meena et al.(2012) reported problematic use upto 25% among school children population. Subharta et al. (2013) specially mentioned about high prevalence of social networking site addiction among college student. Even medical interns are not away from it as mentioned by Dave et al.(2015). However Grover et al. (2010) pointed towards the variation of the prevalence rates suggesting need of cautious approach/evidence based guidelines to identify internet addiction or problematic internet use. In a systematic review and meta-analysis by Davey et al. (2016) Out of total 33 articles included, only 9 studies on PIU in India were taken in meta-analysis; which revealed that although the overall pooled prevalence of "problematic internet use" was lower i.e. 21.6% [95%C.I.=0.2%-63%], despite heterogeneity among studies [(Q=5340, 95% C.I.=99.83 to 99.87], but it was statistically significant ($p<0.0001$) indicating it to be an emerging problem among Adolescents of India. Studies involving higher sample size with variable and heterogenous population with strict inclusion exclusion criteria (both to look for and rule out associated psychiatric comorbidities) are definitely need of the hour considering the telecom revolution India currently going through.

MANAGEMENT: PHARMACOLOGICAL AND NON PHARMAC OPTIONS

Pharmacological Options

Camardese et al. (2015) discussed the various pharmacological options using antidepressants, mood stabilizers, opioid receptor antagonists, or antipsychotics) can alleviate the symptomatic burden in patients with "Internet addiction." We also explore pharmacological interventions that target patterns of comorbidity and underlying psychopathological dimensions (e.g., addiction, impulsivity, obsessive-compulsive spectrum, bipolar spectrum, dissociation, etc.) shared with other behavioural or substance addictions. Successful use of SSRI (maximum dose citalopram 40 mg/day, titrated over a week) with antipsychotic augmentation(second generation antipsychotic quetiapine, upto 200mg/day) has been mentioned as a treatment option for problematic internet use, though the evidence is available as a case report (Atmaca, 2007). Internet addiction as a disorder similar to impulse control and treatment has been postulated accordingly, with known augmenting role of antipsychotics in similar condition. Also, Naltrexone, an opioid antagonist(with highest effect on mu type of receptor) with an established and evidence based role in deaddiction of various addictive substances, has been used in recent times for behavioural addictions including multiple randomized placebo-controlled trials (RCT) and in a meta analysis by Mouaffak et al. (2017) have found statistically significant score improvement under naltrexone versus placebo (fixed effect model: SMD = -0.27, 95% CI [-0.51 to -0.03], z = 2.23; p = 0.025.

TREATMENT STRATEGIES FOR PATHOLOGICAL INTERNET USE

Use of the Internet is legitimate in business and home practice such as in electronic correspondence to venders or electronic banking. Therefore, traditional abstinence models are not practical interventions when they prescribe banned Internet use. The focus of treatment should consist of moderation and controlled use. In this relatively new field, outcome studies are not yet available. However, based upon individual practitioners who have seen Internet addicted patients and prior research findings with other addictions.

Several techniques to treat Internet addiction are (Young,1999): (a) practice the opposite time in Internet use; (b) use external stoppers; (c) set goals; (d) abstain from a particular application; (e) use reminder cards; (f) develop a personal inventory; (g) enter a support group; and (h) family therapy. The first three interventions presented are simple time management techniques. However, more aggressive intervention is required when time management alone will not correct pathological Internet use. In these cases, the focus of treatment should be to assist the patient in developing effective coping strategies in order to change the addictive behavior through personal empowerment and proper support systems. If the patient finds positive ways of coping, then reliance upon the Internet to weather frustrations should no longer be necessary. However, keep in mind that in the early days of recovery, the patient will most likely experience a loss and miss being on-line for frequent periods of time.

Practice the Opposite

Knowing one's internet use pattern and re-arranging the time schedule is among the principle behavioral techniques for internet or online gaming addiction. The clinician should know about:

1. What days of the week do you typically log on-line?
2. What time of day do you usually begin?
3. How long do you stay on during a typical session? and;
4. Where do you usually use the computer?

Following this a new schedule is planned and client is motivated to re-adapt new time patterns of use in an effort to break the on-line habit named as PRACTICE THE OPPOSITE. Simple instructions like advising using internet during the weekends for a user who got used into a daily weekday habit, or planning frequent breaks for a patient who never takes break, checking emails for a person who is used to do the act just after waking up in the morning changing into after reaching office or may be after an hour work there can be useful as early behavioral intervention.

External Stoppers

Another simple technique is to use concrete things that the patient needs to do or places to go as prompters to help log off. If the patient has to leave for work at 7:30 am, have him or her log in at 6:30, leaving exactly one hour before its time to quit. The danger in this is the patient may ignore such natural alarms. If so, a real alarm clock or egg timer may help. Determine a time that the patient will end the Internet session and preset the alarm and tell the patient to keep it near the computer. When it sounds, it is time to log off. Keeping a fixed time to log out (e.g. 30 mins before starting for work or study) or use of actual alarm near the computer can be used as simple yet concrete techniques of external resource of stoppers.

Setting Goals

Many attempts to limit Internet usage fail because the user relies on an ambiguous plan to trim the hours without determining about the remaining on-line slots to use. As avoiding frequent and early relapses should also be kept in the management plan, structured sessions with reasonable goals, perhaps 15 hours instead of a current 30, over the week can make things easier for the user. The next task is schedule those 15 hours into frequent but brief sessions to manage the early craving and withdrawal symptoms. Once patient can successfully achieve a week's target persistently, further decrease in the time can be planned.

Abstinence

If a specific application has been identified and moderation of it has failed, then abstinence from that application is the next appropriate intervention. The patient must stop all activity surrounding that application. This does not mean that patients can not engage in other applications which they find to be less appealing or those with a legitimate use. A patient who finds chat rooms addictive, may need to abstain from them. However, this same patient may use e-mail or surf the World Wide Web to make airline reservations or shop for a new car. Abstinence is most applicable for the patient who also has a history of a prior addiction such as alcoholism or drug use. Patients with a premorbid history of alcohol or drug addiction often find the Internet a physically "safe" substitute addiction, henceforth increasing pattern of use and misuse. However, while the patient justifies the Internet is a "safe" addiction, he or she still avoids dealing with the compulsive personality or the unpleasant situation triggering the addictive behavior. For such cases, patients may feel more comfortable working towards an abstinence goal as their prior recovery involved this model. Incorporating past strategies that have been successful for these patients will empower them to effectively manage the Internet so that they can concentrate and work on their underlying problems.

Reminder Cards

Often patients feel overwhelmed because, through errors in their thinking, they exaggerate their difficulties and minimize the possibility of corrective action. To help the patient stay focused on the goal of either reduced use or abstinence from a particular application, have the patient make a list of the: (a) five major problems caused by addiction to the Internet, with; (b) five major benefits for cutting down Internet use or abstaining from a particular application, which could be difficulties in academic, social or occupational settings. Then, to write the points in a 'card' which patient can carry comfortably all the time, and remind self about his targets and goals. Reassuring the patients that itis well worth it to make their decision list as broad and all-encompassing as possible, and to be as honest as possible is necessary too. This kind of clear-minded assessment of consequences is a valuable skill to learn, one that patients will need later, after they have cut down or quite the Internet, for relapse prevention.

Personal Inventory

Whether the patient is trying to cut down or abstain from a particular application, it is a goodtime to help the patient cultivate an alternative activity. The clinician should have the patient take a personal inventory of what he or she has cut down on, if not have cut out totally, because of the time spent on the Internet. Perhaps the patient is spending less time with family, playing cricket, reading story books, or real dating over online dating. Or, it is an activity that the patient has always put off trying, like joining a fitness center or put off calling an old friend to arrange to have lunch. The clinician should instruct and actively help the patient to make a list of every activity or practice that has been neglected or curtailed since the on-line habit emerged with use of a like rt scale rating for better accountability. This exercise will help the patient become more aware of the choices he or she has made regarding the Internet and rekindle lost activities once enjoyed. This will be particularly helpful for patients who feel euphoric when engaged in on-line activity by cultivating pleasant feelings about real life activities and reduce their need to find emotional fulfillment on-line.

Support Groups

Some patients may be driven towards addictive use of the Internet due to a lack of real life social support. Young (1997) found that on-line social support greatly contributed to addictive behaviors among those who lived lonely lifestyles such as homemakers, singles, the disabled, or the retired. This study also found online behavior often takes grip in a person's life as a substitute for the lack of real life social support. Furthermore, patients who recently experienced situations such as a death of a loved one, a divorce, or a job loss may respond to the Internet as a mental distraction from their real-life problems (Young, 1997). Their absorption in the on-line world temporarily makes such problems fade into the background. If the life events assessment uncovers the presence of such maladaptive or unpleasant situations, treatment should focus on improving the patient's real life social support network. The clinician should help the client find an appropriate support group that best addresses his or her situation. Support groups tailored to the patient's particular life situation will help the patient to make friends who are in a similar situation rather than depending upon on-line cohorts. If a patient leads one of the above mentioned "lonely lifestyles" then perhaps the patient may join a local club, community groups, sports group which will enhance the real life social support. Few hospitals have developed specific treatment module with such recovery groups and offer computer/internet 'Addiction Recovery' services. Addiction recovery groups will address the maladaptive cognitions leading to such feelings and provide an opportunity to build real life relationships that will release their social inhibitions and need for Internet companionship. Lastly, these groups may help the Internet addict to find real life support to cope with difficult transitions during recovery akin to AA sponsors.

Family Therapy

Lastly, family therapy may be necessary among addicts whose marriages and family relationships have been disrupted and negatively influenced by Internet addiction. Intervention with the family should focus on several main areas: (a) educate the family on how addictive the Internet can be; (b) reduce blame on the addict for behaviors; (c) improve open communication about the pre-morbid problems in the family which drove the addict to seek out psychological fulfillment of emotional needs on-line; and (d) encourage the family to assist and being a support rather than turning critical during the process of recovery. A strong sense of family support may enable the patient to look into real life interactions and recovery from Internet addiction.

Hirzallah et al. (2013) proposed a Simple Exercise-to-Play Proposal that would Reduce Games Addiction and Keep Players Healthy especially considering the sedentary lifestyle and physical hazards associated with it. A specially designed treadmill acting as a movement capture device is proposed to capture players' commands for movements. These movements include running, walking, stopping, and turning. In that way, the players enjoy exercising as well as playing the game.

ROLE OF PARENTS AND SCHOOL

Parents

Setting and maintaining a time limit with positive reinforcement for accepted behavior may cause significant change in the targeted behaviors. Children often feel empowered while gaining a sense of mastery or powerfulness with better performance of these games. Overtaking all the cars or shooting the predators are often actually the wish to control things in virtual world if not in actual reality. Giving responsibility like monitoring the class, being the games or cultural coordinator and hence providing them a sense of control or mastery in the actual life can be a useful method. Keeping a connection with the school is also very important. Any academic failure or decline recent change of peers rejection from teachers could be enough stressful for adolescents to turn them into computer screen. We need to understand and not to forget that addiction basically boils down to constant reinforcement (i.e., rewards). An adolescent rarely turns addicted to something unless they are constantly rewarded for the behavior they are engaged in. Online gaming is potentially addictive although the number of people who are truly addicted is small in number. Online gaming addiction comes about by the partial reinforcement effect (PRE) (Griffiths, 2008). This is a critical psychological ingredient of gaming addiction whereby the reinforcement is intermittent (i.e., people keep responding in the absence of reinforcement hoping that another reward is just around the corner). Knowledge about the PRE gives the game designer an edge in designing appealing games. Magnitude of reinforcement (e.g., high points score for doing something in game) is also important. Large rewards lead to fast responding and greater resistance to extinction - in short to more "addiction" (Griffiths, 2008a). Instant reinforcement is also satisfying. online gaming certainly is more addictive than offline gaming, as online gaming involves multiple reinforcements in that different features might be differently rewarding to different people ('the kitchen sink approach'), the often the gamers get trapped in the factor of uncertainty meeting their need of novelty seeking. In video games more generally, the rewards might be intrinsic (e.g., improving your highest score, beating your friend's high score, getting one's name on the "hall of fame", mastering the machine) or extrinsic (e.g., peer admiration) (Griffiths, 2008). In online gaming, there is no end to the game and there is the potential for teenagers to play endlessly against (and with) other real people. This can be immensely rewarding and psychologically engrossing. For a small minority of people this will lead to addiction where online gaming is the single most important thing and that person's life and which the compromise and neglect everything else in their life (Griffiths, 2009). As with all addictions, there is a potential for long-term damage but the good news is that very few people appear to have developed such problems although there is research suggesting that in extreme cases, online gamers can experience all the core signs and symptoms of more traditional addictions such as withdrawal symptoms, conflict with other activities, mood modifying effects, and relapse (Chappell, Eatough, Davies & Griffiths, 2006). Healthy enthusiasms add to life, whereas addictions do the opposite. The vast majority of excessive gamers will say their activity has positive effects for them. There are many people who play excessively without having any negative impact on their life at all although many players experience some signs of addiction without necessarily being addicted (Grüsser, Thalemann, & Griffiths, 2007). Parents can check the content of the gaming activity. It is a positive effort to give the children and adolescents games that are educational rather than violent, and it can be both liked by the individual and therefore successful. Parents usually have control over what their child watches on television - gaming should not be any different. Encouraging group games in place of solitary activities can be tried as a method of 'harm reduction' initially, as research has consistently shown that the main reason for playing online games is for the social element (Griffiths, Davies & Chappell, 2003; 2004). Parents and guardians should always get their children to follow the recommendations by the game manufacturers and/or the service providers (e.g., sit at least two feet from the screen, play games in a well-lit room, never have the screen at maximum brightness, and never engage in gaming when feeling tired). Finally, if all else fails, temporarily prohibit gaming and then allow them to play again on a part-time basis when appropriate.

Not to finish with all negative outcomes, however, in over two decades of examining both the possible dangers and the potential benefits of videogame playing, evidence suggests that in the right context videogames can have positive health and educational benefits to a large range of different sub-groups (Griffiths, 2005; 2008b). There are also recent overviews showing that online gaming can be used in an educationally beneficial context (Defreitas & Griffiths, 2007; 2008). If care is taken in the design, and if they are put into the right context, videogames (both online and offline) have the potential to be used as training aids in classrooms and therapeutic settings, and to provide skills in psychomotor coordination, and in simulations of real life events (e.g., training recruits for the armed forces).

LEGISLATION

The term "internet censorship" it is regarded as an act of control or suppression of the publishing or accessing of information on the Internet. The past few years have seen an explosion in Internet usage in India with approximately a tenth of the country's population now considered active internet users. Excessive internet use often lands up in further risky behavior followed by legal troubles.

In India, laws which apply to or may affect various media are as follows:

1. Telecom and internet sector:
    a. Indian Telegraph Act, 1885.
    b. Indian Wireless Telegraphy Act, 1933.
    c. Regulations, tariff orders and directions which may be issued by telecom policies issued by the government/ regulator.
2. General laws that may be of importance to the above sectors:
    a. Indian Penal Code, 1860.
    b. Copyright Act, 1957.
    c. Indian Contract Act, 1872.
    d. Information Technology Act, 2000. (Telecoms, Media & Internet Laws & Regulations 2017: 10th edition)

Countries such as China have introduced laws to limit the amount of time that adolescents and adults can spend playing online games, and other countries such as Holland and South Korea have seen the opening of dedicated treatment clinics for gaming addiction (Griffiths, 2008). However, the way forward lies not in legislation but in education and prevention. For the vast majority of individuals, online gaming is an enjoyable and harmless activity - at least that is what the empirical evidence says at present. Maybe the situation will change over time and/or research will show there are cultural differences (suggesting different policies in different countries).

CONTROVERSY

Like other diagnostic issues and controversies regarding newly emerging disorders and their validity internet addiction or online gaming addiction is also surrounded by multiple controversies including whether that can be called at all 'an addiction' or not. Researchers has argued that in such way, every leisure activity can come under diagnostic over inclusion and 'forced' disease model about every individual behavior. Doubts has also been expressed about over focusing on individual behavior or behavioral manifestation rather than underlying disease be it mood or anxiety problems/disorder. Internet has been conceptualized as a medium/vehicle rather than the disease supporting the same. However, researchers who majorly considers internet to be gradually turning into a 'mode of disease' itself, argued other internet related behavior like online buying, surfing, creating online social media 'pages' are exclusively internet based behavior, hence particular emphasis should be given on such behaviors.

The major areas of debate remained to be:

- Mental disorder v/smanifestation of another underlying disorder.
- Internet is a medium (vehicle) rather than focus of disorder.
- Addicted to Internet or Internet-related behaviors (e.g., excessive pornography use/gaming/surfing/social networking) (DSM 5, 2013).

FUTURE DIRECTION

Over the past few years, study of the psychological ramifications of the Internet has grown. At the 1997 American Psychological Association convention, two symposia presented research and theories examining the effects of on-line behavior patterns compared to only one poster presentation in the prior year. The emergence of a new psychological journal is being developed that will focus upon aspects of Internet use and addiction. It is difficult to predict the results of these early endeavors. However, it is feasible that with years of collective effort, Internet addiction may be recognized as a legitimate impulse control disorder worthy of its own classification in future revisions of the *Diagnostic and Statistical Manual of Mental Disorders*. Until then, there is a need for the professional community to recognize and respond to the reality of Internet addiction and the threat of its rapid expansion. Surveys have found that about 47 million have ventured on-line and analysts estimate that another 11.7 million are planning to go on-line in the next year (Snider, 1997). With the growing popularity of the Internet, mental health practitioners should respond to the potential for an increased demand in treatment specifically designed to care for the Internet addicted patient. Since this is a new and often laughed about addiction, individuals are reluctant to seek out treatment fearing that clinicians may not take their complaints seriously. Drug and alcohol rehabilitation centers, community mental health clinics, and clinicians in private practice should avoid minimizing the impact to patients whose complaint involves Internet addiction and offer effective recovery programs. Advertisement of such programs both on-line and within the local community may encourage those timid individuals to come forward to seek the help they need. Among university settings and corporations, it would be prudent to recognize that students and employees, respectively, can become addicted to a tool provided directly by the institution. Thus, college counseling centers should invest energy in the development of seminars designed to increase awareness among faculty, staff, administrators, and students on the ramifications of Internet abuse on campus. Lastly, Employee Assistance Programs should educate human resource managers on the dangers of Internet misuse in the work place and offer recovery services for those found to be addicted as an alternative to suspension or termination from employment. To pursue such effective recovery programs, continued research is essential to better understand the underlying motivations of Internet addiction. Future research should focus on how psychiatric illness such as depression or obsessive-compulsive disorder may play a role in the development of pathological Internet use. Longitudinal studies of Internet addicts may reveal how personality traits, family dynamics, or communication skills influence the way people utilize the Internet. Lastly, outcome studies are needed to determine the efficacy of various therapy modalities and compare these outcomes against traditional recovery modalities.

CONCLUSION

The amount and the quality of research in the gaming addiction field has progressed much over the last decade but is still in its infancy compared to other more established behavioral addictions, such as pathological gambling. There is likely to be an even bigger increase in empirical research into problematic video game playing and videogame addiction. This will of course be dependent on both appropriate funding streams and/or whether gaming addiction ends up being included in future psychiatric disorder classifications (e.g., DSM, ICD, etc.). Future research is likely to include more epidemiological and/or general population data on media use, leading to better insights into the onset and course of problematic videogame play and addiction. Given the many different screening instruments that have been developed over the last decade, there is likely to be a refinement of video game addiction measures and greater consensus on its conceptualization, either as a single disorder and/or incorporated into other known disorders (e.g., impulse control disorder). This is also likely to lead to improved assessment tools based on such conceptualization(s). Measures of gaming use and subsequent behavior are likely to diversify in terms of media use, including social networking sites (SNS) and associated Internet resources (Kuss & Griffiths, 2011).

Given the pressure on media enterprises to ‘monetize’ their business and look for different revenue streams, there is likely to be even greater media convergence between gaming and other more profit-making activities such as gambling (King, Delfabbro, & Griffiths, 2010; Griffiths, 2008). Given the well established addictive potential of gambling, this may also have implications for the incidence of video game addiction. Gaming on the move is likely to be a big growth area that may have implications for excessive gaming *via* ‘convenience’ hardware such as handheld gaming consoles, PDA devices, mobile phones, tablet computers, and MP3 players. The world of 2018 onwards will certainly bring many technological fortunes however it’s upon us how we are going to use them best.

REFERENCES

Al-Hantoushi, M., & Al-Abdullateef, S. (2014). Internet addiction among secondary school students in Riyadh city, its prevalence, correlates and relation to depression: A questionnaire survey. *International Journal of Medical Science and Public Health*, *3*(1), 10–15. doi:10.5455/ijmsph.2013.130920131

American Psychiatric Association. (2000). *Diagnostic and statistical manual of mental disorders* (4th ed.). Washington, DC: Author.

American Psychiatric Association. (2013). *Diagnostic and statistical manual of mental disorders* (5th ed.). Arlington, VA: American Psychiatric Publishing.

Atmaca, M. (2007). A case of problematic internet use successfully treated with an SSRI-antipsychotic combination. *Program of Neuro-psychopharmacological and Biological Psychiatry*, *31*(4), 961–962. doi:10.1016/j.pnpbp.2007.01.003 PMID:17321659

Beard, K. W., & Wolf, E. M. (2001). Modification in the proposed di-agnostic criteria for Internet addiction. *Cyberpsychology & Behavior*, *4*(3), 377–383. doi:10.1089/109493101300210286 PMID:11710263

Black, D. W. (1996). Compulsive buying: A review. *The Journal of Clinical Psychiatry*, *57*(8), 50–54. PMID:8698681

Camardese, G., Leone, B., Walstra, C., Janiri, L., & Guglielmo, R. (2015). Pharmacological Treatment of Internet Addiction. In C. Montag & M. Reuter (Eds.), *Internet Addiction. Studies in Neuroscience, Psychology and Behavioral Economics*. Cham: Springer. doi:10.1007/978-3-319-07242-5_10

Caplan, S. E. (2007). Relations among loneliness, social anxiety, and problematic internet use. *Cyberpsychology & Behavior*, *10*(2), 234–242. doi:10.1089/cpb.2006.9963 PMID:17474841

Carbonell, X., Torres-Rodríguez, A., & Fuster, H. (2016). El potencialadictivo de los videojuegos. In E. Echerburua (Ed.), *Abuso de Internet: "antesala para la adicción al juego de azar on-line*. Madrid: Síntesis.

Chakraborty, K., Basu, D., & Kumar, K. (2010). Internet addiction: Consensus, controversies, and the way ahead. *East Asian Archives of Psychiatry*, *20*, 123–132. PMID:22348866

Chambers, R. A., & Potenza, M. N. (2003). Neurodevelopment, impulsivity, and adolescent gambling. *Journal of Gambling Studies*, *19*(1), 53–84. doi:10.1023/A:1021275130071 PMID:12635540

Chappell, D., Eatough, V., Davies, M. N. O., & Griffiths, M. D. (2006). Everquest - It's just acomputer game right? An interpretative phenomenological analysis of online gaming addiction. *International Journal of Mental Health and Addiction*, *4*(3), 205–216. doi:10.100711469-006-9028-6

Charlton, J., & Danforth, I. (2007). Distinguishing addiction and high engagement in the context of online game playing. *Computers in Human Behavior*, *23*(3), 1531–1548. doi:10.1016/j.chb.2005.07.002

Chou, T. J., & Ting, C. C. (2003). The role of flow experience in cyber-game addiction.: The impact of the Internet, multimedia and virtual reality on behavior and society. *Cyberpsychology & Behavior*, *6*(6), 663–675. doi:10.1089/109493103322725469 PMID:14756934

Cole, H., & Griffiths, M. D. (2007). Social interactions in Massively Multiplayer Online Role-Playing gamers. *Cyberpsychology & Behavior*, *10*(4), 575–583. doi:10.1089/cpb.2007.9988 PMID:17711367

Davey, S., & Davey, A. (2014). Assessment of Smartphone Addiction in Indian Adolescents: A Mixed Method Study by Systematic-review and Meta-analysis Approach. *International Journal of Preventive Medicine*, *5*(12), 1500–1511. PMID:25709785

Davey, S., Davey, A., & Singh, J.V. (2016). Emergence of Problematic Internet Use among Indian Adolescents: A Multi Method study. *Journal of Indian Association of Child and Adolescent Mental Health*, *12*(1), 60-78.

Davey, S., Raghav, S. K., Davey, A., Singh, N., & Singh, J. V. (2015). Internet usage patterns among medical interns of Muzaffarnagar: A comprehensive survey analysis. *Asian J Med Sci*, *6*(2), 99–104.

De Freitas, S., & Griffiths, M. D. (2007). Online gaming as an educational tool in learning and training. *British Journal of Educational Technology*, *38*(3), 536–538. doi:10.1111/j.1467-8535.2007.00720.x

De Freitas, S., & Griffiths, M. D. (2008). The convergence of gaming practices with other media forms: What potential for learning? Are view of the literature. *Learning, Media and Technology*, *33*(1), 11–20. doi:10.1080/17439880701868796

Fisher, S. (1994). Identifying video game addiction in children and adolescents. *Addictive Behaviors*, *19*(5), 545–553. doi:10.1016/0306-4603(94)90010-8 PMID:7832013

Gentile, D. (2009). Pathological video game use among youth ages 8 to 18: A national study. *Psychological Science*, *20*(5), 594–602. doi:10.1111/j.1467-9280.2009.02340.x PMID:19476590

Goel, D., Subramanyam, A., & Kamath, R. (2013). A study on the prevalence of internet addiction and its association with psychopathology in Indian adolescents. *Indian Journal of Psychiatry*, *55*(2), 140–143. doi:10.4103/0019-5545.111451 PMID:23825847

Goodman, A. (1992). Sexual addiction: Designation and treatment. *Journal of Sex & Marital Therapy*, *18*(4), 303–314. doi:10.1080/00926239208412855 PMID:1291701

Greenfield, D. (1999). *Virtual addiction: Help for netheads, cyberfreaks, and those who love them.* Oakland, CA: New Harbinger.

Griffiths. (2015). Classification and treatment of behavioral addiction. *Nursing in Practice*. Retrieved from https://www.researchgate.net/publication/273948452

Griffiths, M. (2015). Classification and treatment of behavioral addictions. *Nursing Practice (Edinburgh, Scotland)*, 82.

Griffiths, M. D. (2005). Online therapy for addictive behaviors. *Cyberpsychology & Behavior*, *8*(6), 555–561. doi:10.1089/cpb.2005.8.555 PMID:16332166

Griffiths, M. D. (2008). Diagnosis and management of video game addiction. *New Directions in Addiction Treatment and Prevention*, *12*, 27–41.

Griffiths, M. D. (2009). Online computer gaming: Advice for parents and teachers. *Education for Health*, *27*(1), 3.

Griffiths, M. D., & Cooper, G. (2003). Online therapy: Implications for problem gamblers and clinicians. *British Journal of Guidance & Counselling*, *13*(1), 113–135. doi:10.1080/0306988031000086206

Griffiths, M. D., Davies, M. N. O., & Chappell, D. (2004). Demographic factors and playing variables in online computer gaming. *Cyberpsychology & Behavior*, *7*(4), 479–487. doi:10.1089/cpb.2004.7.479 PMID:15331036

Griffiths, M. D., & Hunt, N. (1998). Dependence on computer games by adolescents. *Psychological Reports*, *82*(2), 475–480. doi:10.2466/pr0.1998.82.2.475 PMID:9621722

Griffiths, M. D., & Nuyens, F. (2017). An overview of structural characteristics in problematic video game playing. *Current Addiction Reports*, *4*(3), 272–283. doi:10.100740429-017-0162-y PMID:28845381

Griffiths, M. D., & Whitty, M. W. (2010). Online behavioral tracking in Internet gambling research: Ethical and methodological issues. *International Journal of Internet Research Ethics*, *3*, 104–117.

Grüsser, S. M., Thalemann, R., Albrecht, U., & Thalemann, C. N. (2005). ExzessiveComputernutzungimKindesalter—ErgebnisseeinerpsychometrischenErhebung. *Wiener Klinische Wochenschrift*, *117*(5-6), 188–195. PMID:15875758

Grüsser, S. M., Thalemann, R., & Griffiths, M. D. (2007). Excessive computer game playing: Evidence for addiction and aggression? *Cyberpsychology & Behavior*, *10*(2), 290–292. doi:10.1089/cpb.2006.9956 PMID:17474848

Haagsma, M. C., Caplan, S. E., Peters, O., & Pieterse, M. E. (2013). A cognitive-behavioral model of problematic online kgaming in adolescents aged 12–22years. *Computers in Human Behavior*, *29*(1), 202–209. doi:10.1016/j.chb.2012.08.006

Hekster, O. (2002). *Commodus: An emperor at the crossroads (Dutch monographs on ancient history and archaeology)*. Amsterdam: Brill Academic Publishers.

Hirzallah, N. (2013). A Simple Exercise-to-Play Proposal that would Reduce Games Addiction and Keep players healthy. *International Journal of Advanced Computer Science and Applications*, *4*(2), 86–91. doi:10.14569/IJACSA.2013.040213

Hussain, Z., & Griffiths, M. D. (2008). Gender swapping and socialising in cyberspace: An exploratory study. *Cyberpsychology & Behavior*, *11*(1), 47–53. doi:10.1089/cpb.2007.0020 PMID:18275312

Hussain, Z., & Griffiths, M. D. (2009). The attitudes, feelings, and experiences of online gamers: A qualitative analysis. *Cyberpsychology & Behavior*, *12*(6), 747–753. doi:10.1089/cpb.2009.0059 PMID:19788376

Kim, J., La Rose, R., & Peng, W. (2009). Loneliness as the cause and the effect of problematic Internet use: The relationship between Internet use and psychological well-being. *Cyber Psycholology and Behaviour*, *12*(4), 451-5.

Kim, K., Ryu, E., Chon, M. Y., Yeun, E. J., Choi, S. Y., Seo, J. S., & Nam, B. W. (2006). Internet addiction in Korean adolescents and its re-lation to depression and suicidal ideation: A question-naire survey. *International Journal of Nursing Studies*, *43*(2), 185–192. doi:10.1016/j.ijnurstu.2005.02.005 PMID:16427966

King, D., Delfabbro, P., & Griffiths, M. (2010). Cognitive behavioral therapy for problematic video game players: Conceptual considerations and practice issues. *Journal of Cyber Therapy and Rehabilitation*, *3*(3), 261–273.

King, D. L., Delfabbro, P. H., & Griffiths, M. D. (2010). The convergence of gambling and digital media: Implications for gambling in young people. *Journal of Gambling Studies*, *26*(2), 175–187. doi:10.100710899-009-9153-9 PMID:19756979

King, D. L., Delfabbro, P. H., & Griffiths, M. D. (2011). The role of structural characteristics in problematic video game play: An empirical study. *International Journal of Mental Health and Addiction*, *9*(3), 320–333. doi:10.100711469-010-9289-y

King, D. L., Delfabbro, P. H., Griffiths, M. D., & Gradisar, M. (2011). Assessing clinical trials of Internet addiction treatment: A systematic review and CONSORT evaluation. *Clinical Psychology Review*, *31*(7), 1110–1116. doi:10.1016/j.cpr.2011.06.009 PMID:21820990

Ko, C. H., Yen, J. Y., Chen, S. H., Wang, P. W., Chen, C. S., & Yen, C. F. (2014). Evaluation of the diagnostic criteria of Internet gaming disorder in the DSM-5 among young adults in Taiwan. *Journal of Psychiatric Research*, *53*, 103–110. doi:10.1016/j.jpsychires.2014.02.008 PMID:24581573

Ko, C. H., Yen, J. Y., Chen, S. H., Yang, M. J., Lin, H. C., & Yen, C. F. (2009, July). 92009). Proposed diagnostic criteria and the screening and diagnosing tool of Internet addiction in college students. *Comprehensive Psychiatry*, *50*(4), 378–384. doi:10.1016/j.comppsych.2007.05.019 PMID:19486737

Ko, C. H., Yen, J. Y., Yen, C. F., Chen, C. S., & Chen, C. C. (2012). The association between Internet addiction and psychiatric disorder: A review of the literature. *European Psychiatry*, *27*(1), 1–8. doi:10.1016/j.eurpsy.2010.04.011 PMID:22153731

Kratzer, S., & Hegerl, U. (2008). Is, "Internet Addiction" a disorder of ist own? A Study on subjects with excessive Internet use. *Psychiatrische Praxis*, *35*, 80–83. doi:10.1055-2007-970888 PMID:17546534

Kuss, D. J., & Griffiths, M. D. (2011). Online Social Networking and Addiction: A review of the psychological literature. *International Journal of Environmental Research and Public Health*, *8*(9), 3528–3552. doi:10.3390/ijerph8093528 PMID:22016701

Kuss, D. J., Griffiths, M. D., & Binder, J. F. (2013). Internet addiction in students: Prevalence and risk factors. *Computers in Human Behavior*, *3*(3), 959–966. doi:10.1016/j.chb.2012.12.024

Kuss, J. D., Griffiths, M., Karila, L., & Billieux, J. (2014). Internet addiction: A systematic review of epidemiological research for the last decade. *Current Pharmaceutical Design*, *20*(25), 4026–4052. doi:10.2174/13816128113199990617 PMID:24001297

Lewis, A., & Griffiths, M. D. (2011). Confronting gender representation: A qualitative study of the experiences and motivations of female casual-gamers. *Aloma: Revista de Psicologia. Ciències de l'Educació i de l'Esport, 28*, 245–272.

Machlis, S. (1997). Gotcha! Computer monitors riding the web wave. *Computerworld*, 1.

Maharana & Rayaprolu. (2016). Internet Censorship In India: Is It Acting Against Freedom Or Is It Serving For The Betterment Of The Community? *Journal of Legal Studies and Research, 2*(1), 81-141.

Meena, P. S., Mittal, P. K., & Solanki, R. K. (2012). Problematic use of social networking sites among urban school going teenagers. *Indian Journal of Psychiatry, 21*(2), 94–97. doi:10.4103/0972-6748.119589 PMID:24250039

Meerkerk, G.J., Van Den Eijnden, R. J. J. M., Vermulst, A. A., & Garretsen, H. F. L. (2009). The Compulsive Internet Use Scale (CIUS): some psychometric properties: the impact of the Internet, multimediaand virtual reality on behavior and society. *Cyber Psychology & Behavior, 12*(1), 1–6.

Mouaffak, F., Leite, C., Hamzaoui, S., Benyamina, A., Laqueille, X., & Kebir, O. (2017). Naltrexone in the Treatment of Broadly Defined Behavioral Addictions: A Review and Meta-Analysis of Randomized Controlled Trials. *European Addiction Research, 23*(4), 204–210. doi:10.1159/000480539 PMID:28877518

Müller, K. W., Glaesmer, H., Brähler, E., Woelfling, K., & Beutel, M. E. (2014). Prevalence of internet addiction in the general population: Results from a German population-based survey. *Behaviour & Information Technology, 33*(7), 757–766. doi:10.1080/0144929X.2013.810778

Murphey, B. (1996). Computer addictions entangle students. *APA Monitor*, 38.

Nael Hirzallah, A. (2013). Simple exercise to play proposal that would reduce game addiction and keep players healthy. *International Journal of Advanced Computer Science and Applications, 2*(2).

Nalwa, K., & Anand, A. P. (2003). Internet addiction in students: A cause of concern. *Cyberpsychology & Behavior, 6*(6), 653–656. doi:10.1089/109493103322725441 PMID:14756932

Newborne, E. (1997). Bosses worry Net access will cut productivity. *USA Today*, p. 4B.

Petry, N. M., & O'Brien, C. P. (2013). Internet gaming disorder and the DSM-5. *Addiction (Abingdon, England), 108*(7), 1186–1187. doi:10.1111/add.12162 PMID:23668389

Pew Internet Research Center. (2003). *Internet use by region in the United States*. Retrieved fromhttp://www.pewinternet.org/reports

Porter, G., Starcevic, V., Berle, D., & Fenech, P. (2010). Recognizing problem video game use. *The Australian and New Zealand Journal of Psychiatry, 44*(2), 120–128. doi:10.3109/00048670903279812 PMID:20113300

Press Release. (1996). *Surf's up! Is productivity down?* Robert Half International.

Quittner, J. (1997, April 14). Divorce Internet Style. *Time*, 72.

Rodriguez, A. T., & Griffiths, M. D. (2017). The Treatment of Internet Gaming Disorder: A Brief Overview of the PIPATIC Program. *International Journal of Mental Health and Addiction*, 1–16. doi:10.100711469-017-9825-0

Rush, B. (1812). *Medical inquiries and observations upon the diseases of the mind.* Philadelphia: Kimber & Richardson.

Sapira, N.A., Lessing, M.C., Goldsmith, T.D., Szabo, S.T., Lazoritz, M., Gold, M.S., & Stein, D.J. (2003). *Problematic internet use: proposed classification and diagnostic criteria.* Academic Press.

Shally, M., & Jensen. (2013). *Mental Health Care Issues in America: An Encyclopedia* (Vol. 1). ABC-CLIO.

Siomos, K. E., Dafouli, E. D., Braimiotis, D. A., Mouzas, O. D., & Angelopoulos, N. V. (2008). Internet addiction among Greek ado-lescent students. *Cyberpsychology & Behavior*, *11*(6), 653–657. doi:10.1089/cpb.2008.0088 PMID:18991535

Slutske, W. S. (2006). Natural recovery and treatment-seeking in pathological gambling: Results of two U.S. national surveys. *The American Journal of Psychiatry*, *163*(2), 297–302. doi:10.1176/appi.ajp.163.2.297 PMID:16449485

Snider, M. (1997, February 11). Growing on-line population making Internet 'mass media.' *USA Today*, p. 1.

Subathra, V., Nimisha, M. M. N., & Hakeem, L. A. (2003). Study on the Level of Social Network Addiction Among College Students. *Social Sciences*, *3*, 354–356.

Swaminath, G. (2008). Internet addiction disorder: Fact or fad? Nosing into nosology. *Indian Journal of Psychiatry*, *50*(3), 158. doi:10.4103/0019-5545.43622 PMID:19742232

Thomas, N. J., & Martin, F. H. (2010). Video-arcade game, computer game and Internet activities of Australian students: Participation habits and prevalence of addiction. *Australian Journal of Psychology*, *62*(2), 59–66. doi:10.1080/00049530902748283

Tonioni, F., D'Alessandris, L., Lai, C., Martinelli, D., Corvino, S., Vasale, M., ... Bria, P. (2012). Internet addic-tion: Hours spent online, behaviors and psychological symptoms. *General Hospital Psychiatry*, *34*(1), 80–87. doi:10.1016/j.genhosppsych.2011.09.013 PMID:22036735

Turel, O., Serenko, A., & Bontis, N. (2011). Family and work-related consequences of addiction to organizational pervasive technologies. *Information & Management*, *48*(2-3), 2–3, 88–95. doi:10.1016/j.im.2011.01.004

Van Rooij, A. J., Schoenmakers, T. M., Vermulst, A. A., Van den Eijnden, R. J. J. M., & Van de Mheen, D. (2011). Online video game addiction: identification of addicted adolescent gamers. Addiction, 106(1), 205–12.

Westwood, D., & Griffiths, M. D. (2010). The role of structural characteristics in video game play motivation: A Q-Methodology Study. *Cyberpsychology, Behavior, and Social Networking*, *13*(5), 581–585. doi:10.1089/cyber.2009.0361 PMID:20950185

Widyanto, L., & McMurran, M. (2004). The psychometric properties of the internet addiction test. *Cyberpsychology & Behavior*, *7*(4), 443–450. doi:10.1089/cpb.2004.7.443 PMID:15331031

Wildt, B. T. (2010). Pathological Internet use and psychiatric disorders: A cross-sectional study on psychiatric phenomenology and clinical relevance of Internet dependency. *European Journal of Psychiatry*, *24*(3), 136–145. doi:10.4321/S0213-61632010000300002

Wood, R. T. A., & Griffiths, M. D. (2007). Time loss whilst playing video games: Is there a relationship to addictive behaviors? *International Journal of Mental Health and Addiction*, *5*(2), 141–149. doi:10.100711469-006-9048-2

Wood, R. T. A., Griffiths, M. D., Chappell, D., & Davies, M. N. O. (2004). The structural characteristics of video games: A psycho-structural analysis. *Cyberpsychology & Behavior*, *7*(1), 1–10. doi:10.1089/109493104322820057 PMID:15006163

Wood, R. T. A., Griffiths, M. D., & Parke, A. (2007). Experiences of time loss among videogame players: An empirical study. *Cyberpsychology & Behavior*, *10*(1), 45–56. doi:10.1089/cpb.2006.9994 PMID:17305447

Yadav, P., Banwari, G., Parmar, C., & Maniar, R. (2013, December). Internet addiction and its correlates among high school students: A preliminary study from Ahmedabad, India. *Asian Journal of Psychiatry*, *6*(6), 500–505. doi:10.1016/j.ajp.2013.06.004 PMID:24309861

Young, K. (1996). Internet addiction: The emergence of a new clinical disorder. *Cyberpsychology & Behavior*, 3.

Young, K. S. (1996). *Caught in the net: how to recognize the signs of Internet addiction—and a winning strategy for recovery*. New York: Wiley.

Young, K. S. (1996). *Internet addiction: The emergence of a new clinical disorder*. Paper presented at the 104th annual meeting of the American Psychological Association, Toronto, Canada.

Young, K. S. (1997). *What makes on-line usage stimulating? Potential explanations for pathological Internet use*. Paper presented at the 105th annual meeting of the American Psychological Association, Chicago, IL.

Young, K. S. (1998). Internet Addiction: The emergence of a new clinical disorder. *Cyberpsychology & Behavior*, *1*(3), 237–244. doi:10.1089/cpb.1998.1.237

Young, K. S. (1999). *Internet Addiction: Symptoms, Evaluation, And Treatment. Innovations in Clinical Practice*. Professional Resource Press. Retrieved from https://pdfs.semanticscholar.org/27f2/4ddc6b37b1242fabecd6f35bc05d248c2059.pdf

Young, K. S. (2004). Internet Addiction: A New Clinical Phenomenon and its Consequences. Center for Online Addiction. *The American Behavioral Scientist*, *48*(4), 402–415. doi:10.1177/0002764204270278

Yu, L., & Shek, D. T. (2013). Internet addiction in Hong Kong adolescents: A three-year longitudinal study. *Journal of Pediatric and Adolescent Gynecology*, *26*(3), S10–S17. doi:10.1016/j.jpag.2013.03.010 PMID:23683821

Chapter 11
Cybersex

Aman Choudhary
Independent Researcher, India

ABSTRACT

Cybersex is often used as a collective term for all sorts of sexually related entertainment, information, and personal contact offers available in computer networks respective "in cyberspace." It is also understood to be a computer-mediated interpersonal interaction in which the participants are sexually motivated, meaning they are seeking sexual arousal and satisfaction. Types are virtual-reality-based cybersex, video-based cybersex, and text-based cybersex. From a technical perspective, two sub-forms of text-based cybersex are differentiated: tinysex and erotic chat. This chapter focuses on various forms of cybersex from commercialization to self-exhibitionism and voyeurism has been explained in terms of commercial and personal cybersex aided by MUD. The chapter concludes with an evaluative view that despite being considered advantageous in a recreative and imaginative alternative for sexual satisfaction, cybersex increases problems an individual goes through along with the family, friends, and other relationships simultaneously elevating infidelity component in stable relationships.

INTRODUCTION

Introduced in the early 1980s and becoming widely popular in 1990s, the internet is powerful – so much so that its existence breaks the binary norms of "good" and "bad". It is impressively diverse – it harbors copious amounts of information on a range of topics including, but not restricted to, the internet itself. Curious as humans are, we wondered if we could find sex over the internet. Turns out, there is plenty of it. And what do they call it? There are various popular terms: netsex, computer sex, Internet sex, cybering, Internet sex, Net-sleazing, modem sex (Döring, 2000).

The *Triple A Engine* was introduced by Cooper et al. (1999a; 1999b) and identifies three characteristics of online environments that support cybersex and sexuality:

1. **Accessibility:** There are millions of easily accessible web pages and large numbers huge numbers of people on social networking sites, in chat rooms, and on private messaging systems, who are available for communicating about sexual matters.

DOI: 10.4018/978-1-5225-4047-2.ch011

2. **Affordability:** Pornography and sexual communication online are cheap, as one only needs a computer and Internet connection to access them.
3. **Anonymity:** Online it is possible to be as anonymous as one chooses to be and people perceive online sexual communication to be anonymous as well (Subrahmanyam, & Šmahel, 2011).

A particularly challenging question to answer is, what is cybersex? In a broad sense of purpose, cybersex is sexually focused communication over the internet. Most often involving two (or more) individuals, connected via a computer or wireless network, cybersex or cybering is exchanging sexually explicit messages with the aim of bonding temporarily in a way that is emotionally and physically gratifying (Hahn, & Harley, 1996).

Cybersex is an umbrella term for describing sexual behaviors which are computer based (Delmonico, David, Griffin, Elizabeth, Moriarity, & Joseph, 2001).

They fall into three general categories:

1. Accessing online pornography, audio, video and text stories.
2. Real time with a fantasy partner.
3. Multimedia software.

Delmonico, Griffin, and Moriarity (2001) suggest that the internet has six attributes – a CyberHex – which make the internet unique among all other media. A combination of these attributes (Intoxicating, Isolating, Integral, Inexpensive, Imposing, Interactive) shapes the internet enormously alluring for someone seeking sexual arousal and satisfaction. It is reported by the individuals that they slip in the "hex" while engaging in cybersex, and these attributes make the internet much more seductive than any other media (Delmonico, David, Griffin, Elizabeth, Moriarity, & Joseph, 2001)

Cybersex is often used as a collective term for all sorts of sexually-related entertainment, information and personal contact offers available in computer Networks respective "in cyberspace". This broad term "cybersex" covers so many different activities and contents that it is of practically no use for the social scientific discourse as long as individual phenomena are not differentiated from one another. In a narrow sense, cybersex is understood to be a computer-mediated interpersonal interaction in which the participants are sexually motivated, meaning they are seeking sexual arousal and satisfaction. Cybersex is not a human-machine interaction and therefore clearly differs from solo sex in that it is a social happening: solitary fantasizing and/or use of erotica do not have to include an active partner, but within the course of cybersexual interactions the participants must continually adapt to one another, they experience consent, rapport and enthusiasm as well as rejection, misunderstanding or violation of personal boundaries. They do not just participate in a shared production of text but also let each other know about their sexual motivation, arousal and perhaps even both masturbate at their computers at the same time. Cybersex is therefore not a conversation about sex, but is a form of sexual encounter in itself (Döring, 2000).

Technical Conditions

A per Döring (2000) Technology driven interpersonal interaction can take place by means of virtual reality technology. These can be primarily attained by online video conferences or digital text exchange. Accordingly, based on the technical conditions under which it takes place, three forms of cybersex can be distinguished, which allow (or does not allow) for specific ways of expressing desires that the partners are seeking. The three forms are: virtual reality-based cybersex, video- based cybersex and text-based cybersex

Virtual Reality-Based Cybersex

Entering into a three-dimensional, audio visual and tactile virtual reality via a full-body data suit and data helmet, expressively for the purpose of cybersex is a scenario that has often been discussed but is still far from being reality. When people are involved in cybersex, they cannot actually kiss each other, but nevertheless the kiss they may send is emotionally vivid and its emotional impact is often similar to that of an actual kiss. Our active role in cyberspace makes this environment more exciting and seductive than that of daydreams, erotic novels, or X-rated movies; hence the temptation to engage in sexual activities is greater. The current band-width of the Net is not wide enough to transmit such huge amounts of data in real time, nor do interface devices currently exist that could provide a pleasant or even orgiastic tele-stimulation of the entire body, including the sexual organs. (Döring, 2000; Branwyn, 1993).

Telegenic Cybersex

This is one of the most common forms of cybersex used where two or more people are interacting with each other in sexual way, like undressing, exposes the private parts and encourage making sexual activities. The interactive revolution in online romantic and sexual relationships has promoted both greater social interaction and more solitary activities. In comparison with standard fantasies, online relationships involve more social activities with other people. However, in comparison with offline relationships, many romantic activities are performed while someone is all alone sitting in front of a computer. Compared with offline masturbation, cybersex is a much more social interaction, as it is done while communicating with another person. While in offline masturbation, orgasm comes courtesy of the person's own hands and mind, in cybersex, orgasm also comes courtesy of another person's mind. Cybersex narrows the gap between masturbation and offline sex, as it involves the active contribution of another person. However, compared with offline sexual relationships, cybersex is less social and it can in fact reduce the need for actual social interactions (Ben-Ze'ev, 2004).

Transcripted Cybersex

Transcripted cybersex is majorly defined as an instant exchange of short and explicit text responses. A computer-mediated chat dialogue transcends into text-based cybersex when the participants describe body features to one another, articulated sexual actions and reactions and make believe of the virtual events as reality. During text-based cybersex participants can neither see nor hear, neither smell, nor taste nor touch each other. Instead, emphasis is often laid on conversion of unspoken expressions into words. Two sub-forms of text-based cybersex are differentiated: tinysex and erotic chat. The term "tinysex" is derived from an early family of MUDs known as TinyMUDs. If a person logs into a MUD via TelNet, WWW or a MUD-Client she is then represented there by a virtual person or a virtual being. Tinysex is the term for transcripted cybersex that takes places in a MUD (Multi User Domain/Dimension/Dungeon) which is safe sex. Erotic chat is a form of transcripted cybersex which takes place with the help of a chat program (Semans, Ann, Winks, & Cathy, 1999). Chat programs are much simpler to use than MUDs and are therefore significantly more popular. Chat forums can be found on online services such as AOL and CompuServe as well as on the Internet, where WebChats, Internet Relay Chat-Channels and the like are available (Döring, 2000; Benedikt, Claire, 1995; Semans, Ann & Winks, Cathy, 1999).

Internalized Social Conditions

The medium is unambiguous about determining how video- or transcripted cybersex proceeds in individual instances. Instead, just like other types of sexual interaction, the individual preferences and skills of the participants and their relationship to one another are decisive. A broad distinction can be made between commercial cybersex and private cybersex, whereby the latter can be part of more or less committed personal relationships (Döring, 2000).

Commercial Cybersex

This is a paid form of cybersex where participants engage in sexual interaction to achieve sexual pleasure and one party (mostly prostitute) offer this service commercially and interested person need to pay money for it.

Personal Cybersex

Personal cybersex includes a mechanism of double-meaning thought process consisting of reciprocal manifestations of desire and mutual sexual enjoyment where economic concerns are not an issue - rather an indirect subject of conversation. Cybersex partners can easily be found in sexually-related video conference rooms, MUDs or chat forums which serve as places to meet and make contact with others and generally are almost free of charge. A significant feature is prohibition of public actions in front of the entire forum. Instead a non-public, person to person connection is used for erotic/sexual interaction after meeting in the forum. Private cybersex is sometimes a matter of brief contacts between strangers, fostering a casual virtual physical relationships without any time constraints. Sometimes, however, cybersex takes place within a gradually developing Net relationship when the participants apparently meet one another on the Net in very different manners (e.g. via online-personal ads or in a scientific mailing list) and gradually become ever more explicit in the expression of their desires during the course of their growing interpersonal attraction and trust. Often, these erotic/sexual cyber-relationships are exclusive, romantic relationships in which actual co-habitation and living is desired. However, like real life, such strong emotional involvement and commitment, despite implying an enormous potential for happiness but also the risk of unhappiness - virtual love is capable of breaking real hearts. Virtually people prefer the status of less committed acquaintance or friendship relationships, especially when those involved already have a satisfying partnership in real world. As exhibitionism becomes one of the key rituals in cybersex participation, people are sometimes familiar with one another's bodies as the individuals on either side of the screen are mutually engaging themselves by exchanging sexually provocative photographs, where nudity is the base. In close online-relationships, personal meetings are frequent, characterised by engagement in meetings outside the virtual world of screen. In addition, people knowing each other personally sometimes fall back on cybersex when separated by distance. As the distance increases, the desire of intimacy elevates, thus resulting in the use of Net for virtual sex engagement driven by their sensory pleasure (Döring, 2000).

Externalized Social Conditions

Net encounters and Net relationships do not exist in and of themselves. They are dependent not only on internal events, but also become a more or less central component of a person's already existing social network. They are often especially relevant to existing partnerships and friendships. In Cybersex and Partnerships, faithfulness in existing partnerships or marriages becomes a virulent issue in connection with cyber-sexual encounters. While some couples explicitly admit to having cyber-sexual encounters by not considering them seriously because of their virtual nature, others are majorly unfavourable towards any distinction between virtual and real unfaithfulness. Some undertake cybersex activities together – voyeurism with one another while having cybersex with a third party or contacting other couples together on the computer. The causative effect created by cybersex on existing relationships, can be described as intimidating, worthless and heartening, yet not often expressed in media, literature or people.

Cybersex and Friendships

Cybersexual contacts and relationships may lead to an estrangement from friends, for example when these friends abstain from the Net and/or laugh at, devaluation or rejection from the online-activities of the person in question. On the other hand, sexual and romantic online-experiences may set off an intimate exchange among on and offline friends from which both the cybersexual contacts and the friendships may benefit. However contrastingly cases may occur where mutual sharing of virtual sex partner can initiate feeling of resentment, aggression and hostility which may be causative to quarrels, aggressive behaviours and intense enemity in real world. Sometimes cyber-sexual contacts are hesitant in simultaneous maintenance of mutually related clients, thus giving rise to conflicts and frustrations in real world situations.

Men and Cybersex

In contemporary societies, new kinds of sexual experience are emerging and sex is taking on new forms and meanings. Online sexual activities are perhaps the most visible manifestation of this. Today people access porn, buy sex toys and seek advice about sex online, and as O'Brien and Shapiro argue, 'sex-related activities can be seen as a major variable in the technological and economic growth and development of the Internet' (O'Brien, & Shapiro, 2004). It is also increasingly common for people to connect and interact sexually with each other online.

As Michael Ross notes, online sexual activity has made it possible for new categories of sexual identity to emerge, such as men who have Internet, but not 'real-life' sex with other men (Ross, 2005). According to Diane Wysocki, cybersex is sought out because it allows people to share sexual fantasies with others and to experience the freedom to take on different sexual personae (Wysocki, 1998). Dennis Waskul has shown that many people who practise cybersex 'claim to learn new sexual techniques, discover new sexual turn-ons, and vicariously experience sexual arousal in ways that they would not, or could not, experience in "real" face-to-face sexual encounters', and because of this they rate their experiences as meaningful and sometimes highly valuable (Waskul, 2003). Don Slater argues that online sex and gender play may in fact work to police sexual desires and to reproduce body ideals which conform to the generic conventions of mainstream heterosexual porn. As Slater indicates, while participants may be aware of the performativity of their online selves, this is often underpinned by a strong belief in a pre-existing 'real self' which finds expression through sexual practices. Other elements of online sexual activity, such as participants' tendency to chat about everyday life, their conceptualization of online encounters as an 'escape' from reality, and their attempts to monitor and make sense of online encounters in terms of everyday rules and ethics, demonstrate that what is really striking about such sexual practices is their 'intimate connection with the mundane' (Rival, Slater, & Miller, 1998). Waskul also finds that in cybersex the body remains important in a symbolic way, particularly in the participants' concerns about the sex, age and appearance of their cybersex partners. Although they may believe that they escape the limits of the physical body in their encounters, their performances occur 'in highly predictable forms' and they tend to reconstruct themselves in line with cultural norms of attractiveness (Waskul, 2003).

Kibby and Costello note that cybersex:

allows for the possibility of rewriting gendered codes of sexuality, in that it blurs the distinction between the subject and the object, the consumer and the consumed, the image and the act (Kibby, & Costello, 2001).

In this sense, although cybersex is clearly constrained by existing gender conventions, it also creates a space where the development of a polymorphous masculine sexuality and the exploration of marginalized sexualities are made possible (Kibby, & Costello, 1999). Communication technologies are understood as extending the recreational possibilities of sexual encounters, allowing a quick intimacy to develop in the conditions of anonymity, physical distance and transience that the Internet makes possible. Such connections have been described as 'more frequent and shallower, more intense and briefer 'than those which take place offline (Kibby, & Costello, 1999). While cybersex is seen as a form of play, with the lack of authenticity that this implies, it may also be viewed as providing 'a kind of missing link between fantasies, desires for intimacy, the traditional role of text in expressing these, and sexuality' (Ross, 2005). The complex interactions between 'person', 'player' and 'personae' across the realms of reality, imagination and fantasy in the role-playing games discussed by Waskul and Lust (2004) suggest a set of possible corresponding relationships, moving us beyond simple notions of 'authentic self' and 'performance', and acknowledging the particular possibilities for experimenting with roles and personae which online interactions open up to its participants (Waskul, & Lust, 2004). Authenticity is both more and less elastic in some of the participants' accounts than previous discussions of cybersex have suggested: not simply a case of expressing the pre-existing real self or escaping it for other selves, but admitting a range of states – playing with roles to achieve a consistency of self-presentation, experimenting with 'mostly-me' personae, losing the self altogether in the pleasure of reciprocation, or developing the 'consistency' and 'credibility' necessary for playful performances. The particular conditions – and joy – of cybersex – the possibility of anonymity coupled with the opportunity for self-disclosure – help to explain how it opens up so readily to a multiplicity of uses. For many men, the significance of communication technologies and of cybersex was that they allowed access to a realm that already existed in their own auto-erotic repertoires, and, more importantly, provided the opportunity to extend their engagements with that realm through a range of interactions. But this opportunity is also related to a set of broader social developments: the use of communication technologies more generally for interaction, the growth of new forms of intimacy, a cultural preoccupation with self-pleasures and the rise of a concept of sex as a type of individualized leisure activity (Attwood, 2009).

SUMMARY

'Cyber' might cover quite a range of interactions beyond the common understanding of cybersex as a form of sexual encounter: for some, it includes activities that are 'sex-like', for others it might be virtual sexual involvement, still others can feel as sexual activity but not sex and refer cybersexual activities as forms of intellectual exercise, rather like chess', 'analogous to flirting', 'just stimulation', or may be 'discreet bar talk'. Majorly men describe a link between their speech and writing in cybersex encounters and other forms of text, for example, porn and are interested in the nature of cybersex as text, whether as a conventionalized framework, as creative expression or as interactive play. This implies in a clear sense that cybersex is perceived as a practice which occupied an unusual cultural position.

ADVANTAGES

Some people believe that cybersex can be used as a compliment to an existing sexual relationship, a safe method of sexual experimentation and an alternative for people with 'unique' sexuality (Daneback, Cooper, & Månsson, 2005); Introverted people, with low self-esteem, unable in sexual companionship and other social misfits derive anonymous sexual pleasure without being judged unnecessarily. Real life spouses, geographically distant, continue to be sexually intimate with the use of their imaginations aided by technology. It can function to prolong the sexual dimension of a relationship in which the partners are devoid of interacting with each other recurrently face to face, due to job or other factors. Also, it can allow partners to work out complexities of sexual life that they feel uneasy in expressing and being vocal while facing each other or taking it to a mediator. Moreover, in cases of long-term ailments (including HIV) engagement in cybersex is a safe way to achieve sexual gratification without putting their partners at any health risks. Often it is considered that cybersex can be a physically safe way for teenagers in their experimental age to quench their sexual thoughts and emotion, more so, it is economically less demanding on the Internet than in real life.

MORAL AND SOCIAL PROBLEMS

Much debate has occurred on the morality or the immorality of cybersex because there are different levels of moral standards for different individuals in different communities across the globe. Orgasm and intimacy as componential factors are typical of sexual relationships and their presence in cybersex makes the participation of any individual, an immoral activity consequently leading to lies, deception and corruption.

The immorality of cybersex is elevated by the broad limits within which the activity can be initiated and maintained. Obviously, this indicates frequent engagement of female children below the age of fifteen in virtual sexual relationships with older men. Cybersex converts from habitual exposure to pornography when the human mind becomes corrupted beyond acceptable societal moral levels. Continuous exposure to cybersex is causative to perversion, forming sexual fantasies in men and women about children which lead to child molestation and sexual exploitation of children. Engagement in sexually provocative activities with children over the cyberspace is promoting traits of paedophilism and exposing children to potential dangers and harm which is as morally unacceptable as child prostitution, among parents, guardians, society and all concerned parties who find cybersex with children an immoral activity.

Cyberspace has created a platform for children to learn sexual information that should be inaccessible until they are adults, where Indirect sexual victimization is the effect of cyber communication. Cybersex is morally unacceptable on a general scale because all adults with fully functional moral and mental faculties would not like to have their children or other people's children exposed to the same (Lanning, 2010).

Another disadvantage of engaging in cybersex on a social level is the degradation of any sexual relationship and satisfaction derived from sexual and emotional contact between the people. Daneback et al. (2005) explains that online affairs turn into offline affairs that cause the breakdown of the family unit which spirals into other negative social effects on both the relating adults and any children they may have. Research has shown that the social effect of cybersex attachment is a leading cause of separation and divorce for affected couples (Callan, Benson, Coward, Davis, Gill, Grant, Percival, Daneback, Cooper, & Mansson, 2010). The nature of expectations that addicts of sexual material in the cyberspace have about their partners, the beliefs and attitudes in the minds of individuals who are continually exposed to cybersex, unconventional sexual practices and their attitudes about love and intimacy drive them to be social aliens. Failure in controlling the outcomes of self activities as far as the children are concerned, then the individual loses self-esteem which causes a wide range of other social problems such as guilt, low self-esteem and criminal activities of sexual origin which make individuals function in a more or less strange manner within social circles. Social effects of cybersex not only influence the individuals that engage in it but their partners and children as well who become socially and psychologically affected to the point that they even need therapy (Goldberg, 2012). His explicit quotation of Young (2001) stating that recreational and pathological users of cybersex develop habits that affect their children and families fades the importance of cybersex as the only recreational option.

PSYCHOLOGICAL PROBLEMS

When comparing extroverts to introverts, the author suggests that the extroverts are more likely to engage in variety of sexual abnormalities than introverts (Barnes, Malamuth, & Check, 1984). This suggests that the more outgoing person would more likely experiment and research on sex which may easily lead them to cybersex and its effects. Sexuality of abnormal nature that triggers people to have sex with children or to be obsessed with sexual activity within the cyber space is associated with psychotic behavior (Barnes, Malamuth, & Check, 1984). The people that engage in abnormal sexual activities may be expressing their emotional and psychological needs for release (Barnes, Malamuth, & Check, 1984). These kinds of people are theorized to be more interested in impersonal sex or aggressive sex (Barnes, Malamuth, & Check, 1984). This suggests that the adventure and excitement that is present in cybersex would be thrilling to psychotic people who may go ahead and express the ideas put in their head during the activity in their offline lives. In extreme cases interacting with a psychotic sexual adventurer can be a dangerous encounter.

MARITAL DYSFUNCTION

Excessive compulsive behavior in sexual activity is a major cause of broken relationships. One of the most fundamental units that may be destroyed as a result of an adult's obsession with cybersex is the family unit. In case one partner is found out or admits that they have a problem with cybersex, marital counselling may be implemented as a method of salvaging the relationship. There are many and frequent cases of marital counselling becoming a necessary factor in relationships as a result of one or both partners being addicted to cybersex or other forms of sexual weaknesses (Mark, 2006).

FUTURE IMPLICATIONS

Cybersex has inspired the sexgineers and artists to come up with new ways to use technology for pleasure and relationships. This market is becoming so enormous that porn might be pushed to the side as more interactive technologies are starting to exist. For example, a Japanese company called Segment introduced a teledildonics system that enables real-time cybersex (using techie toys) with a partner where one can control the speed, intensity and rhythm.

Two new trends are emerging in the cyberspace world that are effecting both the office and the home are- new surveys show that surfing for phonography on the web is a new national pastime on office computer system and, infidelity of cheating spouses is definitely going digital.

Technical Pornography: New Workplace Pass Time

With the advent of internet, people love to surf adult web sites. Worse than that, bulks of them are doing it at work. Nearly, one-fourth of the American work force spends at least an hour and a half of time on the Internet every day. Webmaster Network Strategies recently revealed that the average worker wastes almost two hours per day on their computer. One software company that recently monitored such activity found that 68 percent of it's employees where stopping in at adult rated web sites on company time and on company equipment turning into a criminal one. Some of the materials on many of these X rated sites are illegal. For example, it's illegal to download dirty photos of under aged persons. But the web it full of these types of web sites. The very fact that an employee is downloading dirty photos on company computers is a problem unto itself but it's not the only one. Productivity is also affected. That is, many employees are wasting valuable company time on these activities when they are supposed to be conducting company business. The employer is being raped from a financial standpoint in that the employee is stealing company "on the clock" time.

Infidelity in Virtual World

Divorce cases have always been a mainstay of many private investigative agencies. In the overwhelming majority of divorce cases, the focus is to catch a cheating spouse. But the focus appears to be turning now to cyberspace as the overwhelming majority of infidelity cases now start as an online romance. Many current surveys are now saying that about 50% of all households in the United States have a home computer that's connected to the Internet. People who are otherwise faithful to their spouse are meeting others online in overwhelming numbers and some of these cyber meetings are turning into sexual relationships. The typical profile of such a case starts online in chatrooms that leads to email and then in-person meetings.

Because of this new digital trend, clients are turning to digital discovery services to check out home computers. It's no longer just enough for an investigative service to offer physical surveillance as a means to catch a cheating spouse in the company of their secret lover. Many of these secret relationships are now occurring in cyberspace. Clients are demanding that the investigator survey the ones and zeros contained on the home computer to uncover evidence of cybersex. The numbers of situations like these are on a steep rising curve.

Signs of Digital Infidelity:

- Late night computer usage without relevant work.
- Sudden transaction of passcode folder software so only he/she can access the file.
- Overspending too much time on computer but is unclear about what her/she is doing.
- Subject attempts of changing the tab of computer screen from spouse when he/she enters computer room.
- Subject is trashing explored history instantly.
- A sudden withdrawal from social and marital life seems to have occurred.
- Unexpected changes in sex life.

Only a minority of people see cybersex as involving any emotional connection with partners or discussed the relation between their experiences in chat rooms and their offline lives in any detail where the offline and online worlds were not necessarily organizing principles of understanding. Cybersex relationships have been considered an integrated part of their lives and are understood as a form of human interaction in 'the real world'. Cybersex is considered much more routinely and clearly related to the expression of desires – often discussed in terms of 'fantasy' – rather than their experiences with partner sex or their desire to forge online relationships. This creates different levels of authenticity and honesty, further reinforcing the thought of imaginary roles of being who they like and whatever they like.

REFERENCES

Attwood, F. (2009). 'Deepthroatfucker' and 'Discerning Adonis'. Men and cybersex. *International Journal of Cultural Studies, 12*(3), 279–294. doi:10.1177/1367877908101573

Barnes, G. E., Malamuth, N. M., & Check, J. V. P. (1984). Personality and Sexuality. *Personality Individual Differences, 5*(2), 159-172. Retrieved 25 Sep. 2012, from http://www. personality-project.org/revelle/publications/revelle.issid.07.pdf

Bauman, Z. (2003). *Liquid Love: On the Frailty of Human Bonds*. Cambridge, UK: Polity Press.

Ben-Ze'ev, A. (2012). *Emotions and Morality in Computer-mediated Romantic Relationships*. Retrieved from http://emotionresearch.net/projects/humaine/ws/wp10/presentation-materials/AaronBenZeev-wp10wsMoralityOnlineRelationships-final.pdf

Benedikt, C. (1995). TinySex is Safe Sex. *Infobahn Magazine*. Retrieved from http://www.cwrl.utexas.edu/~claire/texts/thoughts.html

Blair, C. (1998). Netsex: Empowerment through Discourse. In B. Ebo (Ed.), *Cyberghetto or Cybertopia. Race, Class, and Gender on the Internet* (pp. 205–218). Westport, CT: Praeger.

Branwyn, G. (1993). Compu-sex: Erotica for cybernauts. *The South Atlantic Quarterly*, *92*, 779–791.

Butterworth, D. (1996). Wanking in Cyberspace: The Development of Computer Porn. In Feminism and Sexuality. A Reader (pp. 314 320). New York, NY: Columbia University Press.

Daneback, K., Cooper, A., & Mansson, S. (2005). An Internet Study of Cybersex Participants. *Archives of Sexual Behavior*, *34*(3), 321–328. doi:10.100710508-005-3120-z PMID:15971014

Delmonico, D., Griffin, E., & Moriarity, J. (2001). *Cybersex Unhooked: A Workbook for Breaking Free of Compulsive Online Sexual Behaviour*. Wickenburg, AZ: Gentle Path Press.

Döring, N. (2000). Feminist Views of Cybersex: Victimization, Liberation, and Empowerment. *Cyberpsychology & Behavior*, *3*(5), 863–884. doi:10.1089/10949310050191845

Ghoroghi, S., Hassan, S. A., & Ayub, A. F. (2017). The Influence of Religiosity and Risk Taking on Cybersex Engagement among Postgraduate Students: A Study in Malaysian Universities. *International Journal of Social Science and Humanity*, *7*(3), 143–152. doi:10.18178/ijssh.2017.V7.810

Goldberg, D. P. (n.d.). *An Explanatory Study about the Impacts that Cybersex (The Use of the Internet for Sexual Purposes) is Having on Families and the Practices of Marriage and Family Therapists*. Retrieved 25 Sep., 2012, from http://scholar.lib.vt.edu/theses/available/etd- 04262004142455/unrestricted/PeterDGoldberg/Thesis/pdf

Harley, H. (1996). *The Internet Complete Reference* (2nd ed.). Osborne McGraw-Hill.

Kibby, M., & Costello, B. (1999). 'Displaying the Phallus: Masculinity and the Performance of Sexuality on the Internet. *Men and Masculinities*, *1*(4), 352–364. doi:10.1177/1097184X99001004002

Kibby, M., & Costello, B. (2001). Between the Image and the Act: Interactive Sex Entertainment on the Internet. *Sexualities*, *4*(3), 353–369. doi:10.1177/136346001004003005

Lanning, K. V. (2010). *Child Molesters: A Behavioral Analysis. National Centre for Missing & Exploited Children*. Retrieved 25 Sept. 2012, from http://www.missingkids.com/en_US/publications/NC70.pdf.02005.pdfhttp://www.thehopeofsurvivors.com/pdf_files/Pastors_C ybersex_Addiction.pdf

Mark, B. H. (2006). *Sexual Addiction and Marriage and Family therapy: Facilitating Individual and Relationship Healing through Couple Therapy*. Retrieved 25 Sep., 2012, from http://scholar.lib.vt.edu/theses/available/etd04272009102213/unrestricted/MarkBirdDissertation

McRae, S. (1996). Coming Apart at the Seams: Sex, Text and the Virtual Body. In L. Cherny & E. R. Weise (Eds.), *Wired Women. Gender and New Realities in Cyberspace* (pp. 242–264). Seattle, WA: Seal Press.

O'Brien, J., & Shapiro, E. (2004). Doing It" on the Web: Emerging Discourses on Internet Sex. In D. Gauntlett & R. Horsley (Eds.), *Web Studies* (pp. 114–126). London: Arnold.

Rival, L., Slater, D., & Miller, D. (1998). Sex and Sociality: Comparative Ethnographies of Sexual Objectification. *Theory, Culture & Society*, *15*(3), 295–321. doi:10.1177/0263276498015003015

Ross, M. (2005). Typing, Doing, and Being: Sexuality and the Internet. *Journal of Sex Research*, *42*(4), 342–352. doi:10.1080/00224490509552290 PMID:19827239

Semans, A., & Winks, C. (1999). *The Woman's Guide to Sex on the Web*. New York, NY: HarperSanFrancisco.

Slater, D. (1998). Trading Sexpics on IRC: Embodiment and Authenticity on the Internet. *Body & Society*, *4*(4), 91–117. doi:10.1177/1357034X98004004005

Subrahmanyam, K., & Šmahel, D. (2011). Sexuality on the Internet: Sexual Exploration, Cybersex, and Pornography. In *Digital Youth. Advancing Responsible Adolescent Development*. New York, NY: Springer. doi:10.1007/978-1-4419-6278-2_3

Waskul, D. D. (2003). *Personhood in Online Chat and Cybersex*. New York: Peter Lang.

Waskul, D. D., & Lust, M. (2004). Role-playing and Playing Roles: The Person, Player, and Persona in Fantasy Role-playing. *Symbolic Interaction*, *27*(3), 333–356. doi:10.1525i.2004.27.3.333

Wysocki, D. K. (1998). Let Your Fingers Do the Talking: Sex on an Adult Chat-line. *Sexualities*, *1*(4), 425–452. doi:10.1177/136346098001004003

Chapter 12
The Effect of Social Networks on Relationships Outside the Network

Tami Seifert
Kibbutzim College of Education, Technology, and the Arts, Israel

Idit Miara
Kibbutzim College of Education, Technology, and the Arts, Israel

ABSTRACT

This chapter examines the impact of three different aspects of romantic discourse on social networks: romance, identity, and privacy. Qualitative research focused on the influence of the social networks on the opinions and interpersonal behavior of 11 single academics, aged 30-45 years old, men and women who used Facebook as a means for meeting potential romantic partners. The research employed semi-structured in-depth interviews to elicit qualitative data. Results indicate that an intimate, romantic setting cannot exist on the social network. Most users enhanced their identity in order to appear more attractive online. Most of the interviewees clearly felt that they needed to control the exposure of their personal details, and there was a clear indication that privacy does not exist online: it seems to be impossible to limit exposure of the published contents to specific selected audiences. Online romantic relationships are a metonymy for rapidly changing values and social norms in a dynamic global reality.

INTRODUCTION

Technological developments have an indelible impact on the society in which we live, and their influence shapes new norms and rules. The Internet is seen as a world in which new friendships and support networks are formed, so that the user feels involved and supported. Nevertheless, this world often creates a fantastic illusion, and participants may feel a sense of alienation and loneliness.

The dynamics and interactions on social networks (SNs) create a new and varied world of online dating sites and "romantic" encounters. SNs have altered their original function and because of their unique features they have been used to form various types of interpersonal relations. Facebook is open

DOI: 10.4018/978-1-5225-4047-2.ch012

to a community of users and yet it can provide the individual user with a sense of anonymity and invisibility, in other words it can seemingly maintain the user's privacy (Cooper & Sportolari, 1997).

The present study investigated how the virtual world in general and SNs in particular influence romantic interactions and interpersonal behavioral norms outside the network. The research focused on Facebook as a SN that allows the formation of social relationships between couples and investigated the opinions about the existence of romance and privacy in SNs and how SNs influence romantic relationships and social norms outside the network.

Two main questions were derived from this topic to underpin the research:

1. Which characteristics are reported by the interviewees and expressed in their Facebook texts as part of their romantic discourse in encounters between couples?
2. Do the interviewees think that the romantic discourse on Facebook influences romantic discourse outside Facebook and if so, how?

REVIEW OF RELEVANT LITERATURE

Romantic Relationships on the Internet

The last decade has witnessed a revolution in the ways that singles meet other singles. In the "era of isolation", the Internet offers displays of a wide array of eligible single men and women, allowing the user to form romantic encounters and helping to break through gender norms and to form new rules for dating.

The Creation of Romantic Relationships on the Net

The SNs help users to create a self-image (DeVito, Birnholtz & Hancock, 2017; Rettberg, 2017). Consequently, although the romantic connections acquired on the net may be intensive, this does not necessarily testify to any genuine reality. Couple relations on the net often create a fantasy for the user (Mendelson & Papacharissi, 2010). The probability that two people meet on the net is insufficient to ensure that a relationship will be formed. However, geographical space is reduced on the net and this sense of geographical vicinity combined with imagination can help two partners to develop a relationship (Mayers, 1993; Halpern, Katz & Carril, 2017).

The feeling created as a result of the use of the Internet as a tool for acquaintance and to establish a couple relationship is frequently ambivalence. Although romance is usually associated with love and leisure the romantic relationship usually becomes commercialized and practical, contributing to its endurance. Network users today are usually individual, independent persons who seek self-realization (Illouz, 1997). They choose and evaluate their partners through technological means, thus, creating a new situation. This situation allows them to get to know each other through calm conversation at a time when it is suitable and comfortable for both partners. Of course, this conversation lacks the characteristics of normative discourse including meaningful components such as: facial expressions, body language etc.

The development of face-to-face relationships undergoes metamorphosis: from the initial encounter, based on vicinity in space and physical attraction, to the revelation of the potential partner's image and self-exposure (Illouz, 1997). In contrast the development of romantic relationships on the Internet space undergoes an opposite process – while the close relations formed in the initial conversations on chats and/or on Internet pages are often deep, personal and intimate, in face-to-face relationships, physical interaction determines much of the relationship and this intensive exposure may lead to sexual consequences and renewed future search (Wysocki, 1998).

Motives for Couple Relations on Social Networks

In the Internet era, a new persona is created, in a new method for making acquaintances with several characteristics: anonymity and discretion; invisibility; escape, intimacy (Cooper & Sportolari, 1997) and imagination and difference (Amichai-Hamburger & Ben-Artzi, 2000). As a dating site, the SN creates a large alternative space for the shy and unconfident user that is less restricted. This world opens up a new window, facilitating the realization of the desire and ability to become involved. Additionally, the communications media and the technological space apparently protects the user: he/she is kept safe in their interaction with the other user since they are able to gain access to and alter their answers online. This differs from face-to-face dialogs which are conducted as oral "ping-pong" with no possibility to alter answers after they have been voiced (Amichai-Hamburger & Ben-Artzi, 2000). This process alters the acquisition of social observation and dynamic social norms are created outside the technological space (Cooper, McLoughlin & Campbell, 2000). The network user acts in a new world and can create an alternative and different identity than that which he/she holds in human reality.

Activity on the Net: Fictive Identity or Construction of a New Self?

Many philosophers and theorists have discussed the concept of the "self". Kohut (1971) defined the self as a collection of feelings, thoughts, images and ideas that the individual grants to himself/herself. Goffman (1980) claimed that we shape our self-identity according to the situation in which we find ourselves. Invisibility on the Internet has important consequences. It enhances the user's experience of success and self-evaluation (Barak, 2006). However, on the Internet the falsification of identities and unreliable behavior is accepted and even becomes a regular practice. Psychologists estimate that this re-construction of identity allow the user to shape their personality (Turkle, 1995). The persona that appears on the Internet covers itself with masks and different identities, it tries out and examines several identities until the stage when one of the identities becomes an integral and indivisible part of the real self that exists outside the net (Turkle, 1995). Additionally, the use of the network and the time spent on it create a familiarity with a better self and ability to cope with it. Thus, the user is afforded a different experience and a more intelligent ability to examine the "self" (Mckenna & Bargh, 2000). The use of the network exposes aspects of the user's personality that would not be exposed outside this world (Suler, 2004). This manner of activity has been broadened by the world of dating sites, which allows a type of invisibility and self-branding on SNs. One of the networks that has been a trailblazer in this field is a Facebook profile.

FACEBOOK

Facebook: The Privacy Dilemma

In the past, networks had a common character and concept. Today, the SNs have a decentralized character adapted to the individuals who use the network and their character (Wellman, 2003). The depth of connections and relationships on the network vary from what are known as "weak ties" to "strong ties" The substance of the relationships and their strength are defined according to the level of several parameters: (1) intimacy; (2) closeness; (3) length of acquaintance (Granovetter, 1973). It was found that closeness is the main dimension that contributes significantly to the strength of the contact.

The SNs were established in order to reinforce connections existing on the net. Recent research suggests that these networks help to create new connections and opportunities. Relations on the SN can reach a high level of intimacy and familiarity. Continuity is needed following the initial acquaintance on the Internet space to sustain a subsequent relationship between the two network users (Granovetter, 1973). Facebook users will try to find new persons in order to empower their social world in a way that they would not be able to do in actual reality.

Dating Sites

In the last decade, the world of dating sites and ANs has increased its volume and become an integral part of making acquaintances in the modern era. Search engines and SNs help singles to find their partners (Whitty & Carr, 2006). The dating sites in fact fulfill two main purposes: (1) finding romantic contacts for the long-term with a view to marriage and bringing children into the world and; (2) finding romantic sexual partners for short-term relationships for entertainment, pleasure and amusement. The sorting process that the user undergoes is comparatively simple in comparison to that which the prospective dater undergoes outside the Internet. Moreover, the abundant supply of potential partners reaches the surfer in a convenient ready-made package and they just have to leaf through forwards and backwards until they find a suitable candidate (Ben-Ze'ev, 2004).

In studies conducted in the USA, it was found that most users on the dating sites are between ages 30-49. They are mostly academics and their income is above average with greater preponderance of male users (Whitty & Carr, 2006). Studies have found that women and people with lower level education perceive the Internet as an unsafe environment, that can be dangerous and violent. Falsification of many details of the personae of users on these sites is seen by this population as fraudulent and unreliable (Shade, 2002).

In the virtual world, there are other parameters by which the potential partner can be evaluated: writing style, recklessness, spelling mistakes, imagination, creativity, nicknames, pictures etc. The Internet users try to present themselves as attractive and in demand (Connolly, Palmer, Barton, & Kirwan, 2016). It was found that men describing their personality will focus on their personality traits, while women focus on their external appearance. Women will describe themselves as: young, slim, sexy while men describe themselves as romantic and having a good sense of humor (Ben Ze'ev, 2004).

Most of the population that surfs on dating sites does so in order to find a partner for relations outside the network. Relationships that begin on the network, eventually lead to a face-to-face meeting. In some of the cases the users experience disappointment regarding the appearance of the partner during the meeting outside the technological space. Thus, falsification of identity on the net will mostly be expressed by users who do not aspire to form long-term relationships and this form of activity serves them for momentary entertainment and pleasure (Connolly, Palmer, Barton, & Kirwan, 2016). The situation is problematic since the two people do not always have the same goal, meaning that their purpose for using the network may be different. Research has also shown that there are often gaps between the desired characteristics of the partner that the surfer chooses and their prospective partner's requirements (Ben-Ze'ev, 2004).

Facebook: A Platform for Acquaintance Where Identity and Relationships Can Be Built in the Digital Space and Beyond It

Facebook brands those who use it and helps them to construct identities and profiles. In fact, it is a marketing tool for those who use it, the individuals that use the site to create and construct identities. In other words, identity-making is a public process that also includes the construction of the "self" by a person and by the others (Zhao, 2006). The users of the network clothe themselves in different online images forming a dichotomy with their real-life identities beyond the Internet space (Turkle, 1995). This space actually helps them to bypass limitations that exist in face-to-face encounters.

Facebook is actually the ideal environment to examine the construction of identity in an online environment, where relationships are anchored in online communities. It was found that in online dating there is an expectation that users will also engage in structuring identity and will adopt strategies of self-presentation that will help them to protect their anonymity (Connolly, Palmer, Barton, & Kirwan, 2016). This means that the individuals on Facebook will adopt a structured self and not necessarily their real self, which remains hidden. Thus, Facebook users are likely to emphasize things or create an exaggerated form of their possible self, appropriate for the accepted, preferred stereotype outside the online network. In contrast to networks that offer opportunities for dating on the net for those who search solely for momentary romantic relationships, Facebook allows the expansion of existing relationships and acts as an alternative for meeting new acquaintances and the establishment of a romantic couple relationship on the network that will continue outside the network (Zhao, Grasmuck & Martin, 2008). By its very structure, and special profile Facebook has created unique features for the construction of identities. Different goals have developed for identity construction offering different characteristics for its users. Facebook has become a known brand and is marketed today as a broad accessible and available tool for a global audience. Beyond its existence as an online network it has helped to develop different ethical rules that widely influence the dating world and couple hood.

METHODOLOGY

The research aimed to investigate the influence of SNs in general, and specifically of Facebook on couple relationships outside the network.

RESEARCH DESIGN

The research was a qualitative-phenomenological study, dealing with the correlation between participants' external reality, their thinking and feelings and their subjective inner world (Denzin & Lincoln, 1994). The choice of qualitative research enabled the researchers to study how the world of singles' couples is structured in Facebook discourse and the implications of this world on relationships outside the network. Qualitative research aspires to conduct deep investigation into the substance of the studied phenomenon, with an emphasis on the respondents' experiences (Denzin & Lincoln, 1994). Using this methodology, it was possible to elicit and understand the interviewees' meanings and provide interpretation for the experience of couple hood on Facebook and to understand the influence of this experience outside the network.

Sample and Sampling Procedure

The sample in this study was a "convenience sample" and included 11 male and female singles aged between 30-45 years in Israel. They expressed their consent to participate in the research. In order to attain maximum diversity, interviewees were selected from different occupational fields and different geographical regions of Israel (Patton, 1990). The respondents participated in Facebook as a platform on which they could make romantic acquaintances. The interviews were conducted in person at the respondents' homes.

TOOLS USED FOR THE STUDY

A semi-structured in-depth interview (Smith, 1995) specially created for the research by the researchers was used to collect the singles' experiences. The singles were interviewed in person about their activities on Facebook as a platform on which they could make romantic acquaintances. Interview guidelines were employed including a list of questions that served as a tool to remember to focus on the studied subject, in content and to thoroughly exhaust the participants' personal experiences (Patton, 1990). The questions relied on the fact that the Facebook reality is structured by the participants, and the responses to the questions were used to collect data and construct central generalizations that could be transformed into a theoretical attitude (Smith, 1995). The interview encompassed several main areas of interest: (1) the perception of romance, the influence of couple relations on the network on the construction and/or extinction of romance; (2) the meaning and significance of the creation of an identity on the network on the couple's relationship; (3) the Facebook privacy dilemma.

DATA ANALYSIS

The interviews were tape-recorded with the respondents' consent and transcribed. Data analysis was performed by clearly defining the units of analysis and constructing a hierarchy of the repeated contents and themes in the narrative texts, in an attempt to compose a theoretical model (Sabar Ben-Yehoshua, 2001). Qualitative analysis was conducted in stages: the first stage involved repeated holistic readings of all the interviews until the researchers felt that they were familiar with the collected materials. The second stage involved content analysis of the interviews according to "field grounded theory" (Glaser & Strauss, 1967) and main themes and categories were identified. At the third stage the categories were organized into themes with common subjects by relating to the respondents' linguistic elements and images (Lincoln & Guba, 1985). At the last stage, the researchers examined whether there were connections between the different themes through focus and comparison between the contents.

FINDINGS

Three main themes emerged from the interviews: romance, identity and privacy. Categories were derived from these themes. The themes were investigated and received responses from the qualitative interviews. The names of the interviewees reported in the findings are fictive to ensure their anonymity and privacy, for example P1, P2 or P3.

Romance on the Net: Couple or Individual

A central theme that emerged from the interviewees' narratives was their consideration for romance as part of a relationship. They reported that at each state when an intimate situation was created, romance developed. They felt that romance was lacking in SNs. They noted that: physical contact, speech and gestures exchanged between couples create an intimate situation that cannot exist in general on the Internet and in particular on Facebook. It appears from the interviewees' responses that conversations on the Internet are initial discourse that permits the individual to get to know basic identifying details of a prospective partner as a preparation for a meeting outside the Internet.

Intimacy and Privacy In a Romantic Online Conversation

When the interviewees talked about romance they invariably spoke about "intimacy". For most of the interviewees intimacy is formed in a quiet space. A complex situation is created between a couple that meet and get to know each other. According to the interviewees' responses, the intimacy component must exist so that romance can develop. In this manner, intimate cognizance becomes a partnership with someone who is known and familiar. In intimate situations symbiosis forms, allowing the "self" to be shared and bond with parts of the other. Asked about romance on the network, P1 expressed amazement:

I don't think that there is romance on the network. The relationship becomes something that is between interpersonal and publicity, I experience romance when something is intimate. If I make a contact in order to share, that's not romantic.

Thus, intimacy is formed from shared activity between partners who continue romantic discourse in confidentiality. P7 described her first meeting with her partner:

two people who do things together, going to the beach together … holding hands, intimate things, things that you do not share with others, something personal that is not exposed.

Such intimacy was seen as impossible on the network by interviewees who think that it is only possible to perform romantic gestures on the network. P2 thought that the lack of intimacy would harm absolute romance as he sees it:

It's as though someone is making a party or someone proposes marriage during a football game, there are people who see this as something romantic, to propose marriage in front of the whole world. But it's not intimate. There can [only] be romantic gestures on the Internet.

Most of the interviewees emphasized the issue of touch, and giving and taking as conditions for the creation of romance without which romance could not exist. Intimacy was in their opinion created in a real meeting between two people who create reciprocal discourse between them and communication with special qualities.

Difficulties Involved in Creating a Romance on the Network

When the interviewees were asked to define romance, most of them gave a clear definition that included intimacy, shared gestures and containment. Nevertheless, the interviewees were hesitant to declare that romance existed on the network. They felt that there could be no romance without conversation, a face-to-face meeting and gestures of giving and reciprocity between a couple. P8 argued that it was impossible to realize a romantic relationship in the virtual space of the network:

I think that there is no true romance on the network. There is gesturing when one person writes to another, personal matters and personal greetings in posts. [But] I think that it is far more romantic to receive this in a note and not written in the post ...in my opinion the network serves to publish romantic gestures. It's like seeing pictures of diners in a restaurant menu and not really eating the meal.

In her interview, P9 opposed the use of the networks. She did not see the use of technology as an alternative for romantic relationships. P9 found it difficult to understand why she should conduct such a relationship on the network. She told us that she found herself outside the game because she did not approve of such relations. For her, romance did not and could not exist on the Internet:

I am against it, it's shocking, I personally do not like it because there is no courting here and no investment by the man in what is known as romance, it's only to make the initial contact ...when a man invests in me, courts me, invites me for a date, or meals [that can be romantic].

In contrast to P9, P4 does not believe in romantic communication on the network in general, but believes that it can exist to some extent. The network can be used for interpersonal interaction after a continuous period of relations between a couple, and P4 indicates that the network could help to sustain the relationship:

I think that if it takes place let us say after the contact is already established and they already met, for example if they have been going out together for a year, then I think it is personal, even if it's written correspondence.

Although written correspondence may be created after a relationship is established, P4 still does not believe in romantic correspondence on a SN:

there is no romance on the network, it is all shallow communication ... I think it is just a tool for initial acquaintance.

Unlike the other interviewees, P5 found that using the network was effective and efficient. The network opened a window and many possibilities for the user. P5 did not see the Internet as a place where romance developed, however she thought that the network offered many possibilities for meeting people:

I think it's wonderful, because not everyone has ways for meeting people and the network provides them with possibilities they did not otherwise have. In other times you had to go to a club or seek a match through family or friends. Today there are more possibilities on the Internet and that is amazing. Nevertheless, it is not suitable for everyone because there are some who get confused by such a large choice, and there are those who are more stable who are satisfied with what they found on the network and continue on to their real lives.

The evidence from most of the interviewees seems to indicate that there is no romance on the Internet. Romance is seen as created in meetings outside the network. The dialogs on the network provide a springboard from which to begin the relationship and as a basis for getting to know the other person. P4 explained:

[its] just a springboard to form something that will be continued afterwards in a meeting or telephone call.

The interviewees indicated that romance cannot be expressed in a shared space. One of them (P9) thought that her reservation regarding romance on the network was because she had been born and educated during the 1980s, when there was not much exposure to technology, differing from the experience of those who were born into the technological world.

There are some girls who are thrilled when they are proposed marriage and they receive 1000 likes ... I think romance is more personal and private ... perhaps those who did not grow up with the Internet relate to this as something less natural than those who grew up with it.

Initial Encounters on the Network: "Hi, Would You Like to Get to Know Me?"

Most of the interviewees intimated that romantic discourse only exists on the network at the very beginning, in order to make the initial acquaintance. P10 noted:

On the dating sites of the network it is just to make an acquaintance, not for deep conversations, and that's where a decision is made whether to get to get to know someone in more depth or not.

P7 told us:

I went into the site but didn't have any romantic discourse, only exchange of general details, a first dialog that is meant to get to know them, for example what our hobbies are.

Like those interviewees noted above P4 described her conversation on the Internet as the use of a tool to meet her future partner. She told us that she received initial details concerning the partner in the correspondence on the network, but that she had still not managed to form a real connection with someone she met on a SN. She felt that the technological screen formed a wedge between her and her partner:

The network is like a screen, it's not something real unless you channel this just for something real – to meet up ... and that's why I have never met someone new through the network.

In contrast to P4, P2 noted the advantages of a conversation on the network. He indicated that romantic correspondence on the network is advantageous for someone who is introverted and finds it difficult to express their feelings. It offers various opportunities to become acquainted with women with whom they would not talk without the use of Internet. Nevertheless, like P4, P2 only used Facebook for initial acquaintance: *On the Internet it's more a matter of initial meeting and outside the network it's something more concrete and serious*, and he added:

I wasn't good at chatting up girls in person, it requires far more courage to start to talk with a girl in a pub or discotheque ...it's far easier to send a "Hi" or something like that to a thousand girls who live in your vicinity and if ten percent answer you that is already a good start ... first you say "hi" and then you introduce yourself... and tell them something about yourself; 'I live alone ... I have my own apartment ... I am single etc. ... I am looking for something serious, or a one-night stand or something else ... and then she says yes ... and that's how the Internet conversation begins.

In contrast to most of the other interviewees, P3's conversation on Facebook did not only include initial acquaintance with the potential partner. She reported deep conversations that contained experiences and emotions that helped her to get to know her partner:

Yes, there was a guy who contacted me on the site and sent me a message: 'Hi, how are you doing? I'd like to get to know you'. I felt it was a compliment and sent him a message: 'Yes, I'd be happy to get to know you', and that was followed by a ping-pong of questions: where are you from, what do you do? etc. and very quickly we went on to a "chat" conversation and then it became a real conversation through the network and that quickly advanced.

IDENTITY ON THE NETWORK

The interviewees described their identities and the ways in which they were reflected on the dating sites and on the network. It seemed from their evidence that the description of their identity on the network differs from their real identity outside the network. Most of them published selective details for their image on the network.

"If Someone Looks at Me from Behind They Won't Know Who I Am": Basic Identity

Most of the interviewees who were asked to describe how they characterize their identity on Facebook, told us that they only publish basic information, detailing their occupation. Thus, too the pictures that they publish on their profile are selective and displayed only to friends on Facebook. P2 explained:

First of all you being with your personal details, for security reasons you are also prohibited from putting too many personal details on Facebook. You only put in the relevant details ... for example if you went to a low level school you wouldn't mention that ...just like you wouldn't put a place of work that had fired you into your Curriculum Vitae ... I think that finding work and finding a girl are the same thing.

P4 reinforced the words of other interviewees, saying that the construction of a Facebook profile is an important parameter in one's career. She added that Facebook is an accessible means, in which work partners are exposed to pictures and posts that are published there:

It is not always advantageous ... my family has a completely different political opinion so I don't always share discussions with them – on Facebook I am even more cautious, sometimes I prefer not to upload a picture from family events which are not fitting for the character of my friends from college or similar matters ... as if I make a selection and it's not always spontaneous.

Many of the interviewees saw the construction of their initial profile on Facebook as something laconic, without any imagination and providing basic information about their identity. P5 reinforced the words of P2:

I have a Facebook profile that I built from my picture, first and family names and my professional status, where I studied and what my profession is. Most of the details are rather dry ... my identity is far more interesting and complex than appears on the network. I am more reserved and closed on the network.

It seems that the image that the interviewees present on Facebook is not identical to their real identity. The Facebook image is a fantasy and presents facets of their personality that they want to present. P8 talked about his Facebook profile:

I think that it only partially resembles [my identity] since I haven't really participated in the activity for a long time. Let's suppose that I mark likes for some pictures or posts of others, from whom I can perhaps learn something about my opinions but in general it is far from reality. On Facebook I am quite passive and what others publish doesn't really interest me. If I mark likes for friends on the network this is mainly to be considered "a good guy" unless it is something that somebody from my close circle publishes, then I relate to it more seriously and give likes intentionally.

P3 feels that she can choose to present her identity on the network as she wishes. This provides her with confidence as she can choose which details will appear on her profile. She feels that she does not need to expose intimate information that she does not want to share with her network friends:

It gives me confidence since it allows me to express my opinion on subjects that are raised there, it's another platform that creates an experience of identity, where I can expose things and upload pictures from the experiences that occur around me.

The Privacy Dilemma

When the interviewees spoke about privacy, their main theme was their reluctance to share things. The interviewees testified that the right to privacy allows them to act in their private space without exposure to other people. They feel that privacy is built through their ability to selectively choose the details that they decide to expose. Most of the interviewees claimed that there is no privacy on the network. The use of the network was seen by them as an intrusion into their personal world. It seems that most of the interviewees feel that the collaborative element of the SNs clashes with what they understand by the term "privacy". Yet, their participation in SNs stems from their understanding that they are an integral part of the technological circle.

Privacy: Considerations for Controlling Exposure

For some of the interviewees privacy means the ability to control their personal space, where they can determine the rules of the game. P7 related to her desire to expose details of her life. She described "privacy" as *something of yours that you do not wish to expose to everyone ... daily matters that you don't want to share.*

Like other interviewees, P6 related to the word "exposure", which she included as part of her consideration of the term "privacy". She related to the component of "perfection". P6 claimed that exposure of details of her life is influenced by the desire to show an image of perfection to her target audience on the network:

In principle, it means not exposing my feelings ... the less good things. I think that when things are just perfect then there are less filters and when they are less perfect then more care is taken to maintain privacy.

The Network Exposes: Privacy Is Invaded

The interviewees were in a state of dilemma and confusion regarding the definition of the term "privacy" on the net.

You can maintain privacy on the network but you have to be on the alert all the time. Let's say if you publish a post on the iPhone there was a possibility that it would also publish your location, so I closed that possibility. Let's say that yesterday I wanted to note that I was in Tel Aviv, but then I thought, I have lots of friends in Tel Aviv and perhaps they would like to meet me and I wasn't so available for that. If I upload a picture then I flow with that ... those are matters of principle for me. For example when there are articles on a book that I read that I thought of publishing, but then I thought that my family might be hurt by them so I didn't publish them, in other words, that relates more to opinions and attitudes.

Like P4, P7 also considered aspects of exposure on the network. P4 spoke about conflicts and dilemmas when she used the network. She described a situation of deliberation when a gap formed between her desire to share something on the network and her fear that her privacy would be infringed in her world. She spoke about a process that the user undergoes before publishing contents on the network.

There can't be any privacy on the network because the moment that the sites and Facebook began there is no privacy. There are things that you can expose or not expose and at the moment everyone is exposed. If you are not exposed on Facebook then you are exposed on your mobile phone …Yes, if a picture is too exposed I block it or delete it completely. Sometimes for example I leave a picture that I took on my mobile phone and don't publish it.

P11 supported her words, adding:

There may be a sense of privacy but in practice there is no privacy, there is always someone who will analyze the data that you publish on the network and use it.

It seems from P11's words that exposure of personal contents stimulates subjective interpretation of the published contents. This interpretation is dangerous for the publishing person, if the message that they intended to impart was not understood when the contents are shared.

Publishing Contents on the Network: I Am Aware That I Am Exposed

The interviewees were asked to express their feelings concerning their knowledge that others were "nitpicking" whatever they put on their Facebook accounts. Like P4, so too P6 felt that the Facebook contents took on a collaborative dimension. This collaboration meant that the contents were visible to and open to criticism by others. P6 told us that she would choose not to publish pictures on Facebook that she did not wish to expose to a wide public, but rather upload them on to other SNs that maintain the privacy of the people photographed. P5 claimed that the problem created in the framework known as Facebook was the shared friends circle of a member telling something to another member. In this manner, their pictures would be exposed to a broad audience that she was not willing to share this information with. P6 described this:

It doesn't bother me and it doesn't interest me, I take into account that everything that I upload becomes public and I have no control of how it will look, what they will say or remark … [but] when Tamar was born I asked everyone not to upload her photographs on Facebook …I felt that something that this was something that was exclusively mine and not everyone should share in this …until today I won't upload her pictures.

P11 explained that he often encountered dilemmas when he published contents on the network. He examined the materials that he wanted to upload and deliberated before leaving them for a continuous period:

It is not something private for me, sometimes I had opinions about an article that I decided to publish and then I took it down because I had second thoughts about the subject and so I deleted it. …I'm not sure if I could say that I was afraid exactly …like when we sometimes say something that should not be said and then rethink things and perhaps wait before saying it.

P1 supported what the other interviewees had noted. He understood that the information that he chose to publish on the network exposed information from his private life. In his opinion, the contents were open to the use of a wide community to whom he published the information. His words intimate that putting contents on the net should be considered selectively. P1 noted contents that he preferred to delete because of their implications:

I made a photographs competition together with a group of friends on the network and the pictures were silly, in retrospect I regret that they were published ...: so no, today I would not do that, I have matured, it has implications ...you have to sort things before uploading them onto the network. It actually reflects who we are.

On the other hand, he said that there was a tremendous advantage in sharing:

Everyone can know what the consequences will be, the question is whether it is possible to use the information in a bad or good way. There are good consequences, for example if you need help. But again, it is transformed from private to public. There is no privacy and users can exploit the information in a bad way.

The Network: Close Follow-Up

When the interviewees were asked about their observation of their friends' accounts on Facebook, most of them admitted that in their spare time they surf the SNs in general and especially Facebook. Their acquaintances' profiles are interesting and intriguing and the users find themselves "tracking" their friends on the network. P2 explained that with the help of the network he is exposed to the worlds of people whom he knew in the past. He learns about what has happened to them, what their occupations are, their status and sexual preferences:

All sorts of things interest me ...my 'ex's or all sorts of people ... to see if they are married and whether they have children ...someone from my class published that she was a lesbian ... all sorts of things like that.

In contrast to P2, P7 does not track down people from her past. She is occupied with the present status of her current friends. P7 spoke about an additional dimension, her she does not only follow her friends on the network, but also the reactions and feedback that her friends write on the SNs:

I love to look at pictures, [especially] family and if there are reactions to your pictures. I am not on the network everyday but I follow it.

P5 added an observation from a different angle regarding the tracking of friends on Facebook. She explained that she tends to offer friendship only after she has viewed the profile of the user that she intends to approach. She said that there are very specific parameters according to which she chooses her virtual friends, for example: their noted content, age and occupation:

I look at the profiles of other people that I know on Facebook, so I was slightly interested in what is happening to them today, what they experience and then I decide whether to offer them friendship on the network or not.

In her interview P5 said that there is professional dimension to the Facebook search. She learns about her profession by looking at the profiles of her friends on the network. In her interview, it seemed that the P5's cooperation with users creates a professional partnership that broadens the horizons of the area in which she works.

I look at it from a professional level in the field of cosmetics, where they studied and what they do and I look at how they wrote things with their content and then I offered them friendship ... and when others offer me friendship I check what they write and then decide whether to confirm their friendship.

P7 expressed anxiety regarding the exposure of her private details on the Internet and on Facebook. She explained that she does not expose private details because of her desire to maintain confidentiality. She notes that even in situations where friends look at her Facebook account, she feels that her inner world is exposed:

It is harmful, I don't expose all my personal matters ...I feel that they are intruding on my privacy although I only have my close friends on Facebook, they see the pictures and it is not revealed to people who are not my Facebook friends.

P4 talked about another dimension of the implications of personal details to other users. P4 explained that people publish and share information on the network without being aware of the implications. P4 explained that she sometimes feels discomfort about information that she publishes:

I only upload onto Facebook those contents with which I feel comfortable ... I think that each person only publishes what he feels fine to publish ... for example, my friend was once right-wing and since being in the theater she has changed her opinions and become left-wing and two of her brothers cancelled their friendship and when she talks with them they say they can't continue to be her friends on Facebook because she puts up posts that hurt their friends who are right-wing.

In contrast to P4, (P11) agrees that there is a free choice in the very fact of opening and sharing a personal Facebook account. He explained that users should be understanding and know that they expose their details on the network and are exposed:

Those who want to see, let them see, I relate to Facebook as a noticeboard so similar to a noticeboard I have to know that someone will look at it...on the one hand it is intriguing to know who looks while on the other hand I think it can be onerous.

Figure 1 provides a model of the categories and themes that emerged from the findings

Figure 1. Model of categories and themes relating to the influence of social networks on relationships outside the network

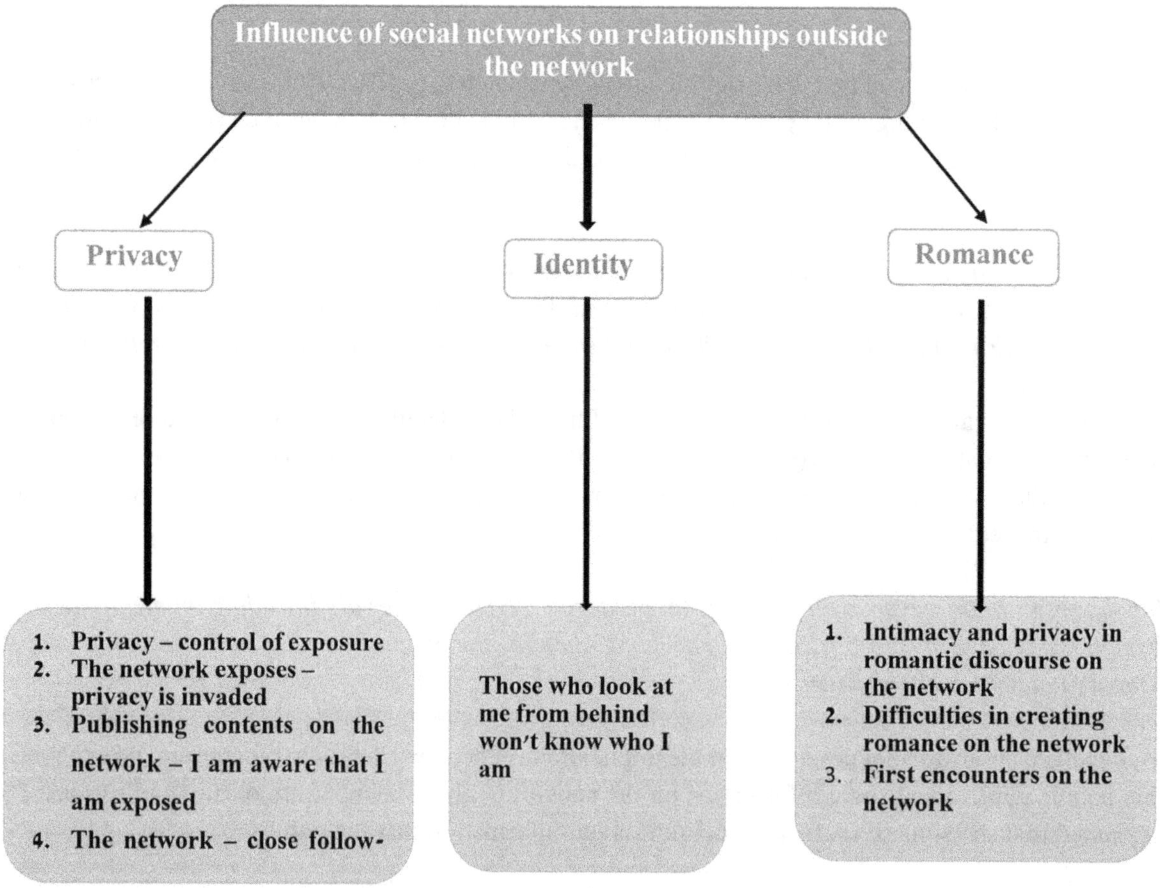

DISCUSSION

This research investigated how the virtual world in general and specifically Facebook influences romantic activities and norms outside the Internet. The main themes that emerged from the initial analysis related to the access to and development of romantic relationships on the network: romance, identity and privacy.

Romance on the Network

The network has in recent years become a key space for romantic and sexual relationships. This space allows surfers to get to know others in order to form serious relationships such as friendship and marriage on the one hand and on the other hand to form random temporary attractions (Ben-Ze'ev, 2004). The research participants were asked about the nature of the connection that was formed between them and their potential partners and they were asked to describe their experiences on the network.

Does Romance Exist on the SN?

The themes that emerged from the research related to the interviewees' consideration of romance. The most outstanding opinion voiced in the findings was that romance did not appear in the virtual space. In the past, romance was seen as a component in the formation of love and it was created in face-to-face encounters (Illouz, 1997). The network users refused to attribute the component of romance to the virtual space and stated that romance on the network transforms an interpersonal act into something commercial. Romance on the network only relates to the initial meeting in which the users get to know who is involved. The intimate context is only created in a closed space, where two partners meet without distractions (at a café, film etc.). For most of the interviewees, romance remained a fantastic dream, in which the couple meet in an intimate environment and get to know each other. In order for "romance" to exist on the network they felt it needed to include four components: (1) two partners who meet face-to-face; (2) a quiet space – a place in which the two partners meet and conduct intimate conversation; (3) a spiritual experience, and; (4) physical contact.

The interviewees emphasized that the second parameter, i.e. the "space" in which a romantic encounter took place was an important component. Mayers (1993) and Illouz (1997) saw modernism as enabling the creation of public meanings in a sphere of consumption and as allowing an authentic development of a relationship between a couple and defined this as "modern romance". The users aspire to engage in classical romance as it existed in the past, before the existence of SNs. Romance according to the evidence from this study can be defined as a face-to-face encounter, in an intimate space that includes physical contact and gestures between two partners such as *going to the beach together…holding hands, intimate things*. According to the findings this is the only way that romance can develop within a relationship. For the interviewees, the network was a place where users could be exposed to potential partners and participate in a dialog, in other words in order to create a romantic relationship two stages were needed:

Stage 1: Initial acquaintance on the network, revealing identifying data and basic familiarity with the "candidate" and for initial acquaintance.

Stage 2: A face-to-face encounter including an intimate conversation between two partners willing to form a relationship:

what happens on the network is not real, it's just a type of courtship and preparation for romance outside the network, romance outside the network is real.

The interviewees negated the possibility of a continuous romance on the network. Dialog in a virtual space that is not shared creates an intimate, experiential and adventurous moment. Even if this acquaintance does not include any physical contact or gestures that the interviewees hoped would be included in a romantic moment, there would be a special, mysterious first meeting for the user.

The findings supported the argument of Illouz (1997) that romance and relationships on the network lack the components that were mentioned above and so there is no complete romantic relationship in the interactive space. The alternatives open to users in order to conduct a relationship are more flexible online; there are many alternatives and they create a new situation. Activities in a modern discourse on the network create a different type of interaction for love life in general and romantic discourse in particular (Illouz, 1997).

Wysocki (1996) argued that romantic relations on the network work in a single direction. The romance begins on the network and continues as interactive interaction. Face-to-face relations are intimate and physical, while romantic discourse that takes place on the Internet is an initial discussion in most cases.

Some of those who surf on the Internet in general and on dating sites in particular arrive "prepared" and motivated to arrange a first meeting. In contrast to the opinion of Wysocki (1996), the findings testify that romantic discourse does not exist on the Internet and an intimate meeting including stroking and intimate gestures are needed for romance:

romance can begin through the network, through a gesture, messages ...but it cannot remain there alone. In my opinion it can strengthen and encourage romance but you need something else beyond the network (P4).

It seems that the findings mostly contradicted and disproved the theory of Visoki. Nevertheless, it seems that after a continuous period of communication when a couple feel confident and their relationship has become more established interactive communication is formed on the SN.

Identity on the Network

The network users dress themselves in masks to create stereotypes to respond to social norms associated with both external appearance and personality characteristics. It was found that these identities develop on the network and alter. Of course, the face-to-face meeting and the path towards it are influenced by the profile and these identities acquired on the SN. However, the meeting in a space outside the network means that the user has to confront their real identity and the potential partner has to accept that real identity.

According to Barak (2006) the "invisibility" afforded by the Internet serves important purposes: the user can attain their goals in this manner. Nevertheless, the user often undergoes a process of symbiosis with the new identity, continuing to wear this mask even in a face-to-face meeting. This manner of behavior seems improper and unreliable. This may be explained because the masks that are worn by the user and the need to change them create an opportunity to examine who their real "self" is (McKenna & Bargh, 2000). In this way the user is able to cope with the search for their real self, find it and cope with it emotionally. The interviewees were asked about the process of construction and the process of coping with the construction of their identities on the network.

Facebook: Self-Presentation

Most of the interviewees altered their identity so that it would be appropriate for the partner that they wanted to "conquer" and/or for the scene for which they wanted to modify their profile. The identities published on Facebook are attractive images that undergo selection. The details that the users chose to define their "self" are subjective details intended to leave a positive impression on the surfing audience. Thus it seems that the interviewees profile is definitely their personal digital footprint.

Goffman (1980), focused his interest on an analysis of the way that people present themselves in their daily life in different social settings. He noted that when a person appears before others, they create a conscious or unconscious definition of the situation and of their identity. It was found that women more than men, tend to falsify their identities and try to adapt them to stereotypes that they think that men would see as attractive (Shade, 2002). According to the present findings, women did indeed alter their profile on Facebook in order to modify themselves to suit the situation and to impress their target audience. However, according to the interview data, it can be seen that this phenomenon also occurs among men. In other words, both sexes create a suitable personal digital footprint for themselves, which is not real, in order to "market" themselves. The users choose to present their identity in the most complimentary manner and to display a facet of their personality that will market an attractive and inviting image to surfers. The surfers understand that before they meet with the potential partner they should transmit pleasantness, beauty, seriousness, reliability, wisdom etc. This is all transmitted through dialog conducted in writing on the network (Ben-Ze'ev, 2004). The surfers understand that their presentation on the network is the first opportunity to create a continuation to a real relationship. The meeting on the network is a springboard to future dialog that will only occur if they succeed in making an impression on the user with whom they conduct an initial conversation. For them their self-presentation resembles an "entry ticket" earned for making a good impression: *you wouldn't put a place of work that had fired you into your Curriculum Vitae.*

According to Amichai-Hamburger and Ben-Artzi (2000), users do not distinguish between the identities they present in the technological space and their identity in actual reality. Nevertheless, according to the present findings the users emphasized that they consciously use fictive identities. As Goffman (1980) claims, people create complementary identities to fit the world in which they belong and the situations in which they exist. The interviewees noted that the details for the construction of their Facebook identities were selected carefully according to the message that they wanted to deliver to other users.

Amichai-Hamburger and Ben Artzi (2000) note that the use of the Internet helps introverted surfers who find it difficult to find partners and romantic relationships outside the network. These users hide and shelter themselves behind the screen. The findings show that indeed the network does provide a real advantage for these introverted surfers who find it difficult to make friendships outside the network and allows them a range of alternative opportunities to meet someone. It is easy to create identities on the Internet, using suitable pictures, a description of a fascinating life and creating a fake identity that does not resemble your true life.

Some of the findings disproved the claim of Amichai et al. (2000). The interviewees noted that they were hesitant to be extensively exposed on SNs in order to meet people. Lack of privacy and the exposure of their profile on Facebook deterred some of the interviewees and created a situation in which they consciously selected the details that they published. The users often fear the consequences of publishing their details. A situation is created in which they meet new people thanks to their Internet personal digital footprint, however the Facebook profile also has a significant disadvantage in the Internet space: *my identity is far more interesting and complex than on the network.*

Privacy on the Network

The network user is in a constant dilemma relating to the choice of details that it is suitable to expose on the network. On the network in general and on Facebook in particular the user enjoys anonymity that is not possible in a face-to-face meeting. The anonymity and privacy create a special situation suitable for introverts. Wellman (2003) assumed that because of their sophisticated technology, the networks are suitable and adapted to the personal character of each user.

Does Privacy Exist on the Network?

It seems that there is privacy on the network and it can be controlled by the user. The user has free choice to choose what to publish in the technological space and who will be the target audience that will view the materials. Brandtza (2010) calls this the "privacy conflict", the gap between efforts to maintain privacy and the desire to publish personal details on the network. The interviewees testified that they choose the details to appear in their profile, which constitutes their personal digital footprint. They decide who will be their "friends", when to react and in what manner. Facebook allows them to expose themselves as eligible singles and to market themselves as experienced professionals. To this extent it is clear that the users can enjoy privacy on the network and it is they who decide exclusively about the publication of their contents.

Nevertheless, the interviewees who used Facebook, also felt that privacy was an illusion on the SN. The network is a shared space in which privacy cannot exist in entirety. Surfers have a feeling of lack of control when their details are exposed to others that they do not know. When the interviewees were asked: "what is privacy for you?" they all expressed a need for control. According to the findings privacy only exists when two basis components exist: (1) control of the choice of contents that they expose and; (2) the ability to choose who will be able to see the contents. The exposure may be performed by a third party. The ownership of a Facebook account is only partial. The user's details can be exposed in a situation in which a friend shows the account of the user to another account holder who is not in the user's community of friends.

The anonymity that characterizes the activity on SNs differs from complex relationships in real life. Being on a SN reduces the difficult coping of persons with a passive, shy or introverted identity. The SNs undergo metamorphosis and alter their purpose, from networks serving collective needs to networks serving individual needs. This fact reflects a change that the networks are undergoing and a change in the individual's consideration of them. In the past, the networks had a common concept. Today, the SNs have a decentralized character that is suited to the user and adapted to its personal character (Wellman, 2003).

IMPLICATIONS

The findings seem to indicate that romance does not exist on the network, rather romantic signs that are expressed in written text. In the modern technological era single can create a romantic space if they adapt the modern tools (the SNs and/or online dating sites) to parameters that they consider romantic. Although the intimate space and physical contact that they expect does not exist on the network, it is possible to create a situation that aspires to intimacy during an initial conversation. The user needs to ensure that they are indeed in a "private" space where they can conduct dialog solely with the proposed partner and that there is no intervention of other partners without their knowledge during the specific conversation. The participant in the conversation should be aware that the identities on the network are built to be "attractive", attempting to create a high-quality image that will be better than those of other candidates on the SN. Awareness of this subject should prevent the user's disappointment in any future face-to-face meeting after the initial acquaintance. Moreover, romantic discourse on the network is influence by behavior outside of the network. In other words, the user will not always aspire to form a serious relationship. In the conversation, the user should define their main goals. The written word and transcription is the user's tool. The dialog should be conducted with care, the style of writing, and words that are chosen, can lead the candidate for a relationship to attain their desired goal. It should also be remembered that the ability to share and publish contents to other participants without the knowledge of the other participant in the conversation on the network limits privacy. Although the first meeting on the network can constitute a "springboard" to a relationship outside the network, the details that are provided by the user should be chosen carefully before knowing the identity of the other side in the dialog. This means that the user should continually be aware of the rules for activity on the network. The network is a space in which conversations take place for various objectives, such conversations have special characteristics that differ from conversations outside the Internet. In order to understand this issue further research should relate to the characteristics of social discourse on the Internet and its contribution to different aspects of our lives.

LIMITATIONS OF THIS STUDY

Since this was a qualitative study with a relatively small sample, the results cannot be generalized to similar circumstances. However, the reader can decide to what extent they are informative for other similar contexts.

Future research should consider a larger sample of respondents with different academic and professional characteristics. In order to derive suitable conclusions for a broader population, further research should relate to a random population of additional singles from different regions and countries. Different populations could be studied including non-academic populations and compared with populations that do not use the SNs.

To summarize, the research and findings described in this paper showed that network surfers idealize their images when presenting themselves on the network in order to be perceived as an attractive and eligible in their search for the ideal partner. The surfers adopt characteristics and attractive features from the images that they know in real life.

The interviewees were asked to define romance on the network. They found it difficult to find its existence on the network. They negated the possibility of creating a romantic situation in the virtual space.

The network personality meets its potential partner in the digital space and from there they can move on to the real world. However, the continuation of this relationship often returns to the network and exists in substance there. Nevertheless, the behavior of the couple on the network is just one of many representations of social aspects in a dynamic changing existence. Dating sites are a metonymy for a whole refreshing world that represents the society in which we live. The SNs began a novel social-personal process which has influenced our lives. At this point in time the digital networks and sites dictate new norms and rules. The open question that remains in this context is whether a long-term study over several years would reveal a different sort of couple relationships.

REFERENCES

Amichai-Hamburger, Y., & Ben-Artzi, E. (2000). The relationship between extraversion, neuroticism, and different uses of the Internet. *Computers in Human Behavior*, *16*(4), 441–449. doi:10.1016/S0747-5632(00)00017-0

Barak, A. (2006). Youth and the Internet: Psychology of "as if" and "like that". [Hebrew]. *Panim*, *37*, 48–58.

Ben-Ze'ev, A. (2004). *Love online: Emotions on the Internet*. Cambridge, UK: Cambridge University Press. doi:10.1017/CBO9780511489785

Connolly, I., Palmer, M., Barton, H., & Kirwan, G. (Eds.). (2016). *An Introduction to Cyberpsychology*. Routledge.

Cooper, A., McLoughlin, I. P., & Campbell, K. M. (2000). Sexuality in cyberspace: Update for the 21st century. *Cyberpsychology & Behavior*, *3*(4), 521–536. doi:10.1089/109493100420142

Cooper, A., & Sportolari, L. (1997). Romance in cyberspace: Understanding online attraction. *Journal of Sex Education and Therapy*, *22*(1), 7–14. doi:10.1080/01614576.1997.11074165

Denzin, N. K., & Lincoln, Y. S. (Eds.). (1994). *Handbook of qualitative research*. Sage Publications.

DeVito, M. A., Birnholtz, J. P., & Hancock, J. T. (2017). Platforms, people, and perception: Using affordances to understand self-presentation on social media. In *CSCW Proceedings of the 2017 ACM Conference on Computer Supported Cooperative Work and Social Computing* (pp. 740-754). ACM.

Glaser, B. G., & Strauss, A. L. (1967). *The discovery of grounded theory: Strategy for qualitative research*. Chicago: Aldine Publishing Company.

Goffman, A. (1980). *Presenting the self in daily life*. Tel Aviv: Reshafim. [Hebrew]

Granovetter, M. S. (1973). The strength of weak ties. *American Journal of Sociology*, *78*(6), 1360–1380. doi:10.1086/225469

Halpern, D., Katz, J. E., & Carril, C. (2017). The online ideal persona vs. the jealousy effect: Two explanations of why selfies are associated with lower-quality romantic relationships. *Telematics and Informatics*, *34*(1), 114–123. doi:10.1016/j.tele.2016.04.014

Illouz, E. (1997). *Consuming the romantic utopia: Love and the cultural contradictions of capitalism*. University of California Press.

Kohut, H. (1971). *The analysis of the self; a systematic approach to the psychoanalytic treatment of narcissistic personality disorders*. New York: International Universities Press.

Lincoln, Y., & Guba, E. G. (1985). *Naturalistic inquiry*. Newbury Park, CA: Sage.

Malach-Feins, A. (2002). *Falling in love: How we choose who to fall in love with?* Tel Aviv: Modan. (in Hebrew)

Mayers, G. (2003). *Social psychology*. McGraw-Hill Ryerson.

McKenna, K. Y., & Bargh, J. A. (2000). Plan 9 from cyberspace: The implications of the Internet for personality and social psychology. *Personality and Social Psychology Review*, *4*(1), 57–75. doi:10.1207/S15327957PSPR0401_6

Mendelson, A. L., & Papacharissi, Z. 2010. Look at us: collective narcissism in college student Facebook photo galleries. In Papacharissi (Ed.), The networked self: Identity, Community and Culture on Social Network Sites (pp. 251–273). New York: Routledge.

Patton, N. Q. (1990). *Qualitative evaluation and research methods* (2nd ed.). Newbury Park, CA: Sage.

Rettberg, J. W. (2017). *Self-Representation in Social Media*. Academic Press.

Sabar Ben-Yehoshua, N. (2001). Ethnography in education. In N. Sabar Ben-Yehoshua (Ed.), Traditions and genres in qualitative research (pp. 100-136). Lod: Dvir. (in Hebrew)

Shade, L. R. (2002). *Gender and community in the social construction of the Internet*. Peter Lang.

Smith, J. A. (1995). Semi-structured interviewing and qualitative analysis. *Rethinking Methods in Psychology, 1*, 8-26.

Suler, J. (2004). The online disinhibition effect. *Cyberpsychology & Behavior*, *7*(3), 321–326. doi:10.1089/1094931041291295 PMID:15257832

Turkle, S. (1995). *Life on the screen: Identity in the age of the Internet*. New York: Simon & Schuster.

Wellman, H., & Cross, D. (2003). Theory of mind conceptual change. *Child Development*, *72*(3), 702–707. doi:10.1111/1467-8624.00309 PMID:11405576

Whitty, M., & Carr, A. N. (2006). *Cyberspace romance: The psychology of online relationships*. Hampshire, UK: Palgrave Macmillan. doi:10.1007/978-0-230-20856-8

Wysocki, D. K. (1996). *Somewhere over the modem: Interpersonal relationships over computer bulletin boards. Sociology*. Santa Barbara: University of California.

Wysocki, D. K. (1998). Let your fingers do the talking. *Sexualities*, *1*(4), 425–452. doi:10.1177/136346098001004003

Zhao, S. (2006). Do Internet users have more social ties? A call for differentiated analyses of Internet use. *Journal of Computer-Mediated Communication*, *11*(3), 844–862. doi:10.1111/j.1083-6101.2006.00038.x

Zhao, S., Grasmuck, S., & Martin, J. (2008). Identity construction on Facebook: Digital empowerment in anchored relationships. *Computers in Human Behavior*, *24*(5), 1816–1836. doi:10.1016/j.chb.2008.02.012

Chapter 13
Romantic Relationships, Online Dating, and Mental Health Issues

Tejaswini Bhave
Deenanth Mangeshkar Hospital and Research Center, India

ABSTRACT

This chapter attempts to present the overview of mental health issues associated with online dating and online romantic relationships with relevant research background. It briefly cautions about the possible risks involved in the world of online dating platforms and later delves into mental health concerns that can emerge out of experiences while selecting a potential partner online, developing a romantic relationship, and being involved in a romantic relationship online. It also discusses safety measures that need to be taken before and while being active on such online dating sites. The chapter draws attention to the specific role of mental health professionals that is needed while dealing with victims of online scams and abuse.

INTRODUCTION

Love and affection are very basic human needs. Romantic relationships are significant part of our lives and contribute in our physical, social and emotional well-being. A good relationship enhances our overall health. (Cohen, Frank, Doyle, Skoner, Rabin, & Gwaltney, 1998), and even help in speedy recovery from various disorders (Kiecolt-Glaser, Loving, Stowell, Malarkey, Lemeshow, Dickinson, & Glaser, 2005). Most of the people find their partners through their social or professional sphere. However, these circles are limited in number and thus the choices can become narrowing. Consequently due to the advent of new technology, people want to widen the scope of finding a more suitable partner and they find the solution in online dating sites.

Using the internet has not just remained a convenience but has become a necessity. With the advancements in technology, today we have plethora of very diverse social networking platforms which are unique in their own way connecting people together online. Social media has revolutionized and digitized human interactions and relationships. Rosenfeld and Thomas (2012) found that the Internet has allowed users to find partners more easily, especially homosexuals and middle-aged people who operate in a "thin market.

DOI: 10.4018/978-1-5225-4047-2.ch013

With the popularity of online dating sites, the stigma of online dating has diminished considerably in the last decade. According to the survey conducted by Smith and Anderson, (2015), overwhelming majority of Americans suggest that online dating is a good way to meet people. Interestingly, more than 15% of adults say that they have used either mobile dating apps or an online dating site at least once in the past. Online dating services are now the second most popular way to meet a partner.

WHAT PERSONALITY CHARACTERISTICS ARE ASSOCIATED WITH THOSE WHO PREFER ONLINE DATING?

1. In a research finding it was concluded that loneliness was found to be one of the major factor that encouraged people to go for online dating. (Lawson & Lake, 2006). The participants reported that they felt less lonely after being a part of the online dating websites.
2. It was observed that individuals scoring higher on the romantic beliefs and especially idealisation of the romantic partner were more vulnerable to being deceived on the online dating sites. These individuals also tended to be more agreeable and more likely to opt for online dating. (Whitty & Buchanan, 2012)

WHAT IS WRONG WITH ONLINE DATING?

In a popular blog post by Ryan Anderson, several warning signals regarding online dating have been put up and they seem to be resonating with reports of Indian newspapers on the same topic (Psychology Today, 2016).

1. People tend to lie about themselves on online dating sites. Out of over 1000 online daters in the USA and UK, 53% confessed that they have lied in their online dating profile; mostly about look, height, financial status. This was an attempt to project an ideal self to attract more partners.
2. It's basically virtual! Smith and Anderson (2015) found out that more than one third of their research participant (online daters) never actually went on a date and those who went found it difficult to connect to the person they had met online.
3. It makes people judgemental. Various online daters confess that they judge the person based on the looks. The apps and websites offer an interface where only the physical aspects of the individual are highlighted so as to make the website more appealing. Naturally the users dismiss the not-so beautiful candidate in just a swipe or a click.

EMERGING MENTAL HEALTH ISSUES RELATED TO ONLINE DATING

However there are some shortcomings of this epidemic of developing romantic relationships. Right from becoming a victim to identity or financial frauds to brief, deceitful and virtual nature of relationships, online dating poses a serious danger to the person's sense of self and his or her relationships with others which in turn lead to many mental health-associated issues.

1. Short and unsuccessful relationships. The very virtual nature of the online dating scene itself suggests that it promises a 'fling'; meaning a very casual, non-committal relationship or so the stigma associated with online dating suggests to people. People are attracted to online dating when they feel lonely or are disappointed by the conventional dating experience or "let some steam off". Thus it becomes apparent that these relationships are not looked upon to be serious and following study attest to that.

A recent study by Paul (2014) showed that couples who met on dating sites are less likely to get married and even further he also pointed through surveys that breakups were more common in couples who met online versus those who met in more traditional set ups. This study asserts that this result is consistent with both married and unmarried couples.

We know that short term and less meaningful relationships that lead to breakups do not contribute to our well-being. Frequent or even one incident of breakup leads to bereavement symptoms including intrusive thoughts and attempts to suppress them and insomnia as well as morbidity factors including broken heart syndrome and immune dysfunction (Field, 2011). In this way online dating can really pose a threat to one's well-being.

2. Online dating scams. As discussed above online dating sites are not safe as in the candidates can put up false information about their looks, financial status, marital status and you have no means to crosscheck this information. A huge number of scams including financial frauds, sexual abuse, internet bullying and blackmailing have mushroomed with the increasing use of online dating websites and apps.

Professor Whitty and Professor Buchanan from the University of Leicester and Westminster have conducted comprehensive studies of the victims of online dating scams. They appraised from a nationally representative sample survey that almost 230,000 people may have been tricked by romance fraudsters in UK only. They assessed the 2 sets of such victims i.e.: 1) those who lost money due to frauds done by online romantic partners, and; 2) non-financial victims.

The victims who had lost money reported significantly higher emotional distress than those who did not lose money. Many non-financial victims too reported high levels of emotional effects. Both set of participants reported experiences of depression, guilt, shame, embarrassment, fear, feeling suicidal, extreme emotional distress, emotionally violated, loss of trust in others, feeling stupid, denial, problems in appetite, sleep and sexual functions.

3. Body Image and Self-Esteem. As discussed above the dating apps and websites bank on the good looks of the candidate and hence the individual with more appealing physical appearance are desired by the opposite gender and they get the most right swipes/likes/interest requests. This creates a problem in how one looks at one's own body and how much importance is attached to looking beautiful.

In a study presented at the annual convention of the American psychological association, researchers explored the psychological effects of a certain popular dating application on a group of 1300 college students. These participants were asked questions based on their appraisal of their own body image and how they compare their looks with others. At the end of this questionnaire they were asked if they used that certain application.

The results showed that individuals using that application had lower levels of self-worth than those who did not use the app. They also reported being less satisfied with their facial features and they were ashamed of their bodies. They also constantly compared themselves with the appearance of others and were self-conscious. Surprisingly, this research even showed that all the findings were true for men and women both, because women tend to judge their own looks negatively (Strubel & Petrie, 2016).

Body dissatisfaction appears to be associated with greater impairment in self-esteem and other aspects of psycho-social functioning in males (Furnham, Badmin, & Sneade, 2002; Wardle & Cooke, 2005).

A longitudinal study examined the relationship between low self-esteem and depression and found that low self-esteem is a causal risk factor for the development of depression. (Robins, Widaman, & Conger, 2014)

4. Too much attention is not good for you! In the world of online dating, the *super like, like, comment, right sweep* is like a tiny dose of positive reinforcement and it is highly pleasurable to the receiving candidate. The rampant world of social media has wired our sense of identity to how we look on our social or dating profile online. People either tend to get more arrogant when they are desired by many people or lose their self-worth because they are rejected or ignored.

An online app user confessed to Times of India how using this app first gave her too many feel good emotions and how she became significantly arrogant and narcissistic. However, when her profile was rejected by a good-looking individual and he said that she was too pretentious she fell in the spiral of self-doubt, low confidence and despair. This shattered her self-worth and she spent hours in the late night to see if anybody has liked her profile or not. The rejection stung her too much and she began crash dieting and her work-life and mental health deteriorated (Times News Network, 2017).

5. Online sexual abuse. Women on various dating websites report the experience of receiving rude, disgusting messages, sexual propositions/requests which if entertained go on to develop sexual abuse. As announced by the UK's national crime agency, online dating related rape has increased by more than 450 percent in last 5 years (2016). The report elaborated that online relationships generally progress at higher rate as compared to offline relationships because in the virtual world people tend to feel free and express their emptions readily. This increased trust leads to individuals taking more risks in the relationship and be willing to participate in vulnerable situations. In these cases previous online flirting, messages with sexual content increase the intimacy between the partners and thus they have higher expectations about sexual activity when they meet for the first time. The offenders use the strategies of persuasion, perseverance and coercion to get the victims agree on the early first date.

This can result into serious mental health problems leading to development of disorders like depression, suicide attempts, Post traumatic stress disorder etc. Research consistently identifies the negative consequences of being a victim of cyber abuse. Victims experience loneliness and social isolation. The person's consequent social withdrawal is likely to lead to low self-esteem and depression. Those who abuse others too are at risk too. They are more likely than non-abusers to engage in a range of maladaptive and antisocial behaviours and at risk of alcohol and drugs dependence, depression and suicidal ideation (Cowie, 2013).

PROTECTING ONE'S WELL-BEING WHILE DATING ONLINE

Now when we are familiar with what dangers online dating poses to our emotional and physical well-being, it becomes mandatory to go through some safety measures candidates need to take before embarking on the journey of online dating. These tips are compiled from various dating websites and cyber security professionals (eharmony.com, Tinder™, OKcupid.com, National Cyber Security Alliance).

Though these measures cannot make the person absolutely immune to the horrors of online dating scams and abuse they can definitely prevent many unwanted situations. It is ultra-important to stay safe online.

1. Use a trusted online dating site or app which has strong customer support, better privacy and those who approve the candidate profile only after checking the claimed information with valid documents or proofs.
2. Check the privacy policy, required details and permissions by the website so as to safeguard your sensitive information and how they handle cases of abuse or scams, features like blocking a profile or disabling instant messaging/ location tracking or the option of reporting a profile are very much necessary.
3. Do not provide sensitive information about yourself and financial details, do not divulge in sharing private and personal details. Do not respond when request of financial details or sexual content are made, block that person and immediately report his profile to concerned authority. Do not exchange private and personal information.
4. Be careful to not disclose your personal mobile numbers immediately. Do not trust blindly.
5. Use a disposable email id for dating sites.
6. Create an honest profile and be specific in your expectations from prospective partners. Do not upload inappropriate pictures or those containing information about your car number, house location etc.
7. Check the person's identity through Google, Facebook or other platforms. Make sure that the name, face and other details are correct.
8. Do not develop too much intimacy online. First meet the person as soon as possible and when your fact check is complete you can slowly develop the relationship.
9. While going on first dates learn to say a firm "No" to any sexual requests, always confide the location details of your date with a known person (family or friend). Meet in public places and avoid long drivways or lonely places. Do not drink too much on the date and be vigilant to any cues of dangers. Confront and ask question when something looks fishy even online and in person.
10. Confide in your near and dear ones about your dating experience online. Do not choose online dating just because you are too lonely, depressed or recently broke up with someone. Make an informed choice.

ROLE OF MENTAL HEALTH PROFESSIONALS

The increasing number of cases of cyber abuse and scams are leaving the victims stranded in the miserable state of anger and disappointment and in many cases their reaction is that of experiencing a trauma. Mental health professionals need to be aware of unique challenges these victims face and they need to prepare themselves to tailor their interventions in such a way that they meet the needs of victims of such abuse.

The study done by Whitty and Buchanan (2012) proposed the shortcomings of the help given by counsellors to such victims. The professionals were inept to understand the nature of the trauma and were quick to judge the victims for being conned financially and emotionally.

The counsellors also did not understand that the victims could not turn to their family and friend for social support and they felt withdrawn and isolated from others.

Hence the mental health professionals need to take care of following aspects as a reflection of Whitty and Buchanman's study;

1. Increasing awareness about such abuse and scams in their working field and spread word of caution. They also need to be approachable to such victims and come out of traditional therapy/counselling set up to meet these victims.
2. Law enforcement agencies need to have strong tie-ups with mental health professionals to facilitate timely referrals and crisis intervention in earlier stage when the victims are vulnerable to suicidal ideation, substance abuse and other such situations.
3. It is necessary to understand that this trauma reaction is similar to the stages of grieving as explained by Kubler-Ross's (1969): denial, bargaining, anger, depression, and acceptance.

The denial stage when unresolved can lead to re-victimization which is much more dangerous. Appropriate interventions need to be employed to fully resolve the grieving response.

4. The increased mistrust towards other people the victims have developed after the trauma can lead to transference issues.
5. Ways of coping with the distress need to be realistic rather than dreamy and farfetched; the professionals need to understand that empowering the victims for a long term is essential rather than for a temporary basis.
6. The professional need to understand the '*double hit*' victim has suffered- the financial loss as well as the loss of a perceived significant relationship.
7. It is necessary to protect the victim from the second wave of being conned.
8. The victims who go through such trauma are often seen to have history of previous sexual abuse and other mental health problems. These vulnerabilities need to be sensitively handled.
9. The victims need to know that professional help is available and professionals need to standards of uphold highest ethical and moral conduct to safeguard the confidentiality and well-being of the victims.

THE POSITIVES OF ONLINE DATING

It goes without saying that even after enlisting many drawbacks of the world of online dating it also has some uses and that is why it is so popular. Finkel and colleagues (2012) discuss the plus points of online dating:

1. **Access:** Online dating equips the individuals with access to many more potential partners than they could often find in their daily lives. This is especially true for individuals interested in partners of a particular type, orientation, lifestyle, or in isolated areas.
2. **Matching:** Many online dating sites offer various types of personality testing and matching. Such matching can help guide individuals toward dating partners who may be more compatible.
3. **Communication:** Online dating offers a number of ways to get to know a possible date before meeting in person. Such computer-mediated communication allows for safe and convenient interaction, without much risk or time commitment. For the busy professional, or the safety-conscious, such communication is an excellent way to "check" potential partners.
4. **Individuals With Social Stigma Attached to Their Particular Condition or Way of Life:** It is difficult for individuals who have social stigma associated with them like homosexuals, people with disability or people having mental illness to find a romantic partner through conventional methods of dating. But these individuals have found it useful to search for a suitable partner through online dating and they are finding meaningful romantic relationships online.

CONCLUSION

In conclusion, it is necessary to understand that both the traditional and online methods have their own advantages and disadvantages but the key to cultivate online romantic relationship is to be cautious while wading through the virtual world. Online dating is a start but meeting the person as soon as possible leads to trust building and rule out dangers of being conned. Considering internet as way to engagement with real human beings and not mistaking it with actual relationship is of utmost importance to protect own mental health and overall well-being.

REFERENCES

Anderson, R. (2016, September 6). The ugly truth about online dating [Web blog post]. Retrieved from www.psychologytoday.com

Cohen, S., Frank, E., Doyle, W. J., Skoner, D. P., Rabin, B. S., & Gwaltney, J. M. (1998). Types of stressors that increase susceptibility to the common cold in healthy adults. *Health Psychology*, *17*(3), 214–223. doi:10.1037/0278-6133.17.3.214 PMID:9619470

Cowie, H. (2013). Cyber bullying and its impact on young people's emotional health and well-being. *The Psychiatrist*, *37*(05), 167–170. doi:10.1192/pb.bp.112.040840

Dating safety. (n.d.). Retrieved from www.tinder.com

Dickinson, S. L., & Glaser, R. (2005). Hostile marital interactions, proinflammatory cytokine production, and wound healing. *Archives of General Psychiatry*, *62*(12), 1377–1384. doi:10.1001/archpsyc.62.12.1377 PMID:16330726

Emerging new threat in online dating -Initial trends in internet dating initiated serious sexual assaults. (2016, May 7). [Web log post]. Retrieved from www.nationalcrimeagency.gov.uk

Field, T. (2011). Romantic Breakups, Heartbreak and Bereavement-Romantic Breakups. *Psychology (Irvine, Calif.)*, *2*(04), 382–387. doi:10.4236/psych.2011.24060

Finkel, E. J., Eastwick, P. W., Karney, B. R., Reis, H. T., & Sprecher, S. (2012). Online dating: A critical analysis from the perspective of psychological science. *Psychological Science in the Public Interest*, *13*(1), 3–66. doi:10.1177/1529100612436522 PMID:26173279

Furnham, A., Badmin, N., & Sneade, I. (2002). Body image dissatisfaction: Gender differences in eating attitudes, self-esteem, and reasons for exercise. *J Psychol*, *136*(6), 581–596. www.okcupid.com. doi:10.1080/00223980209604820 PMID:12523447

Kiecolt-Glaser, J. K., Loving, T. J., Stowell, J. R., Malarkey, W. B., Lemeshow, S., Lawson, H. M., & Leck, K. (2006). Dynamics of internet dating. *Social Science Computer Review*, *24*(2), 189–208. doi:10.1177/0894439305283402

Kübler-Ross, E. (1969). *On death and dying*. New York: Simon & Schuster.

Managing your privacy. (n.d.). Retrieved from www.staysafeonline.org

Orth, U., Robins, R. W., Widaman, K. F., & Conger, R. D. (2014). Is Low Self-Esteem a Risk Factor for Depression? Findings from a Longitudinal study of Mexican-Origin Youth. *Developmental Psychology*, *50*(2), 622 633. doi:10.1037/a0033817 PMID:23895172

Paul, A. (2014). Cyber psychology, behaviour, and social networking. *Oct-Vol.*, *17*(10), 664–667.

Rosenfeld, M. J., & Thomas, R. J. (2012). Searching for a Mate: The Rise of the Internet as a Social Intermediary. *American Sociological Review*, *77*(4), 523–547. doi:10.1177/0003122412448050

Safety tips. (n.d.). Retrieved from www.eharmony.com

Sales, N. J. (2015). *Tinder and the dawn of the dating apocalypse*. Retrieved from http://www.vanityfair.com/culture/2015/08/tinder-hook-up-culture-end-of-dating

Smith, A., & Anderson, M. (2015). *5 facts about online dating*. Pew Research Centre.

Strubel, J. L., & Petrie, T. A. (2016). *Tinder: Swiping self-esteem?* Retrieved from http://www.apa.org

Tiwari, P. (2017, December 7). How dating multiple guys on a popular dating app affected my mental health [Web log post]. Retrieved from https://timesofindia.indiatimes.com

Wardle, J., & Cooke, L. (2005). The impact of obesity on psychological well-being. *Best Practice & Research. Clinical Endocrinology & Metabolism*, *19*(3), 421–440. doi:10.1016/j.beem.2005.04.006 PMID:16150384

Whitty, M. T., & Buchanan, T. (2012). The Online Dating Romance Scam: A Serious Crime. *Cyberpsychology, Behavior, and Social Networking*, *15*(3), 181–183. doi:10.1089/cyber.2011.0352

Chapter 14
Impact of Online Dating, Cyber Stalking, Cybersex, and Pornography on Mental Health

Rejani Thudalikunnil Gopalan
Gujarat Forensic Sciences University, India

ABSTRACT

Online behavior varies according to the purpose and situations and many get involved in intimate relations, like in online dating, which have an impact on the person and his mental health. The chapter focused on the impact of online dating, cyber stalking, cybersex, and pornography on mental health. Though many studied the online dating among adolescents and adults, that of old age group is not yet fully explored especially about their sexual needs. It is worth exploring factors related to risky sexual behaviors among gay and bisexual individuals. Online dating for mentally ill people is an under-researched area. Cyberstalking is an important issue, especially among adolescents and young adults, and cybersex and cyber pornography threatens the safety and mental health in addition to the problems of addiction and child trafficking, and it is linked with high sexual risk behaviors and sex crimes. It is necessary to develop tailored psychotherapeutic and pharmacological interventions by taking into account the complexity and heterogeneity of the problems.

INTRODUCTION

Cyber-psychology is an emerging discipline that focuses on the study of human-machine interaction. It is an area of psychology focusing on the study of *the effects of cyberspace on the behavior of humans and of society in general.* (Grand Dictionnaire de la langue française, 2000). It deals with cyber space interaction and impacts of virtual realities. Virtual reality can be defined as *the application that makes it possible for the user to navigate and to interact in real time with an environment in three dimensions generated by a computer* (Pratt, Zyda, & Kelleher, 1995). Researchers are trying to understand about virtual realities and how it affects human behavior and its pros and cons. Social networking is one of the major topics widely discussed. According to Cambridge dictionary social networking is the use of

DOI: 10.4018/978-1-5225-4047-2.ch014

websites and other internet services to communicate with other people and make friends. Online behavior varies according to the purpose and situations and many get involved in intimate relations, like in online dating. Though it has many positive benefits, it is considered a major risk to mental health issues. This chapter focuses on impact of online dating, cyber stalking, cybersex and pornography on mental health.

ONLINE BEHAVIORS

Mostly the online behaviors are not similar to the actual behaviors of the person in reality depends on the purpose of the interaction. People usually look for companionship and sexual attraction as common relationship goals (Graham, 2011; Masuda, 2003). Many different types of online relationship exists such as internet dating, cybersex, social networking relationships, online gaming, online forums and chat rooms, and Professional relationships. Each type varies according to the purpose and the way of interaction and it will have an impact on the person and his mental health especially interactions related to internet dating, cybersex, social networking relationships, and online gaming. The following section will focus on online dating with special focus on older adults, men engaging in sex with men and bisexuals, and mentally ill individuals; cyber stalking, cybersex and pornography and its relation with mental health.

ONLINE DATING

Online dating is gaining popularity all over the world and many reasons such as increased divorce rate, loneliness, and delayed marriage among many are the reasons for the popularity. Many factors affect the online dating, for example, for men, age, educational level, and self-rated physical attractiveness are important qualities and for women, they are not being overweight, self-rated physical attractiveness, and having a photo (Fiore, 2004). Whyte and Torgler (2017) explored factors that influence matches of online dating participants' stated preference for particular characteristics in a potential partner and compares these with the characteristics of the online daters actually contacted. The nature of online dating facilitates exploration of the differences between stated preference and actual choice by participants, as online daters willingly provide a range of demographics on their ideal partner. They found that factors such as a person's age, their education level, and a more social personality all increase the number of factors they choose in a potential partner that match their original stated preference. Males (relative to females) appear to match fewer characteristics when contacting potential love interests. Conversely, age interaction effects demonstrate that males in their late 60's are increasingly more selective (than females) regarding who they contact. Psychological factors also play a part in engaging online dating. But studies also reported that online dating was unrelated to income and educational level (Valkenburg & Peter, 2007) and gives less accurate information such as men lied more about their height, and women lied more about their weight (Toma, Hancock, & Ellison, 2008). Cali, Coleman, and Campbell (2013) reported that women showed stigma and strong self-protective behavior in online relationship initiation who had never been on a date with someone they had met online was also reported.

The description of profile varies if widower or divorcees seeking partners online. For widowed individuals, online dating sites may function as venues to explore their past experiences and engage in the construction of a post-loss identity or a post-loss "ideal self" (Young & Caplan, 2010). They found that one-third of widowed individuals discussed their loss in their profiles. In addition, about one-third of the widowed profiles included explicit reference to a philosophy of life, and about 16% mentioned sense-making or cognitive reappraisals of their bereavement. Many profiles included some articulation of a vision of a future partnership. Results also revealed a significant correlation between widowed individuals including a backstory and their likelihood of exhibiting sense-making in their profiles. Finally, unlike the widowed users, divorcees provided much briefer mentions of their lost relationships, used less sense-making language, and were less likely to articulate an explicit vision of future partnerships.

Hance, Blackhart, and Dew (2017) found that true self mediated the relationship between rejection sensitivity and online dating site usage. It suggests that rejection-sensitive individuals feel they can more easily represent their "true" selves in online environments, such as online dating sites, which partially explains why they are more likely to engage in online dating. Valkenburg and Peter (2007) reported that respondents between 30 and 50 years old were the most active online daters and people low in dating anxiety were more active online daters than people high in dating anxiety.

Though researches mainly conducted among adolescents and adults regarding online dating, limited knowledge are available on many aspects of online dating among older adults, Men Sex with Men, Bisexuals and people with mental illness. The following section will be focused on these topics.

Older Adults and Online Dating

Online dating has become increasingly popular among older adults following broader social media adoption patterns and the reasons are different for online dating. Usually loneliness and need for companionship were found as reasons for dating and women might value companionship more than men. Older online dating users may be particularly interested in sexual attraction, as sexual desire may motivate active pursuit of new romantic relationships. They value sexual attraction quite highly, though age differences do exist. Men were more likely than women to say the most important reason for dating was to fulfill their sexual needs (Alterovitz & Mendelsohn, 2013; Menkin, Robles, Wiley, & Gonzaga, 2015; Montenegro, 2003).

Adults of different ages may share motivations for companionship and affection, but dating profiles may reveal differences in adults' goals. Theories addressing age-related changes in motivation suggest that younger adults are likely to emphasize themselves, achievements, attractiveness, and sexuality. Older adults are likely to present themselves positively and emphasize their existing relationships and health. Study revealed that older adults were more likely to use first-person plural pronouns (e.g., we, our) and words associated with health and positive emotions. Younger adults were more likely to use first-person singular pronouns (e.g., I, my) and words associated with work and achievement. Findings suggest that younger adults enhance the "self" when seeking romantic partnership. In contrast, older adults are more positive in their profiles and focus more on connectedness and relationships to others (Davis & Fingerman, 2016). Gewirtz-Meydan and Ayalon (2017) examined the visual representations of older people on 39 dating sites intended for the older population and reported that the majority of older men and women were smiling and had a fair complexion, with light eye color and perceived age of younger than 60. Older women were presented as younger and wore more cosmetics as compared with older men.

Wada, Mortenson, and Clarke (2016) examined how relevant Rowe and Kahn's three criteria of successful aging were to older adults' self-portrayals in online dating profiles: low probability of disease and disability, high functioning, and active life engagement. In this cross-sectional study, 320 online dating profiles of older adults were randomly selected and coded based on the criteria. Logistic regression analyses determined whether age, gender, and race/ethnicity predicted self-presentation. Few profiles were indicative of successful aging due to the low prevalence of the first two criteria; the third criterion (active life engagement), however, was identified in many profiles. Native Americans were significantly less likely than other ethnic groups to highlight the first two criteria. Younger age predicted presenting the first criterion. Women's presentation of the third criterion remained significantly high with age. The findings suggest that the criteria may be unimportant to older adults when seeking partners or they may reflect the exclusivity of this construct.

Older women and men expectations about the prospective partners may differ as indicate in their profiles. Because of the dearth of available partners, older women looking to date may have to relax their dating standards to find a dating partner, perhaps accepting a life situation that is not what they had hoped for. However older women may be reluctant to sacrifice an often recently-gained lifestyle free of caregiving obligations. Older men, on the other hand, have a large pool of potential dating partners and do not face the same dilemma. William, Locker, Briley, Ryan, and Scott (2011) compared Internet dating profiles for 100 older adults and 100 younger adults, and found that older adults (and especially older women) were more selective than younger adults when it came to the age, race, religion, income, and height of a prospective dating partner. However, older adults were willing to travel substantially farther than younger adults to meet the right partner. These findings paint a clear picture of older Internet daters as eager to meet the right person, but not desperate to meet just anyone.

Older adults needs and expectations in online dating are different from that of adolescents and young adults. More research is required to understand online dating and mental health issues among them.

Men Having Sex with Men, Bisexuals, and Online Dating

Gay and bisexual men have rapidly taken to using the internet for sexual purposes: for health information seeking, finding sex partners, dating, cybersex, and pornography. Men have adapted to the ever-evolving technological advances that have been made in connecting users to the Internet-from logging on via dial-up modem on a desktop computer to geo-social-sexual networking via handheld devices. The Internet, and specifically mobile technology, is an environment gay and bisexual men are using for sexual purposes, and attracts men with a different demographic profile (Grov, Breslow, Newcomb, Rosenberger, & Bauermeister, 2014; Hospers, Kok, Harterink,& de Zwart, 2005). Internet use provides a vital opportunity for sexual minority youth to learn about sexual desires and pursue partnerships otherwise publicly stigmatized. Young gay men (YGM) benefited online through exploration of their sexual identities, while simultaneously encountering and negotiating sources of risk (Pingel, Bauermeister, Johns, Eisenberg, & Leslie-Santana, 2013). Badal, Stryker, DeLuca and Purcell (2017) reported that more than half of the sample of Men Sex with Men (MSM) were found to be frequent users of dating websites and apps to find partners. Gay and bisexual men (GBM) meeting sexual and romantic partners online has replaced other methods (Prestage, Bavinton, Grierson, Down, Keen, Bradley, & Duncan, 2015).

The presentation of themselves differs whether they are open to public about their orientation or not. Hidden MSM (those who self-label as heterosexual or who hide their same-sex sexual attraction from family, friends, acquaintances, or a female romantic partner) tend to mask their identity on gay chat and dating sites while avoiding offline gay venues. They also focus more strongly on online sexual activities (e.g., masturbating during online chats) when using gay chat and dating sites. However, they spend the same amount of time on these sites, and they use them to initiate offline sexual encounters as often and as fast as open MSM (Lemke & Weber, 2017). Those are open to public about their orientation did not mind to post their nude pictures in their profile. Lemke and Merz (2017) studied the importance of body presentation among men who have sex with men (MSM) by exploring the phenomenon of nude body presentation in online dating environments and found that about two-thirds of the participants declared that they use nude pictures in their dating profiles. The results indicate that the use of nudity is driven by three underlying gratifications: (1) Attracting attention, meaning that nudity is used to accelerate sexual outcomes from online dating use; (2) empowerment, meaning that nudity online serves as an environment for otherwise and elsewhere inhibited forms of body presentation; and (3) self-verification, whereby nudity is used as a means of receiving affirmation from others.

The online behavior is different for guys and bisexuals which are well reflected in online dating. Stigma and social reactions are still strongly present towards these groups in many countries which may be a reason for varied self and body representations in cyberspace.

ONLINE DATING FOR THE MENTALLY ILL

People with mental illness are commonly stigmatized and consequently feel socially isolated. Romantic relationships can be particularly difficult for them to establish and sustain because such relationships typically require more commitment than friendships or even family connections. Hence, many if not most people with mental illness, particularly serious mental illness such as schizophrenia, do not have longstanding romantic relationships. Internet dating has become a popular way to find romantic relationships within the general population. For many people with mental illness, this resource may be especially helpful, because social isolation may impede finding dating connections through friends or family (Virtzberg-Rofe, Rofe, & Rudnick, 2014). More studies are required to understand the expectations, profiles, initiation and maintain relations among people with mental illness.

Online Dating and Mental Health

The reasons for choosing a mate may varies and the question of online dating is actually helpful or not is the major concern for many researchers. Studies have noted that online dating is beneficial to mental health. Whitton, Weitbrecht, Kuryluk, and Bruner (2013) reported that involvement in committed dating relationships may be protective to college student mental health, and highlight the potential of healthy relationship programming to benefit student well-being. Bryce and Fraser (2014) examined the relationship between the evaluation of risk, trust and disclosure of personal information in young peoples' online interactions. A series of 18 focus groups were conducted with young people aged 9–19 years old. The results suggested that the majority of young people have a high level of awareness of the risks and potential outcomes associated with their online behavior. Participants perceived disclosure of personal information to be important for the development of online relationships, and discussed associated strategies for evaluating trust and verifying identity. The study suggests that the perceived benefits associated with the disclosure of personal information and interacting with 'strangers' online may outweigh the perceived risks associated with these behaviors as the result of the importance of peer relationships and the exploration of identity during adolescence.

Many studies found that online dating is detrimental to mental health due to many reasons. The break ups, abuse, and violence may leads to mental health issues. Flach and Deslandes (2017) mentioned high rates of posttraumatic stress disorder substance abuse anxiety, aggressiveness/hostility, sleep disorders, depressive symptoms, self-inflicted violence, and suicidal ideation and suicide attempts, low school performance and delinquent behaviors among victims. They also identified different types of cyber abuse: (1) direct aggression and control; (2) association with other traditional types of intimate partner violence; and (3) interaction between cyber abuse and sexting. Direct aggression involves deliberate behaviors through the use of technologies that allow access to the social media, intended to harm the partner through threats, insults, dissemination of private information, including personal photos and videos, and identity theft through the creation of a false profile for the current or former partner on a social network, and control/monitoring or stalking or invasion of the current partner or former partner's privacy in order to track the last connection or use the partner's password without their consent to check their e-mail, messages, phone contacts, social network, or even to monitor their location with a global positioning system (GPS), through insistent phone contacts, or posting photos and videos intended to humiliate and embarrass the partner or ex-partner.

Zweig, Dank, Yahner, and Lachman (2013) examined the extent of cyber dating abuse-abuse via technology and new media-in youth relationships and how it relates to other forms of teen dating violence. Fifty-two percent of females reported currently being in a dating relationship or having been in one during the prior year. Just over a quarter of youth in a current or recent relationship said that they experienced some form of cyber dating abuse victimization in the prior year, with females reporting more cyber dating abuse victimization than males (particularly sexual cyber dating abuse). One out of ten youth said that they had perpetrated cyber dating abuse, with females reporting greater levels of non-sexual cyber dating abuse perpetration than males; by contrast, male youth were significantly more likely to report perpetrating sexual cyber dating abuse. Victims of sexual cyber dating abuse were seven times more likely to have also experienced sexual coercion (55 vs. 8%) than were non-victims, and perpetrators of sexual cyberdating abuse were 17 times more likely to have also perpetrated sexual coercion (34 vs. 2%) than were non-perpetrators. Studies also have reported that dating abuse is potentially harmful for all youth and may be particularly detrimental for girls (Reed, Tolman & Ward, 2017).

There is a link between cyber dating abuse and engagement in bullying behaviors (Van Ouytsel, Torres, Choi, Ponnet, Walrave, & Temple, 2017). Cyberbullying has emerged as a new form of bullying and harassment, and it has been shown to possess different ramifications from traditional school-yard bullying. This problem has emerged in nations worldwide. Cyber victims have reported various emotional and behavioral symptoms, along with school-related problems (Suzuki, Asaga, Sourander, Hoven, & Mandell, 2012). Chang, Lee, Chiu, Hsi, Huang, and Pan (2013) found that Students with internet risk behaviors were more likely to be involved in cyberbullying and/or cybervictimization; students who had cyberbullying or victimization experiences also tended to be involved in school bullying/victimization. Cyber/school victims and bully-victims were more likely to have lower self-esteem, and cyber/school victims, bullies and bully-victims were at a greater risk for serious depression. Both cyberbullying and school bullying and/or victimization experiences were independently associated with increased depression. In a two-year longitudinal study, Bannink, Broeren, Looij-Jansen, de Waart, and Raat (2014) found that traditional bullying victimization is associated with an increased risk of suicidal ideation, whereas traditional, as well as cyber bullying victimization is associated with an increased risk of mental health problems among girls. These findings stress the importance of programs aimed at reducing bullying behavior, especially because early-onset mental health problems may pose a risk for the development of psychiatric disorders in adulthood. Van Ouytsel et al. (2017) examined the associations between substance use, sexual behaviors, deviant behaviors, self-reported health, and cyber dating abuse perpetration. Having had sexual intercourse or using alcohol or drugs before having sex was significantly linked with cyber dating abuse perpetration, as was poor physical health, and substance use.

Cyber dating poses threats to marriage, both heterosexual and homosexual marriages. The online infidelity mainly begins and maintains through electronic conversations, and it can be specific to one online user or a series of random erotic chat room encounters with multiple online users. As it occurs in secrecy, usually kept hidden from the spouse and breaches trust of married couples, it can be considered as infidelity (Young, 1999; Mileham, 2007). In a large sample study on infidelity in dating relatioships, Martins, Pereira, Andrade, Dattilio, Narcis, and Canavarro (2016) reported that both men and women with a history of infidelity in a prior relationship were more likely to engage in extradyadic involvement (EDI). More positive attitudes toward infidelity, lower relationship satisfaction, lower commitment, and higher quality of alternatives were significantly associated with EDI, regardless of gender. Women reporting infidelity of a partner in a prior relationship were more likely to engage in face-to-face and online emotional EDI; a longer relationship and a younger age at the first sexual encounter were significant correlates of the engagement in face-to-face emotional EDI. Women with higher education were approximately three times more likely to engage in online sexual EDI. Although men and women are converging in terms of overall EDI, men still report higher engagement in physical/sexual extradyadic behaviors, and the correlates of sexual and emotional EDI vary according to gender.

Apart from infidelity, online dating creates distress in marital relation or it may end up with divorce. Spouses feel as betrayed, angry, and hurt by online infidelity (Maheu & Subotnik, 2001). It is also noted that the breakup rates for both marital and non-marital romantic relationships was found to be higher for couples who met online than couples who met through offline venues (Paul, 2014). Technology poses challenges to gay relations such as unrealistic expectations of relationships, inauthentic self-presentation online, sexual primacy over romance, increased opportunities for infidelity, and jealousy and it may cause distress (McKie, Milhausen, & Lachowsky, 2017).

Online dating has impact on the mental health of older people. To understand the positives and negatives of online dating according to the lived experience of older women, Vandeweerd, Myers, Coulter, Yalcin, and Corvin (2016) conducted telephone interviews were conducted with 45 women ages 50+ who date online. Interviews were audio recorded, transcribed verbatim, and thematically team coded. The opportunity to expand one's social network for friendships and romantic partners, the ability to control dating risks and pace of relationship formation, and knowing more about one's partner were significant reported benefits of online dating. Connecting with others via the Internet can decrease social isolation (Wion & Loeb, 2015) but dating online also includes unique risks, such as pervasive lying, attempted financial exploitation in the form of scammers, and unwanted electronic sexual aggression (Vandeweerd, Myers, Coulter, Yalcin, & Corvin, 2016). Health care providers do not always assess dating and sexual health in the older adult population. Nurses are in a position to assess the dating relationships of older patients and can ask targeted questions to determine if patients are in a potentially risky relationship. A non-judgmental attitude and compassionate approach is essential. Knowledge of safe practices, alerting red flags, and available resources are essential tools for gerontological nurses to possess (Wion & Loeb, 2015).

Through e-dating, HIV-positive gay men can avoid abuse, discrimination and sexual rejection but online dating increased the rate of HIV and high risk sexual behavior. Increasingly, gay and bisexual men (GBM) meet casual sex partners online and this has been associated with sexual risk behavior (Prestage, Bavinton, Grierson, Down, Keen, Bradley, & Duncan, 2015). Researchers have portrayed the internet as an inherently risky venue for HIV/STI transmission among young gay men(YGM) (Pingel, Bauermeister, Johns, Eisenberg, & Leslie-Santana, 2013) and young men sex with men (YMSM) in the High Romantic/High Casual group had more unprotected partners (Ogilvie, Taylor, Trussler, Marchand,

Gilbert, Moniruzzaman, & Rekart, 2008; Bauermeister, Leslie-Santana, Johns, Pingel, & Eisenberg, 2011). Some studied noticed that online dating is not significantly increase the risk of unprotected sexual relations. Though HIV-positive MSM were more likely to practice UAI with partners dated online, after correction for partner and partnership characteristics, Heijman, Stolte, Geskus, Matser, Davidovich, Xiridou, and Schim van der Loeff (2016) reported that online partnership acquisition was not associated with a significantly increased risk of unprotected anal intercourse (UAI).

As studies indicated online dating has merits but cannot deny its potential risk to mental health issues and safety. Future studies need to explore it more on personal wellbeing, marriage and relations.

CYBERSTALKING

Cyberstalking is an electronic crime involving a perpetrator using the internet or other high tech communication devices to take advantage of systematic weaknesses, or to exploit a person's vulnerability, including stalking a person online (Stambaugh, Beaupre, Baker, Cassaday, & Williams, 2001). Stalking is a common but variable behaviour which is often associated with psychological and social damage to both victims and perpetrators. The danger of the stalker attacking their victim has understandably dominated the stalking risk assessment literature, but it seems that the major source of harm to the greatest number of victims is not from assault, as might be expected, but from prolonged, unwanted, and unpredictable intrusions that produce a sense of powerlessness and fear (Kamphuis & Emmelkamp, 2005; Pathe´ & Mullen, 1997). Research suggests that the longer stalking continues, the greater the potential for psychological, social, and physical damage, making gauging the potential for persistence an important aspect of stalking risk assessment (Blaauw, Winkel, Arensman, Sheridan, & Freeve, 2002; Hall, 1998; Kamphuis, Emmelkamp, & Bartak, 1998; Pathe, 2002; Purcell, Pathe, & Mullen, 2004; 2005).

The degree of psychosocial damage sustained by any victim or stalker depends on a range of factors, such as personal resilience, existing psychiatric illness, intensity and intrusiveness of the stalking behaviours, and the response of agencies the victim might turn to for support. There is also evidence that stalking duration itself is associated with post-traumatic stress symptoms in some stalking victims. It is noted that prolonged stalking may precipitate cognitive changes in victims, such as more fearful appraisals of others' intentions, and a revised view of their own personal capabilities and level of control. In a prolonged stalking situation, victims may also find it difficult to obtain ongoing assistance and understanding from their usual social supports, which can lead to changes in support networks and the failure of familiar coping strategies. Many victims had major changes in their social and work lives, increased levels of anxiety, intrusive recollections and flashbacks, appetite disturbances and depressed mood, suicidal ruminations, and increased rate in diagnosis of post-traumatic stress disorder (Mullen, Pathe, & Purcell, 2000; Mullen, 1997). David, Coker, and Sanderson (2002) noted that the physical and mental health effects of being stalked were not gender-related. Both male and female victims experienced impaired health, depression, injury, and were more likely to engage in substance abuse than their non-stalked peers. It is therefore in the interests of victims (and stalkers) to intervene and prevent a persistent episode from developing.

To facilitate prompt and targeted interventions, it is essential that clinicians conducting risk assessments can recognize which individual stalkers are most likely to persist. Unfortunately, there is limited information available about the characteristics of stalkers and stalking episodes associated with greater persistence. Currently, the best predictor of stalking duration is the type of prior relationship shared by stalker and victim, with rejected ex-partners thought to be the most persistent, and strangers least (Budd & Mattinson, 2000; Pathe´ & Mullen, 1997; Purcell, Pathé, & Mullen, 2002; Purcell, Pathé, & Mullen, 2004; Tjaden & Thoennes, 1998). Mohandie, Meloy, Green-McGowan, and Williams (2006) identified that ex-intimates as most likely to contact the victim following legal intervention, and strangers least likely; however, they did not record how long the stalking behavior then continued, nor did they attempt to isolate predictors of recidivism. Rosenfeld (2003) did examine factors associated with stalking recidivism in his New York study. He found that ex-intimate partners and those with personality disorders were most likely to be charged with further stalking offences, indicating that these individuals might be more persistent in their stalking behavior. Using the term recidivism tends to conflate the two types of stalking behavior. A persistent stalker is one whose behavior continues in spite of intervention (there may be fluctuations in intensity, but there are no significant periods when the stalker poses a risk but does not intrude). Persistent stalkers are defined by the fact that they continue to harass the victim in the face of interventions intended to make them desist; they do not voluntarily cease their harassment, their aims are merely occasionally thwarted by other parties. A recurrent stalker differs in that they have chosen to cease their previous stalking behavior for some reason. Their motivation to desist may be aided by the presence of a legal injunction, medication, or the victim having a threatening new partner, but for whatever reason, they decide to refrain from intruding upon the victim. The new stalking episode, which may be against the same or a different victim, usually signifies a return to the thought and behavior patterns seen in the previous episode. Often, persistence can only be differentiated from recurrence during a clinical assessment, yet making this determination is important as management strategies may differ significantly between the two groups. For example, the recurrence of stalking behavior may signify noncompliance with antipsychotic medications which, when taken, suppress psychotic symptoms that drive the stalking. Management in such a case could be as (relatively) simple as ensuring the patient complies with medication, preventing a persistent episode from developing (McEwan, Mullen, & MacKenzie, 2009).

Studies have reported different ways the victims dealt with stalkers like ignoring or confronting them, contacting the Internet service provider (ISP) or police, or not returning to the forum in which the cyber stalking took place (Fremauw, Westrup, & Pennypacker, 1997; Working to Halt Online Abuse, 2003).

Since cyber stalking is a relatively new phenomenon compared to stalking, more studies are required to understand its prevention and intervention strategies.

CYBERSEX

Online behaviors, such as cybersex, are linked with online dating. Cybersex is a virtual sex encounter in which two or more people connected remotely via computer network send each other sexually explicit messages describing a sexual experience. It is also called computer sex, Internet sex, netsex and, colloquially, cyber or cybering and in one form, this fantasy sex is accomplished by the participants describing their actions and responding to their chat partners in a mostly written form designed to stimulate their own sexual feelings and fantasies. Cybersex often includes real life masturbation or it can consist merely of sexual arousal induced through electronic communication with another person, or masturbation while engaged on-line. Some would include any sexual activity that occurs while on-line (e.g., while viewing a pornographic Web site) as cybersex (Hahn & Harley, 1996; McGrath & Casey, 2002). Carvalheira and Gomes (2003) noted two trends that people use online chats as a starting place for offline relationships (online anonymity prevents the fear of rejection and social sanctions in real life), and people who want and prefer online sex without any interest in further real contacts. Online environments facilitated access, but also indicated that interest in certain sexual practices could differ between offline and online environments (Craft, 2012). Problematic involvement in cybersex is generally considered to be an excessive and uncontrolled use of online sexual activities associated with tangible negative outcomes and functional impairment. To date, there is no consensus in the literature regarding the conceptualization and labeling of this disorder, or of its diagnosis and assessment (e.g., screening questionnaires and diagnostic criteria)(WBillieux & éry, 2017).

Cybersex is a subcategory of online sexual activities (OSA) and is defined as when two or more people are engaging in sexual talk while online for the purposes of sexual pleasure and may or may not include masturbation. Cybersex is a growing phenomenon with a significant impact on participants but very little research has been done on this subject to date. In a first study to attempt to delineate characteristics of those who engage in cybersex, Daneback, Cooper, and Månsson (2005) collected data through an online questionnaire in Swedish, administered through the Swedish web portal Passagen.se. Out of the total sample (N = 1828), almost a third, both men and women, reported to have engaged in cybersex. A logistic regression analysis showed that age, sex, and sexual orientation were important demographic variables to consider when investigating cybersex. A comparison of interval data showed those engaging in cybersex to have a higher likelihood of spending more time online for OSA and having more offline sex partners than those not engaging in cybersex.

In a large study to compare male and female college students in four countries (Canada, Germany, Sweden, and the U.S.) on their lifetime experiences (prevalence) and frequency of recent experiences with six types of online sexual activities (OSA): sexual information, sexual entertainment, sexual contacts, sexual minority communities, sexual products, and sex work, Döring, Daneback, Shaughnessy, Grov, and Byers (2017) reported that almost half (48.5%) browsing for sexual products, and a substantial minority reported having engaged in cybersex (30.8%). Very few participants (1.1%) paid for online sexual services or received payment (0.5%). In general, participants showed relatively infrequent experience with all types of OSA within the last 3 months. Men showed both higher prevalence and frequency of use of sexually stimulating material online than did women. Overall, students in the four countries were similar in their OSA experiences. Not only adults, adolescents too explore online sexual behavious. Sklenarova, Schulz, Schuhmann, Osterheider, and Neutze (2017) found that adolescents frequently engage in sexual interactions on the internet with only a relatively small number perceiving such contacts as exploitative. In addition, females and adolescents with incomplete family situation, foreign nationality, higher education, homo- or bisexual orientation, and those without perceived social support reported OSS significantly more often.

High-sexual-sensation seekers among university students were more likely than low-sexual-sensation seekers to accept cybersex, multiple sexual partners, and one-night stands (Lu, Ma, Lee, Hou, & Liao, 2014). Although most sex-related online behaviors are not widespread among youth, adolescents who engage in such behaviors are at increased risk for developing negative body and sexual self-perceptions. Private Internet access and less parental rule setting regarding Internet use predicted greater engagement in sex-related online behaviors (Doornwaard, Bickham, Rich, Vanwesenbeeck, van den Eijnden, & ter Bogt, 2014).

In relation with cybersex, Sextortion (threats to expose sexual images to coerce victims to provide additional pictures, sex, or other favors) has been identified as an emerging online threat to youth and it is serious victimizations, and often co-occurred with teen dating violence. Wolak, Finkelhor, Walsh, and Treitman (2017) reported that almost 60% of respondents who were minors when sextortion occurred knew perpetrators in person, often as romantic partners. Most knowingly provided images to perpetrators (75%), but also felt pressured to do so (67%). About one-third were threatened with physical assaults and menaced for >6 months. Half did not disclose incidents, and few reported to police or websites. Perpetrators against minors (vs. adults) were more likely to pressure victims into producing initial sexual images, demand additional images, threaten victims for >6 months, and urge victims to harm themselves. It is also reported that offenders may disclose the interactions to others or public (Carton, 1995).

de Santisteban and Gámez-Guadix (2017) analyzed the prevalence and risk factors associated with both sexual solicitations and interactions of minors with adults as the research on online child sexual victimization has mainly focused on the sexual solicitation of minors (i.e., sexual requests by an adult), with scarce information available on sexual interactions (e.g., cybersex or meeting in person) in which a minor is exploited by an adult. Gender (being female), using video chat, and instant messaging by computer were significant variables for sexual solicitation but not for sexual interaction; participation in online games was significant only for sexual interactions. Finally, minors reporting sexual interactions presented a higher risk profile than those reporting only sexual solicitations.

The anonymity between the participants in cybersex creates many problems. Chiou (2006) examined the effect of anonymity on adolescents' sexual self-disclosure on the internet and it was observed that male adolescents were more likely than females to engage in sexual self-disclosure and to correspondingly respond to cyber partners' sexual disclosure. Results showed that the greater the anonymity, the greater the intent for sexual self-disclosure. Participants exhibited greater reply intent when cyber partners self-disclosed sexual topics with greater intimacy, and the effect of topic intimacy was more pronounced in male participants. The findings suggest that male adolescents tend to adopt a reciprocal strategy in responding to partners' sexual disclosure on the Internet, whereas females tend to employ a conservative strategy. It was concluded that male and female adolescents revealed differential self-presentation and impression management for their sexual self-disclosing and responding on the Internet.

Briggs, Simon, and Simonsen (2011) examined 51 participants convicted of an Internet-initiated sex offense in which they attempted to entice an adolescent into a sexual relationship using an Internet chat room. All participants were convicted of a sex offense and their clinical and behavioral data were obtained from each subject's offense-specific evaluation and chat room transcripts. They found that 90% of the participants were apprehended as a result of an Internet sex sting and the authors conclude that Internet chat room sex offenders constitute a separate group characterized by less severe criminogenic factors than other sex offenders (rapists, child molesters). It can be hypothesized that chat room sex offenders avoid relationships and spend a significant amount of time in online chat rooms as a primary social and sexual outlet, and engage in other sexually compulsive behaviors. Within this offender group, it was discovered that two subgroups exist: a contact-driven group motivated to engage in offline sexual behavior with an adolescent and a fantasy-driven group motivated to engage an adolescent in online cybersex without an express intent to meet offline. The chat room sex offender presents a significant clinical issue to treatment providers as a live victim does not exist. Thus, it is unclear if Internet sex stings prevent incidents of child sexual exploitation and may result in convictions of individuals who may never have abused a child.

Cybersex addiction (CA) has been mostly investigated in heterosexual males. Recent findings have demonstrated an association between CA severity and indicators of sexual excitability, and that coping by sexual behaviors mediated the relationship between sexual excitability and CA symptoms. Strong correlations between CA symptoms and indicators of sexual arousal and sexual excitability, coping by sexual behaviors, and psychological symptoms among homosexual males (Laier, Pekal & Brand, 2015).

In an experimental study on implicit associations in cybersex addiction, Snagowski, Wegmann, Pekal, Laier, and Brand (2015) showed positive relationships between implicit associations of pornographic pictures with positive emotions and tendencies towards cybersex addiction, problematic sexual behavior, sensitivity towards sexual excitation as well as subjective craving. Moreover, a moderated regression analysis revealed that individuals who reported high subjective craving and showed positive implicit associations of pornographic pictures with positive emotions, particularly tended towards cybersex addiction. The findings suggest a potential role of positive implicit associations with pornographic pictures in the development and maintenance of cybersex addiction. In another experimental study, results showed that indicators of sexual arousal and craving to Internet pornographic cues predicted tendencies towards cybersex addiction and problematic cybersex users report greater sexual arousal and craving reactions resulting from pornographic cue presentation. The number and subjective quality of real-life sexual contacts were not associated to cybersex addiction. The results support the gratification hypothesis, which assumes reinforcement, learning mechanisms, and craving to be relevant processes in the development and maintenance of cybersex addiction. The authors suggested that poor or unsatisfying sexual real-life contacts cannot sufficiently explain cybersex addiction but positive reinforcement in terms of gratification plays a major role in cybersex addiction (Laier, Pawlikowski, Pekal, Schulte, & Brand, 2013). Laier, Pekal, and Brand (2014) studied to investigate predictors of cybersex addiction in heterosexual women. Results indicated that Internet Pornograhic Users (IPU) rated pornographic pictures as more arousing and reported greater craving due to pornographic picture presentation compared with Non-Internet pornographic users (NIPU). Moreover, craving, sexual arousal rating of pictures, sensitivity to sexual excitation, problematic sexual behavior, and severity of psychological symptoms predicted tendencies toward cybersex addiction in IPU. Being in a relationship, number of sexual contacts, satisfaction with sexual contacts, and use of interactive cybersex were not associated with cybersex addiction. These results are in line with those reported for heterosexual males in previous studies.

Researchers have argued that similarities to substance dependencies for which approach/avoidance tendencies are crucial mechanisms in cybersex addiction and within an addiction-related decision situation, individuals might either show tendencies to approach or avoid addiction-related stimuli. Individuals with tendencies toward cybersex addiction tended to either approach or avoid pornographic stimuli AND individuals with high sexual excitation and problematic sexual behavior who showed high approach/avoidance tendencies, reported higher symptoms of cybersex addiction (Snagowski & Brand, 2015). Schiebener, Laier, and Brand (2015) supported that reduced executive control over multitasking perormance, when being confronted with pornographic material, may contribute to dysfunctional behaviors and negative consequences resulting from cybersex addiction. However, individuals with tendencies towards cybersex addiction seem to have either an inclination to avoid or to approach the pornographic material.

Online sexual activities (OSA) use can be leads to addiction but it's also reported that it leads to more sexual communications if used recreationally (either individually or with a partner). Negative impacts were also identified, with women more likely to indicate they had less sex as a result of a partner's OSA, and men more likely to indicate they were less aroused by real sex as a result of their own OSA (Grov, Gillespie, Royce, & Lever, 2011). Addiction to cybersex is a growing problems and risk the marriage (Godson & Suzi, 2002). Cybersex can interfere with established relationships, creating problems with trust and intimacy. The powerful emotions involved can cause marital stress, especially when cybersex culminates in an Internet romance. In several known cases, Internet adultery became the grounds for which a couple divorced. Time spent on-line for some can become excessive and possibly meet the criteria for an addiction. This alone can cause problems in a relationship, but, when coupled with either interpersonal virtual relationships or erotic site viewing, the situation can become intolerable for the significant other (McGrath & Casey, 2002). Weinstein, Zolek, Babkin, Cohen, and Lejoyeux (2015) found that pornography, gender, and cybersex significantly predicted difficulties in intimacy and craving for pornography, gender, and difficulties in forming intimate relationships significantly predicted frequency of cybersex use. Men had higher scores of frequency of using cybersex than women (and higher scores of craving for pornography than women). In general, cybersex activity was higher for single participants, although it was also significant for participants with a steady partner (Ballester-Arnal, Castro-Calvo, Gil-Llario, & Giménez-García, 2014).

CYBER PORNOGRAPHY

Cyber pornography users are increasing over the years and many studies have explored the impact of it on mental health. Current knowledge indicates very negative impact on social and psychological levels.

The median age at first pornography viewing was 13 years for men and 16 years for women within the age group of 15 to 29 years. More frequent pornography viewing was associated with male gender, younger age, higher education, non-heterosexual identity, ever having anal intercourse and recent mental health problems. Younger age at first pornography viewing was associated with male gender, younger current age, higher education, non-heterosexual identity, younger age at first sexual contact and recent mental health problems (Lim, Agius, Carrotte, Vella, & Hellard, 2017). Similar finding was reported by Arulogun, Ogbu, and Dipeolu (2016) in which young respondents used the internet for the first time was between the ages of 15-19 years and the main source of information about the internet was friends. Since pornography appeared on the Internet, the accessibility, affordability, and anonymity of consuming visual sexual stimuli have increased and attracted millions of users. Based on the assumption that pornography consumption bears resemblance with reward-seeking behavior, novelty-seeking behavior, and addictive behavior, Kühn and Gallinat (2014) found a significant negative association between reported pornography hours per week and gray matter volume in the right caudate as well as with functional activity during a sexual cue-reactivity paradigm in the left putamen.

Studies have indicated the relation between cyber pornography and addiction. Watching pornography may facilitate problematic use and craving for engagement. Allen, Kannis-Dymand, and Katsikitis (2017) reported the existence of metacognitive processes in the activation of desire thinking and escalation of craving, while indicating that desire thinking has the potential to influence negative affect among problematic pornography users same as in addictive disorders. Using functional magnetic resonance imaging (fMRI), (Gola, Wordecha, Sescousse, Lew-Starowicz, Kossowski, Wypych, Makeig, Potenza, & Marchewka, 2017) examined ventral striatal responses to erotic and monetary stimuli, disentangling cue-related 'wanting' from reward-related 'liking' among 28 heterosexual males seeking treatment for problematic pornography use (PPU) and 24 heterosexual males without PPU. Findings suggest that, similar to what is observed in substance and gambling addictions, the neural and behavioral mechanisms associated with the anticipatory processing of cues specifically predicting erotic rewards relate importantly to clinically relevant features of PPU.

Grubbs, Stauner, Exline, Pargament, and Lindberg (2015) found that perceived addiction to internet pornography is uniquely related to the experience of psychological distress. Self-perceived pornography addiction (SPPA) is reported to affect users and their partners in similar ways, such as increased feelings of isolation and relationship breakdowns (Duffy, Dawson, & Nair, 2016). Brand, Laier, Pawlikowski,

Schächtle, Schöler, and Altstötter-Gleich (2011) found that self-reported problems in daily life linked to online sexual activities were predicted by subjective sexual arousal ratings of the pornographic material, global severity of psychological symptoms, and the number of sex applications used when being on Internet sex sites in daily life. It demonstrated the important role of subjective arousal and psychological symptoms as potential correlates of development or maintenance of excessive online sexual activity.

Researches indicated that exposure to pornographic materials my change sexual behaviours, especially among youngsters. Arulogun, Ogbu, and Dipeolu (2016) reported that post-exposure to pornography influenced on behavior included engagement in oral sex (48.3%), body tattoo (18.3%), having multiple sexual partners (11.6%) and homosexuality (5.0%). More males and frequent users were likely to report a change in sexual behavior. Cyber pornography users represent a heterogeneous population, in which each subgroup is associated with specific sexual outcomes. Vaillancourt-Morel, Blais-Lecours, Labadie, Bergeron, Sabourin, and Godbout (2017) investigated heterogeneity in cyberpornography-related sexual outcomes by examining a theoretically and clinically based model suggesting that individuals who spend time viewing online pornography form three distinct profiles (recreational, at-risk, and compulsive) and to examine whether these profiles were associated with sexual well-being, sex, and interpersonal context of pornography use. Result indicated three distinct profiles: recreational (75.5%), highly distressed non-compulsive (12.7%) and compulsive (11.8%). Recreational users reported higher sexual satisfaction and lower sexual compulsivity, avoidance, and dysfunction, whereas users with a compulsive profile presented lower sexual satisfaction and dysfunction and higher sexual compulsivity and avoidance. Highly distressed less active users were sexually less satisfied and reported less sexual compulsivity and more sexual dysfunction and avoidance. A larger proportion of women and of dyadic users was found among recreational users, whereas solitary users were more likely to be in the highly distressed less active profile and men were more likely to be in the compulsive profile This pattern of results confirms the existence of recreational and compulsive profiles but also demonstrates the existence of an important subgroup of not particularly active, yet highly distressed consumers.

Harkness, Mullan, and Blaszczynski (2015) found that both Internet pornography and general pornography had link with greater unsafe sex practices and number of sexual partners. There is a growing evidence base has identified a relationship between viewing pornography and violent or abusive behavior in young men. Stanley, Barter, Wood, Aghtaie, Larkins, Lanau, and Överlien (2016) reported findings from a large survey of 4,564 young people aged 14 to 17 in five European countries which illuminate the relationship between regular viewing of online pornography, sexual coercion and abuse and the sending and receiving of sexual images and messages, known as "sexting." In addition to the survey, which was completed in schools, 91 interviews were undertaken with young people who had direct experience of interpersonal violence and abuse in their own relationships. Rates for regularly viewing online pornography were very much higher among boys and most had chosen to watch pornography. Boys' perpetration of sexual coercion and abuse was significantly associated with regular viewing of online pornography. Viewing online pornography was also associated with a significantly increased probability of having sent sexual images/messages for boys in nearly all countries. In addition, boys who regularly watched online pornography were significantly more likely to hold negative gender attitudes.

Cheng and Chiou (2017) reported that the high availability of sexual stimuli in cyberspace may be more closely associated with men's cyber-delinquent behavior than previously thought. Sexual abuse and pornography watching are related and Seto and Eke (2017) identified the following behavioral correlates (coded yes/no) of admission of sexual interest in children in the risk tool development sample of 286 men convicted of child pornography offenses: (a) never married (54% of sample); (b) child pornography content included child sexual abuse videos (64%); (c) child pornography content included sex stories involving children (31%); (d) evidence of interest in child pornography spanned 2 or more years (55%); (e) volunteered in a role with high access to children (7%), and; (f) engaged in online sexual communication with a minor or officer posing as a minor (10%).

Perry (2017) studied the potential influence of pornography on marital relationships, more specifically whether pornography consumption at one time predicts marital disruption later on. This article examined whether married Americans who viewed pornography in 2006, either at all or in greater frequencies, were more likely to experience a marital separation by 2012. Binary logistic regression analyses showed that married Americans who viewed pornography at all in 2006 were more than twice as likely as those who did not view pornography to experience a separation by 2012, even after controlling for 2006 marital happiness and sexual satisfaction as well as relevant socio-demographic correlates. The relationship between pornography use frequency and marital separation, however, was technically curvilinear. The likelihood of marital separation by 2012 increased with 2006 pornography use to a point and then declined at the highest frequencies of pornography use. Ancillary analyses, however, showed that this group of married Americans with high frequencies of 2006 pornography viewing and low likelihood of later marital separation was not statistically distinguishable from either abstainers or moderate viewers in terms of marital separation likelihood. In another study Perry and Schleifer (2017) have attempted to determine whether married Americans' pornography use predicted their likelihood of divorce over time and under what social conditions. They employed a doubly robust strategy that combines entropy balancing with logistic regression models and found that the probability of divorce roughly doubled for married Americans who began pornography use between survey waves (N = 2,120; odds ratio = 2.19), and that this relationship held for both women and men. Conversely, discontinuing pornography use between survey waves was associated with a lower probability of divorce, but only for women. Additional analyses also showed that the association between beginning pornography use and the probability of divorce was particularly strong among younger Americans, those who were less religious, and those who reported greater initial marital happiness.

Internet pornography has been regarded as either stimulating sexual aggression or abuse or as serving as a safety valve. This controversy is an important issue in health, media and legal politics. According to empirical studies on pornography in general, soft-core pornography and nonviolent pornography can be regarded as harmless, whereas non-violent hard-core pornography and violent pornography may increase aggression. Individuals with a high risk for sexual aggression show more interest in violent pornography and are stimulated more strongly through such material. Characteristics of internet pornography and cybersex are easy access, anonymity, affordability, wide range and deviation of the material, unlimited market, blurring the borders between consumer and producer, interactive communication, space for experimenting between fantasy and in real-life behavior, virtual identities, easy contact between offender and victim or among offenders, and low risk of apprehension. The phenomenon of "sexual addiction" (or paraphilia- related disorder) is particularly relevant for the problematic use of internet pornography. Beside limiting access to the internet, prevention, and treatment include therapy of comorbid psychiatric disorders and psychological problems (social isolation, bereavement, stress- and anger-management, guilt and shame, childhood traumata, cognitive distortion, victim empathy), psychopharmacotherapy and the enhancement of a more integrative and relationship-oriented sexuality (Hill, Briken, & Berner, 2007).

ADDICTION

Though current chapter in not intended to discuss about addictions related to online behaviors, it is important topic to be mentioned at least briefly. Online social networking sites (SNSs) have gained increasing popularity in the last decade, with individuals engaging in SNSs to connect with others who share similar interests. The perceived need to be online may result in compulsive use of SNSs, which in extreme cases may result in symptoms and consequences traditionally associated with substance-related addictions. In order to present new insights into online social networking and addiction, Kuss and Griffiths (2017) mentioned about ten lessons learned concerning online social networking sites and addiction based on the insights derived from recent empirical research which are as follows:

1. Social networking and social media use are not the same;
2. Social networking is eclectic;
3. Social networking is a way of being;
4. Individuals can become addicted to using social networking sites;
5. *Facebook* addiction is only one example of SNS addiction; (vi) fear of missing out (FOMO) may be part of SNS addiction;
6. Smartphone addiction may be part of SNS addiction; (viii) nomophobia may be part of SNS addiction;
7. There are sociodemographic differences in SNS addiction; and
8. There are methodological problems with research to date (Kuss & Griffiths, 2017).

Mental health practitioners' report increased caseloads of clients whose primary complaint involves the Internet, however, little is known about the incidence, associated behaviors, attitudes of practitioners, and interventions involved related to this relatively new phenomenon. In a study among mental health practitioners, Young, Pistner, O'Mara, and Buchanan (1999) reported an average caseload of nine clients who they classified as Internet-addicted, with a range between 2 and 50 clients treated within the past year. Five general subtypes of Internet addiction were categorized based on the most problematic types of online applications, and they include addictions to cybersex, cyber-relationships, online stock trading or gambling, information surfing, and computer games. Treatment strategies included cognitive-behavioral approaches, sexual offender therapy, marital and family therapy, social skills training, and pharmacological interventions. Based on their client encounters, efforts to initiate support groups and recovery programs specializing in the treatment of Internet addiction were being considered. The current understanding about these disorders and treatment effectiveness are not fully known.

CONCLUSION

Many studies have reported benefits of online dating as well as potential risks and most research on partner preferences has been done with young adults (under 40 years old), but there is growing interest in middle age (age 40-59), young-old (60-74), and even old-old (75+) adults' new romantic relationships. Yet, research on romantic relationship pursuit later in life has been largely restricted to small qualitative studies of young-old adults; with companionship the most widely cited reason for dating (Stevens, 2002). Online dating among old age group is not yet explored especially about their sexual needs. Internet plays lot many roles for gay and bisexual population and it is worth to explore factors related to risky sexual behaviors. The internet can be used for intervention strategies such as dating websites and apps may be effective channels to reach a diverse group of Men Sex with Men with HIV prevention messages and for interventions (Badal, Stryker, DeLuca & Purcell, 2017; Hospers, Kok, Harterink, & de Zwart, 2005).

Online dating for mentally ill people is not under researched area. It is important to explore how is it useful, how well it is affecting their treatment, relapse preventions and recovery, how do they react to break ups of online partners and their coping strategies and this will throw new light on prevention and intervention strategies.

Cyberstalking is an important issue especially among adolescents and young adults and how do they react to these situations are also equally important factor for vulnerability to mental illness. Awareness programs, cyber safety, individual and group based interventions and prevention programs in addition to legal protection are important to tackle the problem.

Cybersex and cyber pornography threats the safety and mental health in addition to the problems of addiction and child trafficking. Though studies reported pornography is less problematic as believed such as little evidence of the association between pornography use and male sexual health disturbances (desire, erectile, or orgasmic difficulties) (Landripet & Štulhofer, 2015), mostly studied reported that it linked with high sexual risk behaviours and sex crimes. Gender egalitarianism, sexual attitude and the allowance of sexual violence in adolescents were influenced by cybersex addiction. Therefore, nursing interventions for prevention and management of cybersex addiction need to be developed and provided to adolescents. In addition, varied programs for teaching sexuality to adolescents should be developed and provided (Koo & Kim, 2007). In a study, Goldberg, Peterson, Rosen, and Sara (2008) reported that most marriage and family therapists felt prepared to diagnose and treat adults with cybersex problems, half felt unprepared to diagnose and treat children and their required college courses were not helpful in preparing them to diagnose and treat cybersex-related problems. New treatment strategies and relapse prevention techniques are needed and needs to be evaluated for their effectiveness.

Online behaviors are prone to addictive disorders and other psychiatric comorbidities, hence it is necessary to develop tailored psychotherapeutic and pharmacological interventions by taking into account the complexity and heterogeneity of the problems. Future studies to intensify the search for understanding of online behaviors, its prevalence, causes and risks, prevention and interventions.

In sum, online behaviors risk mental health but the current understanding of diagnosis; prevention and treatment of online problems are not up to the mark. Treatment for various online issues are still at it preliminary level and the effectiveness of treat programs are not much known. Future studies need to consider these dimensions.

REFERENCES

AARP. (2003). *Lifestyles, Dating, and Romance: A Study of Midlife Singles*. Retrieved from http://assets.aarp.org/rgcenter/general/singles.pdf

Alexy, E. M., Burgess, A. W., & Baker, T. (2005). Internet offenders: Traders, travelers, and combination trader-travelers. *Journal of Interpersonal Violence*, *20*(7), 804–812. doi:10.1177/0886260505276091 PMID:15914702

Allen, A., Kannis-Dymand, L., & Katsikitis, M. (2017). Problematic internet pornography use: The role of craving, desire thinking, and metacognition. *Addictive Behaviors*, *70*, 65–71. doi:10.1016/j.addbeh.2017.02.001 PMID:28214738

Alterovitz, S. S., & Mendelsohn, G. A. (2009). Partner preferences across the life span: Online dating by older adults. *Psychology and Aging*, *24*(2), 513–517. doi:10.1037/a0015897 PMID:19485668

Alterovitz, S. S., & Mendelsohn, G. A. (2013). Relationship goals of middle-aged, young-old, and old-old internet daters: An analysis of online personal ads. *Journal of Aging Studies*, *27*(2), 159–165. doi:10.1016/j.jaging.2012.12.006 PMID:23561281

Arulogun, O. S., Ogbu, I. A., & Dipeolu, I. O. (2016). Influence of internet exposure on sexual behaviour of young persons in an urban district of Southwest Nigeria. *The Pan African Medical Journal*, *25*, 261. doi:10.11604/pamj.2016.25.261.2630 PMID:28293377

Badal, H. J., Stryker, J. E., DeLuca, N., & Purcell, D. W. (2017). Swipe Right: Dating Website and App Use Among Men Who Have Sex With Men. *AIDS and Behavior*, *7*. doi:10.100710461-017-1882-7 PMID:28884248

Ballester-Arnal, R., Castro-Calvo, J., Gil-Llario, M. D., & Giménez-García, C. (2014). Relationship status as an influence on cybersex activity: Cybersex, youth, and steady partner. *Journal of Sex & Marital Therapy*, *40*(5), 444–456. doi:10.1080/0092623X.2013.772549 PMID:24134331

Bannink, R, Broeren, S., van de Looij-Jansen, P.M., de Waart, F.G., & Raat, H. (2014). Cyber and traditional bullying victimization as a risk factor for mental health problems and suicidal ideation in adolescents. *PLoS One*, *9*(4). doi: .10.1371/journal.pone.0094026

Bauermeister, J. A., Leslie-Santana, M., Johns, M. M., Pingel, E., & Eisenberg, A. (2011). Mr. Right and Mr. Right Now: Romantic and casual partner-seeking online among young men who have sex with men. *AIDS and Behavior*, *15*(2), 261–272. doi:10.100710461-010-9834-5 PMID:20953689

Baum, K., Catalano, S., Rand, M., & Rose, K. (2009). *Stalking victimization in the United States*. Washington, DC: U.S. Department of Justice.

Bjorklund, K., Hakkanen-Nyholm, H., Sheridan, L., & Roberts, K. (2010). The prevalence of stalking among Finnish university students. *Journal of Interpersonal Violence*, *25*(4), 684-98.

Blaauw, E., Winkel, F. W., Arensman, E., Sheridan, L., & Freeve, A. (2002). The toll of stalking: The relationship between features of stalking and psychopathology of victims. *Journal of Interpersonal Violence*, *17*(1), 50–63. doi:10.1177/0886260502017001004

Brand, M., Laier, C., Pawlikowski, M., Schächtle, U., Schöler, T., & Altstötter-Gleich, C. (2011). Watching pornographic pictures on the Internet: Role of sexual arousal ratings and psychological-psychiatric symptoms for using Internet sex sites excessively. *Cyberpsychology, Behavior, and Social Networking, 14*(6), 371–377. doi:10.1089/cyber.2010.0222 PMID:21117979

Briggs, P., Simon, W. T., & Simonsen, S. (2011). An exploratory study of Internet-initiated sexual offenses and the chat room sex offender: Has the Internet enabled a new typology of sex offender? *Sexual Abuse, 23*(1), 72–91. doi:10.1177/1079063210384275 PMID:20947699

Bryce, J., & Fraser, J. (2014). The role of disclosure of personal information in the evaluation of risk and trust in young peoples' online interactions. *Computers in Human Behavior, 30*, 299–306. doi:10.1016/j.chb.2013.09.012

Budd, T., & Mattinson, J. (2000). *The extent and nature of stalking: findings from the 1998 British Crime Survey*. Research, Development and Statistics Directorate, London. Retrieved from http://citeseerx.ist.psu.edu/viewdoc/download?doi=10.1.1.527.4457&rep=rep1&type=pdf

Buss, D. M., & Barnes, M. (1986). Preferences in human mate selection. *Journal of Personality and Social Psychology, 50*(3), 559–570. doi:10.1037/0022-3514.50.3.559

Buss, D. M., Shackelford, T. K., Kirkpatrick, L. A., & Larsen, R. J. (2001). A half century of mate preferences: The cultural evolution of values. *Journal of Marriage and the Family, 63*(2), 491–503. doi:10.1111/j.1741-3737.2001.00491.x

Cali, B. E., Coleman, J. M., & Campbell, C. (2013). Stranger danger? Women's self-protection intent and the continuing stigma of online dating. *Cyberpsychology, Behavior, and Social Networking, 16*(12), 853–857. doi:10.1089/cyber.2012.0512 PMID:23849001

Carton, S. (1995). *Internet Virtual Worlds Quick Tour*. Ventana Press.

Carvalheira, A., & Gomes, F. A. (2003). Cybersex in Portuguese chatrooms: A study of sexual behaviors related to online sex. *Journal of Sex & Marital Therapy, 29*(5), 345–360. doi:10.1080/00926230390224729 PMID:14504006

Cattaneo, L., Cho, S., & Botuck, S. (2011). Describing intimate partner stalking over time: An effort to inform victim-centered service provision. *Journal of Interpersonal Violence, 26*(17), 3428–3454. doi:10.1177/0886260511403745 PMID:21810796

Chang, F. C., Lee, C. M., Chiu, C. H., Hsi, W. Y., Huang, T. F., & Pan, Y. C. (2013). Relationships among cyberbullying, school bullying, and mental health in Taiwanese adolescents. *The Journal of School Health, 83*(6), 454–462. doi:10.1111/josh.12050 PMID:23586891

Cheng, W., & Chiou, W.B (2007). *Exposure to Sexual Stimuli Induces Greater Discounting Leading to Increased Involvement in Cyber Delinquency Among Men*. Academic Press. DOI: 10.1089/cyber.2016.0582

Chiou, W. B. (2006). Adolescents' sexual self-disclosure on the internet: Deindividuation and impression management. *Adolescents, 41*(163), 547–561. PMID:17225667

Cox, L., & Speziale, B. (2009). Survivors of stalking. *Affilia, 24*(1), 5–18. doi:10.1177/0886109908326815

Craft, A. J. (2012). Love 2.0: A quantitative exploration of sex and relationships in the virtual world Second Life. *Archives of Sexual Behavior*, *41*(4), 939–947. doi:10.100710508-012-9933-7 PMID:22544305

Daneback, K., Cooper, A., & Månsson, S. A. (2005). An Internet study of cybersex participants. *Archives of Sexual Behavior*, *34*(3), 321–328. doi:10.100710508-005-3120-z PMID:15971014

Das, A., Sharma, M. K., Thamilselvan, P., & Marimuthu, P. (2017). Technology Addiction among Treatment Seekers for Psychological Problems: Implication for Screening in Mental Health Setting. *Indian Journal of Psychological Medicine*, *39*(1), 21–27. doi:10.4103/0253-7176.198939 PMID:28250554

Davis, E. M., & Fingerman, K. L. (2015). Digital Dating: Online Profile Content of Older and Younger Adults. *The Journals of Gerontology. Series B, Psychological Sciences and Social Sciences*, *71*(6), 959–967. doi:10.1093/geronb/gbv042 PMID:26215718

Davis, M., Hart, G., Bolding, G., Sherr, L., & Elford, J. (2006). Sex and the Internet: Gay men, risk reduction and serostatus. *Culture, Health & Sexuality*, *8*(2), 161–174. doi:10.1080/13691050500526126 PMID:16641064

de Santisteban, P., & Gámez-Guadix, M. (2017). Prevalence and Risk Factors Among Minors for Online Sexual Solicitations and Interactions With Adults. *Journal of Sex Research*, 1–12. doi:10.1080/00224499.2017.1386763 PMID:29095040

Doornwaard, S. M., Bickham, D. S., Rich, M., Vanwesenbeeck, I., van den Eijnden, R. J., & ter Bogt, T. F. (2014). Sex-related online behaviors and adolescents' body and sexual self-perceptions. *Pediatrics*, *134*(6), 1103–1110. doi:10.1542/peds.2014-0592 PMID:25404728

Döring, N., Daneback, K., Shaughnessy, K., Grov, C., & Byers, E. S. (2017). Online Sexual Activity Experiences Among College Students: A Four-Country Comparison. *Archives of Sexual Behavior*, *46*(6), 1641–1652. doi:10.100710508-015-0656-4 PMID:26659580

Duffy, A., Dawson, D. L., & das Nair, R. (2016). das Nair, R.Pornography Addiction in Adults: A Systematic Review of Definitions and Reported Impact. *Journal of Sexual Medicine*, *13*(5), 760–777. doi:10.1016/j.jsxm.2016.03.002 PMID:27114191

Finn, J. (2004). A survey of online harassment at a university campus. *Journal of Interpersonal Violence*, *19*(4), 468–483. doi:10.1177/0886260503262083 PMID:15038885

Finn, J. (2004). A survey of online harassment at a university campus. *Journal of Interpersonal Violence*, *19*(4), 468–483. doi:10.1177/0886260503262083 PMID:15038885

Fiore, A. R. T. (2004). *Romantic regressions: An Analysis of Behavior in Online Dating Systems* (Mater Thesis). Retrieved from http://smg.media.mit.edu/papers/atf/fiore_thesis.pdf

Flach, R.M.D., & Deslandes, S.F. (2017). Cyber dating abuse in affective and sexual relationships: a literature review. *Cadernos de Saude Publica, 33*(7). doi: 10.15090/0102-311X00138516

Fremauw, W. J., Westrup, D., & Pennypacker, J. (1997). Stalking on campus: The prevalence and strategies for coping with stalking. *Journal of Forensic Sciences*, *42*(4), 666–669. PMID:9243829

Gewirtz-Meydan, A., & Ayalon, L. (2017). Forever young: Visual representations of gender and age in online dating sites for older adults. *Journal of Women & Aging*, *13*, 1–19. doi:10.1080/08952841.2017.1330586 PMID:28609168

Gola, M., Wordecha, M., Sescousse, G., Lew-Starowicz, M., Kossowski, B., Wypych, M., ... Marchewka, A. (2017). Can Pornography be Addictive? An fMRI Study of Men Seeking Treatment for Problematic Pornography Use. *Neuropsychopharmacology*, *42*(10), 2021–2031. doi:10.1038/npp.2017.78 PMID:28409565

Goldberg, P. D., Peterson, B. D., Rosen, K. H., & Sara, M. L. (2008). Cybersex: The impact of a contemporary problem on the practices of marriage and family therapists. *Journal of Marital and Family Therapy*, *34*(4), 469–480. doi:10.1111/j.1752-0606.2008.00089.x PMID:19017186

Graham, J. M. (2011). Measuring love in romantic relationships: A meta-analysis. *Journal of Social and Personal Relationships*, *28*(6), 748–771. doi:10.1177/0265407510389126

Griffiths, S., Mitchison, D., Murray, S. B., & Mond, J. M. (2017). Pornography use in sexual minority males: Associations with body dissatisfaction, eating disorder symptoms, thoughts about using anabolic steroids and quality of life. *The Australian and New Zealand Journal of Psychiatry*, *1*, 4867417728807. doi:10.1177/0004867417728807 PMID:28891676

Grov, C., Bamonte, A., Fuentes, A., Parsons, J. T., Bimbi, D. S., & Morgenstern, J. (2014). Exploring the internet's role in sexual compulsivity and out of control sexual thoughts/behaviour: A qualitative study of gay and bisexual men in New York City. *Culture, Health & Sexuality*, *10*(2), 107–125. doi:10.1080/13691050701564678 PMID:18247206

Grov, C., Breslow, A. S., Newcomb, M. E., Rosenberger, J. G., & Bauermeister, J. A. (2015). Gay and bisexual men's use of the Internet: Research from the 1990s through 2013. *Journal of Sex Research*, *51*(4), 390–409. doi:10.1080/00224499.2013.871626 PMID:24754360

Grov, C., Gillespie, B. J., Royce, T., & Lever, J. (2011). Perceived consequences of casual online sexual activities on heterosexual relationships: A U. S. online survey. *Archives of Sexual Behavior*, *40*(2), 429–439. doi:10.100710508-010-9598-z PMID:20174862

Grubbs, J. B., Stauner, N., Exline, J. J., Pargament, K. I., & Lindberg, M. J. (2015). Perceived addiction to Internet pornography and psychological distress: Examining relationships concurrently and over time. *Psychology of Addictive Behaviors*, *29*(4), 1056–1067. doi:10.1037/adb0000114 PMID:26372200

Hahn, H. (1996). *The Internet Complete Reference* (2nd ed.). Osborne McGraw-Hill.

Hall, D. M. (1998). The victims of stalking. In J. R. Meloy (Ed.), *The psychology of stalking: Clinical and Forensic Perspectives* (pp. 115–136). San Diego, CA: Elsevier Science. doi:10.1016/B978-012490560-3/50025-6

Hance, M. A., Blackhart, G., & Dew, M. (2017). Free to be me: The relationship between the true self, rejection sensitivity, and use of online dating sites. *The Journal of Social Psychology*, *12*, 1–9. doi:10.1080/00224545.2017.1389684 PMID:29023210

Harkness, E. L., Mullan, B., & Blaszczynski, A. (2015). Association between pornography use and sexual risk behaviors in adult consumers: A systematic review. *Cyberpsychology, Behavior, and Social Networking*, *18*(2), 59–71. doi:10.1089/cyber.2014.0343 PMID:25587721

Heijman, T., Stolte, I., Geskus, R., Matser, A., Davidovich, U., Xiridou, M., & Schim van der Loeff, M. (2016). Does online dating lead to higher sexual risk behaviour? A cross-sectional study among MSM in Amsterdam, the Netherlands. *BMC Infectious Diseases*, *14*, 16,288. doi:10.118612879-016-1637-5 PMID:27295949

Henson, B., Reyns, B. W., & Fisher, B. S. (2011). Security in the 21st century. *Criminal Justice Review*, *36*(3), 253–268. doi:10.1177/0734016811399421

Hill, A., Briken, P., & Berner, W. (2007). Pornography and sexual abuse in the Internet. *Bundesgesundheitsblatt, Gesundheitsforschung, Gesundheitsschutz*, *50*(1), 90–102. doi:10.100700103-007-0114-8 PMID:17177094

Hospers, H. J., Kok, G., Harterink, P., & de Zwart, O. (2005). A new meeting place: Chatting on the Internet, e-dating and sexual risk behaviour among Dutch men who have sex with men. *AIDS (London, England)*, *19*(10), 1097–1101. doi:10.1097/01.aids.0000174457.08992.62 PMID:15958842

Kamphuis, J. H., & Emmelkamp, P. M. G. (1998). Crime-related trauma: Psychological distress in victims of bank robbery. *Journal of Anxiety Disorders*, *12*(3), 199–208. doi:10.1016/S0887-6185(98)00009-7 PMID:9653679

Kamphuis, J. H., & Emmelkamp, P. M. G. (2005). 20 years of research into violence and trauma, Past and future developments. *Journal of Interpersonal Violence*, *20*(2), 167–174. doi:10.1177/0886260504268764 PMID:15601788

Kohm, S. A., & Greenhill, P. (2011). Pedophile crime films as popular criminology: A problem of justice. *Theoretical Criminology*, *15*(2), 195–215. doi:10.1177/1362480610388974

Koo, H. Y., & Kim, S. S. (2007). Relationships among cybersex addiction, gender egalitarianism, sexual attitude and the allowance of sexual violence in adolescents. *Taehan Kanho Hakhoe Chi*, *37*(7), 1202–1211. doi:10.4040/jkan.2007.37.7.1202 PMID:18182882

Koo, H. Y., & Kim, S. S. (2007). Relationships among cybersex addiction, gender egalitarianism, sexual attitude and the allowance of sexual violence in adolescents. *Taehan Kanho Hakhoe Chi*, *37*(7), 202–211. doi:10.4040/jkan.2007.37.7.1202 PMID:18182882

Kühn, S., & Gallinat, J. (2014). Brain structure and functional connectivity associated with pornography consumption: The brain on porn. *JAMA Psychiatry*, *71*(7), 827–834. doi:10.1001/jamapsychiatry.2014.93 PMID:24871202

Kuss, D.J., & Griffiths, M.D. (2017). Social Networking Sites and Addiction: Ten Lessons Learned. *International Journal of Environmental Research and Public Health*, *14*, 311. doi: 10.3390/ijerph14030311

Laier, C., Pawlikowski, M., Pekal, J., Schulte, F. P., & Brand, M. (2013). Cybersex addiction: Experienced sexual arousal when watching pornography and not real-life sexual contacts makes the difference. *Journal of Behavioral Addictions*, *2*(2), 100–107. doi:10.1556/JBA.2.2013.002 PMID:26165929

Laier, C., Pekal, J., & Brand, M. (2014). Cybersex addiction in heterosexual female users of internet pornography can be explained by gratification hypothesis. *Cyberpsychology, Behavior, and Social Networking, 17*(8), 505–511. doi:10.1089/cyber.2013.0396 PMID:25080011

Laier, C., Pekal, J., & Brand, M. (2015). Sexual Excitability and Dysfunctional Coping Determine Cybersex Addiction in Homosexual Males. *Cyberpsychology, Behavior, and Social Networking, 18*(10), 575–580. doi:10.1089/cyber.2015.0152 PMID:26374928

Landripet, I., & Štulhofer, A. (2015). Is Pornography Use Associated with Sexual Difficulties and Dysfunctions among Younger Heterosexual Men? *Journal of Sexual Medicine, 12*(5), 1136–1149. doi:10.1111/jsm.12853 PMID:25816904

Lemke, R., & Merz, S. (2016). The Prevalence and Gratification of Nude Self-Presentation of Men Who Have Sex with Men in Online-Dating Environments: Attracting Attention, Empowerment, and Self-Verification. *Cyberpsychology, Behavior, and Social Networking, 12*, 20. doi:10.1089/cyber.2016.0691

Lemke, R., & Weber, M. (2017). That Man Behind the Curtain: Investigating the Sexual Online Dating Behavior of Men Who Have Sex With Men but Hide Their Same-Sex Sexual Attraction in Offline Surroundings. *Journal of Homosexuality, 64*(11), 1561–1582. doi:10.1080/00918369.2016.1249735 PMID:27754811

Lim, M. S. C., Agius, P. A., Carrotte, E. R., Vella, A. M., & Hellard, M. E. (2017). Young Australians' use of pornography and associations with sexual risk behaviours. *Australian and New Zealand Journal of Public Health, 41*(4), 438–443. doi:10.1111/1753-6405.12678 PMID:28664609

Logan, T., & Walker, R. (2009). Partner stalking. *Trauma, Violence & Abuse, 10*(3), 247–270. doi:10.1177/1524838009334461 PMID:19433407

Lu, H. Y., Ma, L. C., Lee, T. S., Hou, H. Y., & Liao, H. Y. (2014). The link of sexual sensation seeking to acceptance of cybersex, multiple sexual partners, and one-night stands among Taiwanese college students. *The Journal of Nursing Research, 22*(3), 208–215. doi:10.1097/jnr.0000000000000043 PMID:25111114

Maheu, M. M., & Subotnik, R. B. (2001). *Infidelity on the internet: Virtual relationships and real betrayals*. Naperville, IL: Source Books.

Marcum, C. D., Ricketts, M. L., & Higgins, G. E. (2010). Assessing sex experiences of online victimization: An examination of adolescent online behaviors utilizing Routine Activity Theory. *Criminal Justice Review, 35*(4), 412-437.

Martins, A., Pereira, M., Andrade, R., Dattilio, F. M., Narciso, I., & Canavarro, M. C. (2016). Infidelity in Dating Relationships: Gender-Specific Correlates of Face-to-Face and Online Extradyadic Involvement. *Archives of Sexual Behavior, 45*(1), 193–205. doi:10.100710508-015-0576-3 PMID:26194971

Masuda, M. (2003). Meta-analyses of love scales: Do various love scales measure the same psychological constructs? *Japanese Psychological Journal, 45*, 25–37. doi:10.1111/1468-5884.00030

McEwan, T. E., Mullen, P. E., & MacKenzie, R. (2009). A Study of the Predictors of Persistence in Stalking Situations. *Law and Human Behavior, 33*(2), 149–158. doi:10.100710979-008-9141-0 PMID:18626757

McGrath, M., & Casey, E. (2002). Forensic Psychiatry and the Internet: Practical Perspectives on Sexual Predators and Obsessional Harassers in Cyberspace. *The Journal of the American Academy of Psychiatry and the Law*, *30*(1), 81–94. PMID:11931372

McKie, R. M., Milhausen, R. R., & Lachowsky, N. J. (2017). "Hedge Your Bets": Technology's Role in Young Gay Men's Relationship Challenges. *Journal of Homosexuality*, *64*(1), 75–94. doi:10.1080/00918369.2016.1172883 PMID:27042757

Menkin, J. A., Robles, T. F., Wiley, J. F., & Gonzaga, G. C. (2015). Online dating across the life span: Users' relationship goals. *Psychology and Aging*, *30*(4), 987–993. doi:10.1037/a0039722 PMID:26479015

Mileham, B. L. (2007). Online infidelity in Internet chat rooms: An ethnographic exploration. *Computers in Human Behavior*, *23*(1), 11–31. doi:10.1016/j.chb.2004.03.033

Mohandie, K., Meloy, J. R., McGowan, M., & Williams, J. (2006). The RECON typology of stalking: Reliability and validity based upon a large sample of North American stalkers. *Journal of Forensic Sciences*, *51*(1), 147–155. doi:10.1111/j.1556-4029.2005.00030.x PMID:16423242

Mullen, P. E., Pathé, M., & Purcell, R. (2000). *Stalkers and their victims*. New York, NY: Cambridge University Press. doi:10.1017/CBO9781139106863

Ogilvie, G. S., Taylor, D. L., Trussler, T., Marchand, R., Gilbert, M., Moniruzzaman, A., & Rekart, M. L. (2008). Seeking sexual partners on the internet: A marker for risky sexual behaviour in men who have sex with men. *Canadian Journal of Public Health*, *99*(3), 185–198. PMID:18615938

Path, M., & Mullen, P. E. (1997). Article. *The British Journal of Psychiatry*, *170*(1), 12–17. doi:10.1192/bjp.170.1.12 PMID:9068768

Pathé, M., & Mullen, P. E. (2002). The victim of stalking. In J. Boon & L. Sheridan (Eds.), *Stalking and Psychosexual Obsession: Psychological Perspectives for Prevention, Policing and Treatment* (pp. 1–22). West Sussex, UK: Wiley. doi:10.1002/9780470713037.ch1

Paul, A. (2014). Is online better than offline for meeting partners? Depends: Are you looking to marry or to date? *Cyberpsychology, Behavior, and Social Networking*, *17*(10), 664–667. doi:10.1089/cyber.2014.0302 PMID:25226176

Perry, S. L. (2017). Pornography Use and Marital Separation: Evidence from Two-Wave Panel Data. *Archives of Sexual Behavior*, *46*, 549–559. doi:10.100710508-016-0770-y PMID:28936726

Perry, S. L., & Schleifer, C. (2017). Till Porn Do Us Part? A Longitudinal Examination of Pornography Use and Divorce. *Journal of Sex Research*, 1–13. doi:10.1080/00224499.2017.1404959 PMID:28497988

Pingel, E. S., Bauermeister, J. A., Johns, M. M., Eisenberg, A., & Leslie-Santana, M. (2013). "A safe way to explore": Reframing risk on the Internet amidst young gay men's search for identity. *Journal of Adolescent Research*, *28*(4), 453–478. doi:10.1177/0743558412470985 PMID:25525293

Portland State University. (2012). *Prevention of Cyberstalking: A Review of the Literature*. Criminology and Criminal Justice Senior Capstone Project. Retrieved from http://pdxscholar.library.pdx.edu/ccj_capstone/1

Pratt, D. R., Zyda, M., & Kelleher, K. (1995). Virtual reality: In the mind of the beholder. *IEEE Computer, 28*(7), 17–19.

Prestage, G., Bavinton, B., Grierson, J., Down, I., Keen, P., Bradley, J., & Duncan, D. (2015). Online dating among Australian gay and bisexual men: Romance or hooking up? *AIDS and Behavior, 19*(10), 1905–1913. doi:10.100710461-015-1032-z PMID:25777506

Prins, H. (2005). *Mental disorder and violent crime: A problematic relationship*. Probation.

Purcell, R., Pathé, M., & Mullen, P. E. (2002). The prevalence and nature of stalking in the Australian community. *The Australian and New Zealand Journal of Psychiatry, 36*(1), 114–120. doi:10.1046/j.1440-1614.2002.00985.x PMID:11929447

Purcell, R., Pathé, M., & Mullen, P. E. (2004). Stalking: Defining and prosecuting a new category of offending. *International Journal of Law and Psychiatry, 27*(2), 157–169. doi:10.1016/j.ijlp.2004.01.006 PMID:15063640

Purcell, R., Pathé, M., & Mullen, P. E. (2004). Stalking: Defining and prosecuting a new category of offending. *International Journal of Law and Psychiatry, 27*(2), 157–169. doi:10.1016/j.ijlp.2004.01.006 PMID:15063640

Purcell, R., Pathé, M., & Mullen, P. E. (2005). The association between stalking victimization and psychiatric morbidity in a random community sample. *The British Journal of Psychiatry, 187*(05), 416–420. doi:10.1192/bjp.187.5.416 PMID:16260815

Reed, L. A., Tolman, R. M., & Ward, L. M. (2017). Gender matters: Experiences and consequences of digital dating abuse victimization in adolescent dating relationships. *Journal of Adolescence, 59*, 79–89. doi:10.1016/j.adolescence.2017.05.015 PMID:28582653

Regan, P. C., Levin, L., Sprecher, S., Christopher, F. S., & Cate, R. (2000). Partner preferences: What characteristics do men and women desire in their short-term sexual and long-term romantic partners? *Journal of Psychology & Human Sexuality, 123*(3), 1–21. doi:10.1300/J056v12n03_01

Rosenfeld, B. (2003). Recidivism in stalking and obsessional harassment. *Law and Human Behavior, 27*(3), 251–265. doi:10.1023/A:1023479706822 PMID:12794963

Scheibe, S., English, T., Tsai, J. L., & Carstensen, L. L. (2013). Striving to feel good: Ideal affect, actual affect, and their correspondence across adulthood. *Psychology and Aging, 28*, 160–171. doi:10.1037/a0030561

Schiebener, J., Laier, C., & Brand, M. (2015). Getting stuck with pornography? Overuse or neglect of cybersex cues in a multitasking situation is related to symptoms of cybersex addiction. *Journal of Behavioral Addictions, 4*(1), 14–21. doi:10.1556/JBA.4.2015.1.5

Seto, M. C., & Eke, A. W. (2017). Correlates of admitted sexual interest in children among individuals convicted of child pornography offenses. *Law and Human Behavior, 41*(3), 305–313. doi:10.1037/lhb0000240 PMID:28383984

Sklenarova, H., Schulz, A., Schuhmann, P., Osterheider, M., & Neutze, J. (2017). Online sexual solicitation by adults and peers - Results from a population based German sample. *Child Abuse & Neglect*, *76*, 225–236. doi:10.1016/j.chiabu.2017.11.005 PMID:29149683

Smith, P. K., Thompson, F., & Davidson, J. (2014). Cyber safety for adolescent girls: Bullying, harassment, sexting, pornography, and solicitation. *Current Opinion in Obstetrics & Gynecology*, *26*(5), 360–365. doi:10.1097/GCO.0000000000000106 PMID:25136759

Snagowski, J., & Brand, M. (2015). Symptoms of cybersex addiction can be linked to both approaching and avoiding pornographic stimuli: Results from an analog sample of regular cybersex users. *Frontiers in Psychology*, *6*, 653. doi:10.3389/fpsyg.2015.00653 PMID:26052292

Snagowski, J., Wegmann, E., Pekal, J., Laier, C., & Brand, M. (2015). Implicit associations in cybersex addiction: Adaption of an Implicit Association Test with pornographic pictures. *Addictive Behaviors*, *49*, 7–12. doi:10.1016/j.addbeh.2015.05.009 PMID:26026385

Southworth, C., Finn, J., Dawson, S., Fraser, C., & Tucker, S. (2007). Intimate partner violence, Technology, and Stalking. *Violence Against Women*, *13*(8), 842–856. doi:10.1177/1077801207302045 PMID:17699114

Spitzberg, B. H. (2002). The tactical topography of stalking victimization and management. *Trauma, Violence & Abuse*, *3*(4), 261–288. doi:10.1177/1524838002237330

Stambaugh, H., Beaupre, D., Icove, D. J., Baker, R., Cassaday, W., & Williams, W. P. (2000). *State and local law enforcement needs to combat electronic crime*. Retrieved 22 November 2008 from http://www.ncjrs.gov/txtfiles1/nij/183451.txt

Stambaugh, H., Beaupre, D., Icove, D. J., Baker, R., Cassaday, W., & Williams, W. P. (2000). *State and Local Law Enforcement Needs to Combat Electronic Crime*. Washington, DC: U.S. Department of Justice. doi:10.1037/e598132007-001

Stanley, N., Barter, C., Wood, M., Aghtaie, N., Larkins, C., Lanau, A., & Överlien, C. (2016). Pornography, Sexual Coercion and Abuse and Sexting in Young People's Intimate. Relationships. *Journal of Interpersonal Violence*, 1–26. doi:10.1177/0886260516633204 PMID:26951609

Stevens, N. (2002). Re-engaging: New partnerships in late-life widowhood. *Ageing International*, *27*(4), 27–42. doi:10.100712126-002-1013-1

Suzi, G. (2002). *The Sex Book*. Cassell Illustrated.

Suzuki, K., Asaga, R., Sourander, A., Hoven, C. W., & Mandell, D. (2012). Cyberbullying and adolescent mental health. *International Journal of Adolescent Medicine and Health*, *24*(1), 27–35. doi:10.1515/ijamh.2012.005 PMID:22909909

Tjaden, P. G., & Thoennes, N. (1998). *Stalking in America: Findings from the National Violence Against Women Survey*. Washington, DC: US Department of Justice.

Toma, C. L., Hancock, J. T., & Ellison, N. B. (2008). Separating fact from fiction: An examination of deceptive self-presentation in online dating profiles. *Personality and Social Psychology Bulletin*, *34*(8), 1023–1036. doi:10.1177/0146167208318067 PMID:18593866

Vaillancourt-Morel, M. P., Blais-Lecours, S., Labadie, C., Bergeron, S., Sabourin, S., & Godbout, N. (2017). Profiles of Cyberpornography Use and Sexual Well-Being in Adults. *Journal of Sexual Medicine*, *14*(1), 78–85. doi:10.1016/j.jsxm.2016.10.016 PMID:28011208

Valkenburg, P. M., & Peter, J. (2007). Who visits online dating sites? Exploring some characteristics of online daters. *Cyberpsychology & Behavior*, *10*(6), 849–852. doi:10.1089/cpb.2007.9941 PMID:18085977

Van Ouytsel, J., Torres, E., Choi, H. J., Ponnet, K., Walrave, M., & Temple, J. R. (2017). The Associations Between Substance Use, Sexual Behaviors, Bullying, Deviant Behaviors, Health, and Cyber Dating Abuse Perpetration. *The Journal of School Nursing*, *33*(2), 116–122. doi:10.1177/1059840516683229 PMID:28288554

Van Wilsem, J. (2011). Worlds tied together? Online and non-domestic routine activities and their impact on digital and traditional threat victimization. *European Journal of Criminology*, *8*(2), 115–127. doi:10.1177/1477370810393156

Vandeweerd, C., Myers, J., Coulter, M., Yalcin, A., & Corvin, J. (2016). Positives and negatives of online dating according to women 50. *Journal of Women & Aging*, *28*(3), 259–270. doi:10.1080/08952841.2015.1137435 PMID:27191792

Virtzberg-Rofè, D., Rofè, T., & Rudnick, A. (2014). Free online dating site for people with mental illness. *Psychiatric Services (Washington, D.C.)*, *65*(9), 1178. doi:10.1176/appi.ps.650705 PMID:25179191

Wada, M., Mortenson, W. B., & Clarke, H. L. (2016). Older Adults' Online Dating Profiles and Successful Aging. *Canadian Journal on Aging*, *35*(4), 479–490. doi:10.1017/S0714980816000507 PMID:27774918

Weinstein, A. M., Zolek, R., Babkin, A., Cohen, K., & Lejoyeux, M. (2015). Factors Predicting Cybersex Use and Difficulties in Forming Intimate Relationships among Male and Female Users of Cybersex. *Frontiers in Psychiatry*, *6*, 54. doi:10.3389/fpsyt.2015.00054 PMID:25941496

Wéry, A., & Billieux, J. (2017). Problematic cybersex: Conceptualization, assessment, and treatment. *Addictive Behaviors*, *64*, 238–246. doi:10.1016/j.addbeh.2015.11.007 PMID:26646983

White, D., Finneran, C., Sato, K. N., & Stephenson, R. (2014). Sex, HIV, and the Internet: Exploring Variations in the Online Profiles of MSM in the United States. *American Journal of Men's Health*, *8*(4), 289–299. doi:10.1177/1557988313509834 PMID:24232583

Whitton, S. W., Weitbrecht, E. M., Kuryluk, A. D., & Bruner, M. R. (2013). Committed dating relationships and mental health among college students. *Journal of American College Health*, *61*(3), 176–183. doi:10.1080/07448481.2013.773903 PMID:25158015

Whyte, S., & Torgler, B. (2017). Preference Versus Choice in Online Dating. *Cyberpsychology, Behavior, and Social Networking*, *20*(3), 150–156. doi:10.1089/cyber.2016.0528 PMID:28263677

William, D. M., Locker, L. Jr, & Briley, K. (2011). What do older adults seek in their potential romantic partners? Evidence from online personal ads. *International Journal of Aging & Human Development*, *72*(1), 67–82. doi:10.2190/AG.72.1.d PMID:21391407

Wion, R. K., & Loeb, S. J. (2015). Older Adults Engaging in Online Dating: What Gerontological Nurses Should Know. *Journal of Gerontological Nursing*, *41*(10), 25–35, quiz 36–37. doi:10.3928/00989134-20150826-67 PMID:26488252

Wolak, J., Finkelhor, D., Walsh, W., & Treitman, L. (2017). Sextortion of minors: Characteristics and dynamics. *The Journal of Adolescent Health*, *62*(1), 72–79. doi:10.1016/j.jadohealth.2017.08.014 PMID:29055647

Working to Halt Online Abuse (WHOA). (2003). *Online harrassment statistics*. Retrieved May 25, 2007 from http:// www.haltabuse.org/resources/stats/index.shtml

Wykes, M. (2007). Constructing crime: Culture, stalking, celebrity and cyber. *Crime Media, Culture: An International Journal, 3*(2), 158-174. doi:10.1177/1741659007078541

Young, G. D., & Caplan, S. E. (2010). Online dating and conjugal bereavement. *Death Studies*, *34*(7), 575–605. doi:10.1080/07481181003761542 PMID:24482843

Young, H., Turney, C., White, J., Bonell, C., Lewis, R., & Fletcher, A. (2017). Dating and relationship violence among 16-19 year olds in England and Wales: A cross-sectional study of victimization. *Journal of Public Health, 10*, 1–9. doi:10.1093/pubmed/fdx026 PMID:29136181

Young, K., Pistner, M., O'mara, J., & Buchanan, J. (1999). Article. *Cyberpsychology & Behavior*, *2*(5), 475479. doi:10.1089/cpb.1999.2.475

Young, K. S. (1999). The evaluation and treatment of internet addiction. In L. Vande Creek & T. Jackson (Eds.), *Innovations in clinical practice: A source book* (pp. 1–13). Sarasota, FL: Professional Resource Press.

Zou, H., Wu, Z. Yu. J., Li, M., Ablimit, M., Li, F., Pang, L., & Juniper, N. (2010). Sexual risk behaviors and HIV infection among men who have sex with men who use the internet in Beijing and Urumqi, China. *Journal of Acquired Immune Deficiency Syndromes*, *53*(1), S81–S87. doi:10.1097/QAI.0b013e3181c7dd2b PMID:20104115

Zweig, J. M., Dank, M., Yahner, J., & Lachman, P. (2013). The rate of cyber dating abuse among teens and how it relates to other forms of teen dating violence. *Journal of Youth and Adolescence*, *42*(7), 1063–1077. doi:10.100710964-013-9922-8 PMID:23412689

Chapter 15
Empowering Technology Use to Promote Virtual Violence Prevention in Higher Education Context

Miftachul Huda
Universiti Teknologi Malaysia, Malaysia

Budi Rismayadi
Buana Perjuangan University, Indonesia

Aminudin Hehsan
Universiti Teknologi Malaysia, Malaysia

Kamarul Azmi Jasmi
Universiti Teknologi Malaysia, Malaysia

Singgih Basuki
Sunan Kalijaga State Islamic University, Indonesia

Bushrah Basiron
Universiti Teknologi Malaysia, Malaysia

Mohd Ismail Mustari
Universiti Teknologi Malaysia, Malaysia

ABSTRACT

This chapter aims to explore the pattern to use technology as an attempt to promote virtual violence prevention. A literature review from referred journals and books was conducted. The findings reveal that technology use, in particular an effort to solve the emerging issues of violence promotes the solution with an innovative approach designed in HE. With technology use in attempting violence prevention insights, an innovative way to strengthen technology use wisely with underlying the compassionate skills to promote the preventive action of violent forms is needed. Attempts to promote virtual violence prevention in higher education should be combined with empowering technology use to focus comprehensively on encouraging diverse learners with personal and social awareness in digital interaction. This chapter is expected to contribute in dealing with exploring the systematic approach in nurturing the self-awareness and social concern in digital interaction to be potentially applied in HE.

DOI: 10.4018/978-1-5225-4047-2.ch015

INTRODUCTION

In the last decade, the recent feature of communication device has been developed in following the trends adopted across the world. Among them which can be viewed include smartphone application such as WhatsApp, telegram, Facebook and others. Generated with the featured generations of communication, the patterns of delivering information with sophisticated process and more convenient way have been shifted using the new technologies' enhancement. It can be seen in the attempt to enhance the demand for social presence, it is necessary to strengthen digital-mediated communication including WhatsApp, Facebook, telegram, and Instagram with more convenient way to enjoy connecting with other users in the variety of purposes. This particular view points out the design feature to enable individual personality to have the interpersonal relationship which is basically derived from face to face-based communication through the digital model (Huda et al., 2017a). Referring to live interaction tendency, adopting the new paradigm shift with virtual means will lead to the process mode into more efficiency. In terms of the initiative with a rapid development to facilitate the communication patterns, the systematic basis is usually engaged with computer-mediated communication (CMC) for instance (Thurlow, Lengel, & Tomic, 2004) or Instant Messaging (IM) where both will benefit to increase the particular approach to enable the communication basis into interpersonal relationships (Chung & Nam, 2007). As an attempt to utilise the technology tools simultaneously with such benefits like helping the students learning and innovative teaching (Anshari et al, 2017; Ahad & Anshari, 2017; Huda et al, 2017b).

However, since there have been challenging issues such as lack of humanity which comes from the lack of affection in the messages (Berson & Berson, 2005), the orientation basis in addressing the interaction strength refers to the extent that the systematic approach to be applied among the individuals with others should be taken into consideration by addressing the potential values to underlie the interaction basis. Although it has both chances and challenges, especially in the digital age based communication pattern, an entire improvement of technology innovation generated into the particular tools in both visual and audio contents should be simultaneously transmitted with the balance of ethical responsibility (Huda et al., 2017b). This is because the convenient service provided from the certain feature design in the smartphone device would potentially lead to the immoral behaviour such as the pattern risky activities, disclosing personal information where this refers to the problematic online practices (Berson & Berson, 2005). With regard to the impact of such worrying problematic issues, promoting the sense of the way to communicate with others is required necessarily to take concern into morality engaged in the virtual basis. It becomes entirely a pivotal role to deliver the sense of social presence to address the ethical responsibility in underlying the social presence in order to operate the instrument among the users. In the effort to performing the interaction mode basis from live interaction to virtual interaction, the initiative to deliver the information by enabling the medium of social affection within the sense of presence of face-to-face communication refers to the various types belonging to the invention of instant messaging software applications for instance. By proposing a model with the innovative way to empowering technology use to promote virtual violence prevention in higher education context, this chapter attempts to elucidate the stages employed amidst the users in empowering technology use through nurturing innovative approach. It attempts to deal with strengthening awareness of personal and social basis referring to the collaborative skills associated with empathy as the foundation in digital interaction to be framework model of violence actions prevention in the Higher education (HE) setting.

Towards Virtual Violence Prevention in Higher Education

Virtual violence has been an obviously serious issue spread along with social media platform. Among the emergence of the violence issue includes alive bullying and cyberbullying where both indicate the particular category in creating the tendency to lead to the aggressive behaviour which needs to consider with aggressive behaviour. Providing the solution with an innovative approach needs to confirm the way of generating information through social media platform (Wright, 2016). Moreover, the provoking dilemma during the last few decades needs to enhance such kind of thoroughly solving initiation by approaching the supervision extent in guiding the counselling service for instance using the smartphone application (Huda et al., 2017c). In this view, the mediation of providing the service on the feeling impact should be enlarged through the guidance approach in the sense that would lead to transmit the strategy initiation in transforming the entire system within the application. The strategical approach in underlying the way to be good in which the systems can manage the device well referring to the procedural stage needs to enhance the overall consistency in gathering the supervisors valuably with underperforming the continuous development. It addresses to always engage with compassionate feeling in the sense that give insights into such feeling mediated in underlining the curriculum program. The valuable insight may be concerned to play a key role in underpinning the brutal issue of violence. Starting from the leaders and stakeholders of HE, attempts to promote character performance in using the digital device would lead with an in depth trait to create the well conducive circumstance.

In line with addressing the potential insights transmitted into attitudes and beliefs towards the violence issues, the need to maintain the skill approached in consolidating the conflict in strengthening the norm of an appropriate behavioural response should be considered in order to contribute to make the environmental basis in the campus circumstance. In terms of creating the environment with minimising the risk set into achieving the stability with peace co-existence, the initiation of campus policy attempts to provide the platform to promote the violence prevention. In addition to the way which starts from the task and duty, the entire basis of organising the prevention has to be enforced with addressing community law and campus cultural form (Espelage et al., 2013). This attempt with influential basis in enforcing the cultural initiation norm has a point of view in contributing the socialization approach in outlining the prevention insights on the virtual violence. Towards the risk of violence attack in the campus life environment, the way of extending the socialization amongst all members should be associated entirely with making the circumstance typically on the feeling approach basis. This is because this initiative would point out the reason of attempting to maintain the wide range of factors leading to the violence. Such factors related to the human behavioural existence should be addressed in particular approach on the violent event leading to the behaviour circumstance. From the predisposing potential for violent issues, creating the situation to solve violence behaviour has to do with attempts to reduce the tendency in a multi-component initiative of the violence complexity. Referring to the particular risk elements of the violent events for instance, the typical dynamics of campus violence would lead to take into account designing an effort to settle and manage concisely into addressing the arrangement of identifying factors lead to the campus incidents issues (Drysdale, 2010). With this regard, the actual condition is needed to perpetrate adequately in addressing the violence issues along with the settings on the skills for negotiating conflict.

In line with negotiating the conflict initiation, this initiative should start from the basic setting of technology use, since it has been developed with its recent feature as a new medium to assist the human interaction. Moreover, the utilization of technology in every aspect has both chance and challenge respectively. The issue of violence in the virtual basis can be viewed from Social Network Site (SNS) basis in the way which should cater the interaction process among the users wisely in the well performed act. Applied in the violence prevention, the initiative of technology use should be considered in a particular way with addressing the moral integrity for instance compassionate feelings (Huda et al., 2017d). In the interaction process with such potential value in generating the moral engagement, this particular act will potentially lead to drive into the violence prevention insights. Moreover, an example with approaching the development of multimedia perspectives such as smart talk helps people to control emotions using interactive assessment likes animation and games (Moksin et al., 2018; Tang, 2014). In the view of giving solution with approaching such initiatives, violence prevention can be undertaken with a wide range of technology medium. Promoting the knowledge understanding among the users will enable to fully enlarge this initiative in the basis of solution insights.

Challenges of Violence Factor and Virtual Interaction Prevention

About the challenges of virtual violence emerged in the last decades, this worrying issues have been arisen among the youth in both school context (Conoley & Goldstein, 2004) and higher education (Drysdale, 2010). Such violence issues here indicate that the emergence of the behavioural crisis should be taken into serious consideration in solving the systematic programs. The numbers of this challenging issue vary from bullying (Cross et al., 2004) and cyberbullying (DeHue, Bolman, & Völlink, 2008). Moreover, the impact caused from this issue can be viewed into the bullying victimisation (Campbell, 2005). From these forms of examples, there can be indicator for the perpetration among the students, mainly in the higher education (HE) context. In terms of the fact for those involving violence, the most likely the experiential basis seems to be the school-aged students. About the ranging number of violent issues, the complex phenomenon is increasingly seen from both students' interaction and teachers' behavioural performance (Klewin, Tillmann & Weingart, 2003). In this view, both individual and groups have been a similar point of view arising the emergence of conflicts such as miscommunication. The potential risk leading to the issues with the matters on the human interaction refers to the lack of integrity due to coercive or manipulative language that aims to induce fear, guilt, shame, etc. Communication skills need to strengthen the way of looking at the violent modes including the conflict divert in the sense which needs a particular attention among the users (Huda et al., 2017e). This view should be confirmed through clarifying the needs associated with the extent of perceptions, feelings and requests in transforming the rules to give insights in preventing the violence issues. As a result, the violence issue in this view in forming the process of preventive action towards violent forms should be prepared with pointing out an innovative approach in the way to nourish the feeling of compassion together with self-empowerment skills.

In terms of performing the skills of feeling compassionate associated with nurturing the moral values integrated among those involved in the school, the need to point out the factors leading to the violence has to be determined in both individual characteristics and attributes of campus and community environments (Langford, 2004). Among those involved into the multiple influence levels, individual background with social group including institution and community and also public policy can be organized referring to public factors. In this view, the framework of social ecological basis as this model might be enlarged to point out the model of safety basis to cater behavioural circumstance by which to determine the public concern shaped with the societal factors. In terms of strengthening the nature to solve these issues, it is necessary to take serious concern about factors set across the following examples possibly giving insights into influencing the type of violence mainly in HE context. One of them is factors from the personal behaviour involved in the school context including individual factors (Murphy & Van Brunt, 2016). This can be viewed among student and teacher where the awareness of violence issues should be transmitted among them. The following factor is about the inter-individual relationship where the environment has a role to influence the behavioural tendency to others. In this situation, the maturity of beliefs and attitudes about violence issues should be transmitted to response by addressing the norms of appropriate acts. As a result, the institutional regulation needs to consequently accommodate the campus policies with designing the procedures to give insights in preventing the violence existence. Through settings with the high-risk in contributing the solution to minimize the violence issues, creating the campus environment in a conducive way has to be strengthened appropriately. At this point of view, the community engagement becomes a pivotal element to enhance the high rates of awareness to possess mutual understanding about the violence impact.

In line with extending the enforcement of community involvement to tackle violence, creating public policy to maintain the impact of societal influences leading to the negative behavioural extent has to do with enhancing the campus life. This refers to influence potential value which can be managed with the cultural contributions. Through attempting such socialization using the social media for instance, the convergence of elements leading to the violence is required to stabilise the situation by which to make the circumstance well with maintaining the peaceful circumstance among the members (Kardefelt-Winther, 2014). In this view, attempts to predispose the potential element of creating violent behavioural acts in the sense that leads to the situation to some risk of violent events need to accommodate the mutual involvement into the societal level. It can be viewed through consolidating the complexity of violence to emphasise that such efforts might potentially minimise the extent of violence. Towards the initiatives designed with multicomponent in addressing the typical dynamics as an attempt to reduce the violence behaviour, the arrangements in creating the extent of personal behaviour play a significant role in solving any kind of incidents or assault which can give impact to the victim. At this point of view, such factors which can potentially contribute to the violence event should counteract in enhancing the circumstance of campus conditions where to be safety attainment can be achieved.

Featured Technology Improvement and Misbehavior Potential

The design of featured technology improved through such portable devices has a valuable benefit to assist the human life in terms of communication and interaction, business and other purposes. With more convenient in delivering any service, application device is developed to transmit the insightful contribution in underlying the interaction mode basis among the users. Through enhancing to attract the necessary merit in terms of the workplace coordination and organization consolidation, the useful essence especially in the way to support the complex work with the primary use of workplace among the people group needs to gather in discussing the topics designed to transmit the information (Schultze, 2010). It can be used to deliver the information through social media where the user can see from the screen from their mobile phone. With regard to the extent of communication among the users in both physical and virtual mode, the initiative in the workplace setting is seemingly to be more effective in an attempt to establish the sensitive essence within the work groups to enable in helping the workers interact with their peers (Ramirez & Broneck, 2009). In order to getting successful in fostering friendships by increasing communication and connectivity with co-workers, it is necessary to enhance the atmosphere where all the workers may have chance with the means to introduce levity and intimacy into the work place or in any other relation. It is necessary to elaborate the significant participation among others to lead to the organizational communications in the workplace setting with the effective and efficient basis in improving relationships among them.

However, apart from such benefits clearly mentioned above, the challenging issues derive from a wide range of causes varying from the lack of caring in the interaction basis. As a result, the additional impact will result in misbehaviour conduct in the sense that this potency might behave the tendency to the violence. In some cases, the violence issue was caused due to overlapping the activities between university and societal stage with a minimum control in maintaining the good morality (Huda et al., 2017e). In this view, both campus and community traits should construct the initiative in facilitating the circumstance in the sense that generates the violence factors to look at the main root of issues (Murphy & Van Brunt, 2016). The nature of violence in resulting the possibility to influence others needs to be clearly enhanced to provide the prevention insights in accommodating individual, social, institutional and community basis engagement.

Towards the improvement of featured technology, this chance may potentially lead to challenge in the sense that refers to the misbehaviour conduct which traits the potential violence. As a result, attempts to the prevention insights in this view should create the forum among those involved in the programs in order to lead to possess the responsibility awareness since they are together consolidating the response to influence towards the incidents of violence prevention. About the level of individual influence, this initiative refers to violence prevention through dealing or negotiating process among students, staff and lecturers meanwhile for group. It is a responsibility among the group norms with institutional rules to become the bystander response towards the violence incidents. In this view, stakeholder of policy making needs to assure the overall initiative including the rules to combat the violence issues in the way which can be undertaken regularly in evaluating the campus integrity initiation. At this point of view, the extent of communities is necessary to maintain the rules in evaluating the enforcement of community law initiated to violence prevention. With regard to the engagement into the social interactions intimated to take a serious concern of relationships, recent technology advancement and internet strength designed into the mobile application has an important influence on transmitting the communication (Huda et al., 2017f). It points out the extent of technologies leading to the major shift in human social interactions mode. Towards raising the experience of intimacy among interpersonal relationship, the inquiry in looking at the way of these technologies would give an impact into online intimacy and well-being. With this regard, the intimacy prepared in the virtual based-social interactions becomes an outstanding matter to maintain the integrity of experiential interaction basis in the sense that addresses the stages in shaping the online intimacy concern.

In addition, the potential impact caused from the online intimacy among the users in this regard becomes an experiential value to maintain the context of relationship between live interaction and virtual one. With online social interactions, the general sense of shedding the light on the extending level of interactions intimacy to influence the affection among the users should gather the social interactions in online basis with pointing out the components of intimacy in online. Exploring the potential contribution especially for social support with self-disclosure refers to the aims at guiding the directions of online intimacy to indirectly tackle the potential impact being the fundamental attainment of solving initiation . In terms of the access to information in building techno-spatial configurations, sometimes both privileges and discrimination configured by the spatial seclusion could be attributed to affect information-sharing patterns. It can be seen for instance the intimacy basis through practicing technology usage with pointing out the network intimacy coming from personal support among the members

(Sugimoto-Matsuda & Braun, 2014). Apart from this, between disclosure and closeness under internet environment, the challenges may emerge with lending the intimacy, which perceived with the formal tool of computer-mediated communication. For instance, the disclosure of information that is usually kept private defines interactions and relationships as intimate, differentiating them from casual interactions and relationships (Contreras-Castillo, Pérez-Fragoso, & Favela, 2006). As a result, attempts to achieve the mutual sharing of information prepared with the emotions into the intimate romantic interactions are required to possess the awareness about the possible occurrence which may happen. Referring to the network intimacy which may emerge among friends and family members, the challenge may come from the interaction pattern within virtual conversations.

Trough supplying techniques which may be applied to the interpersonal sphere, this awareness will lead to increase the performance of individual basis together with self-censorship or even between users in close relationships. With offering the space of communication pattern more physical distance, the entire concern to the extent additionally users' technology devices with possessing more control enhancement on interpersonal communications is required to be aware of face-to-face based-interaction (Thurlow, Lengel & Tomic, 2004). For example, there is a blocking system tool for most smartphone devices in allowing the users to remove the others from their lists. This is very useful to avoid instant messaging from the ones set out to notify the effects of messenger on interpersonal relationship. With regard to the interpersonal relationship to engage with allowing users to remove other users by blocking system, attempts to set out some of the informants reported with referring to the real-time promoted the way to the communication stage from face to face to the digital touch screen. As popularly known into the interaction mode, it is worthwhile to possibly concern in allowing the people to virtually remain in contact anytime, and anywhere. As a result, effective and social intimacy to promote the steep advancement of frequent conversation actually encourages the desire in creating the atmosphere with focusing on casual environment to be more relaxed to engage into the digital communication (Almunawar et al., 2017). With this regard, interpersonal communication integrated into the face-to-face mode together with digital basis aims to enhance the influences on the relationships to get close among the members including friends, family and colleagues.

Empowering Technology Use to Promote Virtual Violence Prevention in Higher Education Context

Attempts to build the environment by which to empower technology use have been an insightful view to commit in trust and intimacy mainly in the digital world interaction. This initiative has to be enlarged in combatting the virtual violence insights as an attempt to preventive action within HE context. As a pivotal rule in embarking the raise of putting trust in the virtual communication basis, it is necessary to entirely engage the awareness attainment of violence impact amidst the campus life circumstance. This distinctive enhancement needs to convince the recognition with more open to receive an extent of reliability to transmit information clearly. In terms of transferring the set of recognisable values to enhance the basic tenet, this regard attempts to build trust basis in the sense which the reliability to possess the knowledge understanding of violence prevention should be undertaken more attractive with a reciprocal agreement in giving insights into credibility basis. As a result, the technology use with pointing out the influential basis to complete work with keeping credibility outlines the initial point of view as a result of knowing the other users. In the HE context, the students would have their colleagues to transfer information about the academic concern while misbehaviour conduct may be the major issue to solve in building virtual communication integrity (Guinalíu & Jordán, 2016). This includes manual setting of interaction to the digital-based communication with addressing the procedural stage to be easily employed amidst societal life at large. Beyond face to face mode of interaction, the important value in establishing the commitment of putting trust is surely needed to employ the construction ability in the virtual world. With a powerful essence in generating the consistent assumption easily to execute the credential way, formatting the rule of mechanical manner can entirely be engaged into the additional purpose to minimise violence issue. Through attempting the virtual interaction basis, the challenges of embarking violence from featured technology raise need to prepare the strategy with a particular approach in maintaining the awareness of caring based integrity enhancement (Galassi, 2017). With regard to enhancing the sense in attempting the interaction model like instant based communication message, providing this particular approach will eventually need to develop human connection freely and wisely. This significant essence attempts to enlarge assisting the goal-driven initiative by providing the way to help through technology-driven anonymity. To which attempts such initiations need to confirm the particular attention in terms of offering all-important personal touch which is critical in developing intimacy, the key ingredient role of trust has to be entirely involved in the basis of establishing relationships with best practice easily observing communication application amidst the users at large and the students in particular.

In line with protection assurance which the students may undertake to keep from violence issues both from bullying and cyberbullying, attempts to have an initiation to securing system can be set up in the sense which re-energizes the valuable discourse towards prevention insights. Through protecting violence issues, the style of technology use in this view needs to develop the systematic approach in benefiting the valuable contribution as an important attempt considered to determine the prevention enforcement (Huda et al., 2018a; Huda et al., 2018b; Huda, 2018). With this regard, the nature of particular feeling for instance compassionate based empathy becomes a pivotal value with a protective initiation to be integrated amongst the students. As a result, it is considered to give a direction with significant role to drive the communication skills. In this view, the strategies with committing the entire principles communication management to underlie verbal and physical interaction should enlarge transforming environmental basis with strengthening cultural approach amidst the HE context. Attempts to enlarge the integration of mindfulness amongst understanding, feeling and caring essence could enhance making situations to be more empathetic with each other in fostering the compassionate communication (Slonje & Smith, 2008). As a result of assisting the users to get engaged entirely with no particular blaming personal criticisms, promoting the solution to solve the violence issues through being committed to take care with compassionate empathy basis is potentially considered as the way to adopt the technology use with the concern to take aware of the violence issues. Following the way in the adoption of technology use in HE context, determining many factors to lead to violence has to be involved with being careful engagement to build the systematic approach in transmitting information into the users. Concerning generally oriented framework in reducing violence issues, achieving with systematic solution is necessary to point out strengthening the detailed descriptions about the major anti-bullying initiation programs. With regard to behaving awareness in the interaction, the program in presenting caring with compassion in underlying the digital human communication within societal community needs to strengthen the key role in transmitting the way to synergise entire basis of empathy combined with the sympathy enhancement. Through embarking the initiative to strengthen the consciousness in achieving the caring, the necessary act to put integrity with the compassionate skills is required to enlarge the approach in the sense which performs the empathy (Huda et al., 2017d). Enhancing the way to maintain the compassionate basis should give insights to combat violence as an integrated prevention. Towards the specific exploration about caring involvement connected specifically into the bully and cyberbully issue (DeHue, Bolman, & Völlink, 2008; Slonje & Smith, 2008), the initiation to accept the kind of experience would gather the conceptual framework with transmitting the difficult feelings by taking the kindness in recognising the compassion. With referring to the experiential enhancement in acknowledging the element of wisdom, performing self-actualisation more fully to cover the substance is an outstanding value to let the digital interaction committed to the compassionate enhancement.

In line with getting close through social interaction, strengthening the way of technology use should be wisely integrated with feelings compassion in the sense which refers to the empathy (Greeno et al., 2017). This initiative is potentially considered to enhance the consciousness in covering the caring insights together with recognizing the extent of kindness and understanding oneself with others. With a particular essence of caring transmitted into the self-awareness, attempts to enhance the learning process by fully understanding the emotion feeling need to embrace in responding the compassionate-based initiation. It aims to achieve the potential nature with expressing constructively into an additional involvement of feeling compassionate through working with the orientation to the engaged process systematically on online communications basis for instance Social Network Site (SNS). It could become a pivotal element to have a key role in resulting the empowerment of technology use as an attempt to promote virtual violence prevention in HE context. Attempts to promote virtual violence prevention in particular with referring to give insights into designing an innovative solution approach should be enlarged in the combination basis designed in HE context. As a result, strengthening the strategy in the technology use with generating the application on keeping compassionate feeling needs to transmit into the preventive solution insights in predicting the appropriate way in the sense that maintain the convenient essence among the users. In this view, the role of school leader and stakeholders has a key consideration to transmit the core behaviour essence of bullying in which significant supervision as the medium in generating the potential value of compassionate basis needs to bring along with the mediation through pointing out the considerable guidelines (Cross et al., 2004). With this regard, the valuable insight to strengthen critical analysis with underlying to promote the innovative approach would enable individual development in empowering good moral behaviour as the consequent enhancement with a particular attention to feeling compassionate (Huda & Kartanegara, 2015). The initiated way in delivering the process could be significantly engaged into online communications designed into promoting virtual violence prevention in HE context. It is necessary to pay particular attention to make orientation in the technology use wisely with the commitment to enlarge using SNS as a result in empowering self-foundation with entire awareness of misbehaviour potential caused from the featured technology improvement.

Enhancing Interpersonal Interaction With Technology Use in the Digital Age

Enhancing the interpersonal communication with pointing out interpersonal interaction would lead to increase the extent of social relationships with more satisfaction in the virtual world. This can be achieved with attempting to induce the positive mediation in the effort to give insight into the recent relocation to use the communication channel through expressing thoughts together with sharing experience into other users (Espelage et al., 2013). As a result, taking care of the effect which may happen with addressing the mutual understanding would lead directly to increase the users' satisfaction among the individual basis within the interpersonal relationship. Towards the virtual interpersonal relationships in using the technology to engage with building the friendships seems likely to generate the social interaction configured into the quality with a positive effect on their interpersonal relationships in real life. As a result, sustaining the various social relationships among the users in acquainting the extent of relationships should do with tending other users in the way to stress an overall positive impact on personal wellbeing (Maseleno et al., 2017). In terms of strengthening the weak relationships among the users, the use of virtual interaction basis with an effective enhancement to communicate with others should be paid serious attention to enable them maintain the level of trust during the interaction and communication. Considering potential time and cognitive constraints in examining the impact of social network site use (SNS) on social relationships for instance should be considered in particular essence with an entire maintenance to gather long-distance relationship. Between self-identity and social-identity with interpersonal interaction to help the users achieve the ethical responsibility, the extent of intimacy basis inquiry is basically engaged to get access the information delivered across technology tool (Huda et al., 2017; Moksin et al., 2018). It refers to the particular attribution including external events such as interactions with paying serious attention on personal thoughts and feelings strengthened with the modern interpersonal relations and communication.

In line with engaging interaction under the meaningful extent, attempts to get intimated towards the social relationships refer to play a pivotal basis in underlying the key components through influencing general framework illustration. About the social factors leading to cyberbullying for instance, the recent and widespread integration of Internet and mobile communication technologies into daily lives is changing the principal modalities through which we keep in touch with others. With this regard, such critical light of these changes needs to maintain the way of getting interpersonal communication experience in the context of online social engagement could give insights in influencing the outcomes style of digital human. Amidst the digital age where to signify the multiple levels to influence the good feedback including health and wellbeing, social network characteristics size in maintaining social-structural conditions should give an entire governance to always keep on encountering such upstream effects of cultural and socioeconomic factors leading to the violence. With this regard, density and reciprocity become an initial consequence with addressing downstream effects into interpersonal behaviour in the sense that could gather psychosocial mechanisms involving intimate interactions. In terms of getting social interaction to effect ultimately in transmitting behavioural, psychological and physiological pathways, the capacity in directing social connectivity linked more directly to particular outcomes in terms of the social contexts can be considered at multiple levels into the effects of combining the exposition of internet connection. Towards the explosion in enabling social networking with online applications, facilitating the interactions within interpersonal disinhibition to consolidate intimate self-disclosure can potentially enhance the raise of one's social capital in the sense that increased connectivity (Huda et al., 2017g). Through online social networking basis, it needs to necessarily view the mode of meaningful social connections to look at describing the condition of certain aspects of internet-mediated interactions. As a result, increased online disinhibition has to do with increasing self-disclosure-based favour online intimacy. Attempts to promote increased satisfaction in online interpersonal interactions can facilitate meaningful and intimate social interactions in the way that points out highlighting the potential of this medium for cultivating such feeling involving empathy and compassion through high-quality social engagement online.

With regard to outlining the impact of social online communication in digital basis, the entire consideration to be involved with pointing out the extent of online interactions has to bring along with the online resources quality. In terms of the relation to the outcomes in making advanced into the psychological behaviour, attempts to energize the benefits with draw-backs of this social interaction medium need to confirm the sense that synergise technology and human psychology (Loke, 2016). At this point of view, the systematic exploration of online communication to give insights into the digital human interaction within the specific relationship on shedding light on the aim of enhancing interpersonal interaction should point out reintegrating the entire consideration in identifying the potential value in starting points of the extent of knowledge understanding (Huda et al., 2017h). Through this emerging field to identify the stage of understanding the way of digital communication to give a positive feedback in influencing the digital human interaction, the systematic approach to begin with determining the characteristic elements in the digital communication has an entire direction to guide with a fundamental online social interaction. As a result of identifying the stage of multimodal components with online social interactions, attempts to build online social interactions refer to address self-disclosure and social support in the sense that could determine to shed light on the potential contribution of online interaction.

Supporting Technology Use With Engaging Emotional Feeling

The effort to determine the social support in transmitting the technology use wisely to engage into emotional essence has a role to direct with a simultaneous integrity in generating particular attention of perceived support availability. Especially in determining the particular attention to enlarge social engagement, an important mediator with many aspects in covering emotional feeling associated with transmitting instrumental design of informational support would become a point of view attributed to facilitate the social emotional aspects (Huda et al., 2017a). As a result, this initiative referring to the social support in benefitting the digital interactions may help individuals obtain the capability with confidence to use any kind of technology with being consistently careful. It is necessary to address certain aspects of promoting to facilitate self-disclosure interactions with an influential basis of interpersonal communication in the digital age. As an important ability to cope with emotional issues, self-disclosure in enhancing SNS should refer to recognise the significant element to deliver online relationships with an overview in mediating positive feedback concerning online support communities (Huda et al., 2016a). The starting point of instruments developed in assessing meaningful companionship through online relationships requires operationalization to enhance the development of appropriate assessment measured with the actual experience of the different online environments features.

In line with addressing an important accessibility in performing the individual ability to communicate with others, attempts to perceive in expressing different online interactions should begin with ranging from shared communication in the context of live basis to obtain the settings to shared experiences mainly in the digital age. In particular, the way to take advantage of social networks in virtual worlds attempts to focus on online social experience to be more involved with multiple media to gain a clear understanding about digital online communication (Kardefelt-Winther, 2014). As an attempt to develop measures in establishing online interaction models, the extension with an important form to convey the direction in incorporating interpersonal relationship could be undertaken with a better understanding of recognising the necessary involvement into the social interaction (Huda et al., 2017i; Huda et al., 2017j). In this view, the incorporation of accomplishing the existing measurement tools would be modified with addressing the physiological responses in online social experiences. In order to shed light on potential physiological mechanisms, the assessments model would also be important to contribute to health and well-being in determining the way of online experiences (Kross et al., 2013). As a result, examining social interactions in online contexts needs to enhance the practical applicability through which the way of technology use might become an important element to generate psychological practice in the digital era. With being involved into the nature of human social interactions in the digital age, addressing this critical inquiry of violence issues has to be updated to continue the commitment integrity along with continuing to evolve better understanding of the immediate and long-terms effects caused by violence event into the psychological effect.

In addition to the basis of environments with continuously accessible wireless technologies, it is necessary to recognise some of the worrying issues including the tendency growing temptations into misuse behaviour such as cheating, plagiarism, and bullying through the digital technology devices. Through getting early preparatory experiences, the initiation of using computers and mobile phones provide the conjunction with engaging the practicing responses to problematic situations (Almunawar et al., 2017; Huda et al., 2017j). It is worthwhile to be aware of risky situations in order to develop appropriate techniques way adequately though simplistic cautions and authoritative rules (Maseleno et al., 2018). Prepared with the media-saturated culture for instance, the potential value in approaching safety awareness should be enlarged into the basis of comprehensive process with a broader part of safety program. Attempts to understand the particular situation through putting the responsibility awareness are required to prepare the intervention of risk emanated across such efforts with the collaborative basis including understanding the rules with the knowledge to solve wisely (Huda et al., 2016b), and also the knowledge understanding towards the global phenomena committed to the ethical values in the context of advancement and the perfection of the individual and the society at large (Huda et al., 2016c). In the effort to avoid violent situations, engaging the ability in showing the social awareness with personal integrity needs to work together in improving the prosocial decision making demonstrated through interpreting the instruction in interpreting conflict issues by improving their behavioural cues associated with resolution skills. Moreover, the additional initiative by focusing on harm avoidance is entirely engaged into the sensation-seeking behaviours basis in the way which can be obtained through prosocial response (Huda et al., 2017h). In terms of minimizing the clues that would typically lead to the cyberbullying and any other violence issue in cyberspace, it is necessary to enhance the achievement of diminishing the effectiveness of the cognitive component of empathy. This may point out the beneficial inclination through the prevention programs prepared in designing repercussions to safeguard the communication skills basis in the digital age (Schultze, 2010). It is a pivotal view to behave the social responsibility with the ethical values to embed into the behavioral principle (Huda et al., 2016d). It is also an essential component of transmitting the sensitivity of the way of online communications referring to the impact among others in preventing harmful online communication. To be designed in raising the extent of effective internet awareness, the entire initiation may be achieved through the digital literacy together with necessitating the internet safety to accommodate the personal and social replication within the computer interface. Towards the amplification of awareness in frightening in cyberspace, the extent of ability to engage in training with undesirable effort is necessary to expand the making of sense into obtaining the experiential communication basis with more expansive ways of thinking about the sensory data in cyberspace.

Strengthening Responsibility With Social Awareness in Digital Era

As an effort to have responsibility with engaging social awareness, strengthening interaction quality in digital era has to be managed into outlining preventive insights in interfering the initiation associated with prosocial skills integrity. In this view, accessibility into the real-world behaviour through digital device may lead to the opportunity in assisting the human life needs in terms of communication and interaction with others (Sugimoto-Matsuda & Braun, 2014). In attempting to have knowledge understanding both chances and challenges of the violence phenomena popularly among the users, the initiative to broaden the opportunity with more attractive enhancement should engage with pointing out the prevention insight towards abusive behaviours and violent potentials. With this regard, considering the way to make online communication along with transmitting information into others is entirely the initiated accessibility in delivering service into actual purpose. Since the more active users in social media, the more potential to lead to get involved into such violence including bully, threaten and harass and consequently will impact to exploit victims (Wright, 2016). This challenging issue may need to get solved through strengthening responsibility awareness in suggesting the users in having the online activity to avoid the access of potential offenders with being more expansive pool of victims. The consequence is inextricably linked to the strictly pointing out behavioural repercussions with addressing revealed emotional implications where the internet gave the impact apart from the benefiting the imitation through intellectual activity.

Frequently with making such activities through online basis, the contrary act will always happen into the actual purpose, being dramatically increased to point out the social life impact. In this view, transmitting virtual connection to the information delivery may need to have the securing system in order to protect the anonymity status of questionable web page. It is valuable insights into prevention initiation, since this becomes a worrying risky potency to prevent the way in social media use with online communication trough an exposure to the violence potential. With this regard, the risky potency of anonymity should be considered in particular approach to have the relationships in both virtual interaction and live basis. Through pointing out the balance between the two, an exposure of professional and ethical integrity should be an inherent online communication part leading to the violence prevention. In this view, the exploitation coming from increasing the risk for identity deception has to attempt transforming the fluid identity in an online basis to personalise the users with being aware of positive and negative impact. This will result in determining the experiential basis to expand the learning enhancement in the digital age. In terms of the online basis interaction associated with the tendency to diminish self-regulation, self-construction with extending the experiment in engaging the behavioural substance refers to the tendency potentials with an affective feedback to commit to share disclosures to enhance the prevention insights towards aggressive interaction. With this regard, harmful impact inflicted from misbehaviour conduct needs to concern about reducing the cyberspace disregard with the pervasive enlightenment of contributing the initiative negotiated as an anticipated task. In determining the responsibility awareness with an appropriate guideline, getting engaged to keep in working together with directing into a good condition should be enlarged into the digital technology users. Through guiding with a particular supervision, the exertion of technology adoption with process and management skills should be taken appropriately and wisely into consideration in the sense that can point out the adaptive teaching competencies in digital era (Huda et al., 2016a). In particular to supporting the application guideline in big data approach for instance, the extent of responsibility engagement with the multichannel of sources of knowledge aims to extract the new insights of value involved into assessing the insights of adaptive teaching competencies (Huda et al., 2017h). As a result, it is necessary to maintain the way which can lead to the balance orientation into the circumstance in digital era.

In conjunction with connecting the digital communication integrally made a connection into the global understanding of the chance and challenges of SNS, the responsibility engagement can be enhanced through pointing out such moral expertise qualities including mutual safety, comfortability, and privacy concern. Such these should be provided in the way to make a positive feedback from internet literacy with requiring continuum of skills in terms of message delivery from any kind of online device. Attempts to construct the responses towards interpreting perspectives in the way to respond into the others might address the influential basis through combining actions with understanding the nuances of opinions shared especially misperceiving communications in a digital environment. With achieving the competency in the technology basis, learning enhancement can be commenced in the way to see the particular approach through filtering environmental concern set out in order to maximise the knowledge understanding about the violence issue coming from the internet communication impact. As a result, creating the online environment made to carefully engage in enabling the optimal structure should start with building the responsibility based communication skills. With embarking the competency basis on digital technology communication, attempts to rote the basic rules in transmitting the social interaction together with the personal behavioural enhancement need to behave an active engagement in the context of refining the capable skill trait in order to combat the violence potentials.

CONCLUSION

This chapter explored the initiation of technology use with transmitting the responsibility awareness and also interpersonal interaction. With technology use in attempting violence prevention insights, any form in the issue of violence is needed an innovative way to strengthen technology use wisely with underlying the compassionate skills to promote the preventive action of violent forms. Referring to the framework model, attempts to promote virtual violence prevention in higher education context should be combined with empowering technology use to focus comprehensively on encouraging diverse learners with personal and social awareness including empathy, collaborative skills, and conflict literacy as the main foundation in digital interaction. Specifically, this chapter is expected to contribute in dealing with exploring the systematic approach in nurturing the self-awareness and social concern in digital interaction to be potentially applied in HE. This initiative is supposed to enhance in giving awareness of the impact on anti-social behaviour. Elucidating this innovative approach in nurturing compassionate based empathy performances becomes a wide exchange to propose framework model in the effort to prevent violence actions. Among the main strategic strengths for guiding the user's online interaction is empowering technology use to promote virtual violence prevention in higher education context. It refers to enhance interpersonal interaction with technology use in digital age in the way which is supporting technology use with engaging emotional feeling aspect. Followed into strengthening the responsibility with social awareness in digital world towards the potential nature, an additional involvement of enhancing interpersonal interaction with technology use in digital age has to be oriented to the process which could be engaged systematically into online communications. As a result to empowering technology use to promote virtual violence prevention in HE context, engaging emotional feeling responsibility with social awareness entails to point out promoting the solution with an innovative approach designed in HE to generate the preventive solution with predicting the appropriate strategy to be recommended amongst the school leader and stakeholders.

REFERENCES

Ahad, A. D., & Anshari, M. (2017). Smartphone Habits Among Youth: Uses and Gratification Theory. *International Journal of Cyber Behavior, Psychology and Learning*, *7*(1), 65–75. doi:10.4018/IJCB-PL.2017010105

Almunawar, M. N., Anshari, M., Susanto, H., & Chen, C. K. (2017). How People Choose and Use Their Smartphones. *Management Strategies and Technology Fluidity in the Asian Business Sector*, 235.

Anshari, M., Almunawar, M. N., Shahrill, M., Wicaksono, D. K., & Huda, M. (2017). Smartphones usage in the classrooms: Learning aid or interference? *Education and Information Technologies*, 1–17.

Berson, I. R. (2003). Grooming cybervictims: The psychosocial effects of online exploitation for youth. *Journal of School Violence*, *2*(1), 5–18. doi:10.1300/J202v02n01_02

Berson, I. R., & Berson, M. J. (2005). Challenging online behaviors of youth: Findings from a comparative analysis of young people in the United States and New Zealand. *Social Science Computer Review*, *23*(1), 29–38. doi:10.1177/0894439304271532

Bosworth, K., Espelage, D., & DuBay, T. (1998). A computer-based violence prevention intervention for young adolescents: Pilot study. *Adolescence*, *33*(132), 785. PMID:9886006

Campbell, M. A. (2005). Cyber Bullying: An Old Problem in a New Guise? *Australian Journal of Guidance & Counselling*, *15*(01), 68–76. doi:10.1375/ajgc.15.1.68

Conoley, J. C., & Goldstein, A. P. (Eds.). (2004). *School violence intervention: A practical handbook*. Guilford Press.

Contreras-Castillo, J., Pérez-Fragoso, C., & Favela, J. (2006). Assessing the use of instant messaging in online learning environments. *Interactive Learning Environments*, *14*(3), 205–218. doi:10.1080/10494820600853876

Cross, D., Pintabona, Y., Hall, M., Hamilton, G., & Erceg, E. (2004). Validated guidelines for school-based bullying prevention and management. *International Journal of Mental Health Promotion*, *6*(3), 34–42. doi:10.1080/14623730.2004.9721937

DeHue, F., Bolman, C., & Völlink, T. (2008). Cyberbullying: Youngsters' experiences and parental perception. *Cyberpsychology & Behavior*, *11*(2), 217–223. doi:10.1089/cpb.2007.0008 PMID:18422417

Drysdale, D. A. (2010). *Campus attacks: Targeted violence affecting institutions of higher education*. DIANE Publishing.

Espelage, D., Anderman, E. M., Brown, V. E., Jones, A., Lane, K. L., McMahon, S. D., ... Reynolds, C. R. (2013). Understanding and preventing violence directed against teachers: Recommendations for a national research, practice, and policy agenda. *The American Psychologist*, *68*(2), 75–87. doi:10.1037/a0031307 PMID:23294044

Galassi, J. (2017). *Strengths-based school counseling: Promoting student development and achievement*. Routledge.

Greeno, E. J., Ting, L., Pecukonis, E., Hodorowicz, M., & Wade, K. (2017). The role of empathy in training social work students in motivational interviewing. *Social Work Education*, *36*(7), 794–808. do i:10.1080/02615479.2017.1346071

Guinalíu, M., & Jordán, P. (2016). Building trust in the leader of virtual work teams. *Spanish Journal of Marketing-ESIC*, *20*(1), 58–70. doi:10.1016/j.reimke.2016.01.003

Haber, M. G., Cohen, J. L., Lucas, T., & Baltes, B. B. (2007). The relationship between self-reported received and perceived social support: A meta-analytic review. *American Journal of Community Psychology*, *39*(1-2), 133–144. doi:10.100710464-007-9100-9 PMID:17308966

Hawkins, J. D., Smith, B. H., Hill, K. G., Kosterman, R., Catalano, R. F., & Abbott, R. D. (2003). Understanding and preventing crime and violence. In *Taking stock of delinquency* (pp. 255–312). Springer US. doi:10.1007/0-306-47945-1_8

Huda, M. (2018). (accepted for publication). Empowering Application Strategy in the Technology Adoption: Insights from Professional and Ethical Engagement. *Journal of Science and Technology Policy Management.*

Huda, M., Anshari, M., Almunawar, M. N., Shahrill, M., Tan, A., Jaidin, J. H., ... Masri, M. (2016a). Innovative Teaching in Higher Education: The Big Data Approach. *The Turkish Online Journal of Educational Technology*, *15*(Special issue), 1210–1216.

Huda, M., Haron, Z., Ripin, M. N., Hehsan, A., & Yaacob, A. B. C. (2017g). Exploring Innovative Learning Environment (ILE): Big Data Era. *International Journal of Applied Engineering Research*, *12*(17), 6678–6685.

Huda, M., Jasmi, K. A., Alas, Y., Qodriah, S. L., Dacholfany, M. I., & Jamsari, E. A. (2017j). Empowering Civic Responsibility: Insights From Service Learning. In S. Burton (Ed.), *Engaged Scholarship and Civic Responsibility in Higher Education* (pp. 144–165). Hershey, PA: IGI Global; doi:10.4018/978-1-5225-3649-9.ch007

Huda, M., Jasmi, K. A., Basiran, B., Mustari, M. I. B., & Sabani, A. N. (2017h). Traditional Wisdom on Sustainable Learning: An Insightful View From Al-Zarnuji's Ta 'lim al-Muta 'allim. *SAGE Open*, *7*(1), 1–8. doi:10.1177/2158244017697160

Huda, M., Jasmi, K. A., Embong, W. H., Safar, J., Mohamad, A. M., Mohamed, A. K., ... Rahman, S. K. (2017d). Nurturing Compassion-Based Empathy: Innovative Approach in Higher Education. In M. Badea & M. Suditu (Eds.), *Violence Prevention and Safety Promotion in Higher Education Settings* (pp. 154–173). Hershey, PA: IGI Global. doi:10.4018/978-1-5225-2960-6.ch009

Huda, M., Jasmi, K. A., Mohamed, A. K., Wan Embong, W. H., & Safar, J. (2016d). Philosophical Investigation of Al-Zarnuji's Ta'lim al-Muta'allim: Strengthening Ethical Engagement into Teaching and Learning. *Social Science*, *11*(22), 5516–5551.

Huda, M., Jasmi, K. A., Mustari, M. I., Basiron, B., Mohamed, A. K., Embong, W., ... Safar, J. (2017c). Innovative E-Therapy Service in Higher Education: Mobile Application Design. *International Journal of Interactive Mobile Technologies*, *11*(4), 83–94. doi:10.3991/ijim.v11i4.6734

Huda, M., Jasmi, K. A., Shahrill, M., Hehsan, A., Mustari, M. I., Basiron, B., & Gassama, S. K. (2017a). Empowering Children with Adaptive Technology Skills: Careful Engagement in the Digital Information Age. *International Electronic Journal of Elementary Education*, *9*(3), 693–708.

Huda, M., & Kartanegara, M. (2015). Islamic Spiritual Character Values of al-Zarnūjī's Ta 'līm al-Muta 'allim. Mediterranean Journal of Social Sciences, 6(4S2), 229-235.

Huda, M., Maseleno, A., Jasmi, K. A., Mustari, I., & Basiron, B. (2017e). Strengthening Interaction from Direct to Virtual Basis: Insights from Ethical and Professional Empowerment. *International Journal of Applied Engineering Research*, *12*(17), 6901–6909.

Huda, M., Maseleno, A., Muhamad, N. H. N., Jasmi, K. A., Ahmad, A., Mustari, M. I., & Basiron, B. (2018b). Big Data Emerging Technology: Insights into Innovative Environment for Online Learning Resources. *International Journal of Emerging Technologies in Learning*, *13*(1), 23–36.

Huda, M., & Sabani, N. (2018). Empowering Muslim Children's Spirituality in Malay Archipelago: Integration between National Philosophical Foundations and Tawakkul (Trust in God). *International Journal of Children's Spirituality*, • • •, 1–14.

Huda, M., Sabani, N., Shahrill, M., Jasmi, K. A., Basiron, B., & Mustari, M. I. (2017i). Empowering Learning Culture as Student Identity Construction in Higher Education. In A. Shahriar & G. Syed (Eds.), *Student Culture and Identity in Higher Education* (pp. 160–179). Hershey, PA: IGI Global. doi:10.4018/978-1-5225-2551-6.ch010

Huda, M., Shahrill, M., Maseleno, A., Jasmi, K. A., Mustari, I., & Basiron, B. (2017f). Exploring Adaptive Teaching Competencies in Big Data Era. *International Journal of Emerging Technologies in Learning*, *12*(3), 68–83. doi:10.3991/ijet.v12i03.6434

Huda, M., & Siregar, M., Rahman, S.K.A., Mat Teh, K.S., Said, H., Jamsari, E.A., ... Ninsiana, W. (2017b). From Live Interaction to Virtual Interaction: An Exposure on the Moral Engagement in the Digital Era. *Journal of Theoretical and Applied Information Technology*, *95*(19), 4964–4972.

Huda, M., Teh, K. S. M., Nor, N. H. M., & Nor, M. B. M. (2018a). Transmitting Leadership Based Civic Responsibility: Insights from Service Learning. *International Journal of Ethics and Systems*, *34*(1), 20–31.

Huda, M., Yusuf, J. B., Jasmi, K. A., & Nasir, G. A. (2016b). Understanding Comprehensive Learning Requirements in the Light of al-Zarnūjī's Ta'līm al-Muta'allim. *SAGE Open*, *6*(4), 1–14. doi:10.1177/2158244016670197

Huda, M., Yusuf, J. B., Jasmi, K. A., & Zakaria, G. N. (2016c). Al-Zarnūjī's Concept of Knowledge ('ilm). *SAGE Open*, *6*(3), 1–13. doi:10.1177/2158244016666885

Kardefelt-Winther, D. (2014). A conceptual and methodological critique of internet addiction research: Towards a model of compensatory internet use. *Computers in Human Behavior*, *31*, 351–354. doi:10.1016/j.chb.2013.10.059

Keith, S., & Martin, M. E. (2005). Cyber-bullying: Creating a culture of respect in a cyber world. *Reclaiming Children and Youth*, *13*(4), 224.

Klewin, G., Tillmann, K. J., & Weingart, G. (2003). Violence in school. In *International handbook of violence research* (pp. 863–884). Springer Netherlands. doi:10.1007/978-0-306-48039-3_43

Kross, E., Verduyn, P., Demiralp, E., Park, J., Lee, D. S., Lin, N., ... Ybarra, O. (2013). Facebook use predicts declines in subjective well-being in young adults. *PLoS One*, *8*(8), e69841. doi:10.1371/journal.pone.0069841 PMID:23967061

Langford, L. (2004). *Preventing violence and promoting safety in higher education settings: Overview of a comprehensive approach*. Higher Education Center for Alcohol and Other Drug Abuse and Violence Prevention.

Lewis, C., & Fabos, B. (2005). Instant messaging, literacies, and social identities. *Reading Research Quarterly*, *40*(4), 470–501. doi:10.1598/RRQ.40.4.5

Loke, S. W. (2016). Technology Trends: Working Life with 'Smart Things'. In Communicating, Networking, Interacting (pp. 13-20). Springer International Publishing.

Maseleno, A., Pardimin, Huda, M., Ramlan, Hehsan, A., Yusof, Y.M., Haron, Z., Ripin, M.N., Nor, N.H.M., and Junaidi, J. (2018). Mathematical Theory of Evidence to Subject Expertise Diagnostic. *ICIC Express Letters*, *12*(4), 369. doi:10.24507/icicel.12.04.369

Maseleno, A., Huda, M., Siregar, M., Ahmad, R., Hehsan, A., Haron, Z., ... Jasmi, K. A. (2017). Combining the Previous Measure of Evidence to Educational Entrance Examination. *Journal of Artificial Intelligence*, *10*(3), 85–90. doi:10.3923/jai.2017.85.90

Miller, D. (1999). *Principles of social justice*. Academic Press.

Moksin, A. I., Shahrill, M., Anshari, M., Huda, M., & Tengah, K. A. (2018). The Learning of Integration in Calculus Using the Autograph Technology. *Advanced Science Letters*, *24*(1), 550–552.

Murphy, A. L., & Van Brunt, B. (2016). *Uprooting Sexual Violence in Higher Education: A Guide for Practitioners and Faculty*. Taylor & Francis.

Othman, R., Shahrill, M., Mundia, L., Tan, A., & Huda, M. (2016). Investigating the Relationship Between the Student's Ability and Learning Preferences: Evidence from Year 7 Mathematics Students. *The New Educational Review*, *44*(2), 125–138.

Plaga, J. A., Kosnik, W., Lacson, F., Thomas, J., & Whitmore, M. (2016, September). Recent Trends in Human Systems Integration. *Proceedings of the Human Factors and Ergonomics Society Annual Meeting*, *60*(1), 494–498. doi:10.1177/1541931213601112

Pollet, T. V., Roberts, S. G., & Dunbar, R. I. (2011). Use of social network sites and instant messaging does not lead to increased offline social network size, or to emotionally closer relationships with offline network members. *Cyberpsychology, Behavior, and Social Networking*, *14*(4), 253–258. doi:10.1089/cyber.2010.0161 PMID:21067280

Ramirez, A. Jr, & Broneck, K. (2009). IM me': Instant messaging as relational maintenance and everyday communication. *Journal of Social and Personal Relationships*, *26*(2-3), 291–314. doi:10.1177/0265407509106719

Schultze, U. (2010). Embodiment and presence in virtual worlds: A review. *Journal of Information Technology*, *25*(4), 434–449. doi:10.1057/jit.2010.25

Slonje, R., & Smith, P. K. (2008). Cyberbullying: Another main type of bullying? *Scandinavian Journal of Psychology*, *49*(2), 147–154. doi:10.1111/j.1467-9450.2007.00611.x PMID:18352984

Stevens, G., Seedat, S., & van Niekerk, A. (2004). Understanding and preventing violence. *Self, Community & Psychology*, 13-19.

Sugimoto-Matsuda, J. J., & Braun, K. L. (2014). The role of collaboration in facilitating policy change in youth violence prevention: A review of the literature. *Prevention Science*, *15*(2), 194–204. doi:10.100711121-013-0369-7 PMID:23430580

Tang, J. (2014). Graphics, Animation, and Games. In *Beginning Google Glass Development* (pp. 249–295). Apress.

Thurlow, C., Lengel, L., & Tomic, A. (2004). Computer mediated communication. *Sage (Atlanta, Ga.)*.

Valkenburg, P. M., & Peter, J. (2013). The differential susceptibility to media effects model. *Journal of Communication*, *63*(2), 221–243. doi:10.1111/jcom.12024

Wright, M. F. (2016). Cyber Victimization on College Campuses Longitudinal Associations With Suicidal Ideation, Depression, and Anxiety. *Criminal Justice Review*, *41*(2), 190–203. doi:10.1177/0734016816634785

KEY TERMS AND DEFINITIONS

Digital Age: The period of the introduction of the personal computer with subsequent technology in providing the ability to transfer information freely and quickly in human history characterized by the shift from traditional industry. Expanded to include online and social media, the industrial revolution is brought through industrialization into an economy based on information computerization.

Higher Education: A public or non-profit educational institution beyond high school specifically providing by colleges and graduate schools and professional schools. Institution authorized by law to provide a program of education beyond. It is also stated as tertiary education which is in the third stage, third level, and post-secondary education taken to include undergraduate and postgraduate education.

Responsibility With Social Awareness: An entire improvement of technology innovation generated into the particular tools in both visual and audio contents should be simultaneously transmitted with the balance of ethical responsibility. It can usually be identified through the characteristics of intimacy in online social interactions, its multimodal components, and its caveats.

Technology Use: The adoption of reliability with possessing the knowledge to individualize instruction into the collection of techniques, skills, methods, and processes used in the production of goods or services through accomplishing the objectives. For instance, within the computer networks called integrated learning systems, teachers can prescribe individual learning paths for students, where this is called scientific investigation.

Virtual Interaction: An effective enhancement to communicate with others through social network site (SNS) use on social relationships. The consideration in particular essence with an entire maintenance to gather long-distance relationship should be involved with an effective attainment to communicate with others to enable them to maintain the level of trust during the interaction and communication.

Virtual Violence: The kind of behavioral quality which is ethically problematic with aggression leading to the extreme where it refers to violence physically experienced coming from entertainment involving television, video, film, music, computer. In this regard, technology must be utilized for violence prevention and solution.

Compilation of References

AARP. (2003). *Lifestyles, Dating, and Romance: A Study of Midlife Singles*. Retrieved from http://assets.aarp.org/rgcenter/general/singles.pdf

Ahad, A. D., & Anshari, M. (2017). Smartphone Habits Among Youth: Uses and Gratification Theory. *International Journal of Cyber Behavior, Psychology and Learning*, *7*(1), 65–75. doi:10.4018/IJCBPL.2017010105

Ahad, A. D., & Lim, S. M. A. (2014). Convenience or nuisance?: The 'WhatsApp' dilemma. *Procedia: Social and Behavioral Sciences*, *155*(6), 189–196. doi:10.1016/j.sbspro.2014.10.278

Al Mutawa, N., Bryce, J., & Marrington, A.(2015). *Behavioural evidence analysis applied to digital forensics: an empirical analysis of child pornography cases using P2P networks*. Academic Press. 10.1109/ARES.2015.49

Al Mutawa, N., Bryce, J., Franqueira, V. N. L., & Marrington, A. (2016). Forensic investigation of cyberstalking cases using Behavioural Evidence Analysis. *Digital Investigation*, *16*, S96–S103. doi:10.1016/j.diin.2016.01.012

Albury, K. (2015). SelfiesI Selfies, Sexts and Sneaky Hats: Young People's Understandings of Gendered Practices of Self-Representation. *International Journal of Communication*, *9*, 12.

Alexy, E. M., Burgess, A. W., & Baker, T. (2005). Internet offenders: Traders, travelers, and combination trader-travelers. *Journal of Interpersonal Violence*, *20*(7), 804–812. doi:10.1177/0886260505276091 PMID:15914702

Alexy, E. M., Burgess, A. W., Baker, T., & Smoyak, S. A. (2005). Perceptions of cyberstalking among college students. *Brief Treatment and Crisis Intervention*, *5*(3), 279–289. doi:10.1093/brief-treatment/mhi020

Al-Hantoushi, M., & Al-Abdullateef, S. (2014). Internet addiction among secondary school students in Riyadh city, its prevalence, correlates and relation to depression: A questionnaire survey. *International Journal of Medical Science and Public Health*, *3*(1), 10–15. doi:10.5455/ijmsph.2013.130920131

Al-Khateeb, H. M., Epiphaniou, G., Alhaboby, Z. A., Barnes, J., & Short, E. (2017). Cyberstalking: Investigating formal intervention and the role of Corporate Social Responsibility. *Telematics and Informatics*, *34*(4), 339–349. doi:10.1016/j.tele.2016.08.016

Allen, A., Kannis-Dymand, L., & Katsikitis, M. (2017). Problematic internet pornography use: The role of craving, desire thinking, and metacognition. *Addictive Behaviors*, *70*, 65–71. doi:10.1016/j.addbeh.2017.02.001 PMID:28214738

Allen, K. A., Ryan, T., Gray, D. L., McInerney, D. M., & Waters, L. (2014). Social media use and social connectedness in adolescents: The positives and the potential pitfalls. *The Educational and Developmental Psychologist*, *31*(1), 18–31. doi:10.1017/edp.2014.2

Almunawar, M. N., Anshari, M., Susanto, H., & Chen, C. K. (2017). How People Choose and Use Their Smartphones. *Management Strategies and Technology Fluidity in the Asian Business Sector*, 235.

Altan, H. Z. (2015). Sosyal Medyanın Kullanımlar ve Doyumlar Haritası: Youtube, Facebook ve Twitter. In Sosyal Medya Araştırmaları 2: Sosyalleşen Olgular. Konya: Çizgi Publication.

Alterovitz, S. S., & Mendelsohn, G. A. (2009). Partner preferences across the life span: Online dating by older adults. *Psychology and Aging*, *24*(2), 513–517. doi:10.1037/a0015897 PMID:19485668

Alterovitz, S. S., & Mendelsohn, G. A. (2013). Relationship goals of middle-aged, young-old, and old-old internet daters: An analysis of online personal ads. *Journal of Aging Studies*, *27*(2), 159–165. doi:10.1016/j.jaging.2012.12.006 PMID:23561281

American Psychiatric Association. (2000). *Diagnostic and statistical manual of mental disorders* (4th ed.). Washington, DC: Author.

Amichai-Hamburger, Y., & Ben-Artzi, E. (2000). The relationship between extraversion, neuroticism, and different uses of the Internet. *Computers in Human Behavior*, *16*(4), 441–449. doi:10.1016/S0747-5632(00)00017-0

Amichai-Hamburger, Y., & Vinitzky, G. (2010). Social network use and personality. *Computers in Human Behavior*, *26*(6), 1289–1295. doi:10.1016/j.chb.2010.03.018

Amita, V. (2016). *Cyber Crimes & Law.* Central Law Publication. Retrieved from http://www.legalindia.com/cyber-stalking-the-impact-of-its-legislative-provisions-in-india/

Anderson, R. (2016, September 6). The ugly truth about online dating [Web blog post]. Retrieved from www.psychologytoday.com

Anderson, J., Bresnahan, M., & Musatics, C. (2014). Combating weight-based cyberbullying on Facebook with the dissenter effect. *Cyberpsychology, Behavior, and Social Networking*, *17*(5), 281–286. doi:10.1089/cyber.2013.0370 PMID:24690025

Andreassen, C. S. (2015). Online social network site addiction: A comprehensive review. *Current Addiction Reports*, *2*(2), 175–184. doi:10.100740429-015-0056-9

Andreassen, C. S., & Pallesen, S. (2014). Social network site addiction – An overview. *Current Pharmaceutical Design*, *20*(25), 4053–4061. doi:10.2174/13816128113199990616 PMID:24001298

Andreassen, C. S., Pallesen, S., & Griffiths, M. D. (2017). The relationship between addictive use of social media, narcissism, and self-esteem: Findings from a large national survey. *Addictive Behaviors*, *64*, 287–293. doi:10.1016/j.addbeh.2016.03.006 PMID:27072491

Andreassen, S. C., Torscheim, T., & Pallesen, S. (2014). Predictors of use of social network sites at work: A specific type of cyberloafing. *Journal of Computer-Mediated Communication*, *19*(4), 906–921. doi:10.1111/jcc4.12085

Ang, R. P. (2016). Cyberbullying: Its prevention and intervention strategies. In D. Sibnath (Ed.), *Child safety, welfare and well-being: Issues and challenges* (pp. 25–38). Springer. doi:10.1007/978-81-322-2425-9_3

Anshari, M., Almunawar, M. N., Shahrill, M., Wicaksono, D. K., & Huda, M. (2017). Smartphones usage in the classrooms: Learning aid or interference? *Education and Information Technologies*, 1–17.

Aoyama, I., Utsumi, S., & Hasegawa, M. (2011). Cyberbullying in Japan: Cases, government reports, adolescent relational aggression and parental monitoring roles. In Q. Li, D. Cross, & P. K. Smith (Eds.), *Bullying in the global playground: Research from an international perspective*. Oxford, UK: Wiley-Blackwell.

Appel, H., Crusius, J., & Gerlach, A. L. (2015). Social comparison, envy, and depression on Facebook: A study looking at the effects of high comparison standards on depressed individuals. *Journal of Social and Clinical Psychology, 34*(4), 277–289. doi:10.1521/jscp.2015.34.4.277

Argyle, M. (2008). *Social encounters: Contributions to social interaction.* Aldine Transaction.

Aricak, T., Siyahhan, S., Uzunhasanoglu, A., Saribeyoglu, S., Ciplak, S., Yilmaz, N., & Memmedov, C. (2008). Cyberbullying among Turkish adolescents. *Cyberpsychology & Behavior, 11*(3), 253–261. doi:10.1089/cpb.2007.0016 PMID:18537493

Aristotle. (1999). *Nicomachean Ethics.* Indianapolis, IN: Hackett Publishing.

Armstrong, L., Phillips, J. G., & Saling, L. L. (2000). Potential determinants of heavier internet usage. *International Journal of Human-Computer Studies, 53*(4), 537–550. doi:10.1006/ijhc.2000.0400

Arslan, S., Savaser, S., Hallett, V., & Balci, S. (2012). Cyberbullying among primary school students in Turkey: Self-reported prevalence and associations with home and school life. *Cyberpsychology, Behavior, and Social Networking, 15*(10), 527–533. doi:10.1089/cyber.2012.0207 PMID:23002988

Arulogun, O. S., Ogbu, I. A., & Dipeolu, I. O. (2016). Influence of internet exposure on sexual behaviour of young persons in an urban district of Southwest Nigeria. *The Pan African Medical Journal, 25*, 261. doi:10.11604/pamj.2016.25.261.2630 PMID:28293377

Atmaca, M. (2007). A case of problematic internet use successfully treated with an SSRI-antipsychotic combination. *Program of Neuro-psychopharmacological and Biological Psychiatry, 31*(4), 961–962. doi:10.1016/j.pnpbp.2007.01.003 PMID:17321659

Attwood, F. (2009). 'Deepthroatfucker' and 'Discerning Adonis'. Men and cybersex. *International Journal of Cultural Studies, 12*(3), 279–294. doi:10.1177/1367877908101573

Ayas, T., & Horzum, M. B. (2010). *Cyberbullying / victim scale development study.* Retrieved from: http://www.akademikbakis.org

Badal, H. J., Stryker, J. E., DeLuca, N., & Purcell, D. W. (2017). Swipe Right: Dating Website and App Use Among Men Who Have Sex With Men. *AIDS and Behavior, 7.* doi:10.100710461-017-1882-7 PMID:28884248

Baer, M. (2010). Cyberstalking and the Internet Landscape We Have Created. *Virginia Journal of Law & Technology., 15*(154), 153–174.

Bainbridge, W. S. (2012). eAnarchy. *Futures, 44*(9), 823–831. doi:10.1016/j.futures.2012.07.003

Ballester-Arnal, R., Castro-Calvo, J., Gil-Llario, M. D., & Giménez-García, C. (2014). Relationship status as an influence on cybersex activity: Cybersex, youth, and steady partner. *Journal of Sex & Marital Therapy, 40*(5), 444–456. do i:10.1080/0092623X.2013.772549 PMID:24134331

Bannink, R, Broeren, S., van de Looij-Jansen, P.M., de Waart, F.G., & Raat, H. (2014). Cyber and traditional bullying victimization as a risk factor for mental health problems and suicidal ideation in adolescents. *PLoS One, 9*(4). doi: .10.1371/journal.pone.0094026

Barak, A. (2006). Youth and the Internet: Psychology of "as if" and "like that". [Hebrew]. *Panim, 37*, 48–58.

Barbera, L. D., Paglia, L. F., & Valsavoia, R. (2009). Social network and addiction. *Studies in Health Technology and Informatics, 144*, 33–36. PMID:19592725

Bargh, J. A., McKenna, K. Y., & Fitzsimons, G. M. (2002). Can you see the real me? Activation and expression of the "true self" on the Internet. *The Journal of Social Issues*, *58*(1), 33–48. doi:10.1111/1540-4560.00247

Barkan, S. (2006). *Criminology: A sociological understanding* (3rd ed.). Upper Saddle River, NJ: Prentice Hall.

Barker, V. (2009). Older adolescents' motivations for social network site use: The influence of gender, group identity, and collective self-esteem. *Cyberpsychology & Behavior*, *12*(2), 209–213. doi:10.1089/cpb.2008.0228 PMID:19250021

Barlett, C. P., & Gentile, D. A. (2012). Long-term psychological predictors of cyber-bullying in late adolescence. *Psychology of Popular Media Culture*, *2*, 123–135. doi:10.1037/a0028113

Barlett, C. P., Gentile, D. A., Anderson, C. A., Suzuki, K., Sakamoto, A., Yamaoka, A., & Katsura, R. (2013). Cross-cultural differences in cyberbullying behavior: A short-term longitudinal study. *Journal of Cross-Cultural Psychology*, *45*(2), 300–313. doi:10.1177/0022022113504622

Barnes, G. E., Malamuth, N. M., & Check, J. V. P. (1984). Personality and Sexuality. *Personality Individual Differences*, *5*(2), 159-172. Retrieved 25 Sep. 2012, from http://www. personality-project.org/revelle/publications/revelle.issid.07.pdf

Barry, C. T., Doucette, H., Loflin, D. C., Rivera-Hudson, N., & Herrington, L. L. (2017). 'Let me take a selfie': Associations between self-photography, narcissism, and self-esteem. *Psychology of Popular Media Culture*, *6*(1), 48–60. doi:10.1037/ppm0000089

Barthes, R. (1977). *Image-Music-Text*. London: Fontana Press.

Barthes, R. (1981). *Camera Lucida*. New York: Hill and Wang.

Basile, K. C., Swahn, M., Chen, J., & Saltzman, L. (2006). Stalking in the United States: Recent national prevalence estimates. *American Journal of Preventive Medicine*, *31*(2), 172–175. doi:10.1016/j.amepre.2006.03.028 PMID:16829335

Bauermeister, J. A., Leslie-Santana, M., Johns, M. M., Pingel, E., & Eisenberg, A. (2011). Mr. Right and Mr. Right Now: Romantic and casual partner-seeking online among young men who have sex with men. *AIDS and Behavior*, *15*(2), 261–272. doi:10.100710461-010-9834-5 PMID:20953689

Bauman, S., Toomey, R. B., & Walker, J. L. (2013). Associations among bullying, cyberbullying, and suicide in high school students. *Journal of Adolescence*, *36*(2), 341–350. doi:10.1016/j.adolescence.2012.12.001 PMID:23332116

Bauman, S., Underwood, M. K., & Card, N. A. (2013). Definitions: Another perspective and a proposal for beginning with cyberaggression. In S. Bauman, D. Cross, & J. Walker (Eds.), *Principles of cyberbullying research: Definitions, measures, methodology* (pp. 26–40). New York, NY: Routledge.

Bauman, Z. (2003). *Liquid Love: On the Frailty of Human Bonds*. Cambridge, UK: Polity Press.

Baumeister, R. F., & Leary, M. R. (1995). The need to belong: Desire for interpersonal attachments as a fundamental human motivation. *Psychological Bulletin*, *117*(3), 497–529. doi:10.1037/0033-2909.117.3.497 PMID:7777651

Baum, K., Catalano, S., Rand, M., & Rose, K. (2009). *Stalking victimization in the United States*. Washington, DC: U.S. Department of Justice.

Bayar, Y., & Ucanok, Z. (2012). School social climate and generalized peer perception in traditional and cyberbullying status. *Educational Sciences: Theory and Practice*, *12*, 2352–2358.

Bazarova, N. N., & Choi, Y. H. (2014). Self-disclosure in social media: Extending the functional approach to disclosure motivations and characteristics on social network sites. *Journal of Communication*, *64*(4), 635–657. doi:10.1111/jcom.12106

Beard, K. W., & Wolf, E. M. (2001). Modification in the proposed di-agnostic criteria for Internet addiction. *Cyberpsychology & Behavior, 4*(3), 377–383. doi:10.1089/109493101300210286 PMID:11710263

Beckman, L., Hagquist, C., & Hellstrom, L. (2012). Does the association with psychosomatic health problems differ between cyberbullying and traditional bullying? *Emotional & Behavioural Difficulties, 17*(3-4), 421–434. doi:10.1080/13632752.2012.704228

Benedikt, C. (1995). TinySex is Safe Sex. *Infobahn Magazine*. Retrieved from http://www.cwrl.utexas.edu/~claire/texts/thoughts.html

Ben-Ze'ev, A. (2012). *Emotions and Morality in Computer-mediated Romantic Relationships*. Retrieved from http://emotionresearch.net/projects/humaine/ws/wp10/presentation-materials/AaronBenZeev-wp10wsMoralityOnlineRelationships-final.pdf

Ben-Ze'ev, A. (2004). *Love online: Emotions on the Internet*. Cambridge, UK: Cambridge University Press. doi:10.1017/CBO9780511489785

Beran, T. N., Rinaldi, C., Bickham, D. S., & Rich, M. (2012). Evidence for the need to support adolescents dealing with harassment and cyber-harassment: Prevalence, progression, and impact. *School Psychology International, 33*(5), 562–576. doi:10.1177/0143034312446976

BeranuyFargues, M., ChamarroLusar, A., GranerJordania, C., & Carbonell Sánchez, X. (2009). Validación de dos escalas breves para evaluar la adicción a Internet y el abuso de móvil. *Psicothema, 21*(3).

Berkman, L. F., & Glass, T. (2000). Social integration, social networks, social support, and health. *Social Epidemiology, 1*, 137–173. doi:10.1016/S0277-9536(00)00065-4

Berndt, T. J. (1989). Obtaining support from friends during childhood and adolescence. In D. Belle (Ed.), *Children's Social Networks and Social Supports* (pp. 308–331). Oxford, UK: John Wiley & Sons.

Berson, I. R. (2003). Grooming cybervictims: The psychosocial effects of online exploitation for youth. *Journal of School Violence, 2*(1), 5–18. doi:10.1300/J202v02n01_02

Berson, I. R., & Berson, M. J. (2005). Challenging online behaviors of youth: Findings from a comparative analysis of young people in the United States and New Zealand. *Social Science Computer Review, 23*(1), 29–38. doi:10.1177/0894439304271532

Bessiere, K., Pressman, S., Kiesler, S., & Kraut, R. (2010). Effects of internet use on health and depression: A longitudinal study. *Journal of Medical Internet Research, 12*(1), e6. doi:10.2196/jmir.1149 PMID:20228047

Best, P., Manktelow, R., & Taylor, B. (2014). Online communication, social media and adolescent wellbeing:A systematic narrative review. *Children and Youth Services Review, 41*, 27–36. doi:10.1016/j.childyouth.2014.03.001

Bevan, J. L., Gomez, R., & Sparks, L. (2014). Disclosures about important life events on Facebook: Relationships with stress and quality of life. *Computers in Human Behavior, 39*, 246–253. 246-253.doi.org/10.1016/j.chb.2014.07.021. doi:10.1016/j.chb.2014.07.021

Bjorklund, K., Hakkanen-Nyholm, H., Sheridan, L., & Roberts, K. (2010). The prevalence of stalking among Finnish university students. *Journal of Interpersonal Violence, 25*(4), 684-98.

Björklund, K., Häkkänen-Nyholm, H., Sheridan, L., & Roberts, K. (2010). The Prevalence of Stalking Among Finnish University Students. *Journal of Interpersonal Violence, 25*(4), 684–698. doi:10.1177/0886260509334405 PMID:20065315

Blaauw, E., Winkel, F. W., Arensman, E., Sheridan, L., & Freeve, A. (2002). The toll of stalking: The relationship between features of stalking and psychopathology of victims. *Journal of Interpersonal Violence*, *17*(1), 50–63. doi:10.1177/0886260502017001004

Błachnio, A., Przepiorka, A., & Pantic, I. (2016). Association between Facebook addiction, self-esteem and life satisfaction: A cross-sectional study. *Computers in Human Behavior*, *55*, 701–705. doi:10.1016/j.chb.2015.10.026

Black, D. W. (1996). Compulsive buying: A review. *The Journal of Clinical Psychiatry*, *57*(8), 50–54. PMID:8698681

Black, M. C., Basile, K. C., Breiding, M. J., Smith, S. G., Walters, M. L., Merrick, M. T., ... Stevens, M. R. (2011). *National Intimate Partner and Sexual Violence Survey, 2010 summary report*. Atlanta, GA: National Center for Injury Prevention and Control of the Centers for Disease Control and Prevention.

Blair, C. (1998). Netsex: Empowerment through Discourse. In B. Ebo (Ed.), *Cyberghetto or Cybertopia. Race, Class, and Gender on the Internet* (pp. 205–218). Westport, CT: Praeger.

Blossom, J. (2009). *Content Nation: Surviving and Thriving as Social Media Changes Our Work, Our Lives, and Our Future*. Wiley Publishing.

Bocij, P. (2003). Victims of cyberstalking: An exploratory study of harassment perpetrated via the Internet. *First Monday*, *8*(10). doi:10.5210/fm.v8i10.1086

Bocij, P. (2004). *Cyberstalking: Harassment in the Internet age and how to protect your family*. Westport, CT: Praeger Publishers.

Bocij, P., & McFarlane, L. (2002). Online harassment: Towards a definition of cyberstalking. *Prison Service Journal*, *139*, 31–38.

Bocij, P., & McFarlane, L. (2003). Cyberstalking: The Technology of Hate.*The Police Journal: Theory. Practice and Principles*, *76*(3), 204–221. doi:10.1350/pojo.76.3.204.19442

Bocij, P., & McFarlane, L. (2003). The Internet: A Discussion of Some New and Emerging Threats to Young People. *The Police Journal*, *76*(1), 3–13. doi:10.1177/0032258X0307600102

Boies, S. C., Cooper, A., & Osborne, C. S. (2004). Variations in Internet-related problems and psychosocial functioning in online sexual activities: Implications for social and sexual development of young adults. *Cyberpsychology & Behavior*, *7*(2), 207–230. doi:10.1089/109493104323024474 PMID:15140364

Bonanno, R. A., & Hymel, S. (2013). Cyber bullying and internalizing difficulties: Above and beyond the impact of traditional forms of bullying. *Journal of Youth and Adolescence*, *42*(5), 685–697. doi:10.100710964-013-9937-1 PMID:23512485

Bonetti, L., Campbell, M. A., & Gilmore, L. (2010). The Relationship of loneliness and social anxiety with children's and adolescents' online communication. *Cyberpsychology, Behavior, and Social Networking, 13*(3), 279-285. doi: 10.1089=cyber.2009.0215

Boshmaf, Y., Muslukhov, I., Beznosov, K., & Ripeanu, M. (2013). Design and analysis of a social botnet. *International Journal of Computer and Telecommunications Networking*, *57*(2), 556–578. doi:10.1016/j.comnet.2012.06.006

Bosworth, K., Espelage, D., & DuBay, T. (1998). A computer-based violence prevention intervention for young adolescents: Pilot study. *Adolescence*, *33*(132), 785. PMID:9886006

Boulton, M., Lloyd, J., Down, J., & Marx, H. (2012). Predicting undergraduates' self-reported engagement in traditional and cyberbullying from attitudes. *Cyberpsychology, Behavior, and Social Networking, 15*(3), 141–147. doi:10.1089/cyber.2011.0369 PMID:22304402

Boursier, V., & Manna, V. (in press). Problematic linkages in adolescents. Italian adaptation of a measure for Internet-related problems. In B. Bozoglan (Ed.), *Psychological, Social, and Cultural Aspects of Internet Addiction*. Hershey, PA: IGI Global.

Boyd, D. (2009, August 16). Twitter: "pointless babble" or peripheral awareness + social grooming? [Web log post]. Retrieved from http://www.zephoria.org/thoughts/archives/2009/08/16/twitter_pointle.html

Boyd, D. M. &Ellison, N. B. (2007). Social network sites: Definition, history, and scholarship. *Journal of Computer-Mediated Communication, 13*(1), 210-230. doi: 6101.2007.00393.x10.1111/j.1083

Bragazzi, N. L., & Del Puente, G. (2014). A proposal for including nomophobia in the new DSM-V. *Psychology Research and Behavior Management, 7*, 155. doi:10.2147/PRBM.S41386 PMID:24876797

Brand, M., Laier, C., Pawlikowski, M., Schächtle, U., Schöler, T., & Altstötter-Gleich, C. (2011). Watching pornographic pictures on the Internet: Role of sexual arousal ratings and psychological-psychiatric symptoms for using Internet sex sites excessively. *Cyberpsychology, Behavior, and Social Networking, 14*(6), 371–377. doi:10.1089/cyber.2010.0222 PMID:21117979

Branwyn, G. (1993). Compu-sex: Erotica for cybernauts. *The South Atlantic Quarterly, 92*, 779–791.

Briggs, P., Simon, W. T., & Simonsen, S. (2011). An exploratory study of Internet-initiated sexual offenses and the chat room sex offender: Has the Internet enabled a new typology of sex offender? *Sexual Abuse, 23*(1), 72–91. doi:10.1177/1079063210384275 PMID:20947699

Brighi, A., Guarini, A., Melotti, G., Galli, S., & Genta, M. L. (2012). Predictors of victimisation across direct bullying, indirect bullying and cyberbullying. *Emotional & Behavioural Difficulties, 17*(3-4), 375–388. doi:10.1080/13632752.2012.704684

Bromby, M. (2006). Security against Crime: Technologies for Detecting and Preventing Crime. *International Review of Law Computers & Technology, 20*(1-2), 1–5. doi:10.1080/13600860600818235

Brown, C. F., Demaray, M. K., & Secord, S. M. (2014). Cyber victimization in middle school and relations to social emotional outcomes. *Computers in Human Behavior, 35*, 12–21. doi:10.1016/j.chb.2014.02.014

Brown, C. S. D. (2015). Cyber-Attacks, Retaliation and Risk: Legal and Technical Implications for Nation-States and Private Entities. In J. L. Richet (Ed.), *Cybersecurity Policies and Strategies for Cyberwarfare Prevention* (pp. 166–203). Hershey, PA: IGI Global. doi:10.4018/978-1-4666-8456-0.ch008

Brownstein, A. (2000). In the campus shadows, women are stalkers as well as the stalked. *The Chronicle of Higher Education, 47*(15), 4042.

Bryce, J., & Fraser, J. (2014). The role of disclosure of personal information in the evaluation of risk and trust in young peoples' online interactions. *Computers in Human Behavior, 30*, 299–306. doi:10.1016/j.chb.2013.09.012

Budd, T., & Mattinson, J. (2000). *The extent and nature of stalking: findings from the 1998 British Crime Survey*. Research, Development and Statistics Directorate, London. Retrieved from http://citeseerx.ist.psu.edu/viewdoc/download?doi=10.1.1.527.4457&rep=rep1&type=pdf

Buglass, S. L., Binder, J. F., Betts, L. R., & Underwood, J. D. (2017). Motivators of online vulnerability: The impact of social network site use and FOMO. *Computers in Human Behavior, 66*, 248–255. doi:10.1016/j.chb.2016.09.055

Buhrmester, D. (1990). Intimacy of friendship, interpersonal competence, and adjustment during preadolescence and adolescence. *Child Development, 61*(4), 1101–1111. doi:10.2307/1130878 PMID:2209180

Buote, V. M., Wood, E., & Pratt, M. (2009). Exploring similarities and differences between online and offline friendships: The role of attachment style. *Computers in Human Behavior, 25*(2), 560–567. doi:10.1016/j.chb.2008.12.022

Burgess, A. W., & Baker, T. (2002). Cyberstalking. In J. Boon & L. Sheridan (Eds.), *Stalking and psychosexual obsession: Psychological perspectives for prevention, policing and treatment*. Chichester, UK: Wiley. doi:10.1002/9780470713037.ch12

Burke, M., & Kraut, R. E. (2016). The relationship between Facebook use and well-being depends on communication type and tie strength. *Journal of Computer-Mediated Communication, 21*(4), 265–281. doi:10.1111/jcc4.12162

Burke, M., Kraut, R., & Marlow, C. (2011). Social capital on Facebook: Differentiating uses and users. In *Proceedings of the 29th Annual Conference on Human Factors in Computing Systems* (pp. 571–580). New York: ACM Press. 10.1145/1978942.1979023

Burke, M., Marlow, C., & Lento, T. (2010). Social network activity and social well-being. *Postgraduate Medical Journal, 85*, 455–459.

Burke, M., Marlow, C., & Lento, T. (2010, April). Social network activity and social well-being. In *Proceedings of the 28th International Conference on Human Factors in Computing Systems*. New York: ACM.

Burke, S. (2008). *The Death and Return of the Author: Criticism and Subjectivity in Barthes, Foucault and Derrida*. Edinburg, UK: Edinburg University Press.

Burmester, M., Henry, P., & Kermes, L. S. (2005). Tracking Cyberstalkers: A Cryptographic Approach. ACM SIGCAS Computers and Society, 35(3).

Burns, R. M. (2002). Language, tradition, and the self in the generation of meaning. *History of European Ideas, 28*(1-2), 51–75. doi:10.1016/S0191-6599(02)00008-6

Burrow, A. L., & Rainone, N. (2017). How many likes did I get?: Purpose moderates links between positive social media feedback and self-esteem. *Journal of Experimental Social Psychology, 69*, 232–236. doi:10.1016/j.jesp.2016.09.005

Burton, K. A., Florell, D., & Wygant, D. B. (2013). The role of peer attachment and normative beliefs about aggression on traditional bullying and cyberbullying. *Psychology in the Schools, 50*(2), 103–114. doi:10.1002/pits.21663

Buss, D. M., & Barnes, M. (1986). Preferences in human mate selection. *Journal of Personality and Social Psychology, 50*(3), 559–570. doi:10.1037/0022-3514.50.3.559

Buss, D. M., Shackelford, T. K., Kirkpatrick, L. A., & Larsen, R. J. (2001). A half century of mate preferences: The cultural evolution of values. *Journal of Marriage and the Family, 63*(2), 491–503. doi:10.1111/j.1741-3737.2001.00491.x

Butterworth, D. (1996). Wanking in Cyberspace: The Development of Computer Porn. In Feminism and Sexuality. A Reader (pp. 314 320). New York, NY: Columbia University Press.

Butt, S., & Phillips, J. G. (2008). Personality and self reported mobile phone use. *Computers in Human Behavior, 24*(2), 346–360. doi:10.1016/j.chb.2007.01.019

Büyükaslan, A. (2015). Sosyalleşmenin Boyutu. In Sosyal Medya Araştırmaları 2: Sosyalleşen Olgular. Konya: Çizgi Publication.

Cali, B. E., Coleman, J. M., & Campbell, C. (2013). Stranger danger? Women's self-protection intent and the continuing stigma of online dating. *Cyberpsychology, Behavior, and Social Networking*, *16*(12), 853–857. doi:10.1089/cyber.2012.0512 PMID:23849001

Camardese, G., Leone, B., Walstra, C., Janiri, L., & Guglielmo, R. (2015). Pharmacological Treatment of Internet Addiction. In C. Montag & M. Reuter (Eds.), *Internet Addiction. Studies in Neuroscience, Psychology and Behavioral Economics*. Cham: Springer. doi:10.1007/978-3-319-07242-5_10

Cameron, S., & Brown, D. (2015). Investigating and Prosecuting Cyber Crime: Forensic Dependencies and Barriers to Justice. *International Journal of Cyber Criminology*, *9*(1), 55–119.

Campbell, M. A. (2005). Cyber Bullying: An Old Problem in a New Guise? *Australian Journal of Guidance & Counselling*, *15*(01), 68–76. doi:10.1375/ajgc.15.1.68

Caplan, S. E. (2003). Preference for online social interaction: A theory of problematic Internet useand psychosocial well-being. *Communication Research*, *30*(6), 625–648. doi:10.1177/0093650203257842

Caplan, S. E. (2007). Relation among loneliness, social anxiety, andproblematic internet use. *Cyberpsychology & Behavior*, *10*(2), 234–242. doi:10.1089/cpb.2006.9963 PMID:17474841

Cappadocia, M. C., Craig, W. M., & Pepler, D. (2013). Cyberbullying: Prevalence, stability and risk factors during adolescence. *Canadian Journal of School Psychology*, *28*(2), 171–192. doi:10.1177/0829573513491212

Carbonell, X., Torres-Rodríguez, A., & Fuster, H. (2016). El potencialadictivo de los videojuegos. In E. Echerburua (Ed.), *Abuso de Internet: "antesala para la adicción al juego de azar on-line*. Madrid: Síntesis.

Carpenter, C. J. (2012). Narcissism on Facebook: Self-promotional and anti-social behavior. *Personality and Individual Differences*, *52*(4), 482–486. doi:10.1016/j.paid.2011.11.011

Carton, S. (1995). *Internet Virtual Worlds Quick Tour*. Ventana Press.

Carvalheira, A., & Gomes, F. A. (2003). Cybersex in Portuguese chatrooms: A study of sexual behaviors related to online sex. *Journal of Sex & Marital Therapy*, *29*(5), 345–360. doi:10.1080/00926230390224729 PMID:14504006

Caschera, M. C., D'Ulizia, A., Ferri, F., & Grifoni, P. (2012). Towards Evolutionary Multimodal Interaction. In P. Herrero, H. Panetto, R. Meersman, & T. Dillon (Eds.), *On the Move to Meaningful Internet Systems: OTM 2012 Workshops*. Berlin: Springer; doi:10.1007/978-3-642-33618-8_80

Casey, E. (2011). Investigative reconstruction with digital evidence. In E. Casey & B. E. Turvey (Eds.), *Digital evidence and computer crime: forensic science, computers and the internet* (pp. 255–273). Academic Press.

Cassidy, W., Brown, K., & Jackson, M. (2012a). "Making kind cool": Parents' suggestions for preventing cyber bullying and fostering cyber kindness. *Journal of Educational Computing Research*, *46*(4), 415–436. doi:10.2190/EC.46.4.f

Cassidy, W., Brown, K., & Jackson, M. (2012b). "Under the radar": Educators and cyberbullying in schools. *School Psychology International*, *33*(5), 520–532. doi:10.1177/0143034312445245

Castells, M. (2013). Enformasyon Çağı: Ekonomi, Toplum ve Kültür Birinci Cilt: Ağ Toplumunun Yükselişi. Istanbul Bilgi University Publication.

Cattaneo, L., Cho, S., & Botuck, S. (2011). Describing intimate partner stalking over time: An effort to inform victim-centered service provision. *Journal of Interpersonal Violence*, *26*(17), 3428–3454. doi:10.1177/0886260511403745 PMID:21810796

Cavazos-Rehg, P. A., Krauss, M. J., Sowles, S. J., Connolly, S., Rosas, C., Bharadwaj, M., ... Bierut, L. J. (2016). An analysis of depression, self-harm, and suicidal ideation content on Tumblr. *Crisis*, *38*(1), 44–52. doi:10.1027/0227-5910/a000409 PMID:27445014

Cavelty, D. M. (2014). Breaking the cyber-security dilemma: Aligning security needs and removing vulnerabilities. *Science and Engineering Ethics*, *20*(3), 701–715. doi:10.100711948-014-9551-y PMID:24781874

Çetinkaya, A. (2015). Sosyal Medya ve Televizyon İzleme Ölçümü. In Sosyal Medya Araştırmaları 2: Sosyalleşen Olgular. Konya: Çizgi Publication.

Chakraborty, K., Basu, D., & Kumar, K. (2010). Internet addiction: Consensus, controversies, and the way ahead. *East Asian Archives of Psychiatry*, *20*, 123–132. PMID:22348866

Chambers, R. A., & Potenza, M. N. (2003). Neurodevelopment, impulsivity, and adolescent gambling. *Journal of Gambling Studies*, *19*(1), 53–84. doi:10.1023/A:1021275130071 PMID:12635540

Chang, F. C., Lee, C. M., Chiu, C. H., Hsi, W. Y., Huang, T. F., & Pan, Y. C. (2013). Relationships among cyberbullying, school bullying, and mental health in Taiwanese adolescents. *The Journal of School Health*, *83*(6), 454–462. doi:10.1111/josh.12050 PMID:23586891

Chappell, D., Eatough, V., Davies, M. N. O., & Griffiths, M. D. (2006). Everquest - It's just acomputer game right? An interpretative phenomenological analysis of online gaming addiction. *International Journal of Mental Health and Addiction*, *4*(3), 205–216. doi:10.100711469-006-9028-6

Charlton, J., & Danforth, I. (2007). Distinguishing addiction and high engagement in the context of online game playing. *Computers in Human Behavior*, *23*(3), 1531–1548. doi:10.1016/j.chb.2005.07.002

Cheng, W., & Chiou, W.B (2007). *Exposure to Sexual Stimuli Induces Greater Discounting Leading to Increased Involvement in Cyber Delinquency Among Men*. Academic Press. DOI: 10.1089/cyber.2016.0582

Chen, G. M. (2011). Tweet this: A uses and gratifications perspective on how active Twitter use gratifies a need to connect with others. *Computers in Human Behavior*, *27*(2), 755–762. doi:10.1016/j.chb.2010.10.023

Cheng, M., Wu, Y., & Chen, M. (2016). Television Meets Facebook: The Correlation between TV Ratings and Social Media. *American Journal of Industrial and Business Management*, *6*(03), 282–290. doi:10.4236/ajibm.2016.63026

Chiou, W. B. (2006). Adolescents' sexual self-disclosure on the internet: Deindividuation and impression management. *Adolescents*, *41*(163), 547–561. PMID:17225667

Choi, T. R., Sung, Y., Lee, J., & Choi, S. M. (2017). Get behind my selfies: The big five traits and social networking behaviors through selfies. *Personality and Individual Differences*, *10*, 998–1001. doi:10.1016/j.paid.2016.12.057

Chou, H. G., & Edge, N. (2012). "They are happier and having better lives than i am": The impact of using Facebook on perceptions of others' lives. *Cyberpsychology, Behavior, and Social Networking*, *15*(2), 117–122. doi:10.1089/cyber.2011.0324 PMID:22165917

Chou, T. J., & Ting, C. C. (2003). The role of flow experience in cyber-game addiction.: The impact of the Internet, multimedia and virtual reality on behavior and society. *Cyberpsychology & Behavior*, *6*(6), 663–675. doi:10.1089/109493103322725469 PMID:14756934

Chua, T. H., & Chang, L. (2016). Follow me and like my beautiful selfies: Singapore teenage girls' engagement in self-presentation and peer comparison on social media. *Computers in Human Behavior*, *55*, 190–197. doi:10.1016/j.chb.2015.09.011

Church, K., & Oliveira, R. (2013). What's up with whatsapp?: Comparing mobile instant messaging behaviors with traditional SMS. *Proceedings of the 15th international conference on Human-computer interaction with mobile devices and services*, 352-361. 10.1145/2493190.2493225

Chu, Z., Gianvecchio, S., Wang, H., & Jajodia, S. (2010). Who is tweeting on Twitter: human, bot, or cyborg? In *Proceedings of the 26th Annual Computer Security Applications Conference* (pp. 21-30). New York: ACM. 10.1145/1920261.1920265

Clayton, R. B., Osborne, R. E., Miller, B. K., & Oberle, C. D. (2013). Loneliness, anxiousness, and substance use as predictors of Facebook use. *Computers in Human Behavior, 29*(3), 687–693. doi:10.1016/j.chb.2012.12.002

Cohen, S., Frank, E., Doyle, W. J., Skoner, D. P., Rabin, B. S., & Gwaltney, J. M. (1998). Types of stressors that increase susceptibility to the common cold in healthy adults. *Health Psychology, 17*(3), 214–223. doi:10.1037/0278-6133.17.3.214 PMID:9619470

Cohen, S., & Willis, T. A. (1985). Stress, social support, and the buffering hypothesis. *Psychological Bulletin, 98*(2), 310–357. doi:10.1037/0033-2909.98.2.310 PMID:3901065

Cole, H., & Griffiths, M. D. (2007). Social interactions in Massively Multiplayer Online Role-Playing gamers. *Cyberpsychology & Behavior, 10*(4), 575–583. doi:10.1089/cpb.2007.9988 PMID:17711367

Comparcini, D., Simonetti, V., Lupo, R., Galli, F., Bocij, P., & Cicolini, G. (2016). Cyberstalking among Italian nurses: a large multicentric study. *Prof Inferm, 69*(3), 150-158. doi: 10.7429 / pi.2016.693150

Connolly, I., Palmer, M., Barton, H., & Kirwan, G. (Eds.). (2016). *An Introduction to Cyberpsychology*. Routledge.

Conoley, J. C., & Goldstein, A. P. (Eds.). (2004). *School violence intervention: A practical handbook.* Guilford Press.

Contreras-Castillo, J., Pérez-Fragoso, C., & Favela, J. (2006). Assessing the use of instant messaging in online learning environments. *Interactive Learning Environments, 14*(3), 205–218. doi:10.1080/10494820600853876

Cooper, A., McLoughlin, I. P., & Campbell, K. M. (2000). Sexuality in cyberspace: Update for the 21st century. *Cyberpsychology & Behavior, 3*(4), 521–536. doi:10.1089/109493100420142

Cooper, A., & Sportolari, L. (1997). Romance in cyberspace: Understanding online attraction. *Journal of Sex Education and Therapy, 22*(1), 7–14. doi:10.1080/01614576.1997.11074165

Coopersmith, S. (1981). *Self-esteem inventories.* Palo Alto, CA: Consulting Psychologists Press.

Corcoran, L., Connolly, I., & O'Moore, M. (2012). Cyberbullying in Irish schools: An investigation of personality and self-concept. *The Irish Journal of Psychology, 33*(4), 153–165. doi:10.1080/03033910.2012.677995

Correa, T., Hinsley, A. W., & De Zuniga, H. G. (2010). Who interacts on the Web?: The intersection of users' personality and social media use. *Computers in Human Behavior, 26*(2), 247–253. doi:10.1016/j.chb.2009.09.003

Costa, P. T., & McCrae, R. R. (1992). *NEO PI-R professional manual.* Odessa, FL: Psychological Assessment Resources.

Cowie, H. (2013). Cyber bullying and its impact on young people's emotional health and well-being. *The Psychiatrist, 37*(05), 167–170. doi:10.1192/pb.bp.112.040840

Cox, L., & Speziale, B. (2009). Survivors of stalking. *Affilia, 24*(1), 5–18. doi:10.1177/0886109908326815

Craft, A. J. (2012). Love 2.0: A quantitative exploration of sex and relationships in the virtual world Second Life. *Archives of Sexual Behavior, 41*(4), 939–947. doi:10.100710508-012-9933-7 PMID:22544305

Crawford, G. (2015). Is it in the Game? Reconsidering Play Spaces, Game Definitions, Theming, and Sports Videogames. *Games and Culture,* 1-22. Retrieved August 1, 2015, from http://blog.dota2.com/?l=english

Cross, D., Pintabona, Y., Hall, M., Hamilton, G., & Erceg, E. (2004). Validated guidelines for school-based bullying prevention and management. *International Journal of Mental Health Promotion, 6*(3), 34–42. doi:10.1080/14623730.2004.9721937

Csepeli, G., & Nagyfi, R. (2014). Facebook diagnostics: Detection of mental health problems based on online traces. *European Journal of Mental Health, 9*(2), 220–230. doi:10.5708/EJMH.9.2014.2.5

Curelaru, M., Iacob, I., & Abalasei, B. (2009). *School bullying: Definition, characteristics, and intervention strategies.* Lumean Publishing House.

Curtis, L. F. (2012). *Virtual vs. reality: an examination of the nature of stalking and cyberstalking* (Master Thesis). Retrieved from http://citeseerx.ist.psu.edu/viewdoc/download?doi=10.1.1.467.5711&rep=rep1&type=pdf

Daft, R. L., & Lengel, R. H. (1984). Information richness: A new approach to managerial behavior and organizational design. *Research in Organizational Behavior, 6*, 191–233.

Daft, R. L., & Lengel, R. H. (1986). Organizational information requirements, media richness and structural design. *Management Science, 32*(5), 554–571. doi:10.1287/mnsc.32.5.554

Dakanalis, A., Di Mattei, V. E., Bagliacca, E. P., Prunas, A., Sarno, L., Riva, G., & Zanetti, M. A. (2012). Disordered eating behaviors among Italian men: Objectifying media and sexual orientation differences. *Eating Disorders, 20*(5), 356–367. doi:10.1080/10640266.2012.715514 PMID:22985233

Daneback, K., Cooper, A., & Mansson, S. (2005). An Internet Study of Cybersex Participants. *Archives of Sexual Behavior, 34*(3), 321–328. doi:10.100710508-005-3120-z PMID:15971014

Darrach, B. (1970). Meet Shaky: The first electronic person. *Life Magazine, 69*(21), 58B–68B.

Das, A., Sharma, M. K., Thamilselvan, P., & Marimuthu, P. (2017). Technology Addiction among Treatment Seekers for Psychological Problems: Implication for Screening in Mental Health Setting. *Indian Journal of Psychological Medicine, 39*(1), 21–27. doi:10.4103/0253-7176.198939 PMID:28250554

Dating safety. (n.d.). Retrieved from www.tinder.com

Davenport, E. (2008). Social informatics and sociotechnical research – a view from the UK. *Journal of Information Science, 34*(4), 519–530. doi:10.1177/0165551508091011

Davey, S., Davey, A., & Singh, J.V. (2016). Emergence of Problematic Internet Use among Indian Adolescents: A Multi Method study. *Journal of Indian Association of Child and Adolescent Mental Health, 12*(1), 60-78.

Davey, S., & Davey, A. (2014). Assessment of Smartphone Addiction in Indian Adolescents: A Mixed Method Study by Systematic-review and Meta-analysis Approach. *International Journal of Preventive Medicine, 5*(12), 1500–1511. PMID:25709785

Davey, S., Raghav, S. K., Davey, A., Singh, N., & Singh, J. V. (2015). Internet usage patterns among medical interns of Muzaffarnagar: A comprehensive survey analysis. *Asian J Med Sci, 6*(2), 99–104.

Davidow, W. H., & Michael, S. M. (1993). *The Virtual Corporation: Structuring and Revitalizing the Corporation for the 21st Century*. New York: Harper Business.

Davila, J., Hershenberg, R., Feinstein, B. A., Gorman, K., Bhatia, V., & Starr, L. R. (2012). Frequency and quality of social networking among young adults: Associations with depressive symptoms, rumination, and corumination. *Psychology of Popular Media Culture*, *1*(2), 72–86. doi:10.1037/a0027512 PMID:24490122

Davis, E. M., & Fingerman, K. L. (2015). Digital Dating: Online Profile Content of Older and Younger Adults. *The Journals of Gerontology. Series B, Psychological Sciences and Social Sciences*, *71*(6), 959–967. doi:10.1093/geronb/gbv042 PMID:26215718

Davis, K. (2012). Friendship 2.0: Adolescents' experiences of belonging and self-disclosure online. *Journal of Adolescence*, *35*(6), 1527–1536. doi:10.1016/j.adolescence.2012.02.013 PMID:22475444

Davis, L. (2005). *Victimology in South Africa*. Pretoria: Van Schaik.

Davis, M., Hart, G., Bolding, G., Sherr, L., & Elford, J. (2006). Sex and the Internet: Gay men, risk reduction and serostatus. *Culture, Health & Sexuality*, *8*(2), 161–174. doi:10.1080/13691050500526126 PMID:16641064

Day, R. E. (2011). Death of the User: Reconceptualizing Subjects, Objects, and Their Relations. *Journal of the Association for Information Science and Technology*, *62*(1), 78–88. doi:10.1002/asi.21422

De Coster, S., Estes, S., & Mueller, C. (1999). Routine activities and sexual harassment in the workplace. *Work and Occupations*, *26*(1), 21–49. doi:10.1177/0730888499026001003

De Freitas, S., & Griffiths, M. D. (2007). Online gaming as an educational tool in learning and training. *British Journal of Educational Technology*, *38*(3), 536–538. doi:10.1111/j.1467-8535.2007.00720.x

De Freitas, S., & Griffiths, M. D. (2008). The convergence of gaming practices with other media forms: What potential for learning? Are view of the literature. *Learning, Media and Technology*, *33*(1), 11–20. doi:10.1080/17439880701868796

De Goede, I. H., Branje, S., van Duin, J., VanderValk, I. E., & Meeus, W. (2012). Romantic relationship commitment and its linkages with commitment to parents and friends during adolescence. *Social Development*, *21*(3), 425–442. doi:10.1111/j.1467-9507.2011.00633.x

de Santisteban, P., & Gámez-Guadix, M. (2017). Prevalence and Risk Factors Among Minors for Online Sexual Solicitations and Interactions With Adults. *Journal of Sex Research*, 1–12. doi:10.1080/00224499.2017.1386763 PMID:29095040

de Vries, D. A., & Kühne, R. (2015). Facebook and self-perception: Individual susceptibility to negative social comparison on Facebook. *Personality and Individual Differences*, *86*, 217–221. doi:10.1016/j.paid.2015.05.029

de Vries, D. A., Peter, J., de Graaf, H., & Nikken, P. (2016). Adolescents' social network site use, peer appearance-related feedback, and body dissatisfaction: Testing a mediation model. *Journal of Youth and Adolescence*, *45*(1), 211–224. doi:10.100710964-015-0266-4 PMID:25788122

Dean, K. (2000). The Epidemic of Cyberstalking. *Wired News*. Retrieved from http://www.wired.com/news/politics/0,1283,35728,00.html

Dehue, F., Bolman, C., & Vollink, T. (2008). Cyberbullying: Youngsters' experiences and parental perception. *CyberPscyhology& Behavior*, *11*(2), 217–223. doi:10.1089/cpb.2007.0008 PMID:18422417

Dehue, F., Bolman, C., Vollink, T., & Pouwelse, M. (2012). Cyberbullying and traditional bullying in relation to adolescents' perceptions of parenting. *Journal of Cyber Therapy and Rehabilitation*, *5*, 25–34.

Deirmenjian, J. (1999). Stalking in Cyberspace. *The Journal of the American Academy of Psychiatry and the Law*, *27*(3), 407–413. PMID:10509940 deLara, E. W. (2012). Why adolescents don't disclose incidents of bullying and harassment. *Journal of School Violence*, *11*(4), 288–305. doi:10.1080/15388220.2012.705931

Deleuze, G., & Guattari, F. (1994). *What is Philosophy?* London: Verso.

Delmonico, D., Griffin, E., & Moriarity, J. (2001). *Cybersex Unhooked: A Workbook for Breaking Free of Compulsive Online Sexual Behaviour*. Wickenburg, AZ: Gentle Path Press.

Dempsey, A. G., Sulkowski, M. L., Nichols, R., & Storch, E. A. (2009). Differences between peer victimization in cyber and physical settings and associated psychosocial adjustment in early adolescence. *Psychology in the Schools*, *46*(10), 962–972. doi:10.1002/pits.20437

Denzin, N. K., & Lincoln, Y. S. (Eds.). (1994). *Handbook of qualitative research*. Sage Publications.

Derrida, J. (1991). "Eating Well," or the Calculation of the Subject. In E. Cadava, P. Connor, & J. L. Nancy (Eds.), *Who comes after subject* (pp. 96–119). New York: Routlege.

Derrida, J. (1997). *Of Grammatology*. Baltimore, MD: Johns Hopkins University Press.

DeSanctis, G., & Monge, P. (1999). Introduction to the Special Issue: Communication Processes for Virtual Organizations. *Organization Science*, *10*(6), 693–703. doi:10.1287/orsc.10.6.693

Descombes, V. (2004). *Le Complément de Sujet, Enquête sur le fait d'agir de soi-même*. Paris: Gallimard.

Desjarlais, M., Gilmour, J., Sinclair, J., Howell, K. B., & West, A. (2015). Predictors and social consequences of online interactive self-disclosure: A literature review from 2002 to 2014. *Cyberpsychology, Behavior, and Social Networking*, *18*(12), 718–725. doi:10.1089/cyber.2015.0109 PMID:26652672

Desjarlais, M., & Joseph, J. J. (2017). Socially interactive and passive technologies enhance friendship quality: An investigation of the mediating roles of online and offline self-disclosure. *Cyberpsychology, Behavior, and Social Networking*, *20*(5), 286–291. doi:10.1089/cyber.2016.0363 PMID:28418718

Deters, F. G., & Mehl, M. R. (2013). Does posting Facebook status updates increase or decrease loneliness? An online social networking experiment. *Social Psychological & Personality Science*, *4*(5), 579–586. doi:10.1177/1948550612469233 PMID:24224070

Deutsch, A. R. (2012). *A test of a conceptual model of sexual self-concept and its relation to other dimensions of sexuality* (Unpublished doctoral dissertation). The University of Nebraska, Lincoln, NE.

DeVito, M. A., Birnholtz, J. P., & Hancock, J. T. (2017). Platforms, people, and perception: Using affordances to understand self-presentation on social media. In *CSCW Proceedings of the 2017 ACM Conference on Computer Supported Cooperative Work and Social Computing* (pp. 740-754). ACM.

deVries, D. A. (2014). *Social media and online self-presentation: Effects on how we see ourselves and our bodies* (Unpublished doctoral dissertation). University of Amsterdam.

deVries, D. A., & Peter, J. (2013). Women on display: The effect of portraying the self online on women's self-objectification. *Computers in Human Behavior*, *29*(4), 1483–1489. doi:10.1016/j.chb.2013.01.015

Dhir, A., Pallesen, S., Torsheim, T., & Andreassen, C. S. (2016). Do age and gender differences exist in selfie-related behaviours? *Computers in Human Behavior*, *63*, 549–555. doi:10.1016/j.chb.2016.05.053

Diamanduros, T., & Downs, E. (2011). Creating a safe school environment: How to prevent cyberbullying at your school. *Library Media Connection*, *30*(2), 36–38.

Dickinson, S. L., & Glaser, R. (2005). Hostile marital interactions, proinflammatory cytokine production, and wound healing. *Archives of General Psychiatry, 62*(12), 1377–1384. doi:10.1001/archpsyc.62.12.1377 PMID:16330726

Diefenbach, S., & Christoforakos, L. (2017). The selfie paradox: Nobody seems to like them yet everyone has reasons to take them. An exploration of psychological functions of selfies in self-presentation. *Frontiers in Psychology, 8*. doi:10.3389/fpsyg.2017.00007 PMID:28144225

Diener, E., Oishi, S., & Lucas, R. E. (2003). Personality, culture, and subjective well-being: Emotional and cognitive evaluations of life. *Annual Review of Psychology, 54*(1), 403–425. doi:10.1146/annurev.psych.54.101601.145056 PMID:12172000

Diener, E., Suh, E. M., Lucas, R. E., & Smith, H. L. (1999). Subjective well-being: Three decades of progress. *Psychological Bulletin, 125*(2), 276–302. doi:10.1037/0033-2909.125.2.276

Dir, A. L., Cyders, M. A., & Coskunpinar, A. (2013). From the bar to the bed via mobile phone: A first test of the role of problematic alcohol use, sexting, and impulsivity-related traits in sexual hookups. *Computers in Human Behavior, 29*(4), 1664–1670. doi:10.1016/j.chb.2013.01.039

Donovan, F., & Bernier, K. (2009). *Cyber crime fighters: Tales from the trenches*. Indianapolis, IN: Que Publishing.

Doornwaard, S. M., Bickham, D. S., Rich, M., Vanwesenbeeck, I., van den Eijnden, R. J., & ter Bogt, T. F. (2014). Sex-related online behaviors and adolescents' body and sexual self-perceptions. *Pediatrics, 134*(6), 1103–1110. doi:10.1542/peds.2014-0592 PMID:25404728

Döring, N. (2000). Feminist Views of Cybersex: Victimization, Liberation, and Empowerment. *Cyberpsychology & Behavior, 3*(5), 863–884. doi:10.1089/10949310050191845

Döring, N., Daneback, K., Shaughnessy, K., Grov, C., & Byers, E. S. (2017). Online Sexual Activity Experiences Among College Students: A Four-Country Comparison. *Archives of Sexual Behavior, 46*(6), 1641–1652. doi:10.100710508-015-0656-4 PMID:26659580

Douglas, J. E., Ressler, R. K., Burgess, A. W., & Hartman, C. R. (1986). Criminal Profiling from Crime Scene Analysis. *Behavioral Sciences & the Law, 4*(4), 401–421. doi:10.1002/bsl.2370040405

Downing, R. W. (2005). Shoring Up the Weakest Link: What Lawmakers Around the World Need to Consider in Developing Comprehensive Laws to Combat Cybercrime. *Columbia Journal of Transnational Law, 43*, 741–762.

Drahokoupilová, J. (2007). *Cyberstalking*. Available at: http://heinonline.org/HOL/Page?handle=hein.journals/mujlt1&div=36&g_sent=1&collection=journals

Dreßing, H., Bailer, J., Anders, A., Wagner, H., & Gallas, C. (2014). Cyberstalking in a large sample of social network users: Prevalence, characteristics, and impact upon victims. *Cyberpsychology, Behavior, and Social Networking, 17*(2), 61–67. doi:10.1089/cyber.2012.0231 PMID:24106979

Drouin, M., Kaiser, D. H., & Miller, D. A. (2012). Phantom vibrations among undergraduates: Prevalence and associated psychological characteristics. *Computers in Human Behavior, 28*(4), 1490–1496. doi:10.1016/j.chb.2012.03.013

Drysdale, D. A. (2010). *Campus attacks: Targeted violence affecting institutions of higher education*. DIANE Publishing.

Duffy, A., Dawson, D. L., & das Nair, R. (2016). das Nair, R.Pornography Addiction in Adults: A Systematic Review of Definitions and Reported Impact. *Journal of Sexual Medicine, 13*(5), 760–777. doi:10.1016/j.jsxm.2016.03.002 PMID:27114191

Duggan, M. (2015). Mobile messaging and social media 2015. *The Pew Research Center*. Retrieved from http://www.pewinternet.org/2015/08/19/mobilemessaging-and-social media-2015-main-findings/

Duntley, J. D., & Buss, D. M. (2012). The evolution of stalking. *Sex Roles, 66*(5-6), 311–327. doi:10.100711199-010-9832-0

Duval, S., & Wicklund, R. A. (1972). *A theory of objective self awareness*. Oxford, UK: Academic Press.

Dyer, R., Green, R., Pitts, M., & Millward, G. (1995). What's the flaming problem? CMC - deindividuation or disinhibiting? In M. A. R. Kirby, A. J. Dix, & J. E. Finlay (Eds.), *People and computers X* (pp. 289–302). Cambridge, UK: Cambridge University Press.

Eason, K. (2014). Afterword: The past, present and future of sociotechnical systems theory. *Applied Ergonomics, 45*(2), 213–220. doi:10.1016/j.apergo.2013.09.017 PMID:24183568

Ebeling-Witte, S., Frank, M. L., & Lester, D. (2007). Shyness, internet use, andpersonality. *Cyberpsychology & Behavior, 10*(5), 713–716. doi:10.1089/cpb.2007.9964 PMID:17927542

Eden, S., Heiman, T., & Olenik-Shemesh, D. (2013). Teachers' perceptions, beliefs and concerns about cyberbullying. *British Journal of Educational Technology, 44*(6), 1036–1052. doi:10.1111/j.1467-8535.2012.01363.x

Elkind, D., & Bowen, R. (1979). Imaginary audience behavior in children and adolescents. *Developmental Psychology, 15*(1), 38–44. doi:10.1037/0012-1649.15.1.38

Elledge, L. C., Williford, A., Boulton, A. J., DePaolis, K. J., Little, T. D., & Salmivalli, C. (2013). Individual and contextual predictors of cyberbullying: The influence of children's provictim attitudes and teachers' ability to intervene. *Journal of Youth and Adolescence, 42*(5), 698–710. doi:10.100710964-013-9920-x PMID:23371005

Ellison, L. (1999). *Cyberspace 1999: Criminal, criminal justice and the internet*. Fourteenth BI LETA Conference, York, UK. Retrieved from http://www.bileta.ac.uk/99papers/ellison.htm

Ellison, L., & Akdeniz, Y. (1998). *Cyber-Stalking: the Regulation of Harassment on the Internet. In Criminal Law Review* (pp. 29–48). Crime, Criminal Justice and the Internet.

Ellison, N. B., Steinfield, C., & Lampe, C. (2007). The benefits of Facebook "friends": Social capital and college students' use of online social network sites. *Journal of Computer-Mediated Communication, 12*(4), 1143–1168. doi:10.1111/j.1083-6101.2007.00367.x

Elwell, S. J. (2014). The transmediated self: Life between the digital and the analog. *Convergence (London), 20*(2), 233–249. doi:10.1177/1354856513501423

Emerging new threat in online dating -Initial trends in internet dating initiated serious sexual assaults. (2016, May 7). [Web log post]. Retrieved from www.nationalcrimeagency.gov.uk

English, P. (2016). Twitter's diffusion in sports journalism: Role models, laggards and followers of the social media innovation. *New Media & Society, 18*(3), 484–501. doi:10.1177/1461444814544886

Erdur-Baker, O. (2010). Cyberbullying and its correlation to traditional bullying, gender and frequent and risky usage of internet-mediated communication tools. *New Media & Society, 12*(1), 109–125. doi:10.1177/1461444809341260

Espelage, D., Anderman, E. M., Brown, V. E., Jones, A., Lane, K. L., McMahon, S. D., ... Reynolds, C. R. (2013). Understanding and preventing violence directed against teachers: Recommendations for a national research, practice, and policy agenda. *The American Psychologist, 68*(2), 75–87. doi:10.1037/a0031307 PMID:23294044

Every-Palmer, S., Barry-Walsh, J., & Pathé, M. (2015). Harassment, stalking, threats and attacks targeting New Zealand politicians: A mental health issue. *The Australian and New Zealand Journal of Psychiatry, 49*(7), 634–641. doi:10.1177/0004867415583700 PMID:25954019

Fabrigar, L. R., Wegener, D. T., MacCallum, R. C., & Strahan, E. J. (1999). Evaluating the use of exploratory factor analysis in psychological research. *Psychological Methods, 4*(3), 272–299. doi:10.1037/1082-989X.4.3.272

Fanti, K. A., Demetriou, A. G., & Hawa, V. V. (2012). A longitudinal study of cyberbullying: Examining risk and protective factors. *European Journal of Developmental Psychology, 8*(2), 168–181. doi:10.1080/17405629.2011.643169

Fardouly, J., & Vartanian, L. R. (2015). Negative comparisons about one's appearance mediate the relationship between Facebook usage and body image concerns. *Body Image, 12*, 82–88. doi:10.1016/j.bodyim.2014.10.004 PMID:25462886

Feinstein, B. A., Hershenberg, R., Bhatia, V., Latack, J. A., Meuwly, N., & Davila, J. (2013). Negative social comparison on Facebook and depressive symptoms: Rumination as a mechanism. *Psychology of Popular Media Culture, 2*(3), 161–170. doi:10.1037/a0033111

Ferdinand, J. (2015). Building organisational cyber resilience: A strategic knowledge-based view of cyber securitymanagement. *Journal of Business Continuity & Emergency Planning, 9*(2), 185–195. PMID:26642176

Festinger, L. (1954). A theory of social comparison processes. *Human Relations, 7*, 117-140. doi: 10.1177001872675400700202

Festl, R., Schwarkow, M., & Quandt, T. (2013). Peer influence, internet use and cyberbullying: A comparison of different context effects among German adolescents. *Journal of Children and Media, 7*(4), 446–462. doi:10.1080/17482798.2013.781514

Field, T. (2011). Romantic Breakups, Heartbreak and Bereavement-Romantic Breakups. *Psychology (Irvine, Calif.), 2*(04), 382–387. doi:10.4236/psych.2011.24060

Finkel, E. J., Eastwick, P. W., Karney, B. R., Reis, H. T., & Sprecher, S. (2012). Online dating: A critical analysis from the perspective of psychological science. *Psychological Science in the Public Interest, 13*(1), 3–66. doi:10.1177/1529100612436522 PMID:26173279

Finn, J. (2004). A survey of online harassment at a university campus. *Journal of Interpersonal Violence, 19*(4), 468–483. doi:10.1177/0886260503262083 PMID:15038885

Fioravanti, G., Dettore, D., & Casale, S. (2012). Adolescent internet addiction: Testing the association between self-esteem, the perception of internet attributes, and preference for online social ınteractions. *Cyberpsychology, Behavior, and Social Networking, 15*(6), 318–323. doi:10.1089/cyber.2011.0358 PMID:22703038

Fiore, A. R. T. (2004). *Romantic regressions: An Analysis of Behavior in Online Dating Systems* (Mater Thesis). Retrieved from http://smg.media.mit.edu/papers/atf/fiore_thesis.pdf

Fisher, B. S., Cullen, F. T., & Turner, M. G. (2000). *The sexual victimization of college women*. Washington, DC: National Institute of Justice, Bureau of Justice Statistics. doi:10.1037/e377652004-001

Fisher, S. (1994). Identifying video game addiction in children and adolescents. *Addictive Behaviors, 19*(5), 545–553. doi:10.1016/0306-4603(94)90010-8 PMID:7832013

Flach, R.M.D., & Deslandes, S.F. (2017). Cyber dating abuse in affective and sexual relationships: a literature review. *Cadernos de Saude Publica, 33*(7). doi: 10.15090/0102-311X00138516

Floridi, L. (2011). The Construction of Personal Identities Online. *Minds and Machines*, *21*(4), 477–479. doi:10.100711023-011-9254-y

Fogel, J., & Nehmad, E. (2009). Internet social network communities: Risk taking, trust, and privacy concerns. *Computers in Human Behavior*, *25*(1), 153–160. doi:10.1016/j.chb.2008.08.006

Ford, N. (2016). *Do selfies grab our attention? Areas of interest and scan paths of Instagram profiles* (Unpublished honour's thesis). Mount Royal University, Canada.

Foucault, M. (1975). *Discipline and Punish: the Birth of the Prison*. New York: Random House.

Foucault, M. (1977). What is an Author? In D. F. Bouchard (Ed.), *Language, Counter-Memory, Practice* (pp. 124–127). New York: Cornell University Press.

Foucault, M. (1984). Of Other Spaces, Heterotopias. *Architecture, Mouvement, Continuité*, *5*, 46–49.

Foucault, M. (2012). *Order of Things*. London: Routlege.

Fox, J., & Moreland, J. J. (2015). The dark side of social networking sites: An exploration of the relational and psychological stressors associated with Facebook use and affordances. *Computers in Human Behavior*, *45*, 168–176. doi:10.1016/j.chb.2014.11.083

Fremauw, W. J., Westrup, D., & Pennypacker, J. (1997). Stalking on campus: The prevalence and strategies for coping with stalking. *Journal of Forensic Sciences*, *42*(4), 666–669. PMID:9243829

Frison, E., & Eggermont, S. (2016). Exploring the relationships between different types of Facebook use, perceived online social support, and adolescents' depressed mood. *Social Science Computer Review*, *34*(2), 153–171. doi:10.1177/0894439314567449

Furnham, A., Badmin, N., & Sneade, I. (2002). Body image dissatisfaction: Gender differences in eating attitudes, self-esteem, and reasons for exercise. *J Psychol*, *136*(6), 581–596. www.okcupid.com. doi:10.1080/00223980209604820 PMID:12523447

Gadamer, H. G. (2004). *Truth and Method*. London: Continuum.

Galassi, J. (2017). *Strengths-based school counseling: Promoting student development and achievement*. Routledge.

Gamespot. (n.d.). Retrieved July 26, 2016, from http://www.gamespot.com/

Gammack, J., Hobbs, V., & Pigott, D. (2006). *The Book of Informatics*. South Melbourne: Thomson.

Gentile, D. (2009). Pathological video game use among youth ages 8 to 18: A national study. *Psychological Science*, *20*(5), 594–602. doi:10.1111/j.1467-9280.2009.02340.x PMID:19476590

Gentzler, A. L., Oberhauser, A. M., Westerman, D., & Nadorff, D. K. (2011). College students' use of electronic communication with parents: Links to loneliness, attachment, and relationship quality. *Cyberpsychology, Behavior, and Social Networking*, *14*(1-2), 71–74. doi:10.1089/cyber.2009.0409 PMID:20973676

Gewirtz-Meydan, A., & Ayalon, L. (2017). Forever young: Visual representations of gender and age in online dating sites for older adults. *Journal of Women & Aging*, *13*, 1–19. doi:10.1080/08952841.2017.1330586 PMID:28609168

Ghoroghi, S., Hassan, S. A., & Ayub, A. F. (2017). The Influence of Religiosity and Risk Taking on Cybersex Engagement among Postgraduate Students: A Study in Malaysian Universities. *International Journal of Social Science and Humanity*, *7*(3), 143–152. doi:10.18178/ijssh.2017.V7.810

Glaser, B. G., & Strauss, A. L. (1967). *The discovery of grounded theory: Strategy for qualitative research*. Chicago: Aldine Publishing Company.

Glynn, C. J., Huge, M. E., & Hoffman, L. H. (2012). All the news that's fit to post: A profile of news use on social networking sites. *Computers in Human Behavior*, *28*(1), 113–119. doi:10.1016/j.chb.2011.08.017

Goebert, D., Else, I., Matsu, C., Chung-Do, J., & Chang, J. Y. (2011). The impact of cyberbullying on substance use and mental health in a multiethnic sample. *Maternal and Child Health Journal*, *15*(8), 1282–1286. doi:10.100710995-010-0672-x PMID:20824318

Goel, D., Subramanyam, A., & Kamath, R. (2013). A study on the prevalence of internet addiction and its association with psychopathology in Indian adolescents. *Indian Journal of Psychiatry*, *55*(2), 140–143. doi:10.4103/0019-5545.111451 PMID:23825847

Goffman, A. (1980). *Presenting the self in daily life*. Tel Aviv: Reshafim. [Hebrew]

Goffman, E. (1959). *The presentation of self in everyday life*. Westminster, MD: Random House.

Gola, M., Wordecha, M., Sescousse, G., Lew-Starowicz, M., Kossowski, B., Wypych, M., ... Marchewka, A. (2017). Can Pornography be Addictive? An fMRI Study of Men Seeking Treatment for Problematic Pornography Use. *Neuropsychopharmacology*, *42*(10), 2021–2031. doi:10.1038/npp.2017.78 PMID:28409565

Goldberg, D. P. (n.d.). *An Explanatory Study about the Impacts that Cybersex (The Use of the Internet for Sexual Purposes) is Having on Families and the Practices of Marriage and Family Therapists*. Retrieved 25 Sep., 2012, from http://scholar.lib.vt.edu/theses/available/etd- 04262004142455/unrestricted/PeterDGoldberg/Thesis/pdf

Goldberg, P. D., Peterson, B. D., Rosen, K. H., & Sara, M. L. (2008). Cybersex: The impact of a contemporary problem on the practices of marriage and family therapists. *Journal of Marital and Family Therapy*, *34*(4), 469–480. doi:10.1111/j.1752-0606.2008.00089.x PMID:19017186

Gonzales, A. L., & Hancock, J. T. (2011). Mirror, mirror on my Facebook wall: Effects of exposure to Facebook on self-esteem. *Cyberpsychology, Behavior, and Social Networking*, *14*(1-2), 79–83. doi:10.1089/cyber.2009.0411 PMID:21329447

Goode, M. (1995). Stalking: Crime of the nineties? *Criminal Law Journal*, *19*, 21–31.

Goodman, A. (1992). Sexual addiction: Designation and treatment. *Journal of Sex & Marital Therapy*, *18*(4), 303–314. doi:10.1080/00926239208412855 PMID:1291701

Gradinger, P., Strohmeier, D., & Spiel, C. (2009). Traditional bullying and cyberbullying. *The Journal of Psychology*, *217*, 205–213.

Graham, J. M. (2011). Measuring love in romantic relationships: A meta-analysis. *Journal of Social and Personal Relationships*, *28*(6), 748–771. doi:10.1177/0265407510389126

Granovetter, M. S. (1973). The strength of weak ties. *American Journal of Sociology*, *78*(6), 1360–1380. doi:10.1086/225469

Greenfield, D. (1999). *Virtual addiction: Help for netheads, cyberfreaks, and those who love them*. Oakland, CA: New Harbinger.

Greeno, E. J., Ting, L., Pecukonis, E., Hodorowicz, M., & Wade, K. (2017). The role of empathy in training social work students in motivational interviewing. *Social Work Education*, *36*(7), 794–808. doi:10.1080/02615479.2017.1346071

Greenwood, S., Perrin, A., & Duggan, M. (2016, November 11). Social media update 2016: Facebook usage and engagement is on the rise while adoption of other platforms holds steady. *Pew Research Center*. Retrieved from http://www.pewinternet.org/2016/11/11/social-media-update-2016/

Grieve, R., Indian, M., Witteveen, L., Tolan, G. A., & Marrington, J. (2013). Face-to-face or Facebook: Can social connectedness be derived online? *Computers in Human Behavior, 29*(3), 604–609. doi:10.1016/j.chb.2012.11.017

Griffiths, M. D., Kuss, D. J., & Demetrovics, Z. (2014). Social networking addiction: An overview of preliminary findings. *Behavioral addictions: Criteria, evidence and treatment*, 119-141. doi:10.1016/B978-0-12-407724-9.00006-9

Griffiths. (2015). Classification and treatment of behavioral addiction. *Nursing in Practice*. Retrieved from https://www.researchgate.net/publication/273948452

Griffiths, M. (2015). Classification and treatment of behavioral addictions. *Nursing Practice (Edinburgh, Scotland)*, 82.

Griffiths, M. D. (2005). Online therapy for addictive behaviors. *Cyberpsychology & Behavior, 8*(6), 555–561. doi:10.1089/cpb.2005.8.555 PMID:16332166

Griffiths, M. D. (2008). Diagnosis and management of video game addiction. *New Directions in Addiction Treatment and Prevention, 12*, 27–41.

Griffiths, M. D. (2009). Online computer gaming: Advice for parents and teachers. *Education for Health, 27*(1), 3.

Griffiths, M. D. (2012). Facebook addiction: Concerns, criticisms and recommendations. *Psychological Reports, 110*(2), 518–520. doi:10.2466/01.07.18.PR0.110.2.518-520 PMID:22662405

Griffiths, M. D., & Cooper, G. (2003). Online therapy: Implications for problem gamblers and clinicians. *British Journal of Guidance & Counselling, 13*(1), 113–135. doi:10.1080/0306988031000086206

Griffiths, M. D., Davies, M. N. O., & Chappell, D. (2004). Demographic factors and playing variables in online computer gaming. *Cyberpsychology & Behavior, 7*(4), 479–487. doi:10.1089/cpb.2004.7.479 PMID:15331036

Griffiths, M. D., & Hunt, N. (1998). Dependence on computer games by adolescents. *Psychological Reports, 82*(2), 475–480. doi:10.2466/pr0.1998.82.2.475 PMID:9621722

Griffiths, M. D., & Nuyens, F. (2017). An overview of structural characteristics in problematic video game playing. *Current Addiction Reports, 4*(3), 272–283. doi:10.100740429-017-0162-y PMID:28845381

Griffiths, M. D., & Whitty, M. W. (2010). Online behavioral tracking in Internet gambling research: Ethical and methodological issues. *International Journal of Internet Research Ethics, 3*, 104–117.

Griffiths, S., Mitchison, D., Murray, S. B., & Mond, J. M. (2017). Pornography use in sexual minority males: Associations with body dissatisfaction, eating disorder symptoms, thoughts about using anabolic steroids and quality of life. *The Australian and New Zealand Journal of Psychiatry, 1*, 4867417728807. doi:10.1177/0004867417728807 PMID:28891676

Grigg, D. W. (2012). Definitional constructs of cyberbullying and cyber aggression from a triagnulatory overview: A preliminary study into elements. *Journal of Aggression, Conflict and Peace Research, 4*(4), 202–215. doi:10.1108/17596591211270699

Grov, C., Bamonte, A., Fuentes, A., Parsons, J. T., Bimbi, D. S., & Morgenstern, J. (2014). Exploring the internet's role in sexual compulsivity and out of control sexual thoughts/behaviour: A qualitative study of gay and bisexual men in New York City. *Culture, Health & Sexuality, 10*(2), 107–125. doi:10.1080/13691050701564678 PMID:18247206

Grov, C., Breslow, A. S., Newcomb, M. E., Rosenberger, J. G., & Bauermeister, J. A. (2015). Gay and bisexual men's use of the Internet: Research from the 1990s through 2013. *Journal of Sex Research*, *51*(4), 390–409. doi:10.1080/00224499.2013.871626 PMID:24754360

Grov, C., Gillespie, B. J., Royce, T., & Lever, J. (2011). Perceived consequences of casual online sexual activities on heterosexual relationships: A U. S. online survey. *Archives of Sexual Behavior*, *40*(2), 429–439. doi:10.100710508-010-9598-z PMID:20174862

Grubbs, J. B., Stauner, N., Exline, J. J., Pargament, K. I., & Lindberg, M. J. (2015). Perceived addiction to Internet pornography and psychological distress: Examining relationships concurrently and over time. *Psychology of Addictive Behaviors*, *29*(4), 1056–1067. doi:10.1037/adb0000114 PMID:26372200

Grüsser, S. M., Thalemann, R., Albrecht, U., & Thalemann, C. N. (2005). ExzessiveComputernutzungimKindesalter—ErgebnisseeinerpsychometrischenErhebung. *Wiener Klinische Wochenschrift*, *117*(5-6), 188–195. PMID:15875758

Grüsser, S. M., Thalemann, R., & Griffiths, M. D. (2007). Excessive computer game playing: Evidence for addiction and aggression? *Cyberpsychology & Behavior*, *10*(2), 290–292. doi:10.1089/cpb.2006.9956 PMID:17474848

Guilbeault, D. (2016). Growing Bot Security: An Ecological View of Bot Agency. *International Journal of Communication*, *10*, 5003–5021.

Guinalíu, M., & Jordán, P. (2016). Building trust in the leader of virtual work teams. *Spanish Journal of Marketing-ESIC*, *20*(1), 58–70. doi:10.1016/j.reimke.2016.01.003

Gündüz, U., & Pembecioğlu, N. (2015). Sosyal Medya: Mizah, Muhalefet ve Direniş Pratikleri. In Sosyal Medya Araştırmaları 2: Sosyalleşen Olgular. Konya: Çizgi Publication.

Haagsma, M. C., Caplan, S. E., Peters, O., & Pieterse, M. E. (2013). A cognitive-behavioral model of problematic online kgaming in adolescents aged 12–22years. *Computers in Human Behavior*, *29*(1), 202–209. doi:10.1016/j.chb.2012.08.006

Haber, M. G., Cohen, J. L., Lucas, T., & Baltes, B. B. (2007). The relationship between self-reported received and perceived social support: A meta-analytic review. *American Journal of Community Psychology*, *39*(1-2), 133–144. doi:10.100710464-007-9100-9 PMID:17308966

Habermas, J. (1994). Philosophy and Science as Literature? In J. Habermas (Ed.), *Postmetaphysical Thinking: Philosophical Essays* (pp. 205-228). MIT Press.

Habermas, J. (1985). The Theory of Communicative Action: Vol. 1. *Reason and the Rationali-zation of Society*. Boston: Beacon Press.

Haferkamp, N., Eimler, S. C., Papadakis, A. M., & Kruck, J. V. (2012). Men are from Mars, women are from Venus? Examining gender differences in self-presentation on social networking sites. *Cyberpsychology, Behavior, and Social Networking*, *15*(2), 91–98. doi:10.1089/cyber.2011.0151 PMID:22132897

Haferkamp, N., & Krämer, N. C. (2011). Social comparison 2.0: Examining the effects of online profiles on social-networking sites. *Cyberpsychology, Behavior, and Social Networking*, *14*(5), 309–314. doi:10.1089/cyber.2010.0120 PMID:21117976

Hall, D. M. (1998). The victims of stalking. In J. R. Meloy (Ed.), *The psychology of stalking: Clinical and Forensic Perspectives* (pp. 115–136). San Diego, CA: Elsevier Science. doi:10.1016/B978-012490560-3/50025-6

Halpern, D., Katz, J. E., & Carril, C. (2017). The online ideal persona vs. the jealousy effect: Two explanations of why selfies are associated with lower-quality romantic relationships. *Telematics and Informatics*, *34*(1), 114–123. doi:10.1016/j.tele.2016.04.014

Hance, M. A., Blackhart, G., & Dew, M. (2017). Free to be me: The relationship between the true self, rejection sensitivity, and use of online dating sites. *The Journal of Social Psychology*, *12*, 1–9. doi:10.1080/00224545.2017.1389684 PMID:29023210

Hargittai, E. (2008). Whose space? Differences among users and non-users of social netwrok sites. *Journal of Computer-Mediated Communication*, *13*(1), 276–297. doi:10.1111/j.1083-6101.2007.00396.x

Harkness, E. L., Mullan, B., & Blaszczynski, A. (2015). Association between pornography use and sexual risk behaviors in adult consumers: A systematic review. *Cyberpsychology, Behavior, and Social Networking*, *18*(2), 59–71. doi:10.1089/cyber.2014.0343 PMID:25587721

Harley, H. (1996). *The Internet Complete Reference* (2nd ed.). Osborne McGraw-Hill.

Harman, G. (2013). *Tool-Being: Heidegger and the Metaphysics of Objects*. Chicago: Open Court.

Harmon, R. B., Rosner, R., & Owens, H. (1995). Obsessional harassment and erotomania in a criminal court population. *Journal of Forensic Sciences*, *40*(2), 188–196. doi:10.1520/JFS15339J PMID:7602275

Harrison, C. (2006). Cyberspace and child abuse images. *Affilia*, *21*(4), 365–379.

Hart, M. (2017). Being naked on the Internet: Young people's selfies as intimate edgework. *Journal of Youth Studies*, *20*(3), 301–315. doi:10.1080/13676261.2016.1212164

Hawkins, J. D., Smith, B. H., Hill, K. G., Kosterman, R., Catalano, R. F., & Abbott, R. D. (2003). Understanding and preventing crime and violence. In *Taking stock of delinquency* (pp. 255–312). Springer US. doi:10.1007/0-306-47945-1_8

Heijman, T., Stolte, I., Geskus, R., Matser, A., Davidovich, U., Xiridou, M., & Schim van der Loeff, M. (2016). Does online dating lead to higher sexual risk behaviour? A cross-sectional study among MSM in Amsterdam, the Netherlands. *BMC Infectious Diseases*, *14*, 16,288. doi:10.118612879-016-1637-5 PMID:27295949

Hekster, O. (2002). *Commodus: An emperor at the crossroads (Dutch monographs on ancient history and archaeology)*. Amsterdam: Brill Academic Publishers.

Helliwell, J. F., Huang, H., & Harris, A. (2009). International differences in the determinants of life satisfaction. In R. Tridip, E. Somanathan, & D. Bhaskar (Eds.), *New and enduring themes in development economics* (pp. 3–40). Singapore: World Scientific. doi:10.1142/9789812839428_0001

Henson, B., Reyns, B. W., & Fisher, B. S. (2011). Security in the 21st century. *Criminal Justice Review*, *36*(3), 253–268.

Hill, A.L., Rand, D.G., Nowak, M.A., & Christakis, N.A. (2010). Emotions as infectious diseases in a large social network: the SISa model. *Proceeding of Biological Science, 277*(1701), 3827–3835. doi: 10.1098/rspb.2010.1217

Hill, A., Briken, P., & Berner, W. (2007). Pornography and sexual abuse in the Internet. *Bundesgesundheitsblatt, Gesundheitsforschung, Gesundheitsschutz*, *50*(1), 90–102. doi:10.100700103-007-0114-8 PMID:17177094

Hinduja, S., & Patchin, J. W. (2007). Offline consequences of online victimization. *Journal of School Violence*, *6*(3), 89–112. doi:10.1300/J202v06n03_06

Hinduja, S., & Patchin, J. W. (2008). Cyberbullying: An exploratory analysis of factors related to offending and victimization. *Deviant Behavior*, *29*(2), 129–156. doi:10.1080/01639620701457816

Hinduja, S., & Patchin, J. W. (2010). Bullying, cyberbullying, and suicide. *Archives of Suicide Research, 14*(3), 206–221. doi:10.1080/13811118.2010.494133 PMID:20658375

Hinduja, S., & Patchin, J. W. (2012). Cyberbullying: Neither and epidemic nor a rarity. *European Journal of Developmental Psychology, 9*(5), 539–543. doi:10.1080/17405629.2012.706448

Hinduja, S., & Patchin, J. W. (2013). Social influences on cyberbullying behaviors among middle and high school students. *Journal of Youth and Adolescence, 42*(5), 711–722. doi:10.100710964-012-9902-4 PMID:23296318

Hirzallah, N. (2013). A Simple Exercise-to-Play Proposal that would Reduce Games Addiction and Keep players healthy. *International Journal of Advanced Computer Science and Applications, 4*(2), 86–91. doi:10.14569/IJACSA.2013.040213

Hitchcock, J. A. (2000). Cyberstalking. *Link-Up, 17*(4). Retrieved from http://www.infotoday.com/lu/ju100/hitchcock.htm

Holland, G., & Tiggemann, M. (2016). A systematic review of the impact of the use of social networking sites on body image and disordered eating outcomes. *Body Image, 17*, 100–110. doi:10.1016/j.bodyim.2016.02.008 PMID:26995158

Horrocks, C. (2000). *Marshall McLuhan and virtuality*. Cambridge: Icon Books.

Hospers, H. J., Kok, G., Harterink, P., & de Zwart, O. (2005). A new meeting place: Chatting on the Internet, e-dating and sexual risk behaviour among Dutch men who have sex with men. *AIDS (London, England), 19*(10), 1097–1101. doi:10.1097/01.aids.0000174457.08992.62 PMID:15958842

Hu, Y., Manikonda, L., & Kambhampati, S. (2014). What we instagram: A first analysis of instagram photo content and user types. In *Proceedings of AAAI International Conference on Web and Social Media.* (pp. 595-598). Ann Arbor, MI: AAAI. Retrieved from http://www.aaai.org/ocs/index.php/ICWSM/ICWSM14/paper/viewFile/8118/8087

Huang, Y., & Chou, C. (2010). An analysis of multiple factors of cyberbullying among junior high school students in Taiwan. *Computers in Human Behavior, 26*(6), 1581–1590. doi:10.1016/j.chb.2010.06.005

Huda, M., & Kartanegara, M. (2015). Islamic Spiritual Character Values of al-Zarnūjī's Ta 'līm al-Muta 'allim. Mediterranean Journal of Social Sciences, 6(4S2), 229-235.

Huda, M. (2018). (accepted for publication). Empowering Application Strategy in the Technology Adoption: Insights from Professional and Ethical Engagement. *Journal of Science and Technology Policy Management.*

Huda, M., Anshari, M., Almunawar, M. N., Shahrill, M., Tan, A., Jaidin, J. H., ... Masri, M. (2016a). Innovative Teaching in Higher Education: The Big Data Approach. *The Turkish Online Journal of Educational Technology, 15*(Special issue), 1210–1216.

Huda, M., Haron, Z., Ripin, M. N., Hehsan, A., & Yaacob, A. B. C. (2017g). Exploring Innovative Learning Environment (ILE): Big Data Era. *International Journal of Applied Engineering Research, 12*(17), 6678–6685.

Huda, M., Jasmi, K. A., Alas, Y., Qodriah, S. L., Dacholfany, M. I., & Jamsari, E. A. (2017j). Empowering Civic Responsibility: Insights From Service Learning. In S. Burton (Ed.), *Engaged Scholarship and Civic Responsibility in Higher Education* (pp. 144–165). Hershey, PA: IGI Global; doi:10.4018/978-1-5225-3649-9.ch007

Huda, M., Jasmi, K. A., Basiran, B., Mustari, M. I. B., & Sabani, A. N. (2017h). Traditional Wisdom on Sustainable Learning: An Insightful View From Al-Zarnuji's Ta 'lim al-Muta 'allim. *SAGE Open, 7*(1), 1–8. doi:10.1177/2158244017697160

Huda, M., Jasmi, K. A., Embong, W. H., Safar, J., Mohamad, A. M., Mohamed, A. K., ... Rahman, S. K. (2017d). Nurturing Compassion-Based Empathy: Innovative Approach in Higher Education. In M. Badea & M. Suditu (Eds.), *Violence Prevention and Safety Promotion in Higher Education Settings* (pp. 154–173). Hershey, PA: IGI Global. doi:10.4018/978-1-5225-2960-6.ch009

Huda, M., Jasmi, K. A., Mohamed, A. K., Wan Embong, W. H., & Safar, J. (2016d). Philosophical Investigation of Al-Zarnuji's Ta'lim al-Muta'allim: Strengthening Ethical Engagement into Teaching and Learning. *Social Science, 11*(22), 5516–5551.

Huda, M., Jasmi, K. A., Mustari, M. I., Basiron, B., Mohamed, A. K., Embong, W., ... Safar, J. (2017c). Innovative E-Therapy Service in Higher Education: Mobile Application Design. *International Journal of Interactive Mobile Technologies, 11*(4), 83–94. doi:10.3991/ijim.v11i4.6734

Huda, M., Jasmi, K. A., Shahrill, M., Hehsan, A., Mustari, M. I., Basiron, B., & Gassama, S. K. (2017a). Empowering Children with Adaptive Technology Skills: Careful Engagement in the Digital Information Age. *International Electronic Journal of Elementary Education, 9*(3), 693–708.

Huda, M., Maseleno, A., Jasmi, K. A., Mustari, I., & Basiron, B. (2017e). Strengthening Interaction from Direct to Virtual Basis: Insights from Ethical and Professional Empowerment. *International Journal of Applied Engineering Research, 12*(17), 6901–6909.

Huda, M., Maseleno, A., Muhamad, N. H. N., Jasmi, K. A., Ahmad, A., Mustari, M. I., & Basiron, B. (2018b). Big Data Emerging Technology: Insights into Innovative Environment for Online Learning Resources. *International Journal of Emerging Technologies in Learning, 13*(1), 23–36.

Huda, M., & Sabani, N. (2018). Empowering Muslim Children's Spirituality in Malay Archipelago: Integration between National Philosophical Foundations and Tawakkul (Trust in God). *International Journal of Children's Spirituality*, ▪ ▪ ▪, 1–14.

Huda, M., Sabani, N., Shahrill, M., Jasmi, K. A., Basiron, B., & Mustari, M. I. (2017i). Empowering Learning Culture as Student Identity Construction in Higher Education. In A. Shahriar & G. Syed (Eds.), *Student Culture and Identity in Higher Education* (pp. 160–179). Hershey, PA: IGI Global. doi:10.4018/978-1-5225-2551-6.ch010

Huda, M., Shahrill, M., Maseleno, A., Jasmi, K. A., Mustari, I., & Basiron, B. (2017f). Exploring Adaptive Teaching Competencies in Big Data Era. *International Journal of Emerging Technologies in Learning, 12*(3), 68–83. doi:10.3991/ijet.v12i03.6434

Huda, M., & Siregar, M., Rahman, S.K.A., Mat Teh, K.S., Said, H., Jamsari, E.A., … Ninsiana, W. (2017b). From Live Interaction to Virtual Interaction: An Exposure on the Moral Engagement in the Digital Era. *Journal of Theoretical and Applied Information Technology, 95*(19), 4964–4972.

Huda, M., Teh, K. S. M., Nor, N. H. M., & Nor, M. B. M. (2018a). Transmitting Leadership Based Civic Responsibility: Insights from Service Learning. *International Journal of Ethics and Systems, 34*(1), 20–31.

Huda, M., Yusuf, J. B., Jasmi, K. A., & Nasir, G. A. (2016b). Understanding Comprehensive Learning Requirements in the Light of al-Zarnūjī's Ta'līm al-Muta'allim. *SAGE Open, 6*(4), 1–14. doi:10.1177/2158244016670197

Huda, M., Yusuf, J. B., Jasmi, K. A., & Zakaria, G. N. (2016c). Al-Zarnūjī's Concept of Knowledge ('ilm). *SAGE Open, 6*(3), 1–13. doi:10.1177/2158244016666885

Hughes, D. J., Rowe, M., Batey, M., & Lee, A. (2012). A tale of two sites: Twitter vs. Facebook and the personality predictors of social media usage. *Computers in Human Behavior, 28*(2), 561–569. doi:10.1016/j.chb.2011.11.001

Hussain, Z., & Griffiths, M. D. (2008). Gender swapping and socialising in cyberspace: An exploratory study. *Cyberpsychology & Behavior, 11*(1), 47–53. doi:10.1089/cpb.2007.0020 PMID:18275312

Hussain, Z., & Griffiths, M. D. (2009). The attitudes, feelings, and experiences of online gamers: A qualitative analysis. *Cyberpsychology & Behavior, 12*(6), 747–753. doi:10.1089/cpb.2009.0059 PMID:19788376

Hutchins, B. (2008). Signs of meta-change in second modernity: The growth of e-sport and the World Cyber Games. *New Media & Society*, *10*(6), 851–869. doi:10.1177/1461444808096248

Hutton, S., & Haantz, S. (2003). *Cyber stalking*. Retrieved from http://www.nw3c.org

Illouz, E. (1997). *Consuming the romantic utopia: Love and the cultural contradictions of capitalism*. University of California Press.

Ingram, S. (1998). If the Profile Fits: Admitting Criminal Psychological Profiles into Evidence in Criminal Trials. *Journal of Urban and Contemporary Law*, *54*, 239–266.

Jaimesa, A., & Nicu, S. (2007). Multimodal human–computer interaction: A survey. *Computer Vision and Image Understanding*, *108*(1-2), 116–134. doi:10.1016/j.cviu.2006.10.019

Jang, H., Song, J., & Kim, R. (2014). Does the offline bully-victimization influence cyberbullying behavior among youths? Application of general strain theory. *Computers in Human Behavior*, *31*, 85–93. doi:10.1016/j.chb.2013.10.007

Jelenchick, L. A., Eickhoff, J. C., & Moreno, M. A. (2013). Facebook depression?"Social networking site use and depression in older adolescents. *The Journal of Adolescent Health*, *52*(1), 128–130. doi:10.1016/j.jadohealth.2012.05.008 PMID:23260846

Jenson, B. (1996). *Cyberstalking: Crime, enforcement and personal responsibility of the on-line world*. S.G.R. MacMillan. Retrieved from http://www.sgrm.com/art-8.htm

Jin, S. A. A., & Phua, J. (2014). Following celebrities' tweets about brands: The impact of Twitter-based electronic word-of-mouth on consumers' source credibility perception, buying intention, and social identification with celebrities. *Journal of Advertising*, *43*(2), 181–195. doi:10.1080/00913367.2013.827606

Joinson, A. (1998). Causes and implications of behavior on the Internet. In J. Gackenbach (Ed.), *Psychology and the Internet: Intrapersonal, interpersonal, and transpersonal implications* (pp. 43–60). San Diego, CA: Academic Press.

Joinson, A. N. (2001). Self-disclosure in computer-mediated communication: The role of self-awareness and visual anonymity. *European Journal of Social Psychology*, *31*(2), 177–192. doi:10.1002/ejsp.36

Joinson, A. N. (2004). Self-esteem, interpersonal risk, and preference for e-mail to face-to-face communication. *Cyberpsychology & Behavior*, *7*(4), 472–478. doi:10.1089/cpb.2004.7.472 PMID:15331035

Joinson, A. N., McKenna, K., Postmes, T., & Reips, U. D. (Eds.). (2007). *The oxford handbook of Internet psychology*. Oxford, UK: Oxford University Press.

Jose, P. E., Ryan, N., & Pryor, J. (2012). Does social connectedness promote a greater sense of well-being in adolescence over time? *Journal of Research on Adolescence*, *22*(2), 235–251. doi:10.1111/j.1532-7795.2012.00783.x

Joseph, J. J. (2017). *Examining mediating and moderating factors in the relationship between Facebook use and subjective well-being* (Unpublished honour's thesis). Mount Royal University, Canada.

Joseph, J. J., & Desjarlais, M. (2017, April). *The relationship between Facebook and subjective well-being: The mediating roles of social comparison and social connectedness*. Poster presented at the 49th Banff International Conference on Behavioural Science, Banff, AB.

Judovitz, D. (1988). *Subjectivity and representation in Descartes: The origins of modernity*. Cambridge, UK: Cambridge University.

Kamphuis, J. H., & Emmelkamp, P. M. G. (1998). Crime-related trauma: Psychological distress in victims of bank robbery. *Journal of Anxiety Disorders*, *12*(3), 199–208. doi:10.1016/S0887-6185(98)00009-7 PMID:9653679

Kamphuis, J. H., & Emmelkamp, P. M. G. (2000). Stalking—A contemporary challenge for forensic and clinical psychiatry. *The British Journal of Psychiatry*, *176*(03), 206–209. doi:10.1192/bjp.176.3.206 PMID:10755065

Kamphuis, J. H., & Emmelkamp, P. M. G. (2005). 20 years of research into violence and trauma, Past and future developments. *Journal of Interpersonal Violence*, *20*(2), 167–174. doi:10.1177/0886260504268764 PMID:15601788

Kant, I. (2009). *An Answer to the Question: What is Enlightenment?* London: Penguin.

Kara, T. (2013). *Sosyal Medya Endüstrisi. Beta Publication.*

Kardefelt-Winther, D. (2014). A conceptual and methodological critique of internet addiction research: Towards a model of compensatory internet use. *Computers in Human Behavior*, *31*, 351–354. doi:10.1016/j.chb.2013.10.059

Karmen, A. (2012). *Crime victims: an introduction to victimology.* Cengage Learning.

Kato, Y. (2015). A generation gap on mobile phone communication: The sense of discomfort experienced by digital natives when communicating with digital immigrants. *Journal of Information and Media Studies*, *1*, 31–44.

Kato, Y., & Kato, S. (2015). Reply speed to mobile text messages among Japanese college students: When a quick reply is preferred and a late reply is acceptable. *Computers in Human Behavior*, *44*, 209–219. doi:10.1016/j.chb.2014.11.047

Kato, Y., & Kato, S. (2016a). Mobile phone use during class at a Japanese women's college. In M. N. Yildiz & J. Keengwe (Eds.), *Handbook of Research on Media Literacy in the Digital Age* (pp. 436–455). Hershey, PA: IGI Global. doi:10.4018/978-1-4666-9667-9.ch021

Kato, Y., & Kato, S. (2016b). Mobile phone placement during lectures and dependency on LINE and text messaging: Survey of students at a women's university in Japan. *Journal of Socio-Informatics*, *8*(1), 28–40.

Kato, Y., Kato, S., & Chida, K. (2012). Reply timing and emotional strategy in mobile text communications of Japanese young people: replies to messages conveying four different emotions. In S. D. Long (Ed.), *Virtual Work and Human Interaction Research* (pp. 99–114). Hershey, PA: IGI Global. doi:10.4018/978-1-4666-0963-1.ch006

Kato, Y., Kato, S., & Chida, K. (2013). Reply timing as emotional strategy in mobile text communications of Japanese young people: focusing on perceptual gaps between senders and recipients. In J. E. Pelet & P. Papadopoulou (Eds.), *User Behavior in Ubiquitous Online Environments* (pp. 1–18). Hershey, PA: IGI Global.

Katz, J. E., & Crocker, E. T. (2015). Selfies| Selfies and photo messaging as visual conversation: Reports from the United States, United Kingdom and China. *International Journal of Communication*, *9*, 1861–1872. Retrieved from http://ijoc.org/index.php/ijoc/article/view/3180/1405

Keith, S., & Martin, M. E. (2005). Cyber-bullying: Creating a culture of respect in a cyber world. *Reclaiming Children and Youth*, *13*(4), 224.

Kennedy, M. A., & Taylor, M. A. (2010). Online Harassment and Victimization of College Students. *Justice Policy Journal*, *7*, 1–21.

Kibby, M., & Costello, B. (1999). 'Displaying the Phallus: Masculinity and the Performance of Sexuality on the Internet. *Men and Masculinities*, *1*(4), 352–364. doi:10.1177/1097184X99001004002

Kibby, M., & Costello, B. (2001). Between the Image and the Act: Interactive Sex Entertainment on the Internet. *Sexualities*, *4*(3), 353–369. doi:10.1177/136346001004003005

Kiecolt-Glaser, J. K., Loving, T. J., Stowell, J. R., Malarkey, W. B., Lemeshow, S., Lawson, H. M., & Leck, K. (2006). Dynamics of internet dating. *Social Science Computer Review*, *24*(2), 189–208. doi:10.1177/0894439305283402

Kienlen, K. K. (1998). Developmental and social antecedents of stalking. In J. R. Meloy (Ed.), *The psychology of stalking: Clinical and forensic perspectives* (pp. 52–65). San Diego, CA: Elsevier Science. doi:10.1016/B978-012490560-3/50022-0

Kienlen, K. K., Birmingham, D. L., Solberg, K. B., & O'Regan, J. T. (1997). A comparative study of psychotic and non-psychotic stalking. *The Journal of the American Academy of Psychiatry and the Law*, *25*(3), 317–334. PMID:9323658

Kiesler, S., Siegel, J., & McGuire, T. W. (1984). Social psychological aspects of computer mediated communication. *The American Psychologist*, *39*(10), 1123–1134. doi:10.1037/0003-066X.39.10.1123

Kim, J., La Rose, R., & Peng, W. (2009). Loneliness as the cause and the effect of problematic Internet use: The relationship between Internet use and psychological well-being. *Cyber Psychololoy and Behaviour*, *12*(4), 451-5.

Kim, J., LaRose, R., & Peng,W. (2009). Loneliness as the cause and the effect of problematic internet use: The relationship between internet use and psychological well-being. *CyberPsychology & Behavior, 12*(4), 451-455. doi: 10.1089=cpb.2008.0327

Kim, H. H. (2016). The impact of online social networking on adolescent psychological well-being (WB): A population-level analysis of Korean school aged-children. *International Journal of Adolescence and Youth*, 1–13. doi:10.1080/02673843.2016.1197135

Kim, H. S., Sherman, D. K., & Taylor, S. E. (2008). Culture and social support. *The American Psychologist*, *63*(6), 518–526. doi:10.1037/0003-066X PMID:18793039

Kim, J. W., & Chock, T. M. (2015). Body image 2.0: Associations between social grooming on Facebook and body image concerns. *Computers in Human Behavior*, *48*, 331–339. doi:10.1016/j.chb.2015.01.009

Kim, J. W., & Chock, T. M. (2017). Personality traits and psychological motivations predicting selfie posting behaviors on social networking sites. *Telematics and Informatics*, *34*(5), 560–571. doi:10.1016/j.tele.2016.11.006

Kim, J., & Lee, J. R. (2011). The Facebook paths to happiness: Effects of the number of Facebook friends and self-presentation. *Cyberpsychology, Behavior, and Social Networking*, *14*(6), 359–364. doi:10.1089/cyber.2010.0374 PMID:21117983

Kim, K., Ryu, E., Chon, M. Y., Yeun, E. J., Choi, S. Y., Seo, J. S., & Nam, B. W. (2006). Internet addiction in Korean adolescents and its re-lation to depression and suicidal ideation: A question-naire survey. *International Journal of Nursing Studies*, *43*(2), 185–192. doi:10.1016/j.ijnurstu.2005.02.005 PMID:16427966

King, S. A. (1996). *Is the Internet Addictive, or Are Addicts Using the Internet?* Retrieved February 18, 2006, from Web site: http://webpages.charter.net/stormking/iad.html

King, D. L., Delfabbro, P. H., & Griffiths, M. D. (2010). The convergence of gambling and digital media: Implications for gambling in young people. *Journal of Gambling Studies*, *26*(2), 175–187. doi:10.100710899-009-9153-9 PMID:19756979

King, D. L., Delfabbro, P. H., & Griffiths, M. D. (2011). The role of structural characteristics in problematic video game play: An empirical study. *International Journal of Mental Health and Addiction*, *9*(3), 320–333. doi:10.100711469-010-9289-y

King, D. L., Delfabbro, P. H., Griffiths, M. D., & Gradisar, M. (2011). Assessing clinical trials of Internet addiction treatment: A systematic review and CONSORT evaluation. *Clinical Psychology Review*, *31*(7), 1110–1116. doi:10.1016/j.cpr.2011.06.009 PMID:21820990

King, D. L., Delfabbro, P. H., Kaptsis, D., & Zwaans, T. (2014). Adolescent simulated gambling via digital and social media: An emerging problem. *Computers in Human Behavior*, *31*, 305–313. doi:10.1016/j.chb.2013.10.048

King, D., Delfabbro, P., & Griffiths, M. (2010). Cognitive behavioral therapy for problematic video game players: Conceptual considerations and practice issues. *Journal of Cyber Therapy and Rehabilitation*, *3*(3), 261–273.

Klewin, G., Tillmann, K. J., & Weingart, G. (2003). Violence in school. In *International handbook of violence research* (pp. 863–884). Springer Netherlands. doi:10.1007/978-0-306-48039-3_43

Kling, R. (2000). Learning About Information Technologies and Social Change: The Contribution of Social Informatics. *The Information Society*, *16*(3), 217–232. doi:10.1080/01972240050133661

Köbler, F., Riedl, C., Vetter, C., Leimeister, J. M., & Krcmar, H. (2010). Social connectedness on Facebook – An explorative study on status message usage. In *Proceedings of the 16th Americas Conference on Information Systems* (*Vol. 247*, pp. 12-15). Lima, Peru: Academic Press.

Ko, C. H., Yen, J. Y., Chen, S. H., Wang, P. W., Chen, C. S., & Yen, C. F. (2014). Evaluation of the diagnostic criteria of Internet gaming disorder in the DSM-5 among young adults in Taiwan. *Journal of Psychiatric Research*, *53*, 103–110. doi:10.1016/j.jpsychires.2014.02.008 PMID:24581573

Ko, C. H., Yen, J. Y., Chen, S. H., Yang, M. J., Lin, H. C., & Yen, C. F. (2009, July). 92009). Proposed diagnostic criteria and the screening and diagnosing tool of Internet addiction in college students. *Comprehensive Psychiatry*, *50*(4), 378–384. doi:10.1016/j.comppsych.2007.05.019 PMID:19486737

Ko, C. H., Yen, J. Y., Yen, C. F., Chen, C. S., & Chen, C. C. (2012). The association between Internet addiction and psychiatric disorder: A review of the literature. *European Psychiatry*, *27*(1), 1–8. doi:10.1016/j.eurpsy.2010.04.011 PMID:22153731

Kochenderfer-Ladd, B., & Pelletier, M. (2008). Teachers' views and beliefs about bullying: Influences on classroom management strategies and students' coping with peer victimization. *Journal of School Psychology*, *46*(4), 431–453. doi:10.1016/j.jsp.2007.07.005 PMID:19083367

Kocsis, R. N. (2006). *What Is Criminal Profiling?* Springer. doi:10.1007/978-1- 59745-109-3_1

Kohm, S. A., & Greenhill, P. (2011). Pedophile crime films as popular criminology: A problem of justice. *Theoretical Criminology*, *15*(2), 195–215. doi:10.1177/1362480610388974

Kohut, H. (1971). *The analysis of the self; a systematic approach to the psychoanalytic treatment of narcissistic personality disorders*. New York: International Universities Press.

Koo, H. Y., & Kim, S. S. (2007). Relationships among cybersex addiction, gender egalitarianism, sexual attitude and the allowance of sexual violence in adolescents. *Taehan Kanho Hakhoe Chi*, *37*(7), 1202–1211. doi:10.4040/jkan.2007.37.7.1202 PMID:18182882

Kowalski, R. M., & Limber, S. P. (2007). Electronic bullying among middle school students. *The Journal of Adolescent Health*, *41*(6), 22–30. doi:10.1016/j.jadohealth.2007.08.017 PMID:18047942

Krämer, N. C., Feurstein, M., Kluck, J. P., Meier, Y., Rother, M., & Winter, S. (2017). Beware of selfies: The impact of photo type on impression formation based on social networking profiles. *Frontiers in Psychology*, *8*. doi:10.3389/fpsyg.2017.00188 PMID:28261129

Krämer, N. C., & Winter, S. (2008). Impression management 2.0: The relationship of self-esteem, extroversion, self-efficacy, and self-presentation within social networking sites. *Journal of Media Psychology*, *20*(3), 106–116. doi:10.1027/1864-1105.20.3.106

Krasnova, H., Wenninger, H., Widjaja, T., & Buxmann, P. (2013). *Envy on Facebook: A hidden threat to users' life satisfaction?* Paper presented at the 11th International Conference on Wirtschaftsinformatik (WI), Leipzig, Germany.

Kratzer, S., & Hegerl, U. (2008). Is, "Internet Addiction" a disorder of ist own? A Study on subjects with excessive Internet use. *Psychiatrische Praxis*, *35*, 80–83. doi:10.1055-2007-970888 PMID:17546534

Kraut, R., Patterson, M., Lundmark, V., Kiesler, S., Mukopadhyay, T., & Scherlis, W. (1998). Internet Paradox: A social technology that reduces social involvement and psychological well-being? *The American Psychologist*, *53*(9), 1017–1031. doi:10.1037/0003-066X.53.9.1017 PMID:9841579

Kross, E., Verduyn, P., Demiralp, E., Park, J., Lee, S. D., Lin, N., ... Ybarra, O. (2013). Facebook use predicts declines in subjective well-being in young adults. *PLoS One*, *8*(8), e69841. doi:10.1371/journal.pone.0069841 PMID:23967061

Kübler-Ross, E. (1969). *On death and dying*. New York: Simon & Schuster.

Kühn, S., & Gallinat, J. (2014). Brain structure and functional connectivity associated with pornography consumption: The brain on porn. *JAMA Psychiatry*, *71*(7), 827–834. doi:10.1001/jamapsychiatry.2014.93 PMID:24871202

Kuss, D. J., & Griffiths, M. D. (2011). Online social networking and addiction: A review of the psychological literature. *International Journal of Environmental Research and Public Health*, *8*(12), 3528–3552. doi:10.3390/ijerph8093528 PMID:22016701

Kuss, D. J., & Griffiths, M. D. (2017). Social networking sites and addiction: Ten lessons learned. *International Journal of Environmental Research and Public Health*, *14*(3), 311. doi:10.3390/ijerph14030311 PMID:28304359

Kuss, D. J., Griffiths, M. D., & Binder, J. F. (2013). Internet addiction in students: Prevalence and risk factors. *Computers in Human Behavior*, *3*(3), 959–966. doi:10.1016/j.chb.2012.12.024

Kuss, J. D., Griffiths, M., Karila, L., & Billieux, J. (2014). Internet addiction: A systematic review of epidemiological research for the last decade. *Current Pharmaceutical Design*, *20*(25), 4026–4052. doi:10.2174/13816128113199990617 PMID:24001297

Kuyucu, M. (2015). Sosyal Medyada Mahremiyet: Türkiye'deki Twitter Kullanıcılarının Mahremiyet Anlayışı. In Sosyal Medya Araştırmaları 2: Sosyalleşen Olgular. Konya: Çizgi Publication.

Kwan, G. C. E., & Skoric, M. M. (2013). Facebook bullying: An extension of battles in school. *Computers in Human Behavior*, *29*(1), 16–25. doi:10.1016/j.chb.2012.07.014

Kyriacou, C. (2017). Dealing with cyberbullying by pupils. In All Party Parliamentary Group on Bullying (Ed.), *Evidence presented at meetings of the All Party Parliamentary Group on Bullying 2011-2016* (pp. 21-22). London: All Party Parliamentary Group on Bullying.

Laftman, S. B., Modin, B., & Ostberg, V. (2013). Cyberbullying and subjective health: A large-scale study of students in Stockholm, Sweden. *Children and Youth Services Review*, *35*(1), 112–119. doi:10.1016/j.childyouth.2012.10.020

Laier, C., Pawlikowski, M., Pekal, J., Schulte, F. P., & Brand, M. (2013). Cybersex addiction: Experienced sexual arousal when watching pornography and not real-life sexual contacts makes the difference. *Journal of Behavioral Addictions*, *2*(2), 100–107. doi:10.1556/JBA.2.2013.002 PMID:26165929

Laier, C., Pekal, J., & Brand, M. (2014). Cybersex addiction in heterosexual female users of internet pornography can be explained by gratification hypothesis. *Cyberpsychology, Behavior, and Social Networking*, *17*(8), 505–511. doi:10.1089/cyber.2013.0396 PMID:25080011

Laier, C., Pekal, J., & Brand, M. (2015). Sexual Excitability and Dysfunctional Coping Determine Cybersex Addiction in Homosexual Males. *Cyberpsychology, Behavior, and Social Networking*, *18*(10), 575–580. doi:10.1089/cyber.2015.0152 PMID:26374928

Landripet, I., & Štulhofer, A. (2015). Is Pornography Use Associated with Sexual Difficulties and Dysfunctions among Younger Heterosexual Men? *Journal of Sexual Medicine*, *12*(5), 1136–1149. doi:10.1111/jsm.12853 PMID:25816904

Langford, L. (2004). *Preventing violence and promoting safety in higher education settings: Overview of a comprehensive approach*. Higher Education Center for Alcohol and Other Drug Abuse and Violence Prevention.

Lanning, K. V. (2010). *Child Molesters: A Behavioral Analysis. National Centre for Missing & Exploited Children*. Retrieved 25 Sept. 2012, from http://www.missingkids.com/en_US/publications/NC70.pdf.02005.pdfhttp://www.the-hopeofsurvivors.com/pdf_files/Pastors_C ybersex_Addiction.pdf

Latour, B. (1987). *Science in action: How to follow scientists and engineers through society*. Cambridge, MA: Harvard University Press.

Laukyte, M. (2017). Artificial agents among us: Should we recognize them as agents proper? *Ethics and Information Technology*, *19*(1), 1–17. doi:10.100710676-016-9411-3

Lazuras, L., Barkoukis, V., Ourda, D., & Tsorbatzoudis, H. (2013). A process model of cyberbullying in adolescence. *Computers in Human Behavior*, *29*(3), 881–887. doi:10.1016/j.chb.2012.12.015

League of Legends. (n.d.). Retrieved August 1, 2015, from http://gameinfo.eune.leagueoflegends.com/en/game-info/get-started/what-is-lol/

Lee, E., Lee, J., Moon, J. H., & Sung, Y. (2015). Pictures speak louder than words: Motivations for using Instagram. *Cyberpsychology, Behavior, and Social Networking*, *18*(9), 552–556. doi:10.1089/cyber.2015.0157 PMID:26348817

Lee, J. A., & Sung, Y. (2016). Hide-and-seek: Narcissism and "Selfie"-related behavior. *Cyberpsychology, Behavior, and Social Networking*, *19*(5), 347–351. doi:10.1089/cyber.2015.0486 PMID:27028460

Lemke, R., & Merz, S. (2016). The Prevalence and Gratification of Nude Self-Presentation of Men Who Have Sex with Men in Online-Dating Environments: Attracting Attention, Empowerment, and Self-Verification. *Cyberpsychology, Behavior, and Social Networking*, *12*, 20. doi:10.1089/cyber.2016.0691

Lemke, R., & Weber, M. (2017). That Man Behind the Curtain: Investigating the Sexual Online Dating Behavior of Men Who Have Sex With Men but Hide Their Same-Sex Sexual Attraction in Offline Surroundings. *Journal of Homosexuality*, *64*(11), 1561–1582. doi:10.1080/00918369.2016.1249735 PMID:27754811

Lenhart, A. (2015). *Teens, social media & technology overview 2015*. Retrieved from: http://www.pewinternet.org/2015/04/09/teens-social-media-technology-2015/

Lenhart, A., Purcell, K., Smith, A., & Zickuhr, K. (2010). *Social Media & Mobile Internet Use among Teens and Young Adults. Pew internet & American life project*. Washington, DC: Millennials.

Lévy, P. (1997). *Cyberculture. Rapport au Conseil de l'Europe dans le cadre du projet "Nouvelles technologie: coopération culturelle et communication"*. Paris: Odile Jacob.

Lewis, A., & Griffiths, M. D. (2011). Confronting gender representation: A qualitative study of the experiences and motivations of female casual-gamers. *Aloma: Revista de Psicologia. Ciències de l'Educació i de l'Esport*, *28*, 245–272.

Lewis, C., & Fabos, B. (2005). Instant messaging, literacies, and social identities. *Reading Research Quarterly*, *40*(4), 470–501. doi:10.1598/RRQ.40.4.5

Libera, A. (2007). *Archéologie du sujet, I. Naissance du sujet*. Paris: Vrin.

Libera, A. (2008). *Archéologie du sujet, II. Quette de l'Identité*. Paris: Vrin.

Lim, M. S. C., Agius, P. A., Carrotte, E. R., Vella, A. M., & Hellard, M. E. (2017). Young Australians' use of pornography and associations with sexual risk behaviours. *Australian and New Zealand Journal of Public Health, 41*(4), 438–443. doi:10.1111/1753-6405.12678 PMID:28664609

Lincoln, S. R. (2009). *Mastering Web 2.0: Transform Your Business Using Key Website and Social Media Tools*. Kogan Page.

Lincoln, Y., & Guba, E. G. (1985). *Naturalistic inquiry*. Newbury Park, CA: Sage.

Li, Q. (2007). Bullying in the new playground: Research into cyberbullying and cybervictimization. *Australian Journal of Educational Technology, 23*, 435–454.

Li, Q. (2008). A cross-cultural comparison of adolescents' experience related to cyberbullying. *Educational Research, 50*(3), 223–234. doi:10.1080/00131880802309333

Liu, C. Y., & Yu, C. P. (2013). Can Facebook use induce well-being? *Cyberpsychology, Behavior, and Social Networking, 16*(9), 674–678. doi:10.1089/cyber.2012.0301 PMID:24028138

Livingstone, S. (2008). Taking risky opportunities in youthful content creation: Teenagers' use of social networking sites for intimacy, privacy and self-expression. *New Media & Society, 10*(3), 393–411. doi:10.1177/1461444808089415

Lobinger, K., & Brantner, C. (2015). Selfies| In the eye of the beholder: Subjective views on the authenticity of selfies. *International Journal of Communication, 9*, 1848–1860.

Logan, T., & Walker, R. (2009). Partner stalking. *Trauma, Violence & Abuse, 10*(3), 247–270. doi:10.1177/1524838009334461 PMID:19433407

Loke, S. W. (2016). Technology Trends: Working Life with 'Smart Things'. In Communicating, Networking, Interacting (pp. 13-20). Springer International Publishing.

Lopez-Fernandez, O., Honrubia-Serrano, L., Freixa-Blanxart, M., & Gibson, W. (2014). Prevalence of problematic mobile phone use in British adolescents. *Cyberpsychology, Behavior, and Social Networking, 17*(2), 91–98. doi:10.1089/cyber.2012.0260 PMID:23981147

Lou, L. L., Yan, Z., Nickerson, A., & McMorris, R. (2012). An examination of the reciprocal relationship of loneliness and Facebook use among first-year college students. *Journal of Educational Computing Research, 46*(1), 105–117. doi:10.2190/EC.46.1.e

Lucas, M., Mekary, R., Pan, A., Mirzaei, F., O'Reilly, É. J., Willett, W. C., ... Ascherio, A. (2011). Relation between clinical depression risk and physical activity and time spent watching television in older women: A 10-year prospective follow-up study. *American Journal of Epidemiology, 174*(9), 1017–1027. doi:10.1093/aje/kwr218 PMID:21984659

Lu, H. Y., Ma, L. C., Lee, T. S., Hou, H. Y., & Liao, H. Y. (2014). The link of sexual sensation seeking to acceptance of cybersex, multiple sexual partners, and one-night stands among Taiwanese college students. *The Journal of Nursing Research, 22*(3), 208–215. doi:10.1097/jnr.0000000000000043 PMID:25111114

Luor, T., Lu, H. P., Wu, L. L., & Tao, Y. H. (2010). The effect of emoticon in simplex and complex task-oriented communication: An empirical study of Instant Messaging. *Computers in Human Behavior, 26*(5), 889–895. doi:10.1016/j.chb.2010.02.003

Lup, K., Trub, L., & Rosenthal, L. (2015). Instagram# instasad?: Exploring associations among instagram use, depressive symptoms, negative social comparison, and strangers followed. *Cyberpsychology, Behavior, and Social Networking, 18*(5), 247–252. doi:10.1089/cyber.2014.0560 PMID:25965859

Lyndon, A., Bonds-Raacke, J., & Cratty, A. D. (2011). College students' Facebook stalking of ex-partners. *Cyberpsychology, Behavior, and Social Networking, 14*(12), 711–716. doi:10.1089/cyber.2010.0588 PMID:21732735

Machackova, H., Dedkova, L., & Mezulanikova, K. (2015). Brief report: The bystander effect in cyberbullying incidents. *Journal of Adolescence, 43*, 96–99. doi:10.1016/j.adolescence.2015.05.010 PMID:26070168

Machackova, H., Dedkova, L., Sevcikova, A., & Cerna, A. (2013). Bystanders' support of cyberbullied schoolmates. *Journal of Community & Applied Social Psychology, 23*(1), 25–36. doi:10.1002/casp.2135

Machlis, S. (1997). Gotcha! Computer monitors riding the web wave. *Computerworld*, 1.

Maharana & Rayaprolu. (2016). Internet Censorship In India: Is It Acting Against Freedom Or Is It Serving For The Betterment Of The Community? *Journal of Legal Studies and Research, 2*(1), 81-141.

Maheu, M. M., & Subotnik, R. B. (2001). *Infidelity on the internet: Virtual relationships and real betrayals.* Naperville, IL: Source Books.

Malach-Feins, A. (2002). *Falling in love: How we choose who to fall in love with?* Tel Aviv: Modan. (in Hebrew)

Managing your privacy. (n.d.). Retrieved from www.staysafeonline.org

Manago, A. M., Graham, M. B., Greenfield, P. M., & Salimkhan, G. (2008). Self-presentation and gender on MySpace. *Journal of Applied Developmental Psychology, 29*(6), 446–458. doi:10.1016/j.appdev.2008.07.001

Manago, A. M., Taylor, T., & Greenfield, P. M. (2012). Me and my 400 friends: The anatomy of college students' Facebook networks, their communication patterns, and well-being. *Developmental Psychology, 48*(2), 369–380. doi:10.1037/a0026338 PMID:22288367

Manago, A. M., Ward, L. M., Lemm, K. M., Reed, L., & Seabrook, R. (2015). Facebook involvement, objectified body consciousness, body shame, and sexual assertiveness in college women and men. *Sex Roles, 72*(1-2), 1–14. doi:10.100711199-014-0441-1

Manna, V., & Boursier, V. (2015a, September). *Selfie and Sexting: risky opportunities for teens on web and apps. Some preliminary results.* Paper presented at 17th National Meeting of the Italian Association of Psychology, Section of Clinical and Dynamic Psychology, Milazzo, Italy.

Manna, V., & Boursier, V. (2015b, November). *Social media connectedness, sexual exploration and self-presentation. Measuring adolescents' expectancies towards sexting and selfie.* Paper presented at the 8th International and 13th National Congress of Clinical Psychology, Granada, Spain.

Manna, V., & Boursier, V. (2017, July). *I am a sexual person: measuring sexual self-concept and attitudes towards sexuality among adolescents. An Italian study.* Paper presented at the 15th European Congress of Psychology, Amsterdam, The Netherlands.

Manovich, L. (2001). *The Language of New Media.* Cambridge: MIT Press.

Maple, C., Short, E., & Brown, A. (2011). *Cyberstalking in the United Kingdom An Analysis of the ECHO Pilot Survey.* Retrieved from http://paladinservice.co.uk/wp-content/uploads/2013/12/ECHO_Pilot_Final-Cyberstalking-in-the-UK-University-of-Bedfordshire.pdf

Marcum, C. D., Ricketts, M. L., & Higgins, G. E. (2010). Assessing sex experiences of online victimization: An examination of adolescent online behaviors utilizing Routine Activity Theory. *Criminal Justice Review*, *35*(4), 412-437.

Marcum, C. D., Ricketts, M. L., & Higgins, G. E. (2010). Assessing sex experiences of online victimization: An examination of adolescent online behaviors utilizing Routine Activity Theory. *Criminal Justice Review*, *35*(4), 412–437. doi:10.1177/0734016809360331

Marion, D., Laursen, B., Zettergren, P., & Bergman, L. R. (2013). Predicting life satisfaction during middle adulthood from peer relationships during mid-adolescence. *Journal of Youth and Adolescence*, *42*(8), 1299–1307. doi:10.100710964-013-9969-6 PMID:23771820

Mark, B. H. (2006). *Sexual Addiction and Marriage and Family therapy: Facilitating Individual and Relationship Healing through Couple Therapy*. Retrieved 25 Sep., 2012, from http://scholar.lib.vt.edu/theses/available/etd04272009102213/unrestricted/MarkBirdDissertation

Martins, A., Pereira, M., Andrade, R., Dattilio, F. M., Narciso, I., & Canavarro, M. C. (2016). Infidelity in Dating Relationships: Gender-Specific Correlates of Face-to-Face and Online Extradyadic Involvement. *Archives of Sexual Behavior*, *45*(1), 193–205. doi:10.100710508-015-0576-3 PMID:26194971

Maseleno, A., Pardimin, Huda, M., Ramlan, Hehsan, A., Yusof, Y.M., Haron, Z., Ripin, M.N., Nor, N.H.M., and Junaidi, J. (2018). Mathematical Theory of Evidence to Subject Expertise Diagnostic. *ICIC Express Letters*, *12*(4), 369. doi:10.24507/icicel.12.04.369

Maseleno, A., Huda, M., Siregar, M., Ahmad, R., Hehsan, A., Haron, Z., ... Jasmi, K. A. (2017). Combining the Previous Measure of Evidence to Educational Entrance Examination. *Journal of Artificial Intelligence*, *10*(3), 85–90. doi:10.3923/jai.2017.85.90

Mason, K. (2008). Cyberbullying: A preliminary assessment for school personnel. *Psychology in the Schools*, *45*(4), 323–348. doi:10.1002/pits.20301

Masuda, M. (2003). Meta-analyses of love scales: Do various love scales measure the same psychological constructs? *Japanese Psychological Journal*, *45*, 25–37. doi:10.1111/1468-5884.00030

Matheson, K. (1991). Social cues in computer-mediated negotiations: Gender makes a difference. *Computers in Human Behavior*, *7*(3), 137–145. doi:10.1016/0747-5632(91)90003-J

Matheson, K., & Zanna, M. P. (1988). The impact of computer-mediated communication on self-awareness. *Computers in Human Behavior*, *4*(3), 221–233. doi:10.1016/0747-5632(88)90015-5

Mayers, G. (2003). *Social psychology*. McGraw-Hill Ryerson.

McAndrew, F. T., & Jeong, H. S. (2012). Who does what on Facebook? Age, sex, and relationship status as predictors of Facebook use. *Computers in Human Behavior*, *28*(6), 2359–2365. doi:10.1016/j.chb.2012.07.007

McCain, J. L., Borg, Z. G., Rothenberg, A. H., Churillo, K. M., Weiler, P., & Campbell, W. K. (2016). Personality and selfies: Narcissism and the dark triad. *Computers in Human Behavior*, *64*, 126–133. doi:10.1016/j.chb.2016.06.050

McCann, J. T. (2000). A descriptive study of child and adolescent obsessional followers. *Journal of Forensic Sciences*, *45*(1), 195–199. doi:10.1520/JFS14660J PMID:10641939

McCormick, R. (2013). *League of Legends' eSports finals watched by 32 million people*. Retrieved June 8, 2016, from http://www.theverge.com/2013/11/19/5123724/league-of-legends-world-championship-32-million-viewers

McEwan, T. E., Mullen, P. E., & MacKenzie, R. (2009). A study of the predictors of persistence in stalking situations. *Law and Human Behavior*, *33*(2), 149–158. doi:10.100710979-008-9141-0 PMID:18626757

McFarlane, L., & Bocij, P. (2003). An exploration of predatory behavior in cyberspace: Towards a typology of cyber-stalkers. *First Monday*, *8*(9), 1–12. doi:10.5210/fm.v8i9.1076

McGrath, M., & Casey, E. (2002). Forensic Psychiatry and the Internet: Practical Perspectives on Sexual Predators and Obsessional Harassers in Cyberspace. *The Journal of the American Academy of Psychiatry and the Law*, *30*(1), 81–94. PMID:11931372

McGuire, T. W., Kiesler, S., & Siegel, J. (1987). Group and computer-mediated discussion effects in risk decision making. *Journal of Personality and Social Psychology*, *52*(5), 917–930. doi:10.1037/0022-3514.52.5.917

McKenna, K. Y. A., & Bargh, J. A. (2000). Plan 9 from cyberspace: The implications of the internet for personality and social psychology. *Personality and Social Psychology Review*, *4*(1), 57–75. doi:10.1207/S15327957PSPR0401_6

McKenna, K. Y., Green, A. S., & Gleason, M. E. (2002). Relationship formation on the Internet: What's the big attraction? *The Journal of Social Issues*, *58*(1), 9–31. doi:10.1111/1540-4560.00246

McKie, R. M., Milhausen, R. R., & Lachowsky, N. J. (2017). "Hedge Your Bets": Technology's Role in Young Gay Men's Relationship Challenges. *Journal of Homosexuality*, *64*(1), 75–94. doi:10.1080/00918369.2016.1172883 PMID:27042757

McKinley, N. M., & Hyde, J. S. (1996). The objectified body consciousness scale development and validation. *Psychology of Women Quarterly*, *20*(2), 181–215. doi:10.1111/j.1471-6402.1996.tb00467.x

McKinnon, M. (2015, January 12). 2015 Canadian social media usage statistics. *Canadians Internet*. Retrieved from http://canadiansinternet.com/2015-canadian-social-media-usage-statistics/

McLean, S. A., Paxton, S. J., Wertheim, E. H., & Masters, J. (2015). Photoshopping the selfie: Self photo editing and photo investment are associated with body dissatisfaction in adolescent girls. *International Journal of Eating Disorders*, *48*(8), 1132–1140. doi:10.1002/eat.22449 PMID:26311205

McQuade, C. S., Colt, P. J., & Meyer, B. N. (2009). *Cyber bullying: Protecting kids and adults from online bullies*. Westport, CT: Praeger.

McRae, S. (1996). Coming Apart at the Seams: Sex, Text and the Virtual Body. In L. Cherny & E. R. Weise (Eds.), *Wired Women. Gender and New Realities in Cyberspace* (pp. 242–264). Seattle, WA: Seal Press.

Meena, P. S., Mittal, P. K., & Solanki, R. K. (2012). Problematic use of social networking sites among urban school going teenagers. *Indian Journal of Psychiatry*, *21*(2), 94–97. doi:10.4103/0972-6748.119589 PMID:24250039

Meerkerk, G.J., Van Den Eijnden, R. J. J. M., Vermulst, A. A., & Garretsen, H. F. L. (2009). The Compulsive Internet Use Scale (CIUS): some psychometric properties: the impact of the Internet, multimediaand virtual reality on behavior and society. *Cyber Psychology & Behavior*, *12*(1), 1–6.

Mehdizadeh, S. (2010). Self-presentation 2.0: Narcissism and self-esteem on Facebook. *CyberPsychology, Behavior, and Social Networking, 13*(4), 357-364. doi: 10.1089=cyber.2009.0257

Meier, E. P., & Gray, J. (2014). Facebook photo activity associated with body image disturbance in adolescent girls. *Cyberpsychology, Behavior, and Social Networking*, *17*(4), 199–206. doi:10.1089/cyber.2013.0305 PMID:24237288

Meloy, J. R. (1996). Stalking (obsessional following): A review of some preliminary studies. *Aggression and Violent Behavior*, *1*(2), 147–162. doi:10.1016/1359-1789(95)00013-5

Meloy, J. R. (1998). The Psychology of stalking. In J. R. Meloy (Ed.), *The psychology of stalking: Clinical and forensic perspectives* (pp. 2–21). San Diego, CA: Elsevier Science. doi:10.1016/B978-012490560-3/50020-7

Meloy, J. R., & Gothard, S. (1995). Demographic and clinical comparison of obsessional followers and offenders with mental disorders. *The American Journal of Psychiatry, 152*(2), 25826. PMID:7840361

Ménard, K. S., & Pincus, A. L. (2012). Predicting overt and cyber stalking perpetration by male and female college students. *Journal of Interpersonal Violence, 27*(11), 2183–2207. doi:10.1177/0886260511432144 PMID:22203630

Mendelson, A. L., & Papacharissi, Z. 2010. Look at us: collective narcissism in college student Facebook photo galleries. In Papacharissi (Ed.), The networked self: Identity, Community and Culture on Social Network Sites (pp. 251–273). New York: Routledge.

Menkin, J. A., Robles, T. F., Wiley, J. F., & Gonzaga, G. C. (2015). Online dating across the life span: Users' relationship goals. *Psychology and Aging, 30*(4), 987–993. doi:10.1037/a0039722 PMID:26479015

Michalos, A. C. (1985). Multiple discrepancies theory (MDT). *Social Indicators Research, 16*(4), 347–413. doi:10.1007/BF00333288

Mileham, B. L. (2007). Online infidelity in Internet chat rooms: An ethnographic exploration. *Computers in Human Behavior, 23*(1), 11–31. doi:10.1016/j.chb.2004.03.033

Miller, B. N., & Morris, R. G. 2012. Cyber-related violence. In Violent offenders: Theory, research, policy and practice. London: Jones & Bartlett Learning.

Miller, D. (1999). *Principles of social justice.* Academic Press.

Miller, G. (1999). Gore to release cyberstalking report, call for tougher laws. *Latimes.com.* Retrieved from http://www.latimes.com/news/ploitics/elect2000/pres/gore

Miller, T., Lawrence, G. A., McKay, J., & Rowe, D. (2001). *Globalization and Sport: Playing the World.* London: SAGE Publications Ltd.

Ministry of Internal Affairs and Communications. (2015). *White paper 2015: Information and communications in Japan.* Retrieved November 12, 2016, from http://www.soumu.go.jp/johotsusintokei/whitepaper/eng/WP2015/2015-index.html/

Ministry of Internal Affairs and Communications. (2016). *White paper 2016: Information and communications in Japan.* Retrieved January 15, 2015, from http://www.soumu.go.jp/johotsusintokei/whitepaper/eng/WP2016/2016-index.html/

Mitchell, K. J., Ybarra, M., & Finkelhor, D. (2007). The relative importance of online victimization in understanding depression, delinquency, and substance use. *Child Maltreatment, 12*(4), 314–324. doi:10.1177/1077559507305996 PMID:17954938

Mitchell, K., Becker-Blease, K., & Finkelhor, D. (2005). Inventory of problematic Internet experiences encountered in clinical practice. *Professional Psychology, 36*(5), 498–509. doi:10.1037/0735-7028.36.5.498

Mitchell, K., Finkelhor, D., & Wolak, J. (2001). Risk factors for and impact of online sexual solicitation of youth. *Journal of the American Medical Association, 285*(23), 3011–3014. doi:10.1001/jama.285.23.3011 PMID:11410100

Mitchell, K., Finkelhor, D., & Wolak, J. (2003). The exposure of youth to unwanted sexual material on the Internet: A national survey of risk, impact and prevention. *Youth & Society, 34*(3), 300–358. doi:10.1177/0044118X02250123

Mitchell, K., Finkelhor, D., & Wolak, J. (2007). Youth Internet users at risk for the more serious online sexual solicitations. *American Journal of Preventive Medicine, 32*(6), 532–537. doi:10.1016/j.amepre.2007.02.001 PMID:17533070

Mohandie, K., Meloy, J. R., McGowan, M., & Williams, J. (2006). The RECON typology of stalking: Reliability and validity based upon a large sample of North American stalkers. *Journal of Forensic Sciences*, *51*(1), 147–155. doi:10.1111/j.1556-4029.2005.00030.x PMID:16423242

Moksin, A. I., Shahrill, M., Anshari, M., Huda, M., & Tengah, K. A. (2018). The Learning of Integration in Calculus Using the Autograph Technology. *Advanced Science Letters*, *24*(1), 550–552.

Moncura, W., Orzecha, K. M., & Nevilleb, F. G. (2016). Fraping, social norms and online representations of self. *Computers in Human Behavior*, *63*, 125–131. doi:10.1016/j.chb.2016.05.042

Moon, J. H., Lee, E., Lee, J., Choi, T. R., & Sung, Y. (2016). The role of narcissism in self-promotion on Instagram. *Personality and Individual Differences*, *10*, 122–125. doi:10.1016/j.paid.2016.05.042

Morrison, K. (2001). Predicting Violent Behavior in Stalkers: A Preliminary Investigation of Canadian Cases in Criminal Harassment. *Journal of Forensic Sciences*, *46*(6), 1403-1410. 10.1520/JFS15163J

Mouaffak, F., Leite, C., Hamzaoui, S., Benyamina, A., Laqueille, X., & Kebir, O. (2017). Naltrexone in the Treatment of Broadly Defined Behavioral Addictions: A Review and Meta-Analysis of Randomized Controlled Trials. *European Addiction Research*, *23*(4), 204–210. doi:10.1159/000480539 PMID:28877518

Mouttapa, M., Valente, T., Gallagher, P., Rohrbach, L. A., & Unger, J. B. (2004). Social network predictor of bullying and victimization. *Adolescence*, *39*, 315–335. PMID:15563041

Mowshowitz, A. (1999). The switching principle in virtual organization. In P. Sieber & J. Griese (Eds.), *Organizational Virtualness and Electronic Commerce* (pp. 9–20). Simova Verlag.

Mowshowitz, A., & Kawaguchi, A. (2005). Quantifying the switching model of virtual organization. *Journal of Information Technology Theory and Application*, *6*(4), 53–74.

Mullen, P. E., Pathé, M., & Purcell, R. (2000). *Stalkers and their victims*. Cambridge, UK: Cambridge University Press. doi:10.1017/CBO9781139106863

Mullen, P. E., Pathé, M., Purcell, R., & Stuart, G. W. (1999). A study of stalkers. *The American Journal of Psychiatry*, *156*, 1244–1249. PMID:10450267

Müller, K. W., Glaesmer, H., Brähler, E., Woelfling, K., & Beutel, M. E. (2014). Prevalence of internet addiction in the general population: Results from a German population-based survey. *Behaviour & Information Technology*, *33*(7), 757–766. doi:10.1080/0144929X.2013.810778

Murphey, B. (1996). Computer addictions entangle students. *APA Monitor*, 38.

Murphy, A. L., & Van Brunt, B. (2016). *Uprooting Sexual Violence in Higher Education: A Guide for Practitioners and Faculty*. Taylor & Francis.

Muscanell, N. L., & Guadagno, R. E. (2012). Make new friends or keep the old: Gender and personality differences in social networking use. *Computers in Human Behavior*, *28*(1), 107–112. doi:10.1016/j.chb.2011.08.016

Muthen, L. K., & Muthén, B. O. (2010). Mplus user's guide, v. 6.1. Los Angeles, CA: Muthen and Muthen, UCLA.

Nael Hirzallah, A. (2013). Simple exercise to play proposal that would reduce game addiction and keep players healthy. *International Journal of Advanced Computer Science and Applications*, *2*(2).

Nalwa, K., & Anand, A. P. (2003). Internet addiction in students: A cause of concern. *Cyberpsychology & Behavior*, *6*(6), 653–656. doi:10.1089/109493103322725441 PMID:14756932

Natus Vincere. (n.d.). Retrieved July 21, 2016, from http://navi-gaming.com/en

Nesi, J., & Prinstein, M. J. (2015). Using social media for social comparison and feedback-seeking: Gender and popularity moderate associations with depressive symptoms. *Journal of Abnormal Child Psychology*, *43*(8), 1427–1438. doi:10.100710802-015-0020-0 PMID:25899879

Newborne, E. (1997). Bosses worry Net access will cut productivity. *USA Today*, p. 4B.

O'Brien, J., & Shapiro, E. (2004). Doing It" on the Web: Emerging Discourses on Internet Sex. In D. Gauntlett & R. Horsley (Eds.), *Web Studies* (pp. 114–126). London: Arnold.

O'Connell, R., Barrow, C., & Sange, S. (2002). *Young peoples use of chat rooms: Implications for policy strategies and programs of education*. Retrieved November 1, 2005, from http://www.uclan.ac.uk/host/cru/ publications.htm

O'Hara, K., Massimi, M., Harper, R., Rubens, S., & Morris, J. (2014). Everyday dwelling with WhatsApp. *Proceedings of the 17th ACM conference on Computer supported cooperative work & social computing*, 1131-1143.

O'Keeffe, G. S., & Clarke-Pearson, K. (2011). The impact of social media on children, adolescents, and families. *Pediatrics*, *127*(4), 800–804. doi:10.1542/peds.2011-0054 PMID:21444588

Oberst, U., Wegmann, E., Stodt, B., Brand, M., & Chamarro, A. (2017). Negative consequences from heavy social networking in adolescents: The mediating role of fear of missing out. *Journal of Adolescence*, *55*, 51–60. doi:10.1016/j.adolescence.2016.12.008 PMID:28033503

Ogilvie, E. (2000). *Cyberstalking, trends and ıssues in crime and criminal justice*. Retrieved from http://www.aic. gov.au

Ogilvie, G. S., Taylor, D. L., Trussler, T., Marchand, R., Gilbert, M., Moniruzzaman, A., & Rekart, M. L. (2008). Seeking sexual partners on the internet: A marker for risky sexual behaviour in men who have sex with men. *Canadian Journal of Public Health*, *99*(3), 185–198. PMID:18615938

Oldmeadow, J. A., Quinn, S., & Kowert, R. (2013). Attachment style, social skills, and Facebook use amongst adults. *Computers in Human Behavior*, *29*(3), 1142–1149. doi:10.1016/j.chb.2012.10.006

Olenik-Shemesh, D., Heiman, T., & Eden, S. (2012). Cyberbullying victimisation in adolescence: Relationships with loneliness and depressive mood. *Emotional & Behavioural Difficulties*, *17*(3-4), 361–374. doi:10.1080/13632752.2012.704227

Olweus, D. (1993). *Bullying at school. What we know and what we can do*. Malden, MA: Blackwell Publishing.

Orth, U., Robins, R. W., Widaman, K. F., & Conger, R. D. (2014). Is Low Self-Esteem a Risk Factor for Depression? Findings from a Longitudinal study of Mexican-Origin Youth. *Developmental Psychology*, *50*(2), 622–633. doi:10.1037/a0033817 PMID:23895172

Othman, R., Shahrill, M., Mundia, L., Tan, A., & Huda, M. (2016). Investigating the Relationship Between the Student's Ability and Learning Preferences: Evidence from Year 7 Mathematics Students. *The New Educational Review*, *44*(2), 125–138.

Pantic, I. (2014). Online social networking and mental health. *Cyberpsychology, Behavior, and Social Networking*, *17*(10), 652–657. doi:10.1089/cyber.2014.0070 PMID:25192305

Pantic, I., Damjanovic, A., Todorovic, J., Topalovic, D., Bojovic-Jovic, D., Ristic, S., & Pantic, S. (2012). Association between online social networking and depression in high-school students: Behavioral physiology viewpoint. *Psychiatria Danubina*, *24*, 90–93. PMID:22447092

Park, S., Lee, S. W., Kwak, J., Cha, M., & Jeong, B. (2013). Activities on Facebook reveal the depressive state of users. *Journal of Medical Internet Research*, *15*(10), 1–15. doi:10.2196/jmir.2718 PMID:24084314

Patchin, J. W., & Hinduja, S. (2006). Bullies move beyond the schoolyard: A preliminary look at cyberbullying. *Youth Violence and Juvenile Justice*, *4*(2), 148–169. doi:10.1177/1541204006286288

Pathé, M. (2002). *Surviving stalking*. London: Cambridge University Press. doi:10.1017/CBO9780511544200

Pathé, M., & Mullen, P. E. (2002). The victim of stalking. In J. Boon & L. Sheridan (Eds.), *Stalking and Psychosexual Obsession: Psychological Perspectives for Prevention, Policing and Treatment* (pp. 1–22). West Sussex, UK: Wiley. doi:10.1002/9780470713037.ch1

Path, M., & Mullen, P. E. (1997). Article. *The British Journal of Psychiatry*, *170*(1), 12–17. doi:10.1192/bjp.170.1.12 PMID:9068768

Patton, C. L., Nobles, M. R., & Fox, K. A. (2010). Look who's stalking: Obsessive pursuit and attachment theory. *Journal of Criminal Justice*, *38*(3), 282–290. doi:10.1016/j.jcrimjus.2010.02.013

Patton, N. Q. (1990). *Qualitative evaluation and research methods* (2nd ed.). Newbury Park, CA: Sage.

Paul, A. (2014). Cyber psychology, behaviour, and social networking. *Oct-Vol.*, *17*(10), 664–667.

Paul, A. (2014). Is online better than offline for meeting partners? Depends: Are you looking to marry or to date? *Cyberpsychology, Behavior, and Social Networking*, *17*(10), 664–667. doi:10.1089/cyber.2014.0302 PMID:25226176

Paulhus, D. L., & Vazire, S. (2007). The self-report method. Handbook of Research Methods in Personality Psychology, 1, 224-239.

Paullet, K. L., Rota, D. R., & Swan, T. T. (2009). Cyberstalking: An exploratory study of students at a mid-Atlantic university. *Issues in Information Systems*, *2*, 640–649.

Pavot, W., & Diener, E. (2004). The subjective evaluation of well-being in adulthood: Findings andimplications. *Ageing International*, *29*(2), 113–135. doi:10.100712126-004-1013-4

Peichi, C. (2008). New Media for Social Change: Globalisation and the Online Gaming Industries of South Korea and Singapore. *Science, Technology & Society*, *13*(2), 303–323. doi:10.1177/097172180801300207

Pelosi, A., Zorzi, G., & Corsano, P. (2014). The Body Image Control in Photos questionnaire (BICP). *BPA-Applied Psychology Bulletin (Bollettino di Psicologia Applicata)*, *62*(269).

Perren, S., Dooley, J., Shaw, T., & Cross, D. (2010). Bullying in school and cyberspace: Associations with depressive symptoms in Swiss and Australian adolescents. *Child and Adolescent Psychiatry and Mental Health*, *4*(1), 1–10. doi:10.1186/1753-2000-4-28 PMID:21092266

Perry, S. L. (2017). Pornography Use and Marital Separation: Evidence from Two-Wave Panel Data. *Archives of Sexual Behavior*, *46*, 549–559. doi:10.100710508-016-0770-y PMID:28936726

Perry, S. L., & Schleifer, C. (2017). Till Porn Do Us Part? A Longitudinal Examination of Pornography Use and Divorce. *Journal of Sex Research*, 1–13. doi:10.1080/00224499.2017.1404959 PMID:28497988

Petherick, W. (2001). *Cyberstalking: Obsessional pursuit and the digital criminal*. Retrieved from http://www.crimelibrary.com/criminology/cyberstalking/index.html

Petrocelli, J. (2005). Cyber stalking. *Law and Order*, *53*(12), 56–58.

Petry, N. M., & O'Brien, C. P. (2013). Internet gaming disorder and the DSM-5. *Addiction (Abingdon, England), 108*(7), 1186–1187. doi:10.1111/add.12162 PMID:23668389

Pew Internet Research Center. (2003). *Internet use by region in the United States*. Retrieved fromhttp://www.pewinternet.org/reports

Pew Research Center. (2017, January 12). Social media fact sheet. *Pew Research Center.* Retrieved from http://www.pewinternet.org/fact-sheet/social-media/

Phua, J., Jin, S. V., & Kim, J. (2017). Uses and gratifications of social networking sites for bridging and bonding social capital: A comparison of Facebook, Twitter, Instagram, and Snapchat. *Computers in Human Behavior, 72*, 115–122. doi:10.1016/j.chb.2017.02.041

Pinch, T., & Bijker, W. (1986). Science, relativism and the new sociology of technology: Reply to Russell. *Social Studies of Science, 16*(2), 347–360. doi:10.1177/0306312786016002009

Pingel, E. S., Bauermeister, J. A., Johns, M. M., Eisenberg, A., & Leslie-Santana, M. (2013). "A safe way to explore": Reframing risk on the Internet amidst young gay men's search for identity. *Journal of Adolescent Research, 28*(4), 453–478. doi:10.1177/0743558412470985 PMID:25525293

Pittman, M. (2015). Creating, consuming, and connecting: Examining the relationship between social media engagement and loneliness. *The Journal of Social Media in Society, 4*, 66–98. Retrieved from http://www.thejsms.org/tsmri/index.php/TSMRI/article/view/92

Pittman, M., & Reich, B. (2016). Social media and loneliness: Why an Instagram picture may be worth more than a thousand Twitter words. *Computers in Human Behavior, 62*, 155–167. doi:10.1016/j.chb.2016.03.084

Plaga, J. A., Kosnik, W., Lacson, F., Thomas, J., & Whitmore, M. (2016, September). Recent Trends in Human Systems Integration. *Proceedings of the Human Factors and Ergonomics Society Annual Meeting, 60*(1), 494–498. doi:10.1177/1541931213601112

Pollet, T. V., Roberts, S. G., & Dunbar, R. I. (2011). Use of social network sites and instant messaging does not lead to increased offline social network size, or to emotionally closer relationships with offline network members. *Cyberpsychology, Behavior, and Social Networking, 14*(4), 253–258. doi:10.1089/cyber.2010.0161 PMID:21067280

Pornari, C. D., & Wood, J. (2010). Peer and cyber aggression in secondary school students: The role of moral disengagement, hostile attribution bias, and outcome expectancies. *Aggressive Behavior, 36*(2), 81–94. doi:10.1002/ab.20336 PMID:20035548

Porter, G., Starcevic, V., Berle, D., & Fenech, P. (2010). Recognizing problem video game use. *The Australian and New Zealand Journal of Psychiatry, 44*(2), 120–128. doi:10.3109/00048670903279812 PMID:20113300

Portland State University. (2012). *Prevention of Cyberstalking: A Review of the Literature*. Criminology and Criminal Justice Senior Capstone Project. Retrieved from http://pdxscholar.library.pdx.edu/ccj_capstone/1

Pratt, D. R., Zyda, M., & Kelleher, K. (1995). Virtual reality: In the mind of the beholder. *IEEE Computer, 28*(7), 17–19.

Prensky, M. (2001a). Digital natives, digital immigrants. *On the Horizon, 9*(5), 1–6. doi:10.1108/10748120110424816

Prensky, M. (2001b). Digital natives, digital immigrants, part II: Do they really think differently? *On the Horizon, 9*(6), 1–6. doi:10.1108/10748120110424843

Press Release. (1996). *Surf's up! Is productivity down?* Robert Half International.

Prestage, G., Bavinton, B., Grierson, J., Down, I., Keen, P., Bradley, J., & Duncan, D. (2015). Online dating among Australian gay and bisexual men: Romance or hooking up? *AIDS and Behavior, 19*(10), 1905–1913. doi:10.100710461-015-1032-z PMID:25777506

Prins, H. (2005). Mental disorder and violent crime: A problematic relationship. *Probation Journal, 52*(4), 333–357. doi:10.1177/0264550505058033

Prins, H. (2005). *Mental disorder and violent crime: A problematic relationship.* Probation.

Przybylski, A. K., Murayama, K., DeHaan, C. R., & Gladwell, V. (2013). Motivational, emotional, and behavioral correlates of fear of missing out. *Computers in Human Behavior, 29*(4), 1841–1848. doi:10.1016/j.chb.2013.02.014

Purcell, R., Pathé, M., & Mullen, P. E. (2002). The prevalence and nature of stalking in the Australian community. *The Australian and New Zealand Journal of Psychiatry, 36*(1), 114–120. doi:10.1046/j.1440-1614.2002.00985.x PMID:11929447

Purcell, R., Pathé, M., & Mullen, P. E. (2004). Stalking: Defining and prosecuting a new category of offending. *International Journal of Law and Psychiatry, 27*(2), 157–169. doi:10.1016/j.ijlp.2004.01.006 PMID:15063640

Purcell, R., Pathé, M., & Mullen, P. E. (2005). The association between stalking victimization and psychiatric morbidity in a random community sample. *The British Journal of Psychiatry, 187*(05), 416–420. doi:10.1192/bjp.187.5.416 PMID:16260815

Quittner, J. (1997, April 14). Divorce Internet Style. *Time*, 72.

Ramirez, A. Jr, & Broneck, K. (2009). IM me': Instant messaging as relational maintenance and everyday communication. *Journal of Social and Personal Relationships, 26*(2-3), 291–314. doi:10.1177/0265407509106719

Re, D. E., Wang, S. A., He, J. C., & Rule, N. O. (2016). Selfie indulgence: Self-favoring biases in perceptions of selfies. *Social Psychological & Personality Science, 7*(6), 588–596. doi:10.1177/1948550616644299

Reed, L. A., Tolman, R. M., & Ward, L. M. (2017). Gender matters: Experiences and consequences of digital dating abuse victimization in adolescent dating relationships. *Journal of Adolescence, 59*, 79–89. doi:10.1016/j.adolescence.2017.05.015 PMID:28582653

Regan, P. C., Levin, L., Sprecher, S., Christopher, F. S., & Cate, R. (2000). Partner preferences: What characteristics do men and women desire in their short-term sexual and long-term romantic partners? *Journal of Psychology & Human Sexuality, 123*(3), 1–21. doi:10.1300/J056v12n03_01

Reinecke, L., & Trepte, S. (2014). Authenticity and well-being on social network sites: A two-wave longitudinal study on the effects of online authenticity and the positivity bias in SNS communication. *Computers in Human Behavior, 30*, 95–102. doi:10.1016/j.chb.2013.07.030

Report on Cyberstalking. (1999, August). *Cyberstalking: A new challenge for law enforcement and industry.* A Report from the Attorney General to The Vice President. Retrieved from http://www.usdoj.gov/criminal/ cybercrime/cyberstalking.htm

Rettberg, J. W. (2017). *Self-Representation in Social Media.* Academic Press.

Reyns, B. W. (2010). A situational crime prevention approach to cyberstalking victimization: Preventive tactics for Internet users and online place managers. *Crime Prevention and Community Safety, 12*(2), 99–118. doi:10.1057/cpcs.2009.22

Reyns, B. W., Henson, B., & Fisher, B. S. (2011). Being pursued online: Applying cyberlifestyle- routine activities theory to cyberstalking victimization. *Criminal Justice and Behavior, 38*(11), 1149–1169. doi:10.1177/0093854811421448

Ricoeur, P. (1990). *Time and Narrative.* Chicago: University of Chicago Press.

Ricoeur, P. (1992). *Oneself as another.* Chicago: University of Chicago Press.

Rideout, V. J., Roberts, D. F., &Foehr, U. G. (2005). *Generation M: Media in the lives of 8-18-year-olds: Executive summary.* Menlo Park, CA: Henry J. Kaiser Family Foundation.

Ridgway, J. L., & Clayton, R. B. (2016). Instagram unfiltered: Exploring associations of body image satisfaction, Instagram #selfie posting, and negative romantic relationship outcomes. *Cyberpsychology, Behavior, and Social Networking, 19*(1), 2–7. doi:10.1089/cyber.2015.0433 PMID:26779659

Riva, G. (2016). *I social network.* Bologna, Italy: Il mulino.

Rival, L., Slater, D., & Miller, D. (1998). Sex and Sociality: Comparative Ethnographies of Sexual Objectification. *Theory, Culture & Society, 15*(3), 295–321. doi:10.1177/0263276498015003015

Robins, R. W., & Beer, J. S. (2001). Positive illusions about the self: Short-term benefits and long-term costs. *Journal of Personality and Social Psychology, 80*(2), 340–352. doi:10.1037/0022-3514.80.2.340 PMID:11220450

Rodriguez, A. T., & Griffiths, M. D. (2017). The Treatment of Internet Gaming Disorder: A Brief Overview of the PIPATIC Program. *International Journal of Mental Health and Addiction,* 1–16. doi:10.100711469-017-9825-0

Rogers, M. (2003). The role of criminal profiling in the computer forensics process. *Computers & Security, 22,* 292-298. doi: 10.1016/s0167-4048(03)00405-x

Rogers, M.K. (2015). Psychological profiling as an investigative tool for digital forensics. *Digital Forensics Threatscaes and Best Practices,* 45-58. DOI:10.1016/B978-0-12-804526-8.00003-4

Rosenfeld, B. (2003). Recidivism in stalking and obsessional harassment. *Law and Human Behavior, 27*(3), 251–265. doi:10.1023/A:1023479706822 PMID:12794963

Rosenfeld, M. J., & Thomas, R. J. (2012). Searching for a Mate: The Rise of the Internet as a Social Intermediary. *American Sociological Review, 77*(4), 523–547. doi:10.1177/0003122412448050

Rosen, L. D. (2007). *Me, Myspace, and I: Parenting the Net Generation.* New York: Palgrave Macmillan.

Rosen, L. D., Whaling, K., Rab, S., Carrier, L. M., & Cheever, N. A. (2013). Is Facebook creating "iDisorders"? The link between clinical symptoms of psychiatric disorders and technology use, attitudes and anxiety. *Computers in Human Behavior, 29*(3), 1243–1254. doi:10.1016/j.chb.2012.11.012

Ross, M. (2005). Typing, Doing, and Being: Sexuality and the Internet. *Journal of Sex Research, 42*(4), 342–352. doi:10.1080/00224490509552290 PMID:19827239

Rui, J. R., & Stefanone, M. A. (2013). Strategic image management online: Self-presentation, self-esteem and social network perspectives. *Information Communication and Society, 16*(8), 1286–1305. doi:10.1080/1369118X.2013.763834

Rush, B. (1812). *Medical inquiries and observations upon the diseases of the mind.* Philadelphia: Kimber & Richardson.

Rutter, D. R. (1984). *Looking and seeing the role of visual communication in social interaction.* Chichester, UK: John Wiley & Sons.

Rutter, D. R. (1987). *Communicating by telephone.* Oxford, UK: Pergamon Press.

Rutter, D. R., Stephenson, G. M., & Dewey, M. E. (1981). Visual communication and the content and style of conversation. *British Journal of Social Psychology, 20*(1), 41–52. doi:10.1111/j.2044-8309.1981.tb00472.x PMID:7237005

Ryan, T., Chester, A., Reece, J., & Xenos, S. (2014). The uses and abuses of Facebook: A review of Facebook addiction. *Journal of Behavioral Addictions*, *3*(3), 133–148. doi:10.1556/JBA.3.2014.016 PMID:25317337

Ryan, T., & Xenos, S. (2011). Who uses Facebook? An investigation into the relationship between the Big Five, shyness, narcissism, loneliness, and Facebook usage. *Computers in Human Behavior*, *27*(5), 1658–1664. doi:10.1016/j.chb.2011.02.004

Sabar Ben-Yehoshua, N. (2001). Ethnography in education. In N. Sabar Ben-Yehoshua (Ed.), Traditions and genres in qualitative research (pp. 100-136). Lod: Dvir. (in Hebrew)

Safety tips. (n.d.). Retrieved from www.eharmony.com

Sahin, M. (2010). Teachers' perceptions of bullying in high schools: A Turkish study. *Social Behavior and Personality*, *38*(1), 127–142. doi:10.2224bp.2010.38.1.127

Sales, N. J. (2015). *Tinder and the dawn of the dating apocalypse*. Retrieved from http://www.vanityfair.com/culture/2015/08/tinder-hook-up-culture-end-of-dating

Salmela-Aro, K., Upadyaya, K., Hakkarainen, K., Lonka, K., & Alho, K. (2017). The dark side of Internet use: Two longitudinal studies of excessive Internet use, depressive symptoms, school burnout and engagement among Finnish early and late adolescents. *Journal of Youth and Adolescence*, *46*(2), 343–357. doi:10.100710964-016-0494-2 PMID:27138172

Sampasa-Kanyinga, H., & Lewis, R. F. (2015). Frequent use of social network sites is associated with poor psychological functioning among children and adolescents. *Cyberpsychology, Behavior, and Social Networking*, *18*(7), 380–385. doi:10.1089/cyber.2015.0055 PMID:26167836

Sánchez-Carbonell, X., Beranuy, M., Castellana, M., Chamarro, A., & Oberst, U. (2008). La adicción a Internet y al móvil:¿ moda o trastorno? *Adicciones*, *20*(2), 149. doi:10.20882/adicciones.279 PMID:18551228

Sapira, N.A., Lessing, M.C., Goldsmith, T.D., Szabo, S.T., Lazoritz, M., Gold, M.S., & Stein, D.J. (2003). *Problematic internet use: proposed classification and diagnostic criteria*. Academic Press.

Scheibe, S., English, T., Tsai, J. L., & Carstensen, L. L. (2013). Striving to feel good: Ideal affect, actual affect, and their correspondence across adulthood. *Psychology and Aging*, *28*, 160–171. doi:10.1037/a0030561

Schiebener, J., Laier, C., & Brand, M. (2015). Getting stuck with pornography? Overuse or neglect of cybersex cues in a multitasking situation is related to symptoms of cybersex addiction. *Journal of Behavioral Addictions*, *4*(1), 14–21. doi:10.1556/JBA.4.2015.1.5

Schmitz, A., Yanenko, O., & Hebing, M. (2012). Identifying artificial actors in E-dating: A probabilistic segmentation based on interactional pattern analysis. In W. Gaul, A. Geyer-Schulz, L. Schmidt-Thieme, & J. Kunze (Eds.), *Challenges at the Interface of Data Analysis, Computer Science, and Optimization. Studies in Classification, Data Analysis, and Knowledge Organization* (pp. 319–327). Berlin: Springer. doi:10.1007/978-3-642-24466-7_33

Schreiber, M. (2015). Seeking blame in a Kawasaki teen's death. *The Japan Times*. Retrieved January 15, 2017, from http://www.japantimes.co.jp/news/2015/03/14/national/media-national/seeking-blame-kawasaki-teens-death/#.WYVJGYTyiUk

Schroeder, R. (2007). An overview of ethical and social issues in shared virtual environments. *Futures*, *39*(6), 704–717. doi:10.1016/j.futures.2006.11.009

Schultze, U. (2010). Embodiment and presence in virtual worlds: A review. *Journal of Information Technology*, *25*(4), 434–449. doi:10.1057/jit.2010.25

Scott, D. J., Coursaris, C. K., Kato, Y., & Kato, S. (2009). The exchange of emotional context in business communications: A comparison of PC and mobile email users. In M. M. Head & E. Li (Eds.), Mobile and ubiquitous commerce: Advanced e-business methods: volume 4 of advances in electronic business series (pp. 201-219). Hershey, PA: IGI Global.

Scott, D. J., Kato, Y., Kato, S., & Liu, S. (2012). Comparing computer and mobile phone use by American and Japanese university students. *Proceedings of World Conference on E-Learning in Corporate, Government, Healthcare, and Higher Education (E-Learn) 2012*, 1912-1917.

Seigel, J. (1994). The human subject as a language-effect. *History of European Ideas, 18*(4), 481–495. doi:10.1016/0191-6599(94)90081-7

Semans, A., & Winks, C. (1999). *The Woman's Guide to Sex on the Web.* New York, NY: HarperSanFrancisco.

Seto, M. C., & Eke, A. W. (2017). Correlates of admitted sexual interest in children among individuals convicted of child pornography offenses. *Law and Human Behavior, 41*(3), 305–313. doi:10.1037/lhb0000240 PMID:28383984

Sevcikova, A., Machackova, H., Wright, M. F., Dedkova, L., & Cerna, A. (2015). Social support seeking in relation to parental attachment and peer relationships among victims of cyberbullying. *Australian Journal of Guidance & Counselling, 15*, 1–13. doi:10.1017/jgc.2015.1

Shabir, G., Hameed, Y. M. Y., Safdar, G., & Gilani, S. M. F. S. (2014). The Impact of Social Media on Youth: A Case Study of Bahawalpur City. *Asian Journal of Social Sciences & Humanities, 3*(4), 132–151.

Shade, L. R. (2002). *Gender and community in the social construction of the Internet.* Peter Lang.

Shally, M., & Jensen. (2013). *Mental Health Care Issues in America: An Encyclopedia* (Vol. 1). ABC-CLIO.

Shapka, J. D., & Law, D. M. (2013). Does one size fit all? Ethnic differences in parenting behaviors and motivations for adolescent engagement in cyberbullying. *Journal of Youth and Adolescence, 42*(5), 723–738. doi:10.100710964-013-9928-2 PMID:23479327

Shariff, S., & Hoff, D. L. (2007). Cyber bullying: Clarifying legal boundaries for school supervision in cyberspace. *International Journal of Cyber Criminology, 1*, 76–118.

Sheldon, P. (2008). The relationship between unwillingness-to-communicate and students' Facebook use. *Journal of Media Psychology, 20*(2), 67–75. doi:10.1027/1864-1105.20.2.67

Sheldon, P., & Bryant, K. (2016). Instagram: Motives for its use and relationship to narcissism and contextual age. *Computers in Human Behavior, 58*, 89–97. doi:10.1016/j.chb.2015.12.059

Sheridan, L., & Grant, T. (2007). Is cyberstalking different? *Psychology, Crime & Law, 13*(6), 627–670. doi:10.1080/10683160701340528

Shin, Y., Kim, M., Im, C., & Chong, S. C. (2017). Selfie and self: The effect of selfies on self-esteem and social sensitivity. *Personality and Individual Differences, 111*, 139–145. doi:10.1016/j.paid.2017.02.004

Short, J. A., Williams, E., & Christie, B. (1976). *The social psychology of telecommunications.* London: Wiley.

Siegel, J., Dubrovsky, V., Kiesler, S., & McGuire, T. W. (1986). Group processes in computer-mediated communication. *Organizational Behavior and Human Decision Processes, 37*(2), 157–187. doi:10.1016/0749-5978(86)90050-6

Siibak, A., &Hernwall, P. (2011). 'Looking like my favourite Barbie': Online Gender Construction of Tween Girls in Estonia and in Sweden. *Studies of Transition States and Societies, 3.*

Sijtsema, J. J., Ashwin, R. J., Simona, C. S., & Gina, G. (2014). Friendship selection and influence in bullying and defending. *Effects of moral disengagement. Developmental Psychology*, *50*(8), 2093–2104. doi:10.1037/a0037145 PMID:24911569

Silde, A. (2013). *Profiling the Cyberstalker* (Master Thesis). Retrieved from file:///C:/Users/HP/Downloads/67-1-209-1-10-20140623%20(5).pdf

Simoncic, T. E., Kuhlman, K. R., Vargas, I., Houchins, S., & Lopez-Duran, N. L. (2014). Facebook use and depressive symptomatology: Investigating the role of neuroticism and extraversion in youth. *Computers in Human Behavior*, *40*, 1–5. doi:10.1016/j.chb.2014.07.039 PMID:25861155

Sinwelski, S., & Vinton, L. (2001). Stalking: The constant threat of violence. *Affilia*, *16*(1), 46–65. doi:10.1177/08861090122094136

Siomos, K. E., Dafouli, E. D., Braimiotis, D. A., Mouzas, O. D., & Angelopoulos, N. V. (2008). Internet addiction among Greek ado-lescent students. *Cyberpsychology & Behavior*, *11*(6), 653–657. doi:10.1089/cpb.2008.0088 PMID:18991535

Sissing, S. K. (2013). *A criminological exploration of cyber stalking in South Africa* (Master Thesis). Retrieved from http://uir.unisa.ac.za/bitstream/handle/10500/13067/dissertation_sissing_sk.pdf?sequence=1

Sjurso, I. R., Fandream, H., & Roland, E. (2016). Emotional problems in traditional and cyber victimization. *Journal of School Violence*, *15*(1), 114–131. doi:10.1080/15388220.2014.996718

Sklcnarova, II., Schulz, A., Schuhmann, P., Osterheider, M., & Neutze, J. (2017). Online sexual solicitation by adults and peers - Results from a population based German sample. *Child Abuse & Neglect*, *76*, 225–236. doi:10.1016/j.chiabu.2017.11.005 PMID:29149683

Slater, A., Tiggemann, M., Hawkins, K., & Werchon, D. (2011). Just one click: A content analysis of advertisements on teen web sites. *The Journal of Adolescent Health*, *50*(4), 339–345. doi:10.1016/j.jadohealth.2011.08.003 PMID:22443836

Slater, D. (1998). Trading Sexpics on IRC: Embodiment and Authenticity on the Internet. *Body & Society*, *4*(4), 91–117. doi:10.1177/1357034X98004004005

Slonje, R., & Smith, P. K. (2008). Cyberbullying: Another main type of bullying? *Scandinavian Journal of Psychology*, *49*(2), 147–154. doi:10.1111/j.1467-9450.2007.00611.x PMID:18352984

Slutske, W. S. (2006). Natural recovery and treatment-seeking in pathological gambling: Results of two U.S. national surveys. *The American Journal of Psychiatry*, *163*(2), 297–302. doi:10.1176/appi.ajp.163.2.297 PMID:16449485

Smith, A. (2011, November 15). Why Americans use social media friends. *Pew Research Center*. Retrieved from http://www.pewinternet.org/2011/11/15/why-americans-use-social-media/

Smith, A., & Anderson, M. (2015). *5 facts about online dating*. Pew Research Centre.

Smith, J. A. (1995). Semi-structured interviewing and qualitative analysis. *Rethinking Methods in Psychology, 1*, 8-26.

Smith, A., & Williams, K. D. (2004). R U there? Ostracism by cell phone text messages. *Group Dynamics*, *8*(4), 291–301. doi:10.1037/1089-2699.8.4.291

Smith, H. J., Dinev, T., & Xu, H. (2011). Information privacy research: An interdisciplinary review. *Management Information Systems Quarterly*, *35*(4), 989–1015. doi:10.2307/41409970

Smith, P. K., Del Barrio, C., & Tokunaga, R. S. (2013). Definitions of bullying and cyberbullying: How useful are the terms? In S. Bauman, D. Cross, & J. Walker (Eds.), *Principles of cyberbullying research: Definitions, measures, methodology* (pp. 26–40). New York, NY: Routledge.

Smith, P. K., Mahdavi, J., Carvalho, M., Fisher, S., Russell, S., & Tippett, N. (2008). Cyberbullying: Its nature and impact in secondary school pupils. *Journal of Child Psychology and Psychiatry, and Allied Disciplines*, *49*(4), 376–385. doi:10.1111/j.1469-7610.2007.01846.x PMID:18363945

Smith, P. K., Thompson, F., & Davidson, J. (2014). Cyber safety for adolescent girls: Bullying, harassment, sexting, pornography, and solicitation. *Current Opinion in Obstetrics & Gynecology*, *26*(5), 360–365. doi:10.1097/GCO.0000000000000106 PMID:25136759

Smutny, Z. (2016). Social informatics as a concept: Widening the discourse. *Journal of Information Science*, *42*(5), 681–710. doi:10.1177/0165551515608731

Snagowski, J., & Brand, M. (2015). Symptoms of cybersex addiction can be linked to both approaching and avoiding pornographic stimuli: Results from an analog sample of regular cybersex users. *Frontiers in Psychology*, *6*, 653. doi:10.3389/fpsyg.2015.00653 PMID:26052292

Snagowski, J., Wegmann, E., Pekal, J., Laier, C., & Brand, M. (2015). Implicit associations in cybersex addiction: Adaption of an Implicit Association Test with pornographic pictures. *Addictive Behaviors*, *49*, 7–12. doi:10.1016/j.addbeh.2015.05.009 PMID:26026385

Snider, M. (1997, February 11). Growing on-line population making Internet 'mass media.' *USA Today*, p. 1.

Sorokowska, A., Oleszkiewicz, A., Frackowiak, T., Pisanski, K., Chmiel, A., & Sorokowski, P. (2016). Selfies and personality: Who posts self-portrait photographs? *Personality and Individual Differences*, *90*, 119–123. doi:10.1016/j.paid.2015.10.037

Sorokowski, P., Sorokowska, A., Frackowiak, T., Karwowski, M., Rusicka, I., & Oleszkiewicz, A. (2016). Sex differences in online selfie posting behaviors predict histrionic personality scores among men but not women. *Computers in Human Behavior*, *59*, 368–373. doi:10.1016/j.chb.2016.02.033

Sorokowski, P., Sorokowska, A., Oleszkiewicz, A., Frackowiak, T., Huk, A., & Pisanski, K. (2015). Selfie posting behaviors are associated with narcissism among men. *Personality and Individual Differences*, *85*, 123–127. doi:10.1016/j.paid.2015.05.004

Sourander, A., Brunstein, A., Ikonen, M., Lindroos, J., Luntamo, T., Koskelainen, M., ... Helenius, H. (2010). Psychosocial risk factors associated with cyberbullying among adolescents: A population-based study. *Archives of General Psychiatry*, *67*(7), 720–728. doi:10.1001/archgenpsychiatry.2010.79 PMID:20603453

Southworth, C., Finn, J., Dawson, S., Fraser, C., & Tucker, S. (2007). Intimate partner violence, Technology, and Stalking. *Violence Against Women*, *13*(8), 842–856. doi:10.1177/1077801207302045 PMID:17699114

Souza, F., de Las Casas, D., Flores, V., Youn, S., Cha, M., Quercia, D., & Almeida, V. (2015). Dawn of the selfie era: The whos, wheres, and hows of selfies on Instagram. In *Proceedings of the 2015 ACM Conference on Online Social Networks* (pp. 221-231). Palo Alto, CA: ACM Press. 10.1145/2817946.2817948

Spitzberg, B. H. (2002). The tactical topography of stalking victimization and management. *Trauma, Violence & Abuse*, *3*(4), 261–288. doi:10.1177/1524838002237330

Spitzberg, B. H., & Cupach, W. R. (2007). The state of the art of stalking: Taking stock of the emerging literature. *Aggression and Violent Behavior*, *12*(1), 64–86. doi:10.1016/j.avb.2006.05.001

Spitzberg, B. H., & Hoobler, G. (2002). Cyberstalking and the technologies of interpersonal terrorism. *New Media & Society*, *4*(1), 71–92. doi:10.1177/14614440222226271

Spitzner, L. (2002). *Honeypots: Tracking hackers*. Addison Wesley.

Sproull, L., & Kiesler, S. (1986). Reducing social context cues: Electronic mail in organizational communication. *Management Science*, *32*(11), 1492–1512. doi:10.1287/mnsc.32.11.1492

Srnicek, N. (2017). *Platform Capitalism*. Cambridge, UK: Polity Press.

Stambaugh, H., Beaupre, D., Icove, D. J., Baker, R., Cassaday, W., & Williams, W. P. (2000). *State and local law enforcement needs to combat electronic crime*. Retrieved 22 November 2008 from http://www.ncjrs.gov/txtfiles1/nij/183451.txt

Stambaugh, H., Beaupre, D., Icove, D., Baker, R., Cassaday, W., & Williams, W. (2000). *State and local law enforcement needs to combat electronic crime*. U.S. Department of Justice, Office of Justice Programs, National Institute of Justice. Retrieved from U.S. Government website: https://www.ncjrs.gov/pdffiles1/nij/183451.pdf

Stambaugh, H., Beaupre, D., Icove, D., Baker, R., Cassaday, W., & Williams, W. (2001). *Electronic crime needs assessment for state and local law enforcement*. Retrieved September 1, 2005 from http://www.ojp.usdoj.gov/nij/pubs-sum/186276.htm

Stambaugh, H., Beaupre, D., Icove, D. J., Baker, R., Cassaday, W., & Williams, W. P. (2000). *State and Local Law Enforcement Needs to Combat Electronic Crime*. Washington, DC: U.S. Department of Justice. doi:10.1037/e598132007-001

Stanley, N., Barter, C., Wood, M., Aghtaie, N., Larkins, C., Lanau, A., & Överlien, C. (2016). Pornography, Sexual Coercion and Abuse and Sexting in Young People's Intimate. Relationships. *Journal of Interpersonal Violence*, 1–26. doi:10.1177/0886260516633204 PMID:26951609

Statista Facts on Social Networks. (n.d.). Available online: https://www.statista.com/topics/1164/social-networks/

Statista. (2016). *Most popular global mobile messenger apps 2016*. Retrieved January 10, 2017, from http://www.statista.com/statistics/258749/most-popular global mobile-messenger-apps/

Statista. Average Numbers of Hours Per Day Spent by Social Media Users on all Social Media Channels as of 4th Quarter 2015, by Country. (n.d.). Available online: https://www.statista.com/statistics/270229/usage-duration-of-social-networks-by-country/

Stats (2016, September 30). Stats. *Facebook Newsroom*. Retrieved from http://newsroom.fb.com/company-info/

Steers, M. L. N., Wickham, R. E., & Acitelli, L. K. (2014). Seeing everyone else's highlight reels: How Facebook usage is linked to depressive symptoms. *Journal of Social and Clinical Psychology*, *33*(8), 701–731. doi:10.1521/jscp.2014.33.8.701

Stephenson, P. R., & Walter, R. D. (2011). *Toward cyber crime assessment*. Cyberstalking 6th Annual symposium on information assurance (ASIA'11)

Stevens, G., Seedat, S., & van Niekerk, A. (2004). Understanding and preventing violence. *Self, Community & Psychology*, 13-19.

Stevens, N. (2002). Re-engaging: New partnerships in late-life widowhood. *Ageing International*, *27*(4), 27–42. doi:10.100712126-002-1013-1

Stoll, L. C., & Block, R. Jr. (2015). Intersectionality and cyberbullying: A study of cybervictimization in a Midwestern high school. *Computers in Human Behavior*, *52*, 387–391. doi:10.1016/j.chb.2015.06.010

Stone, G. (1981). Appearance and the self: A slightly revised version. In G. Stone & H. A. Farberman (Eds.), *Social psychology through symbolic interaction* (2nd ed.; pp. 187–202). New York, NY: Wiley.

Strawhun, J., Adams, N., & Huss, M. T. (2013). The assessment of cyberstalking: An expanded examination including social networking, attachment, jealousy, and anger in relation to violence and abuse. *Violence and Victims*, *28*(4), 715–730. doi:10.1891/0886-6708.11-00145 PMID:24047049

Strohmeier, D., Aoyama, I., Gradinger, P., & Toda, Y. (2013). Cybervictimization and cyberaggression in Eastern and Western countries: Challenges of constructing a cross-cultural appropriate scale. In S. Bauman, D. Cross, & J. L. Walker (Eds.), *Principles of cyberbullying research: Definitions, measures, and methodology* (pp. 202–221). New York: Routledge.

Strubel, J. L., & Petrie, T. A. (2016). *Tinder: Swiping self-esteem?* Retrieved from http://www.apa.org

Subathra, V., Nimisha, M. M. N., & Hakeem, L. A. (2003). Study on the Level of Social Network Addiction Among College Students. *Social Sciences*, *3*, 354–356.

Subrahmanyam, K., & Lin, G. (2007). Adolescents on the net: Internet use and well-being. *Adolescence*, *42*(168), 659–677. PMID:18229503

Subrahmanyam, K., & Šmahel, D. (2011). Sexuality on the Internet: Sexual Exploration, Cybersex, and Pornography. In *Digital Youth. Advancing Responsible Adolescent Development.* New York, NY: Springer. doi:10.1007/978-1-4419-6278-2_3

Sugimoto-Matsuda, J. J., & Braun, K. L. (2014). The role of collaboration in facilitating policy change in youth violence prevention: A review of the literature. *Prevention Science*, *15*(2), 194–204. doi:10.100711121-013-0369-7 PMID:23430580

Suler, J. (2004). The online disinhibition effect. *Cyberpsychology & Behavior*, *7*(3), 321–326. doi:10.1089/1094931041291295 PMID:15257832

Sullivan, H. S. (1953b). Preadolescence. In H. S. Perry & M. L. Gawel (Eds.), *The Interpersonal Theory of Psychiatry* (pp. 245–262). New York: Norton.

Suls, J., Martin, R., & Wheeler, L. (2002). Social comparison: Why, with whom, and with what effect? *Current Directions in Psychological Science*, *11*(5), 159–163. doi:10.1111/1467-8721.00191

Sung, Y., Lee, J., Kim, E., & Choi, S. M. (2016). Why we post selfies: Understanding motivations for posting pictures of oneself. *Personality and Individual Differences*, *97*, 260–265. doi:10.1016/j.paid.2016.03.032

Superdata. (2016). *Playable media & games market research.* Retrieved June 8, 2016, from https://www.superdataresearch.com/

Suzi, G. (2002). *The Sex Book.* Cassell Illustrated.

Suzuki, K., Asaga, R., Sourander, A., Hoven, C. W., & Mandell, D. (2012). Cyberbullying and adolescent mental health. *International Journal of Adolescent Medicine and Health*, *24*(1), 27–35. doi:10.1515/ijamh.2012.005 PMID:22909909

Swaminath, G. (2008). Internet addiction disorder: Fact or fad? Nosing into nosology. *Indian Journal of Psychiatry*, *50*(3), 158. doi:10.4103/0019-5545.43622 PMID:19742232

Szablewicz, M. (2016). A Realm of Mere Representation? "Live" E-Sports Spectacles and the Crafting of China's Digital Gaming Image. *Games and Culture*, *11*(3), 256–274. doi:10.1177/1555412015595298

Tandoc, E. C. Jr, Ferrucci, P., & Duffy, M. (2015). Facebook use, envy, and depression among college students: Is facebooking depressing? *Computers in Human Behavior*, *43*, 139–146. doi:10.1016/j.chb.2014.10.053

Tangen, D., & Campbell, M. (2010). Cyberbullying prevention: One primary school's approach. *Australian Journal of Guidance & Counselling*, *20*(02), 225–234. doi:10.1375/ajgc.20.2.225

Tang, J. (2014). Graphics, Animation, and Games. In *Beginning Google Glass Development* (pp. 249–295). Apress.

Taylor, N. (2015). Play to the camera: Video ethnography, spectatorship, and e-sports. *Convergence (London)*, ▪▪▪, 1–16.

Taylor, T. L. (2012). *Raising the Stakes: The Professionalization of Computer Gaming*. Cambridge, MA: The MIT Press.

Thapa, A., & Kumar, R. (2011). Cyber staking: crime and challenge at the cyberspace. *International Journal of Computing and Business Research*, *2*(1).

Thomas, N. J., & Martin, F. H. (2010). Video-arcade game, computer game and Internet activities of Australian students: Participation habits and prevalence of addiction. *Australian Journal of Psychology*, *62*(2), 59–66. doi:10.1080/00049530902748283

Thurlow, C., Lengel, L., & Tomic, A. (2004). Computer mediated communication. *Sage (Atlanta, Ga.)*.

Tiggemann, M., & Miller, J. (2010). The Internet and adolescent girls' weight satisfaction and drive for thinness. *Sex Roles*, *63*(1-2), 79–90. doi:10.100711199-010-9789-z

Tiggemann, M., & Slater, A. (2013). NetGirls: The Internet, Facebook, and body image concern in adolescent girls. *International Journal of Eating Disorders*, *46*(6), 630–633. doi:10.1002/eat.22141 PMID:23712456

Tiggemann, M., & Slater, A. (2014). NetTweens: The Internet and body image concerns in preteenage girls. *The Journal of Early Adolescence*, *34*(5), 606–620. doi:10.1177/0272431613501083

Ting, H., Wong, W. P. M., de Run, E. C., & Lau, S. Y. C. (2015). Beliefs about the use of Instagram: An exploratory study. *International Journal of Business and Innovation*, *2*, 15–31.

Tiwari, P. (2017, December 7). How dating multiple guys on a popular dating app affected my mental health [Web log post]. Retrieved from https://timesofindia.indiatimes.com

Tjaden, P. G., & Thoennes, N. (1998). *Stalking in America: Findings from the National Violence Against Women Survey*. Washington, DC: US Department of Justice.

Tobin, S. J., Vanman, E. J., Verreynne, M., & Saeri, A. K. (2015). Threats to belonging on Facebook: Lurking and ostracism. *Social Influence*, *10*(1), 31–42. doi:10.1080/15534510.2014.893924

Tokunaga, R. S., & Aune, K. S. (2015). Cyber-Defense: A Taxonomy of Tactics for Managing Cyberstalking. *Journal of Interpersonal Violence*, *32*(10), 1451–1475. doi:10.1177/0886260515589564

Toledano, S., Werch, B. L., & Wiens, B. A. (2015). Domain-specific self-concept in relation to traditional and cyber peer aggression. *Journal of School Violence*, *14*(4), 405–423. doi:10.1080/15388220.2014.935386

Toma, C. L., Hancock, J. T., & Ellison, N. B. (2008). Separating fact from fiction: An examination of deceptive self-presentation in online dating profiles. *Personality and Social Psychology Bulletin*, *34*(8), 1023–1036. doi:10.1177/0146167208318067 PMID:18593866

Tonioni, F., D'Alessandris, L., Lai, C., Martinelli, D., Corvino, S., Vasale, M., ... Bria, P. (2012). Internet addic-tion: Hours spent online, behaviors and psychological symptoms. *General Hospital Psychiatry*, *34*(1), 80–87. doi:10.1016/j.genhosppsych.2011.09.013 PMID:22036735

Totura, C. M. W., MacKinnon-Lewis, C., Gesten, E. L., Gadd, R., Divine, K. P., Dunham, S., & Kamboukos, D. (2009). Bullying and victimization among boys and girls in middle school: The influence of perceived family and school contexts. *The Journal of Early Adolescence*, *29*(4), 571–609. doi:10.1177/0272431608324190

Tromholt, M. (2016). The Facebook experiment: Quitting Facebook leads to higher levels of well-being. *Cyberpsychology, Behavior, and Social Networking*, *19*(11), 661–666. doi:10.1089/cyber.2016.0259 PMID:27831756

Turel, O., Serenko, A., & Bontis, N. (2011). Family and work-related consequences of addiction to organizational pervasive technologies. *Information & Management*, *48*(2-3), 2–3, 88–95. doi:10.1016/j.im.2011.01.004

Turkle, S. (1995). *Life on the screen: Identity in the age of the Internet*. New York: Simon & Schuster.

Turk, M. (2014). Multimodal interaction: A review. *Pattern Recognition Letters*, *36*(2), 189–195. doi:10.1016/j.patrec.2013.07.003

Turvey, B. E. (2011). A history of criminal profiling. In B. E. Turvey (Ed.), *Criminal profiling: An introduction to behavioural evidence analysis* (pp. 3–40). Oxford, UK: Elsevier.

Twitch.tv. (n.d.). Retrieved June 1, 2016, from http://www.twitch.tv/p/about

Tyler, J. R., & Tang, J. C. (2003). When can I expect an email response? A study of rhythms in email usage. *Proceedings of the Eighth European Conference on Computer Supported Cooperative Work (ECSCW2003)*, 239-258. 10.1007/978-94-010-0068-0_13

U.S. Department of Justice. (2000). *The electronic frontier: The challenge of unlawful conduct involving the use of the Internet*. Report of the President's Working Group on Unlawful Conduct on the Internet. Washington, DC: Author. Retrieved March 20, 2003, from http://www. usdoj.gov/criminal/cybercrime/unlawful.htm

Utz, S., Muscanell, N., & Khalid, C. (2015). Snapchat elicits more jealousy than Facebook: A comparison of Snapchat and Facebook use. *Cyberpsychology, Behavior, and Social Networking*, *18*(3), 141–146. doi:10.1089/cyber.2014.0479 PMID:25667961

Vaillancourt-Morel, M. P., Blais-Lecours, S., Labadie, C., Bergeron, S., Sabourin, S., & Godbout, N. (2017). Profiles of Cyberpornography Use and Sexual Well-Being in Adults. *Journal of Sexual Medicine*, *14*(1), 78–85. doi:10.1016/j.jsxm.2016.10.016 PMID:28011208

Valenzuela, S., Halpern, D., & Katz, J. E. (2014). Social network sites, marriage well-being and divorce: Survey and state-level evidence from the United States. *Computers in Human Behavior*, *36*, 94–101. doi:10.1016/j.chb.2014.03.034

Valenzuela, S., Park, N., & Kee, K. F. (2009). Is there social capital in a social network site? Facebook use and college students' life satisfaction, trust and participation. *Journal of Computer-Mediated Communication*, *14*(4), 875–901. doi:10.1111/j.1083-6101.2009.01474.x

Valkenburg, P. M., & Peter, J. (2007). Online communication and adolescent well-being: Testing the stimulation versus the displacement hypothesis. *Journal of Computer-Mediated Communication*, *12*(4), 1169–1182. doi:10.1111/j.1083-6101.2007.00368.x

Valkenburg, P. M., & Peter, J. (2007). Who visits online dating sites? Exploring some characteristics of online daters. *Cyberpsychology & Behavior*, *10*(6), 849–852. doi:10.1089/cpb.2007.9941 PMID:18085977

Valkenburg, P. M., & Peter, J. (2009). Social consequences of the Internet for adolescents a decade of research. *Current Directions in Psychological Science*, *18*(1), 1–5. doi:10.1111/j.1467-8721.2009.01595.x

Valkenburg, P. M., & Peter, J. (2011). Online communication among adolescents: An integrated model of its attraction, opportunities, and risks. *The Journal of Adolescent Health, 48*(2), 121–127. doi:10.1016/j.jadohealth.2010.08.020 PMID:21257109

Valkenburg, P. M., & Peter, J. (2013). The differential susceptibility to media effects model. *Journal of Communication, 63*(2), 221–243. doi:10.1111/jcom.12024

Valkenburg, P. M., Peter, J., & Schouten, A. P. (2006). Friend networking sites and their relationship to adolescents' well-being and social self-esteem. *Cyberpsychology & Behavior, 9*(5), 584–590. doi:10.1089/cpb.2006.9.584 PMID:17034326

Valkenburg, P. M., Schouten, A. P., & Peter, J. (2005). Adolescents' identity experiments on the Internet. *New Media & Society, 7*(3), 383–402. doi:10.1177/1461444805052282

Van Baren, J., IJsselsteijn, W. A., Markopoulos, P., Romero, N., & De Ruyter, B. (2004). Measuring affective benefits and costs of awareness systems supporting intimate social networks. In Nijholt, A., & Nishida, T. (Eds.), *Proceedings of the 3rd Workshop on Social Intelligence Design* (*Vol. 2*, pp. 13-19). Academic Press.

Van Dreunen, J. (2011). *A Business History of Video Games: Revenue Models from 1980 to Today. The Game Behind the Video Game: Business, Regulation, and Society in the Gaming Industry*. New Brunswick, NJ: Academic Press.

Van Ouytsel, J., Torres, E., Choi, H. J., Ponnet, K., Walrave, M., & Temple, J. R. (2017). The Associations Between Substance Use, Sexual Behaviors, Bullying, Deviant Behaviors, Health, and Cyber Dating Abuse Perpetration. *The Journal of School Nursing, 33*(2), 116–122. doi:10.1177/1059840516683229 PMID:28288554

Van Rooij, A. J., Schoenmakers, T. M., Vermulst, A. A., Van den Eijnden, R. J. J. M., & Van de Mheen, D. (2011). Online video game addiction: identification of addicted adolescent gamers. Addiction, 106(1), 205–12.

Van Wilsem, J. (2011). Worlds tied together? Online and non-domestic routine activities and their impact on digital and traditional threat victimization. *European Journal of Criminology, 8*(2), 115–127. doi:10.1177/1477370810393156

Vandeweerd, C., Myers, J., Coulter, M., Yalcin, A., & Corvin, J. (2016). Positives and negatives of online dating according to women 50. *Journal of Women & Aging, 28*(3), 259–270. doi:10.1080/08952841.2015.1137435 PMID:27191792

Vasicek, Z. (2012). *Jak se delaji filosofie* [How are the philosophies being formed]. Prague: Triada.

Vaterlaus, J. M., Barnett, K., Roche, C., & Young, J. A. (2016). "Snapchat is more personal": An exploratory study on Snapchat behaviors and young adult interpersonal relationships. *Computers in Human Behavior, 62*, 594–601. doi:10.1016/j.chb.2016.04.029

Verduyn, P., Lee, D. S., Park, J., Shablack, H., Orvell, A., Bayer, J., & Kross, E. (2015). Passive Facebook usage undermines affective well-being: Experimental and longitudinal evidence. *Journal of Experimental Psychology: General, 144*, 480-488. doi: 2062/10.1037/xge0000057

Verma, S. K., & Raman Mittal, R. (2004). *Legal Dimension of Cyberspace*. New Delhi: Indian Law Institute.

Virtzberg-Rofè, D., Rofè, T., & Rudnick, A. (2014). Free online dating site for people with mental illness. *Psychiatric Services (Washington, D.C.), 65*(9), 1178. doi:10.1176/appi.ps.650705 PMID:25179191

Vogel, E. A., Rose, J. P., Roberts, L. R., & Eckles, K. (2014). Social comparison, social media, and self-esteem. *Psychology of Popular Media Culture, 3*(4), 206–222. doi:10.1037/ppm0000047

Wada, M., Mortenson, W. B., & Clarke, H. L. (2016). Older Adults' Online Dating Profiles and Successful Aging. *Canadian Journal on Aging, 35*(4), 479–490. doi:10.1017/S0714980816000507 PMID:27774918

Wade, A., & Beran, T. (2011). Cyberbullying: The new era of bullying. *Canadian Journal of School Psychology*, *26*(1), 44–61. doi:10.1177/0829573510396318

Wallace, B. (2000). Stalkers find a new tool—The Internet e-mail is increasingly used to threaten and harass, authorities say. *SFGate News*. Retrieved from http://sfgate.com/cgi-bin/article_cgi?file=/chronicle/ archive/2000/07/10/MN39633.DTL

Walther, J. B. (1992). Interpersonal effects in computer-mediated interaction: A relational perspective. *Communication Research*, *19*(1), 52–90. doi:10.1177/009365092019001003

Walther, J. B. (1996). Computer-mediated communication: Impersonal, interpersonal, and hyperpersonal interaction. *Communication Research*, *23*(1), 3–43. doi:10.1177/009365096023001001

Walther, J. B. (2007). Selective self-presentation in computer-mediated communication: Hyperpersonal dimensions of technology, language, and cognition. *Computers in Human Behavior*, *23*(5), 2538–2557. doi:10.1016/j.chb.2006.05.002

Walther, J. B., Anderson, J. F., & Park, D. W. (1994). Interpersonal effects in computer-mediated interaction: A meta-analysis of social and antisocial communication. *Communication Research*, *21*(4), 460–487. doi:10.1177/009365094021004002

Walther, J. B., & Burgoon, J. K. (1992). Relational communication in computer-mediated interaction. *Human Communication Research*, *19*(1), 50–88. doi:10.1111/j.1468-2958.1992.tb00295.x

Walther, J. B., & Tidwell, L. C. (1995). Nonverbal cues in computer-mediated communication, and the effect of chronemics on relational communication. *Journal of Organizational Computing and Electronic Commerce*, *5*(4), 355–378. doi:10.1080/10919399509540258

Wang, R., Yang, F., & Haigh, M. M. (2017). Let me take a selfie: Exploring the psychological effects of posting and viewing selfies and groupies on social media. *Telematics and Informatics*, *34*(4), 274–283. doi:10.1016/j.tele.2016.07.004

Wardle, J., & Cooke, L. (2005). The impact of obesity on psychological well-being. *Best Practice & Research. Clinical Endocrinology & Metabolism*, *19*(3), 421–440. doi:10.1016/j.beem.2005.04.006 PMID:16150384

Waskul, D. D. (2003). *Personhood in Online Chat and Cybersex*. New York: Peter Lang.

Waskul, D. D., & Lust, M. (2004). Role-playing and Playing Roles: The Person, Player, and Persona in Fantasy Role-playing. *Symbolic Interaction*, *27*(3), 333–356. doi:10.1525i.2004.27.3.333

Weinstein, A. M., Zolek, R., Babkin, A., Cohen, K., & Lejoyeux, M. (2015). Factors Predicting Cybersex Use and Difficulties in Forming Intimate Relationships among Male and Female Users of Cybersex. *Frontiers in Psychiatry*, *6*, 54. doi:10.3389/fpsyt.2015.00054 PMID:25941496

Weiser, E. B. (2015). #Me: Narcissism and its facets as predictors of selfie-posting frequency. *Personality and Individual Differences*, *86*, 477–481. doi:10.1016/j.paid.2015.07.007

Weisskirch, R. S., & Delevi, R. (2011). 'Sexting' and adult romantic attachment. *Computers in Human Behavior*, *27*(5), 1697–1701. doi:10.1016/j.chb.2011.02.008

Wellman, H., & Cross, D. (2003). Theory of mind conceptual change. *Child Development*, *72*(3), 702–707. doi:10.1111/1467-8624.00309 PMID:11405576

Wenninger, H., Krasnova, H., & Buxmann, P. (2014). Activity matters: Investigating the influence of Facebook on life satisfaction of teenage users. In M. Avital, J. M. Leimeister, & U. Schultze (Eds.), *Twenty Second European Conference on Information Systems* (pp. 1–18). Tel Aviv, Israel: ECIS.

Wéry, A., & Billieux, J. (2017). Problematic cybersex: Conceptualization, assessment, and treatment. *Addictive Behaviors, 64*, 238–246. doi:10.1016/j.addbeh.2015.11.007 PMID:26646983

Westwood, D., & Griffiths, M. D. (2010). The role of structural characteristics in video game play motivation: A Q-Methodology Study. *Cyberpsychology, Behavior, and Social Networking, 13*(5), 581–585. doi:10.1089/cyber.2009.0361 PMID:20950185

White, D., Finneran, C., Sato, K. N., & Stephenson, R. (2014). Sex, HIV, and the Internet: Exploring Variations in the Online Profiles of MSM in the United States. *American Journal of Men's Health, 8*(4), 289–299. doi:10.1177/1557988313509834 PMID:24232583

White, W. E., & Carmody, D. (2014). Preventing Online Victimization College Students' Views on Intervention and Prevention. *Journal of Interpersonal Violence*. doi:10.1177/0886260515625501

Whitton, S. W., Weitbrecht, E. M., Kuryluk, A. D., & Bruner, M. R. (2013). Committed dating relationships and mental health among college students. *Journal of American College Health, 61*(3), 176–183. doi:10.1080/07448481.2013.773903 PMID:25158015

Whitty, M. T., & Buchanan, T. (2012). The Online Dating Romance Scam: A Serious Crime. *Cyberpsychology, Behavior, and Social Networking, 15*(3), 181–183. doi:10.1089/cyber.2011.0352

Whitty, M., & Carr, A. N. (2006). *Cyberspace romance: The psychology of online relationships*. Hampshire, UK: Palgrave Macmillan. doi:10.1007/978-0-230-20856-8

Whyte, S., & Torgler, B. (2017). Preference Versus Choice in Online Dating. *Cyberpsychology, Behavior, and Social Networking, 20*(3), 150–156. doi:10.1089/cyber.2016.0528 PMID:28263677

Widyanto, L., & McMurran, M. (2004). The psychometric properties of the internet addiction test. *Cyberpsychology & Behavior, 7*(4), 443–450. doi:10.1089/cpb.2004.7.443 PMID:15331031

Wildt, B. T. (2010). Pathological Internet use and psychiatric disorders: A cross-sectional study on psychiatric phenomenology and clinical relevance of Internet dependency. *European Journal of Psychiatry, 24*(3), 136–145. doi:10.4321/S0213-61632010000300002

William, D. M., Locker, L. Jr, & Briley, K. (2011). What do older adults seek in their potential romantic partners? Evidence from online personal ads. *International Journal of Aging & Human Development, 72*(1), 67–82. doi:10.2190/AG.72.1.d PMID:21391407

Williams, R., & Edge, D. (1996). The social shaping of technology. *Research Policy, 25*(6), 865–899. doi:10.1016/0048-7333(96)00885-2

Wilson, K., Fornasier, S., & White, K. M. (2010). Psychological predictors of young adults' use of social networking sites. *CyberPsychology, Behavior, and Social Networking, 13*(2), 173-177. doi: 10.1089=cyber.2009.0094

Wilson, R. E., Gosling, S. D., & Graham, L. T. (2012). A review of Facebook research in the social sciences. *Perspectives on Psychological Science, 7*(3), 203–220. doi:10.1177/1745691612442904 PMID:26168459

Wion, R. K., & Loeb, S. J. (2015). Older Adults Engaging in Online Dating: What Gerontological Nurses Should Know. *Journal of Gerontological Nursing, 41*(10), 25–35, quiz 36–37. doi:10.3928/00989134-20150826-67 PMID:26488252

Wolak, J., Finkelhor, D., Walsh, W., & Treitman, L. (2017). Sextortion of minors: Characteristics and dynamics. *The Journal of Adolescent Health, 62*(1), 72–79. doi:10.1016/j.jadohealth.2017.08.014 PMID:29055647

Wong, D. S., Chan, H. C. O., & Cheng, C. H. (2014). Cyberbullying perpetration and victimization among adolescents in Hong Kong. *Children and Youth Services Review*, *36*, 133–140. doi:10.1016/j.childyouth.2013.11.006

Wood, R. T. A., & Griffiths, M. D. (2007). Time loss whilst playing video games: Is there a relationship to addictive behaviors? *International Journal of Mental Health and Addiction*, *5*(2), 141–149. doi:10.100711469-006-9048-2

Wood, R. T. A., Griffiths, M. D., Chappell, D., & Davies, M. N. O. (2004). The structural characteristics of video games: A psycho-structural analysis. *Cyberpsychology & Behavior*, *7*(1), 1–10. doi:10.1089/109493104322820057 PMID:15006163

Wood, R. T. A., Griffiths, M. D., & Parke, A. (2007). Experiences of time loss among videogame players: An empirical study. *Cyberpsychology & Behavior*, *10*(1), 45–56. doi:10.1089/cpb.2006.9994 PMID:17305447

Working to Halt Online Abuse (WHO). (2003). *Online harassment statistics*. Retrieved May 25, 2007 from http://www.haltabuse.org/resources/stats/index. shtml

Working to Halt Online Abuse (WHOA). (2003). *Online harrassment statistics*. Retrieved May 25, 2007 from http://www.haltabuse.org/resources/stats/index.shtml

Working to Halt Online Abuse. (2011). *Online Harassment/Cyberstalking Statistics*. Retrieved from http://www.haltabuse.org/resources/stats/index.shtml

Wortham, J. (2013, October 19). My Selfie, Myself. *The New York Times*. Retrieved from http://www.nytimes.com/2013/10/20/sunday-review/my-selfie-myself.html

Wright, J. A., Burgess, A. G., Burgess, A. W., Laszlo, A. T., McCrary, G. O., & Douglas, J. E. (1996). A typology of interpersonal stalking. *Journal of Interpersonal Violence*, *11*(4), 487–502. doi:10.1177/088626096011004003

Wright, K. B., Rosenberg, J., Egbert, N., Ploeger, N. A., Bernard, D. R., & King, S. (2013). Communication competence, social support, and depression among college students: A model of Facebook and face-to-face support network influence. *Journal of Health Communication*, *18*(1), 41–57. doi:10.1080/10810730.2012.688250 PMID:23030518

Wright, M. F. (2013). The relationship between young adults' beliefs about anonymity and subsequent cyber aggression. *Cyberpsychology, Behavior, and Social Networking*, *16*(12), 858–862. doi:10.1089/cyber.2013.0009 PMID:23849002

Wright, M. F. (2014a). Cyber victimization and perceived stress: Linkages to late adolescents' cyber aggression and psychological functioning. *Youth & Society*.

Wright, M. F. (2014b). Predictors of anonymous cyber aggression: The role of adolescents' beliefs about anonymity, aggression, and the permanency of digital content. *Cyberpsychology, Behavior, and Social Networking*, *17*(7), 431–438. doi:10.1089/cyber.2013.0457 PMID:24724731

Wright, M. F. (2014c). Longitudinal investigation of the associations between adolescents' popularity and cyber social behaviors. *Journal of School Violence*, *13*(3), 291–314. doi:10.1080/15388220.2013.849201

Wright, M. F. (2015). Cyber victimization and adjustment difficulties: The mediation of Chinese and American adolescents' digital technology usage. *Cyberpsychology (Brno)*, *1*(1), 1. Retrieved from http://cyberpsychology.eu/view.php?cisloclanku=2015051102&article=1

Wright, M. F. (2016). Cyber Victimization on College Campuses Longitudinal Associations With Suicidal Ideation, Depression, and Anxiety. *Criminal Justice Review*, *41*(2), 190–203. doi:10.1177/0734016816634785

Wright, M. F. (in press). Adolescents' cyber aggression perpetration and cyber victimization: The longitudinal associations with school functioning. *Social Psychology of Education*.

Wright, M. F., Kamble, S., Lei, K., Li, Z., Aoyama, I., & Shruti, S. (2015). Peer attachment and cyberbullying involvement among Chinese, Indian, and Japanese adolescents. *Societies (Basel, Switzerland)*, *5*(4), 339–353. doi:10.3390oc5020339

Wright, M. F., & Li, Y. (2012). Kicking the digital dog: A longitudinal investigation of young adults' victimization and cyber-displaced aggression. *Cyberpsychology, Behavior, and Social Networking*, *15*(9), 448–454. doi:10.1089/cyber.2012.0061 PMID:22974350

Wright, M. F., & Li, Y. (2013a). Normative beliefs about aggression and cyber aggression among young adults: A longitudinal investigation. *Aggressive Behavior*, *39*(3), 161–170. doi:10.1002/ab.21470 PMID:23440595

Wright, M. F., & Li, Y. (2013b). The association between cyber victimization and subsequent cyber aggression: The moderating effect of peer rejection. *Journal of Youth and Adolescence*, *42*(5), 662–674. doi:10.100710964-012-9903-3 PMID:23299177

Wykes, M. (2007). Constructing crime: Culture, stalking, celebrity and cyber. *Crime, Media, Culture*, *3*(2), 158–174. doi:10.1177/1741659007078541

Wysocki, D. K. (1996). *Somewhere over the modem: Interpersonal relationships over computer bulletin boards. Sociology*. Santa Barbara: University of California.

Wysocki, D. K. (1998). Let Your Fingers Do the Talking: Sex on an Adult Chat-line. *Sexualities*, *1*(4), 425–452. doi:10.1177/136346098001004003

Yadav, P., Banwari, G., Parmar, C., & Maniar, R. (2013, December). Internet addiction and its correlates among high school students: A preliminary study from Ahmedabad, India. *Asian Journal of Psychiatry*, *6*(6), 500–505. doi:10.1016/j.ajp.2013.06.004 PMID:24309861

Ybarra, M. L., Diener-West, M., & Leaf, P. (2007). Examining the overlap in internet harassment and school bullying: Implications for school intervention. *The Journal of Adolescent Health*, *1*(6), 42–50. doi:10.1016/j.jadohealth.2007.09.004 PMID:18047944

Ybarra, M. L., & Mitchell, K. J. (2004). Online aggressor/targets, aggressors, and targets: A comparison of associated youth characteristics. *Journal of Child Psychology and Psychiatry, and Allied Disciplines*, *45*(7), 1308–1316. doi:10.1111/j.1469-7610.2004.00328.x PMID:15335350

Young, K. S. (1996). *Internet addiction: The emergence of a new clinical disorder*. Paper presented at the 104th annual meeting of the American Psychological Association, Toronto, Canada.

Young, K. S. (1997). *What makes on-line usage stimulating? Potential explanations for pathological Internet use*. Paper presented at the 105th annual meeting of the American Psychological Association, Chicago, IL.

Young, K. S. (1999). *Internet Addiction: Symptoms, Evaluation, And Treatment. Innovations in Clinical Practice*. Professional Resource Press. Retrieved from https://pdfs.semanticscholar.org/27f2/4ddc6b37b1242fabecd6f35bc05d248c2059.pdf

Young, G. D., & Caplan, S. E. (2010). Online dating and conjugal bereavement. *Death Studies*, *34*(7), 575–605. doi:10.1080/07481181003761542 PMID:24482843

Young, H., Turney, C., White, J., Bonell, C., Lewis, R., & Fletcher, A. (2017). Dating and relationship violence among 16-19 year olds in England and Wales: A cross-sectional study of victimization. *Journal of Public Health*, *10*, 1–9. doi:10.1093/pubmed/fdx026 PMID:29136181

Young, K. (1996). Internet addiction: The emergence of a new clinical disorder. *Cyberpsychology & Behavior*, 3.

Young, K. S. (1996). *Caught in the net: how to recognize the signs of Internet addiction—and a winning strategy for recovery*. New York: Wiley.

Young, K. S. (1998). Internet Addiction: The emergence of a new clinical disorder. *Cyberpsychology & Behavior*, *1*(3), 237–244. doi:10.1089/cpb.1998.1.237

Young, K. S. (1999). The evaluation and treatment of internet addiction. In L. Vande Creek & T. Jackson (Eds.), *Innovations in clinical practice: A source book* (pp. 1–13). Sarasota, FL: Professional Resource Press.

Young, K. S. (2004). Internet Addiction: A New Clinical Phenomenon and its Consequences. Center for Online Addiction. *The American Behavioral Scientist*, *48*(4), 402–415. doi:10.1177/0002764204270278

Young, K., Pistner, M., O'mara, J., & Buchanan, J. (1999). Article. *Cyberpsychology & Behavior*, *2*(5), 475479. doi:10.1089/cpb.1999.2.475

Yousef, W. S. M., & Bellamy, A. (2015). The impact of cyberbullying on the self-esteem and academic functioning of Arab American middle and high school students. *Electronic Journal of Research in Educational Psychology*, *23*(3), 463–482.

Yu, L., & Shek, D. T. (2013). Internet addiction in Hong Kong adolescents: A three-year longitudinal study. *Journal of Pediatric and Adolescent Gynecology*, *26*(3), S10–S17. doi:10.1016/j.jpag.2013.03.010 PMID:23683821

Zhao, S. (2006). Do Internet users have more social ties? A call for differentiated analyses of Internet use. *Journal of Computer-Mediated Communication*, *11*(3), 844–862. doi:10.1111/j.1083-6101.2006.00038.x

Zhao, S., Grasmuck, S., & Martin, J. (2008). Identity construction on Facebook: Digital empowerment in anchored relationships. *Computers in Human Behavior*, *24*(5), 1816–1836. doi:10.1016/j.chb.2008.02.012

Zhou, Z., Tang, H., Tian, Y., Wei, H., Zhang, F., & Morrison, C. M. (2013). Cyberbullying and its risk factors among Chinese high school students. *School Psychology International*, *34*(6), 630–647. doi:10.1177/0143034313479692

Zona, M. A., Sharma, K. K., & Lane, A. J. (1993). Comparative study of erotomanic and obsessional subjects in a forensic sample. *Journal of Forensic Sciences*, *38*(4), 894–903. PMID:8355005

Zou, H., Wu, Z. Yu. J., Li, M., Ablimit, M., Li, F., Pang, L., & Juniper, N. (2010). Sexual risk behaviors and HIV infection among men who have sex with men who use the internet in Beijing and Urumqi, China. *Journal of Acquired Immune Deficiency Syndromes*, *53*(1), S81–S87. doi:10.1097/QAI.0b013e3181c7dd2b PMID:20104115

Zweig, J. M., Dank, M., Yahner, J., & Lachman, P. (2013). The rate of cyber dating abuse among teens and how it relates to other forms of teen dating violence. *Journal of Youth and Adolescence*, *42*(7), 1063–1077. doi:10.100710964-013-9922-8 PMID:23412689

About the Contributors

Rejani Thudalikunnil Gopalan is currently working as Professor and Head of Clinical Psychology, Amity University, Jaipur, India. She was working as a faculty in Gujarat Forensic Sciences University prior to this appointment. She is a specialist in child and adolescent mental health issues and has closer to two decades work experience as Clinical Psychologist, Faculty and administrator. She served as member of doctoral committee and board of studies, editorial board member of many reputed journals and edited handbook and books. She has won many prestigious awards for her contribution in mental health area. Traumas and abuses, especially sexual abuse, addictive disorders, childhood mental health issues, school mental health, cyber crimes, mental health issues in convicted criminals and juveniles are her predominant areas of research. Her specialized services extended to clinical consultation and therapeutic remedies for the group including adults and children with mental illness in Prison and juvenile homes along with court related disputes.

***

Bushrah Basiron is a senior lecturer of comparative religion, digital innovations, learning and contemporary issues in digital age at Universiti Teknologi Malaysia (UTM). She has been working in teaching for more than fifteen years.

Singgih Basuki is senior lecturer at religious ethics and digital ethics at Islamic State University Sunan Kalijaga, Indonesia. He has been working in teaching and research in his field for more than fifteen years.

Tejaswini Bhave is a Pune based clinical psychologist currently working as a health psychologist at the Deenanath Mangeshkar Hospital and Research center, Pune. She has completed her M.Phil in clinical Psychology from the Gujarat Forensic Sciences University and her M.A. in clinical psychology with a university gold medal from Savitribai Phule Pune University. Her interest areas include preventive psychotherpay and positive psychology.

Valentina Boursier graduated in Clinical Psychology, PhD in Gender Studies, Researcher at Naples University "Federico II", Psychotherapist for Children and Adolescents, Member of the Winnicott's Institute (iW) and of the Italian Psychoanalytical Psychotherapy Society for Children and Adolescents (SIPsIA). Her occupational fields and research areas are Clinical Psychology and Development Psychoanalysis, Gender Studies, Feminine Identity, Maternity and motherhood, Mother-Infant interactions, Children's psychopathology prevention, Direct observation for training, intervention and clinical research tools. One specific study direction focus on the web use and misuse among parents as e-health users and adolescents, underlying related risks and opportunities.

Müge Çelik Örücü received her MS in Psychology from Middle East Technical University in 1994 and she got her degree as a Clinical Psychologist in 1997. She worked at METU Medical Centre (MC) for 15 years. She had internationally recognized certificates of EMDR, Cognitive-Behavioral Therapy and PREPaRE Crisis Intervention program and motivational interviewing. In 2005 she got her Ph.D from METU Department of Educational Sciences in Psychological Counseling and Guidance program. She is working as an associate professor in the Faculty of Education, Guidance and Psychological Counseling program at TED University. She writes and presents widely on stress management, school climate, crisis intervention, motivational interviewing and sibling relationships.

Aman Choudhary is currently a clinical trainee, pursuing M.Phil Clinical Psychology fromGFSU (Gujarat Forensic Sciences University), Gandhinagar, Gujarat. After achieving first class bachelor's degree in Psychology from St.Xavier's College, Ahmedabad, the author went on to study M.Sc Neuropsychology from GFSU and passed out in 2016 with distinction. His work experience counts teaching at Amity University, Gurgaon for 9 months where he taught subjects of his interest in Physiological Psychology to Therapies. He has been a gold medalist in undergraduate degree dissertation and worked on various projects on cyberpsychology during M.Sc degree. His work was praised at various levels in conferences entitled him to get the best paper award and acknowledgment at different seminars.

Malinda Desjarlais has a PhD from Brock University in Ontario, Canada. She is currently an Associate Professor in the Department of Psychology at Mount Royal University in Calgary, Alberta, Canada. Her research interests include the use of digital technology and its impact on social and cognitive development.

Luka Druks is an Engineer of Media Communications currently focusing on marketing and design in a startup ecosystem. He used to work for the World Champion E-sports team Natus Vincere as Content Manager. With his existing enthusiasm for video games, he fell in love with the industry quickly. Even though he is not working in the industry any more, he is still active in the industry. He completed his Degree in Media Communications at the Faculty of Electrical Engineering and Computer Science at the University of Maribor Currently, he is in charge of Marketing and Design for a startup called InstantAPI.

Aminudin Hehsan is senior lecturer at Centre for Fiqh Research in Science and Technology (CFiRST) Faculty of Islamic Civilisation (FTI), Universiti Teknologi Malaysia.

Lucijana Herceg is currently completing her Bachelor of Arts degree in Psychology with a minor in Sociology at Mount Royal University. She is currently assisting in conducting research on selfie-posting behavior under the supervision of Dr. Malinda Desjarlais.

Miftachul Huda is a researcher at Faculty of Islamic Civilisation, Universiti Teknologi Malaysia. His research interest includes digital ethics, educational studies, innovation, Islamic studies. He has been experienced in working on research for more than five years. Contributing several works, he is currently the member of the advisory editorial board in some international journals. Traveling in some countries with scholarly intent makes him extensive experience on his research expertise in international trend and issues. Thus, he commits to contributing his knowledge to the benefit of society through professional and social activities.

Václav Janoščík is a pedagogue, researcher and curator; he is currently an assistant professor at the Academy of Fine Arts, and Academy of Performing Arts (Photography Departement), he is head of Visual Arts program at UMPRUM and a lecturer at other Prague-based universities. He focuses on contemporary philosophy and theory of media and art, nonetheless he keeps engaged in other diverse fields. In this respect it is interdisciplinarity, dialogue (between theory and arts) and the critical aspects of art which form his main interest. He edited several collective monographs, most recently the collective monograph entitled Objekt (2015), translating some key text from speculative realism, and Reinventing Horizons (2016), an international book featuring texts aiming at redefinition of current means in art, technology, academia, and society. He has curated several international exhibitions such as Cities and Velocities (2016 Brussels, BOZAR) or a section of Moscow Biennale of Young Art (2014 Moscow, MMOMA).

Kamarul Azmi Jasmi is a senior lecturer of Civilisation Studies,,Innovations, Islamic Education and Qualitative Research Approach at Universiti Teknologi Malaysia (UTM). He has been working in teaching for more than fifteen years and published books and referred journals. He committed to continue his research and teaching as his contribution to the society through the professional and social activities.

Jessica J. Joseph received a Bachelor of Arts Honours degree in Psychology from Mount Royal University in 2017. She completed her Honours thesis on Facebook Depression under the supervision of Dr. Malinda Desjarlais. Her research and presentation experience has focused on the use of social interactive technology and the effects on users' friendships and subjective well-being.

Shogo Kato is an Associate Professor in the School of Arts and Sciences, Tokyo Woman's Christian University in Japan. He earned a Ph.D. from Tokyo Institute of Technology in 2005. His general research interests include educational technology; the application of behavior science, psychology, and information and communication technology (ICT) to educational scenes. Dr. Kato is particularly interested in the emotional aspects in virtual community, such as Internet bullying. His newest book chapter is as follows: Kato, Y., & Kato, S. (2016). Mobile phone use during class at a Japanese women's college. In M. N. Yildiz & J. Keengwe (Eds.), Handbook of Research on Media Literacy in the Digital Age, (pp.436-455 as Chapter 21). Hershey, PA: IGI Global.

Yuuki Kato is an Associate Professor at Sagami Women's University, Faculty of Arts and Sciences, Department of Information and Media Studies in Japan. He earned a Ph.D. from Tokyo Institute of Technology in 2005. His general research interests include educational technology; the application of behavior science, psychology, and information and communication technology (ICT) to educational scenes. Dr. Kato is particularly interested in the emotional aspects in technology-mediated human communications. His newest article is as follows: Kato, Y., & Kato, S. (2015). Reply speed to mobile text messages among Japanese college students: When a quick reply is preferred and a late reply is acceptable. Computers in Human Behavior, 44, 209-219.

Valentina Manna, PhD, post-doctoral fellow at Naples University, is clinical psychologist and post-graduate student in Psychoanalyitic Psychotherapy of the child, adolescent and parents (Winnicott Institute,ASNE-SIPsIA). She mostly works with schoolers and preschoolers, also being engaged as educator at a nursery school. She was project manager in several national/international projects about prevention of risk in childhood and adolescence, equal opportunities and gender issues. She was awarded (2015) by the Italian Order of Psychologists for the project Dear Sibling, addressed to young siblings of children with Down Syndrome. She has been enrolled in home visiting programs for at-risk-children, and currently runs help-desks for parents. She is vice president of Roots in Action Association, active in the field of psychosocial interventions for children with disabilities and developmental disorders. Her research interests, presented at international conferences and publications, include sibling relationships in disabilities, psychodynamic observation, videobservation/videofeedback, identity processes and technologies in adolescence, and infant psychoanalysis.

İrem Metin Orta received her Ph. D. degree in Psychology from Middle East Technical University and currently works in the Department of Psychology at Atilim University, Turkey. Her recent interests include cyberloafing, social media use, attitudes, sexism, homophobia, emotions, vicarious embarrassment, early attachment, maternal sensitivity, attachment-based interventions. She has published several papers in journals including Sex Roles, Personality and Individual Differences, Social Behavior and Personality, Infant and Child Development, and Turkish Psychological Reports.

Idit Miara Shepaich is a consultant and moderator of workshops at Haifa University. In recent years, Idit has specialized in training and developing technological systems. She also heads a volunteer program that matches children from underprivileged backgrounds with university students who act as their tutors. Idit holds a master's degree (M.Ed.) from Kibbutzim College of Education in Information Technology (2013-2015), and a B.A in Hebrew Literature and General History from Haifa University (2001-2004). She has a teaching certificate, specializing in Hebrew literature (2005), and a certificate in training program development from Haifa University (2010).

Mohd Ismail Mustari is an associate professor of on digital innovation and Islamic education at Universiti Teknologi Malaysia (UTM). He has been working in teaching for more than fifteen years.

Yasuyuki Ozawa is a college student majoring in developmental psychology at Meisei University, Faculty of Education. He is now a co-researcher of Yuuki Kato and Shogo Kato and engaged in research on communication using text messengers such as LINE text messenger application. His research interests are in the area of human behavioral and psychological aspects in social media.

Budi Rismayadi is senior lecturer at Faculty of Economics and Business, University of Singaperbangsa Karawang, Indonesia. He has many experienced position as chairman in one of the High School of Economics Science in 2004 to 2008, and had served as chairman of the Institute for Research and Community Service (LPPM) University of Singaperbangsa Karawang in 2009 to 2014, and currently serves as Dean of the Faculty of Business and Social Sciences at the University of Buana Perjuangan Karawang, Indonesia. He is also active in various professional activities as a board of Private College Association commissariat IV A West Java, and active as a member of the Association of Indonesian Lecturers.

Gülşah Sari works as an Assistant Professor at the Department of Radio Television and Cinema, Abant Izzet Baysal University, Turkey. She became a PhD in İstanbul University, Department of Radio Television and Cinema in 2016. She holds a master degree in Marmara University, department of Cinema in 2010. Her recent interests include television, cinema, product placement, social media and advertising. She has published several paper in journals including advertising, product placement, transmedia and cinema.

Tami Seifert is currently a senior lecturer at Kibbutzim College of Education, Tel-Aviv. She has a PhD in Urban Studies and Instructional Design and Technology from Old Dominion University (Virginia, USA) in 2001. She earned both her B.Sc and M.Sc from Tel-Aviv University. Between 2003 and 2005 she completed a post-doctorate from Tel-Aviv University on implementation of handheld computers in education. She served as head of the Department of Educational Computing, the head of Academic ICT and vice-director of the Teacher Training for Graduates Program at Kibbutzim College of Education (2007-2014). Courses Tami has taught in the past five years include: Innovative Technologies in Education, Online Education, The Design of Online Instruction: From Planning to Assessment, Social Networking in Educational Contexts, Application of Video in Teaching. Courses Tami has taught in the past five years include: Innovative Technologies in Education, Online Education, The Design of Online Instruction: From Planning to Assessment, Social Networking in Educational Contexts, Application of Video in Teaching. She promotes and advises digital literacy among faculty.

Zdenek Smutny is Assistant Professor at Faculty of Informatics and Statistics, University of Economics, Prague and also Project Manager at Telematix Group. He graduated in informatics and media studies and as a scholar, he focuses on online marketing management and a wide concept of social informatics: interaction between ICT and humans at the organizational (micro) and society (macro) level and ICT applications in the social sciences.

Tina Tomazic graduated from the Faculty of Economics and Business and earned, in a marketing field, a Master's of Science in Economics and Business Sciences. She became a PhD at a Philosophical Faculty in the field of Information and Communication Science. She is working as an Assistant Professor at the Institute of Media Communications, University of Maribor in Slovenia. During her work she has participated actively in scientific conferences in this country and abroad and has published numerous books and articles, which have appeared in significant journals (as Industrial Management & Data Systems and Lex localis). She participated in a targeted Research Project on the Impact of Digital Technologies Slovenian AV production in the light of Europe 2020.

Noémia Bessa Vilela, Ph.D. Candidate, is a Senior Research Assistant at the Faculty of Law, University of Maribor, and a Founding member and Researcher at IJP – Portucalense Institute for Legal Research, at University Portucalense Infante D. Henrique in Porto, Portugal where she also assists the Rectorate in the Internationalization process. She undertakes research in Law, mostly comparative European Law, Civil Procedure and Human Rights. She has been part of several EU projects and Networks. She also published a few book chapters and scientific papers in both Portuguese and International Journals. Having professional interest in the field of Human Rights, Noémia is also part of the Executive Board of the Observatory for Human Rights in Portugal, where she also acts as a rapporteur.

Michelle F. Wright is a research associate at Penn State University and a postdoctoral research fellow at Masaryk University in Brno, the Czech Republic. Her research focus is on the contextual factors which influence children's, adolescents', and young adults' involvement in aggressive behaviors, with a special interest in social goals, peer status, and cultural values. She has published on these topics, with her most recent work focused on culture and anonymity, and their role in cyberbullying among adolescents.

Index

A

Addiction 21-22, 26, 30, 32, 39, 41, 50, 174-193, 244, 254-256, 258-260
Adolescence 41, 50, 176, 248
Advertising 84-85, 88-89, 91-94, 175
Anonymity 29, 40, 42, 65-66, 110, 127, 131, 133, 153-154, 163-164, 173, 206, 214-215, 217, 219, 231-232, 252, 254, 256, 258, 279, 284
Anxiety 21-23, 27-28, 32, 39, 127, 131, 135, 163, 173, 175, 179, 185, 192, 227, 246, 248, 251
Assessment 11, 25, 43-44, 105, 125, 182-183, 188-189, 193, 251-253, 275, 282
Attachment 21-22, 28-29, 39, 83, 128, 133-135, 158, 162, 173, 208

B

Behavioral Addiction 174, 176
Body Control Image in Photos 55
Body image control 40-41, 44, 50
Broadcasting 86, 89, 94, 96, 107

C

Collectivism 173
Commercial cybersex 204
Communication 1, 8-12, 14, 19, 21-29, 31-32, 64-67, 75-76, 82, 89-92, 96-99, 106, 110-111, 113-115, 126-128, 133, 135, 138, 141-143, 154, 160, 164, 174, 185, 189, 193, 202, 206, 208, 220-221, 230, 251-252, 258, 273, 275-277, 279-285, 291
Communication Tools in Japan 82
Computer-Mediated Communication 26, 65, 138, 273, 278
Confirmatory Factor Analysis (CFA) 46, 55
Criminal profiling 136-137
Culture 5, 86, 89-90, 96, 283
Cut Off Value 55
Cyber Stalking 127-129, 131-133, 135, 137-138, 142-143, 244-245, 252
Cyberbullying 21, 29, 32, 39, 107, 153-165, 173, 249, 274-275, 279, 281, 283
Cybersex 201-210, 244-245, 247, 252-256, 258-260
Cyberstalking 126-127, 129-138, 142-144, 244, 251, 260

D

Depression 21-25, 29, 32, 39, 104-108, 110-111, 113-116, 125, 131, 158, 163, 175, 185, 193, 238-240, 249, 251
Digital Age 273, 280-285, 290
Digital Immigrants 67, 82
Digital Natives 67, 82

E

E-sports 84-94
Exploratory Factor Analysis (EFA) 55
Externalizing Difficulties 173

F

Facebook 9, 12, 19, 21-32, 42-44, 47, 50, 65, 82-83, 87, 90-92, 98, 100, 104-111, 113-116, 125, 132, 138, 157, 213-219, 222-223, 225-228, 230-232, 273
Facebook Contentment 104-108, 110-111, 114-115, 125
Facebook Depression 23, 104-108, 110-111, 113-114, 116, 125
Forensic investigation 126, 135, 137
Fragmentarization 1-2, 4, 6-7, 9-10, 13-14

G

Gaming 84-86, 88-90, 93-94, 155, 158, 174, 176-178, 185, 187, 190-193, 245

Gender 29-31, 40, 43-44, 47-48, 51, 99, 131, 133-134, 136, 143, 154, 158, 178, 205-206, 214, 246, 250, 254, 256-257, 260

H

Higher Education Context 272-273, 278, 285

I

Identity 6, 9-11, 31, 40-42, 44, 47-51, 127, 142, 153-155, 185, 205, 213, 215, 217-219, 222-224, 228, 230-233, 237, 245, 247-249, 256, 284
Individualism 173
Infidelity 201, 209-210, 250
Internet Use 23-24, 28, 47, 65, 138, 174, 177-188, 191-193, 247, 253
Internet-Based Services 2, 7-14, 18-19

K

Kimola 96, 99

L

Line Messenger Application 68, 76, 82
LINE's Read Receipt Status 83
LINE's Unread Receipt Status 83
Loneliness 21-22, 24-26, 28-29, 32, 39, 106-108, 110, 114, 158, 163, 173, 175, 185, 213, 239, 245-246

M

Management 9, 11, 24, 30, 42, 44, 110, 133, 138, 144, 174-175, 186-187, 252, 254, 260, 279, 284
Marketing 1-2, 10-14, 19, 84-85, 89, 99, 217
Mental Health 21-23, 25, 29, 32-33, 105, 107, 115-116, 138, 143, 162, 173-174, 185, 192, 236-237, 239, 241-242, 244-245, 247-251, 256, 259-260
Mental health professionals 143, 236, 241
Monitoring 30, 32, 96, 98-99, 127, 138, 142, 159-160, 164, 173, 184, 190, 249

N

Natus Vincere 84-86, 90-92
Negative Social Comparison 109, 114-116, 125
Net Use 51
Nonverbal Cue 64
Normative Belief 173

O

Offenders 126-128, 132-135, 144, 254, 258, 284
Online Behaviors 127, 138, 160-161, 164, 179, 189, 244-245, 248, 252-253, 259-260
Online Dating 188, 213, 217, 232, 236-238, 240, 242, 244-248, 250-252, 259-260
Online disinhibition effect 154, 163-164
Online Gaming 86, 155, 158, 174, 177-178, 185, 187, 190-192, 245
Online Social Networking 21-25, 32-33, 259, 281

P

Parental Mediation and Monitoring 160, 173
Parenting Style 159, 173
Passive Facebook Use 104-110, 115-116, 125
Peer Attachment 158, 162, 173
Peer Contagion 161, 173
Personal cybersex 201, 204
Personality 21-22, 24, 26, 30-31, 39, 42, 128, 134, 136-137, 175, 178-179, 185, 188, 193, 215-216, 223, 230-231, 233, 237, 245, 252, 273
Pornography 30, 207, 209, 244-245, 247, 256-258, 260
Positive Social Comparison 109, 125
Prevention 25, 126, 129, 137-139, 144, 161, 165, 188, 191, 252, 258, 260, 272-275, 277-280, 283-285, 291
Privacy 27, 31, 44, 48, 141, 144, 213-214, 216, 218-219, 224-228, 231-233, 249, 285
Pro-Victim Attitudes 173
Psychosocial Functioning 104-105, 107, 115
Public Relations 84-85, 88, 90, 92-94

R

Reply Speed 75
Risk Measure 55
Romance 209, 213-214, 218-221, 228-230, 232-233, 238, 250, 255

S

Selective Presentation 110, 116
Self-Disclosure 23, 66, 110-111, 116, 206, 254, 277, 281-282
Self-Esteem 21-23, 25-27, 32, 39, 41, 106-115, 125, 132, 164, 175, 185, 207-208, 239, 249
Self-exhibitionism 201

Selfies 40, 42-44, 47-49, 51, 56, 105-106, 110-113, 115, 125
Self-Portrait 41, 47-48, 50, 56
Series 4, 87, 96, 98-100, 103, 113, 248, 250
Smartphone 40-42, 47-48, 65, 67, 75, 83, 112, 125, 273-274, 278
Social Anxiety 21-23, 28, 32, 39, 179
Social cognitive theory 163
Social Comparison Theory 109-110
Social Connectedness 106-108, 114, 116, 125
Social Exclusion 155, 173
Social Media 2, 7, 18, 22-23, 30-32, 41, 43-44, 47-48, 50-51, 56, 65, 82, 87-89, 96-100, 103-105, 111-114, 116, 157, 192, 236, 246, 249, 274, 276, 284, 290
Social Networking Sites 15, 21-24, 39-44, 48, 50-51, 89-92, 94, 98, 100, 104-105, 107, 110, 113-114, 131-132, 135, 142, 186, 193, 213, 215, 228, 259, 282
Speed of Reply 64, 75-76, 83
Stalking 29, 126-139, 142-143, 244-245, 249, 251-252
Stickers 83
Subjective Wellbeing 21, 125
Subjective Well-Being 22, 26-27, 32, 39, 105-110, 112-116
Subjectivity 1-4, 6-15, 18
Surveillance 43-44, 47, 50, 106, 114, 210
Survey 64, 68-69, 75-76, 130, 132, 184, 210, 237-238, 257-258

T

Technology Use 153, 158, 160, 164, 272-275, 278-280, 282, 285, 290
Television 91, 96-99, 103, 190, 291
Text Messaging 67-68, 75-76, 82-83, 153
Traditional Face-to-Face Bullying 155, 158, 161, 163, 165, 173
Turkish television series 96
Typologies 126-127, 129, 137, 144

V

Victims 29, 126, 128, 130-136, 138, 142-144, 153-158, 160, 162-164, 173, 236, 238-239, 241, 249, 251-254, 284
Video-based cybersex 201
Virtual Environment 2-3, 5-9, 11-14, 18-19, 131
Virtual Interaction 273, 275, 279, 281, 284, 291
Virtual Reality 2, 18, 202-203, 244
Virtual reality-based cybersex 203
Virtual Violence 272-275, 278, 280, 285, 291
Virtual violence prevention 272-274, 278, 280, 285
Virtual World 2, 48, 190, 204, 209, 214, 216, 228, 242, 279-280
Voyeurism 201, 205

W

Well-Being 22-24, 26-28, 32-33, 39, 104-116, 236, 238, 240, 242, 248, 257, 277, 282

www.ingramcontent.com/pod-product-compliance
Lightning Source LLC
LaVergne TN
LVHW062134300926
849161LV00010B/2528
* 9 7 8 1 5 2 2 5 4 0 4 7 2 *